THE ENCYCLOPEDIA OF MODERN HISTORY

'Consider that forty centuries of history look down
on you from these monuments!'—Napoleon to his
soldiers before the Battle of the Pyramids, 1798

THE ENCYCLOPEDIA OF MODERN HISTORY

Hamlyn

LONDON · NEW YORK · SYDNEY · TORONTO

The birth of modern mankind interpreted by a great 20th-century artist, Salvador Dali

Key to Contributors

The publishers wish to acknowledge their gratitude to Professor James Joll, Stevenson Professor of International History at the London School of Economics and Political Science, University of London, for his advice in preparing this work for publication. The publishers' thanks are also due to Professor Ragnhild Hatton, Dr R. J. Bullen and Walter Laqueur for their assistance and suggestions.

Executive editor: James Clark

Introductory essays

M. B.   **Dr Michael Biddiss**
University of Leicester

K. B.   **Professor Ken Bourne**
The London School of Economics & Political Science

P. H.   **Dr Peter Hatton**

W. J. M.   **Dr Wolfgang J. Mommsen**
Director of the German Historical Institute, London

R. A. C. P.   **Dr Alastair Parker**
The Queen's College, Oxford

S. S.   **Dr Simon Schama**
Brasenose College, Oxford

L. S.   **Professor Leonard Schapiro**
The London School of Economics & Political Science

D. C. W.   **Professor Donald Watt**
The London School of Economics & Political Science

J. E. V.   **Professor The Lord Vaizey of Greenwich**
Brunel University

First published in Great Britain 1978 by
The Hamlyn Publishing Group Limited
London · New York · Sydney · Toronto
Astronaut House, Hounslow Road
Feltham, Middlesex

Created, designed and produced by Trewin Copplestone
Publishing Limited, London

ISBN 0 600 33184 9

Printed in Italy by New Interlitho Spa, Milan

Key to Contributors

Contributors

C. G. A.   **Dr Christopher G. Abel**
Lecturer in Latin American History, University College, London

A. P. A.   **Professor Anthony Adamthwaite**
University of Loughborough

D. G. C. A.   **D. G. C. Allan**
Curator-Librarian, Royal Society of Arts

P. A. A.   **Dr Percy Allum**
Reader in Politics, University of Reading

M. S. A.   **Professor M. S. Anderson**
Professor of International History, London School of Economics & Political Science

D. G. B.   **Dr David G. Blackbourn**
Dept of History, Queen Mary College, London

B. J. B.   **Brian J. Bond**
Reader in War Studies, King's College, London

C. E. B.   **Constantine Brancovan**
Dept of History, University of Manchester

E. B.   **Professor Ernest Braun**
Head of Technology Policy Unit, University of Aston

W. H. B.   **Dr W. H. Brock**
Victorian Studies Centre, University of Leicester

D. R. B.   **Dr David R. Brooks**
Dept of History, Queen Mary College, London

A. H. B.   **Archie Brown**
Lecturer in Soviet Institutions, Oxford

P. S. B.   **Paul S. Butterworth**
Dept of Physics & Astronomy, University College, London

M. V. C.   **Manuel V. Cabral**
St Antony's College, Oxford

R. C.   **Richard Clogg**
School of Slavonic & East European Studies, London

P. R. C.   **Dr Paul R. Corner**
Director of the Centre for the Advanced Study of Italian Society, University of Reading

P. L. C.   **Dr Philip Cottrell**
Dept of Economic & Social History, University of Leicester

M. L. D.   **Dr Michael L. Dockrill**
Lecturer in War Studies, University College, London

S. G. B.   **Sarah Graham-Brown**

R. F. H.   **Robert F. Holland**
Lecturer in Imperial History, Institute of Commonwealth Studies, London

G. A. H.   **Dr Geoffrey Hosking**
Senior Lecturer and Chairman of the History Dept, University of Essex

M. C. K.   **Michael Kaser**
Professorial Fellow, St Antony's College, Oxford

D. K.   **Dr David Kirby**
School of Slavonic & East European Studies, London

L. K.   **Dr Lionel Kochan**
Bearstead Reader in Jewish History, University of Warwick

B. L. M.   **Bernard L. Myers**
Royal College of Art, London

R. F. L.   **Professor R. F. Leslie**
Professor of Modern History, Queen Mary College, London

G. L. L.   **Dr Geoffrey L. Lewis**
Lecturer in Turkish, Oriental Institute, Oxford

P. H. L.   **Dr Peter H. Lyon**
Institute of Commonwealth Studies, London

J. S. M.   **Dr J. S. McClelland**
Dept of Politics, University of Nottingham

R. P. M.   **Professor Roger P. Morgan**
Head of European Centre for Studies in Democratic Politics, Policy Studies Institute, London

E. M.   **Eric McGraw**
Director, Population Concern

P. M.   **Dr Peter Morris**
Dept of Politics, University of Nottingham

T. M.-P.   **Thomas Munch-Petersen**
Dept of Scandinavian Studies, University College, London

I. H. N.   **Dr Ian H. Nish**
Reader in International History, London School of Economics & Political Science, London

B. N. P.   **Dr B. N. Pandey**
School of Oriental and African Studies, London

L. P.   **Dr László Péter**
Lecturer in Hungarian History, School of Slavonic & East European Studies, London

A. N. P.   **Dr Andrew N. Porter**
Dept of History, King's College, London

J. F. P.   **John F. Preston**
Dept of Physics and Astronomy, University College, London

P. P.   **Dr Paul Preston**
Dept of History, Queen Mary College, London

M. C. R.   **Dr M. C. Ricklefs**
School of Oriental and African Studies, London

M. R.   **Dr Michael Riff**
School of History, University of Leeds

A. R.   **Adam Roberts**
Lecturer in International Relations, London School of Economics & Political Science

G. S.   **George Schöpflin**
Dept of Politics, London School of Economics & Political Science

H. S.   **Dr Harold Shukman**
University Lecturer in Russian History, Oxford

A. S.   **Dr Alan Sked**
Dept of International History, London School of Economics & Political Science

R. S.   **Robert Skidelsky**
Head of the Dept of History, Philosophy and European Studies, Polytechnic of North London

W. H. S.   **Dr Liam Smith**
Goldsmiths' College, London

R. B. S.   **Dr Ralph B. Smith**
School of Oriental and African Studies, London

M. S.   **Melvyn Stokes**
Lecturer in American History, University College, London

T. V. T.   **Trevor Vaughan Thomas**
School of Slavonic & East European Studies, London

P. W.   **Dr Peter Warwick**

D. C. W.   **Professor Donald Watt**
Professor of International History, London School of Economics & Political Science

M. B. Y.   **Dr Michael B. Yahuda**
Lecturer in International Relations, London School of Economics & Political Science

How To Use This Book

Each double-page opening in this encyclopedia throws a spotlight on a particular event or phase in modern history, providing the reader with a concentrated survey of the main trends of the time. The reader can therefore find a starting-point anywhere in the book and extend his knowledge of other, related areas of modern history by reading either forwards or backwards step by step from that article.

There are two ways of adding the articles together to make a continuous introduction to an area of interest to the reader – whether in following the history of an individual country or region over a period of time, or in comparing developments throughout Europe or the world at a particular moment. These alternatives are shown in the arrangement of the contents list on pages 6 and 7. For example, on the one hand, all the articles on the USA, or on France, can be noted and read one after the other, as they form a continuous account of each country's political development and changing place in the world during the 200 years covered by this book. On the other hand, each of the sections, which groups together a number of articles, constitutes an international survey of a recognizable phase, for example, the years between the two world wars, or the late Victorian age, when the British Empire was the dominant world power.

Because of the current importance of America as the world's leading economy and a nuclear super-power, separate sections have been provided to bring together the articles dealing with the growth of the USA from the beginning of the modern period.

It is not necessary for the reader to know dates already or to be able to identify the historical personalities, for he can refer to the Index at the beginning of the book, where all relevant names are listed (with dates of birth and death), as well as a page number referring to the article that contains the main mention of the person or event, and to any other subject articles where the same name occurs by way of cross-reference.

A valuable feature of the contents is the coverage, all the way through, of most of the areas of the world that make the news today, even though they may have been quite marginal in world affairs a hundred or more years ago. The world outside Europe and North America – including China, Japan, South America, southern Africa – was once lumped together under the label 'overseas and colonial', but the reader will find articles on all of them from the early 19th century onwards. The encyclopedia, in correcting the Europe-centred view of world history, also does justice to the history of the advanced nations of the Commonwealth – Australia, Canada, New Zealand – which can be read in parallel with the account of the rise and decline of the mother country as a world power.

The Further Reading list, with headings that relate to the subject areas covered in the articles, is the key to a more detailed knowledge of the regions, periods and international problems dealt with.

Contents

Index   *10*

The Birth of the Modern World   *18*
Science and Social Change   1700–1770   *20*

The First Modern Democracies   *22*
American Discontents   1763–1774   *24*
From Protest to Revolution   1774–1776   *26*
The War of Independence   1776–1781   *28*
France and America   1776–1783   *30*
The Ancien Régime in France   1760–1788   *32*
The French Revolution   1789–1792   *34*
The First Republic   1792–1799   *36*
General Bonaparte   1793–1799   *38*

The Age of Napoleon   *40*
Napoleon's Battles and Conquests   1800–1815   *42*
Napoleon's Political System   1799–1813   *44*
Russia in the Age of Napoleon   1801–1825   *46*
British Sea Power Established   1793–1815   *48*

Industrial Revolution   *50*
The Railroads   1800–1845   *52*
Medicine and Public Health   1800–1860   *54*

Reaction in Europe   *56*
Revolution and Counter-Revolution   1789–1821   *58*
Trade Unions in Britain   1790–1836   *60*
Italy   1796–1831   *62*
The German States   1815–1848   *62*
France's Monarchies   1813–1848   *64*
Aftermath of the Peninsular War   1807–1874   *66*
Russia, the 'Policeman of Europe'   1825–1855   *68*
The Nordic Countries   1807–1848   *69*

Nationalism and Reform   *70*
Britain: Reform, Chartism,
   Free Trade   1830–1860   *72*
Ireland   1800–1860   *74*
The Nordic Countries   1848–1905   *75*
Freedom for Greece   1821–1881   *76*
Independence for Belgium   1799–1939   *77*
The Risorgimento and Liberal Italy   1831–1880   *78*
Hungary   1848–1849   *80*
Poland   1794–1864   *80*
Liberals and Nationalists in Germany   1813–1848   *82*
The Year of Revolutions   1848–1849   *84*
The Decline of the Ottoman Empire   1800–1918   *86*
The Revolutions in Spanish America   1810–1828   *88*
Independence in Spanish America   1828–1870   *90*
Brazil: Colony, Empire and Republic   1807–1889   *90*

Jefferson to Lincoln   *92*
Slavery and the Union   1776–1861   *94*
The War between the States   1861–1865   *96*
Aftermath of Civil War   1865–1877   *98*

The Balance of Power in Europe   *100*
High Victorian Britain   1860–1890   *102*
Britain and the Empire   1850–1903   *104*
Napoleon III: an Adventure   1848–1870   *106*
Austria's Decline   1848–1910   *108*
The Forging of a German State   1848–1888   *110*
Russia between Serfdom
   and Constitution   1861–1905   *112*
Spain: the Restoration System   1874–1909   *114*
Portugal: from Liberalism
   to Corporativism   1851–1933   *115*

The Making of the Second British Empire   *116*
Canada   1759–1867   *118*
India under the Company   1760–1858   *120*
South Africa up to the Greak Trek   1795–1837   *122*
Australasia   1770–1860   *124*

Exploration, Expansion and Imperialism   *126*
The End of Imperial China   1839–1912   *128*
The Opening of Japan   1853–1900   *130*
The Scramble for Africa   1800–1900   *132*
The East Indies   1830–1945   *134*
Indochina   1800–1941   *136*
Canada   1867–1939   *138*
Australasia   1860–1945   *140*
Egypt and the Sudan   1798–1918   *142*
The Indian Empire: Congress v. Raj   1858–1935   *144*
Southern Africa   1837–1910   *146*

The Great Republic   *148*
USA, Coast to Coast   1783–1869   *150*
American Capitalism   1860–1918   *152*
Voices of Reform and Protest   1870–1918   *154*
'Teddy' Roosevelt and the Big Stick   1898–1905   *156*
American Power   1860–1918   *158*
Mexico: from 'Porfiriato'
   to Revolution   1876–1917   *160*

Intellectual Climates in the 19th Century   *162*
Scientific Enquiry   1800–1913   *164*
Romanticism and Nationalism   1750–1900   *166*
Early Socialism and Anarchism   1830–1848   *168*
The Age of Exhibitions   1851–1914   *170*

Great Power Rivalries   *172*
Britain and Ireland   1906–1914   *174*
France: the Third Republic   1871–1914   *176*
Wilhelmine Germany   1888–1914   *178*
Italy: Growing Pains   1880–1915   *180*
The Russo-Japanese War   1904–1905   *182*
Russia in Crisis   1905–1914   *184*
New Perceptions   1905–1914   *186*
The Last Summer   1914   *188*

Contents

The First World War — 190
Stalemate in the West — 1914–1918 — 192
Dismemberment of the
 Ottoman Empire — 1915–1918 — 194
Italy Comes In — 1915 — 196
The Easter Rising — 1916 — 196
America In, Russia Out — 1917–1918 — 198

The Russian Revolution — 200
From February to the Death of Lenin — 1917–1924 — 202
Trotsky and Stalin — 1924–1929 — 204

The Inter-War Years — 206
Versailles and the Peace Conference — 1919–1920 — 208
Britain between the Wars — 1919–1939 — 210
France: Versailles to Vichy — 1918–1940 — 212
The World Depression — 1929–1933 — 214
The Roosevelt Era — 1933–1940 — 216
The Atatürk Revolution — 1923–1939 — 218
Spain — 1909–1931 — 219
Republican China — 1912–1945 — 220
Stalin and the Five Year Plans — 1929–1941 — 222
The Weimar Republic — 1919–1923 — 224
Poland — 1918–1944 — 224
Greece — 1919–1940 — 225
The Fascist Régime in Italy — 1922–1939 — 226
The Ascent of Hitler — 1923–1937 — 228
The Spanish Civil War — 1936–1939 — 230
Towards the Second World War — 1937–1939 — 232
Japan, China — 1931–1939 — 234
Germany, Poland, Russia — 1938–1939 — 234

The Second World War — 236
The Triumph of Blitzkrieg — 1939–1941 — 238
Rommel in Africa — 1941–1943 — 240
The Nordic and Baltic Lands — 1918–1945 — 241
The Tide Begins to Turn — 1941–1943 — 242
The Pacific War — 1942–1945 — 244
The Axis Smashed — 1942–1945 — 246

The Post-War World — 248
Years of Hope — 1945–1948 — 250
The 'Cold War' — 1948–1962 — 252
A Watershed: Suez and Hungary — 1956 — 254
Britain after Churchill — 1955– — 256
US Economic and Foreign Policy — 1953– — 258
De Gaulle and After — 1944– — 260
West Germany — 1945– — 262
Belgium — 1940– — 263
Italy — 1943– — 264
The Partition of India — 1935–1947 — 266
Decolonization (I) — 1957–1968 — 268
Decolonization (II) — 1945–1962 — 270
Malaysia — 1957– — 272
Indochina — 1941–1954 — 272
The Vietnam War — 1954–1973 — 274
Indonesia and the Philippines — 1945– — 276
Canada — 1939– — 278
Australasia — 1945– — 280
Japan — 1945– — 282
Economic Communities in Europe — 1952– — 284

The Red East — 286
The USSR after Stalin — 1953– — 288
The German Democratic Republic — 1945– — 290
Poland — 1945– — 291
Czechoslovakia — 1945– — 292
Hungary — 1945– — 293
Rumania, Bulgaria, Albania — 1945– — 294
Yugoslavia — 1944– — 296
The People's Republic of China — 1949– — 298

The Non-Aligned World — 300
South America: the Major
 Economies — 1945– — 302
Mexico — 1917– — 304
Chile — 1900– — 305
Demagogue Dictators: Castro and
 Perón — 1945– — 306
Independent Africa — 1957– — 308
India — 1948– — 310
Pakistan and Bangladesh — 1948– — 312
Burma and Sri Lanka — 1947– — 314

The Middle East and the Arab World — 316
Israel: Political Issues — 1948– — 318
Israel and the Arab World — 1947– — 320
Egypt and the Sudan — 1918– — 322
Turkey since Atatürk — 1939– — 324
The Fertile Crescent — 1918– — 326
Northern Africa — 1945– — 328
Desert Arabia — 1918– — 330
Iran — 1918– — 332
OPEC and Oil Power — 1960– — 333

The 1970s — 334
The Return of Democracy — 1974–1976 — 336
The White Rearguard in Africa — 1968– — 338
Inter-Communal Wars — 1969– — 340
Political Terrorism — 1970– — 342
The Space Programmes: USA and
 USSR — 1960– — 344
World Population and Resources — 1975– — 346

Further Reading — 348

Recommended Films — 350

Acknowledgements — 352

Index

Principal entries are indicated in **bold**.

ATOM BOMB

Abbas I (1813–54) 142
Abbas II (1874–1944) 143
Abboud **323**
Abd al-Krim (1882?–1963) 271
Abd al Qadir (el-Kader) (c. 1807–83) **270**, 271
Abdul-illah (1913–58) 327
Abdul Rahman, Taku (1903–73) 272
Abdul Razak, Tun (b. 1922) 272
Abdulhamid II (1842–1918) 86
Abdullah (1882–1951) **330**
Acts:
  Agricultural Adjustment (US) **216**
  Alien (US) 92
  Banking (US) 216
  British North America (UK) 119, 138
  Canada (UK) 119
  Canadian Citizens (Can.) **278**
  Chapultepec (US) 246
  Civil Rights (US) 98
  Coal Mines (UK) 175
  Coercion (UK) **24–5**, 26, 27
  Colonial Development (UK) 210
  Combination (UK) **60–1**
  Constitution (UK) 124
  Devolution (as Bills) (UK) 256
  Education (UK) **105**, 174
  Elkins (US) 155
  Enabling (Ger.) 232
  Glass-Steagall (US) 216
  Government of India (UK) 145, **266**
  Hepburn (US) 155
  Immigration (US) 159
  Land (UK) 103
  Meat Inspection (US) 155
  Medical (UK) 54·
  National Health (UK) 175
  National Industrial Recovery (US) **216**
  National Insurance (UK) **175**
  Navigation (UK) 73
  Parliament (UK) 174
  Pure Food and Drug (US) 155
  Quebec (UK) **25**
  Reform (UK) **72**, 102
  Revenue (UK) **24**
  Stamp (UK) **24**
  Securities (US) 216
  Sedition (US) 92
  Social Security (US) 217
  Unemployment (UK) 210
  Wagner (US) 217
Action Party 264
Adams, John (1735–1826) 26, 31
Adams, Samuel (1722–1803) 24
Addams, Jane (1860–1935) 155
Adelphi (Italian) 62
Adenauer, Konrad (1876–1967) **262**

African National Congress 338
Agadir crisis 271
Aguinaldo, Emilio (1869–1964) **134**, 156
Albert (1819–61) 170, 171
Alexander I (1777–1825) 42, **46–7**, 69, 81
Alexander II (1818–81) 68, 81, **112–13**
Alexander III (1845–94) 113
Alfonso XII (1857–85) 66, 114
Alfonso XIII (1886–1941) 219
Ali Pasha (1744?–1822) 76
Allende, Salvador (1908–73) 305
Amadeo of Savoy (1845–90) 66
Amin, Idi (b. 1925?) 309
Anarchism **168–9**
Angry Brigade 342
Anti-Corn Law League **73**
Anti-Fascist People's Freedom League **314**
Apartheid **338**
Appeasement 232–3, 235
April Laws **80**
Arab Socialist Union 322
Arabi Pasha 142
Arakcheev, A. A. (1769–1834) **47**
Aramburu, P. E. (1903–70) 342
Arif, Abdu'Salam 327
Arnold, Benedict (1741–1804) 28, 29
Asquith, Herbert (1852–1928) 155, 174–5, 196, 210
Assad, Hafez al- (b. 1928) 326
Aswan Dam 254, 322
Atatürk, Kemal (1881–1938) **86–7**, 194, **218**, 225, 324
Atom bomb 245, 247
Attlee, Clement (1883–1967) **250–1**, 267
Ausgleich, Austria-Hungary 109
Awami League 312
Ayub Khan, Muhammad (1907–74) **312**

BASTILLE

Baader-Meinhof gang 342
Ba'ath Party **326**, **327**
Babeuf, Gracchus (1760–97) **37**, 58, 84, **169**
Bach, Alexander (1813–93) 108
Bailly, Jean (1736–93) 35
Baker, Ray Stannard (1870–1946) 155
Bakunin, Mikhail (1814–76) 114, 168, **169**
Balewa, Abubaker Tafawa (1912–66) 308
Balfour, Arthur (1848–1930) 320
Bandaranaike, Sirimavo (b. 1916) **315**
Barnave, Antoine (1761–93) 35
Barras, Paul de (1755–1829) 38
Bastille 22, **34**
Batista, Fulgencio (1901–73) 306
Battles and sieges:
  Acre 39
  Adowa 180
  Antietam 96
  Aspern 42
  Atlantic 239, **242–3**
  Aubers Ridge 192

Auerstädt **42**, 44
Austerlitz **42**, 44
Bautzen 43
Blood River 146
Borodino 42
Boyacá 89
Brandywine 31
Bull Run 96
Bunker Hill 27
Caporetto 196
Chancellorsville 97
Chicamauga 96, 97
Colenso 147
Concord 26
Copenhagen 75
Coral Sea **244**
Ctesiphon 194
Custozza 84
Dien Bien Phu 252, 260, 272
Dogali 180
El Alamein **240**, 242
Eylau 42
Festubert 192
Fredericksburg 97
Friedland 42, 44
Gallipoli 140
Germantown 29
Gettysburg 97
Guadalajara 231
Jarama 231
Jena **42**, 44, 166
Kut el Amara 194
Ladysmith 147
Leipzig 43
Lexington 26
Liao-yang 183
Ligny 43
Long Island 28
Loos 192
Lützen 43
Mafeking 147
Magenta 106
Magersfontein 147
Marengo 39, 41, **42**
Megiddo 194
Midway **244**
Mukden 183
Majuba 146
Navarino 76–7, 142
Neuve-Chapelle 192
New Cold Harbor 97
Nile 39, 48
Omdurman 143
Paardeberg 147
Petersburg 97
Port Arthur 182–3
Prinsloo 147
Quatre Bras 43
Pyramids 39
Rivoli 38
Sadowa (Königgrätz) 71, 108
Samar Island 245
San Jacinto 150
Saratoga 31
Sedan 106
Shiloh 96
Solferino 106
Sollum 240
Somme 193
Stalingrad **242**
Stones River 96
Stormberg 147
Tal al-Kabir 142
Te-li-ssu 182
Titusville 158
Tobruk 240
Toulon 36, 38
Trafalgar 48, 67, 183

Trenton 28, 30
Tsushima 183
Ulm 44
Valley Forge 28, 29, 31
Valmy 37
Verdun 193
Vicksburg 97
Vittorio Veneto 196
Wagram **43**, 45, 61, 77
Yorktown **29**, 31
Ypres 192
Baudouin (b. 1930) 263
Bay of Pigs 306
Beck, Jozef (1899–1944) 224
Begin, Menachem (b. 1913) 318, 319, 321
Bellamy, Edward (1850–98) 154
Ben Barka, Mehdi 329
Ben Bella, Ahmad (b. 1919) **329**
Ben-Gurion, David (1886–1973) **318–19**
Beneš, Eduard (1884–1948) 233, **292**
Bentham, Jeremy (1748–1832) **20–1**, 168
Berchtold, Leopold von (1863–1942) **188–9**
Berenguer, Damaso (1873?–1953) **219**
Beresford, William (1768–1854) 67
Beria, Lavrenti (1899–1953) 288
Berlin
    Congress 87, 341
    Wall 252, 262, 290
Berlinguer, Enrico 265
Bernadotte, Jean-Baptiste (1763–1844) **69**
Bernard, Claude (1813–78) **55**
Betancourt, Romulo (b. 1908) 302
Bethmann, Theobald (1856–1921) 178
Beveridge Report 175, 237
Bevin, Ernest (1881–1951) 251
Bhutto, Zulfikar Ali (b. 1928) **312–13**
Biko, Steve 339
Bismarck, Otto von (1815–98) 41, 71, 84, **101**,
    106, 110, 132, 172, 176, **178–9**, 187
Black September 342
Blanc, Louis (1811–82) 168
Blanco, Carrero 337
Blanqui, Louis-Auguste (1805–81) 168
Blitzkrieg **238–9**
'Bloody Sunday' massacre **184**
Blücher, Gebhard von (1742–1819) 43
Blum, Léon (1872–1950) 212
Bolívar, Simon (1783–1830) **88–9**, 116–17
Bolsheviks **113**, 184, **200–3**, 222
Bonapartism **65**
Bonifacio, Andrés 134
Booth, Charles (1840–1916) 104
Botany Bay 124
Botha, Louis (1862–1919) 147
Boulanger, Georges (1837–91) 176
Boulanger affair, the 212
Boumedienne, Houari (b. 1932?) **329**
Bourguiba, Habib (b. 1903) 271, **328–9**
Bowring, John (1792–1872) 136
Boxer Uprising, the **129**, 131, 182
Bragg, Braxton (1817–76) 96
Brandt, Willy (b. 1913) 262
Brezhnev, Leonid (b. 1906) 287, **289**
Briand, Aristide (1862–1932) 212
Brienne, Étienne de (1727–94) **33**
Brissot, Jacques (1754–93) 36
Brown, John (1800–59) 95
Brüning, Heinrich (1885–1970) 228
Bryan, William Jennings (1860–1925) 154
Buddhism 136, 275, 314, 315
Budi Otomo 134
Buenorotti, Filippo 169
Bukharin, N. I. (1888–1938) **205**, 288
Bulganin, N. A. (b. 1895) 288
Bülow, Bernhard von (1849–1929) 178
Burke, Edmund (1729–97) **58–9**, 166
Butler, R. A. (b. 1902) 254

CHURCHILL

Cabral, Costa (1796–1854) 67
Caciques **114**, 119, 230
Caetano, Marcelo (b. 1906) **336**, 339
Cairo Agreements 340
Caldera, Rafael (b. 1916) 302
Calhoun, John C. (1782–1850) 94
Calles, P. E. (1877–1945) 304
Calonne, Charles de (1734–1802) 33
Camara, Dom Helder 303
Campbell-Bannerman, Henry (1836–1908) 147,
    174
Campo Formio, Peace of 39
Canalejas, José (1854–1912) 219
Canning, George (1770–1827) 60, 117
Canningites 61
Cánovas del Castillo, Antonio (1828–97) **114**
Caprivi, Georg von (1831–99) 178
Carbonari 62, 78
Cárdenas, Lazaro (1895–1970) **304**
Carlism **66**
Carlo Alberto (1798–1849) 84
Carlos, Don (1788–1855) **66**
Carlsbad Decrees **56**, **62**
Carnot, Lazare (1753–1823) 38
Carol (1893–1953) 294
Carson, Edmund (1854–1935) 174
Carter, Jimmy (b. 1924) 289, 335
Casement, Roger (1864–1916) **196**
Castro, Fidel (b. 1926) **306–7**
Castro, Raul (b. 1916) 306
Catherine the Great (1729–96) 59, 68
Catholicism, Catholics 25, 35, 51, 61, 74, 77, 79,
    103, 106, 174, 228, **340**
Catholic Centre Party 110, 178, 228
Cavour, Camillo (1810–61) 71, **78**, 106
Central African Federation **338–9**
Central Treaty Organization 327
Centre Union 336
Chamberlain, Joseph (1836–1914) 103, 104, **105**,
    147, 174
Chamberlain, Neville (1869–1940) 210, 233, 278
Chambord, Comte de (1820–83) 65
Charles, Archduke 42
Charles III of Spain (1716–88) **88**
Charles IV of Spain (1748–1819) 66
Charles X of France (1757–1836) **64–5**, 270
Charles XIV of Sweden: *see* Bernadotte
Chartism **72**, 74, **168**, 170
Cheka, the 203, 222
Chervenkov, Vúlko 295
Chiang Kai-shek (1887–1975) **221**, 234, 252, 258,
    272
Chifley, Ben (1885–1951) **280**
Chou-En-lai (1898–1976) 283
Christian Democrat Parties 262 (Germany); 305
    (Chile); **264–5** (Italy)
Christian Social Party (Austria) 109
Churchill, Winston (1874–1965) 174, 187, 240,
    243, **246–7**, 250, 254, 256, 266–7, 278, 336
Cientificos 160
Clemenceau, Georges (1841–1929) **208**, 212
Cleveland, Grover (1837–1903) 153
Clinton, Henry (1738?–95) 28
Cobbett, William (1766–1835) 72
Cobden, Richard (1804–65) 73

Comecon **285**, 287, 294
Cominform 251, 286, 297
Comintern 204, 210, 220, 222, **223**, 228, 251
Common Market: *see* European Economic
    Community
Communist League 85
Communist Manifesto **84–5**
Communist Parties **134**, 212, **221**, **222–3**, **224**,
    226, 228, 231, 232, 241, 250, 251, 252, **255**, 258,
    259, 260, **261**, **264–5**, 268, **272**, **274–5**, 285, 287,
    288–9, 290, **292**, 293, 294, 295, 296–7, 302, 303,
    305, 307, 314, 322, 327, 336, 337, 340
Compromise **94–5** (US), **109** (Austro-Hungarian)
Comte, Auguste (1798–1857) **162**, 164
Condorcet, Marie de (1743–94) 23
Confederation of Autonomous Rightist Groups,
    Spanish **230**
Confédération Générale du Travail 169, 176
Confederation, German **62**, 75, 84, 108
Conferences: Algeciras 271
    Bandung 268, 301
    Cairo 246
    Geneva 210, 232, 258, 259, 286
    Imperial Economic 210
    Inter-American 302
    Potsdam 291
    Round Table 145, 266
    on Security and Cooperation in Europe 289
    Simla 266–7
    Yalta 246–7
Confucianism 128, 136, 220
Congresses: All-India National 144
    Basel 169
    Berlin 87, 341
    Communist Party 204, 288
    Pan-Africanist 338
    Tucumán 89
    Vienna **56**, 58, **62**, 67
Congress Party **266–7**, **310**
Conservative Parties **102–3**, **104–5**, **174–5**, **196**,
    210, **254**, **256** (Britain); **114**, 219 (Spain); **138**,
    278 (Canada); 160 (Mexico); 196 (Italy)
'Conspiracy of Equals' 169
Constantine II (b. 1940) **336**
Constitutions: American 58, **92**, **94**, **98**
    Belgian 77
    Burmese **314**
    Canadian **138**
    Filipino 276
    French 39, **44–5**, 58, 64–5, **106**, **176**, **260**, 269
    Greek **76–7**, 336
    Hanoverian 62
    Hungarian 255
    Indian 310
    Iranian 332
    Israeli 318
    Japanese 131, 282
    Mexican **161**, 304
    Ottoman 86
    Pakistani **312–13**
    Polish 224, 291
    Portuguese 115, 336
    Russian 289
    Siamese 137
    Spanish **66**
    Sri Lankan 315
    Turkish 324
Continental Association 26
Conventions: Algeciras 157
    Alvensleben 108
    Anglo-German naval 232
    Cyprus 341
    Plombières 106
Cooke, Jay (1821–1905) 152, 159
Cooperative Commonwealth Federation Party
    138
Cooperative Societies 61
COPEI 302

Index

Corn Laws **73**, 74
Corporativism **115**, 169, 336
Corresponding Societies 60
Council of Europe 251
Country Party **280**
Craig, William (b. 1924) 340
Cripps, Stafford (1889–1952) 266, 267
Crispi, Francesco (1819–1901) 180
Cromer, Lord (1841–1917) **142–3**
Cronje, Piet (1840–1911) 147
Cultuurstelsel 134

DE GAULLE

Daladier, Edouard (1884–1970) 233
d'Alembert, Jean (1717–83) 166
Dalhousie, Lord (1812–60) 121
d'Annunzio, Gabriele (1863–1938) 226
Danton, Georges (1759–94) 37
Danzig (Gdansk) 224, 234, 291
Dato, Eduardo (1850–1921) 219
Davis, Jefferson (1808–89) **96**
Davout, Louis (1770–1823) 42
Deák, Ferenc (1803–76) 80
Deane, Silas (1737–89) 30–1
Debré, Michel 261
Debs, Eugene V. (1855–1926) 155
Decembrists **47**
Declarations: 'Anti-Colonialist', the 268
    of Independence, Unilateral (Rhod.) 269
    of Independence (US) 22, 26, **27**, 28, 30, **92**
    of Rights and Grievances 26
    of the Rights of Man and the Citizen 22, **34**, 58
    of Rio de Janeiro 246
Decolonization 249, **268–71**, 308–9, 329
De Gasperi, Alcide (1881–1954) **264**
De Gaulle, Charles (1890–1970) **246**, 247, 256, **260–1**, 268, 269, 271, 284, 329
Delgado (1909–50) 336
Dej, Gheorghe Gheorghui- (1901–65) 294
de Maistre, Joseph (1755–1821) **59**, 64
Demirel, Süleyman (b. 1924) 324
Democratic Action **302**
Democratic Movement for Change 319
Democratic Party 95, 98, 154–5, **216–17**
de Polignac, Prince (1780–1847) 64
Depression, the 103, 114, 138, **140**, **141**, 152, 154, 158, 159, 207, **210**, 212, **214–15**, 216, 219, 228, 241
Depretis, Agostino (1813–87) 79
Desai, Morarji (b. 1896) **310**
d'Estaing, Comte (1729–94) 29
Destour Party 271
Détente 252, 258, 294, 299, 339
De Valera, Eamonn (1882–1975) 196
de Wet, Christian (1854–1922) 147
Dewey, George (1837–1917) 134
Dewey, John (1859–1952) 155
d'Holbach, Paul (1723–89) 58
Díaz, Porfirio (1830–1911) **160–1**
Dickinson, John (1732–1808) 27
Diderot, Denis (1713–84) 22, 58
Diefenbaker, John (b. 1895) 278
Dimitrov, Georgi (1882–1949) 295

Dingane 123, 146
Dinwiddie, Robert (1693–1770) 28
Directory, the 37, **38–9**, 169, 170
Disraeli, Benjamin (1804–81) 101, **102**, 146
Djilas, Milovan (b. 1911) 297
Dönitz, Karl (b. 1891) 239, 243
Douglas, Stephen (1813–61) 94, 95
Doumer, Paul (1857–1932) 137
Drake, Edwin (1819–80) 158
Dreyfus, Alfred (1859–1935) **176–7**
Dubček, Alexander (b. 1921) **292**, 294
Du Bois, W. E. B. (1868–1963) 268
Dulles, John Foster (1888–1959) 252, 322
Dumas 46, **184**
Dumoriez, Charles (1739–1823) 37
Dunkirk **238–9**
Durham, Lord (1792–1840) 119
Dylan, Bob (b. 1941) 342

'EVITA'

EAM/ELAS 336
Eanes, Ramalho 336
East India Company 24, **120–1**, 127 (Brit.), **122** (Dutch)
Easter Rising, the **196**
Ecevit, Bülent (b. 1925) **325**
Eden, Anthony (1897–1977) **254**
Eisenhower, Dwight D. (1890–1969) 240, 252, 258, 259, 322
El Agheila 240
El Alamein 240, 242
Engels, Friedrich (1820–95) **85**, 168
Enlightenment, the 19, 31, 46, 47, **58–9**, 85, 88, **162**, **166–7**, 168
Enosis 341
EOKA 341
Erhardt, Ludwig (b. 1897) **262**
Espartero, Baldomero (1792–1879) 66
Estonia 241
'Eurocommunism' 287
European Coal and Steel Community 258, 284
European Economic Community **256**, **258**, 260, 261, 263, 279, 280, 281, 283, **284**, 285, 337
European Free Trade Area 256
Evian Agreement 271, 329

FASCISM

Fabians, the 169
Faisal (b. 1905) 322, **331**, *see also* Feisal
Falange Party **230–1**
Fanelli, Giuseppe 114
Farmers' Union 154

Faruq (1920–65) 322
Fascism 77, 115, 169, 212, 223, **226**, 254, 264, 265, 290, 299, 303, 307, 336
Fashoda (Kodok) 132, 143
Faulkner, Brian (1921–77) 340
Federation of Labour, American **153**, 155
Feisal I (1885–1933) 326, 327, 330
Feisal II (1935–58) 327
Ferdinand, Emperor (1793–1875) 62, 108
Ferdinand II (1816–85) 84
Ferdinand VII (1784–1833) **66**, 88
Ferguson, Adam (1723–1816) 85
Ferry, Jules (1832–93) 176
Fichte, Johann (1762–1814) 59, **166–7**
Fisk, Jim (1834–72) 152
Fiume 226
Ford, Henry (1863–1947) 158
Fouché, Joseph (1763–1820) 39
Fourier, Charles (1772–1837) **168**
Framework Agreement 278
Francis (Franz) I (1708–65) 62
Franco, Francisco (1892–1975) 226, **231**, 336, **337**
Franjieh (Frangiya) 326, 340
Frankfurt Parliament 83
Franklin, Benjamin (1706–90) **26–7**, **30–1**
Franz Ferdinand (1863–1914) 188
Franz Josef I (1830–1916) 80, **108–9**
Fraser, Malcolm (b. 1930) 280
Frederick II (1712–1786) 32
Free Democratic Party 262
Free Officers' Movement **322**, 323
Frei, Eduardo (b. 1911) 305
Fremont, John C. (1813–90) 95
Friedman, Milton (b. 1912) 215
Friedrich Wilhelm III (1770–1840) 62
Friedrich Wilhelm IV (1795–1861) 62, 84, 106, 110
Friendly Societies 61
Friendly Society of Agricultural Workers 61
Front de la Libération Nationale **270–1**, 328, 329
Front de Libération du Québec 342

GENOCIDE

Gadsden Purchase, the 151
Gage, Thomas (1721–87) 25, 26
Galton, Francis (1822–1911) 165
Gandhi, Mohandas K. (1869–1948) **144–5**, 169, 267
Gandhi, Indira (b. 1917) **310**, 313, 315
Garibaldi, Giuseppe (1807–82) **78**
Garrison, William Lloyd (1805–79) 94
Garvey, Marcus (1887–1940) 268
Gates, Horatio (1728–1806) 29
Gaullist Party 260, 261
Gdynia 291
General Union of Workers **219**
'General Will', The **58**
General Zionist Party 318
Geneva Agreements 274
    Conferences 210, 232, 258, 259, 286
Gentz, Friedrich von (1764–1832) 59
George I of Greece 77
George II of Greece 225
George V of Great Britain (1865–1936) 174
George, Henry (1839–97) 154
German colonies 179
Gerö, Ernö (b. 1898) 293

Gierek, Edward (b. 1913) 291
Gil Robles, José María 230
Giolitti, Giovanni (1842–1928) **180**
Girondins 35, 36, 37
Giscard d'Estaing, Valéry (b. 1926) **261**
Gladstone, William Ewart (1809–98) **102–3**, 127
Glubb, John (Pasha) (b. 1897) 330
Godwin, William (1756–1836) **168**
Goldman, Emma (1869–1940) 169
Golitsyn, A. N. (1773–1844) 46
Gompers, Samuel (1850–1924) 153
Gomulka, Wladyslaw (b. 1905) 252, 291, 293
Gonçalves, Vasco 336
Gorchakov, Alexander (1798–1883) 112
Gordon, Charles (1833–85) 143
Göring, Hermann (1893–1946) **232**, 239, 242
Gottwald, K. (1896–1953) 292
Goulart, João (b. 1918) **303**
Gould, Jay (1836–92) **152**
Gowon, Y. (b. 1934) **308**
Grant, Ulysses (1822–85) **96–7**, 171
Grasse, Françoise de (1722–88) 31
Great Trek, The **123**
Green, Nathanael (1742–86) 29
Grenville, George (1712–70) 24
Grey, Edward (1862–1933) **188**
Grey, George (1812–1898) 141
Grimond, Joseph (b. 1913) 254
Grivas, George (1898–1974) 341
Guderian, Heinz (1888–1954) 239
Guernica 231
Guevara, Ernesto 'Che' (1928–67) 306, 342
Guizot, François (1787–1874) 65

HITLER

Haile Selassie (1892–1975) 309
Halifax, Lord (1881–1959) 232
Hallstein, Walter 284
Halsey, William (1882–1959) **244–5**
Hamilton, Alexander (1757?–1804) 92
Hanover Professors, The 62
Hansson, Per-Albin (1885–1946) 241
Harper's Ferry 95
Harriman, Edward H. (1848–1909) 152
Hartington, Lord (1833–1908) 103, 104
Hassan II (b. 1929) **329**
Hastings, Warren (1732–1818) 121
Hay, John (1838–1905) 157
Hayes, Rutherford (1822–93) 98
Hearst, William Randolph (1863–1951) 156
Heath, Edward (b. 1916) 256
Hegel, Friedrich (1770–1831) 59, 84
Helou, Charles (b. 1911?) 326
Helsinki Agreement 289
Herder, Johann von (1744–1803) **166**
Herut Party 318
Hewitt, Abram S. (1822–1903) 158
Hidalgo, Miguel (1753–1811) **89**
Hijackings 321, **342–3**
Hindenburg, Paul von (1847–1934) 198, 228, 232
Hiroshima 245, 247
Hitler, Adolf (1889–1945) 207, 212, 223, 224, 225, 226, **228–9**, 231, **232–4**, 238–41, 242, 246
Ho Chi Minh (1890–1968) 268, **272**, 274
Hohenlohe, Chlodwig (1819–1901) 178
Holy Alliance, the **46**, 67, 80
Home Rule 174–5, 196
Honecker, Erich (1892–1955) 290

Hong Kong 128, 134, 242
Hoover, Herbert (1874–1964) 216
Hopkins, Harry (1890–1946) 217
Houphouet-Boigny, Félix (b. 1905) **269**
Howe, William (1729–1814) 28
Hoxha, Enver (b. 1908) **295**
Huerta, Victoriano (1854–1916) **161**
Hume, Joseph (1777–1855) 60
Husak, Gustav (b. 1913) **292**
Husein, Sharif 330, 331
Hussain (b. 1935) 330, 342

ISRAEL

Ibn Saud, Abdul-Aziz (1880?–1953) **331**
Ibrahim Pasha (1789–1848) 76, 142
Idris (b. 1890) 328
Independent Social Democratic Party 224
Independent Liberal Party 318
Immigration 75, **278–9**, 281, 318, 320
Inflation 199, 256, 283, 290, 291, 302, 303, 305, 307, 319, 323, 324, 325, 340
Inönü, Ismet (1884–1969) **324**
Institutionalized Revolutionary Party **304**
International Bank for Economic Cooperation 285
International Workers of the World 153, 169
Ioannidis (b. 1924) **336**
Irish Party **103**, 174
Ironsi 308
Isabella II (1830–1904) **66**
Islam 86, 87, 121, 143, 144–5, 218, 266–7, 270, 308, 312, 318, 324–5, 326, 328, 331, 340
Ismail (1830–95) **142**
Istiqlal Party 271, 329
Ito (1841–1909) 130
Iturbide, Agustin (1783–1824) 89
Iwakura, Tomomi (1825–83) 130

JEFFERSON

Jackson, Thomas (1824–63) **96–7**
Jacobinism 35, 36, 37, 58, 62, 166
Jahn, Fredrich (1778–1852) 82
Janata Party **310**
Jayawardene, J. R. **315**
Jay, John (1745–1829) 31
Jefferson, Thomas (1743–1826) **26**, 27, 92, 150, 152
Jews, Judaism 81, 86, 184, 228, 263, 318
Jiménez, Marcos Pérez (b. 1914) 302
Jinnah, Mohammad Ali (1876–1948) 144, **266–7**, **312**
Dom João VI (1767–1826) **67**, **90**
Johnson, Andrew (1808–75) **98**
Johnson, Lyndon B. (1908–73) 259, 275, 341
Jones, William (1764–94) 144
Joseph II (1741–90) 32, 35
Juan Carlos (b. 1938) **337**

Juárez, Benito (1806–1972) 160
Jumblat, Kamal 340
Junot, Andoche (1771–1813) 38, 67
Justice Party 324

KIERKEGAARD

Kádár, János (b. 1912) 255, 293
Kadet Party, Russia 184
Kaganovich, L. M. (b. 1893) 288
Kamenev, L. B. (1883–1936) **204**
Kankrin, E. F. (1774–1845) 68
Kant, Immanuel (1724–1804) **166**
Kapp, Wolfgang (1858–1922) 224
Karamanlis, Constantine (b. 1907) **336**
Kassavubu **308**
Katipunan 134
Kaunda, Kenneth (b. 1924) 269, 339
Kemal, Mustafa *see* Atatürk
Kennedy, John Fitzgerald (1917–63) 252, 258, 306, 307
Kenyatta, Jomo (1893?–1978) 269
Kerensky, Alexander (1881–1970) **202–3**
Keynes, John Maynard (1883–1946) 210, 215
Khadafi (Gadaffi) Mu'ammar (b. 1941) **328**
Khalid **331**
Khrushchev, Nikita (1894–1971) 252, 255, 258, 286, **288–9**, 293, 294, 298, 307
Khuri 326
Kierkegaard, Søren (1813–55) 162
Kiesinger, Kurt Georg (b. 1904) **262**
Kissinger, Henry (b. 1923) 275
Kluck, August von 192
Knights of Labor **153**
Kornilov, Lavr 203
Kosciuszko, Tadeusz (1746–1817) 80
Kossuth, Lajos (1802–94) **80**
Kosygin, Alexei (b. 1904) **289**
Kropotkin, Peter (1842–1921) **169**
Kruger, Paul (1825–1904) **146–7**
Ku-Klux-Klan 98
Kulturkampf **110**
Kuo Min Tang (KMT) **220–1**
Kuropatkin, Alexei (1848–1925) **182–3**

LINCOLN

La Harpe, Frederic de (1754–1838) 46
Labour Parties **140**, **280** (Australia); **141**, **281** (New Zealand); **174–5**, 210, 254, **256**, 267 (Britain); 324 (Turkey); *see also* Socialist Parties
Labour Democratic Party 264
Lafayette, Marquis de (1757–1834) 29, **31**, 37, 65
La Follette, Robert (1855–1925) 154
Laos 275
Latvia 241

Index

Laurel, José (1891–1959) 134
Laurens, Henry (1724–92) 31
Laurier, Wilfrid (1841–1919) **138**
Lavon, Pinchas (1904–76) 319
Latifundios **114**
Lawrence, T. E. (1888–1935) 194, 326
League of Nations 138, 209, **210**, 218, 223, 226, 232, 234, 250, 320, 326
Le Chapelier 35
Le Duc Tho (b. 1911) 275
Lee, Arthur (1740–92) 30
Lee Kuan Yew (b. 1923) 272
Lee, Robert E. (1807–70) **96–7**, 98
Legitimists, France **65**
Lenin, Vladimir Ilych (1870–1924) 113, 200, **202–3**, 204, 205, 222, 223, 268, 299
Leningrad 239, 241; *see also* Petrograd *and* St Petersburg
Leo XIII (1810–1903) 176
Leopold, Prince (1853–84) 55
Leopold II, Emperor (1747–92) 35
Leopold I (of Belgium) (1790–1865) 77
Leopold II (of Belgium) (1835–1909) 127, **132**
Leopold III (b. 1901) 77, **263**
Lerdo, Miguel (d. 1861) 160
Liaquat Ali Khan (1895–1951) 312
Liberal-Democratic Party, Japan 282
Liberal-Country Coalition, Australia **280**
Liebknecht, Karl (1871–1919) 224
Likud Party 319
Lincoln, Abraham (1809–65) 92, **95**, **96**, 97, **98**
Linlithgow, Lord (1887–1952) **266–7**
Lin Piao (1908–71) 299
Liston, Robert (1742–1836) 55
Lithuania 241
Liu Shao-ch'i (1898?–1973?) 299
Liverpool, Lord (1770–1828) 60
Lloyd George, David (1863–1945) 104, 155, 174–5, 196, **208–9**, **210**
Lloyd, Henry Demarest (1847–1903) 154
Lloyd, Selwyn (1904–78) 256
Lon-Nol (b. 1913) 275
Louis XVI (1754–93) 31, **32–7**
Louis XVIII (1755–1824) 45, **64**
Louis-Philippe (1773–1850) **64–5**, 106
Louisbourg 118
Louisiana 92, 94, 98, 150
Lovett, William (1800–77) 72
Luanda 132
Ludendorff, Erich (1865–1937) 198, 224
Lueger, Karl (1844–1910) 109
Luftwaffe, the **238–9**
Lumumba, Patrice (1926–61) **308**
Luthuli, Albert (1898?–1967) 338
Luxemburg, Rosa (1870–1919) 224
Lyautey, Louis (1854–1934) 271
Lytton, Lord (1871–1947) 234

MARX
Mably, Bonnot de (1709–85) 58
MacArthur, Douglas (1880–1964) **244–5**, 252, 282
Macaulay, Lord (1800–59) 121
McCulloch, J. R. (1789–1864) 60

Macdonald, John A. (1815–91) **138**
Mackenzie King, William Lyon (1874–1950) **138**, 278
Mackenzie, William Lyon (1795–1861) 118–19
McKinley, William (1843–1901) 156
Macmillan, Harold (b. 1894) 254, 256, 268
Madero, Francisco (1873–1913) **161**
Madison, James (1751–1836) 150
Magnitsky, M. L. 46
Magsaysay, Ramon (1907–57) 276
Mahdi, the (1844?–85) **143**
Mahmud II (1784–1839) 76, 86
Makarios, Archbishop (1913–77) 336, **341**
Malatesta, Errico (1850–1932) 169
Malenkov, Georgi (b. 1901) **288**
Manin, Daniele (1804–57) 78
Manstein, Erich von (1887–1973) 242
Mao Tse-tung (1893–1976) **221**, 259, 287, **298–9**
Mapai Party **318–19**
Marat, Jean-Paul (1743–93) 35
Marcos, Ferdinand (b. 1917) 276
Maria Cristina (1806–78) **66**
Marie Antoinette (1755–93) 35, 37
Maritz, Gerrit (1876–1940) 123
Marmont, Auguste (1774–1852) 38
Maronites 340
Marshall, George (1880–1959) **250–1**
Marshall, John (1755–1835) 92
Marshall Plan **251**, 264, 285
Martov 113
Marx, Karl (1818–83) 70, **84–5**, 113, 162, 168, 169, 170
Marxism 222, 296, 297, 305, 314, 339
Marxism-Leninism 250, 289, 307
Masaryk, T. G. (1850–1937) 232
Matteotti, Giacomo (1885–1924) 226
Mau Mau rebellion **269**
Maurras, Charles (1868–1952) 212
Mazzini, Giuseppe (1805–72) 71, **78**, 106
Meade, George (1815–72) 96, 97
Meir, Golda (b. 1898) 319
Méline, Félix (1838–1912) 176
Mendelianism 165
Menderes, Adnan (1899–1961) **324**
Mendizabel, Juan Alvarez (1790–1853) 66
Mensheviks **113**, 184, 203
Menzies, Robert G. (1894–1978) **280**
Metaxás, Ioannis (1871–1941) 225
Methuen, Lord (1845–1932) 147
Metternich, Klemens von (1773–1859) **56**, 59, 62, 66, 66, 71, 80, 82, 84, 101, 108
Mfecane, the **123**
Miguel, Dom (1802–56) **67**
Mill, John Stuart (1806–73) 73
Mindszenty, József (b. 1892) 255
Minh Mang (1792–1841) 134
Minto, Lord (1845–1914) 145
Mirabeau, Honoré de (1749–91) **34**, 35
Mirs **112**, 184
Missionaries 123, 127, 129, **132**, 136
Mitterrand, François (b. 1916) **261**
Mobutu, Sese Seko (b. 1930) **308**
Mohammed (Mehmet) Ali (1769?–1849) 76, **142**, 331
Molotov, V. M. (b. 1890) 288
Moltke, Helmuth von (1848–1916) 189, 192
Monnet, Jean (b. 1888) 284
Monroe, James (1758–1831) 157
Montgomery, Richard (1738?–75) 28
Morelos, José Maria (1765–1815) 89
Morgan, John P. (1837–1913) 152, **159**
Moro, Aldo (1916–1978) 265
Morris, William (1834–96) 169
Moscicki, Ignacy (1867–1946) 224
Moshesh (c. 1786–1870) 123
Mosley, Oswald (b. 1896) 210
Mountbatten, Lord (b. 1900) **267**, 272
Movement, Party of 65

Mugabe, Robert 339
Muhammad V (1910–61) 271, 329
Mujibur Rahman (1920–1975) **312**, **313**
Müller, Johannes (1752–1809) 22, 59
Munich Agreement **233**, 234
Musadiq (Mossadegh), Muhammad 332
Muslim Brotherhood Party **322**
Muslim League **144**, **266–7**
Mussolini, Benito (1883–1945) **226**, 231, 233, **246**, 264
Mutiny, Indian **120**
Muzorewa, Abel (b. 1925) 339
Mzilikazi (c. 1790–1868) 123

NASSER
Naguib, Mohammed (b. 1901) 322
Nagy, Ferenc (b. 1903) 255
Nagy, Imre (1896–1958) 252, **255**, **293**
Napoleon I (1769–1821) 37, **38–45**, 48, 56, 58, 64, 66, 67, 68, 69, 80–1, 82, 88, 90, 120, 134, 150, 169
Napoleon III (1808–73) 71, 78, 84, **106**, 170–1, 176
Narayan, J. P. (b. 1902) 310
Narvaez, Ramón (1800–68) **66**
Nasser, Gamal Abdul (1918–70) **254**, 320, **322–3**, 326, 327, 331
National Committee of the Homeland, Greece 225
National Confederation of Labour, Spain, **219**
National Economic Development Council 256
National Liberal Federation of India 144, 145
National Organization of Greek Fighters 341
National Party **281** (Australia), 305 (Chile), **338** (South Africa)
National Peasant Party, Hungary 255
National Radical Union, Greece 336
National Socialist Party *see* Nazism
Nationalism **70–91**, **166–7**
Navarro, Carlos Arias **337**
Nazism 212, 225, **228**, **232–3**, 260, 262, 290
Necker, Jacques (1732–1804) 33
Nehru, Jawaharlal (1899–1964) 145, **266–7**, 268, **310**
Nenni, Pietro (b. 1891?) 264
Neto, Antonio (b. 1922) 307
Neurath, Constantin von (1873–1956) 232
New Deal, the **216–17**
Ne Win (b. 1911) **314**
New Zealand Association 124
Ngo Dinh Diem (1901–63) 259, 274, 275
Nguyen Van Thieu (b. 1923) **275**
Nice 106
Nicholas I (1796–1855) **68**, 84
Nicholas II (1868–1917) 189, 199
Nimitz, Chester (1885–1966) 244
Nixon, Richard (b. 1913) 252, 259, 275, 282, 294, 298
Nkomo, Joshua (b. 1917) 339

Nkrumah, Kwame (1909–72) 268, 269
Non-Aligned Countries, Group of 300–1, 304
North Atlantic Treaty Organization 252, 258, 263, 278, 325, 336
North, Lord (1732–92) 24, 27, 31
Noske, Gustav (1868–1946) 224
Novalis, Friedrich (1772–1801) 59
Novotny, Antonin (1904–75) **292**
Nuclear weapons 186, 237, **245**, 247, 249, 283, 288, 299, 310, 335
Numairi (Nimeiry), Jaafar 323
Nuri es-Said (1888–1958) 327
Nyerere, Julius (b. 1922) 269

ORANGE ORDER

O'Connor, Fergus (1794–1855) **72**
O'Donnell, Leopold (1809–67) 66
Oil 259, 279, **283**, 284, **302**, 303, 304, 321, 325, 327, 328, 329, 330, **331–3**
Ojukwe (b. 1933) **308**
Ollivier, Emile (1825–1912) 106
Olmütz (Olomouc) 84
Onn, Datuk Hussein 272
Organisation de l'Armée Secrète 271
Organization of African Unity 309
Organization for European Economic Cooperation 251, 285
Organization of Petroleum Exporting Countries **333**
Orlando, V. E. (1860–1952) 209
Orleanism **65**
Ortega y Gasset, José (1883–1955) 114
Osmeña, Sergio (1878–1961) 134
Otto (1815–67) 77
Owen, Robert (1771–1858) **168**

POLLUTION

Pacts: Anti-Comintern 232
   Baghdad 310, 322, 330
   Lebanese National 326
   Nazi-Soviet 223, 225
   Polish-German Non-Aggression 224, 232
   Russo-German Non-Aggression 234
   Sino-American 298
   'of Steel' 226, 234

Warsaw: see Warsaw Treaty Organization
Western European Union 251
Paine, Thomas (1737–1809) **27, 59**
Pais, Sidónio (1872–1918) **115**
Paisley, Ian (b. 1926) 340
Palestine Liberation Organization **320, 321**
Palmerston, Lord (1784–1865) 80, 84, 128
Panama Canal 149, **156–7**
Paoli, Pasquale (1725–1807) 38
Papadopoulous, George (b. 1919) **336**
Papandreou, George (b. 1919) 336
Papen, Franz von (1880–1969) 228
Papineau, Louis Joseph (1786–1871) 119
Parnell, Charles Stewart (1846–91) **103**
Parti Québecois 278, 279
Pasternak, Boris (1890–1960) 289
Pathet Lao 274, **275**
Paul I (1754–1801) 46
Paulus, Fredrich von (b. 1890) **242**
Pearl Harbor 242, 272
Pearson, Lester (1897–1972) **278**
Peasant Party (Poland) 291
Pedro I (Dom Pedro) (1798–1834) **67, 90**
Pedro II (1825–91) **91**
Peel, Robert (1788–1850) 60, 61, 72, 74, 102
People's Parties 232, 312, 313
Périer, Casimir (1717–1832) 65
Perón, Eva Duarte (1919–52) **307**
Perón, Isabel **307**
Perón, Juan (1895–1974) **307**
Perry, Matthew (1794–1858) 130
Peters, Carl (1856–1918) 179
Petrograd 199, 202–3; see also St Petersburg
Phalangist Party 340
Phibunsongkram 137, 272, 274
Philippe Egalité (1747–93) **64**
Phnom Penh 275
Pilsudski, Josef (1867–1935) 224
Pinchot, Gifford (1865–1946) 155
Pinilla, Gustavo Rojas (b. 1900) 302
Pinochet, Auguste (b. 1915) **305**
Pitt, William (1708–78) 26
Pitt, William (1759–1806) 48
Pius VII (1740–1823) 45
Pius IX (1792–1878) 78, 106
Place, Francis (1771–1854) 60, 72
Plaid Cymru 256
Plekhanov, George (1857–1918) **113**
Podgorny, Nikolai (b. 1903) 289
Poincaré, Henri (1854–1912) 165
Poincaré, Raymond (1860–1934) 212
Politburo, the 204, 288, 289
Polk, James K. (1795–1849) 151
Pollution 346
Pompidou, Georges (1911–74) **261**
Poor Law 175
Pope, John (1822–92) 96
Popular Front 212 (France), 230 (Spain), 305 (Chile)
Population, world **346**
Populist Party, USA **154**
Poqo 338
'Porfiriato' **160–1**
Potgieter, Hendrik (1808–75) 123
Potsdam 246, 247
   Agreement 250
   Conference 291
Powderley, Terence (1849–1924) 153
Pretorius, Andries (1819–1901) 146
Pridi, Panomyong (b. 1900) 274
Primo de Rivera, José Antonio (1903–36) 231
Primo de Rivera, Miguel (1870–1930) **219**
Princip, Gavrilo (1895–1918) 188
Progressive Party 110, 318
Progressivism **154–5**
Protestantism 25, 74, 77, 174–5, 228, **340**
Proudhon, Pierre-Joseph (1809–65) 168, **169**
Pullman strike 153

'THE QUEEN'

Qasim (Kassem) 327
Quadruple Alliance 46
Quezon, Manuel L. (1878–1944) 134

RHODES

Rabin, Yitzhak (b. 1922) 319
Radetzky, Joseph (1766–1858) 84
Radic, Stjepan (1871–1928) 296
Radical Party **212**
Rajk, László (1906–49) 293
Rakosi, Matyas (1892–1971) **255, 293**
Rashid Ali al-Ghailani (b. 1892) **327**
Rasputin, Gregor (1872?–1916) 199
Rassemblement Démocratique Africaine **269**
Redmond, John (1856–1918) 174, 196
Republican Party (USA) 95, 98, 155, 217
Republican People's Party (Turkey) 218, 324–5
Retief, Piet 123, 146
Revere, Paul (1735–1818) 26
Revolutions: see also Wars:
   American **24–31**, 33, **58–9**, 118, 124, 200
   Chinese **220–1**, 298, **299**
   French 31, 33, **34–7**, 41, 42, 48, 54–5, 56, **58–9**, 62, 64–5, 68, 82, 118, 166–7, 168, 169, 171, 200
   European 58–9, 84–5
   in German states 82–3
   Hungarian 68, 249, **255**, 258, 287
   Mexican **89**, 150, **160–1**
   in Ottoman Empire **86–7**, 142
   Russian 47, 68, **112–13**, **184**, 199, **200–5**, 220, 222, 226, 241
Reza Khan (1877–1944) 332
Reza Pahlavi, Muhammad (b. 1919) 332
Rhodes, Cecil (1853–1902) 132, **146–7**
Rhodesian Front 339
Ricardo, J. E. S. (1772–1823) 73
Riego, Rafael de (1785–1823) 66

Index

Riel, Louis (1844–85) **138**
Risorgimento, the **78–9**
Robespierre, Maximilien de (1758–94) 23, 36, **37**, 58
Rockefeller, John D. (1839–1937) **152**, 154
Rockingham, Lord (1730–82) 24
Romanticism 41, **162**, **166–7**
Rommel, Erwin (1891–1944) **240**, 242, 322
Roosevelt, Franklin Delano (1882–1945) 207, **216–17**, 246, 247, 306
Roosevelt, Theodore (1859–1919) 134, 149, **155–7**, 183, 187
Rosecrans, William (1819–98) 96
Rote Armeé Fraktion (RAF) 342
Rousseau, Jean-Jacques (1712–78) 58, 59, 85, **166**, 168
Roux, Abbé (d. 1794) 37
Rowntree, Joseph (1836–1925) 104
Roxas, Manuel (1894–1948) 134
Runciman, Lord (1870–1949) 233
Runich, D. P. 46

STRIKE

Sadat, Anwar al- (b. 1918) **321**, 323
Sagasta, Práxedes Mateo (1825–1903) 114
Said (1822–63) 142
Saint Just, Louis de (1767–94) 37
St Laurent, Louis 278
St Petersburg
    Protocol of 76
Saint-Simon, Henri de (1760–1825) 70, **168**
Salazar, Antonio de Oliveira (1889–1970) **115**, 169, 303, 336
Salisbury, Robert Cecil, Lord (1830–1903) **103–5**
San Martin, José de (1778–1850) **89**
Sans-culottes **36–7**
Sarajevo 188
Sarekat Islam 134
Sato, Eisaku (b. 1901) 283
Saud (1902–69) **331**
Schacht, Hjalmar (1877–1970) **232**
Scheel, Walter (b. 1919) 262
Schleicher, Kurt von (1882–1934) 228
Schleiden, Matthias (1804–81) 55
Schlieffen Plan **198**
Schönerer 109
Scientific developments **20–1**, 51, **52–5**, 109, 163, **164–5**, **186**, **344–5**
Seddon, 'King Dick' (1845–1906) 141
Séguin, Marc (1786–1875) 53
Selim III (1761–1808) 86
Senghor, Léopold (b. 1906) 269
Serfdom, Russian 46, 47, 68, **112–13**
Sétif 270
Shaka (1773–1828) **123**
Shamoun 326
Sharpeville 338
Shastri, Lal Bahadur (1904–66) 310
Sherman, William (1820–91) **96–7**
Shihab (Chehab) 326
Sidqi, Bakr (d. 1937) 327
Sieyès, Abbé (Emmanuel) (1758–1836) 33, 39, 58, 166
Sihanouk, Norodom (b. 1922) 274, 275
Sikorski, Igor (1889–1972) 186

Sikorski, Wladyslaw (1881–1943) 225
Simonstown 147
Simpson, James (1811–70) 55
Sithole, Ndabaningi (b. 1920) 339
Slavery 90, **91**, **94–5**, 98, 122, **132**
Smallholders' Party 255
Smith, Adam (1723–90) 73, 168
Smith, Ian (b. 1919) **339**
Smuts, J. C. (1870–1950) **147**
Smyrna (Izmir) 225
Sobhuza (b. 1899) 123
Sobukwe, Robert 338
Social Credit Party 138
Social Democrat Parties 110, 178, **224**, 232, 250, **262** (Germany); 109 (Austria)
Social Democratic Labour Party, Russian **113**, 290
Socialism 155, **168–9**, 204, 286, 309
Socialist Parties **155** (USA); **180**, **196**, **226**, **264–5** (Italy); **212**, **261** (France); 283 (Japan); 305 (Chile); *see also* Labour Parties
Socialist Programme Party, Burma **314**
Socialist Revolutionary Party **113**, 184, 203
Socialist Unity Party 250, **290**
Socialist Workers' Party, Hungarian 293
Soshangane 123
Sotelo, José Calvo (1892–1936) 231
South-East Asia Treaty Organization 310
Soviets **184**, **202–3**
Soweto 339
Spartacists **224**
Speransky, M. M. (1772–1839) 46
Spinola, Antonio (b. 1910) 336
Spionkop 147
Sri Lanka Freedom Party **314–15**
Stakhanovites 222
Stalinism 255, **288–9**, 290, 293, 294, 295
Stalin, Joseph (1879–1953) 203, **204–5**, 221, **222–3**, 239, 247, 250–1, 252, 255, 258, 286, 288–9, 293, 295, 296, 336
Stark, John (1728–1822) 29
Stauning, Torvald (1873–1942) 241
Stavisky Affair, the 212
Steffens, Lincoln (1866–1936) 155
Stevens, Thaddeus (1792–1868) 98
Stolypin, Petr (1863–1911) **184**
Strategic Arms Limitation Talks 258
Stresemann, Gustav (1878–1929) 212, 228
Suárez, Adolfo **337**
Sucre, Antonio José de (1793–1830) 89
Suez Canal 102, **142–3**, 194, 196, **254**, 278, 310, 320, 321, **322–3**, 330
Suharto 276
Sukarno (1901–70) 134, **272**, **276**
Sumner, Charles (1811–74) 98
Sun Yat-sen (1867–1925) 129, **220–1**
Szczecin (Stettin) 291
Széchenyi, István 80

Taft, William Howard (1857–1930) 149, **155**
Taiping Uprising, the **128**
Talal 330
Talleyrand, Charles de (1754–1838) 35, 39
Tanaka, Kakuei (1863–1929) **283**
Tarbell, Ida (1857–1944) 155
Tawfiq 142
Terror, the 23, 36, **37**, 39, 65
    Red 203
    Stalin's **222–3**
Terrorism **112–14**, 145, 219, 231, 262, **265**, 305, 320, 340, **342–3**
Teschen (Cieszyn) 81
Thiers, Adolphe (1797–1877) 65, **176**
Tildy, Zoltán 255
Tin U 314
Tirpitz Plan **179**

TERRORISM

Tisza, Stephen (1861–1918) 189
Tito, Josip (b. 1892) 246, 247, 251, 286, 295, **296–7**, 298, 336
Tocqueville, Charles de (1805–59) 70
Togliatti, Palmiro (1893–1964) 264
Tolpuddle Martyrs, the **61**
Tolstoy, Leo (1828–1910) 162, 169
Torres, Camilo **302**
Tory Party **60–1**, **102**; *see also* Conservative Party
Touré, Sékou 269
Townshend, Charles (1725–67) 24
Trade unions **60–1**, 72, 77, 140, 153, 168, 169, 174, **175**, 176, 184, 215, **219**, 223, 228, 256, 264, 280, 282, 302, 303, 304, 305, 307, 319, 324, 336
Treaties: Adams-Onis 150
    Amiens 39, 44, 122, 150
    Anglo-Iraqi 326
    Anglo-Japanese commercial 131
    Ashburton-Webster 151
    Brest-Litovsk 203
    Cobden-Chevalier 106
    Indo-Soviet Friendship 310
    Lausanne 218, 341
    London 76, 84, 196
    Nanking 128
    Neuilly 208
    North Atlantic 252
    Nuclear Test Ban 258
    Paris **31**, 68, **118**
    Peace with Japan **282**
    Rapallo 223
    Riga 224
    Rome 284
    Saigon 136
    Saint-Germain 208
    San Stefano 295
    Sèvres 208, 326
    Shimonoseki **131**
    Tientsin 137
    Tilsit 42, 69
    Trianon 208
    Versailles **208–9**, 224, 228
    Vienna 64
    Waitangi **124**
Triple Alliance 101, 180, 196
Trotsky, Leon (1877–1940) 202, **203**, 204, **222**, 288
Trudeau, Pierre (b. 1919) 278
Truman, Harry S. (1884–1972) **250–1**, 252, 282
Trumbull, Lyman (1813–96) 98
Tseng Kuo-fan 128
Tshombe, Moïse (1918–69) **308**
Tupamaros 342
Turner, Nat (rising) (1800–31) **94**

UNITED NATIONS

U-boats 198, **239**, **243**
Ulbricht, Walter 290
Umkonto we Sizwe 338
Unamuno, Miguel de (1864–1936) 114
U Nu **314**
Unemployment 210, 214–15, 216, 217, 228, 232, 239, 256, 303, 305, 307, 340
Union National des Forces Populaires 329
Union Nationale 138
Union of Liberation 112
Unionist Party 104–5, **174–5**, **196**
Unionist Party, Ulster **340**
United Empire Loyalists 118
United Liberation Front, Tamil 315
United National Party **314–15**
United Nations Organization 249, **250**, 252, 258, 259, 267, 268, 278, 282, 293, 299, 301, 304, 308, 320, 321, 322, 323, 324, 325, 328, 329, 330, 346
United Workers' Party, Polish 291
Uys, Piet 123
Uvarov, Sergey (1785–1855) 68

VIETNAM WAR

Vanderbilt, Cornelius (1794–1877) 152
Vargas, Getulio (1883–1954) **303**
Varlet, Jean 37
Velasco 303
Venizelos, Eleftherios (1864–1942) 77, **225**
Veracruz 161
Vergennes, Charles de (1717–87) 30, 31
Versailles Peace Conference **208–9**, 220, 226
Verwoerd, Hendrik (1869–1966) 338
Victor Emmanuel II (1820–78) 106
Victoria (1819–1901) 55, 102, 103, 171
Vienna, Congress of **56**, 58, **62**, 67
Viet Minh 272, 274
Villa, 'Pancho' 161
Villèle, Jean Baptiste de (1773–1854) 64
Vogel, Julius (1835–99) 141
Voltaire, François de (1694–1778) 18, 19, 58
Voortrekkers **123**, 146
Vorster, Balthazar **339**
Vyshnegradsky 112

WOODROW WILSON

Wafd Party 322
Wakefield, Edward (1796–1862) **124**
Wang Ching-wei 234
Warren, Joseph (1741–75) 24
Wars: Aceh 134
   Afghan 102, 120
   African 336, 339
   American, of Independence **24–31**, 33, **58–9**, 118, 124, 200
   American-Mexican 94, 151
   Arab-Israeli 249, **319–21**, 322–3
   Arab-Egyptian 142
   Austro-Hungarian **80**
   Austro-Danish 110
   Austro-Prussian 106, 108
   Balkan 77, 87, 173, 188, 294, 295
   British-Afghanistan 102, 120
   British-French 60, 118, 150
   Burmese 120
   Civil: American 66, 92, **94–8**, 142, 151, 154, 158, 217
      Angolan **339**
      Argentinian 307
      Biafran 249, **308**
      Chinese **221**, 252
      Colombian **302**
      Cuban **306**
      Ethiopian 249, **309**
      Finnish **241**
      Greek 76, **250–1**, 336
      Hungarian **80**
      Indian **267**
      Japanese **130**
      Lebanese 326, **340**
      Nigerian 249, **308**
      Northern Irish **340**, 342
      Portuguese **67**
      South African 101, **104**, 117, **147**
      Spanish **66**, 219, 226, **230–1**, 336, 337
      Spanish American **88–90**
      Yemeni 249, 322, 331
      Zaire 249, **308**
   'Cold' 252, 258–9, 264, 268, 298
   Crimean 68, 78, 81, 106, 108, 110, 171
   Franco-Algerian **270–1**
   Franco-Austrian 36–7
   Franco-Italian 106
   Franco-Prussian 36–7, **106**, 110
   Franco-Vietnamese **136–7**
   Indo-Chinese **136–7**, 252, 310
   Indo-Pakistan 249, 267, 310, 312
   Korean **252**, 258, 260, 282, **298**, 322, 325
   Maori 124, 141
   Napoleonic **38–9**, **42–3**, 44, 45, **48**, 56, 77, 118, 122
   Opium 116, **128**, 299
   Russo-Japanese 101, 157, **182–3**, 184
   Russo-Polish **81**, 224
   Russo-Turkish 86, 112
   Sino-Japanese **131**, **221**, **234**
   Spanish American 131, 148, 156
   Vietnam 249, 258, **259**, 272, **274–5**, 280, 281, 343
   World, First 75, 77, 86, 96, 115, 127, 138, 140, 141, 143, 144–5, 153, 155, 157, 159, 173, 175, 180, 182, 184, 186, **188–99**, 207, **208–9**, 210, 212, 214, 218, 219, 220, 223, 224, 225, 232, 241, 294, 295, 332
   World, Second 77, 134, 137, 138, 141, 210, 214, 217, 221, 225, 226, **232–47**, 249, **250–1**, 258, 260, 262, 263, 264, 266, 272, 278, 282, 294, 295, 296, 322, 324, 328, 332, 336
   Zulu 102, 117, **123**, 146
Warsaw Treaty Organization 252, 258, 287, 291, 293, 294
Washington, George (1732–99) 27, **28–9**, 31
Weathermen 342
Weizmann, Chaim 318
Welfare schemes, state 51, 141, **174**, **175**, 210, 237, 256, 281, 290, 304, 305, 307, 309, 315, 322, 330
Wellington, Duke of (1769–1852) 42, **61**, 74
Whig Party 72, **102**
White, Henry (1850–1927) 157
Whitlam, Gough (b. 1916) **280**
Whitlock, Brand (1869–1934) 154
Wilhelm I (1797–1888) **110**
Wilhelm II (1859–1941) 110, 171, **178–9**, 189
Willem I (1772–1843) 77
Wilson, Harold (b. 1916) 256
Wilson, Woodrow (1856–1924) 149, **154–5**, 198, **208–9**
Witte, Sergei (1849–1915) 112, 184
Working Men's Association, London 72
Wu Ch'ang 129

YALTA

Yahya Khan 312
Yalta Conference 246, 247
Yamamoto (1883–1943) 244
Yenan 221
Yüan Shih-k'ai (1859–1916) **220**

ZAPU

Zaglul, Saad 322
Zapata, Emilio (1877?–1919) 161
Zapotocky 292
Zemstvos **112**, 184
Zhivkov, Todor **295**
Zia ul-Haq, Mohammad 312, **313**
Ziaur Rahman **313**
Zimbabwe African People's Union 339
Zimbabwe African Nationalist Union 339
Zinoviev, Grigori (1883–1936) **204**, 210
Zionism 318
Zog (1895–1961) 295

In the second half of the 18th century thinking Europeans embraced the prospect of modernity and the future with new ebullience. Armed with reason and science, they believed fatalism would be routed and replaced by the breezy confidence that educated man could master his fortune. Even the perennial scourges of penury, disease and massacre would retreat before the advance of prosperity and enlightenment.

To be sure, this Elysian vision would not be realized at once. 'The world marches *slowly* to its wisdom,' the *philosophes* wrote, well aware that the worlds of knowledge and credulousness co-existed in peculiar juxtaposition. In 1771 Voltaire reminded his acolytes that 'more than half the world remains populated by two-footed animals living in a horrible condition . . . barely enjoying the gift of speech, living and dying practically without knowing it.'

Given time, though, and the gradual diffusion of knowledge, all that might be changed. And some of it already was. The last major visitation of bubonic plague was at Marseilles in 1722. The exterminating famines of the 17th century would never return and infant mortality was falling because of better and more balanced nutrition. The radius of ignorance was shrinking all the time with the opening up of new communications on turnpike roads and canals.

The apostles of modernity saw themselves as engaged into two major enterprises. The first was to clear away the clutter of inherited barbarities, superstitions and unreasoned dogma.

The second enterprise was to replace myth with a body of scientific propositions and laws, testable by logic and observation, that would make the true workings of both the material and the human world discernible to all reasoning men. In this way only the nature of the prime mover would remain obscure.

The political economists believed that all they were doing was uncovering the laws of nature pertaining to man's function as *homo*

economicus. Remove the artificial constraints imposed by ramshackle despotisms, and human welfare would flower of its own accord. The other major axiom of the time, that of utility, could point in the opposite direction of more, not less government. Given that the end of government was to secure happiness, its legitimacy might have to rest on the degree to which it promoted the 'greatest happiness of the greatest number'.

Was the modern world, then, to be one in which the individual, free and educated, would find his allotted role in the scheme of things, or one in which he would be steered to it by a body of omniscient legislators? None of the philosophers yet knew, and few were agreed about priorities. But Voltaire was at least sure that 'Everything I see scatters the seeds of a revolution which will definitely come. . . . The Enlightenment has gradually spread so that it will burst into light at the first opportunity and then there will be a fine uproar.' *S. S.*

THE BIRTH OF THE MODERN WORLD

**Below, from left to right:
Voltaire, Rousseau, Diderot, Tom Paine.**

Science and Social Change

The Swedish botanist Carl von Linné, Latinized as Linnaeus for the publication of his scientific work, produced his revolutionary system for the classification of plants in a series of works from 1730. Hitherto the families of plants and animals had been established by physical likeness and comparative anatomy. Linnaeus held that physical or morphological similarities in nature may be the result of environmental conditioning of unrelated species, and consequentially 'accidental'. He showed that plants and animals were only truly related if they could interbreed, and thus his classification had a sexual basis.

Linnaeus's *Philosophia Botanica* of 1750 was translated into English by a country doctor and amateur scientist, Erasmus Darwin of Lichfield in the industrial north midlands of England. Darwin was strongly influenced by Linnaeus's ideas, and attempted to apply them further in two directions.

The first was to use Linnean classification to describe the works of man. Darwin's long, didactic poem 'The Botanic Garden' is as much about science, machines and industry as it is about plants and their use, full of classical imagery and allegory. Darwin's stated intention was to 'enlist the imagination under the Banner of Science'. The strange subtitle, 'The Loves of the Plants', is a direct reference to Linnaeus's classification, and by it Darwin attempted to demonstrate that ideas and inventions also evolve and interbreed.

The other was to take the idea of evolution further in his *Zoonomia* ('laws of animal life'), in which Darwin outlined a theory of natural selection which would later be developed by his grandson, Charles Darwin. In turn, Charles Darwin saw his theory of evolution and natural selection applied, too, in social science, politics and economics with far-reaching consequences in the 20th century.

The idea of classification was fundamental to the 18th century and onwards. Agreed terms, names and labels were essential to the development of science and technology and the interchange of knowledge. Systems of classification of all knowledge and phenomena were applied, in encyclopedias, in libraries, and in industry and society. Even feelings were not exempt, and the science of aesthetics, or the description of response to art, music and poetry, was born.

Traditionally, the scientist or 'philosopher', as he was commonly known, had been an observer and commentator, carefully looking at both the world of nature and the works of man alike, and drawing abstract conclusions of general principles or laws from what he saw. The engineer was the practical man, who could build bridges and buildings without knowing the rules of statics and dynamics, build mills and machines and sail ships against the wind without knowing the forces involved, while the scientist watched him and analysed his work.

At the beginning of the 18th century, the roles of scientist and engineer changed dramatically, and it may be said that the steam engine was the first invention to be derived from applying scientific theory rather than from practical experiment. A shortage of timber, and then of coal, had led to deeper mining. Pumps were needed to keep the mines clear of water. Experimenters such as Evangelista Torricelli in Italy and Otto von Guericke in north Germany had carried out vital measurements and demonstrations of the vacuums and the force of atmospheric pressure. Simultaneous inventions to use these forces quickly followed in other parts of Europe, including the use of steam to form a vacuum by condensation.

The most practical of these inventions was the engine built in 1712 by Thomas Newcomen, an English ironmonger. Although referred to as a steam engine, it was more properly a vacuum engine, for it was the weight of atmospheric air bearing upon the surface of a very large piston that provided the working force for his machine. He used the simple technology of his day. He combined a distiller's copper boiler with a cylinder from a cannon foundry. All his piping came from domestic plumbing. A millwright built the engine beam, a mason the engine frame, and a blacksmith made all the ironwork. Newcomen used a very low steam pressure, just equal to the atmosphere, and kept his cylinder airtight with a packing of wet tow. The engine was crude but, unlike its more sophisticated competitors, it worked.

Even more important than the commercial impact of the first steam-driven pump was the effect that it had on the mind and imagination. From now on the scientist would be involved practically in the development of technology as a researcher and innovator. It was a turning point, the first vital step in the Industrial Revolution.

Jeremy Bentham, an English materialist who tried to apply rational science to the organization of society, held that ultimately the only reliable instinct in man was that of self-preservation at all costs, a law of nature for the preservation of the species. However, no individual could survive against the forces of nature without cooperation. Thus Bentham envisaged an ideal social structure based upon enlightened self-interest and coined the phrase 'for the greatest happiness of the greatest number'.

He believed that all institutions should be judged by their utility to this given end, and put forward an elaborate table of aims and motives. Bentham's influence was strong in two fields. The first was that of education, which he saw as the foundation of reformed society. He was instrumental in founding University College, London, as a secular institution free from church control, and his utilitarian principles were a guiding factor in the growth of state education in Britain in the 19th century.

His second field of influence was in architecture. Bentham conceived the idea of the 'panoptikon', literally a 'see-all' building as the physical embodiment of his principles of enlightened control. Perhaps unfortunately, his main influence here was, and still is, in prison buildings. The basic plan is star shaped, or concentric. The centre of control is the physical centre of the building. From here authority is delegated through successive levels. The supervisor can see exactly what his subordinates or their charges are doing at any one time, down to the remotest individual at the furthest end.

Bentham proposed his panoptikon as being ideal for mills and factories for the centralized control of systems of production by division of labour and standardization of parts, but the most familiar example of Benthamite architecture is the centralized library, epitomized by that designed by Sydney Smirke for the reading room of the British Museum, London.

This, a later addition to the new classical building designed by Sydney's elder brother Sir Robert Smirke, is a purely industrial utilitarian structure. Surmounted by an

D'Alembert and other brilliant intellectuals gathering round Diderot, editor of the 'Encyclopédie', at his salon attended by aristocratic patrons of enlightened views (painting by Lemounier, 1760)

Voltaire, tireless pamphleteer against ignorance and the abuse of privilege, dictates while getting dressed

iron dome 106 feet high with no internal supports, the plan is concentric. Readers' tables radiate like the spokes of a wheel, along which a clear view is afforded of each reader at work. At the centre is the librarian's desk, with an outer system of circular desks for assistants in order of seniority. The outermost ring was to house the catalogue as well as being the issuing desk. Round the walls of the circular building the book stacks are arranged in galleried tiers. Classified, indexed and docketed, all could be controlled from the one centre point in an orderly way. The Benthamite system was to influence exhibition buildings and department stores down to the present day.

B. L. M.

THE FIRST MODERN

The modern nation state was born in the fire and passion of revolution, two hundred years ago. Its enthusiasts, who in America and Europe brandished their optimism in the face of the moth-eaten monarchies they had so spectacularly humiliated, were emphatic about the new age they were ushering in. A universal regeneration, they announced, would make free citizens out of craven subjects, enlightened men out of ignorant and superstitious brutes, and in place of arbitrary despotisms and bloated aristocracies would institute the rule of the people: virtuous, just, humane, wise and patriotic.

'God,' said the Swiss historian Johannes Müller on hearing of the fall of the Bastille, 'wishes to electrify the human race.' But many other celebrants would have echoed the belief of the philosopher Diderot that after primitive man, pagan man and Christian man, there

would follow the age of rational man. The application of the human intellect, unfettered by deference to thrones and altars, would now achieve an unprecedented transformation in the condition of humanity. Hunger, poverty and disease would recede before the inexorable advance of science and industry and even war, hitherto the deadly chess game of tyrants, would be precluded by the revolt of the pawns. 'If we succeed,' wrote the poet André Chenier, 'the destiny of Europe will be changed.'

Only a small part of these lofty expectations was destined to be fulfilled. The American Declaration of Independence and the French Declaration of the Rights of Man enshrined for posterity the essential axioms of modern democracy, most notably the *assumption* that men were born free and equal and that the only legitimate authorization for government derived from their consent. However much governing

DEMOCRACIES

élites dissented from that presumption, all would have to take account of the potency of its message to those without democratic rights. But away from the realm of ideas, the blood-spattered history of the French Revolution turned the stomachs of many of its original supporters, as well as stiffening the resistance of its most determined opponents. The Reign of Terror, which devoured many of the early heroes of liberty, bequeathed to subsequent generations of moderates and liberals the queasy apprehension that revolutions were exterminating angels, beckoning with a beacon of light in one hand and a razor-edged sword in the other. As French armies rampaged across Europe, Robespierre's warning that 'no one loves armed missionaries' was alarmingly vindicated, and the continent became embroiled not in a crusade of peoples against despots but in a protracted resistance to French hegemony.

If the flamboyant promise of the Revolution died with its apostles on the guillotine and the battlefield, its most compelling dreams remained to haunt the new century and the modern world. The inspirational summons of the Marseillaise, the subterranean rumble of a great volcanic lava flow that one day would erupt and sweep away the accumulated corruption of centuries, continued to trouble the sleep of the powerful from that day to this. The philosopher-turned-revolutionary Marquis de Condorcet himself perished at the hands of revolutionary proscription, but his utopian promise remained imperishable. 'The moment will come,' he wrote 'when the sun will shine only on free men who recognize no master other than their reason; when tyrants and slaves, priests and their stupid or hypocritical instruments will exist only in history or on the stage.'

S. S.

American Discontents

Between the 'Glorious Revolution' of 1688 and the end of the Seven Years War in 1763, France and Britain fought four wars for European and colonial supremacy. The last of the series ended with Britain as the dominant power in North America. France was forced to give up her claims to Canada and to all land east of the Mississippi River. In the years that followed, however, the British slowly came to realize that this elimination of French influence had been a mixed blessing. So long as a French threat existed, the American colonists were closely bound to Britain by their need for protection. After 1763, with this tie weakened, the colonists became increasingly fractious. In particular, they raised strong objection to the attempt on the part of several British ministers to make them shoulder part of the financial burden of imperial defence.

To the British government, this seemed a not unreasonable request. French power might have been broken, but there were still Indians menacing the western frontier. British troops had had to be used to put down Pontiac's Indian rebellion of 1763–66, when it had seemed that the colonies were incapable of cooperating among themselves even in their own defence. The Indian problem overlapped with several other issues that were to be causes of friction between the American colonists and Britain in the years after the Seven Years War. One was the control and regulation of the lucrative fur trade. Another, even more important, was British policy over land and future settlement. A royal proclamation of 1763 barred settlers from the trans-Allegheny territory until the Indians there had been pacified and a comprehensive approach to the settlement of the area had been worked out. British ministers were obviously alive to the dangers of indiscriminate settlement by the colonists.

The response of the American colonists to the various attempts made to tax them between 1764 and 1773 varied considerably. The duties on imported sugar and other commodities imposed in the Revenue Act of 1764 were annoying to many Americans, who responded by boycotting products taxed under the Act, but these duties caused nothing like the furore provoked by the Stamp Act of 1765. The difference between the two methods of raising money was crucial. The colonies were part of the British commercial system: they received enormous benefits from this position, and had never sought to question the competence of Parliament to legislate for the colonies on questions of trade; the Revenue Act was only another, albeit somewhat arbitrary, exercise of this power. The Stamp Act was something quite different: it was the first direct tax ever to be imposed on the colonies by Parliament, and as such encountered intense opposition. The representatives of nine colonies met in congress in New York to debate the issue of 'no taxation without representation'. In the meantime, non-importation associations among the colonists and the actions of the more violent 'Sons of Liberty' managed to render the Stamp Act completely ineffective. In the midst of all this controversy, the Grenville ministry which had passed the Act fell, and a new government headed by Lord Rockingham repealed the Stamp Act in March 1766. Lest this be taken by the colonists as a sign of weakness, or of surrender to outside pressures, Parliament at the same time affirmed its right to legislate for the colonies on all matters.

The next conflict between the colonists and the govern-

The fiasco of the Stamp Act satirized in the 'Pennsylvania Journal' of 31 October 1765

ment in London was precipitated in 1767 when Charles Townshend, chancellor of the exchequer, tried to reduce the British land tax through collecting duties in the colonies on imported English paper, paint, lead and tea. American opposition to the Townshend duties was much less violent and coordinated than was opposition to the Stamp Act, but they did provide radicals such as Samuel Adams and Joseph Warren with an issue to exploit. A fatal affray between British redcoats and Bostonians on 5 March 1770 – the so-called 'Boston Massacre' – seemed a heaven-sent opportunity for further propaganda to a man like Adams, who had already decided in his own mind that any British authority whatever over the colonies was inadmissible. Unfortunately for the radicals, the new British government headed by Lord North, acting on the very same day as the 'Boston Massacre' took place, repealed the offending duties – except that on tea.

The 'Intolerable' (Coercion) Acts

By the summer of 1770, therefore, the tiny minority of Americans who wanted to throw off the British yoke completely were without an important issue to exploit. All they could do was to utilize the solitary surviving tea duty as a focus for opposition, and the British government played into their hands by granting a monopoly on all tea imported into the colonies to the powerful East India Company. Colonial resistance to this tea monopoly took many forms, and by far the most dramatic was that devised by Sam Adams. During the night of 16 December 1773, members of the 'Sons of Liberty', unconvincingly disguised as Indians, boarded three tea ships in Boston harbour and threw their cargoes into the sea. The 'Boston Tea Party' accomplished just what Adams himself had hoped: the North ministry interpreted it as a direct challenge to parliamentary authority and reacted accordingly.

In May and June 1774, Parliament passed a series of Acts that were sweeping in scope and coercive in intent. One closed the port of Boston to all commerce until the tea was paid for. Another radically altered the Charter of Massachusetts by removing the most liberal features of the colony's government. A third provided for the transportation of certain classes of legal offenders to England

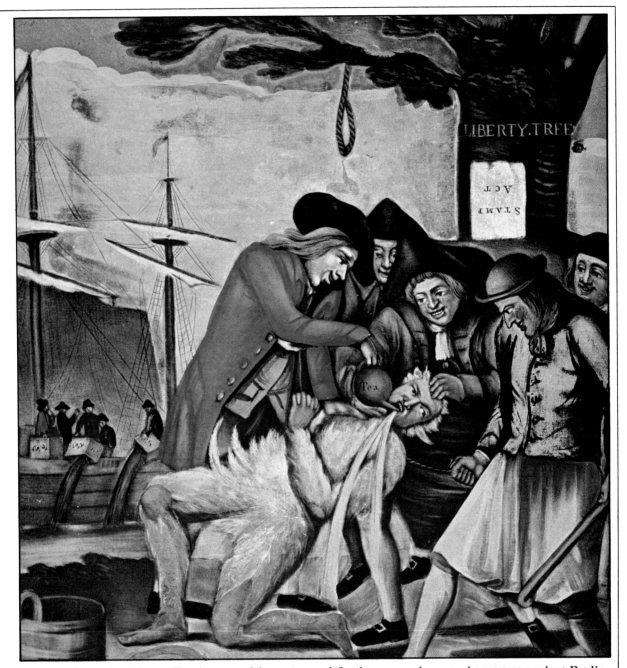

Beneath Boston's 'Liberty Tree' angry citizens tar and feather an excise man in protest against Parliament's extension of the Stamp Act to America. The 'Boston Tea Party' is in progress in the background

for trial. A fourth appointed the British military commander in America, General Gage, Governor of Massachusetts and ominously authorized the quartering of troops in private homes.

The Coercion Acts were quickly followed by the Quebec Act of 1774, which greatly extended the boundaries of Quebec Province and tried to appease French inhabitants by enlarging the privileges of the Roman Catholic Church. Although not punitive in intent, the Act was seen by many Americans as a deliberate check to their expansion westwards and as a 'Romish' threat to their Protestant religious liberties. The Act was certainly ill-timed, and served to push many more American colonists towards a breach with the mother country. Taken all together, in fact, the legislation of 1774 had a disastrous effect on colonial relations. The British government's attempt at coercion, far from isolating Massachusetts, served only to bring the colonies closer together, for in May 1774, at a meeting at the Raleigh Tavern in Williamsburg, members of the Virginia Assembly called for a congress of all the British American colonies. From this root grew the famous first Continental Congress. *M. S.*

From Protest to Revolution

The first Continental Congress

Most of the 55 men from 12 of the 13 colonies (Georgia abstaining) who assembled in Philadelphia on 5 September 1774 had no desire for complete independence from Britain. Their primary concern was to defend what they conceived to be the liberties of American colonists within the British Empire. Yet within two years of the meeting of this first Continental Congress, the colonies had declared their independence and were engaged in a war to secure it. Only the course of events between 1774 and 1776 can explain this abrupt change of policy.

Congress first applied itself to retaliatory measures against the Coercion Acts. Remembering the lessons of 1765–66, it resorted to economic sanctions, adopting stringent agreements on non-importation and non-consumption of British goods and the non-exportation of American produce to England. To supervise the effectiveness of these sanctions, Congress created an extra-legal body, the Continental Association. Congress also passed a Declaration of Rights and Grievances addressed to the people of Britain and the colonies, and for good measure added a petition to the king. Both of these stopped well short of challenging the authority of Parliament over commerce. On 22 October 1774, Congress adjourned, resolving to meet again in the following May if the grievances it articulated had not been resolved.

Two developments took place in the intervening months. One was the failure of William Pitt the Elder (Lord Chatham), leading the opposition to the government's American policy, to secure the repeal of the Coercion Acts and the removal of British troops. The second was that during this period, men like John Adams and Thomas Jefferson for the first time began openly to question the view that Parliament had an intrinsic right of legislating for the colonies. By the spring of 1775, the colonists were drifting further and further away from their loyalty to the mother country. It would need only one spark to provoke a conflagration. The attempt of General Gage, the royal governor of Massachusetts, to seize powder and military supplies that were being gathered by an openly revolutionary committee at Concord, provided that spark. Warned by Paul Revere, the minutemen of Massachusetts tried to stop the British force at Lexington on 19 April 1775. Eight Americans died in an exchange of fire: in retrospect, these were the opening shots of the revolutionary war.

When the second Continental Congress assembled in Philadelphia three weeks later, it was evident that the colonial revolt was gathering momentum and that the colonists themselves were unbowed by the British threat of military retaliation. One of the members of this congress was Thomas Jefferson, a Virginia lawyer and planter, who was eventually to be the principal draftsman of the Declaration of Independence. Jefferson's pamphlet, *A Summary View of the Rights of British America* (1774), had already marked him out as a leading patriot with increasingly radical views on the course to be followed by the colonists. Another member was Benjamin Franklin, journalist, scientist and inventor, who for many years had served Pennsylvania and several other colonies as their

agent in London. During his time in England, Franklin had worked hard for a reconciliation between Britain and her colonies, but after the Coercion Acts were passed in 1774 he came to favour outright American independence. Franklin too was to be a member of the committee that, with Jefferson, drafted the Declaration of Independence.

Within Congress, however, there were still many men who believed that the colonists had not yet reached the end of the path of conciliation. John Dickinson persuaded his colleagues to send another petition for redress to the king. But the real temper of Congress can be gauged from the forthright *Declaration of the Causes and Necessity of Taking up Arms*, written jointly by Dickinson and Jefferson. At the same time, Congress took the Massachusetts militia into its service and set the seal on its determination to resist British intimidation by appointing George Washington commander-in-chief of the armed forces of the colonies. In June 1775, the first serious military clash occurred when the British garrison in Boston, increasingly isolated and surrounded by unfriendly colonists, made a frontal attack on Bunker Hill. They gained their objective, but suffered many casualties in the process.

In the year that separated Bunker Hill from the Declaration of Independence, the British government made no effort to conciliate the colonists. Quite the reverse, in fact, for the North ministry applied further sanctions. In August 1775 a royal proclamation declared the colonies to be in a state of rebellion, and in December all trade and intercourse with the colonies was suspended by Parliament. In January 1776, before the news of this last step reached America, Thomas Paine published his pamphlet *Common Sense*. Paine, born in Thetford, England, had been encouraged by Franklin to migrate to America and try his hand at journalism. He was a radical with a gift for agitation and polemics. In his pamphlet, he argued that it was impractical for an island 3000 miles away to dominate an entire continent, that monarchy was an essentially corrupt form of government, and that the colonies should declare their independence from Britain because the British government was hampering their economic growth through taxes and restrictions upon trade. *Common Sense* was one of those works which, by their timing, influence the course of history: it became an almost instant best-seller and rallied many undecided Americans to the cause of independence.

The spring of 1776 saw bitter feuding in some states between loyalists and advocates of revolution. Indeed, the Americans never attained unanimity on the question of independence either before or during the revolutionary war. Loyalist sentiment remained surprisingly strong: New York, for example, provided more men to fight for Britain than it ever did for the revolutionary armies. Some families were rent by the dispute: Benjamin Franklin signed the Declaration of Independence – his natural son William was the last royal governor of New Jersey.

Left: A contemptuous London caricature ('yankee doodles intrenchment near Boston, 1776') mocking the supposedly craven militia, their puritan preachers (''Tis old Oliver's cause, no monarchy nor laws') a drunken General Israel Putnam, the Liberty Tree flag and the motto 'Death or liberty'.

The best-liked American republican, and the most welcome in London and Paris, where he was equally at home, was the Boston-born, Philadelphia printer, journalist, scientist and statesman, Benjamin Franklin (painting by David Martin, 1767)

The Fourth of July

During the early months of 1776, aided by the increasingly fast tempo of events, the advocates of full independence consolidated their position and began to come out on top. In March, the legislature of North Carolina instructed its delegates to Congress to seek a declaration of independence and foreign alliances. Congress itself responded to the parliamentary interdiction on all trade with the colonies by throwing open American ports to the commerce of the world. In May, news arrived that 12,000 German mercenaries would soon be arriving in America to confront the recalcitrant colonists. In June, Congress debated the subject of independence, and finally, on 2 July, at last declared the US to be a sovereign, independent nation. Two days later, it adopted Jefferson's celebrated Declaration of Independence. But to declare independence was one thing: to succeed in maintaining it quite another. Several years of war now lay ahead before Britain could finally be forced to recognize the final loss of her American colonies. *M. S.*

The War of Independence

The fact that the USA succeeded in establishing its independence by force of arms owes much to the courage and determination of one man: George Washington. A Virginia-born planter, Washington had been commissioned by Governor Dinwiddie as a major in the state's militia. He fought well in the Seven Years War against the French, and led the Virginia forces in the successful attack on Fort Duquesne in 1758. The following year he was elected to the Virginia House of Burgesses, where he served for many years. In 1774, he was present at the meeting in Raleigh Tavern that issued the call for the first Continental Congress. Washington himself was a member both of this first Congress and its successor. In June 1775, he was appointed head of all the colonists' armed forces. During the revolutionary war itself, he commanded a heterogeneous, undisciplined force whose size fluctuated alarmingly according to the season of the year. In the hard winter of 1777–78, when the Continental Army had shrunk to less than 5000 men quartered at Valley Forge, only Washington's own indomitable will stood in the way of absolute military collapse. Congress frequently saddled him with incompetent subordinates. Worse, it failed to keep him furnished with adequate supplies and basic equipment for his army. Since Congress was unable to tax the colonists directly, it had to resort to the practice of requisitioning supplies from individual states which might or might not comply. Experience repeatedly proved how useless this procedure was.

1775–1777

There had been military operations even before the Declaration of Independence. In particular, Richard Montgomery and Benedict Arnold had launched an attack on Canada in the closing weeks of 1775. They captured Montreal but failed in a desperate attack on Quebec in the middle of a blinding snowstorm on the last night of 1775. The British did not have things all their own way: an attack on Charleston in June 1776 was repulsed, and the British commanders, Sir Henry Clinton and Lord Cornwallis, were forced to withdraw. They were in time, however, to join Sir William Howe in his successful attack on New York. After the Battle of Long Island, Washington was forced to retreat away from New York City, which became a British base for the rest of the war. Followed at a more leisurely pace by Howe, Washington moved back across New Jersey into Pennsylvania with his dwindling, demoralized army.

It was evident to Washington by December 1776 that without some bold stroke on his part the war was as good as lost. On Christmas Day 1776 he ferried his army across the Delaware River and in the next few days won two decisive, if small-scale, victories at Trenton (26 December 1776) and Princeton (3 January 1777). Despite the encouragement these provided to the American cause, neither was enough to stem the British advance. Howe wintered in New Jersey and in the summer of 1777 began his attack on Philadelphia with a force greatly superior to

NEW HAMPSHIRE

MASSACHUSETTS
RHODE ISLAND
CONNECTICUT
NEW YORK

PENNSYLVANIA
NEW JERSEY
DELAWARE
MARYLAND

VIRGINIA

Charlottesville

Yorktown

NORTH CAROLINA

Charlotte

King's Mountain

SOUTH CAROLINA

Charleston

GEORGIA

The Thirteen Colonies

Cornwallis's march 1781

Battle sites

anything Washington could muster. All Washington could do, in fact, was to delay him for a few days at Brandywine Creek on 9 September. Just over two weeks later the British entered Philadelphia. Washington's attack on Germantown in early October was gallant but unsuccessful, and his army spent a difficult winter at Valley Forge while the British were comfortably in Philadelphia.

On the northern front, in the meantime, things had been going rather better for the Americans. Burgoyne, the British commander, advanced down the Hudson River from Canada. In August 1777, he was beaten at Bennington by John Stark and his Green Mountain Boys. For an irregular army, nothing ever succeeds like success: the news of Bennington brought a flood of enlistments into the New England militia. When Burgoyne resumed his interrupted march southwards, he encountered stiffer and stiffer resistance. In October 1777, he was forced to surrender his whole army of 5000 men to General Gates at Saratoga. This, the most decisive British defeat of the war, was significant in other ways. More than anything else, it was responsible for bringing France into the war.

1778-1781

The year 1778 was, for the most part, a year of indecisive military engagements in which neither side obtained a distinct advantage. In December, however, the British scored a striking success when they captured Savannah and went on to recover most of the rest of Georgia. A British assault on Charleston, South Carolina, failed; but so, too, did a French attempt under the Comte d'Estaing to recover Savannah. The mixed record of their success in 1779 encouraged the British to adopt a new strategy. They began to plan an ambitious operation to capture Charleston, to resurrect loyal governments in the Carolinas with the aid of local Tories, and to force the surviving American forces to retreat into Virginia where they could be dealt with almost at leisure. The new southern campaign began well for the British when they captured Charleston by amphibious assault in May 1780. Five thousand five hundred men surrendered in the worst American disaster of the revolutionary war. More bad news was to follow: Lord Cornwallis inflicted a crushing defeat on American reinforcements under Gates at Camden, South Carolina, in August. Fortunately for the Americans, Congress at this juncture finally gave Washington the power to appoint his own commander in the south, and he selected Nathanael Greene of Rhode Island. Greene was a gifted general and, although hampered by limited resources, he at once began a masterly campaign that recovered much of the interior of South Carolina.

Meanwhile, Cornwallis marched northwards into Virginia where the Marquis de Lafayette (an American major-general) and Benedict Arnold (who had changed sides and now supported the British) were fighting each other inconclusively. At the beginning of August, Cornwallis settled down with his forces on the sea-coast at Yorktown, and set out to fortify the town. Ironically, he seems to have intended his military base at Yorktown to be of assistance to the British navy in controlling Chesapeake Bay. Instead, he found himself besieged by a joint French-American army of 15,000 men. With less than half that number, Cornwallis was at a grave disadvantage, but what made his position untenable was the temporary ascendancy gained by the French navy over the whole of Chesapeake Bay. For once, a British army looked in vain for succour to the sea. Recognizing the inevitable, Cornwallis surrendered his entire army on 17 October 1781, bringing the war effectively to an end.   *M. S.*

The button of the New York Volunteers (NYV), still stamped with the British crown

Left: George III's equestrian statue in New York being toppled by 'patriot' citizens

France and America

Without French help, it is almost inconceivable that the American colonists could have achieved their independence. Almost from the very beginning of the revolutionary war, most of the military supplies that kept the Continental Army in the field came from France. If this aid had not been forthcoming, it is difficult to see how the victories of Trenton, Princeton and Saratoga would have been possible.

The fact that France, a colonial power governed by an absolutist monarchy, should find herself supporting a colonial revolt by avowed republicans is one of the ironies of history. But to many astute French observers, the difficulties that arose between Britain and her colonies after 1763 provided a welcome opportunity for France to gain her revenge for the humiliations incurred by the Seven Years War. The two foreign ministers of these years, the Duc de Choiseul, who left office in 1770, and the Comte de Vergennes, who succeeded him, urged that if relations between Britain and her colonists in America reached breaking point, France should provide aid and assistance to the insurgents by all means short of open war. This was the policy pursued by France between 1776 and 1778.

In the spring of 1776, Congress sent Silas Deane to Paris in order to procure supplies and munitions. The French quickly agreed to American requests for aid, although insisting that their help be kept secret. Arms and supplies were channelled to the Americans through the medium of a bogus company organized by Beaumarchais, famous as the author of *The Barber of Seville* (and later, in 1784, of the insolent *Marriage of Figaro*).

After the Declaration of Independence in July, Benjamin Franklin and Arthur Lee were dispatched to join

Washington's French ally, Comte de Rochambeau, helps direct the final assault on Yorktown, October 1781. Lafayette stands in the background between them (painting by M. Conder)

Deane in Paris with instructions to seek further aid, and to offer France a treaty of amity and commerce with the US. Franklin landed in France in December 1776. No better choice of emissary could have been made. His reputation as a scientist and author preceded him and, with his combination of diplomatic experience and New World simplicity, he quickly became a popular figure on the French social scene. But for all his personal success, Franklin could not budge the French government from its determination to furnish only covert aid to the colonists.

Lafayette

To many young Frenchmen, deeply imbued with the ideas of the Enlightenment, the American revolution was a deeply exciting event. One of them, the Marquis de Lafayette, a young officer in the French army, did more than merely approve: despite the opposition of his family and the king, he arranged through Silas Deane for a commission in the Continental Army. Lafayette left for America in April 1777 and in July met with the Continental Congress. On agreeing to serve without pay and without a specific command, he was appointed a major-general in the American army. In August he met George Washington for the first time, and this proved to be the beginning of a life-long friendship. It is probable that Congress had entertained considerable doubts about this young foreign adventurer, despite his previous military experience. These doubts, however, were largely erased at the Battle of Brandywine in September, when Lafayette fought well and was wounded. In December 1777, he was given his own command. He spent the winter of 1777–78 with Washington at Valley Forge, and then led an unsuccessful expedition into Canada. Lafayette managed to extricate his men through a well-executed and orderly retreat, and emerged from the débâcle with his reputation, if anything, higher. In the succeeding months, he came to play an increasingly important role in the war, both as a military commander and as a symbol of the Franco-American alliance that became a reality in May 1778.

France's military aid to the colonists justified this complacent design for a monument to Louis XVI as 'liberator' of America and the high seas

Open intervention by France

The French decision to abandon their policy of secret aid in favour of open support and an inevitable war with Britain was the result of two factors. One was the news of the Battle of Saratoga, which for the first time seems to have convinced the French government that the colonists were capable of maintaining their independence by force. The second, astutely exploited by Franklin, was the suspicion that the chastened British might now offer generous enough terms to end the war on some basis short of independence. In January 1778, American and French representatives sat down together to negotiate treaties of alliance and commerce. Congress enthusiastically ratified both treaties in May. In June 1778 hostilities broke out between Britain and France when their fleets met in battle. Thereafter, French forces came to play an increasingly important part in the war. It was the presence of Comte de Grasse's fleet in Chesapeake Bay in 1781 that led directly to the decisive British surrender at Yorktown.

After Yorktown, it was only a question of time before peace came. What had begun, on Britain's part, as an attempt to suppress a rebellion, had developed into a world war: Spain entered the fighting as a French ally in 1779, and Holland declared war on Britain in 1780. News of the surrender of Yorktown reached a war-weary England in February 1782, and North's ministry, the surviving obstacle to peace, fell a month later. In April, unofficial contacts began between Britain and the American peace commissioners: Franklin, John Jay and John Adams. In the succeeding months, it became clear to the Americans – and clearest of all to Jay – that the interests of the US and France were far from identical. So far as possible, de Vergennes wanted to limit the US to the eastern seaboard of North America: if any country was to possess the enormous area of land between the Appalachian Mountains and the Mississippi River, he preferred that it should be France's ally, Spain. Consequently, acting on their own initiative and disobeying their instructions to coordinate peace efforts with France, the American commissioners – now joined by Henry Laurens – secretly negotiated a preliminary treaty of peace, which they signed on 30 November 1782.

The Treaty of Paris

The preliminary treaty, which became definitive in September 1783 after France and Spain had also made peace, embodied generous terms for the US. Britain not only recognized American independence, but also gave the new country a vast domain stretching from Canada south as far as the 31st parallel, and from the Atlantic to the Mississippi River. Franklin, by skilful diplomacy, managed to mollify de Vergennes for the American initiative in making peace, but nothing could disguise the fact that France was one of the biggest losers from the American War of Independence. She got nothing for her efforts apart from a few West Indian islands, an unfulfilled hope of large new American markets, and an empty treasury. Only five years after the final recognition of the independence of the American republic, financial bankruptcy compelled the government of Louis XVI to summon the States-General and thereby set in motion the train of events that led to the French Revolution in 1789. *M. S.*

The Ancien Régime in France

France was the richest and most populous country of Western Europe, with 26 million people in the 1780s. It was an overwhelmingly agrarian society. Land was the main source of wealth and between a quarter and a third of the land was owned by the peasantry. Most peasants were free men and farmed their own land. Nevertheless, they found it hard to feed themselves because individual holdings were small and peasant farmers lacked the knowledge and capital to make improvements. Large-scale famine was no longer a threat but life was still precarious from one harvest to the next.

Society was divided into three traditional orders: the clergy or First Estate; the nobility or Second Estate; and everyone else was part of the Third Estate. Within these orders there was great diversity of conditions. As well as a clerical élite of wealthy upper clergy, the First Estate included many poor parish priests. The Second Estate ranged from the Princes of the Blood and older aristocracy to the comparatively poor provincial nobility. It is estimated that in the 1780s there were between 200,000 and 250,000 noble males in France. The most heterogeneous group was the Third Estate (*le Tiers État*), ranging from tramps and landless labourers to well-to-do magistrates, bankers and merchants. What distinguished the First and Second Estates was their privileged position. The Church was exempt from tax. Clergy, rich and poor alike, were disciplined in Church courts. The clergy controlled education, hospitals and much poor relief. The nobility were exempt from some taxation and enjoyed a monopoly of leading occupations – army, diplomacy and the Church.

In theory, France was an absolute monarchy ruled by Louis XVI (1774–92). In practice, royal power was circumscribed by a number of privileged bodies: the Church, some provincial Estates and the law courts. The Church was the greatest landowner and had a strong sense of its own corporate power and identity. It retained its privilege of holding meetings of the Clerical Assembly every five years and resisted direct taxation by the state. Some of the most recently acquired provinces had kept their local Estates. These were not representative bodies in a modern sense. The Estates of Artois in the north-west, for example, represented only the upper clergy and leading nobility. For the Crown they constituted a hindrance because they bargained with the government about taxation.

The 'parlements'

The chief challenge to royal absolutism came from the dozen appeal courts, or *parlements*. The judges who were nobles could not be removed by the Crown. As guardians of traditional law they claimed the right to advise the king on the limits of his authority. The king could make laws and enforce their registration but the *parlements* retaliated by calling judicial strikes and provoking popular feelings against royal officials. The king would then exile the members of the recalcitrant *parlements* to small provincial towns. However, rather than go on and risk the break-

down of the judicial system the royal government negotiated a compromise. In the second half of the 18th century the *parlements* grew increasingly assertive, claiming to be guardians of a shadowy medieval constitution and employing terms such as 'nation' or 'citizen' instead of 'kingdom' and 'subject'.

Louis XVI might have followed the example of the 'enlightened despots' of that time, Frederick II of Prussia and Joseph II of Austria, by riding roughshod over the *parlements* and Estates. He had a powerful professional army, but he lacked the education and temperament to do so. Surrounded by the great nobility at Versailles he shared their outlook and assumptions. He made no attempt either to rule or to delegate his power to a chief minister, nor could he count on the service of a loyal bureaucracy. The kingdom was administered by royal officials known as *intendants*, who were often nobles for whom it was easy to identify with the local nobility. An *intendant* would seek to place a son in the local *parlement* or to arrange a good match for a daughter as his way of establishing a limited local influence.

The Achilles heel of royal absolutism was faulty finance. The monarchy's efforts to stave off bankruptcy aroused the opposition of the privileged orders and led directly to

Right: Grudgingly convoked, and seated by their due degrees and orders, the States General of France were opened 5 May 1789 in Versailles, not to dissolve until the Revolution was an accomplished fact

the revolution of 1789. Successive wars since the later years of the reign of Louis XIV, culminating in the effective French intervention in the American War of Independence in 1778–81, created a large annual deficit. In 1788, at the end of the *ancien régime*, over three-quarters of the annual state expenditure was being spent on defence and the service of the public debt. The accumulation of a vast debt was only part of the problem. The tax collection machinery did not work. The raising of indirect taxes, of which the salt tax (*gabelle*) was the most hated, was leased out to the 'farmers-general', a group of powerful financiers, in return for a fixed payment to the Crown which could only be increased once in six years. By 1787–1788 the possibilities of raising additional revenue through borrowing were virtually exhausted. The only way out of the *impasse* was for the monarchy to tap the wealth of the clergy and nobility, who largely escaped direct taxation.

Underlying the financial predicament was a deep economic crisis. A rapid rise in population was not followed by any significant increase in agricultural production, but instead fuelled a long-term inflation of food prices. As a protection against inflation, some landlords adopted a more businesslike and systematic exploitation of manorial dues. The burden of direct and indirect taxes bore heavily on the peasantry, and when the harvest of 1788 turned out to be a catastrophe, many were living in want and misery.

In 1787, Calonne, minister of finance since 1783, proposed radical reforms which included a tax on all land. His programme was rejected by an Assembly of Notables. The attempt of his successor, de Brienne, to implement the essentials of the programme also aroused the opposition of the privileged orders. In desperation, de Brienne restricted the judicial powers of the *parlements*. But the *coup d'état* provoked widespread unrest in the provinces. On 5 July 1788 de Brienne announced the calling of the Estates General and on 8 August, the date of its meeting was fixed for 1 May 1789. In August de Brienne was replaced by Necker, a Swiss banker. Necker recalled the *parlements* from exile but it was too late for conciliation. Millions of Frenchmen recognized the need for a transformation of France's political structure. In opposition to the conservative aristocracy a 'patriotic' or 'national' party had emerged. Prominent among its leaders was the Abbé Sieyès. In 1789 Sieyès published a pamphlet *What is the Third Estate?* 'The Nation', he wrote, 'exists before all things . . . its will is always legal.'   *A. A.*

The French Revolution

The attack on traditional political, legal and social institutions had begun in 1789 with the summoning of the States General to resolve the monarchy's financial crisis. The States General was an assembly of representatives of the three legal orders of French society – the clergy, the aristocracy and everybody else. The Third Estate very quickly made it clear that it did not accept this ordering, but saw itself as representing the whole nation. Under the leadership of an aristocrat, Honoré, Comte de Mirabeau, it constituted itself the National Assembly on 19 June. The following day, excluded from its usual hall, it repaired to an indoor tennis court (Jeu de Paume) and there passed the famous Tennis Court Oath by which it undertook not to dissolve until France had a constitution. On 9 July, it gave itself powers as the Constituent Assembly to draw up that constitution. Louis XVI was unable to stop the actions of the Third Estate, but fears that he was planning an attack on it led, on 14 July, to the storming of the Bastille prison at Paris. The importance of the date lies less in the frightfulness of the old prison (it contained a mere handful of inmates, most of whom promptly had to be locked up again on account of their madness) than in the destruction of a symbol of royal despotism and arbitrary imprisonment, and in the alliance of the wealthy leaders of the Third Estate with the Paris poor that brought it about. Popular disorder was being used, not repressed. In August the 'great fear' occurred, an extraordinary series of uprisings in the provinces that led to the destruction by the peasants of many of the legal documents defining their feudal status and obligations. This led on 4 August to the formal renunciation by the aristocracy of its privileges. On 26 August the National Assembly promulgated the Declaration of the Rights of Man and of the Citizen, which affirmed the principle of civil equality. The summer of 1789 had thus witnessed a successful challenge to the old order. Louis's failure to resist it was symbolized by the enforced transfer of the royal family in October from Versailles to Paris.

The task facing the Constituent Assembly in 1790 was to create a new administrative and political order. This involved the replacement of the old administrative units, the provinces, with 83 departments and some 44,000 communes, the basic unit of local government. At the same time, France's chaotic system of justice was reformed and humanized. The leaders of the Assembly wanted a constitution to regulate political power, but they also wanted strong government and they certainly did not want that government to be exercised by, or in the hands of, the urban poor. Thus, the constitution of 1791 provided for a monarch whose executive powers were limited and whose veto could be overturned; for a legislative assembly with absolute powers over the budget and the right to initiate laws; and for a franchise qualification that, though generous by the standards of the time, nevertheless excluded the poor of France. Louis publicly accepted the constitution and the leading personalities in the Assembly (Mira-

The Third Estate, assembled in the tennis court at Versailles, swears it will not dissolve until France has a constitution, 20 June 1789 (engraving by Berthault)

beau and Talleyrand, and others such as Bailly, Le Chapelier and Barnave) were extremely anxious to work with him. The aim was for a constitutional monarchy that would prevent any further social disturbance and bring the revolution to a close.

The revolution did not, however, come to an end and the national unity that had appeared to exist in 1789 was short-lived. This was due to growing tensions between groups on the left and the right (descriptive categories that date from the revolutionary period). The Legislative Assembly of October 1791 was dominated by the educated middle class, but its leadership came from a group known as the Girondins (the core of them were deputies from the Gironde department), who wanted a more radical assertion of revolutionary policy. Already the still more radical Club des Jacobins had come into existence. In Paris the springing up of political clubs testified to the growing political awareness of the poorer citizen and men like Jean-Paul Marat started to preach, by word and in print, that the revolution had not gone far enough, that inequality had social as well as political origins. Such an idea was anathema to the majority of the Constituent Assembly, who were further alarmed by continued peasant unrest and food riots in the towns. The problem of financing the revolution had led in 1789–90 to decisions by the Constituent Assembly to sell Church lands to guarantee France's currency and then to promulgate the Civil Constitution of the Clergy, which increased the power of the state over Church organization. These measures split the clergy, some of whom refused to take an oath of loyalty to the constitution. This was the beginning of over a hundred years of hostility between many French Catholics and the supporters and followers of the revolution. Above all, the monarchy ceased to be a focus of unity and became a source of disagreement. As early as 1789 the king's brothers and other aristocrats had fled from France and used their self-imposed exile to try to stir up the European monarchies against the revolution. Louis's wife, Marie Antoinette, was sister of two Holy Roman Emperors, Joseph II and Leopold II, and she bitterly resented the concessions made by her husband to the Constituent Assembly. So, privately, did Louis himself. In 1791 the royal family attempted to escape from France to join the loyal émigrés on the Rhine (the Flight to Varennes). They were recognized and brought back in humiliation to Paris. The monarchy remained, but its prestige was gravely compromised in the eyes of the increasingly radical population of Paris. By 1792 a divorce was becoming evident between loyalty to the king and loyalty to the revolution. The Girondins urged a war against Austria as a means of forcing Louis to come out unequivocally for the revolution and against his exiled brothers. Louis did indeed commit France to war against the emperor on 20 April 1792, but many of his supporters hoped for a military defeat that would discredit the revolution and restore royal authority. Instead, the war was to lead to the destruction of the monarchy and to a second revolution.

P. M.

Danton, the fiery orator: champion of revolutionary war, but guillotined as a 'moderate'

An emblem of the days of hope: nation, law and king united under the constitution of 1791

The First Republic

In the summer of 1792 the French Revolution entered its most radical phase, which was to last until July 1794. Many of the most famous events, groups and individuals associated with the Revolution – the execution of the king, the Terror, the Jacobins and *sans-culottes*, Robespierre – are found in this two-year period. The break with France's past appeared to be total and was emphasized in October 1793 by the replacement of the old calendar with a completely new one, Year 1 of which dated from the establishment of the Republic.

It was the war with Austria and Prussia that precipitated events. This war was far from being the normal 18th century conflict between monarchs over territory – rather was it a struggle concerning the very existence of France and the survival of the Revolution. Moreover, the fight was not just between Frenchmen and foreigners, for it became clear that those Frenchmen who opposed the course the Revolution was taking were prepared to take advantage of the Prussian invasion to challenge the revolutionary leadership: the outbreak of war in April provoked counter-revolutionary movements in many regions, notably the south (as in Toulon). This internal conflict should not simply be viewed as one between rich and poor – many wealthy men had bought church or *emigré* land and had a vested interest in the Revolution's survival – but

it was dramatized as one between the patriotic, common man (the *sans-culotte* or, as one might say, the 'no silken breeches') and the treacherous, aristocratic man.

The Girondin leader Brissot had hoped that the war would force Louis XVI to submit to the Revolution, but it looked at first more likely that it would destroy the Revolution and restore royal supremacy. The Prussians' advance, the statement of their commander that the Parisians would be held responsible for the safety of the royal family, and the well-founded belief that the Court was in touch with the invader all combined to create intense political excitement in Paris. In early July National Guards started to arrive in Paris from the provinces. They were inflamed by the revolutionary ardour they met there and on 10 August combined with the *sans-culottes* in an attack on the king's residence at the Tuileries. The constitutional monarchy was henceforth doomed and with it the Legislative Assembly. Louis was suspended and the government decided to summon a National Convention (which was to be elected by universal suffrage) to draw up a new constitution. At the same time the Commune of Paris was taken over by radicals, who would henceforth act as a watchdog on government.

All this was radical enough, but it did not solve the problem of winning the war and it did not satisfy the *sans-*

culottes that counter-revolutionary defeatism had been crushed. Suspicion of royalist treachery, fed by the desertion to the Austrians of Lafayette in August, led to the September massacres in which over a thousand prisoners in Paris were murdered. At the same time the oratory of Danton inspired thousands of Parisians to march to the defence of the Revolution. In the months that followed, the French, having defeated the Prussians at Valmy (20 September), thereafter swept beyond France's borders into Germany and the Austrian Netherlands. Revolutionary euphoria led the newly elected Convention to declare that France was ready to support any people trying to obtain its liberty from despotism. At home, the monarchy was abolished and Louis XVI was put on trial for treason. On 21 January 1793 he was guillotined.

Revolutionary successes were short lived. To the conflict with Austria and Prussia was added, in February 1793, war with England and Holland, and later with Spain. The French advance against the Austrians came to a halt and in April General Dumoriez, the favourite of the Girondins, also deserted. At home, the winter of 1792–1793 was marked by disturbances in both countryside and towns. Men like the Abbé Roux and Varlet were arguing at Paris for comprehensive economic controls. In the western departments (the Vendée region) a full-scale re-

bellion broke out in defence of the old order, especially of the Catholic Church. The Convention that had to deal with all these problems was rent by enmities between two groups, the Girondins and the Montagnards, which, although they formed a minority of the Convention's membership, dominated its proceedings by the viciousness of their rivalries. These owed less to policy than to personality, and neither group was in favour of the economic radicalism of the sans-culottes.

The most prominent Montagnards, Robespierre and Saint Just, stood for an intensification of the conflict against the 'enemies of the revolution' (including food hoarders) and were prepared to go along with the sans-culottes. Between 31 May and 2 June 1793 another Paris insurrection led to the arrest of the Girondin leaders.

There followed the period known as the Terror. The legend of Robespierre's ruthlessness is so well established that it is important to realize that the basis of his power, a sub-committee of the Convention known as the Committee of Public Safety, had been set up as early as April and the revolutionary tribunal (to deal with traitors) even earlier. The period of rule by Robespierre and his Jacobin followers brought the virtual elimination of foreign invaders from French soil, the strengthening of France's armies and the re-establishment of central authority over the rebellious provinces. The Committee of Public Safety introduced price controls and rationing to protect the poor. Its social policy has been described as enlightened and benevolent, but with this benevolent virtuousness went a growing ferocity towards the 'enemies of virtue'. Towns like Lyons and Nantes witnessed the mass execution of political prisoners, and in the last six weeks of Robespierre's rule 1376 people were guillotined in Paris alone. Whereas earlier victims of the Terror had been notable reactionaries like Marie Antoinette, later ones included some leaders of Robespierre's erstwhile champions, the sans-culottes, and Danton himself. Eventually, the Convention rounded on Robespierre before he could round on it. He was executed, with his closest followers, on 28 July (9 Thermidor) 1794. The next day his supporters in the Commune of Paris were also guillotined.

The five years that separate the fall of Robespierre from the triumph of Bonaparte were marked by continued political instability. The 'Thermidorean' reaction resulted in the freeing of many prisoners, but also in a 'white terror' that caused the death of thousands of poor people, and in a royalist revival. Political power fell into the hands of successful businessmen, war contractors and profiteers; wealth, not virtue, was now fashionable. The Constitution of 1795 greatly restricted the franchise while creating an executive of five members, the Directory. In 1796 Gracchus Babeuf acquired a place in the history of socialism (but brought about his own death) by unsuccessfully attempting to overthrow the government and install a communist form of society. Increasingly, the army commanders, whose military successes in Europe financed the government at home, dominated political life. In 1799 one of them, General Bonaparte, seized power.   P. M.

Enough is enough: Barras, for the National Convention, carries out the arrest of the already wounded Robespierre (inset: sketched from the life by David) on the night of 27 July 1794

General Bonaparte

Napoleon Buonaparte's father was one of Paoli's lieutenants in the Corsican war of independence against the Genoese. After the cynical French take-over of the island in 1769, the Buonapartes sided with the French and were friendly enough with the French *intendant* for rumours to spread that the Frenchman was Napoleon's real father. It was through his good offices that the young Napoleon was supplied with a patent of nobility and a free education at the best military schools in France. His provincial accent and odd physical appearance had already invited comment from his fellow students of the *haute noblesse*, but it was the incorporation of Corsica into France in 1789, and not the *ancien régime*'s 'cascade of contempt' for him that made Napoleon, if not a revolutionary, at least a product of the Revolution. At first Napoleon, like many Corsicans, had seen the Revolution as an opportunity to reassert Corsican independence, but when the National Assembly gave Corsicans all the rights of Frenchmen, the whole Buonaparte family threw in their lot with the new order.

A series of fortunate accidents brought him to prominence at the siege of Toulon. A posting to Italy had brought him to the city, where the artillery commander had been one of only three casualties in the first action of the siege. A friend and fellow Corsican, in Toulon by chance, offered Napoleon the command of the artillery while a letter from Paris offering the command to a more senior officer (Napoleon was a captain) went astray. He met Barras and Robespierre's brother, Augustin, who

were impressed by his energy and competence; the Minister of War, Carnot, was impressed by his plans; he worked with Junot, who was to become the emperor's chief-of-staff, and Marmont, who was to become one of his marshals. The British were repulsed at the end of 1793. Thereafter, Napoleon's luck held. A feigned illness kept him out of the Vendée war, that graveyard of reputations; he avoided the guillotine after the fall of Robespierre despite a period under arrest. 1795 found him a brigadier-general in Paris with an entrée into the social life of the Directory through Barras and an introduction to Josephine de Beauharnais. It was a love match with great conveniences on both sides. She was a woman of the world perhaps just beginning to fade; he represented a future. The crisis of 13 Vendémiaire, when General Buonaparte's guns round the Tuileries palace provided the 'whiff of grapeshot' that stopped the revolt of the Parisian *sections* against the Law of the Two-Thirds (by which the Legislative Council was to be packed by co-option from the outgoing Convention) brought Napoleon closer to the Directory. He was appointed Commanding-General of the Army of Italy in March 1796.

The war in Italy was against Sardinia (Piedmont) and Austria. Bonaparte's job (he de-Italianized his name by dropping the 'u') was to win victories that would secure concessions on the Rhine, where the war was going badly, and to make the war pay. A whirlwind campaign, ending at the battle of Rivoli, took the Napoleonic army to within

Bonaparte's victory over the Mamelukes in the Battle of Pyramids (21 July 1798) gave him glory in the eyes of France, but his control of Egypt was lost when Nelson destroyed his fleet at Abukir, 1–2 August

a hundred miles of Vienna by January 1797. Systematic looting propped up the finances of the Directory (and provided his sisters with handsome dowries). The victory was so complete that the war in Italy could no longer be regarded as a sideshow, and observers noted that Napoleon's headquarters at the palace of Mombello began to resemble a court, with the intrigues being provided by the Bonaparte family against Josephine, of whom 'Madame Mère', the mother of Napoleon and his brethren, had never approved. Bonaparte conducted himself at the Peace of Campo Formio more like a prince than the Directors' general.

The return to Paris was a triumph. He was made 'Commander of the Army of England', but there was little hope of an invasion. He chose to command the expedition to Egypt, the Directory being perhaps relieved to see him out of the way. The Mamelukes were thrashed at the Battle of the Pyramids (1798), Egypt was organized as a French colony, and an advance into Syria was begun to force the Ottoman Sultan into an alliance. This was intended as a prelude to threatening British interests in India through alliances with native princes, but the destruction of the French fleet by Nelson at the Battle of the Nile, and the repulse of the army from the siege of Acre, cut the French off from home, and confined them to Egypt. The Army of Egypt could now be saved only by a victory on land in Europe. Napoleon had other pressing reasons for returning to France. Russia, Austria and

Britain were on the offensive, Italy was lost again, an Anglo-Russian expedition had invaded Holland, and Josephine had a lover.

He returned to France in October 1799, heard Josephine's side of the story before Madame Mère could get to him, and forgave her. He found the Directory quarrelling with the Legislative Councils and at its wit's end for money. The Vendée guerrilla war was about to escalate. The left was calling for a military dictatorship and a return of the Terror, while Sieyès, Talleyrand, Fouché and the moderates wanted an end to the corrupt incompetence of the Directory and a stronger executive to fight the war. Bonaparte was courted from all sides; he had only to choose. Sieyès, inevitably, prepared the ground. He and his friends were looking for a general and expected to 'manage' Bonaparte to their own ends. Bonaparte did not show up well in the coup d'état of 18 Brumaire itself. His brother, Lucien Bonaparte, as president of the Council of Five Hundred, had to persuade them not to declare his brother an outlaw, but when a rump of the Legislative Councils appointed a provisional executive of three (Sieyès, Ducos, Bonaparte), Napoleon was able to insist that the Second and Third Consuls should be advisory only. The Constitution of 1800 made him First Consul for 10 years; after the Peace of Amiens (1802) he made himself Consul for life, and after Marengo (1804) he declared a hereditary empire. *J. S. M.*

An 'incroyable' in the fashion of the Directoire period, 1795-99

Bonaparte defended by grenadiers during his coup d'état of 18 Brumaire (9-10 November 1799)

THE AGE OF NAPOLEON

When Napoleon crossed the River Niemen in 1812 at the head of an army of some 430,000 troops speaking among themselves a dozen tongues, he was the sovereign of 87 million souls. Nothing like his empire had been seen since the days of Alexander or Charlemagne, to whom he was constantly likening himself. Just three years later all that was left was the rock in the Atlantic to which the British had pinned him, and the gorgeous fabric of memories and legends from which he would bequeath to posterity the image of the fallen Prometheus, hunted down for daring to steal fire from the heavens.

Some of his phenomenal success he owed to good fortune, as at the Battle of Marengo; some to the fatuousness and division among his enemies. His gift for felicitous timing, both in war and politics, was extraordinary. But his real genius was utterly modern: it lay in an incomparable grasp of the roots of power in a post-revolutionary world. As a charismatic manipulator of allegiance he was peerless; his intuitive comprehension of the psychology of mass motivation marks him out as the formative virtuoso of modern dictatorship.

There were five cardinal elements in his strategy. Firstly, he saw that the French Revolution had obliterated the mystique of royal authority without supplying an adequate substitute to assuage the popular craving for some incarnation of national identity. If the 'sovereign people' were reluctant to worship themselves, he was fully prepared to let them worship France through his own person, endowed, as he fully believed it was, with the talisman of destiny. Secondly, he understood that the Revolution had exposed a painful contradiction between the claims of liberty and the claims of equality. Until they were both subsumed in some larger political entity France could never properly mobilize its colossal potential of talent and power. So he determined to sacrifice those freedoms held in high regard only by a minority to the equality desired by the masses. Thirdly, he pandered to what Chateaubriand described as the inordinate collective vanity of the French, knowing (like Bismarck after him) that spectacular military success silenced political qualms. By emphasizing his community with the common soldiery he identified the entire nation with his own feats of arms. Fourthly, he inherited from the past century the as yet largely untested axiom that bureaucratic efficiency and the rule of law would purify despotism of the taint of arbitrariness. Finally, he knew that the modern world was not yet so liberated from its old magic as to dispense entirely with ceremony and ritual. By reinstating the forms of religion without reactivating their power to do political mischief he was neutralizing one of the principal causes of instability in the Old Régime.

All of this foundered on the magnitude of Bonaparte's own ego. During the height of his power he showed absolutely no inclination to moderate his ambition in the cause of peace or even to stabilize his own achievement by a modicum of prudence in war and diplomacy.

Did his epoch destroy more than it built? The balance-sheet is difficult to draw up. Although this was a period of almost incessant war, the fatalities from battle were, by modern standards, light. The 3 per cent of Frenchmen who lost their lives for him over 15 years were far fewer than those who would have died from one year of dearth or epidemic. It is more difficult to quantify the miseries of economic deprivation, requisitions, conscription that became commonplace at this time. If he brought on the destruction of French Atlantic commerce, he laid the basis for Belgian industrialization; if he ruined Bordeaux, he brought carriages over the Simplon and the Corniche. As for the celebrated Codes, these endured, shorn of nearly all of the Revolution's most liberal provisions regarding, for example, the rights of women and illegitimate children. He reduced the intellectual (though not the scientific) life of France to such a degree of stultification that even the Bourbons marked a refreshing change.

Napoleon's significance for the modern world may lie rather in what he was than what he wrought. His career represents the ultimate in Romantic egotism; 'I would not be God,' he is reported as having once remarked; 'that would be a cul-de-sac.' After Napoleon, the 19th century would try very hard to settle for less dangerous brilliance. *S. S.*

Napoleon, in his coronation robes

Napoleon's Battles and Conquests

Napoleon's military achievement

Napoleon was no innovator either in tactics or in weapons, but from his first independent command in Italy in 1796, when aged only 26, he fully exploited the possibilities of the new kind of decisive warfare which he inherited. The previous 20 years had witnessed considerable improvements in roads and artillery and, most important, the beginnings of the system of dividing an army in the field into formations containing units of all arms that were strong enough to fight independently until reinforced. To these developments the French Revolution added particular military advantages of its own, including young and ambitious generals, larger numbers of troops inspired by a revolutionary fervour and rapid mobility dictated by a need to live off the land. Napoleon's genius lay in the charisma of his leadership and in his unrivalled ability to control widely dispersed formations and concentrate them at the decisive point. But he had no magic formula for victory, and as his enemies gradually learned to counter his methods he was obliged to rely increasingly on weight of numbers. He managed to defy the odds for so long chiefly because his opponents failed to coordinate their efforts.

The Reconquest of Italy

Marengo was not one of Napoleon's best-managed battles. In trying to outmanoeuvre the Austrians in northern Italy in 1800 he split his army into three detachments and stumbled on the main Austrian corps on 14 June with only 18,000 men against the Austrians' 30,000. He was saved from defeat by the return of Desaix and a gallant charge by Kellerman. Napoleon's severe losses – ten per cent were offset by the Austrians' acceptance of an armistice.

Austerlitz and Jena

In 1805 and 1806, Napoleon (now titled emperor) and his armies reached their peak of efficiency – a perfect blend of experience and élan. Thwarted in his plans to invade England, he rushed his divisions from Boulogne to the upper Rhine and so outmanoeuvred the Austrian commander Mack that he surrendered with 30,000 men at Ulm on 21 October 1805. By 1 December, Napoleon had left Vienna to confront the Russian and Austrian armies on a seven-mile front at Austerlitz. The French appeared to be outnumbered but Napoleon brought up reinforcements from great distances. Both French wings gave ground but then Napoleon boldly attacked in the centre to win perhaps his greatest victory. The enemy lost 25,000 men as against 9000 French casualties. Austria abandoned the coalition.

Prussia, which had remained neutral during this campaign, unwisely challenged France in the autumn of 1806. On 14 October, Prussia suffered overwhelming defeats at the twin battles of Jena and Auerstädt. At Jena, Napoleon threw 85,000 troops against what he wrongly thought to be the enemy's main army, gaining a victory over an inferior force only after heavy fighting. Meanwhile, Davout's corps, 27,000 strong, was outnumbered almost two to one by the Duke of Brunswick's army, but Davout first blocked the Prussians' attempt to retreat and then routed them in a counter-attack. It was this brilliant victory at Auerstädt which ensured Prussia's collapse. It became a French satellite until 1812.

Russia and Spain

Russia had intervened too late to save Prussia and was now facing Napoleon alone. He took the gamble of a winter campaign in East Prussia and Poland and, although he triumphed, there were signs that he was overtaxing French manpower and industrial resources. On 8 February 1807, French and Russians fought a bloody draw at Eylau in a snowstorm with the former losing 15,000 men. French morale slumped as supplies grew short and the wounded suffered terrible deprivation, 700 miles from home. With new levies, Napoleon raised his army to 300,000 in the spring and crushed the Russians in another costly battle at Friedland on 14 June. The Treaty of Tilsit (7 and 9 July 1807) with Alexander I followed, leaving Napoleon apparently master on the continent of Europe.

However, the French armies with which Napoleon attempted to extend his boycott of British goods to the Iberian Peninsula in November 1807 provoked a national rebellion in Spain and Portugal in the summer of 1808. From then onwards, this took the form of guerrilla operations combined with the campaigns of Wellington's army, with the result that Napoleon's armies were increasingly overstretched and weakened by the 'Spanish ulcer'.

Wagram

Encouraged by French reverses in Spain and the promise of British support, Austria again risked war early in 1809. This seemed a reasonable gamble but the Archduke Charles's dispersed offensives and lethargic movements enabled the French to brush his defences aside and enter Vienna on 13 May. The Austrians rallied on the left bank of the River Danube at Aspern and Napoleon's daring attempt to attack across the river failed after two days of fighting. Although the Austrian casualties were higher they could claim a victory over Napoleon. Seven weeks later, on 5 and 6 July, the French attacked successfully across the Danube at Wagram but still failed to secure a decisive victory. Although the Austrians requested an armistice their army remained in being.

To Moscow and back

In 1812 Napoleon committed a fatal error in invading Russia. He assembled a cosmopolitan army of nearly 600,000 men which, because of its size, was far too large to supply in such a poor country. A decisive battle was essential but Borodino, on 7 September, was a stalemate

Murat, one of Napoleon's favourite marshals

Napoleon's ambition to be the 'light of his age' was all cannon-flash, and went up in gunsmoke - a caricature of 1815

Russians now took their toll to the extent that only about 50,000 troops survived.

Napoleon's enemies now scented victory and in 1813 Prussia rejoined the Alliance to expel him from Germany. On 2 and 20 May 1813, Napoleon beat the joint Prussian and Russian armies at Lützen and Bautzen, but now it was his turn to seek an armistice. When this expired Austria, too, joined the alliance. Napoleon kept them at bay until mid-November but the Battle of Leipzig from 16 to 19 November turned into a rout with total French losses of 200,000 men. Even then, by brilliant defensive manoeuvres, Napoleon resisted in France until 31 March 1814, when the Allies' entry into Paris sealed his fate.

Waterloo

The Waterloo campaign added a costly postscript to Napoleon's career. He again stole a march on the enemy, splitting the Prussian centre at Ligny on 16 June 1815, but with only about 130,000 men against potential Allied forces of 700,000 he needed an immediate, decisive victory. Wellington denied him this at Quatre Bras and the arrival of Blücher's Prussians on 18 June completed the French rout.

B. J. B.

with huge losses approximately equal. The French entered Moscow on 16 September, but after five weeks in the devastated city the French retreated. Winter and the

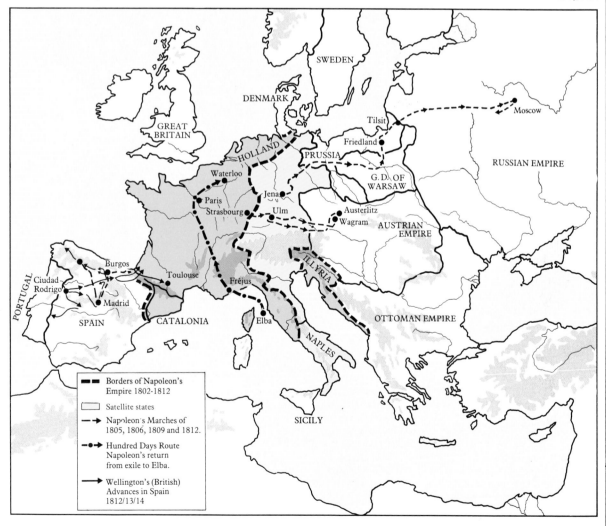

Borders of Napoleon's Empire 1802-1812

Satellite states

Napoleon's Marches of 1805, 1806, 1809 and 1812.

Hundred Days Route Napoleon's return from exile to Elba.

Wellington's (British) Advances in Spain 1812/13/14

Napoleon's Political System

Clary

Carlo - Maria Buonaparte ~ Letizia Ramolino

The

Désirée Julie ~ Joseph

Napoléon I ~ 1 Joséphine
(1 de Beauharnais)
2 Marie Louise
(Habsburg)

Lucien

Elise
Baciocchi

~Bernadotte

Napoléon II
Roi de Rome
l'Aiglon

From 1799 to 1815 European politics were dominated by Napoleon Bonaparte. His military and diplomatic victories made France the dominant land power in Europe; his ambitions made him the centre of all its diplomatic and military activity. His actions profoundly modified the geographical and administrative arrangements of Europe, and he came to represent a new kind of leadership.

When Bonaparte engineered the coup d'état of 1799, he was already France's best-known general, and France had been at war with most of Europe for seven years. With the exception of the Peace of Amiens (signed with England in 1802), war would continue throughout the period of Napoleon's rule. At the height of his power Napoleon was, quite simply, the master of Europe. In the campaigns of 1805–7 he defeated Austria at Ulm and Austerlitz, Prussia at Jena and Auerstädt, and Russia at Friedland. He then made agreements with Russia, with Austria (later marrying a Habsburg princess) and with other smaller states. France governed, as part of France, all Germany west of the Rhine, western Italy down to the borders of Naples, and the Illyrian provinces. At St Helena Napoleon was to claim that the aim of his foreign policy had been to create European unity; in fact, his motives were always the strategic interests of France and the dynastic interests of his family. Like a clan leader, he placed members of his family on the thrones of a series of satellite states. Brother Louis became king of Holland; brother Jérôme, king of Westphalia; brother Joseph was king of Naples and, after

1808, king of Spain; sister Caroline married General Murat, who took over Naples.

The fascination of Bonaparte does not, however, reside solely in the extent of his conquests. It rests too on the changes he brought to the form and style of government. Wherever he passed in Europe, feudalism was abolished and Italy, Belgium and the Rhineland all adopted the Code Napoleon as the foundation of their law. In France itself the administrative structure of the late 20th century is still based on the arrangements made by Napoleon in the early 19th. The principles of that structure owe much more to a belief in the need for efficient government than to a desire for democratic decision-taking. Napoleon described himself as a son of the Revolution, but he saw his task as ending the instability of revolutionary politics and he had no faith at all in representative institutions. Authority had to come from above. In 1804 he proclaimed himself emperor, but his attitude towards the relative roles of executive and legislature was already clear in the Constitution of 1799. This created three assemblies, membership of which was essentially obtained by nomination rather than election. The Tribunate discussed government bills but did not vote on them, the Legislative Body did the reverse, and the Senate, the most prestigious of them all, as well as the most timid, gave its 'consent'. It is a measure of Bonaparte's dislike of even minor criticism that when the Tribunate began to show signs of independent judgement, he dissolved it. The Ministry of

Family

Louis ~ Hortense de Beauharnais

Pauline
1 Gen. Leclerc
2 C. Borghese

Caroline ~ J. Murat

Jérôme

Napoléon III
(Louis-Napoléon)

Police of this 'new ruler' was as ubiquitous as the police services of the reactionary Habsburg emperor, and the most famous of all his administrative creations – the corps of prefects, one for every department – has become a symbol of central suspicion of local political activity.

Nevertheless, it would be wrong to concentrate exclusively on the repressive aspects of the system. Napoleon was determined that government should be both efficient and concerned with the well-being of the governed. The Ministry of the Interior had a wide-ranging competence over economic and social life (including the gathering of statistical information) and its membership, small by today's standards, impressed contemporaries with its bureaucratic size. Elsewhere, Napoleon created the Bank of France (1800), completed the codification of France's laws, created the Conseil d'Etat (1799) to provide a corps of expert administrators and law-drafters, and instituted the *Université* (1806) as a higher education system with control over secondary education, and consolidated the Institut de France as a centre of research. Moreover, he realized that he could not command obedience as a right and that it was necessary to gain the support of individuals and groups. High office came to depend on merit as well as on birth, and the introduction of the Légion d'Honneur and of a new aristocracy were evidence of his attempt to create loyalty. In 1802 the Concordat with Pope Pius VII sought to reintegrate Catholics into the national community. He was ready to employ in government both former republicans and former emigrés.

The failure of Napoleon was less that of his governmental system than of himself and his dynastic hopes. Externally, his attempt to defeat Britain by an economic blockade (the Continental System) was not only unsuccessful in itself, but was greatly resented by other countries whose trade suffered. The failure to subdue Spain dented France's reputation for invincibility and her enemies were, above all, encouraged by the catastrophic failure of Napoleon's invasion of Russia in 1812. This defeat led to Prussia and Austria joining with Britain and Russia against him. For the first time since 1793 France was herself invaded. Napoleon's generalship was as brilliant as ever, but he could not defeat the determination of his enemies combined with the apathy of his subjects. Conscription could not be enforced, and bad harvests led to subsistence riots. Many of the businessmen, civil servants and dignitaries who had benefited from his régime now felt it more prudent to sacrifice the emperor than to join him in a last ditch stand. In 1814 Paris was not defended and Napoleon's own Senate pronounced his deposition. The emperor exchanged rule over France for rule over Elba. In March 1815, however, he once again asserted his claim to govern France. His internal opponents fled, chief among them the restored Bourbon King Louis XVIII, but his external enemies were more determined. At the battle of Waterloo, the career of Napoleon Bonaparte ended.

P. M.

Russia in the Age of Napoleon

Russia entered the 'Age of Napoleon' a centralized, multi-national empire, the largest state in Europe and already an important element in the intricate network of European alliances and alignments. Her two most characteristic institutions, and the 'twin pillars' of her political and social order – autocracy and serfdom – had undergone no fundamental change since the reign of Peter the Great (1682–1725). With the gentry enjoying social and economic privileges but no political rights as such, and in the absence of a real bourgeoisie, the autocrat remained unhindered by conventional checks on his prerogatives. Serfdom, on which the predominance of the gentry largely rested, was still much more akin to slavery, with the landlord exercising unlimited authority over the person of his serf, who could indeed be described as his 'baptized property'.

The fundamental task facing the Russian autocracy in this period was the introduction of radical reforms in the governmental system, so as to adapt to new conditions and demands and to avoid the arbitrariness and unpredictability that had characterized the reign of Paul I (1796–1801), in whose overthrow Alexander I (1801–25) had been involved. Educated by the Swiss revolutionary La Harpe in the spirit of the Enlightenment, Alexander showed throughout his reign a genuine interest in constitutional and liberal reforms. But he tended to combine it with a firm commitment to the principle of unlimited autocracy, and it is this coexistence of two diametrically opposed principles within Alexander that gives a basic unity to a reign that it is otherwise tempting to divide into two contrasting halves: a liberal one until Napoleon's invasion of Russia in 1812, in which the main emphasis is on domestic affairs, and a conservative one until 1825 in which the emperor is almost exclusively involved in European affairs.

In the first half the intense discussion and planning of reforms, especially in the period 1807–12, when M. M. Speransky was Alexander's main adviser, led to some important and lasting changes being made in the fields of education and administration. The statute of 1804, the most liberal of the century, acknowledged the need for the widest spread of education and gave Russia her first coherent, all-embracing school system. The establishment (1802) and reorganization (1811) of ministries as central administrative organs, based upon the principle of monocratic authority and with a clear division of responsibility, and the creation of the State Council (1810) as an advisory legislative body to the emperor, introduced some badly needed order and clarity into the governmental structure. But Alexander remained a confirmed autocrat and he never implemented the rest of Speransky's ambitious and complex plan, for its provisions – especially the projected legislative state *duma* (parliament) – would quite clearly have limited his autocratic powers.

This same suspicion of fundamental change when considering practical implementation rather than abstract discussion robbed Alexander's peasant legislation of its potential effectiveness. The decree on free agriculturists (1803) made it possible for the gentry to emancipate its serfs with land, but left any such attempt to the private initiative of the individual serf-owner, while in the Baltic provinces, a landless emancipation (1816–19) led to the emergence of a peasantry, juridically free, but economically still dependent upon its former masters.

Tsar Alexander I (engraved from a painting by G. Kügelgen)

From 1812 the complexities of the international situation and disenchantment with slow progress at home led Alexander to devote himself almost exclusively to foreign affairs. Following his defeat of Napoleon and the subsequent campaigns (1812–15), Russia reached the peak of her power and prestige in Europe, with Alexander as one of the main architects of 'Congress Diplomacy', which successfully kept the peace in Europe for decades. The Holy Alliance (1815), of which Alexander was the author – a grandiose but nebulous attempt to base international relations on justice, Christian charity and peace – and the Quadruple Alliance (1815), which turned it into a pure interventionist doctrine, were also symptomatic of the growing conservatism and religious revival in Europe in reaction to the precepts of the Enlightenment. In Russia it manifested itself in an almost mystical feeling of intense national pride, the popularity of bible societies and the determination of the government to uphold the status quo.

A new ministry of 'Spiritual Affairs and Education' headed by Prince A. N. Golitsyn began a crusade against 'free-thinking' in education, with the universities of Kazan and St Petersburg being intellectually mutilated by the obscurantist activities of their respective curators, M. L. Magnitsky and D. P. Runich.

There were still some administrative changes in this period, but, again no basic reforms, although Alexander did not lose interest in liberal constitutional projects, at home or abroad, until he became alarmed at the political implications of the military uprisings in Spain, Piedmont and Naples (1820), the mutiny in his own Semenovsky guards regiment (1820) and the proliferation of secret societies. The *éminence grise* of the reign was now the conservative general Count A. A. Arakcheev, but this cannot be called the 'Era of Arakcheev'. Alexander remained in full control of domestic policy, and their relationship rested exclusively on Arakcheev's loyalty and ability to be the faithful executor of his master's wishes, whether liberal or conservative. This can be seen in his readiness to draw up a proposal for the emancipation of the serfs, and at the same time to set up the notorious 'military

Above: The burning of Moscow before Napoleon's eyes, September 1812 (painting by A. F. Smirnov)
Below: 'Visit to a Cossack Encampment in the Champs Elysées' (painting by A. I. Sauerweid, 1814)

colonies', an ill-fated attempt to create a new class of peasant-soldiers by combining peacetime farming with military service.

The reign of Alexander I ended in general disappointment. Serfdom and unlimited autocracy were still Russia's fundamental characteristics and the glaring contrast between this reality and the promise of the 'wonderful beginning of the Alexandrine years' led some 500 noble officers (supported by 3000 soldiers) to stage the first attempt at political revolution in Russia. The 'Decembrists' – so-called because they mutinied on 14 December 1825, during the succession crisis following the childless Alexander I's death, in the hope of installing a liberal provisional government – were steeped in the tradition of the Enlightenment and early 19th century European liberalism. They had been greatly influenced by the campaigns of 1812–15 and their direct contact with western Europe. Unlike past peasant uprisings and palace revolutions, they had clear political goals and were united in advocating the abolition of autocracy and serfdom. Although they failed – they were too small a minority, lacking general support, unity and, above all, a proper organization – the Decembrists succeeded in highlighting what was wrong with unreformed Russia and opened up a rift between the government and educated public opinion that was to have grave consequences for the rest of the 19th century. *C. B.*

British Sea Power Established

Toulon

Some people in Britain could welcome the upheavals in France in 1789 as a weakening either of autocracy or of the power of an old rival; others saw in them no more than an unpleasant domestic conflict. But as violence and republicanism increased, and the French armies defeated the Austrians and moved into the Low Countries in 1792–93, the forces of revolution seemed to present a serious threat to Britain's internal stability, trade and national security. The Younger Pitt's government, with neither navy nor army in a state of readiness, had no wish for conflict, but France's declaration of war on 1 February 1793 left no alternative. Underestimating French strength, Britain engaged in a series of uncoordinated offensives of which the blockade and capture of Toulon by Admiral Hood in August 1793 was the most dramatic. It only proved, however, that a combination of British naval forces and local French royalists could neither hold Toulon nor use it as a base for further advances without military aid. As this did not arrive, the British, after destroying the French warships, retreated in December, leaving Toulon to the young Napoleon Bonaparte. Toulon was symbolic both of Allied failures to cooperate in military matters and of Britain's dependence on her naval resources for success against the French.

Press gangs and mutinies

Naval victories alone saved Britain from invasion, and enabled her both to obtain essential supplies and cripple enemy trade. Late in 1797, however, the situation was extremely gloomy, and despite Jervis's defeat of the Spanish fleet (in alliance with the French) off Cape St Vincent in February, victory was some way off. Discontent among British seamen ran high, for conditions of pay, food and leave were appalling. Naval recruitment was never easy, and in wartime the press-gang appeared as a feared and familiar feature of life in many ports. Such gangs, using force or fraud, were used to get men aboard to make up crews enabling ships to sail. Not surprisingly, unwilling and ill-used sailors mutinied in April 1797 off Spithead, refusing to man the Channel Fleet. Their demands were rapidly met, but in May a second mutiny at the Nore was sternly suppressed.

Egypt and the Mediterranean

Discipline was restored none too soon. Between spring 1796 and summer 1798, Napoleon shifted his war effort to the Mediterranean, invading Italy, forcing Spain on to his side, and compelling the British to quit Elba, Corsica and Malta. British interests in the Mediterranean were considerable. At all times a major artery of British trade, it provided, too, a vital link with her overland route to India and the East; now in war it was crucial to her contacts with her allies, Austria and Naples. Napoleon's expedition to Egypt in June 1798 threatened to create a French, Middle-Eastern, empire and to extinguish British interests. Despite the danger that the removal of vessels from the English Channel or its approaches might revive the possibility of invasion, Pitt decided that the Mediterranean had to be reopened, and sent a squadron after Napoleon. The French fleet was eventually located in Aboukir Bay at the mouth of the River Nile, and largely destroyed (Battle of the Nile, 1 August 1798). A skilful victory, it restored Britain's national self-confidence, restored a degree of British control of Mediterranean waters, stranded Napoleon for 15 months and French forces for far longer, and gave the coalition powers time to pull themselves together.

Nelson

Horatio Nelson was perhaps the greatest of those naval officers whose qualities as commanders, and successes in battle, restored national as well as naval morale after the mutinies of 1797, and established beyond question Britain's command of the seas. Born on 29 September 1758, one of the country gentry of Norfolk and therefore with little of the sea in his blood, he nevertheless joined the navy when 12 years old. Careful study, powerful ambition, prolonged unemployment and an uneasy marriage, all combined to give direction to his natural impetuosity. Brilliant but previously untried tactics of his own against the French at Cape St Vincent first brought him renown, and he confirmed his reputation as a commander at Aboukir Bay – the first of a trio of victories, each destined to mark a turning point in the war. In 1800, following a series of French military successes, the League of Baltic States began to restrict British trade and shipping. Britain's reply was to attack Copenhagen, where Nelson, on 2 April 1801, ignored his commander and destroyed the Danish fleet, and so hastened the collapse of northern hostility. His final contribution occurred in 1805, as the British tried to pin down the French and restrain Napoleon's renewed aggression. As the French left Cadiz for a diversionary attack on British-backed Naples, Nelson caught and thrashed their fleet at the Battle of (Cape) Trafalgar on 21 October. Although he was killed in the action, Nelson's victory permanently finished French naval threats, and set Britain on the path to sustained military involvement on the continent of Europe.

Far-flung outposts

By 1806, while Napoleon was at the height of his power in Europe, Britain had effectively driven the French from the seas. British control was reinforced by the seizure of territory or strategic bases on the world's principal trading routes. On this world scale, the conflict with Napoleon continued the pattern of earlier Anglo-French wars for empire and trade. Fear of France added impetus to territorial expansion in India, and well before Trafalgar Britain had captured Trinidad, Tobago and Dutch Guiana. Between 1802 and 1815, the Cape of Good Hope, Mauritius and Ceylon were acquired, and were kept at the final peace settlement. Such formal acquisitions were matched elsewhere by an informal expansion of British trade, in the Far East and in Latin America. While other rival empires of the Dutch and Spanish had been irreparably damaged, Britain emerged in 1815 with a worldwide network of trade and territory, resting on her naval supremacy.

A. N. P.

Right: The chain of bases on vital trade routes left in British hands at the post-Napoleonic peace settlements

HMS 'Brunswick' in a desperate engagement with 'Vengeur' and 'Achille', 1 June 1794 (painting by Nicholas Pocock). Inset: England's darling, Horatio Nelson

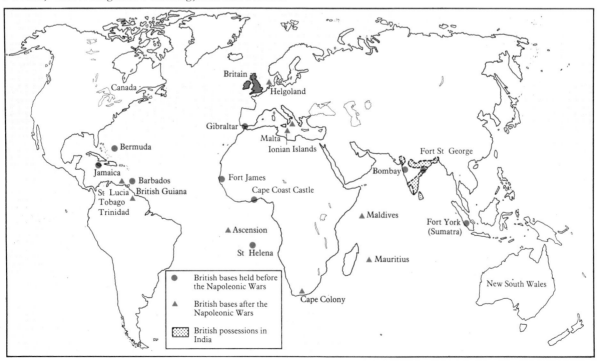

Isambard Kingdom Brunel

INDUSTRIAL

Most of the new processes in the manufacture of iron, textiles and chemicals demanded the constant supervision of workers, and only offered geographical and economic advantages to employers if the labour force were gathered together into a few large factories. This fact, together with the displacement of agricultural labourers and small farmers from the land by changing methods of agricultural practice, caused urbanization. The social effects of urbanization were felt more dramatically in Britain than elsewhere, partly because of its religious division into Anglicanism and Dissent, partly because of the waves of Irish immigration and partly because it led the world in industrialization. From the 1830s onwards novelists like Dickens and Mrs Gaskell, critics like Carlyle and fact-finding parliamentary commissions probed 'the condition of England'. Consequently, important steps were taken by Parliament to reduce the tensions in society: the granting of emancipation to Roman Catholics and Nonconformists, the encouragement of emigration to Canada and Australia, the prevention of exploitation of women and children in factories, and the creation of systems of mass elementary and technical education by 1870. The result of these changes was a class-conscious society: an aristocracy with dwindling powers, a largely unskilled and religiously indifferent labour force that was becoming conscious of its political weight and bargaining power, and a powerful, prosperous middle class.

Upon the face of the land itself a new force in communications was burrowing and tracing its network of steel rails. As the 'iron roads' spread, they both destroyed and transformed towns and cities, and created easy routes for the mass transport of goods and people. They increased personal initiative through mobility, and made possible the new idea of mass holidays. They imposed a uniform system of time-keeping throughout each nation and the world.

Population pressures had such dire consequences on the health of both privileged and poor that state intervention in hygiene proved essential. This provided opportunities for the social advancement of middle class engineering and medical experts. Their advice and practice had, in turn, important implications for the curriculum of schools and universities and gave a higher status to scientific education in an industrial society. *W. H. B.*

REVOLUTION

The Railroads

Until the 1830s the 'railway', or 'railroad', remained essentially a method of conveyance of materials for the mining industry. It had been developed in central Europe during the later Middle Ages, the first recorded use of small trucks on wooden rails being in the Tyrol in 1530. Railways, also called tramways, were in operation in England from at least the 16th century and their numbers grew rapidly after 1700 with the beginnings of industrialization particularly to connect coal mines with rivers, canals or tidewater. Early guidance systems were primitive and the first positive evidence of the employment of a flanged wheel is in 1733 on a line joining a quarry at Prior Park, Bath, with the River Avon. The first cast-iron wheel was patented in England in 1731 and iron rails were first used at Coalbrookdale in 1767. Initially, rails were laid upon continuous lengths of timber laid lengthways, but in 1789 William Jessop developed a system of short lengths of cast-iron rail, joined with laps and pins, and supported by spaced stone blocks. Wooden ties or sleepers were introduced with Thomas Barnes's modification of Jessop's methods in which the rails abutted and were supported by chairs. In 1800 there were a variety of horse-drawn railway systems, the major alternative to the flanged-edge rail being the plate-way which had a flange on the inside edge of the rail itself. It was used mainly in the collieries and ironworks of the north Midlands and south Wales and had the advantage that ordinary carts could be drawn on it without modification. Cast iron was brittle and from the 1820s was replaced by wrought iron, following John Birkinshaw's discovery of a method of rolling wedge-shaped wrought-iron rails, coupled with the development at the Bedlington ironworks, Northumberland, of a way of producing them in long lengths.

The steam revolution

Steam power, like the railway, was also a product of the mining industry, being employed initially for pumping. It was first applied to locomotion in 1769 by a Frenchman, Nicholas Cugnot in France. James Watt took out a patent for a self-propelling engine in the same year and a refined version of it was built by his pupil William Murdoch in 1785. Watt's engines were low pressure, i.e. up to 5lb/sq. in. Richard Trevithick followed a different course, the application of high pressure with the steam exhausted directly into the atmosphere. He built a road vehicle embodying these principles in 1801, a railway engine in 1804 – the *Pen-y-darran* – which was a modified prime mover for an ironworks hammer, and four years later demonstrated publicly his ideas with *Catch-me-who-can* which ran on a circular track at Bloomsbury, London. His de-

signs were developed further on the northern coalfields by George Stephenson and his son Robert, Hedley and Blenkinsop. There was concern over whether smooth wheels could gain purchase on smooth rails and in 1811 Blenkinsop built a two-cylinder engine with a drive consisting of a geared wheel which engaged a rack fitted to the track. George Stephenson and Nicholas Wood found that the gear drive was unnecessary, dispensed with it, but otherwise retained Blenkinsop's practice for their *Puffing Billy*. During the 1810s this pair of colliery engineers made considerable advances in establishing the basic technology of the steam engine. Their Killingworth colliery engine had direct drive from the pistons to the wheels via connecting rods and crankpins while the exhaust steam was taken up through the smokebox which both quietened the engine and gave additional draught on the boiler fire. *Locomotion*, the original engine of the Stockton & Darlington railway, was an advanced version of the Killingworth colliery type built by George Stephenson. Although the first steam-powered public railway, the Stockton & Dar-

Right: Civil engineering work (tunnels, viaducts), on a scale not seen since Roman times, accompanied the spread of the rail network in the 1840s

lington used a mixture of horses, stationary engines and steam locomotives for traction, its running costs soon showed that the steam engine was cheaper than the horse and that the locomotive was more economic than the stationary engine. Doubts over the economics of steam locomotion continued, however, until the mid-1830s, one consequence being the Rainhill Trials of 1829 for an engine for the Liverpool & Manchester.

The trials were won by Robert Stephenson's *Rocket*, a locomotive which marked further progress in design. It had a multi-tubular boiler, developed by Stephenson in England and independently by Marc Séguin in France, together with inclined outside cylinders. *Northumbrian* was the first engine of the Rocket class to have a proper tender and a firebox not only surrounded by water but also totally enclosed in the rear end of the boiler barrel. Stephenson's next series of locomotives was the Planet class, with inside cylinders in front below the smokebox and outside sandwich frames, supplemented by light inside frames. Stephenson's influence in the 1830s and early

1840s pervaded both Britain and elsewhere in the world of which one effect was the subsequent near universality of his gauge of 4ft 8½in. In 1841 his long-boiler type appeared which was an attempt to obtain a better exchange of heat in the boiler without raising the centre of gravity of the locomotive, which was then thought to be undesirable. Although the ride of the engine was poor as a result of a short wheel-base, it was taken up both in Britain and on the Continent. At the same time, Stephenson perfected his mechanical valve gear which allowed the easy reversing of the locomotive and the ability to adjust, while running, the point of the piston stroke at which the admission of steam to the cylinder was cut off.

Advances in locomotive design were coupled with some improvements in rolling-stock. The prototype of the modern compartment coach made its appearance in the early 1830s but only for first-class passengers.

The spread of rail networks
Railways were opened in the USA in 1827, in France in 1828, in Germany in 1835, in Belgium and Canada in 1836, in Austria in 1837, in Russia in 1838 and in Holland and Italy in 1839. Where steam locomotives were employed, they were initially usually British, often Stephenson types. The pioneer Belgian line, the Brussels & Malines, had Stephenson engines built by Tayleaur at the Vulcan foundry while the first domestically constructed Belgian locomotive, *Le Belge* of 1835, was erected by Cockerill, a firm of English origins, to a Stephenson design. Similarly *Der Adler*, the locomotive of the first German line, was a Stephenson engine.

English locomotives were also exported to North America. The *Stourbridge Lion* of 1829 was built by Foster, Raistrick but proved to be too heavy for the Delaware & Hudson Canal and was converted into a stationary engine. *John Bull* was a Stephenson engine employed in 1831 by the Camden & Amboy, a company founded by the sons of Colonel John Stevens, the pioneer of American steam locomotives. Unfortunately the locomotive left the lightly laid tracks, a problem which was cured by fitting a leading pony truck. This marked one of the important early American divergences in design practice and, whereas in England the 0-6-0 coupled engine became almost a standard, especially for goods workings, in America the Baldwin works were producing the forerunners of the ubiquitous 4-4-0 in large numbers by the end of the 1830s. This difference arose out of American engineers accepting gradients far more severe than Stephenson's recommendation of a maximum of 1 in 330, and out of their use of the flat-footed rail spiked to the tie or sleeper, rather than the double-headed rail held in chairs.   *P. C.*

Below: Rolling stock of the 1830s for 2nd class passengers and livestock

Medicine and Public Health

The earliest form of state medicine was vaccination. In 1798, Edward Jenner had demonstrated that smallpox could be prevented by inoculating a healthy subject with material from a cowpox scab. Despite the dangers of cross-infection from arm-to-arm vaccination with unsterilized needles, the British government repeatedly, but unsuccessfully, tried to make vaccination compulsory during the 19th century. It was Jenner's method which convinced Louis Pasteur and other microbiologists that the body possessed natural immunological agents which could be stimulated by mild doses of a disease (vaccine therapy). Pasteur's most important demonstration of this principle came in 1885 when he prevented an outbreak of rabies by using attenuated vaccine.

Until the 19th century, there were traditional demarcation lines drawn between the upper rank of the medical profession, the physicians, who were university-educated and ranked in society as 'gentlemen', and the surgeons and apothecaries who were trained by apprenticeship and accorded the status of tradesmen. By 1850, however, the physicians' hegemony had been challenged and the modern division of labour between general practitioners and consultant surgeons and physicians had become established. The General Medical Council was established in Britain in 1858 as a consequence of the Medical Act of that year which called for a legal register of all qualified practitioners.

As a consequence of the institutional reforms made pos-

Louis Pasteur, to whom we owe 'pasteurizing'

The cartoonist Gillray lampoons anti-vaccination agitation in 1802 with the supposed effects of cow-pox inoculation

sible by the French Revolution, young French doctors were able to implement new ideas and practices. Avoiding dogmatism, and stressing clinical signs and symptoms, these practitioners extended the sensory equipment of the profession by introducing the stethoscope and the clinical thermometer, and by the use of percussion of the chest and back. Such techniques were introduced into other countries during the 1820s and 1830s by students attracted to Paris by its clinical reputation – a point used by George Eliot in characterizing Lydgate in her novel *Middlemarch* (1871–72). By the 1860s, using vivisection as a basic tool of physiological investigation, C. Bernard had established the existence of an 'internal environment' (homeostasis) whereby an animal controls its own metabolism through a complex series of interacting regulatory mechanisms – the unravelling of which has provided the programmes of research for physiologists, biochemists and pathologists ever since.

Medical research

In the German states the competitive character of the universities and their healthy financial endowment by their governments, produced a close relationship between biological research and hospital medicine. Using the achromatic microscope developed in England in 1829, M. Schleiden and T. Schwann showed that the common elements of growth and nutrition in plants and animals were the cells. This enabled R. Virchow in the 1860s to explain disease in terms of the pathology of cells and establish the microscope as an important tool of research. Earlier, in 1840, Justus Liebig, through his book *Animal Chemistry*, had laid the foundations of biochemistry by demonstrating how organic chemistry might be used to unravel the metabolic pathways of food as it was transformed into energy, animal heat, tissues and excreta.

Liebig's view that disease was due to oxidation, or putrefaction, of tissues was very influential, but until the principle of antisepsis was established by J. Lister in 1867 the air-tight binding of wounds with surgical dressings did little to reduce mortality. During the 1860s, Pasteur showed that various vinous fermentations and all so-called spontaneous generations were due to the presence in the air of minute living particles which he and others termed germs, microbes or bacteria. Since such life was destroyed by the application of heat or disinfectants, it occurred to Lister that if surgical sepsis was caused by microbes, it could be prevented by spraying wounds with a carbolic acid solution and using impregnated dressings. Much else of the impedimenta of modern aseptic surgery, including rubber gloves and soluble ligatures, was also developed by Lister. Although his innovations came too late to reduce the appalling casualty rate of the Franco-Prussian War (1870), antisepsis (together with anaesthesia) had revolutionized surgery by the 1880s.

In 1846, accompanied by publicity from the weekly journal *The Lancet*, Robert Liston used ether to anaesthetize patients undergoing amputations. In Edinburgh, J. Simpson adopted ether in obstetric operations but, perturbed by its effects (nausea and vomiting), he made a systematic search of volatile chemicals for a better alternative. In November 1847 he discovered the narcotic effects of chloroform and successfully promoted its wider adoption. Its analgesic properties were noticed by the London physician John Snow, who administered chloroform to Queen Victoria during the birth of Prince Leopold in 1853. Anaesthesia made longer and more difficult operations possible, but until the advent of antisepsis, surgeons continued to expect an operative mortality rate of 10 per cent and a post-operative sepsis rate of over 60 per cent.

Snow is also remembered for his demonstration in 1848 of the water-borne character of cholera, though its bacteriological cause was not discovered until 1884 by the German bacteriologist Robert Koch. Cholera, typhoid, typhus, diphtheria, scarlet fever and smallpox were all endemic, and although they struck both rich and poor alike, they were associated in medical minds with the dirty, crowded conditions of the sprawling industrial cities. It was therefore inevitably believed that 'dirt' caused disease, which was spread through the atmosphere by prevailing weather conditions. Such a miasmatic theory of disease, which was right for the wrong reasons, led E. Chadwick to promote a campaign for sanitary engineering to remove sewage from homes and towns in drains, to supply constant pure water to houses, to pave streets and to provide areas for municipal cemeteries.

Whereas the early 19th-century doctor had few prophylactic aids at his command other than traditional blood-letting and a few drugs, by the end of the century the removal of health hazards by better sanitation, the improved education of doctors in the basic sciences, the development of anaesthesia and asepsis and, above all, the emergence of the bacteriological theory of disease, seemed to promise longevity and the complete eradication of disease from society. Bacteriologists were soon proved over-confident, for, with the dawn of the 20th century, the nutritional, endocrinal and virus basis of many unconquered diseases became apparent. *W. H. B.*

An excursion in the Paris sewers - Victorians took pride in their new sanitary engineering

The confrontation between the forces of continuity and change has never been more open and extensive than during the years from 1789 to 1848. The earlier part of this period, dominated by the French Revolution and the Napoleonic Wars, constituted an epoch of unprecedentedly huge upheaval. Bonaparte himself, even while seeking to convert chaos into order, brought cold comfort to truer conservatives. The latter enjoyed a spell of better fortune only after 1815, the year in which the Vienna Congress completed its attempt at restoring stability to Europe.

The 1815 settlement aimed to reassert wherever feasible the principle of hereditary dynastic kingship, and also gave hope to the defenders of traditional aristocratic and ecclesiastical authority. Most particularly, it attempted to establish bulwarks against any re-emergence of France as a major disruptive force. The peacemakers wished to construct such a balance of power as would preserve Europe from further general warfare. A scheme for regular international meetings, concerned to promote whatever would be 'most salutary for the repose and prosperity of the nations and for maintaining the peace of Europe', broke down within a decade. British enthusiasm especially had waned, as it became evident that the more autocratic governments of Russia, Austria and Prussia were interpreting this 'Congress System' as a charter for reactionary intervention in the internal affairs of smaller countries.

This post-Napoleonic era is associated always with the name of Klemens von Metternich, foreign minister of Austria from 1809 and chancellor from 1821. The Carlsbad Decrees of 1819, which he helped to impose upon all the states of the new German confederation, typify his efforts to stifle the organization and expression of progressive dissent.

The values that Metternich symbolized were endangered not only by movements intended to promote liberal, nationalist and even socialist causes. Less conscious forces of a more social than political kind, such as the very rapid growth of population and of industrial activity, also played a vital role in eroding the conservative order. The revolutionary disturbances of 1830 turned out to be merely the prelude for still more widespread turmoil in 1848. Even though the rejoicing of European liberals at the flight of Metternich was premature, none could deny that with his exile a distinctive epoch had come to an end. _M. D. B._

REACTION IN EUROPE

From left to right: Dom Miguel of Portugal, Ferdinand VII of Spain, Charles X of France, Frederick William III of Prussia, Frederick VI of Denmark, Metternich, Emperor Ferdinand I of Austria, Tsar Nicholas I of Russia

Revolution and Counter-Revolution

To think there was a simple cause-and-effect relationship between the Enlightenment and the American and French revolutions would be naïve. Both revolutions had complex political, social and economic roots reaching back for at least a century, yet the political activists in each country were men of their own time. Inevitably their actions, in one way or another, embodied the main currents of contemporary thought. In both upheavals we can see the influence on them of such late 17th- and 18th-century thinkers as John Locke, Charles de Montesquieu or Voltaire, of the encyclopedist Denis Diderot, the Franco-German materialist Paul d'Holbach, the proto-socialist Bonnot de Mably. It was only natural, for example, that the American colonists should seek moral support for their rebellion in Locke's widely influential *Two Treatises on Civil Government* (1690) with its propositions of human goodness and the natural right to freedom, and its justification of revolution in some circumstances, or look for counsel on the framing of their constitution in *The Spirit of Laws* (1748) of de Montesquieu, with its advocacy of checks and balances in the exercise of sovereignty. Similar influences can be recognized in the earlier stages of the French Revolution, especially in the language of the *Declaration of the Rights of Man* (1789). In France, moreover, the rationalist and anti-clerical inheritance of the *philosophes* and the physiocrats of the Enlightenment is to be seen in much of the legislation of the Revolution as well as the Napoleonic period: for instance, the *Civil Constitution of the Clergy* (1790), the administrative and fiscal reforms carried out under the National Assembly, the replacement of the Gregorian with a Republican calendar and the great codification of French civil law, the *Code Napoléon* (1804–07).

Rousseau

At the same time, much of what went on in France, or elsewhere in Europe for that matter, between the Revolution and the Bourbon restoration of 1814 ran counter to the ideals of the Enlightenment. The Abbé Sieyès, in what is certainly the best-known pamphlet of the French Revolution, *What is the Third Estate?* (1789), by identifying the people with the government, put forward a notion of popular sovereignty in which any checks on governmental authority were removed. Yet even a cursory reading of the political writings of Locke or the *philosophes* – especially de Montesquieu – would reveal a strong bias in the Enlightenment for built-in institutional restraints on the exercise of sovereignty. For them, the naked exercise of authority meant the demise of personal liberty, an ideal almost universally cherished in the Enlightenment. It is doubtful whether even the great propagandist of freedom, Jean Jacques Rousseau, renounced this ideal. His definition of the 'General Will' refers to that which all the people in a given polity would will if they were only acting in the common interest. It is an ideal will, exercised to frame general laws only. He does not suggest that it should operate in the everyday administration of government.

Because of the way he wrote, however, Rousseau is easily misinterpreted or misrepresented. For example, equating the General Will with the direct action of the people, Maximilien Robespierre, the leader and chief ideologue of the Jacobins, justified his party's use of the revolutionary mob against its opponents. Once in power,

of course, Robespierre and his colleagues found themselves in the opposite position of having to suppress the popular force they had invoked.

Burke

Although in the eyes of extremists even to the left of Robespierre – the *enragés*, the *Hébertistes*, Babeuf and others – the revolution in France had not gone far enough, the actions of the National Assembly, let alone of the Jacobins, aroused fear and repulsion amongst conservatives throughout Europe. The best-known ideological critique of the upheaval in France came from the Irish political writer and Whig member of the British Parliament, Edmund Burke. Despite its title, he wrote the *Reflections on the Revolution in France* (1790) in response to what he perceived to be the growth of radicalism in his own party, thus directing his arguments towards a British rather than a French or European audience. The *Reflections*, nevertheless, was soon translated into the major European languages, and to this day continues as one of the major statements of conservative ideology in the Western world. In his concern to point out the dangerous nature of the events in France, Burke clearly espoused a political philosophy and a view of history which rejected the concept of natural rights and the rule of reason. According to Burke, the usurpers of authority in France, in attempting to apply the principles of science to a re-organization of society and political life, had ignored the organic nature of history and the more subtle, less tangible aspects of the human personality. For him, customs and habits were not simply relics of past cultures and social forms, but expressions of the cumulative experience of mankind. Put simply, he believed that human rights do not exist apart from society and, furthermore, that they evolve with the passage of time. To tamper with the fabric of society, as was being done in France was, according to his analysis, to destroy the matrix within which change could take place. Reform, he was to declare, could thus only take place by building upon established institutions.

In spite of the inherently conservative nature of this doctrine, its emphasis on the organic and individualistic nature of society occasionally led Burke to take up positions of a seemingly progressive nature on some of the major issues of his day. He called for restraint in British rule over Ireland and India on the grounds that the native

Joseph de Maistre (left) and Edmund Burke (right), ideologists of the Right

institutions and culture should be respected, and he pleaded the case of the colonists in America by defending their inherited rights as Englishmen.

The *Reflections* did not go unnoticed in radical circles. The most famous polemical reply to Burke came from the radical publicist Thomas Paine, who had taken an active part in the American Revolution, and was shortly to become involved in the French Revolution. In his pamphlet *The Rights of Man* (1791), Paine upheld the notion of natural rights to the point of arguing that man has the inviolable and inalienable right to oppose tyranny.

Burke's views found an echo in Europe. The Empress Catherine of Russia congratulated him personally on his work. Significantly, Friedrich von Gentz, later to become secretary to Metternich and the Vienna Congress, translated the *Reflections* into German in 1793.

De Maistre

Although very much a thinker in his own right, Joseph de Maistre quoted Burke extensively. Leaving his native Savoy when it was annexed by the revolutionary army of France, he spent his years of exile first in Germany and then at the imperial court in St Petersburg. Like Burke, he rejected the political reasoning of the *philosophes*, on whom he blamed the convulsion in France. Political ideas could not be deduced, as they did, from a set of first principles, but were, according to his *Essay on the Generative Principle*, to be based on evidence gleaned from history and experience, and to be evaluated on the basis of whether they were 'beneficial' or 'harmful'. In this aspect of his thought, de Maistre was thinking along similar lines to the 'utilitarians' and foreshadowing the American pragmatic school of philosophy.

Like Burke, he also believed that the thinkers of the Enlightenment had neglected the instinctive side of man's make up. For example, man, according to de Maistre, constantly craves for authority. In destroying the monarchy and the Church, the revolutionaries had removed the two most important pillars of French society. What is more, in his view, they had vandalized the work of God. In this sense, de Maistre quite clearly saw the French Revolution as a manifestation of evil, which he thought of as being in a constant duel with the good in man.

Because of the strong anti-rationalist current in his thought (most clearly seen in *The St Petersburg Dialogues*, 1821), de Maistre has usually been classified together with such other late 18th- and early 19th-century writers in German as the nationalist Fichte, the Swiss historian Müller, the philosopher Hegel and the novelist Novalis, as well as with the man who in his eyes was an arch-villain of the period, Rousseau. De Maistre's influence on conservative thought in general is, like Burke's, unmistakable, but it was through his insistence on the cardinal importance of divine revelation and the role of the Catholic Church in interpreting and implementing revelation that he became one of the intellectual authorities of ultramontanism, the extreme centralizing and papal absolutist tendency in 19th-century Catholicism.   *M. R.*

In their first fresh enthusiasm the people of France celebrated the Revolution by planting 'liberty trees' in the presence of the mayor and the National Guard, to the sounds of music and song

Trade Unions in Britain

The Combination Acts

In response to an increase in urban and industrial unrest as the Napoleonic wars hit Britain's economy, the Combination Acts were passed in 1799 and 1800 by Parliament, whose members, while they had little knowledge of the circumstances and passions of working men, were also fearful of a repetition in Britain of the excesses of revolutionary France. Although many, especially employers, welcomed the additional opportunity provided by these Acts to prevent the further growth of trade unions and so to depress wages, in practice the Acts proved singularly ineffective for this purpose. The Acts not only established comparatively minor penalties for offenders, but also prohibited employers' combinations and offered arbitration in disputes. Although these clauses were not exploited, they also emphasize the place of the Combination Acts as the last in a series of restrictive measures passed since 1794. These – temporary suspension of habeas corpus, the limitations imposed on all public meetings, the redefinition of 'treason', and the suppression of the political Corresponding Societies – marked the banding together of men of different shades of political opinion in defence of property and the status quo. There was little possibility – and even less conception – of any government controlling the economic changes moulding Britain's new industries and urban centres. While war, bad harvests and high prices (as in 1794–95) imposed additional strains, the navy and army were mobilized to meet the French.

Other domestic resources for maintaining law and order were pitifully small. Repressive legislation and penal deterrence seemed to be the only course.

As memories of revolutionary uproar receded, and the varied popular disturbances of 1815–20 (the machine-wrecking Luddite Movement, the Spa Fields and Peterloo demonstrations) died away, the scene was set for the repeal of the Combination Acts. In 1822, the reconstruction of Lord Liverpool's Tory administration had brought forward not only the popular George Canning but also other younger and less obstructive Tories, like Sir Robert Peel at the Home Office. Government and people relaxed in proportion as general economic conditions improved and unemployment declined. Relative prosperity stimulated the growth of the workmen's combination ('trade union' was a term only slowly coming into fashion), especially in skilled trades such as printing, where labour was most likely to be in short supply. However, pressure for legislative reform came less from trade unionists themselves than from those who believed that unions were unnecessary and who felt that, once the irritant of prohibition was removed, workmen would soon realize this for themselves. Under the influence of Francis Place, a leading London artisan, J. R. McCulloch the economist and the radical MP Joseph Hume, the House of Commons first appointed a select committee to enquire into the working of the Acts, and then legislated to repeal them on the basis of the committee recommendations. Although the com-

The 'Peterloo' massacre, 16 August 1819, drawn by Cruikshank

mittee members and witnesses were carefully chosen by the reformers, there seems little reason to doubt their view that repeal of unenforceable legislation would remove an obstacle to better industrial relations. A new Act admitted the principle of combination for the fixing of wages and hours and, with further reinforcement in 1825, invoked penalties only for violence and intimidation in pursuit of a combination's goals.

Wellington's ministry

If many of the reforms of the Tory administration of the early 1820s took place against a backcloth of economic improvement, renewed economic difficulties underlay both the hardening of political attitudes and the fragmentation of the Tory Party during Wellington's ministry of 1828–30. Many landowners felt that inadequate protection was being given to agriculture, felt hard pressed by taxation and resented Wellington's refusal to do more for them. Merchants and industrialists also felt that their interests were neglected. The Canningites or 'liberal' Tories (Canning himself had died in 1827) clashed with Wellington over the question of how to deal with two parliamentary constituencies found guilty of electoral corruption, and resigned from the Government. The opposite wing of the Tory Party was outraged by Wellington's and Peel's decision in 1829, in the face of practical difficulties in Ireland, to pass a Roman Catholic Emancipation Bill abolishing many of the restrictions on Catholics' rights to hold public office or be elected to Parliament. Finally, when Wellington, in an attempt to revive his Party, declared his opposition to further political reform and his admiration for the existing constitution, he only united critics from left and right, inside and outside Parliament, against him. In 1830 the long dominance of British politics by conservative forces was broken, in part by economic and social pressures for change, in part through the lack of political skills demonstrated by the military victor of Waterloo.

The 'Tolpuddle martyrs'

The years after 1825 witnessed the rapid growth of working-class organizations. These were of three main types: the Friendly Societies, providing such facilities as pensions or medical expenses, in return for regular subscriptions; the Cooperative Societies, devoted (until the 1840s) to the founding of self-sufficient communist communities; and the trade unions. Middle-class successes, especially in the struggle for political reform between 1830 and 1832, left many working-class people feeling deserted and with a heightened sense of their own separate interests. These feelings now inspired attempts, particularly among the trade unions, to establish national organizations – for groups of trades, like the Operative Builders' Union, or, in the case of the Grand National Consolidated Trades Union of 1834, for all trades. The Friendly Society of Agricultural Labourers formed at Tolpuddle in Dorset in October 1833, was therefore one among many such societies; only its treatment by local magistrates was exceptional. After a questionable trial, its leader, George Loveless, and five members were sentenced under one of the restrictive Acts of the 1790s to transportation to Australia, for administering unlawful oaths to unionists. The sentences were confirmed by the Whig Government. This severity is partly explained by the refusal of the authorities to countenance the formation of agricultural unions, when rural unrest, arson and rioting were widespread. Not until the 1870s were such unions successful. However, the outcry and demonstrations of sympathy provoked by the Tolpuddle case produced a pardon for the 'martyrs' in 1836, and their return to England, where sufficient money had been collected to provide most of them with farms of their own. *A. N. P.*

The Dorset farm labourers known as the Tolpuddle Martyrs after their conviction and transportation for administering 'unlawful oaths' in forming a Friendly Society in 1833

Italy   1796-1831   The German States

For the states of Italy, as for many other parts of Europe, the French Revolution constituted a fundamental breach with the past. The libertarian ideas proclaimed by the revolutionary armies in 1796–97 had a profound impact on states accustomed for centuries to varying degrees of absolutist rule, either foreign or local. Direct domination of Italy by the French between 1796 and 1814 served not only to disseminate new ideas, but also brought many of the features of Napoleonic rule – administrative reform, new legal codes, and an attack on feudalism and the established privileges of the church. Many rulers fled, and new and larger states were formed and annexed to France, the name 'Italy' being used officially for the first time. The pope was removed to France and the Papal States were taken over. Paradoxically, the immense stimulus given to both intellectual and economic activity by the French invasion also helped to generate anti-French sentiment. Conscription and heavy taxation were partially responsible, but it was also clear that continued French domination accorded badly with the libertarian ideals of the Revolution.

Secret societies (in the north the Adelphi, in the south the Carbonari, or 'charcoal burners') were formed to organize anti-French feeling. They had little impact prior to the defeat of Napoleon, but the restoration of the old absolute rulers and the general reaction of governments against Napoleonic ideas were a motive for the societies to continue in existence after 1815. In 1820–21 risings were organized against Austrian occupation in the north, and against the Bourbon despotism in Naples and Sicily, while in 1831 there was a similar rising in the Duchy of Modena (an Austrian dependency). In all cases, however, poor organization and the force of Austrian arms prevented the realization of the liberal, constitutional aims of the insurgents.   *P. R. C.*

Armed carbonari on patrol, led by police officers, 1821

The Congress of Vienna radically simplified the map of Germany, confirming the disappearance during the Napoleonic period of many petty principalities and ecclesiastical territories. The German Confederation which emerged consisted of 39 states, of which the largest were Austria and Prussia and represented a halfway-house between the old Holy Roman Empire (extinguished in 1806) and the future Prussian-dominated Reich. Within the states a more or less severe absolutism was in force, resting on bureaucracies and police forces larger and usually more efficient than they had been in the later 18th century. In Austria, documentation was required to travel from one province to another, letters were opened (including the correspondence of the Imperial Family) and police spies attended lectures and sermons to detect signs of 'Jacobin' sentiment. In Prussia, too, administrative reforms were successful not only in wiping out the large criminal bands which began to disappear after 1815, but in permitting a state surveillance of political life and literary output.

There was a cycle to repression. It reached a peak in the years after the Carlsbad Decrees of 1819, a series of measures for the control of political expression, pushed through the federal diet of the Confederation following the murder by a radical student of August von Kotzebue, a minor dramatist of reactionary views and part-time tsarist spy. It increased in intensity again in the 1830s, after revolution in France had provided a stimulus to the German liberal opposition, culminating in 1837 in the constitution of Hanover being revoked and seven professors dismissed on political grounds. Surveillance was a constant, however, along with pre- and post-publication censorship. The heavy-handed interference of the absolutist state in the lives of its citizens was not confined to overtly political matters. In Bavaria, it was decreed in 1838 that men sporting the moustache, alleged badge of radicalism, should be arrested and shaved, while, in Bremen, doctors worked under the aegis of the 'health police commission'. This preoccupation with public order at all levels was characteristic of the German absolutist states before 1848.

Representative institutions to provide a check on State power were absent or ineffectual. In Austria, neither the Emperor Francis (Franz) I nor his simple-minded successor Ferdinand would countenance constitutional checks on their authority. Political life was moribund and, as one contemporary remarked, administration had taken the place of government. Metternich did encourage provincial diets, but largely in order to head off potentially liberal and nationalist demands by fostering a sense of local cultural identity. In Prussia, too, Friedrich Wilhelm III refused to introduce the constitution earlier promised his subjects; and the eight provincial diets in the state lacked any real authority. The accession of Friedrich Wilhelm IV in 1840 did more to raise liberal expectations than to satisfy them. In the smaller states of the south there were parliaments which met regularly, but they remained essentially debating clubs through which petitions were transmitted to await the pleasure of the ruler. The suffrage qualifications were extremely restrictive; and here, as in all the German states, government newspapers and officials were used as a matter of course to influence the outcome of elections.   *D. G. B.*

Carl Spitzweg's gentle satire of a petty principality in the 1830s: 'The Visit of His Highness'

France's Monarchies

The Treaty of Vienna of 1815 exiled the Emperor Napoleon to St Helena as *General* Bonaparte to show that the old Europe was to be restored, but nothing could ever be the same again. The restored Louis XVIII had two alternatives: he could try to reconcile to the restored Bourbons those who had acquired lands and titles after the Revolution, which meant keeping the extreme royalists in check, or he could pretend the Revolution had never happened, pursue an extreme royalist policy and risk the revolution happening again. The royalist policy would have meant returning their estates to the nobility, an end to constitutional monarchy, restoration of the power and property of the Church and revenge on the revolutionaries (a term which might include almost anybody who had served in some official capacity since 1789), especially those who had supported Napoleon during the 'Hundred Days' of 1815. But that would only be the beginning. Since 1789 France had acquired a codified set of laws, a uniform currency, codified weights and measures, a centralized system of government based on *départements* that had replaced the old provinces, a more equitable distribution of the land and a great military tradition – not to mention new national symbols, the tricolour flag and the *Marseillaise*. To undo all that would have meant a revolution almost as radical in its way as the Revolution of 1789. Instead, Louis granted the French a charter in which he agreed to govern with the aid of a two-tier legislature, the lower house of which was to be chosen from an electorate of 100,000. The religious orders were allowed to return, encouraged by those aristocrats who had shaken off their Voltairean rationalism and now believed, with de Maistre, that the Revolution had been a judgement of God upon the nation.

In 1824 Louis was succeeded by his brother Charles. His chief minister, Villèle, engineered a majority for the 'ultras' (the extreme royalists) in the Chamber, reimbursed émigrés out of public funds, made a bishop minister of education, muzzled the press and introduced a bill to make sacrilege punishable by death. Such extremism was more than even the moderate royalists could stomach, and an alliance began to form inside and outside the Chamber of republicans, Bonapartists, liberals, constitutionalists and disgruntled royalists that made a clash between the government and the Chamber inevitable. The clash came soon after the 'ultra' Prince de Polignac became prime minister in August 1829. In March 1830 the chamber passed a vote of no confidence. The king supported Polignac, and, in what was virtually a coup d'état, the July Ordinances were issued, silencing the press, dissolving the Chamber and announcing new elections with the electorate reduced by three-quarters. The Chamber stood firm. Demonstrations in Paris, where the royalist forces were weak, by students, workers and the National Guard, and the appointment by the Chamber of Louis-Philippe, Duke of Orléans, as Lieutenant-General of the kingdom, might have induced Charles to compromise, or at least to play for time, but he appears to have thought the July Ordinances would be enough. At the back of everyone's mind was the

Charles X as priest, 'aristo', censor and gendarme (cartoon by Ruckert)

The barricades of Paris in July 1830, when the people replaced Charles X by Louis-Philippe

Revolution of 1789 and the Terror of 1793. For moderates like the liberal historian, Adolphe Thiers, 1789 had been a great lost opportunity for France to acquire an English-style constitutional monarchy, and the Terror had been the result. Louis-Philippe would be the ideal constitutional monarch: the feud between the Orléans and Bourbon branches of the royal family was legendary; old Philippe Égalité, his father, had supported the revolution; Louis-Philippe (who was 57 in 1830) had been in exile and knew how constitutional monarchy worked; he was rich, but had known poverty; he was a family man, thrifty, had simple tastes, dressed in the English manner (top hat and umbrella) and patronized good causes. Charles had no option but to confirm his appointment. He abdicated in favour of his son, but the Chamber appointed Louis-Philippe king on the grounds that 'the throne of France is vacant'. It had been a remarkably *political* revolution; the 1820s had been a time of relative plenty.

The 'July Monarchy' lasted until 1848. The citizen king, as he was called, still had to solve the problems tackled by Louis and ignored by Charles. The revolution of 1830 divided the aristocracy into Legitimists (calling for the return of Charles' grandson, the Comte de Chambord) and Orleanists (supporting Louis-Philippe). It pleased the pro-English bourgeoisie, but monarchy was still monarchy. Bonapartists and republicans could bide their time and bid for the support of the industrial workers, who, after the strike of the Lyons silk workers in 1832, could be in no doubt on whose side the Orleanist

monarchy would stand in the industrial troubles occurring in a rapidly industrializing France. The Orleanists were themselves divided between the Party of Movement (Lafayette, Laffite, Thiers) and the Party of Resistance (the Duc de Broglie, Casimir Périer and Guizot, the king's favourite and prime minister 1840–48). But Louis-Philippe's policy of letting France become what the rest of Europe wanted her to be – prosperous, bourgeois, debt-paying and law-abiding – was frustrated by the Napoleonic legend and an old-fashioned bread crisis. The homely virtues of Orleanism could not compete with the panâche of Bonapartism (carefully fostered by the great Napoleon's nephew, Louis-Napoleon, and the novelists Balzac and Stendhal) unless times were good.

1846 saw a bad harvest all over Europe. This led in France, as elsewhere, to a rise in bread prices that so reduced the purchasing power of workers that demand for industrial goods fell, which in turn caused an industrial slump in 1847–48. The government of Guizot appeared to be helpless, and the republicans, joined by the socialist followers of Saint-Simon and Louis Blanc, decided that this was the moment to re-enact the events of 1789 and 1830 in Paris. When the government banned a great banquet of protest scheduled for 22 February 1848, there was a huge demonstration. Louis-Philippe dismissed Guizot, but even a government headed by Thiers would not satisfy the rioters of Paris. A republic was proclaimed at the Hôtel de Ville. The National Guard would not support the king, who abdicated in favour of his son.

J. S. M.

The comfortable bourgeois Louis-Philippe, suspected of imperialist ambitions

Aftermath of the Peninsular War

Within five months of invading Spain in December 1807, Napoleon had so skilfully exploited intrigues between Charles IV and his son Ferdinand as to leave the decrepit Spanish monarchy in a state of humiliation and collapse. Yet Ferdinand VII's surrender on 5 May 1808 marked the beginning, not the end, of the war of independence against the French. Army officers and people joined in six years of fanatical guerrilla war against the invader, thereby establishing a tradition of spontaneous violence as a method of 'saving' the fatherland. At the same time, prosperous middle-class liberals, merchants and financiers from the great trading ports, set about using the ideas that had been brought to Spain on French bayonets to modernize the country. In 1812, they set up a Cortes, or Parliament, at Cadiz and elaborated a Constitution which attacked the aristocratic, ecclesiastical and regional privileges which they saw as the cause of Spain's backwardness. The revolt against the old semi-feudal monarchy also spread to the American colonies, where independence movements in Mexico and Venezuela were quickly followed by others in Chile and Peru.

With the defeat of Napoleon, Ferdinand VII was restored and quickly tried to resurrect the traditional monarchy. He overthrew the Cortes of Cadiz and began preparations to reconquer the colonies. However, in the war against the French, the army had become a liberal stronghold. Officers had no desire to die in South American jungles and in January 1820, the army backed a *pronunciamiento*, or coup d'état, by Major Rafael Riego. There followed a short period of liberal rule, but the attempt to rebuild the Constitution of Cadiz was undermined first by frequent royalist plots and then, in April 1823, by a French invasion. The conservative monarchies of Europe, inspired by Metternich, could not tolerate the subversive example of Spanish liberalism and by October 1823, Ferdinand VII had been restored. Nevertheless, severely weakened by the loss of empire, and plunged into a severe financial crisis by the cessation of American silver deliveries, the Crown failed to crush the liberals.

Indeed, in the last decade of Ferdinand VII's reign, until his death in 1833, the most serious opposition he suffered came from the ultra-reactionary royalists who wanted to see the liberals persecuted and a return to the days of the inquisition. Since these diehards gathered around the king's brother, Don Carlos, who aspired to the throne, the monarchy was driven to look for allies among the enemies of such reactionary clerical absolutism. When Ferdinand died, the Carlists rose against his widowed queen, Maria Cristina, acting as regent for their daughter Isabella II. They had their support in the Church and the conservative smallholding peasantry of Navarre and the Basque country. The queen turned to the liberals for support and their alliance was clinched in the Constitution of 1837 drawn up by her prime minister, Juan Alvarez Mendizabal. Its most important feature was the *desamortización*, or disentailment, of Church and aristocratic land, whereby it was freed to be saleable on the commercial market, arguably the most important event in the history of 19th-century Spain. Not only did it strengthen the monarchy but it also drew the teeth of the liberals as a progressive, modernizing force.

Merchants and financiers hastened to buy the vast tracts suddenly put on the open market. Instead of investing their capital in industrialization, they used it to buy their way into the landed oligarchy. In the process, they worsened the terrible agrarian problem of the *latifundios*, the great estates of the south, worked by an army of almost starving landless labourers. The incorporation of the liberals into the old order was accompanied by a royal rapprochement with the Carlists. The war ended in stalemate, since the Carlists were impregnable in their mountain strongholds of Navarre, though unable to win a definitive victory on the Castilian Plain. In 1839, they surrendered in return for incorporation into the regular army, which in consequence became far more conservative. Once the Vatican accepted the *desamortización* of ecclesiastical land in return for regular payments to the clergy, the union of the Spanish upper classes around the throne was complete. Church, army, financial bourgeoisie and landed oligarchy were, by the 1840s, linked together in a single coalition.

With a frivolous queen, Isabella II (reigning from 1843), the country was ruled by a series of military strong-men. Between 1840 and 1868, generals Espartero, Narvaez and O'Donnell monopolized political power and kept down proletarian and peasant discontent with a repressive fierceness. To this end, Narvaez founded the Civil Guard in 1844. On his death-bed, General Narvaez said 'I have no enemies . . . I have shot them all.' As the self-appointed guardian of order, the army inevitably came into conflict with the lower classes. With population growth in the middle of the century increasing pressure on the land, unskilled labourers flocked to the towns, where, in an unemployed mob, they were highly sensitive to increases in bread prices. Hardly less wretched was the situation of the urban lower middle class of teachers, officials and shopkeepers. Conditions were worst in the Catalan textile industry which produced all the ills of nascent capitalism – long hours, child labour, overcrowding and low wages. When the American Civil War cut off supplies of cotton in the 1860s, the consequent unemployment combined with a depression in railway construction to drive the urban working class to desperation.

In 1868, this popular discontent combined with a movement of middle-class and military resentment of the monarchy. Queen Isabella had begun to surround herself with clerical and ultra-conservative advisers and to ignore the Constitution. A number of *pronunciamientos* by liberal army officers combined with urban riots led to the overthrow of the queen in 1868. The two movements were ultimately contradictory. The liberals were terrified to find that their constitutionalist rebellion had awakened a revolutionary movement of the masses. To make matters worse, a rebellion began in Spain's richest surviving colony, Cuba, which was to last for 10 years, and Carlist subversion recommenced in the north. The chosen replacement monarch, Amadeo of Savoy, abdicated in despair in 1873. In the ensuing vacuum, a republic was established after a number of working-class risings. The consequent threat to the established order was intolerable to the army which rose in December 1874 to establish Alfonso XII, Isabella's son, as king. Yet again, Spanish liberalism had opted for order in preference to liberty. The army had reasserted its claim to be the arbiter of Spanish politics and the great coalition of the upper classes was firmly back in possession of power. *P. P.*

Portugal

The Portuguese ruling classes and the regent (later João VI) had not been unwilling, in 1800, to co-operate with Napoleon against the British, but Napoleon's decision, after the Battle of Trafalgar (1805) to extend the continental blockade against British trade to Spain and Portugal changed all that. Portugal having refused to comply, he sent Marshal Junot with French forces through Spain to occupy Portugal in November 1807. The royal family (Braganza) and the court embarked for the safety of the colony of Brazil and, as it became known that the French had proposals for partitioning Portugal with their Spanish allies, the support of Britain was sought under an old treaty. The price paid for this in the ensuing Peninsular War (1802–12) proved to be extremely high. Not only was the country devastated to an extent unknown in previous wars and her resources either destroyed or diverted to Brazil, but also the Portuguese government was forced to open the Brazilian trade – and later the Portuguese trade itself – to British competition under treaties of 1808 and 1810. The Congress of Vienna, after Napoleon's fall, gave Portugal a considerably diminished place in the international scene compared to the relatively powerful and wealthy one that had been hers prior to the Napoleonic Wars.

These circumstances account largely for the long period of social, economic and political crises that the country witnessed throughout the next decades. Liberals and patriots joined forces in August 1820, during an absence of General William Beresford, the British organizer of the Portuguese army, to expel the regency and impose a constitution on the still absent João VI. The king had to return, leaving behind his elder son, Pedro, who became an independent emperor in 1822. The revolution thus failed in its aim of regaining full control over Brazil, and, faced with the resistance of the traditionalist propertied classes and the non-involvement of the rural masses, the constitutional régime quickly collapsed. By 1828 royal absolutism had been restored by the king's younger son, Miguel, who was the candidate Metternich sponsored for the throne, as part of that European network of absolute monarchs mutually supporting one another that was called the 'holy alliance'.

The liquidation of feudalism had already progressed too far for Portuguese society to succumb entirely to Miguel's reactionary intentions, particularly among the powerful merchant bourgeoisie and the rising manufacturers in the cities. On the other hand, the liberals, now led by Miguel's elder brother, Pedro, who had abdicated as emperor of Brazil in 1830, benefited from the world-wide shift away from absolutism in the early 1830s, and eventually defeated the 'Miguelists' in 1834 with the armed support of Britain, France and Spain. But the liberals' ascendancy and initial reforms only began another long-drawn-out, though limited, civil war, this time between the two main liberal factions, consisting roughly of the 'high bourgeoisie' of merchants and financiers on the one hand, and on the other the industrialists, big agriculturalists and the professions, supported by the urban artisans, civil servants and junior army officers.

These factions were in and out of power for more than a decade in a series of coups d'état. In the early 1840s, under the dictatorship of Costa Cabral, the general framework of a modern state was established, but the plans for modernizing taxation led first to a revolt of the northern peasantry and later to another brief civil war. This was ended in the summer of 1847 by international intervention, but the settlement of that year did not allow for the rising economic and political interests of the middle classes. A final coup d'état in April 1851, leading to an enlarged franchise, eventually restored a balance of power and set the pattern for Portuguese liberalism for the next decades.   *M. V. C.*

Dom Pedro, Emperor of Brazil, 1822–30

Dona Maria II, Queen of Portugal in the 1830s

Russia, the 'Policeman of Europe'

The Decembrist mutiny that accompanied his accession in 1825 made a deep impression on the new emperor, Nicholas I, who became the unswerving champion of legitimism and traditional order and the resolute opponent of any political change. Abroad, with the increasing polarization of European politics, it was the conservative monarchies of central Europe – Austria and Prussia – who became his logical allies. As a result of his determination to save Europe and Russia from the 'many-headed hydra' of revolution – best seen in his suppression of the Hungarian revolution in 1849 – Russia now came to be seen, in liberal and radical circles, as the 'policeman of Europe'.

At home Nicholas governed according to the three fundamental principles formulated by Count S. S. Uvarov (minister of education 1833–49): orthodoxy, autocracy and nationality, a tripartite theory later known as 'Official Nationality', which was part of the general reaction of the European Right against the consequences of the French Revolution and Napoleon. The 'system' of Nicholas I consisted of a deep distrust of educated public opinion and the gentry (whose political decline begins in this period), and an accelerated transition from the gentry-state of Catherine II in the late 18th century to a military-bureaucratic one based on an almost unprecedented growth in the personal power of the autocrat. This power was exercised through a series of supra-legal agencies that operated outside the established state machinery and independently of it. Most important among these were various *ad hoc* committees, which discussed specific administrative reforms in almost conspiratorial fashion, and the several sections of His Imperial Majesty's Own Chancellery, of which the most famous was the Third Section – the security police.

Nicholas was not opposed to administrative reforms and it would be inaccurate to regard this period as one of total stagnation – at least until the panic period of 1848–55 set in, with its exaggerated restrictions on education and travel and its obscurantist censorship. For the first time since 1649 Russian law was codified, and there was a significant improvement in the condition and status of the peasants living on state and crown lands who made up over a third of the total peasant population. These reforms combined a modicum of elected self-government with the principle of state tutelage and for the first time related the amount of tax paid by the peasant to the potential income from the land held. Above all, these reforms constituted the first step towards an eventual reorganization of the condition and status of the peasantry as a whole. Despite the fact that Nicholas I opposed serfdom, there was little real change in the situation of the privately-owned serfs, mainly because the government feared the consequences of a sudden emancipation. Nevertheless, three principles became accepted in official circles that signalled a shift away from the absolute power of the landlord and were bound to affect any future discussions of serfdom: (1) the peasants were not to be seen as the private property of the landlord; (2) they would have to be emancipated *with* land; (3) state intervention in landlord-peasant relations was justified in the name of popular welfare.

Trade and industry made little progress in this period. The important monetary reforms, the heavily protectionist tariffs and the first Russian railways did not form part of a coherent plan of development. There was no real inter-

vention by the state in this field because, once again, Count Kankrin (minister of finance, 1823–44) and Nicholas I feared the social and political consequences of change: in this case the emergence of an industrial proletariat.

The same distrust applied to education. It was placed firmly under state control and made to conform to the existing social structure. Yet, paradoxically, standards were maintained and, despite severe censorship, intellectual and literary activity flourished. Two intellectual trends in particular crystallized during this period in an attempt to answer the crucial question of the age: 'whither Russia?' The Slavophiles rejected the Westernizing reforms of Peter the Great, idealized the Muscovite past and stressed the peculiarities of Russian development. The Westerners admired Peter as a radical reformer and were more sympathetic to the idea of the applicability to Russia of the general pattern of European development.

The administrative reforms and partial improvements of this period were not sufficient to maintain Russia as a great power, and the Crimean War (1853–56) exposed her as the 'giant with feet of clay'. She could not mobilize, equip or transport her army adequately and was defeated by the combined forces of Britain, France and Turkey on her own home ground. The 'system' of Nicholas I lay in ruins, the Treaty of Paris (1856) greatly reduced Russia's influence in Europe, and at home the need for drastic reforms became more obvious than ever. The lesson was quickly learnt, and the new emperor, Alexander II (1855–1881), set in motion the process that was to culminate in the 'great reforms' of the 1860s.　　　　*C. E. B.*

A 'Punch' caricature of Nicholas I, on the occasion of Britain declaring war on Russia, March 1854

The Nordic Countries

The Nordic countries, like other parts of Europe, were strongly affected by the upheavals of the Napoleonic period. During these years state boundaries in the Nordic area were radically altered and Finland and Norway set on the road towards separate nationhood. The kingdoms of Denmark and Sweden had long been independent states and each had experienced periods of pre-eminence in the Baltic region, though both had been reduced to the status of powers of the second rank by the beginning of the 19th century. Finland and Norway, on the other hand, had enjoyed no such recent tradition of independence and had been under Swedish and Danish rule respectively for many centuries.

Russia had long had a strategic interest in Finland, which lay close to the imperial capital of St Petersburg, and the agreement that Tsar Alexander I and Napoleon concluded at Tilsit in 1807 gave Russia an opportunity for expansion at Sweden's expense and with the consent of Europe's dominant power. In 1808–9 Russia conquered Finland and Sweden was obliged by the peace treaty to surrender Finland to Russia. The tsar was anxious to win the loyalty of his new subjects and treated the Finns generously. Finland was not integrated into the Russian empire but became an autonomous grand duchy within it. The tsar, as Grand Duke, exercised wide prerogatives, but the Finns retained their traditional rights and privileges, and acquired their own central administration, manned by Finnish citizens.

The loss of Finland was a bitter blow to Sweden and many Swedes hoped that it could be reversed. However,

Jean-Baptiste Bernadotte, one of Napoleon's marshals who had surprisingly been elected Crown-Prince of Sweden in 1810, persuaded his new countrymen to renounce any ideas of regaining Finland and to seek, in association with Napoleon's enemies, to acquire Norway in compensation from Denmark, France's ally since 1807. The breach between Napoleon and Alexander gave Bernadotte his opportunity: he joined the coalition against France and secured from his allies a promise that Sweden would receive Norway. Denmark was obliged to surrender Norway to Sweden in January 1814. The Norwegians, however, would not accept their transfer to Sweden, and they met in a parliamentary assembly to declare their country's independence and to draw up a constitution. Swedish troops invaded Norway and forced the Norwegians to accept union with Sweden. Bernadotte, like the tsar, acted cautiously. The terms of the union were negotiated, not imposed, and afforded wide autonomy for Norway. The following hundred years or so were to show that autonomy under a new ruler would be far more conducive to the development of a Finnish and Norwegian national identity than integration within Sweden and Denmark had been.   *T. M.-P.*

Jean-Baptiste-Jules Bernadotte, marshal of France, made Prince of Ponte Corvo by Napoleon, and elected heir-apparent to the Swedish throne in 1810. He succeeded in 1818 as Charles XIV of Sweden

Commentators in the middle of the 19th century were fond of comparing the forces of historical change to that awesome industrial engine, the locomotive. At a time when Brunel's paddle steamer, *Great Western*, had crossed the Atlantic in two weeks it seemed as inconceivable for modernization to be arrested as for a train to be stopped on its tracks by a horse and cart. All the great thinkers and writers of the time – Saint-Simon, Marx, Carlyle, de Tocqueville – assumed history to be rushing to some indeterminate 'modern' rendezvous. The important thing was to keep in step with progress, lest an idea, or a class, or a nation, or even an empire be doomed to become an anachronism. Even the arch-conservative Tsar Nicholas I listened patiently to imprisoned Decembrist revolutionaries, so as to better understand their apocalyptic view of the future.

For those outside the charmed circles of the powerful and the rich – revolutionaries, soldiers of fortune, hunted writers and journalists, workers or peasants – the task was to accelerate the process of change so that it would sweep aside the forces of repression. However many setbacks, fiascos or comic opera uprisings they endured, they consoled themselves that history would be their vindication. For those on the other side of the barricades – landowners, bankers, functionaries, generals, professors, entrepreneurs – the task was to make change compatible with the preservation of political, social and even international peace.

The means to be adopted varied according to differing national traditions and recent histories. The British ruling élite, blessed with a resilient constitution and only too aware of the massive social changes liberated by the industrial revolution, averted political upheaval in 1832 by enfranchising the respectable elements of the middle class. Elsewhere the path of liberalism was less smooth. Liberals, when pitchforked into power by the incapacity of traditional monarchies to cope with the crises of social and economic change, faced a practical test of their insistence that constitutions and

Bismarck

Kosciusko

Cavour

NATIONALISM ANI

free economies would pacify grievances. The history of 1848 (especially in Germany) witnessed the bankruptcy of that assumption. When the limited concessions offered by provisional revolutionary administrations failed to appease the angry and the hungry, liberals found themselves stranded between radical revolutionaries on the one hand, and the gathering forces of conservative reaction on the other. Even where, as in France, manhood suffrage was instituted, it came as a shock to discover a massive popular preference for the charismatic authoritarianism of Louis Napoleon over free speech, free votes and parliaments full of lawyers.

Metternich had seen all nationalists, liberals and democrats as part of the same seditious ragbag – a conviction strengthened by the effusions of Mazzini, calling 'nationality the role assigned by God to a people in the work of humanity'. But the impotence of the national ideal in Italy and Germany in 1848 in the face of superior power gave more discriminating conservatives the cue that they might well pre-empt liberal claims to be the exclusive guardians of national destiny. Money, the allegiance of an army, the nerve to rule unconstitutionally if need be, and the guile to exploit international power competition delivered the nationalist cause to masters of *realpolitik* like Cavour and Bismarck.

By the 1860s it was more or less accepted that the nation states, each bound together by language, territory and history, would be the 'natural' constituent units into which Europe would resolve itself. This sense was fostered by a great repertoire of cultural activities: folk histories, opera, poetry, congresses of 'national' scientists and professors. The gradual crystallization of a 'Europe des patries' spelled the doom of the old multinational dynastic empires – the Habsburg and the Ottoman. Just how and when they would finally collapse was unclear, but that they would was being confidently predicted even before Bismarck's trouncing of Austria at Sadowa-Königgrätz (1866).   *S. S.*

Garibaldi

Bolívar

Kossuth

REFORM

Britain: Reform, Chartism, Free Trade

The Reform Acts

When the Whigs took office in 1830, everywhere there were demands for the reform of Parliament. Existing arrangements were felt to produce governments insufficiently responsive to the needs of the country and its principal interest-groups. The distribution of seats and voting qualifications – based on the idea of representing important and distinct communities, whether county or town – had changed little since the 17th century. As the wealth of the nation had grown and been redistributed, as new towns like Manchester or Halifax sprang up and old ones (especially in the south and west) declined, people felt that these new communities and forms of wealth should have their national importance acknowledged by being given votes and parliamentary seats. A widespread popular movement outside Parliament was led by middle-class radicals like Thomas Attwood of Birmingham who founded a widely-imitated Political Union to organize the agitation. Many a working man backed it, expecting that, somehow, parliamentary reform would improve his lot – that it would, as William Cobbett said, 'put bread and cheese into his satchell instead of infernal cold potatoes'.

In order to restore middle-class respect for government and stem the unrest, the Great Reform Act of 1832 was passed. Although the dominance of landowners and of the south survived, new towns received seats and decayed, old boroughs were disfranchised; the electorate was increased, and borough voting qualifications standardized by allowing adult male occupants of houses worth £10 a year to vote. Anomalies remained but – given agriculture's importance for the bulk of the population, and the continuing preoccupation with local communities rather than numbers of heads – the reform was arguably sound, if cautious. However, working-class hopes of political participation and improved circumstances were entirely dashed. Parliamentary reform was followed in 1834–1835 by reform of local government. Subsequent attempts were made to change this structure, but the next Reform Act in 1867 adhered to very similar guiding principles.

Chartism

Persistent economic hardship, the virtual collapse of the trade union movement by 1837, and dissatisfaction with the political reforms of 1832–35, gave rise to the working-class Chartist movement. In 1836, William Lovett formed the London Working Mens' Association (LWMA) 'to seek by every legal means to place all classes of society in possession of equal political and social rights'. Seeing political changes as the essential prelude to social reform, the LWMA published in 1838 its 'People's Charter', drafted with the help of the radical publicist Francis Place. It demanded universal male suffrage, annual Parliaments, equal electoral districts, abolition of property qualifications for MPs, payment of MPs and the secret ballot. Enthusiasm for the Charter, and for a national petition to Parliament supporting it, was widespread. However, divisions split the movement, especially between moderates favouring peaceful persuasion and those willing to advocate physical violence if opposed. It was also difficult to coordinate provincial Chartist activity. Parliament's re-fusal to consider the petition, the collapse of the 1839 national Chartist Convention and imprisonment of its leaders marked its first failure. No greater success attended either Lovett's attempt to win middle-class support for his principles, or the second national petition organized by the movement's new leader, the Irish ex-MP and publisher of the *Northern Star*, Feargus O'Connor. Renewed depression in 1846 ushered in the final phase, but again O'Connor, talking of land reform and organizing a third petition, achieved little save a large meeting on Kennington Common in London. O'Connor gradually became insane and the movement faded away. Like other popular movements between 1830 and 1850, Chartism directed attention to the economic and social plight of the working classes, and reinforced a growing tradition of working-class solidarity; its tragic history was that of unrealistic hopes founded on inadequate resources.

The last great Chartist demonstration on Kennington Common, London, 10 April 1848

Free Trade

The erratic, uncontrolled process of urbanization and industrial expansion which underlay middle- or working-class demands for reform also inspired the gradual abolition of that system of legislation, devised since the 17th century, which protected British trade, industry, shipping and agriculture against foreign competition. A growing industrial economy, relying on raw-material imports and the export of manufactures, in quantities which its colonial territories could neither provide nor purchase, necessitated free trade. Economists from Adam Smith to J. E. S. Ricardo and John S. Mill provided theoretical arguments for abolishing laws restricting trade, but, as with other reforms, sustained agitation was necessary before vested interests were overcome. Most vigorous was the protest against the Corn Laws introduced in 1815. These attempted to limit imports in order to keep up the prices paid to British farmers. The Anti-Corn Law League, founded in 1838 and led by Richard Cobden, argued that free trade in such basic foods would mean cheaper food, less unemployment, more manufactures exported and more efficient British agriculture. Its single goal, its middle-class finance, and its careful organization, made it a model pressure group. Landed opinion split on the question, and Sir Robert Peel's repeal of the Corn Laws in 1846 owed a considerable indirect debt to League propaganda. Despite resistance, all restrictions on foreign ships trading to British ports disappeared with the repeal of the Navigation Acts in 1849, and the final triumph of free-trade principles – which contributed much to Britain's mid-century prosperity – was marked by the abolition of duty on sugar (1854) and timber (1860).

A. N. P.

Ireland

The Union of Ireland with England in 1800 was widely seen as the inevitable response to the Irish Rebellion of 1798, the only way of securing England against Franco-Irish Catholic intrigues. In persuading the Irish parliament to vote away its existence, Britain (in theory) took responsibility for governing an over-populated country with a poverty-ridden peasantry, its depressed trade and few natural resources. In practice, few Englishmen knew anything of Ireland at first hand, and Ireland suffered practical neglect. For most Irishmen, British government was identified with the injustice of tithes for an alien Church, and oppression by Protestant landlords. The latter were naturally anxious to protect their own living standards, and were indirectly as much the victims of Ireland's poverty as their tenants. As population increased and farms were subdivided by inheritance, only death, emigration or radical reform of the ecclesiastical and land systems promised any relief. To most Englishmen, Ireland meant a land of violence threatening to disrupt their own lives, and which raised issues productive of political crisis: Irish agitation brought on Wellington's decision for Catholic emancipation in 1829; Irish famine, Peel's repeal of the Corn Laws and Irish emigration stimulated Chartism in England. In Ireland the potato famine of 1846–48 meant far more – one million dead, and more than two million emigrants within 15 years. But population decrease did little to calm agrarian violence, and British governments, preoccupied with these symptoms, postponed considering fundamental changes until the 1860s.

A. N. P.

'Ejectment' of an Irish tenant by armed forces of the law in the 1840s

The Nordic Countries

During the 19th century nationalist sentiment had a strong impact on the Nordic countries. The kingdom of Denmark had in the past been a major power in northern Europe and had acquired many subjects who were not Danish-speaking. Norway was lost in 1814 and further losses followed. Schleswig-Holstein was the first area to present difficulties. Holstein and southern Schleswig were German-speaking, while northern Schleswig was inhabited by Danes. To add to the complications, Holstein, though under the Danish crown, was included in the German Confederation (1815–66). The growth of separatist aspirations among the Germans of Schleswig-Holstein led to an ultimately unsuccessful revolt in the two provinces in 1848 and in 1864 to war between Denmark on the one hand and Prussia and Austria on the other. Denmark was defeated and forced to surrender all of Schleswig-Holstein. The final resolution of the problem was achieved in 1920 when the northern part of Schleswig was returned to Denmark after a plebiscite in the province. In the later part of the century nationalist feelings in favour of self-rule developed in Denmark's north Atlantic territories – Iceland and the Faroe Islands – both areas with distinct languages and traditions of their own. The outcome of long struggles with the central government in Copenhagen was the achievement of complete independence by Iceland in 1944 and of autonomy by the Faroes in 1948.

For the first 90 years or so of the grand duchy of Finland, the Russians by and large respected Finnish autonomy. Under Russian rule, a Finnish identity developed that was quite distinct from feelings of Swedish nationality. The dominance of the Swedish-speaking élite was felt to detract from Finland's national character, and gradually, after about 1850, members of the élite began to 'finnify' themselves.

The Finns were loyal subjects of the tsar until, at the end of the 19th century, the Russians sought to integrate Finland more fully into their empire. This policy alienated the Finns, but it was not until the Bolshevik Revolution in 1917 that the Finns finally declared their country's independence.

By this time Norway had broken away from Sweden. The union between the two countries had functioned smoothly for much of the 19th century, but it could not accommodate the Norwegian striving for greater independence. The union broke up in 1905 and Norway became a new kingdom under a Danish prince.

At the beginning of the 19th century the Nordic countries were overwhelmingly agrarian societies, unable to cope with the considerable population growth they experienced. In the course of the century there was heavy emigration to Minnesota and other mid-west states of the USA, particularly from Sweden (about a million) and Norway (about 730,000). However, the second part of the century, particularly after 1870, was also a period of industrialization and urbanization in the Nordic countries. Their industrial development was comparatively late in European terms, but it had transformed the nature of society by the outbreak of the First World War. This process was least apparent in Finland, where real industrialization occurred only after 1945. The beginnings of an urban, industrial society were accompanied by the foundation of social democratic parties, as in other European countries, during the last 30 years of the 19th century. By 1914 social democracy had become a very significant political force in the Nordic countries.

Denmark–Norway had long been an absolute monarchy, while in Sweden–Finland, though a parliamentary tradition existed, the king governed the country. The Norwegians created their own constitution and parliament in 1814, and both continued to exist under the union with Sweden. Absolutism lasted in Denmark until 1848 and was followed by the introduction of a constitution and parliamentary institutions. In Denmark, Norway and Sweden a prolonged struggle between conservative and liberal forces finally led to the acceptance of the principle that governments should be drawn from the majority group in parliament and that the latter should be elected by universal suffrage. Political democracy was not established in Finland until after independence from Russia through the constitution of 1919.   *T. M.-P.*

Danish defence works ('Dannewerk') after storming – with propagandistic effect – by the Prussians, 1864

Freedom for Greece

The Greeks were the first of the subject peoples of the Ottoman Empire to gain full independence. The rediscovery by the Greeks in the 18th century of their historical heritage, the development of Greek commerce and the contacts that resulted with Western Europe and the development of education all contributed to the development of Greek nationalism. These national aspirations were given articulation by the *Philiki Etairia* (friendly society). It laid the organizational framework of the revolt that broke out in February 1821 with the invasion of the Danubian principalities by a Greek army.

The invasion was soon suppressed, but an uprising that broke out shortly afterwards in the Peloponnese met with greater success. The insurgent Greeks were able to exploit the fact that substantial Ottoman forces were tied down in an attempt to suppress the Muslim Albanian warlord Ali Pasha of Jannina. They were also able to call upon the martial skills of the *klephts* (bandits), who for centuries had been at odds with the Ottoman authorities, and on the Greek mercantile marine. The Greeks received little encouragement from the Great Powers, who feared an upset in the balance of power, although the Greek cause attracted the support of liberal opinion in Europe, and volunteers flocked to Greece to help the insurgents.

In the early years the Greeks met with considerable success in largely clearing the Peloponnese and a part of mainland Greece of Turks. Early in 1821 they promulgated a remarkably liberal constitution, which for the most part existed on paper only. Conflict between Greeks of different regions and between traditionalists and westernizers resulted in much internal dissension, which at times erupted into open civil war. The Greek cause took a serious turn for the worse when the Ottoman Sultan Mahmud II was able to enlist the support of Mehmet Ali of Egypt, whose son, Ibrahim, early in 1825 landed in the Peloponnese at the head of a substantial army. The Great Powers intervened for fear that continued hostilities would upset the fragile power balance in the eastern Mediterranean. By the Protocol of St Petersburg Britain and Russia agreed to mediate between the warring parties and to create an autonomous Greek state. This initiative was joined by the French and by the Treaty of London of July 1827 the three powers agreed to send a fleet to impose an armistice. The combined allied fleet destroyed the combined Turco-Egyptian fleet at Navarino in October 1827.

Greek insurgents resisting government cavalry from a tower in Thebes, 1833

Independence for Belgium

Kingdom of
Greece in 1830

Acquisitions to
1881

Acquisitions to
1913

This victory ensured that some form of independent Greece would come into existence, but it was not until 1832 that the boundaries of the new state were recognized. At the same time Britain, France and Russia installed the 17-year-old Otto of Wittelsbach as king. The new state contained only a quarter of the Greeks under Ottoman dominion. As a consequence the 'Great Idea', the vision of uniting all the Greeks of the region within the bounds of a single state, dominated Greek foreign, and indeed domestic, policy for the best part of a century after independence.

Thessaly and a part of Epirus were incorporated into Greece in 1881, but the major extension of Greek territory occurred during the Balkan wars of 1912–13. The Dodecanese islands were not ceded to Greece until 1947, while the largely Greek-inhabited island of Cyprus passed from Turkish to British rule in 1878. Greece enjoyed parliamentary government after King Otto was forced to grant a constitution in 1843. A highly democratic constitution was promulgated in 1864 during the reign of King George I, but the country's political development was impeded by clientelist politics, in which personalities counted for much more than policies, and by the tendency for the army to intervene directly in the political process. A further element of political instability was added by the quarrel between the prime minister, Eleftherios Venizelos, and King Constantine I as to whether Greece should align herself with the Entente powers or remain neutral during the First World War. The resulting 'national schism' divided the country into rival and, at times, warring camps.   *R. C.*

Belgium

By 1799 the French revolutionary armies had gained control of the parts of the Low Countries ruled by Austria (the Austrian Netherlands), which correspond roughly to present-day Belgium. The southern region, being French-speaking, was easily assimilated as departments of France. With the collapse of Napoleon's empire after Waterloo (fought on Belgian soil) the victorious powers united Belgium with Holland under the Dutch monarch, Willem I, to provide a stable barrier to future French expansion,

and to create a state large enough to have a strong economy. Unfortunately, the union was weakened by the linguistic division between French and Flemish speakers and by religious difficulties: the predominantly Protestant Dutch despised the Catholic Belgians of both languages as priest-ridden, and, since they had always been ruled by foreigners (Burgundians, Spanish, Austrians, French), as lacking in national sense. The Belgians equally disliked the Dutch, and felt the financial burdens of the union to be unfair. Willem I tried to stimulate economic development, but in spite of prosperity the Belgians felt that the Dutch dominated the commercial structure, and that they provoked quarrels with the Catholic Church.

By 1830 economic and political discontent led to a riot in Brussels, which the Dutch handled so badly that it developed into a full-scale movement for separatism. In 1831 a Belgian kingdom emerged with an international guarantee of neutrality; the king, Leopold of Saxe-Coburg, widower of George IV's daughter, represented English influence (already considerable economically), and as a result Belgium tended to have a 'special relationship' with England. Modern Belgium is thus really a political contrivance. With its linguistic divisions and a lack of historical statehood, its existence is due to its position at the economic crossroads of northern Europe, virtually controlling the outlet to the sea of the central European bloc. This has made it too rich a prize for the European states to allow any one of them to dominate the trade and commerce of the region at the expense of the others.

Although Leopold granted a liberal constitution, property and literacy tests restricted the franchise until 1893 to roughly 5 per cent of the population. In many respects, however, the parliamentary government was liberal, even towards the Flemings, who by the 1860s were demanding a bilingual state as opposed to an officially French-speaking one. With a highly industrialized and prosperous economy, Belgium seemed to have achieved stability. Rising living standards among the working people led to recognition of trades unions in 1866, and by 1885 a militant socialist party, pressing for social legislation, had achieved considerable workers' protection, so that by the end of the century continuing stability seemed to be guaranteed. There was, however, industrial unrest in the period before 1914 and the linguistic problem had produced a hardening of attitudes as the government seemed determined to 'gallicize' the Flemings.

The violation of Belgian neutrality in 1914 and the country's sufferings under German occupation in the war produced great sympathy, and although Belgium emerged in 1919 with only a slight increase in territory, it commanded respect. Unfortunately, the general European decline in prosperity in the 1920s affected Belgium, and exacerbated internal problems. In spite of many linguistic concessions, the Flemings produced a national separatist movement, which, by the 1930s, displayed fascist characteristics and looked to Germany for support. On the eve of the Second World War many in Belgium were convinced that a new order was necessary to restore prosperity and provide social justice, and this weakening of support for the constitutional parliamentary state helped to produce the collapse of the country in 1940, when King Leopold III was forced to surrender to the Germans.

W. H. S.

Italy: the Risorgimento and Liberal Italy

The failure of the risings organized by the Carbonari and others between 1820 and 1831 prompted a new approach. In 1831 Giuseppe Mazzini formed the movement 'La Giovine Italia' (Young Italy), clearly dedicated to a unified Italy with republican democratic institutions. 'La Giovine Italia' was far more prepared than the secret societies had been to try to establish links with the mass of the population. In practice unsuccessful as a revolutionary organizer in the period before 1848, Mazzini did proclaim the cause of a united Italy throughout Europe and gained considerable sympathy for it. Within Italy, however, his slogan of 'God and the people' appeared too radical for moderate opinion, and by the 1840s deep divisions had emerged between the mystical and romantic vision of Mazzinianism and the more conservative anti-Austrian feeling of a developing bourgeoisie held back by Austrian domination. Such divisions were to prove crucial during the uprising against Austria in 1848. Although initially successful, the revolt petered out as a result of delays, fear on the part of the moderates of too radical a change in the political structure of Italy, and the ambitions of the king of Piedmont, more anxious to further the interests of the dynasty of Savoy than to pursue the objective of a unified Italy. Even Pius IX, welcomed on his election in 1846 as a liberal and anti-Austrian pope, withdrew from the struggle in disillusion at an early stage and rapidly went over to a more reactionary stance. By 1849 only the Roman Republic, inspired and defended by Mazzini and Garibaldi, and the Venetian Republic, led by Daniele Manin, continued to offer resistance. Both were subdued by force of arms during the course of the year. France – now ruled by Louis-Napoleon – saw to it that the pope was reinstated, while the Austrians restored their authority in Venice. The first major effort of the 'resurgence' (risorgimento) of Italy left matters no better than they had been before.

Despite his dramatic achievements in 1848–49, Mazzini and the republican and democratic tradition steadily lost influence during the 1850s as the politics of subversion and insurrection came to seem ever less realistic. Instead, the bourgeois liberal – but socially conservative – influence of the rapidly developing northern state of Piedmont (technically the kingdom of Sardinia) came to dominate the movement against Austria. Instrumental in this transition was Count Cavour, the major force in Piedmontese politics from 1852 until his death in 1861. Convinced of the value of economic and political liberalism, Cavour exploited the changed outlook in Europe after the revolutions of 1848 to bring Piedmont and the Italian question to the attention of the powers. Piedmontese participation in the Crimean War earned the sympathy of the French, and it was to Napoleon III that Cavour turned for support in the final battles in which Austria was defeated in 1859. Although he had originally considered that only the unification of the north was possible, Cavour had his hand forced by the independent initiative of Garibaldi and his Thousand in their audacious expedition to foment a rising in the south in 1860. By careful political manoeuvring, however, the Piedmontese statesman managed to exploit the success of Garibaldi's 'Red Shirts', while at the same time ensuring that unification was neither frustrated by foreign intervention nor turned into a social revolution exploding from the south.

The problems facing the new nation were enormous. The

Giuseppe Mazzini in exile in the 1860s

country was formed of areas largely unknown to each other, often with diverse political traditions and different levels of economic development. In addition there was the profound social division between the relatively small political class that had dominated the risorgimento and the mass of workers and peasants who had been excluded from participation in the formation of the new state. The first measures of national government did little to heal these divisions. Administrative centralization, imposed after 1861 on the Piedmontese model, created resentment at what seemed excessive influence of Piedmont on the structures of the new state. The pressing problems of defence and the need to balance a national budget severely in deficit as a result of the debts incurred during the wars of unification (and in the expensive war for the acquisition of the Veneto in 1866), had the result that to many Italians the new state meant only conscription or the highest level of taxation in Europe. In the south resentment at the impositions of national government boiled over into a series of revolts against the authorities that assumed the form of established brigandage. Only through use of the army was state authority restored during the 1860s. The gulf between government and people was

Garibaldi at Catafalmi, Sicily, in 1860, declares to Nino Bixio: 'Here we shall make One Italy, or die!'

exacerbated after the conquest of Rome in 1870 when the pope, offended at the loss of his domains to Italy, declared by the *non expedit* of 1874 that Catholics were not to participate in the activities of the liberal Italian state upon pain of religious sanctions.

The dominance of a small political class produced conservative policies more concerned with efficient administration and financial stability than with reform, and nobody took the initiatives needed to overcome these social and religious differences. Even the fall in 1876 of the parliamentary formation known as the 'Right' (a largely northern aristocratic group with landowning and financial interests) changed little. The advent of the so-called 'Left', although it brought the representatives of southern landowners and northern industrial bourgeoisie into the government, produced no fundamental change of policy. The political game that the Italians called *trasformismo*, of which Agostino Depretis – the champion of the 'Left' between 1876 and 1887 – was a master, made parliamentary majorities dependent on shifting alliances based on personal loyalties or on political corruption rather than on commitment to principle.   *P. R. C.*

Daniele Manin, defender of the Venetian republic

The Hungarian national movement emerged in the early 19th century and in a short time transformed political life in the kingdom, then part of the Habsburg Empire. The movement was led by the nobility and its ultimate aim was the creation of a separate Hungarian state into which Croatia-Slavonia and Transylvania, with their Slav and Rumanian inhabitants, would merge.

Ferenc Kazinczy modernized the Hungarian language (previously Latin had been in official use) and that prompted an upsurge of literature in which Mihály Vörösmarty and Sándor Petöfi were outstanding. The movement soon turned to politics. The diet was once more convoked in 1825, marking the beginning of the Reform Era. Legislation replaced Latin by Hungarian (Magyar) in public life and education in the 1830s. Count István Széchenyi, a wealthy Catholic aristocrat from western Hungary, initiated economic and social reforms, including the reform of serfdom. The movement took a sharp turn with the ascendancy of Lajos Kossuth over Hungarian politics. A lawyer turned journalist from the impoverished Lutheran highland nobility, Kossuth launched the *Pesti Hirlap* (*Pest News*) in January 1841, making it the rallying point of the radical nationalists. Kossuth attacked the 'Viennese Government', asserted Hungary's constitutional rights for greater separation from Austria, inspired 'Magyarization' throughout the land and demanded radical social measures including the abolition of serfdom.

Lajos Kossuth, governor of a briefly independent Hungary, 1849

The Hungarians (Magyars) were a minority within the limits of the Kingdom of Hungary and in opposition to their aspirations the Croats, Serbs, Slovaks and Rumanians in the kingdom had their own national movements demanding the right to use their own language as well as cultural and political recognition.

On 3 March 1848, after the revolution in Paris, Kossuth was the first to denounce 'the Metternich system' in revolutionary terms that reverberated throughout the empire. Hungary now became the pacesetter of revolution: the April Laws abolished serfdom, declared legal equality, modernized Parliament and set up an 'independent and responsible' government at Buda-Pest, with authority over Hungary, Croatia and Transylvania. The government headed by Count Batthyány, and in which Kossuth was the driving force, became embroiled in conflicts with the nationalities and the Habsburg Court simultaneously. Civil war broke out: Baron Jellačić, *ban* (Viceroy) of Croatia, and General Windischgrätz with an imperial army invaded Hungary. The Buda-Pest National Assembly gave control to a Committee of National Defence dominated by Kossuth. In April 1849, the Assembly declared Hungary an independent republic. On 21 May the new emperor, Franz Joseph, reached agreement with the tsar for Russian forces to cross into Austria–Hungary and help suppress the Hungarian republic. This was The Holy Alliance doing its work for the last time. The Russians began to enter Hungary on 18 June. A hastily assembled army and the skill of its commanding general, Görgey, delayed defeat by the combined imperial armies of Austria and, later, her ally Russia until August. Kossuth – elected governor by the National Assembly after the declaration of Hungarian independence in April – had to flee to Turkey. After Palmerston had saved his life by preventing Kossuth's extradition which Austria had demanded, the ex-governor was hailed by the public in Britain and America as a champion of liberty. He lived in exile in England and Italy. Kossuth denounced the Settlement (*Ausgleich*) reached between Ferenc Deák, the Hungarian political leader and the Austrian government in 1867, as an act of folly that tied Hungary's fate to the sinking ship of the Habsburg dynasty. No other Hungarian has ever left (or is likely to leave) as deep an imprint on the Hungarian political character as did Kossuth.   *L. P.*

Poland

Polish territory had been shared out in 1772 by Russia, Prussia and Austria, and again in 1793 by Russia and Prussia. The insurrection of 1794 under Tadeusz Kościuszko was an effort by the lower ranks of Polish noble society (the *szlachta*) to restore the remaining state to its former size, but its failure led to the final partition of 1795 and the extinction of Poland by Russia, Prussia and Austria. A brief revival occurred in 1807 when Napoleon established a duchy of Warsaw from Polish territories taken by Prussia. The duchy was enlarged in 1809 by the annexation of the province of Western Galicia, Austria's gain under the partition of 1795. The peace settlement of

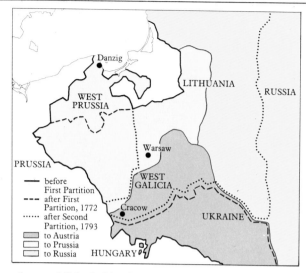

before First Partition
after First Partition, 1772
after Second Partition, 1793
to Austria
to Prussia
to Russia

1815 established a kingdom of Poland out of the territories of the Duchy of Warsaw, less the western area of Poznania, which was assigned to Prussia as the Grand Duchy of Posen. Cracow was made a free city, but it was annexed by Austria in 1846. The kingdom of Poland was linked with Russia by Tsar Alexander I being named its king, but the *Code Napoléon*, imposed upon the Duchy of Warsaw by Napoleon, continued to be the basis of its legal system.

From 1815 until 1918 the whole of Poland remained under foreign domination. The Prussian portions, including Poznania, West Prussia and Mazuria, were mainly agricultural, but in Upper Silesia, which was to become highly industrialized, there was a gradual development of Polish nationalism. Austrian Poland (the kingdom of Galicia and Lodomeria) was inhabited by Poles in the western regions, but by a mixture of Poles and Ukrainians in the eastern areas, which was to give rise to rival national revivals during the 19th century. Economically, Austrian Poland was very poor owing to the extreme sub-division of peasant holdings. There was a sizeable Polish population in the Czech industrial area of Teschen (Cieszyn). Cracow was to become a centre of learning and arts for all Poles, while the capital, Lemberg (Lwów), was also important in this respect.

The bulk of the Polish territories was engulfed by Russia, including beside the kingdom of Poland, the provinces of north-western and south-western Russia, where the Polish population amounted rarely to more than 10 per cent of the population. The other national elements were the native Lithuanians, Byelorussians and Ukrainians. The Jewish population, concentrated in the towns, amounted to 10 per cent of the entire population. The first clash between Poles and Russians occurred in the rising of November 1830, but the war led to defeat in 1831, followed by the abolition of the constitution of the kingdom of Poland and the imposition of much stricter Russian control. The progressive wing of Polish society sought to achieve independence by appealing to the peasants, who were to be given their freeholds and liberated from labour service without being required to pay the landlords' redemption dues. The reaction of the propertied classes was to adopt the 'organic work' policy, by which Poland was first to build up its economic resources before seeking independence. A rising was attempted in Cracow and western Galicia in February 1846, but collapsed owing to the hostility of the Polish peasants, who killed about 2000 of the insurgents. In 1848 the Austrian authorities granted the peasants freeholds to the arable lands in anticipation of further disorders. After the Crimean War, Alexander II adopted a policy of compromise in the kingdom of Poland, but a major insurrection broke out in January 1863. To bring it to an end, the Russian government outbid the insurgents in 1864 by granting the peasants their freeholds without the obligation of making redemption payments.

The rest of the 19th century was the period of 'triloyalism', each constituent part of Poland accepting the fact of foreign domination. Prussian Poland was a conservative area in which the Poles had to resist germanization. Some local autonomy was enjoyed by Galicia in the years 1867–1914, but Austrian Poland remained backward. The kingdom of Poland and Western Russia was subjected to intensive russianizing. The agrarian reforms of 1864 had impoverished the landed gentry, and so there was a large migration from the countryside to the towns. Industrialization was fast, centred in Łódź, Warsaw, Częstochowa, Białystok and the Dąbrowa basin, and by 1900 Russian Poland accounted for about 12 per cent of the industrial capacity of all Russia. *R. F. L.*

Thomas Stothard's portrait of Tadeusz Kosciuszko, revolutionary commander in America and Poland

Liberals and Nationalists in Germany

Nationalism and liberalism in pre-1848 Germany had many roots. What they had in common was the distance separating them from the mass of the population in a society still predominantly rural, and governed in its attitudes by the petty 'particularism' of the small state (Kleinstaaterei) and the parochialism of the small town.

Nationalism defined in terms of cultural, linguistic and ethnic characteristics was a property of the élite. In Austria, indeed, cultural revivals in Bohemia and the southern Slav lands were deliberately and cynically fostered by Metternich as a counterweight to the demands of German and Hungarian nationalists and the spectre of liberal reform. Elsewhere, certainly, this kind of cultural nationalism was rather less spurious. Just as the Romantic movement had a powerful impact on German literature, philosophy and legal theory, so also it placed its stamp on German nationalism. Ernst Moritz Arndt, for example, had a mystical belief in the particular purity of the German language and race. Like 'Father' Jahn, whose gymnastic drill was intended to prepare German students for the coming national struggle, he contrasted German nationalism with the supposedly less virile, more cosmopolitan variety, particularly that espoused by the effete French.

Such views gained currency among many students and writers, but later events have led to an overestimation of their relative significance. German nationalism before 1848 was also fed directly by the example of the French Revolution and Napoleon, and by the experience in west and south-west Germany of French occupation. This strain of nationalism was revived by the events of 1830 in France, and was clearly evident at gatherings like that in Hambach in 1832, when democratic nationalists raised the black-red-gold tricolour and drank toasts to the sovereignty of the people and the brotherhood of nations.

While Romantic nationalists were illiberal, nationalism and liberalism were commonly, in fact, seen as two sides of the same coin by the academics and other middle-class professional men who opposed both absolutism and particularism. Some stressed French ideas of the liberty of the individual; others looked to British institutions (the balance of power between legislature, executive and judiciary; trial by jury) for their model.

Paradoxically, liberal appetites were also being fed involuntarily by the actions of these states themselves. The absolutist state had at its head the ruler, backed by a powerful bureaucracy and army: it denied the claims of other institutions and groups like the Church, aristocracy or privileged town corporation to stand between ruler and subject. In trimming the wings of a group like the aristocracy they were creating the preconditions for the liberal ideal of a sovereign state of equal citizens, while they continued to resist the constitutionalism which would have involved some transfer of power to the middle-class liberals.

Similarly, in their economic policies, states like Prussia and Baden were helping to undermine the very order they stood for. The classic liberal demands for freedom before the law of all citizens and the free disposability of property required the emancipation of the peasantry and the dismantling of the old restrictive guild system. These reforms, with their origins in the period of French occupation, were largely pushed through in the years before 1848, although the pattern varied from state to state. This, too,

Delegates to the All-German National Assembly entering St Paul's Church, Frankfurt, 18 May 1848

heightened liberal opposition; for if men were free to buy and sell in the open market, and old restrictions were to be removed in the economic sphere, what was to stop them being implemented in the political sphere as well?

Emancipation of the peasantry and abolition of the guilds were, like the direct fostering of industry, intended to strengthen the absolutist state. Instead, they undermined the old economic and social order, without – before 1848 – putting anything in its place. A rapidly rising population created pressure on the land and the formation of unemployed or underemployed 'dangerous classes' in the towns. When successive harvest failures and a manufacturing slump coincided in the 1840s, the grievances of impoverished peasants, depressed artisans and the urban unemployed fused temporarily to create a revolutionary situation. It was to this movement, itself evidence of governmental failure even to keep order, that a middle-class already frustrated in its national and liberal demands attached itself in 1848.

The revolutions in the German states bore the seeds of their own failure. Made possible because of the initial loss of nerve by Germany's rulers, they were compromised not only by the absence of any one focal point but also by the diversity of the forces which produced them. A national assembly was elected and it began meeting on 18 May 1848. Yet even the suffrage arrangements for this assembly varied in the different states. Moreover, the men who de-

Menzel's oil sketch of the victims of the March 1848 rebellion lying in state in Berlin

bated the future of Germany at the Frankfurt parliament were divided on the question of the shape the future German state should assume, with the principal split separating pro-Prussian ('lesser German') and pro-Austrian ('greater German') nationalists. They were sharply divided, too, over political issues, between radical democrats and those who wished merely to extract a constitutional earnest of future good intentions from Germany's rulers. Above all, the Frankfurt parliament, and the liberal ministries which had sprung up in the individual states in the spring of 1848, failed to harness the revolutionary currents of a popular movement whose aims veered away from their own prim constitutionalism.

Lacking internal unity or popular support, the provisional German government in Frankfurt was a government in name only. It had no revenue and no armed forces. It collapsed when Germany's rulers recovered their nerve. The old order was re-established in Prussia and Austria in the autumn of 1848, and by the spring of the following year popular rebellion had been crushed or ebbed away in fruitless, undirected struggles. *D. G. B.*

The German Confederation 1815
The Austrian Empire
Prussia

The Year of Revolutions

The fall of Louis-Philippe in Paris on 24 February 1848 was not the first signal that Europe was about to experience a year of revolutions. For example, the king of Naples, Ferdinand II, had already been forced to concede a constitution on 12 January. However, it was events in Paris and, in particular, their echo in Vienna – where Metternich was dismissed on 13 March – that really sparked off the conflagration, for with the fall of these two old men, the European order established in 1815 had truly collapsed and the politics of the Continent entered a state of flux.

What would happen next depended on a number of factors, but in particular on the foreign policies of Britain (Palmerstone was foreign secretary) and France, and on the military strength remaining at the disposal of the 'Northern Courts' (Austria, Prussia and Russia). In the last resort, the question of the day would be decided, in Bismarck's phrase, not by the votes and resolutions of majorities but by iron and blood. Thus, as soon as it became clear that France and Britain would pursue moderate policies and that the Northern Courts could and would defend their interests militarily, the victory of the counter-revolution was assured.

France in 1848, in the throes of setting up the Second Republic, was simply not prepared to risk a war over political changes in Italy or Germany, and British policy was aimed primarily at safeguarding the peace of Europe and the international standing of the Habsburg monarchy. Thus, although the British (like the French) were pre-pared to advise the Austrians to give up Lombardy, where the population was in revolt, on the grounds that Austrian occupation of that part of Italy constituted a drain on Austrian strength, they were not prepared to go further in supporting 'revolutionary' aims in Europe and certainly would not countenance the independence of Hungary. In any case, once Field Marshal Radetzky had defeated the Piedmontese under King Carlo Alberto at Custozza (24 July) and imposed an armistice, it was clear that the Austrians would suppress the revolutions by force. Given the support of Tsar Nicholas I of Russia, this was a policy that could be successfully pursued in Hungary also.

International relations in 1848 centred around three problems: the future of Italy, the future of Germany and the future of Hungary, with all three countries seeking national unity and independence from Habsburg control. The first of these problems was easily solved. The Piedmontese and other Italians rejected the Austrian terms, with the result that Radetzky could regroup his forces and crush the Italians militarily.

The German problem proved more difficult. In Schleswig-Holstein, where the Danes (themselves in the process of establishing a constitution) were trying to annex the two duchies fully to Denmark, Prussia had intervened in support of the German population. But under pressure from Britain and Russia, Prussia was forced to sign the Malmö armistice of 26 August with Denmark, and in 1852 the Treaty of London confirmed Danish possession of the duchies, albeit with separate status. In Posen (Poznan), Prussia in the end conceded nothing to the Polish minority and in Germany as a whole a stalemate was reached when in November 1850 King Friedrich Wilhelm IV of Prussia agreed at Olmütz (Olomouc) to resurrect the old German Confederation of 1815, thus accepting Habsburg leadership again. The result was that Germany reverted to the situation that prevailed before 1848. The Hungarian question was solved when the Russians agreed in April 1849 to help the Austrians crush the armies of independent Hungary. Thus, the Habsburgs were able to survive the challenges of the year of revolutions.

1848 has, therefore, been well described as a 'turning point at which history failed to turn'. Europe had suffered a profound social shock, and in international affairs the 'man of destiny' – Louis-Napoleon, president of France, and soon (1852) to be the Emperor Napoleon III – had come to the fore, and was to be the catalyst for change in international affairs in the 1850s.   *A. S.*

The Communist Manifesto

By the 1840s Paris was once again the revolutionary 'kitchen' of Europe. In the wake of the July Revolution of 1830 memories of the republic, as well as Babeuf's 'Conspiracy of Equals', revived, only to acquire a new dimension with the beginnings of industrialization in France and elsewhere on the Continent. What is more, an increasing number of foreign workers and political dissidents from all over Europe were flocking to Paris and other French cities, seeking better economic opportunities or a refuge from tyranny. One of these was the young German intellectual Karl Marx. He came to Paris in 1843, disenchanted with the prevailing philosophy of Friedrich Hegel and committed to the idea of imbuing nascent French socialism with a German theoretical framework.

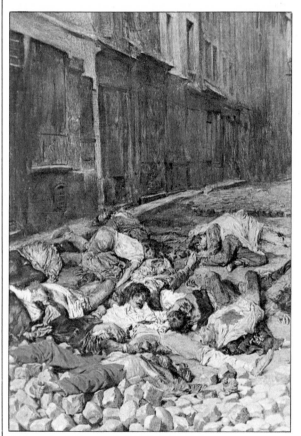

After the failure of the rising

In becoming acquainted with the main ideas and personalities of the radical groups that had come into being in Paris, Marx not only made valuable contacts for the future, but became further convinced of the necessity of giving the radical movement a truly ideological focus. It was in this period that his life-long association with Friedrich Engels began. Engels, who had just returned from a stint of working in the Manchester branch of his family's cotton manufacturing business, was able to relate to Marx his experience of the practical workings of the capitalist system, and make him aware of the importance of economics as part of any comprehensive theory of society. Although Engels' stay in Paris only lasted two weeks, the two men spent most of their time with each other and at the end decided to collaborate on a polemic against the 'Young Hegelians'.

Hardly had Marx completed the text than he was expelled from France. He moved to Brussels, and from there he visited England with Engels to gain first-hand knowledge of the economic processes about which he was writing and to make contacts among German and other radicals living in London. Among those whom he met were the leaders of the quasi-underground League of the Just, which in 1847, after it had changed its name to the Communist League, asked Marx and Engels to prepare for them a manifesto.

At about the same time Marx and Engels began work on *The German Ideology* (which was published posthumously in 1932). Following the thinking of such late Enlighten-ment figures as Rousseau and Adam Ferguson, they viewed history as a social process. Their doctrine of 'dialectical materialism' (a term they themselves did not use) maintained that society transformed itself in relation to its own particular material environment and heritage, the essence of which was embodied in man's relationship to the forces of production. The process of change moves blindly and man is not immediately conscious of what is happening. Only by studying its course, according to Marx and Engels, could one determine the 'logic of history'. The oppressed class in society, being conscious of its condition, had the historic function of forcing change.

Having formulated his ideology of class struggle, Marx was intent on obtaining as broad an acceptance of its basic principles in the working class movement as possible. He hoped to do this through the network of communist correspondence committees that he and Engels had helped to establish. Marx soon found himself in a series of partly ideological and partly personal debates. By the time he and Engels got down to writing the *Communist Manifesto*, Marx had not only come to terms with his philosophical past and confronted the opposition in the new-born socialist movement, but had also assimilated the thinking of the British liberal economists. Despite being published in German for an organization with a largely German membership, the *Manifesto* was, in calling on workers all over the world to unite in the struggle against oppression, internationalist in outlook. *M. R.*

Marx and Engels checking sheets of the 'Rheinische Zeitung' (painting by Shapiro)

The Decline of the Ottoman Empire

In 1800 the Ottoman Empire was a huge multi-national monarchy stretching from Belgrade to Basra, from Egypt to the Caucasus, with an archaic administration and a complex social structure based largely upon the religious allegiances, to Islam, Judaism or various forms of Christianity, of its extremely variegated population. By 1918 it was on the point of becoming a relatively small republic confined territorially to Asia Minor, with a secularized government and administrative system and a population for the most part ethnically Turkish. This transformation was produced by two forces. The first of these was a drive, intermittent, stoutly opposed and often ineffective in the first half of the 19th century but gathering force in its later decades, towards internal reform that aimed at making the empire strong and efficient enough to hold its own in a dangerously competitive state-system. The second was nationalism, showing itself first in the Balkans, then hesitantly in the Arab world and finally among the Turks themselves. As it gained ground it split off parts of the empire as new national states, or threatened to do so, so that by 1918 the Ottoman Empire was in effect dead and the Turkish republic soon to be born.

The need to equip the empire with a modern army and thus enable it to withstand increasingly dangerous pressures from outside had already been felt before the end of the 18th century. The efforts of Sultan Selim III in this direction ended, however, with his deposition and murder in 1807. Only the brutal crushing in 1826 by Mahmud II of the Janissaries, a privileged military corps deeply opposed to reform, opened the way to substantial military change. The strengthened and modernized army that evolved from the 1830s and 1840s showed its potential in

the resistance that it offered to outside attack during the Russo-Turkish war of 1877–78, and the Dardanelles campaign of 1915. Efforts at reform in other spheres also took shape in the middle decades of the 19th century, notably in a decree of 1839 that provided for the drawing up of a penal code and reform of the tax system, while another of 1856 proclaimed religious equality throughout the empire (an idea totally irreconcilable with the old régime) as well as various economic improvements and the abolition of tax-farming and bribery. The obstacles to effective reform were formidable. Religious conservatism, economic weakness, poor communications and a lack of trained officials all meant that progress was slow. In 1875 the combination of heavy military and naval expenditure with inelastic revenue led to government bankruptcy. However, the reign of Abdulhamid II (1876–1909) saw, in spite of the timidity of the sultan, considerable material improvement, notably in the development of railways and telegraphs, which made control of the empire by the central government more effective.

Military, administrative, legal and economic improvements were associated with a growing demand, from the 1860s onwards, for changes in the political structure of the empire and for a constitution. In 1876 a constitution was adopted, though this was in effect overthrown by Abdulhamid early in 1878. A generation later, mounting discontent provoked by repeated losses of territory and the interference of the powers in the internal affairs of the empire provoked the Young Turk revolution of 1908. This was essentially a movement of disgruntled army officers; Mustafa Kemal, later president and creator of the Turkish republic, was one of its members. The Com-

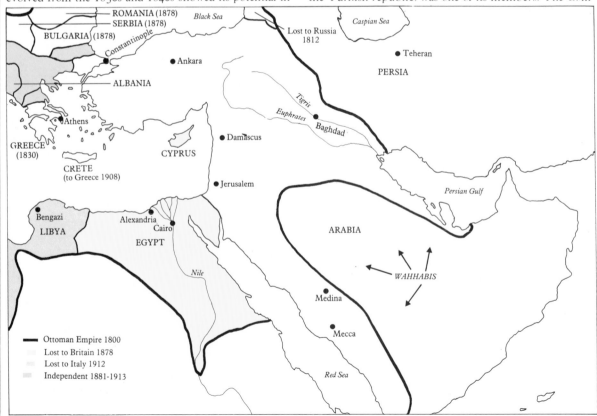

mittee of Union and Progress, the most important of the organizations associated with the revolution, continued to be the leading political influence in the empire until the collapse of 1918; and the Young Turks, in spite of weaknesses and failures, paved the way for the emergence of modern Turkey.

The disintegrating effects of nationalism were first clearly seen in the Greek revolt of 1821, which by 1832 had produced a small independent Greek state. (The earlier Serb rebellion of 1804 was social and religious rather than national, though it led to the emergence of an autonomous principality under Turkish suzerainty.) In 1859 the Danubian principalities of Moldavia and Wallachia, for centuries under Turkish suzerainty, united under a single ruler, the crucial step towards the creation of modern Rumania. In 1878, at the Congress of Berlin, the independence of Serbia, Rumania and the small state of Montenegro was internationally recognized. The Bulgars, hitherto scarcely understood to exist as a separate nation, began to assert their claims in the 1860s and 1870s. By the mid-1880s an autonomous Bulgarian state under theoretical Turkish suzerainty existed, though it was not formally independent until 1908. The collapse of Turkish territorial power in Europe and the triumph of small-state nationalism was completed by the Balkan wars of 1912–13, a complex series of struggles that left the empire with eastern Thrace as its only European possession.

Arab nationalism was slower to develop and a much less serious threat than that of the Balkan peoples. By the later 19th century and the first years of the 20th a few Arab intellectuals and small groups of political emigrés in western Europe were beginning to put forward demands of this kind. Moreover, the years before 1914 saw a marked development of the newspaper press, always an important vehicle for nationalist emotions, in the Arab provinces. Down to the First World War, however, few Arab leaders aimed at more than greater autonomy for these provinces. A common Muslim faith provided an important link between Arabs and Turks, which was lacking in the Balkans.

Repeated nationalist challenges by the other peoples of the empire inevitably at length produced nationalism among the Turks themselves. This development becomes clear only in the last years of this period, when the idea of a Turkish nation as distinct from the multi-national Ottoman Empire and the world-wide Islamic religion finally develops. Pan-Turkish or 'Turanian' ambitions, aiming at the union of all Turkish-speaking peoples – including, therefore, those in Transcaucasia (Baku) and central Asia (Turkestan) – proved impossible to realize. The foundations of the modern Turkish nationalism of the 1920s and later, however, had been laid by the time of the First World War.

M. S. A.

Abdul Hamid II, shortly before his deposition in 1909
Inset: A French view of the 'Eastern Question', 1908

The Revolutions in Spanish America

The festering resentments of the élites of native-born whites in Spanish America burst into open rebellion when Napoleon Bonaparte occupied Spain and ousted Ferdinand VII. Resentments against Spain had accumulated over two generations. Charles III, a vigorous monarch with an eye for talented ministers, undertook a drastic reform programme aimed at rationalizing and streamlining the Spanish empire. Charles was concerned, above all, to raise tax revenues by invigorating the languishing Spanish American economies. His success heightened tensions throughout the empire. The Creoles were angered by new taxes, by the efficient collection of old ones, and by exclusion from the most lucrative – official – posts. The intermediate strata of *mestizos* (half-white, half-Indian) and *mulatos* (half-white, half-black) were allowed some limited social mobility but were still excluded from occupations restricted to Creoles and Spaniards. The Indians in corporate communities were the main victims of the imperial overhaul: mineowners and landowners tried to extract forced labour from the Indians and encroached upon their land. The black slaves were also hard-pressed: new profits from sugar cane encouraged the planters to demand a more brutal work routine and to deny the slaves the privacy of family huts and the independence of small garden plots.

The new prosperity meant that the Creole élite could travel more widely. After three centuries of insulation from events in Europe – the Reformation, the 'scientific revolution' and the Enlightenment – the Creole élite was exposed to international trends. Increasingly the Creoles became conscious of a separate Spanish American identity.

The occupation of Madrid by Napoleon left the Creole élites in a quandary. Their main objectives were to preserve public order and to avoid any political radicalization that might inflame the lower classes and culminate in a race war. Independence was, therefore, perceived as a defensive and conservative measure. Soon, however, rivalries between cities and factions culminated in a series of inconclusive civil wars between republican and royalist movements.

In 1811 Simon Bolívar, the son of a Venezuelan cocoa-planter who had prospered under Charles III, emerged as the outstanding republican leader in the Andes. He exhorted the republicans to seize the initiative from the resurgent royalists; and modelling his strategy and tactics upon those of Napoleon, he swooped on Carácas from the Andes and restored the republic. In 1814–15 the royalists, encouraged by the reactionary turn of events in Spain, were again on the offensive. In Venezuela they used undercover agents to inflame the resentments of the *llaneros* (plainsmen) against the élite of Carácas. The atrocities committed by the *llanero* Legion of Hell compelled Bolívar to retaliate with guerrilla tactics. Bolívar suffered setbacks and withdrew into the Andes to slowly reassemble his forces. He recaptured Venezuela and, in the most spectacular campaign to date, set out to capture New Granada, and later took the road to Bogotá. The route was arduous: the troops endured tropical rainfall

The glorious memory of 'El Libertador' is kept fresh on the lid of the Bolívar brand of Havana cigars

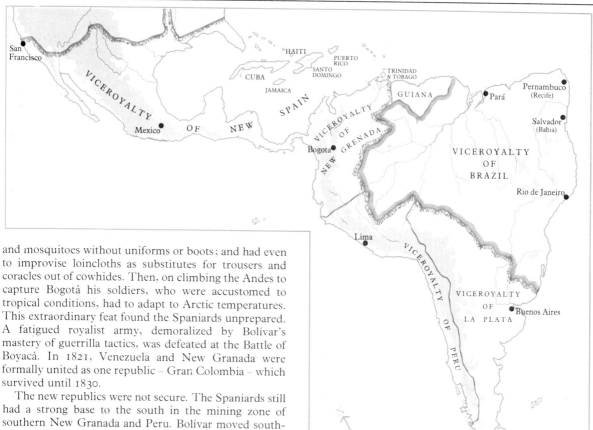

and mosquitoes without uniforms or boots; and had even to improvise loincloths as substitutes for trousers and coracles out of cowhides. Then, on climbing the Andes to capture Bogotá his soldiers, who were accustomed to tropical conditions, had to adapt to Arctic temperatures. This extraordinary feat found the Spaniards unprepared. A fatigued royalist army, demoralized by Bolívar's mastery of guerrilla tactics, was defeated at the Battle of Boyacá. In 1821, Venezuela and New Granada were formally united as one republic – Gran Colombia – which survived until 1830.

The new republics were not secure. The Spaniards still had a strong base to the south in the mining zone of southern New Granada and Peru. Bolívar moved southwards to consolidate the republican position.

In 1822, Bolívar met General José de San Martín at the port of Guayaquil in Ecuador. San Martín was an outstanding professional soldier, probably unequalled in reputation in the southern half of South America, a constitutiónalist liberal of some monarchist sentiments and a freemason. In 1816 he was prominent in the Congress of Tucumán where the independence of the River Plate region was uncompromisingly declared. Recognizing the value of recruits from the underprivileged social strata, San Martín set out to abolish Indian tribute and forced labour and to accelerate the emancipation of the Negro slaves. More willing to negotiate with royalists than the republican Bolívar, San Martín, after being recognized as 'Protector of Peru', contemplated the possibility of an independent monarchy in Peru with a Spanish prince as ruler. This solution was unacceptable to Bolívar. Although the content of the conversation at Guayaquil remains a matter of speculation, San Martín appears to have been willing to put himself under Bolívar's command in exchange for help with consolidating his own position in Peru and Upper Peru. Certainly, the risk of a personality clash was avoided, and Bolívar went ahead to complete the independence process in Peru. After a gruelling Andean campaign, Bolívar's second-in-command, Antonio José de Sucre, finally defeated the royalists at Ayacucho in 1824; and it remained only for him to undertake some mopping-up operations in Upper Peru, which had already declared its own independence, taking the name Bolivia after its liberator.

The process of independence in Mexico was scarcely related to that in South America. Independence was first declared in Mexico by conservative Creoles determined at all costs to preserve their privileged position with regard to the *mestizos*, *mulatos* and Indians. But revolutionary language – of liberty, fraternity and equality – soon aroused the feelings of the lower classes. Warfare in Europe had obstructed the export of Mexican silver and caused an unemployment crisis and agricultural slump in the mining zone of the Bajio. Miguel Hidalgo, a Creole parish priest who associated himself with the plight of his illiterate parishioners, formed a movement of peasants and miners that threatened the ruling class in the Bajío. This radical movement failed to win sympathizers in other parts of Mexico and was annihilated by an army sent from Mexico City. Another priest, José Maria Morelos, took up Hidalgo's banner and with a smaller and better-disciplined army, posed a more serious challenge to the Creole élite. But Morelos had no success either in building more than a regional movement, and was defeated by the superior arms of the Creoles. In the early 1820s the Spanish Liberals who were in the ascendancy in Spain tried to impose a reform programme on Mexico that jeopardized the Creole position. The Creole élite resisted these innovations to a man, declared independence to be final and absolute, and chose one of their own number, Agustín Iturbide, as emperor. The empire was short-lived: Mexico was finally declared a republic in 1826. *C. G. A.*

The revolutions left a legacy of economic uncertainty and political instability throughout most of ex-Spanish America. Trade routes were broken, labour supplies dislocated, mines abandoned and often flooded, and livestock slaughtered. In the early 1820s enthusiastic investors in the City of London made generous loans to the successor states, but soon lost confidence when all the new states but one defaulted. Not only did the investors of international capital abandon the continent but stocks of domestic capital had also been dissipated in the struggle for independence. There were few opportunities for economic expansion. Only two regions in the whole continent prospered in the aftermath of independence: one was still a Spanish colony, Cuba, which flourished on sugar cane produced by slave labour until abolition in 1886; the other was the cattle-ranching zone of Buenos Aires, which profited from exports of salt beef to the slave plantations of Brazil and Cuba. Most of ex-Spanish America was condemned to half a century of stagnation and recession until a new wave of European and US investment began to reactivate its economies in the 1870s.

Economic uncertainty was matched by political instability. The new states confronted enormous obstacles in the struggle for order and stability. Poverty diminished revenues. Few states were able to finance the reforms that all thought imperative, such as the construction and maintenance of new mule trails and cart roads, railway and port development, and an efficient mail service. Poverty also meant that the former leaders of armies in the struggles for independence, the *caudillos*, fought greedily for control over state budgets. No government had the resources to iron out the family and municipal feuds and the regional antagonisms that were inherited from the wars of independence which obstructed the efficient working of each state.

Much of ex-Spanish America was torn by civil war in the 1840s and 1850s. Centralists demanding the concentration of resources in the national capital battled with federalists demanding its dispersal in the regional cities. Civilians who demanded representative government clashed with the military autocrats. Political lines began to crystallize in the late 1840s with the formation of Liberal and Conservative parties on roughly European lines. Liberals demanded the secularization of Church wealth and state control over education, the elimination of the privileges of those serving in the army and the formation of citizen militias under close civilian surveillance, and the dismantling of all 'colonial relics' – monopolies, protective tariffs and obligatory communities for the Indians. Conservatives argued that the Church had been a vital, creative force throughout Spanish-American history and that its properties and influence in education should be left undisturbed. They dismissed alternatives to a central army as inefficient and anarchic aberrations. They looked to protectionism as a means of developing local industries, and insisted on the special protected status of the Indians. The European revolutions of 1848 had repercussions throughout Spanish America. Young patricians born after independence were impatient for change. Dazzled by imported visions of an overnight transformation of society, they took up arms against the established order. A series of savage civil wars postponed the possibility of peaceful economic change for a generation.   *C. G. A.*

The independence of Brazil in 1822 owed more to events in Portugal than to those in Brazil itself. Tensions between metropolis and colony had mounted in the 18th century: the Brazilian economy, flourishing on a basis of sugar cane, cotton and minerals, came to yield more revenue to the Braganza dynasty in Lisbon than to the stagnant Portuguese economy. Brazilian planters bitterly resented the fact that they were taxed heavily but were not consulted over imperial policy.

In 1807, Portugal succumbed to invasion by Napoleon. The Portuguese court fled to Rio de Janeiro and Brazil enjoyed a *de facto* independence. King João VI raised Brazil to the status of a kingdom in 1815, and there was an unprecedented boom in Anglo-Brazilian trade stimulated in part by the removal of Lisbon as an intermediary. In the 1820s it was evident that the status of metropolis and colony had been reversed. After the defeat of the French in the Napoleonic Wars the Portuguese Cortes tried to reassert control over Brazil. The attempt met with a unanimous resistance from the Brazilian propertied interests whose stubbornness was reinforced by the examples of the US and the Hispanic-American republics. In 1821, Dom João hastily returned to Lisbon to counteract republican initiatives, and left his son Pedro as regent in Rio. In 1822 Dom Pedro, concerned both to placate the Brazilian propertied classes and to preserve Brazil within the Braganza patrimony, declared independence with himself as Emperor Pedro I. Brazilian independence was entirely defensive and conservative: the dynastic empire survived and the interests of the propertied classes were never, as in the Spanish dominions in America, threatened

Negro slaves washing for diamonds in Brazil

by class and racial violence.

The empire survived in Brazil until as late as 1889. For most of this period (1830–89) it was ruled by Pedro II, a 'liberal' monarch by European standards who forestalled republican advances by making concessions to planters and the professional class.

Liberation was not, in any sense, complete. The slave population of Brazil (perhaps as many as five million in 1800) outnumbered the free. In the 1820s the British, spurred on by humanitarian pressure-groups and by sugar-planters in the British Caribbean islands, took drastic action to curb the slave trade on the Atlantic. By the 1830s the Brazilian sugar producers (concentrated in the north-east of the country) were in crisis, finding it harder to replenish their slave labour force and losing their pre-eminence in sugar production in cane in Cuba and sugar beet in Europe. These difficulties coincided with the rise of coffee in the south of Brazil and a shift of economic gravity from the north-east to the south. By the 1850s Brazil was already aspiring to be the world's leading coffee producer, but expanding production was obstructed by an inadequate supply of labour. Newly impoverished sugar-planters sold off their slaves to the coffee estates: and the more resilient sugar-producers transferred their assets southwards and moved their slaves with them. It seemed, briefly, that prosperity from coffee would give the institution of slavery a new lease of life, but several circumstances combined to demolish this assumption: the high death-rate among slaves and continued difficulties in replenishing the labour force, the reluctance of European immigrants to work alongside slaves, manumission in the Paraguayan War of 1864–70, the craving of urban professionals for Brazil to be acknowledged as a modern power, and European humanitarian pressures. But probably unsentimental managerial calculations were primarily responsible for the abolition of slavery. Coffee entrepreneurs came slowly to the conclusion that free labour was more productive than slave labour, and that the latter was ill-adapted both to the need for semi-skilled workers on the plantations and in frontier society as a whole. Slavery was slowly phased out: in 1850, Pedro II introduced legislation to prohibit slave imports; in 1871 the children of slave mothers were freed; in 1888 slavery was formally abolished – but by that date the institution had virtually withered away.

The transition from colony to republic was slow. By the late 1880s a strong republican movement of planters and professionals were united against the empire. They regarded monarchy as an outdated institution incompatible with a modern state, and looked askance at Dom Pedro's heir-apparent. Ultimately, the liberal empire sealed its own fate by allowing a republican movement to organize itself. The republicans found allies in the officer corps who were disenchanted with low salaries and small budgets, and ousted Dom Pedro in a bloodless coup. The main lines for the subsequent development of Brazil were now established. A small élite of planters, professionals and military officers dominated a political system in which the working class and peasants had few opportunities to participate. These 'whites' held sway in a multi-racial society characterized not by a legal colour-bar but by more subtle practices of racial discrimination.   *C. G. A.*

Conditions in the 19th-century coffee industry in Brazil - collecting the beans

Thomas Jefferson

JEFFERSON TO LINCOLN

From the signing of the Constitution in 1787 to the end of Reconstruction in 1877 most of the issues of American politics centred around two problems. The first of these was the nature of the line to be drawn between federal authority and that of the respective states. Thomas Jefferson believed in the 'strict construction' of the federal Constitution: only those powers specifically granted to the federal government in the Constitution could be validly exercised. (In the purchase of Louisiana, it may be noted, Jefferson went against the grain of his own convictions.) The opposing view was well expressed by Alexander Hamilton, the first Secretary of the Treasury, who argued that to have an effective, efficient government, the Constitution should be interpreted in a broad way so as to enhance federal authority. In 1819 the Supreme Court under Chief Justice John Marshall endorsed Hamilton's ideas of 'loose' construction or 'implied' powers. Controversy over the precise boundaries between federal and state authority arose as early as 1798, over the Alien and Sedition Acts.

The second problem concerned the way in which the promised guarantee of 'life, liberty, and the pursuit of happiness' in the Declaration of Independence was to be interpreted. Few Americans in the early years of the 19th century would have accepted, for example, that this applied to Indians. Before the Civil War there was a widespread conviction – in the North as well as in the South – that it should not apply to slaves of African descent. Before the three Constitutional amendments of the Reconstruction years – the 13th, abolishing slavery, the 14th, defining the Negro as a citizen of the US for the first time, and the 15th, seeking to guarantee him the vote – the black man in the US existed in a kind of constitutional limbo.

States' rights stood firmly in the path of any attempt to end slavery or clarify the status of the black man in American society. The contradiction between states' rights, as guaranteed in the Constitution, and human rights, as promised in the Declaration of Independence, finally brought on a long and bloody civil war between the sections. The North, at least initially, fought not to abolish slavery but to preserve the Union: this was, after all, a period in which nations like Germany and Italy were being unified. Only after considerable early reverses in the war did Lincoln, after much hesitation, issue his provisional proclamation of emancipation, which promised liberty to those black slaves living in the rebellious states. The Northern victory on the battlefield gained the Negro his freedom; it did not, as Reconstruction was to show, establish him as a citizen in the fullest sense of the word. In the dark days after the collapse of Reconstruction in 1877 the American black learned a bitter truth: the only freedoms he could enjoy were those a predominantly white society was willing to accord him.   *M. S.*

Abraham Lincoln. Inset, top: Jefferson Davis; left, General Ulysses S. Grant; right, General Robert E. Lee.

Slavery and the Union

Slavery and colonization in America went hand in hand almost from the beginning. The first African slaves were landed at Jamestown, Virginia, as early as 1619. Even before the end of the 17th century, slavery had become an established feature of colonial society apart from New England. By 1700, South Carolina had a total population of around 5000, half of them black slaves.

The existence of slavery was a distinct embarrassment to Americans of the revolutionary generation, who declared their independence with the assertion 'that all men are created equal'. The constitution drawn up in 1787 reflected this embarrassment. It decreed that non-voting slaves were to count as three-fifths of a person in apportioning representatives between the states. Slaves who escaped from one state to another were to be returned, although Congress should have the power to abolish the slave trade itself after 1808. Nowhere in the Constitution did the actual words 'slave' or 'slavery' occur; the Founding Fathers preferred to use circumlocutions like persons 'held to service or labour'. Many of them hoped for the decline and eventual abolition of the whole system.

Not only did slavery not die out, it became a steadily more important factor in the southern economy. The most important reason for this was Eli Whitney's invention of the cotton gin in the 1790s, which spread cotton cultivation across the south during the early years of the 19th century. This accentuated the economic cleavage between sections that had existed since colonial times. The North had begun to be a centre of manufacturing and commerce comparatively early, while the South remained wedded to the cultivation of tropical crops like cotton, rice, tobacco and sugar. Northern attempts to secure national banking legislation, and protective tariffs for its industry, were regarded with profound suspicion by Southerners determined to protect their own economic interests. The first major product of this increased sectional feeling was the Compromise of 1820, which sought to maintain a political balance between North and South by admitting Missouri to the Union as a slave state and Maine as a free one. It also prohibited slavery in areas north of the line 36° 30′ in land acquired through the Louisiana Purchase of 1803.

Some Southerners protested at this limitation, but they were a distinct minority. Even in the 1820s, there were more societies calling for the abolition of slavery in the South than there were in the North. This situation began to change at the end of the decade; 1831 saw two significant events. One was the Nat Turner rising in Virginia, the first serious slave insurrection since colonial times. This prompted considerable fear in the South over the social consequences of abolition and led to a tightening up of the whole slave system. The second event was the publication, in Boston, of William Lloyd Garrison's abolitionist journal, *The Liberator*. In the years that followed, slavery as a system came under increasing attack by Northern abolitionists. Southerners reacted in an increasingly united way in defence of what many, from the 1830s on, referred to fondly as their 'peculiar institution'. John C. Calhoun of South Carolina even went so far as to describe slavery as 'a positive good' on the floor of the US Senate in 1837.

In defending slavery, the South was turning its back on trends in the rest of the world. The trade in slaves had been abolished within the British Empire in 1807. British

Abolitionist propaganda in the 1840s

The genial southern view, in the famous 'Darktown' series of coloured prints

liberals like William Wilberforce then turned their attention to abolishing slavery itself. They succeeded in 1833 when the British Parliament abolished slavery throughout the colonies and compensated the slave-owners. Unfortunately for the South, slavery there was protected by the constitutional rights of the states against any attempt at abolition by the federal government, so that the British kind of compensated emancipation was not possible.

The 'Compromise' and the Republican Party

American expansionism, particularly into those vast areas seized from Mexico as a result of the war of 1846–48, wrought a change in the Southern defence of slavery. Hitherto, southerners had only sought to defend slavery where it already existed. In the 1840s they began to realize that unless the South was allowed to spread its system into new lands, all future states coming into the Union would be free, and eventually there would be enough of them to pass a constitutional amendment abolishing slavery. Southerners would only accept the admission of California into the Union as a free state in 1850 if the new territories of Utah and New Mexico had no restrictions on slavery and were equally open to Northern and Southern settlement. The people of the territories themselves would decide whether they would enter the Union as free or slave states. This was the principle of the Compromise of 1850.

Despite a strong pro-Union reaction in the South during 1850–51, the Compromise broke down very quickly. In 1854, Senator Stephen A. Douglas pushed a bill through Congress organizing the territories of Kansas and Nebraska, once again leaving the question of slavery

1860 Republican Party campaign flag. Hamlin was vice-president during the Civil War

to be decided by the settlers themselves. Not only did this lead to a violent struggle for supremacy in Kansas between pro- and anti-slavery factions, it prompted the emergence of a new Republican Party, pledged to resist any further expansion of slavery. In 1856, the Republicans came very close to electing their first presidential candidate, John C. Fremont.

Both Northern and Southern opinion hardened during the 1850s, as the bonds of Union continued to crack. Harriet Beecher Stowe's novel, *Uncle Tom's Cabin* (1852), convinced many Northerners of the intrinsic evil of slavery. In 1859, John Brown's raid on Harper's Ferry re-kindled the old southern fear of slave insurrection. By 1860, in fact, the only real bond of Union left was the Democratic Party. When that, too, split at Charleston in April, it became a foregone conclusion that the candidate of the purely northern Republican Party would win the presidency. That candidate, Abraham Lincoln, had first come to national prominence through his campaign against Douglas for the Senate in 1858. His platform not only called for an end to slavery expansion, it supported all the other things that the South had for so long resisted: higher tariffs, banking legislation and cheap western homesteads. To the Southern states, therefore, Lincoln's election seemed an assertion of impending northern dominance. Rather than accept this, they preferred to secede from the Union. *M. S.*

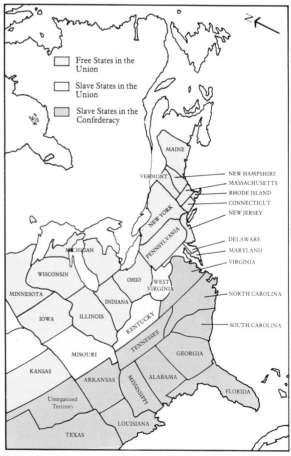

Free States in the Union

Slave States in the Union

Slave States in the Confederacy

The War between the States

The American Civil War was the first great conflict of the industrial age and, as such, displayed many of the technological, economic and political features which were to revolutionize war in the 20th century. Superior military leadership enabled the much weaker Confederacy to keep the Union forces at bay for four years, but victory ultimately went to the stronger industrial power. This was also an ideological conflict of rival cultures and nationalisms inflamed by the issue of slavery. The North fought to preserve the Union, the South (the Confederacy) for independence. In a conflict between peoples there was no room for compromise. In spite of about 150 major actions there was no decisive battle. The conflict was won by attrition of the Confederacy's manpower, economy and will to fight.

Both sides had to experiment with their high-command systems. Jefferson Davis had more military experience than Abraham Lincoln, but he lacked the latter's flair in human relations and failed to coordinate the war efforts of the individual states comprising the Confederacy. Lincoln took time to create an effective command system and the men to run it, but from March 1864 he enjoyed an excellent understanding with his leading generals – Grant, Sherman and Meade.

The rival armies had to be largely improvised from scratch. Most of the 16,000 regulars remained with the Union in 1861 but many of the best officers, including Lee, Jackson and Longstreet, joined the Confederacy. Nearly a fifth of the latter's five million whites became soldiers, at first by volunteering, but later by conscription of all fit men between the ages of 17 and 50. Blacks were also conscripted but seldom, in contrast to the Union, used in battle. From a population of over 20 million, the Union recruited nearly $2\frac{1}{2}$ million in all. By 1864 sheer weight of numbers was beginning to tell, particularly as the Confederacy suffered acute supply problems.

The outstanding tactical feature of the war was the rapid development of firepower. The standard muzzle-loading smoothbore musket (the Springfield) was gradually replaced by breechloading magazine rifles, and primitive machine guns were introduced. Though both sides pressed home frontal attacks with astonishing resolution, murderous firepower forced them increasingly to shelter in trenches until, by 1864, the Virginian theatre of war foreshadowed the Western Front in the First World War. Similarly, cavalry was employed as mounted infantry using carbines instead of swords.

Communications were of vital importance in such a vast, underpopulated country. At sea, the Confederacy improvised a navy and successfully defied the Union attempt at blockade, but its ports were gradually reduced by land or amphibious actions until by early 1865 it was practically isolated. Similarly, inland, the Union steadily tightened its grip on the great rivers such as the Tennessee, Ohio and Mississippi. Finally, this was the first war in which railroads were of decisive strategic importance. The Union had far more rail tracks and rolling stock than the Confederacy and used them better. The Union's greatest feat in this respect was to transport 23,000 troops with guns 1200 miles in seven days in September 1863 to reinforce Rosecrans at Chickamauga. By contrast, the Confederacy did not take over and use the railroads as a strategic network until February 1865, two months before final defeat.

Union and Confederate strategies were different. The Union attempted to strangle the enemy by simultaneous offensives in the eastern and western theatres and at sea. The Confederacy could not afford to rely on static territorial defence because it needed to capture wavering border states like Kentucky and Missouri and also to impress Union and European public opinion with its military superiority. Moreover, the Union and Confederacy both believed that the capture of the enemy's capital (Washington and Richmond respectively) would end the war. On 21 July 1861, the Union advance on Richmond was routed at the first major encounter at Bull Run.

1862

Major campaigns were fought in east and west, the Confederates decisively repelling further attempts to take Richmond, but the Union making gains along the Mississippi, Cumberland and Tennessee rivers. Grant's advance in the west was checked at the bloody, drawn, Battle of Shiloh on 6 April, but the same day the Union seized New Orleans. Late in the year, the Confederate General Bragg crossed Kentucky to the Ohio but was beaten at the Battle of Stones River, Tennessee. This was the furthest north the Confederates advanced in that theatre. Meanwhile, Lee and Jackson, after crushing Pope's force at the second Battle of Bull Run, boldly advanced into Maryland, only to be checked by McLellan's superior numbers at Antietam – the bloodiest one-day battle in the whole war.

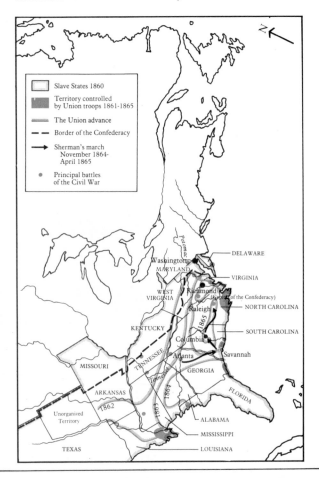

	Slave States 1860
	Territory controlled by Union troops 1861-1865
	The Union advance
---	Border of the Confederacy
→→	Sherman's march November 1864-April 1865
•	Principal battles of the Civil War

The year ended with another brilliant victory for Lee and Jackson at Fredericksburg, Virginia, where the Union lost 15,000 men.

1863

The Confederate effort reached its peak and began to wane. Grant at last opened up the whole Mississippi for the Union on 4 July by capturing Vicksburg. Simultaneously, the Confederates were being pushed out of Tennessee – despite a victory at the most murderous battle of Chickamauga. In Virginia, Lee and Jackson won perhaps their greatest victory at Chancellorsville on 3 May, driving back an attack by Northern forces more than twice as large as their own, but Jackson was killed. Lee once more advanced into enemy territory, only to be halted by Meade at the three-day Battle of Gettysburg, Pennsylvania, from 1 to 3 July. Simultaneous defeats at Gettysburg and Vicksburg ended Confederate prospects of victory: their only hope now lay in Union war-weariness.

1864-1865

Now led by determined generals in Grant, Sherman and Sheridan, the Union closed in on the shrinking Confederacy from all sides. On 2 June, Grant's army suffered terrible slaughter at New Cold Harbor only five miles from Richmond, but he advanced resolutely to besiege the capital and Petersburg, Virginia. Sheridan, after de-

feating the last Confederate raid on Washington, devastated the Shenandoah Valley. Between May and July, Sherman made his famous march through Georgia to Atlanta, cutting the Confederacy in half. Then, in November and December, he continued to Savannah, Georgia. By the end of the year, the Confederacy comprised only the Carolinas and Georgia, and the Union naval blockade was almost complete. Lincoln's re-election also ended any hopes of a compromise peace. The last phase of Southern resistance was heroic but futile. Grant at last forced Lee out of Richmond and accepted his surrender at Appomattox on 9 April 1865.   *B. J. B.*

Confederate romantic patriotism

Lincoln towering above his generals and staff of the Union army. Inset: The dead after Gettysburg

Aftermath of Civil War

Lincoln's magnanimity

When Robert E. Lee surrendered at Appomattox on 9 April 1865, there were already two very different Union (Northern) views over the kind of peace that was to follow. The first was associated with President Abraham Lincoln. It began with his Proclamation of Amnesty and Pardon in December 1863, and found its most moving expression in his second inaugural speech of 4 March 1865. Lincoln, 'with malice toward none' and 'charity for all', sought to bind up the nation's wounds and reconcile the two sections by a policy of magnanimity towards the defeated South. The second view of what should follow the end of hostilities was that held by congressional radicals like Thaddeus Stevens of Pennsylvania and Charles Sumner of Massachusetts. These men believed that to allow the Southern states back into the Union with the same rights and privileges they had enjoyed in 1860 would set at naught all the gains of the war period.

Lincoln never had the opportunity of putting his plan to the test. His assassination in mid-April brought Vice-President Andrew Johnson to the presidency (1865–69). Not only was Johnson inexperienced and impulsive, he was not even a Republican. A states-rights Democrat from the border state of Tennessee, he had been put on the Republican ticket with Lincoln in 1864 in an attempt to attract bi-partisan support. Nevertheless, despite all his personal and political disadvantages, Johnson tried very hard to put what he conceived to be Lincoln's plan of reconstruction into effect. He exercised the presidential power to pardon in a most liberal way and made determined efforts to organize provisional governments in the Southern states. By the time Congress met in December 1865, the President felt able to announce that the process of restoring rebel states to the Union was complete.

What President Johnson declared as the end of Reconstruction proved to be just the beginning. Congress voted not only to exclude representatives elected by the Southern states, but also to set up a Joint Committee of Fifteen from both houses to oversee the reconstruction process. In the months that followed, the intransigence of the South, aided and increasingly abetted by Johnson, gave the Congressional radicals the lever they required to attempt a fundamental reconstruction of Southern society. The passage in many Southern state legislatures during the fall of 1865 of 'Black Codes' regulating the status of newly-freed slaves, seemed to many Northerners a deliberate attempt to circumvent the new freedom for Negroes proclaimed by Lincoln and written into the Constitution with the ratification of the Thirteenth Amendment in December 1865. Congressional moderates, led by Lyman Trumbull of Illinois, attempted to make the position of the ex-slaves more secure by renewing the life of the Freedmen's Bureau set up in March 1865 for a further two years, and by passing a Civil Rights Act. In February 1866, Johnson vetoed both bills as unconstitutional exercises of Congressional power since the South was still unrepresented in either the House or the Senate. Congress responded by re-passing both bills.

In April 1866, the Joint Committee of Fifteen issued its report proposing a Fourteenth Amendment to the Constitution. This would define, for the first time, the nature of United States citizenship and enable the federal government to protect citizens whose rights were threatened by their own states. Negroes desperately needed such federal protection. Race riots at Memphis in May 1866 and at New Orleans in July indicated their extreme vulnerability to violence on the part of Southern whites. It was against this sombre background that Johnson launched his own bid for popular support in the Congressional fall elections of 1866. In his much-derided 'swing around the circle', Johnson's undignified and vituperative attacks on leading radical politicians cost him the last vestiges of Northern support. Pro-Johnson candidates were buried in a Republican landslide.

Radical Reconstruction

By the spring of 1867, every Northern state had ratified the Fourteenth Amendment while every Southern state (encouraged by Johnson) had rejected it. The Republicans in Congress took up this challenge. By a series of Acts, beginning in March 1867, they used their two-thirds majority in both houses of Congress to impose radical reconstruction by military means on the South. The army was to supervise elections for new constitutional conventions, after which new state governments would be elected on a franchise that discriminated against ex-Confederates. In several states, including South Carolina, Mississippi and Florida, black voters now outnumbered white. During the course of Reconstruction, the Southern state governments were composed of blacks, native 'scallawags' (collaborators) and Northern 'carpetbag' adventurers. Once the Southern states had ratified the Fourteenth Amendment, and also the Fifteenth, which sought to guarantee the Negro's right to vote, Congress formally readmitted them and allowed their newly-elected senators and representatives to take their seats.

Radical Reconstruction lasted, at most, ten years. In many states it ended well before the disputed presidential elections of 1876 and President Rutherford Hayes's decision to remove the last federal troops from the South. What the radicals attempted in a few short years, in fact, was little less than a revolution in race relations. Through the Freedmen's Bureau they sought to secure economic independence for the Negro by giving him abandoned or confiscated land. This policy was wrecked by Johnson's pardoning policy: Southern whites, after receiving a presidential pardon, claimed back all their former rights and property, including land. Attempts to educate the Negro were more successful. But the radicals had to administer a policy that provoked constant white opposition, much of it violent. The Ku-Klux-Klan, the organization seeking supremacy of whites over blacks, flourished during the early days of radical Reconstruction and Mississippi was 'redeemed' from radical control through violence and intimidation by its native whites in 1875. Nor could the radicals always be sure of Northern support for their plans: many Northern whites were quickly frustrated by what they saw as the slow progress of the black man in the South. By the 1876 election, only South Carolina, Louisiana and Florida still had federal garrisons. When they, too, were withdrawn in the spring of 1877, the Republican régimes in those states collapsed and radical Reconstruction came to an abrupt end.   *M. S.*

Right: A memento of short-lived Radical Reconstruction in Louisiana, 1868

Comic map of Europe c. 1871

THE BALANCE OF POWER

uropean international relations in the second half of the 19th century were dominated by the creation of the German Empire and the system Bismarck developed to preserve it. Disraeli pronounced the balance of power 'entirely destroyed' in 1871. But he was wrong. Rather, England looked to Germany to replace Austria as its defence against Russia and France, while both Russia and Austria also looked to Berlin for help against each other in the Balkans.

Bismarck accepted this central role for Germany, not eagerly but with relief. For in this way, he calculated, he could fend off any hostile coalition and play off Austria against Russia in the Balkans, and England against France overseas. But Bismarck's 'system', like Metternich's before it, had two fatal flaws: it offered no ultimate solutions to Europe's problems and it depended too much upon the genius of a single individual. After his dismissal in 1890, his successors too often overplayed their hand when confronted with the problems he had always exploited but never solved. They soon drove Russia into an alliance with France, gradually undermined Italy's attachment to the Triple Alliance and made Britain increasingly apprehensive of German ambitions in Europe and the wider world. All the powers sought to ease internal tensions by vigorous policies of colonial and, therefore, naval expansion – and in so doing worsened their external tensions. Germany in particular relied too much on exploiting Anglo-French and Anglo-Russian rivalry in Africa, the East, and the Mediterranean. By the end of the century the British had already decided they could no longer bear the strain of so much competition, even in naval power. As the Boer War found them so isolated in Europe, and Germany set her price for friendship too high, they had eased the strain by appeasing the USA and allying with Japan. It was, in turn, the Russo-Japanese War that forced the next stage in the process. That war exposed to Russia and to France the weaknesses and the dangers of their alliance. It threatened, in particular, to involve the ally of Russia in a conflict with the ally of Japan. So there followed in 1904 the entente between England and France, and in 1907 the entente between England and Russia.

By the end of the 20th century's first decade Europe was not yet divided into two armed camps. However, the 'eastern question' remained, almost where Bismarck had left it in 1878, with no room for manoeuvre. _K. B._

IN EUROPE

High Victorian Britain

Whig into 'Liberal', Tory into 'Conservative'

Both parties were originally dominated by landed interests. Industrialization brought changes as manufacturing and commercial groups initially joined the Whigs as traditionally the party of reform. A paternalistic Whig view of themselves as defenders of popular liberties, against central government's abuse of power, was replaced by an individualistic reforming ideology. Government power should be used to increase the individual's freedom to advance himself, by providing education and removing outdated legal restrictions. Tory adjustment from unqualified defence of existing institutions was slower, despite Peel's Tamworth Manifesto of 1834, announcing a cautious willingness to consider all reforms on their merits. However, the terms 'Liberal' and 'Conservative' had come to be commonly used by 1868 and, if a bias towards industry and religious nonconformity or towards land and Anglicanism, respectively, persisted, both parties attracted support from all classes. Parliamentary reform in 1867 and 1884–85 further enlarged the electorate and re-drew constituency boundaries. Especially in urban seats, professional constituency associations replaced older forms of influence and control, and made the individual MP dependent on their finance and hard work. The annual party conferences developed and became the vehicle for those who wished to dictate policy to party leaders. After 1890, the Conservatives became increasingly the party of property, and the Liberals modified their libertarian ethic to allow a greater role for state action to improve working-class conditions.

Disraeli

Benjamin Disraeli, Jewish by origin, outwardly Anglican and an author, was first noted as leader of 'Young England', a group of romantic escapists favouring a revival of feudal ideas of mutual responsibility between the aristocracy and the lower orders. His talent, ambition and hatred of Peel brought him joint leadership of the protectionist majority of the divided Conservative Party after 1846. For resisting free trade, the Conservatives were dubbed the 'stupid party' and remained 20 years in Opposition. Disraeli had to restore their reputation as a governing party. He therefore adopted Peel's principles, and skilfully engineered the passage of the 1867 Reform Act by a Conservative minority government. Still rejected by the electorate in 1868, he had Party organization overhauled, and in speeches in 1872–73, referring vaguely to social reform and empire, painted the Conservatives as the party of stability and patriotism. Mounting Liberal unpopularity helped him win power easily in 1874. As prime minister, Disraeli's interest lay in foreign affairs. His attachment to British rule in India and concern to protect her trade routes led him to buy shares in the Suez Canal Company, acquire Cyprus from the Turks, yet to defend Turkish misrule in the Balkans, thereby infuriating Liberals and humanitarians. War in South Africa and Afghanistan, near war with Russia, were seen as the results of Disraeli's 'imperialism', and the Conservatives were ousted from office in 1880.

Gladstone

William Ewart Gladstone, perhaps Britain's most distinguished 19th-century politician began his career as a

Benjamin Disraeli, photographed for Queen Victoria at Osborne, July 1878

William Nicholson's striking, icon-like image of the 'Widow of Windsor', Queen Victoria

Conservative influenced by Peel, but broke with the protectionists and in 1865 became leader of the Liberals. A great chancellor of the exchequer, he was at his best in domestic affairs, presiding over the Liberal reforms of 1868–74 in elementary education, the army, civil service and trade unions, and the universities. His unrealistic vision of European cooperation in an age of rising

William Gladstone at the time of his last ministry, 1892–94

Charles Stewart Parnell, in 1886, at the height of his influence at Westminster

nationalism, his hostility to imperial expansion and support for colonial self-government brought him into conflict with Disraeli, and many – especially Queen Victoria – questioned his ability to safeguard British interests. His attempts to settle Ireland through ecclesiastical and land reforms in 1868, 1870 and 1881, and the rise of radical Liberal social reformers also turned many into Conservatives. But Gladstone's religious fervour and single-minded devotion to 'great moral causes', which won much popular acclaim and helped him defeat the 'unprincipled' Disraeli in 1880, were combined with a conservative attachment to existing institutions. Affectionately known as the Grand Old Man, he resisted over-rapid reform and remained an advocate of limited, cheap and efficient central government. He thus helped the Liberals to preserve a commitment to individual freedom while they devised ways of tackling the economic and social problems of the 1880s and 1890s. *A. N. P.*

Irish 'Home Rule'
Ireland formed one of the main issues in British politics during the 1880s and early 1890s. Though Ireland had enjoyed a representation of a hundred and more MPs at Westminster since 1800, it had never been fully assimilated to the rest of Great Britain. Its largely agricultural economy and the predominance of Catholicism kept it distinct, and it continued in practice to be administered by English civil servants, who made full use of the exceptional powers given them by coercive legislation. Nationalist agitation came to a head in the early 1880s. The world agricultural depression hit Ireland with particular severity, and caused widespread rent strikes as well as violence by Irish tenants against their frequently absentee English landlords. Gladstone attempted to remedy the situation by imposing rent controls through the Land Act of 1881, but this proved too late to stop the growth of Parnell's Irish Parliamentary Party, which demanded autonomy, or Home Rule, for Ireland, and which reinforced its claim by winning 86 seats in the general election of 1885.

Despairing of any other solution, Gladstone himself now came out for Home Rule, but his action split the Liberal Party irrevocably. Old-style Whigs such as Lord Hartington, as well as energetic radicals like Joseph Chamberlain, considered that Home Rule for Ireland would imperil the security of the empire at its very centre, and they joined with the Conservatives to defeat the first Home Rule Bill in 1886. Gladstone's followers were overwhelmed at the general election of that year, and a Conservative government under Lord Salisbury took office, supported by former Liberals, such as Hartington and Chamberlain, who had now left their party over the Irish issue. Salisbury's government tried to bribe away Irish discontent by loans and public relief works. Gladstone attacked this as a waste of public money and made much of the government's continuing failure to solve the problem of Ireland. For a time it seemed that Gladstone might recover all his old popularity, but the Liberal revival was dented by Parnell's involvement in divorce proceedings, which discredited the Irish cause with many potential sympathizers. When Gladstone did manage to return to power again in 1892 it was with only a small majority. His second Home Rule Bill in 1893 was decisively rejected by the House of Lords, and, following his retirement in 1894 at the age of 84, Liberals were pleased to abandon, for the time being, a preoccupation with Irish affairs that had caused them so much trouble and unpopularity. *D. R. B.*

Britain and the Empire

Britons in the 1850s and 1860s were extremely self-confident. In escaping revolutionary upheaval since 1815, they appeared with their form of liberal democracy to have hit on the perfect type of political organization. Their industrial and commercial supremacy was plain for the world to see. They saw their success as evidence of Divine approval for their Christian Protestant nation. In their disputes with West African or Chinese rulers they found it hard to understand why their presence might not be welcomed, their habits, customs and merchandise not admired. National pride was never far removed from aggressive assertions of superiority. Non-European resistance to British blandishments prompted the assumption that such peoples were morally degraded, perhaps incapable of appreciating true worth, and therefore inferior. Ideas of racial types or hierarchy were not new, but received apparent support from Charles Darwin's evolutionary theory as, too, did international competition. If the mid-century expansion of British trade and control was so justified, the late-century acquisition of a territorial empire had additional roots. The growth of European economic rivalry bred British defensiveness, resentment and fear of being cut off from markets, raw materials and trade routes. Expansion and imperial economic development were necessary to survival. The mid-century idea of a great federated empire reflecting Anglo-Saxon virtues became entwined with the emphasis on imperial consolidation and belief in the necessity of size if Britain were to remain a world power. *A. N. P.*

New problems emerged to challenge politicians during the 1890s. On the domestic front there was growing concern over the extent of ill-health and deprivation among the population, as revealed by the surveys of Booth and Rowntree. The Liberals, however, were not well placed to take advantage of social reform sentiment. Traditionally they were opposed to anything involving increased government expenditure. They much preferred political to social reform, and during their period in office from 1892 to 1895 they contented themselves – apart from an expansion of Death Duties – with a measure for the democratization of parish councils. In 1895 the Conservatives under Lord Salisbury returned to power with a massive majority. (They were now called 'Unionists', as the government included former Liberals, such as Hartington and Chamberlain, who had left their party in order to preserve the Union with Ireland.) A modicum of social reform was attempted, but generally the Unionist government considered that Britain's well-being depended on the maintenance of the imperial position overseas.

In his earlier period in office Salisbury had ensured a sizeable share for Britain in the carve-up of tropical Africa among the European powers. By the late 1890s events were moving towards a crisis in South Africa. This part of the world had long possessed strategic importance in the minds of British statesmen, particularly as it lay on one of the routes to India. Recent discoveries of gold and diamonds had added much more to its significance, especially as the gold deposits lay in areas ruled by the Afrikaners (or Boers), who resolutely refused to submit their independent, but impoverished, republics to British imperial control. Britain was anxious to bring these areas into an enlarged southern African fief, partly on the grounds that

Empire-builder Frederick Lugard, who made Uganda and Nigeria British, seen by 'Spy'

much of the gold-mining was being carried out by British engineers and settlers. The Boers were likewise determined to preserve their freedom, and the outcome was only settled by the South African War of 1899–1902.

The war against the Boers in a sense marked the high point of Britain's imperial age. The Unionists took the opportunity to appeal to the country on a tide of victory in the 'khaki election' of 1900, and were returned to power in a surge of patriotic enthusiasm. The Liberals were divided at the time over whether or not to support the war, the young David Lloyd George being among those who were labelled 'pro-Boers' from their opposition to British expansionism. Despite the eventual success of the war, there were grounds for disquiet in the minds of Britain's leaders. Rarely had Britain found herself so isolated in the diplomatic arena, most world opinion being on the side of the Boers. Also, the menace of Germany was becoming increasingly apparent, for that new nation had already outstripped Britain in most areas of economic performance, and was now starting construction on a large fleet that could only be designed to challenge the Royal Navy. The events of the following years are to a considerable extent explained by this sense of British insecurity. Until this

The idea of empire: Young Cubs 'Well done, Dad! We'll stick to you!' British Lion 'Thank you, my Boys! I never doubted it!' ('Punch', 1896)

The immaculate pose of Joseph Chamberlain, with orchid buttonhole, was his political trade-mark

time, Britain had avoided foreign alliances and had preferred to remain in what Salisbury had called 'splendid isolation', but in 1902 Britain concluded an alliance with Japan in order to safeguard imperial possessions in the Far East. In 1904 Britain ended many years of bad relations with France by a settlement of outstanding colonial disputes generally known as the *Entente cordiale*.

At home, the Unionist government also recognized the need for greater 'national efficiency' and passed an important education act in 1902. All schools (except the purely private) were to be placed under the jurisdiction of local authorities in order to give them readier access to public funds, and thus the modern framework of education in the United Kingdom was established. But it was Joseph Chamberlain who launched the most dramatic initiative in domestic policy. Since becoming Colonial Secretary in 1895 he had striven both to develop Britain's tropical possessions as economic assets, and to tie the white 'dominions' closer to the mother country, so that the British Empire should present a stronger and more cohesive unit in an increasingly unsettled world. In 1903 he startled fellow politicians by producing a plan for an imperial 'common market'. Its implementation would depend on a reimposition of tariff barriers against foreign imports, and the Liberals seized on this as a retreat from the sacred principles of free trade that were at the time broadly regarded as a cornerstone of British prosperity. They were also able to demonstrate that Chamberlain's proposals would involve an increase in the cost of food and other necessities. Unionist popularity waned dramatically and by-election results foreshadowed a reversal of political fortunes.   *D. R. B.*

Napoleon III: an Adventure

Louis-Napoleon Bonaparte was elected president of France in 1848 with 71 per cent of the poll under an electoral law that enfranchised all males over 25. He came from nowhere, having spent the Louis-Philippe years either in gaol for a ludicrous Bonapartist conspiracy in 1836 or in England. All that was otherwise known of him was that he believed in national self-determination for Italy and Germany, and had written books on poverty and the Napoleonic legend. But in 1848 his was the only name that was widely known. Louis-Napoleon represented all things to all men: to the soldiers, he represented the glories of the Empire; to the peasantry, he stood for law and order; to the workers, he could pose as the exterminator of poverty; to royalists, he could be a stop-gap before the return of the real king; to Republicans the name of Bonaparte promised a revision of the settlement imposed on France by the Allies in 1815. And Catholics could reconcile themselves to a Bonaparte on whose orders the French troops, ostensibly sent to Rome to support the republic of Mazzini, had restored Pope Pius IX.

Like most French constitutions, the constitution of November 1848 failed to provide for clashes between the president and the Assembly. Instead, it forbade the re-election of the president, leaving an ambitious incumbent with the alternatives of either a return to obscurity or recourse to a coup d'état. Louis-Napoleon had only to choose his time – and he succeeded brilliantly. When Paris woke up on 2 December 1851, the party leaders had already been arrested and the Chamber occupied. Posters already on the walls accused the Assembly of treason. Universal suffrage was restored, a new constitution was promised, and the new order was to be confirmed by a plebiscite that, before the month was out, voted 7,481,000 for, with only 647 against or abstaining. Resistance was unco-ordinated, and mass arrests, imprisonment and deportation did the rest. It was a remarkably modern operation.

Because the Second Empire collapsed with France's defeat in the war of 1870 there is a tendency to see Louis-Napoleon as an adventurer who used foreign policy successes to compensate for domestic failures. Yet a Bonaparte without an active foreign policy was a contradiction in terms for those who had chosen him as the instrument for restoring the frontiers of 1814, and he was already on record as wanting 'to do something for Italy'. When France emerged from the Crimean War on the winning side, with the peace treaty signed in Paris (1856), Louis-Napoleon could believe that France was the diplomatic centre of Europe. His later involvement in Italy was not a gamble, but a nicely calculated policy in which France's new-found prestige could be used to satisfy the claims of principle (he had been accused of dragging his feet over Italian unification) and national interest (a grateful and preferably weak Italy would cede Nice and Savoy). The Plombières agreement with Cavour (June 1858) committed France to intervention in north Italy to expel the Austrians, and to support for a loose Italian confederation under the presidency of the pope. But the Italy that emerged from the costly war of 1859 was united under King Victor Emmanuel II (with Venetia still Austrian), and the pope was confined to 'Rome and a garden'. Nor was Italy grateful, for Louis-Napoleon had appeared to hold back in the war. At home, Catholics were outraged

at the treatment of the pope, and concessions to liberalism (press freedom, freedom of speech, increased provision for secular education) alienated some of his closest supporters while they whetted the appetites of others for a truly liberal empire.

The Cobden-Chevalier free-trade treaty (1860) patched up relations with Britain, which had been upset by France's acquisition of Nice and Savoy, and Louis-Napoleon could claim that the settlement after the Austro-Prussian War of 1866 was a diplomatic triumph because France had acted as peacemaker and had made Austria hand over Venetia to Italy. His claims of a triumph were, however, made to sound thin by the deliberate snub he received from Bismarck when he asked for territorial adjustments in France's favour on the Rhine. He had already offered empty support to the Polish insurgents in 1863 and to the Danes in the dispute with Prussia over Schleswig-Holstein. He again compromised with the opposition in 1867, having left his protégé the Emperor Maximilian to his fate in Mexico after initial support by a French army, which lost 6000 men from battle and disease. Despite these failures, the experiment of a constitutional empire, initiated in 1860, with the ex-republican Emile Ollivier as prime minister, was still able to command overwhelming support in a plebiscite a year before the Franco-Prussian War.

Louis Napoleon was already a sick man when Bismarck persuaded the king of Prussia's cousin to accept the offer of the Spanish throne in 1870. A German king on the Spanish throne would plainly be unacceptable to France, and Louis-Napoleon's representations to Prussia secured the withdrawal of the Hohenzollern candidate. From then on it appears that the Ollivier government, not Louis-Napoleon, made the running, demanding a formal guarantee that the candidature would never be renewed. This was too much for King Friedrich Wilhelm, and Bismarck doctored the famous Ems telegram to make it appear that there had been a mutual display of rudeness between the king and the French ambassador in Berlin. Paris demanded war, which was declared on 19 July 1870. The defeat at Sedan, the capture of the emperor and his exile in England quickly followed.

Louis-Napoleon began, like Napoleon I, by trying to win battles in order to make foreign policy but, having been sickened by the casualties at Magenta and Solferino in 1859, he ended by trying to make foreign policy by simply meddling. Only the fiasco of installing Maximilian as emperor of Mexico could be regarded as an adventure in an age taught by Bismarck that war was still an efficient instrument of policy. France could easily forgive a Bonaparte for making war, but could not forgive Louis-Napoleon for doing it badly. *J. S. M.*

Louis-Napoleon towards the end of his reign as the Emperor Napoleon III, already marked by illness and fatigue

Austria's Decline

The Emperor Ferdinand was persuaded to abdicate in 1848 in favour of the 18-year-old Franz Josef. Highly conscientious, but hidebound and unimaginative, Franz Josef presided over an empire whose unifying principle was dynastic rather than territorial, cultural or ethnic, and which in the 70 years of his reign was progressively torn apart by national antagonisms, fuelled in later years by bitter economic and social conflicts. Throughout these years the rulers of Austria, with the emperor at their head, responded to events rather than initiating them, muddling through to the end by means of a series of tactical accommodations and concessions which left increasingly little room for manoeuvre.

The year 1848 brought a challenge to the empire from nationalists in Hungary, Italy and Bohemia, which led to temporary concessions and a brief experiment in constitutionalism; but with the pacification in turn of these uprisings (in Hungary with the help of the tsar), and the crushing of revolution in Vienna itself, a new, centralizing absolutism was established under Alexander Bach. While an elaborate spy system was maintained and concessions were made to the Church, the work of 'Bach's hussars' was also, in an administrative sense, reforming the legal system and judiciary, and overhauling the bureaucracy. Roads and railways were built. Yet Austria remained overcommitted in her far-flung empire, both militarily and financially, as her eclipse by Prussia over the leadership of

Germany showed.

Until the end of the 1850s there was stalemate over this issue. Austria had quickly snuffed out a Prussian diplomatic initiative, and had resurrected a shadowy version of Metternich's German Confederation, within which the two great powers watched each other suspiciously, over the heads of the lesser German states. French support for Italian national aspirations, however, brought about military defeat in 1859 and the loss of Lombardy. The reverse was not only damaging in itself: it highlighted both Austrian diplomatic isolation following her vacillation during the Crimean War, and the inherent instability of the multi-racial empire.

The reaction was a further bout of energetic centralization, coupled with a token constitutionalism which nevertheless opened the future possibility of national struggles being fought out on the parliamentary stage. Making a final attempt to bid for German leadership, however, Austria failed. Running a poor second to Prussia economically, isolated diplomatically from Russia following the Alvensleben Convention of 1863 (the anti-Polish pact between Russia and Prussia following the Polish rising in that year) and outwitted by Bismarck over Schleswig-Holstein, Austria was eventually manoeuvred in 1866 into a losing war with Prussia.

The defeat at Sadowa (Königgrätz) not only excluded Austria definitively from Germany, but also brought the

The Habsburg archdukes with their brother, the Emperor Franz Josef, in the 1860s. The hapless-looking Maximilian (in naval uniform) was destined to die before a Mexican firing squad. The others are Karl Ludwig (father of the later crown prince Franz Ferdinand, assassinated at Sarajevo) and Ludwig Victor

loss of Venetia, for Prussia had formed an alliance with the new kingdom of Italy three months previously. As a result, the centre of gravity of Austrian domestic and foreign problems moved to the eastern and south-eastern parts of the empire and to the Balkans in particular. Unlike 1848 and 1859, moreover, the Austrian reaction to 1866 was not further centralization: it was a reversion, under far more difficult circumstances, to that cynical balancing act above the conflicting nationalities which had characterized the absolutist immobilism of pre-1848.

To prevent Hungarian secession after defeat, Austria agreed by the 'Compromise' (*Ausgleich*) of 1867 to allow the Magyars joint hegemony with the German-speaking Austrians as a 'master-nation' within what now became the Dual Monarchy. This entailed an indefinite blocking of the aspirations of the southern Slav peoples, who were cast upon the untender mercies of the Magyars. Generally, although the Polish aristocracy of Galicia continued to be favoured by Vienna as a necessary political support, the *Ausgleich* was an anti-Slav arrangement. In particular, Czech nationalists were both embittered and spurred on by the deal with Hungary, and in subsequent years they began to turn every decision over a railway line, school or administrative post into a national issue of principle. Finally, power-sharing with the Magyars also created grievances among the Germans of the empire, and Schönerer's virulent German nationalist movement,

founded in the 1880s, was in the following decade especially to cause violent parliamentary disruption.

Democratic modifications of the parliamentary suffrage in 1873 and 1905 served largely to frustrate rather than strengthen government. In addition, governments were faced with the emergence of two mass parties which, although not committed to the break-up of imperial unity, were fundamentally opposed (for different reasons) to the dynastic and bureaucratic temper of Franz Josef and his ministers: Social Democracy, and the Christian Social Party of Karl Lueger, which by means of demagogic weapons like anti-semitism had succeeded in mobilizing the Viennese lower middle class and the German-speaking Catholic peasantry. These parties joined in the game of demanding official favours and spoils.

It is against this background that one must view the cultural vitality of Vienna in the last years before 1914: the originality of Freud, Ernst Mach and Karl Kraus, paralleled in the musical sphere by Mahler, Schönberg, Webern and Berg, and in creative writing by Hofsmannsthal, Musil, Broch and Trakl. Like the flowering of the 'Weimar culture' in Germany in the 1920s, this creative cornucopia was accompanied at the political level by mounting tensions and governmental paralysis; a combination which also found its reflection in the fateful foreign policy of the Austrian empire. *D. G. B.*

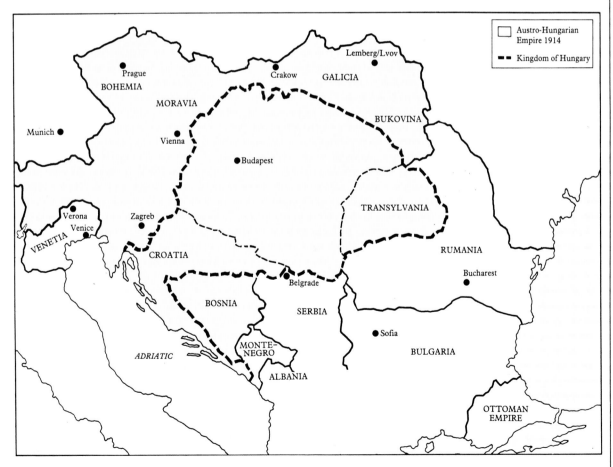

The Forging of a German State

The unification of Germany by Prussia rather than by Austria was the result not only of superior diplomacy, but also of Prussia's greater economic, social and political dynamism particularly since the absorption of the Rhineland province at the post-Napoleonic peace settlement. Austrian economic reforms in the 1850s did not bear fruit until later; in Prussia advance was heady. As industrial output rose in all key branches and communications within the Prussian-led customs union (*Zollverein*) improved, Prussia became increasingly attractive to a growing middle class which was both liberal and nationalist, and beginning to form political and other organizations which demanded a unified Germany. These included the German National Association, the Progressive Party, the chambers of commerce and groups like the German Association of Jurists.

Prussia had nevertheless made no positive bid for German leadership in the 1850s, taking no part in the Crimean War and failing in 1859 to come to the aid of her nominal ally, Austria. In fact, Wilhelm I, who succeeded Friedrich Wilhelm IV in 1861, faced two serious problems: at home, a constitutional conflict over control of the purse strings; and abroad, a renewed attempt by Austria to take the initiative over the German question. Wilhelm I's appointment of Otto von Bismarck as his chief minister was an attempt to spike the guns of opponents in both cases.

Bismarck's domestic and foreign policies during the 1860s were interdependent. Bismarckian diplomacy and Prussian arms were used to compromise Austria in the war with Denmark over Schleswig-Holstein, to exploit this opening to exclude Austria finally from Germany in 1866, and to neutralize the one power capable of preventing the southern German states from falling into Prussian hands by defeating France in 1870. This made possible the creation of a 'lesser German' state in which Prussia was dominant. At the same time, diplomatic and military success served a domestic function. The fighting against Denmark was 'stage-managed' to create maximum impact on opinion at home; Prussian success against Austria persuaded the liberals to vote for the Indemnity Bill which retrospectively sanctioned four years of illegal taxation, thus concluding the constitutional conflict; and the lightning success of the Franco-Prussian War put the seal of popular enthusiasm on Bismarck's achievements.

The 'second Reich'

The establishment of the German empire should not, however, be seen simply as a 'revolution from above' over German liberalism. Liberalism and nationalism were intimately connected, and the very establishment of a nation-state could be regarded by liberals as a blow struck against out-moded particularism and conservatism (including Prussian conservatism) in general. Moreover, the newly established Reichstag was elected by universal suffrage, and in the 1870s Bismarck, as chancellor, ruled with a liberal majority, enacting legislation which they approved: economic legislation, for example, and the expulsion of the Jesuits, greater state control of education and other measures which formed part of that struggle against the Catholic Church known as the *Kulturkampf* (a word coined by a liberal).

Yet Prussia dominated the new Germany; and within Prussia an inequitable three-class franchise remained,

Legend:
- Prussia in 1815
- Acquisitions 1815-66
- Boundary of North German Confederation 1866
- Boundary of German Empire 1871

while bureaucracy and army retained their positions, based on the unbroken power of the conservative Junker landowners. Liberals might have hoped gradually to remove these and other features of the empire which did not accord with their expectations. But the closing years of the 1870s showed how much they remained the victims of Bismarck's political guile. The introduction of an anti-socialist law in 1878 and a shift to the right in economic policy the following year allowed Bismarck to divide and weaken the liberals. This was accompanied by a vigorous purging of liberal elements in the Prussian bureaucracy. By 1880 the politics of the empire were more firmly embedded in authoritarianism than at the beginning.

The new state was institutionally and politically consolidated in the 1880s. The role of the imperial government increased; the *Kulturkampf* was wound up; participation in elections rose; and the national minorities within the empire – Poles, Danes and Alsatians – began to vote for German-based rather than separatist parties. But unresolved contradictions remained at every level: between Prussia and the Reich; between the three-class franchise in the former and universal suffrage in the latter; and between the new mass parties which were emerging in the Reichstag and the repressive bedrock of imperial politics. The Catholic Centre Party, to which Bismarck remained fundamentally unreconciled, consistently won a quarter of the seats in the Reichstag; while neither the carrot of social legislation nor the stick of the anti-socialist law was able to arrest the growth of the Social Democratic Party. When Wilhelm II became kaiser in 1888, therefore, the reich had been formally consolidated; but the political system created by Bismarck was threatening to become unworkable. *D. B.*

Bismarck in the Reichstag building with Baron von Schönhausen beneath a plaque that declares 'A nation's most sacred right is to exist and be recognized as such'

Russia between Serfdom and Constitution

Russian society's fundamental problem in this period was the situation of the peasants. Their emancipation from serfdom (decreed 19 February 1861) left them *with* land, in the form of an allotment made to each household through the village commune (*mir*). However, this allotment was often smaller than the household's previous holding, and it had to be paid for over a period of 49 years. Emancipation thus strengthened the *mir* and bound peasants to it at a time when the rural population was growing fast and was being heavily taxed. The result was over-population, chronic poverty and occasional famine. In spite of this, individual peasants were often able to leave the village and seek work in industry or transport for at least part of the year, while still remaining attached to the *mir*, and they formed a substantial proportion of the rapidly growing industrial labour force.

Between the 1880s and 1900 very fast expansion took place in all branches of heavy industry, financed largely by the state and foreign investors, and protected by high tariffs imposed by finance ministers Vyshnegradsky (1887–92) and Witte (1892–1903). The new factories adopted the latest Western technology and were often very large: this meant the concentration of huge numbers of raw workers and 'worker-peasants' in the largest cities, a worry to the police and the Ministry of the Interior.

The reforms accompanying the emancipation of the serfs changed Russia's social structure in other respects too, leading to the formation of a large professional stratum, which, like the working class, had no place in the old official hierarchy of social 'estates' or *sosloviya*. The landed gentry were hard-hit by being deprived of their free labour. A few made a successful transition to commercial agriculture, but many stagnated or declined economically, and about 40 per cent of them sold their estates and joined the landless nobility of government service, the army or the professions. The new elected local government assemblies (*zemstvos*, introduced in 1864), the new Western-style law courts (established in the judicial reforms of 1864), the modern conscript army (introduced in 1874), and the enormously expanded educational system all needed to employ well-trained professional men in unprecedented numbers.

The emergence of this new professional class increased the importance of public opinion and strengthened the demands for a limitation of the autocracy through some kind of elected parliament. In the 1870s these demands tended to express themselves in the form of pan-slavism: the notion that Russia should help to emancipate its Slav 'brethren' from despotic Austrian and Turkish rule. When anti-Turkish revolts took place in Bosnia-Herzegovina and Bulgaria in 1875–76, the pan-slavs put pressure on the government to intervene on behalf of the rebels. Volunteers, supported by public subscription, went to fight for the 'gallant Serbs'. Alexander II and his foreign minister, Gorchakov, were reluctant to yield to this public pressure, for they wanted to defend peace, stability and the monarchical principle throughout Europe, but eventually they acceded and Russia declared war on Turkey in April 1877. This democratic involvement did not, however, lead to any relaxation of autocracy at home. After a lull caused by the assassination crisis of 1881 (see below), constitutional pressure on the government resumed during the late 1890s and early 1900s, coming from *zemstvos*, professional associations and, to some extent, the nobility. The Union of Liberation, established abroad in 1903, attempted to co-ordinate these efforts, and in the autumn of 1904 organized a campaign of 'constitutional banquets' to press the demand for a parliament on the government. Together with the growing number of similarly minded *zemstvo* congresses, these passed into the general revolutionary agitation of 1905.

In contrast to the peaceful methods of the constitutionalists, the revolutionaries (also drawn in the main from the professional strata) were prepared to use violence. Demands for a violent overthrow of the autocracy and the establishment of a socialist society appeared in student circles in 1861, and there was an attempt on the tsar's life in 1866. During the early 1870s thousands of young idealists 'went to the people', flocking peacefully out to live in villages and preach socialism to the peasants. Most peasants were uncomprehending, and some handed the students over to the police; the government then gave them long and well-publicized trials for subversion. Some socialists drew from this experience the lesson that it was necessary to organize and to use violence. In 1879 they formed *Naródnaya Volyá* (the People's Will), an elaborate conspiratorial organization covering many provincial towns as well as the major cities. They made their main

Tsar Alexander II, the Emancipator, 1858, three years after his accession

George Valentinovich Plekhanov, the father of Russian Marxism

Telling the serfs they are now free: the 'Regulations Concerning Peasants' being read on the Prozorov estate, Moscow province, in 1861

aim the assassination of Alexander II, and this they achieved, after a number of attempts, on 1 March 1881. Their triumph was, however, pyrrhic, for nothing changed in Russian society as a result, except that Alexander III, the new emperor, strengthened the powers of the security police, establishing the Okhrana to coordinate the investigation of political crime, and placing most of Russia under 'emergency rule'.

The non-terrorists, notably George Plekhanov, in exile in Switzerland, argued from this fiasco that the revolutionaries must wait for the 'objective conditions' of revolution, as seen by Marx, to mature, through the creation of a truly revolutionary class, the urban proletariat. Plekhanov's writings laid the foundations for the establish-

ment of the Russian Social Democratic Labour Party (RSDRP) in 1898. The ideas of *Naródnaya Volyá* were also revived, in the formation of the Socialist Revolutionary Party (SR) in 1901. Both parties had their headquarters abroad, but numerous branches inside Russia. The RSDRP split at its second congress (Brussels–London, 1903) into a so-called 'minority' (Menshevik) faction led by Martov, which favoured a loose organization designed to attract mass working-class membership, and a 'majority' (Bolshevik) faction led by Lenin, which, at least in theory, favoured a smaller, more professional and more disciplined party. The SR and the RSDRP both came to play an important organizational part in the 1905 revolution.

G. A. H.

Spain: the Restoration System 1874-1909

Alfonso XII's adviser, Antonio Cánovas del Castillo, was the architect of a political system whose main objective was to prevent a repetition of the instability which had terrified the ruling classes in the interregnum. A fervent admirer of English politics, Cánovas aimed to build a long period of stable two-party parliamentary government. Two parties were formed: the Conservatives led by Cánovas himself, and the Liberals, led by Práxedes Mateo Sagasta. They were fairly similar in that they each represented sectors of the landed oligarchy – the Conservatives were supported by the olive-growers of the south, the Liberals by the wheat-growers of the centre and north. In an ostensibly democratic system, the monopoly of politics by these narrow groups was guaranteed by polling frauds. The northern bourgeoisie was barely represented within the system but was, for the moment, content to devote its activities to economic expansion in an atmosphere of stability. The large majority of the population was deprived of legal channels for its aspirations.

Liberal and Conservative governments followed one another with soporific regularity. When results were not faked in the Ministry of the Interior, they were fixed at a local level by political bosses, known as *caciques* (a South American Indian word meaning 'chief'). In the northern smallholding areas, the *cacique* was usually a money lender, a bigger landowner, a lawyer – or even a priest – who had mortgages on the small farms. In the areas of the great estates or *latifundios*, Castile, Extremadura, Andalusia, the *cacique* was the landlord or his agent, the man who decided who worked and therefore who did not starve. The 1890s were a period of economic depression which exacerbated the grievances of the lower classes, especially in the countryside. Land hunger was creating a growing demand for change, the more so as the southern labourers came under the influence of anarchism. Introduced in 1868 by Giuseppe Fanelli, an Italian disciple of Bakunin, the anarchist message of justice and equality found eager converts among the starving day-labourers or *braceros*. They took part in outbreaks of sporadic violence, crop-burnings and strikes. In 1891, an army of *braceros*, armed only with sticks and scythes but driven by hunger, seized the town of Jerez. Anarchism also took root in the small workshops of the highly fragmented Catalan textile industry.

The system came under increasing strain from strikes and acts of anarchist terrorism. The police reacted with great brutality and, in reprisal, anarchists assassinated Cánovas in 1897. An even more crippling blow came in the following year when the Spanish navy was annihilated in the Philippines and Cuba by the Americans and the remnants of empire were lost. The disaster of 1898 had a catastrophic effect, particularly in Catalonia, as Cuba had been a protected market for Catalan products.

The 'generation of '98', as they were known, blamed the disaster on the corrupt system. Their ideas had considerable impact. Immensely important political thinkers, such as José Ortega y Gasset and Miguel de Unamuno, called for the regeneration of Spain. By 1910, republicans, Catalan nationalists and socialists were fighting against electoral corruption and winning seats in the larger towns. Moreover, after the murder of Cánovas and the death of Sagasta in 1903, the two oligarchical parties began to break up into factions scrambling for patronage. With the return of political instability, the army also began to return to the centre of the stage.

The situation came to a head in 1909. The central government was using provocateurs to create disorder in Barcelona. As part of the Spanish attempt to colonize Morocco, the army was involved in a series of costly wars against the tribes of the Rif. In July 1909, defending iron mines popularly supposed to be Jesuit property, Spanish troops suffered a heavy defeat. The government saw this as an opportunity to provoke disorder in Catalonia in order to justify an assertion of its power. Working-class conscripts from Barcelona were called up and the city rose in revolt. From 25 July to 1 August, the 'Tragic Week', there was mob rule and over 40 ecclesiastical buildings were burnt. This was followed by an implacable repression and executions ran into the hundreds. It was the beginning of the end for the restoration system. *P. P.*

Alfonso XII, proclaimed king after the restoration of the Spanish monarchy in 1875

Portugal: Liberalism to Corporativism   1851-1933

The 1851 coup had brought about a lasting truce between the dominant social and political groups in Portugal. The 'regeneration' period benefited at first from the world-wide economic expansion of the time. Politically, the system was a poor imitation of British parliamentarianism, with a very limited franchise, and abuses like patronage and jerrymandering. It nevertheless survived the national crises of the rest of the century. These were the advent of working-class politics in the late 1860s, and the major crises of the early 1890s, when the British ultimatum of January 1890 – demanding that the Portuguese should desist from moves to link their two African territories through central Africa – combined with several financial disasters to produce a challenge to the Braganza dynasty in the republican revolt of January 1891. Although the political system survived the latter crisis, it meant a break with liberal economic policies, as well as the enfranchisement of the working classes. There was also seen the first manifestation of modern authoritarian nationalism.

The latter tendencies were reinforced in the first decade of the 20th century by economic and financial difficulties and increasing social unrest. The republican party capitalized both on this and on the anti-monarchist and anti-clerical feelings of the urban lower-middle classes. On 5

Antonio de Oliveira Salazar

October 1910 the monarchy was removed with surprisingly little bother. As soon as the republicans took over, the divisions of Portuguese society reappeared, and the party split into as many factions as there were possible attitudes and solutions to the crisis. The leadership of a more militant working class passed to the revolutionary syndicalists and the anarchists, adding to the difficulties of the new régime, which did no better than the monarchy in overcoming the problems of the liberal state. The First World War produced a further split, between neutralists and interventionists. Britain had her eye on the German ships interned in Portuguese harbours, and applied successful pressure on the interventionist side. Portugal joined the Allies in 1916. The dictatorship of Sidónio Pais, who ruled the country for one year after his coup in December 1917, was a more serious sign of authoritarian tendencies. His régime was also the first European dictatorship of the modern type – with populist appeal, personal charisma of the leader and the cult of youth – and in its social and political measures a clear precursor of corporativism and fascism.

The end of the war and the assassination of Pais in 1918 were followed by another period of political instability. In 1926, in view of the collapse of the authority of parliament, the armed forces at last united to put an end to Portuguese liberalism. On 28 May a military dictatorship was installed, but it could not establish itself on a permanent footing or provide solutions to the country's problems until the military dictators had given way two years later to the new breed of right-wing authoritarian politician led by Antonio de Oliveira Salazar. Differing from conservative dictatorships of that time, Salazar's system meant a complete break with all liberal machinery for popular representation and arbitration. He replaced them with institutions that, coupled to various social and economic devices aimed at isolationism abroad and at restricting competition and wage bargaining at home, formed the framework of the 'Corporative State'. This was formalized in a new authoritarian constitution of 1935. The establishment of corporative institutions and economic autarky (self-sufficiency) together with ruthless repression of all political dissent explains the success of Salazar's rule for more than 40 years.   *M. V. C.*

The young Alfonso XIII, born king of Spain in 1886, after his father's death in 1885

THE MAKING OF THE SECOND BRITISH EMPIRE

In 1783 Britain recognized the independence of the United States of America; nevertheless, thereafter trade between them expanded greatly. So British commerce did not require a formal protected empire and the 'old colonial system' died. Belief in free trade led Britain to value small possessions that were potential market places for their areas – Singapore, Hongkong and Trinidad. Eighteenth-century industrial Britain invested massively overseas, but only about a sixth of that investment was within the Empire.

In the wars between 1793 and 1815 Britain asserted an unchallengeable control of the seas. This not only produced colonial gains at the peace, but also enabled Britain to enforce her interests throughout the world, as the use of naval power in the 1840–42 Opium War with China proved, for example. The naval supremacy had political implications: Bolívar explained that 'only England, mistress of the seas, can protect us from the united forces of European reaction.' But it was informal influence, not empire, that British foreign secretary George Canning contemplated when he said in 1824: 'Spanish America is free and if we do not mismanage our affairs sadly, she is English.'

The loss of the 13 North American colonies left Britain with an abiding realization of the futility of coercing white settlers. Australasia, Canada and South Africa, also colonies of white settlement, grew so fast under the British flag that by 1837 she possessed a second British Empire whose nature resembled that of the lost American colonies. This situation resulted from many factors, including having dictated the non-European clauses of the 1815 peace, renewed emigration from Britain (especially in the 1820s and 1830s) and domination of the eastern trade routes.

However, this Empire did not consist solely of white settlers and island entrepôts. Frontier wars had caused territorial expansion in South Africa and more extensively in India. By 1850 the whole sub-continent was under British control (her frontier wars were now against Burma, Persia and Afghanistan). British India was a bulwark of Britain's power: by 1914 her troops had fought from China to Kenya, and she made Victoria an empress rather than a queen; this and much more was highly valued. Yet the British government regarded India as an exceptional case, the product of trade protection by a trading company. In 1850 Britain did not desire to imperialize large areas with non-white populations, yet she had founded an empire with a mixed complexion. *P. H. S. H.*

Background, the Taj Mahal. Insets, left to right: Hongkong; Indian village, Canada; Table Mountain, South Africa.

Canada

The word 'Canada' derives from a Huron–Iroquois word, *kanata*, and first appeared in print in the account by Jacques Cartier, the French navigator, of his explorations in 1534–35 around the vast estuary area of the St Lawrence River. Until 1867 Canada was a variable label and was used to designate only part of what eventually was to become the whole independent Canada of today. The indigenous human history of Canada should properly begin with Eskimos and Indians (in Canada today these people are more often called the Inuit and Dene respectively), but until recently the story has been written principally in terms of European incursions, explorations, settlements and developments. The first Europeans to land in Canada were Vikings from Scandinavia, about AD 1000, but it was about another 500 years before a persistent European impact began to be made. In 1497, soon after the explorations of Columbus much further south, the Italians John and Sebastian Cabot explored the coast of Newfoundland on behalf of their patron, Henry VII, King of England. They laid claim to the eastern shore, but they had, of course, no idea of the overall shape and size of the nearby continent. In 1534 Jacques Cartier explored the mouth of the St Lawrence – which the French later called 'the river of Canada'. It was not until after 1600, however, that permanent settlement began to take root. In 1604 Samuel de Champlain established a base at Port Royal (present-day Annapolis) in Nova Scotia. In 1608 he constructed a fort at Quebec, on the St Lawrence, and called the surrounding countryside New France. Subsequently, Frenchmen sailed right up the St Lawrence River, while others filtered northwards up the Mississippi from the French settlements bordering the north-east coasts of the Caribbean, seeking to outflank the English colonies of the tidewater lands in the south and in New England.

Between the 1750s and 1815 Britain and France were mostly at war or at readiness for war with each other, and colonial North America enacted its own versions of Anglo-French clashes and rivalries that were simultaneously raging in Europe and in south Asia. From 1756 to 1763 the Seven Years War raged in Europe, and the American aspect of this conflict, the French and Indian War, settled the outcome of the local British and French rivalries. In 1758 the ambitiously conceived French fortress of Louisbourg fell to the British; in 1759 James Wolfe's forces captured Quebec; in 1760 Montreal surrendered. By the Peace of Paris (1763) all New France east of the Mississippi, apart from New Orleans, was ceded to Britain. In what now became the province of Quebec, 60,000 French Canadians became British subjects.

The American War of Independence, 1776–83, was a civil war within the British empire of North America. With the launching of the United States and British recognition of its independence (1783) came the confirmation and enhancement of the importance of the loyalist colonies to Britain, and about 40,000 of what were known as the United Empire Loyalists left the USA to resettle northwards within the British realms. The French Revolutionary and Napoleonic Wars (1792–1815) deeply affected North America. War changed trans-Atlantic trade patterns, but ultimately confirmed the territorial dispositions of 1763 and 1783. Out of the British blockade of France and similar war measures arose the War of 1812 between Britain and the USA; for Americans this seemed an opportunity to liberate the remaining British colonies to their north, while for Canadians it was a war of defence against invaders. The war ended in stalemate, but that eventually fructified into a form of stability that facilitated new growth. In 1821 British North America, that is to say, the colonies of Nova Scotia, New Brunswick, Lower Canada (Quebec) and Upper Canada, had a population of about 750,000 people. By 1851 there were 2,300,000, with the majority of the new immigrants in Upper Canada (Ontario).

Social and political changes in Upper and Lower Canada led to increased agitation for governmental changes, and this was fuelled by economic discontents and funnelled by rebellious new leaders – notably William

The Citadel, Quebec, in the early 19th century

Lyon Mackenzie in Upper Canada and Louis Joseph Papineau in Lower Canada. Rebellions in Upper and in Lower Canada in 1837 were quashed. Then Lord Durham, nicknamed Radical Jack, was sent out as Governor-General and Royal Commissioner to enquire into the causes of the rebellions and to make recommendations. The extensive Durham Report of 1839 made many proposals, including the union of Upper and Lower Canada and parliamentary government. Even so, the confederation of Canada as formulated in the British North America Act of 1867 did not emerge swiftly and smoothly out of an easily forged consensus of provinces and people. After the Durham Report there ensued more than 25 years of controversies, piecemeal attempts at reform (including a Canada Act of 1840) and intermittent, at times acute, tension with the USA. There was a series of conferences and eventually much opposition to confederation in the Maritime Provinces (Nova Scotia, New Brunswick and Prince Edward Island). Prince Edward Island, with Newfoundland, adamantly boycotted the proposed federation. The new union was hammered out basically between Ontario and Quebec, and incorporated no less than 72 resolutions from Quebec. The four British North American colonies of Nova Scotia, New Brunswick, Canada East (formerly Lower Canada, i.e. Quebec) and Canada West (formerly Upper Canada, i.e. Ontario) joined together to form the Canadian Confederation on 1 July 1867, when the Dominion of Canada was officially born. *P. H. L.*

India under the Company

The English East India Company (founded in 1600 and dissolved in 1874) started to acquire and rule Indian territories outside its main trading posts of Madras, Calcutta and Bombay in 1765. The great Mughal empire had just disintegrated into numerous independent kingdoms, while in England the industrial revolution was getting under way. By 1849 the Company had succeeded in bringing under its direct rule the whole of what came to be called British India, and in extending its paramountcy over nearly 600 princely states. Factors that urged the Company to continue extending its boundaries were 'French competition' (Napoleon's scheme to take India) and the 'Russian threat'. The latter became real after the defeat of Napoleon in 1815, and led the Company into making its last two major conquests (Sind and the Punjab) in the 1840s, and fighting two Afghan wars (1839–42, 1878–79) in order to keep Afghanistan out of the Russian sphere of influence. Security motives mainly lay behind the three

Burmese wars of 1826, 1852 and 1886. Burmese aggression on India's north-east frontiers provoked the Company into waging the first war, while the build-up of French influence in Indochina stirred the British into annexing the remainder – Upper Burma – in 1886, thereby bringing the whole of Burma under the British pale.

Turning this vast land of several nationalities into a single state was the first achievement of the British raj. It was not a unique achievement in the context of 4000 years of Indian history, but it was unique in the kind of political, legal, social and economic changes that the British Empire introduced into India. Almost all of these took place during the Company's rule from 1765 to 1858, when British administrators in India displayed confidence, missionary zeal and enterprise.

The Company's rule in India, however, came to an end with the Indian uprising of May 1857, which engulfed the whole of northern India for just over a year, until June

An Hon. East India Company official receiving the attentions of a British Resident's Indian household

The shattered interior of the Sikandra Bagh, Lucknow, after the fighting, 1857

1858. This was sparked off when the Indian soldiers in the Company's service discovered that the cartridges that they had to bite before loading were greased with cow and pig fat – unclean for both Hindus and Muslims. But the deeper reason was a growing protest against the coming of Western ways on the part of traditional India. The recent reforms of the great governor-general, Lord Dalhousie (1848–56), had both aggravated the Indian soldiers' suspicions and discontent, and created a class of deposed and dispossessed feudal lords. When these feudal elements joined the mutineers in proclaiming the nominal Mughal emperor (whose sovereignty had shrunk to the four walls of his Delhi palace) as their ruler, the mutiny became an Indian revolt. However, the uprising, which the British held to be the consequence of several innovations they had made in the political and social life of the country, dampened the reforming spirit of the Company days and, consequently, the direct rule of Westminster over India, commencing in 1858, became cautious and conservative.

Constitutional law was a new phenomenon for India, as the country had hitherto been ruled only by personal government. It was a surprise for Indians to realize that the high and mighty sahebs who ruled India were accountable to still higher authorities in London, by whom they could not only be removed from office, but even, as in the case of Warren Hastings, be impeached. Another innovation in the political arena was the creation of the legislative bodies at the central and provincial levels. During the first

half of the 19th century they were appointed and consisted only of British officials, but during the second half, Indians came to be nominated to them, and in 1892 the elective principle was at last introduced. The British in fact excelled in keeping the liberal stream of politics alive in their imperial holdings by progressively grooming their legislative bodies into self-governing institutions. Perhaps the most important British innovation was the establishment of the rule of law. The independence of the judiciary and the introduction of English law began with the establishment of the Supreme Court in 1774, and by 1872 India had one of the best legal systems in the world. The Indian Criminal and Civil Codes, based on the principles of English law, came to be administered by highly trained judges and counsellors, most of whom were Indians.

The introduction of English education in 1835 was to have significant impact, particularly on the upper and middle ranks of Indian society. The British intended, as Macaulay (then a member of the Governor-General's executive council) put it, to form a class of Indians who might be interpreters between the British and the millions of Indians, a class of persons Indian in blood and colour, but English in tastes, opinions, morals and intellect. However, this class of English-educated Indians, numbering about 55,000 in 1885, became more than an interpreter – it claimed to be representative of the Indian people and began asking first for a share in political power, and eventually for the whole of it. *B. N. P.*

South Africa up to the Great Trek

The Cape of Good Hope was first sailed round by the Portuguese at the end of the 15th century, but it was not until shortly after 1652, the year in which the Dutch East India Company established a revictualling station there for its passing sailing vessels, that the region became an outpost of European settlement. Between 1657 and 1707 Dutch, German and French Huguenot settlers arrived at the Cape – the forbears of the Afrikaner (or Boer) people of South Africa. The economy of the new colony was founded upon cereal-farming, viticulture and, further into the Cape's hinterland, stockraising. Labour was provided both by slaves, originally imported by the Company from East and West Africa, Madagascar, Indonesia and other Asian centres, and by the progeny of unions between white settlers, their slaves and the indigenous Khoikhoi people (Hottentot), whose descendants now make up South Africa's two million coloured (mixed-race) population. Attempts by the East India Company to closely regulate the lives of the immigrants failed and many settlers moved away from Cape Town and its neighbourhood, and during the 18th century a new frontier society grew up that was based on freedom from governmental control, individualism, companionship with one's own kind and observance of the Calvinist faith of the Dutch Reformed Church.

British occupations of the Cape

Control of the colony by the Dutch East India Company finally ended in 1795 when, following the French invasion of The United Netherlands, the British occupied the Cape with the agreement of the House of Orange. Britain's initial occupation lasted only until 1803, when, by the Treaty of Amiens, the Cape was transferred to the Batavian Republic (as The United Netherlands had been renamed by Napoleon). However, in 1806, Britain again took control of the colony, mainly for strategic reasons, and this time with permanent occupation in mind.

Even before her possession of the Cape was ratified by the peace treaties that ended the Napoleonic Wars, Britain embarked upon the creation of a colony that was British in spirit. In 1807 the slave trade at the Cape was formally brought to a halt.

Matters which, under Company administration, had largely been governed by unwritten convention were regularized and made subject to legislation. The status and terms of employment of 'coloured' workers were enshrined in law. The system of justice was revised, regular court circuits introduced in 1811, and their sittings made public two years later. The English language was encouraged in schools and made compulsory in courts of law, Presbyterian Scotsmen were appointed to occupy the pulpits of the Dutch Reformed Church, and efforts were made to attract English immigrants. In 1820 some 5000 settlers arrived in the eastern Cape to take up farms each of 100 acres. In 1825 an element of democracy was introduced by the creation of separate Advisory Councils in

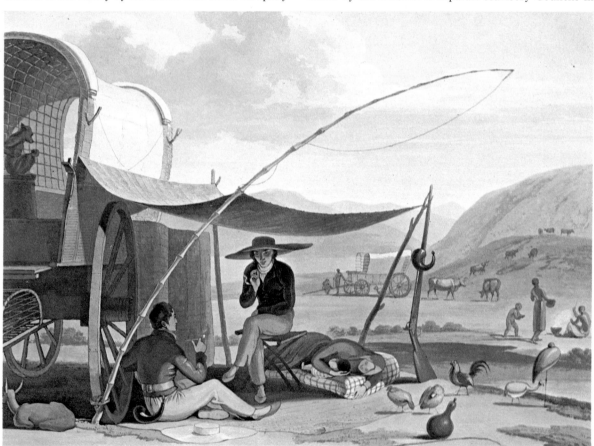

Samuel Daniell's contemporary observation of the 'Halt of a Boors Family' at the time of the Great Trek

Cape Town and Grahamstown, and later a Legislative Council was established with a small number of nominated unofficial members. In 1828, the freedom of the press was guaranteed by ordinance, and in the same year 'coloured' people were freed from having to carry passes and given the right to own land, and their rights as workers defined.

Many of the reforms introduced by Britain were bitterly opposed by Afrikaner settlers, especially those living far into the Cape's interior. Frontiersmen and their families had grown accustomed to the casual, remote and sometimes corrupt administration of a trading company, and new efforts to regulate their lives were unwelcome. Attempts by Britain to control and restrict landholding were regarded as an affront to the settlers' way of life, since men had come to expect, almost as a birthright, the availability of 6000-acre farms for their exclusive use. Considerable annoyance was provoked, too, by the introduction of measures that made it possible for 'coloured' servants to take their employers to court and win cases against them. Activities on behalf of the 'coloured' communities by some of the early missionaries to South Africa, such as James Read and John Philip of the London Missionary Society, further threatened to turn upside down the world the Afrikaners knew. Their disillusionment was made more complete by the British government's apparent lack of concern for the predicament of settlers on the eastern frontier in their regular and often bitter clashes over land with the Bantu-speaking Xhosa people, who were pastoralists like themselves, but more densely settled than the Khoisan groups further west, and better organized and more menacing than the other natives the settlers had hitherto encountered.

The Great Trek

For many Afrikaners the final straw came in 1836 when Queen Adelaide Province, situated between the Keiskamma and Kei rivers, was handed back to the Xhosa since it was considered by Britain to be too expensive to defend and administer. Already, the possibility of moving further into the interior away from British control had been discussed among the frontier communities, and within weeks of the decision to abandon Queen Adelaide Province, families had begun to form themselves into organized parties, sold their farms and, accompanied by their 'coloured' servants, set out to trek north across the Orange River and away from a system of government that seemed oppressive, wrong-headed and insensitive to their needs. While most Afrikaners chose to stay in the Cape, prepared to endure British authority rather than trek away north to an unknown destiny, other families joined the exodus during the winter months, so that the Voortrekkers, as the members of the Great Trek became known, eventually numbered some 6000 whites. Under the leadership of frontiersmen with military experience, such as Hendrik Potgieter, Piet Uys, Gerrit Maritz and Piet Retief, they began a journey that would involve them in frequent and fierce struggles with the African peoples of the interior, and would lead as well to further harassment from the British. But it was a journey, too, that would ultimately bear fruit in the establishment of the independent Afrikaner republics of the Transvaal and Orange Free State.

The Mfecane

At the same time that relations between the British and Boers in the Cape were becoming progressively more difficult, a revolution was taking place in African affairs beyond the Cape's frontiers. Until the end of the 18th century the Bantu-speaking peoples of southern Africa mostly comprised small independent chiefdoms, but as the African population grew, chiefdoms became consolidated into larger political units, and competition for land on which to graze their cattle became more fierce. Fighting became more frequent and intense. One African group, the Zulu in Natal, led by a brilliant military strategist and tactician, Shaka, successfully expanded its boundaries so that by 1826 all its rivals in southeast Africa had been vanquished. The Zulu were able to do this by creating a large, well-disciplined and mobile standing army, and by replacing their main weapon, the long throwing spear, with a short stabbing spear (or assegai), which was used by warriors at close quarters. The efficiency of the assegai was demonstrated many times in battle. In military engagements Shaka favoured a tactical movement known as 'the horns of the buffalo', in which the wings of the Zulu army advanced around the flanks of the enemy thereby preventing an organized retreat from a ruthless frontal assault.

Some defeated African chiefs and their followers, rather than submit to Shaka's tyrannical rule, embarked on journeys that took them hundreds of miles to the north. Soshangane fled to Gazaland in Mozambique, Zwangandaba to the shores of Lake Nyasa and Mzilikazi to the high veld and, ultimately, to Mashonaland (Rhodesia). Some groups, such as the Mfengu, migrated south and increased the pressure of population on the Cape Colony's eastern frontier. Other refugee leaders, such as Sobhuza of the Swazi and Moshesh of the Basuto, forged new nations (now Swaziland and Lesotho) strong enough to withstand the Zulu. This period of intense African military activity and nation-building has become known as the *Mfecane*, an African word which means 'the crushing of peoples'. In 1828 Shaka was assassinated and succeeded by Dingane, the Zulu chief with whom the Voortrekkers had to deal when they crossed the Drakensberg Mountains into Natal. *P. W.*

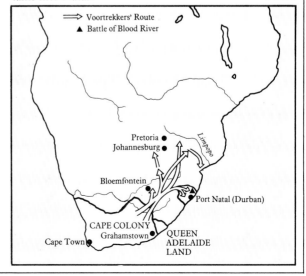

123

Australasia

Although Australia had long been inhabited by peoples of Negroid stock, the history of Australia is really all 'modern', and dates from Captain James Cook's arrival at Botany Bay in 1770. His return to England came at a critical juncture when the British government, prevented by the American revolutionary war from sending convicts to the transatlantic colonies, was looking for alternative outlets. In 1787, therefore, Governor Philip was commissioned to set up a new penal colony, and, accompanied by over 600 prisoners, a military contingent and a few civilians, he arrived at Botany Bay in January 1788. Within a week this group had moved up the coast to Sydney Cove, which became the focus of settlement.

Cut off from a regular source of supply and unused to Australian conditions, the colony, which was called New South Wales, was desperately short of key resources in its early years. Not surprisingly, at this stage influence was possessed by those enjoying official positions rather than by those who had wealth, since in such primitive conditions of society money had only a minor role to play. In particular, a clique of officers largely succeeded in forming a closed hierarchy that attempted, with varying success, to dominate the governor. Gradually, a merchant and farmer interest developed to challenge the earlier pattern of power. By 1800 some Sydney traders were already transacting business with Tahiti and even China. Farm settlements, especially after 1800, spread out across the Bathurst Plains. After 1810, a more integrated economic system became discernible, so that metal money replaced the old paper notes and in 1817 the first commercial bank opened in Sydney.

The aboriginal inhabitants shortly became victims of this colonial society. Settlers appropriated their lands, and when the aboriginals refused to be transformed into a labour force, they were simply pushed into the outback. The main factor dictating the pace of this appropriation of native land was the growth of the pastoral industry. Fine-quality Spanish sheep had been introduced on the Australian grazing lands at a time when European woolproducers were failing adequately to supply the British textile manufacturers, and when marine technology was making it cheaper to transport cargoes between England and Australia than between England and Europe.

The post-1820s were the heyday of the 'squatter', the man who took his sheep beyond existing settlements and resided on the empty lands technically owned by the Crown. This 'squattocracy' rapidly became a rich landed gentry, and controlling their activities emerged as the major problem facing the local administrators in Sydney and the imperial authorities in London. These authorities preferred a more geographically limited, manageable and efficient form of expansion than that provided by sheepranching. It was in this context that the ideas and propaganda of Gibbon Wakefield took on great significance. Wakefield, particularly in his book *The Art of Colonization* (1829), advocated the sale, rather than the free gift, of land to settlers. The revenue was to be used to assist the immigration of 'free' (that is, non-convict) labourers, who would be constrained by high land prices to work on arable farms close to the towns. In this way the hierarchical social system of Britain would be reproduced in a colonial setting.

The colony of South Australia began along these lines in 1836. These objectives, however, clashed with the vested interests which wished land to remain free and 'squattable', and so the 1830s and 1840s witnessed a political conflict between the British government, with its Wakefieldian views, and dominant groups in the Australian colonies. Ultimately, the facts of local conditions were bound to overcome the merely political preferences of the British government.

While the squatters were winning this battle, other economic groups were growing in scale and influence. Agriculturalists, such as wheat producers, businessmen and even manufacturers were accumulating capital, and in the boom conditions that followed the gold 'strikes' of the early 1850s, above all in Victoria, they thrived as populations, and markets expanded. In this increasingly complex economic society some mechanism was required to regulate affairs and provide some measure of the strength of different interests, and so it was during the 1850s that the colonies demanded and received responsible government. New South Wales, for example, received its Constitution Act in 1856, and in the following years the political institutions of mass democracy, such as manhood suffrage and the secret ballot, were adopted by most of the Australian colonies.

New Zealand

Captain Cook had circumnavigated New Zealand on the same journey that took him to Botany Bay, but the settlement of New Zealand proved much slower. In many senses it was only a frontier of the more dynamic growth of the Australian colonies. The relative compactness of the Maori tribes partly explains this, but gradually a merchanting presence (gun-sellers and whalers, for example) grew up, and the disintegrative effects of the European traders' interaction with the Maoris forced a reluctant British government to appoint a Resident in 1833.

The colonizing process gathered pace as Wakefield and his aristocratic-radical backers in Britain (keen to find outlets for those pauperized by industrial change at home) set up a New Zealand Association in 1837. Whereas previously European merchants and Maoris could, despite occasional disputes, construct mutually beneficial relationships, settlers and Maoris were bound sooner or later to clash on the central issue of land ownership. The Treaty of Waitangi in 1840, which annexed New Zealand as a colony, was a step in the British government's attempt to control and stabilize this situation. By the Waitangi Treaty, the Maoris were guaranteed the ownership of their lands, which only the British Crown could purchase.

As settler communities spread (Nelson was established in 1841, Otago in 1848 and Canterbury in 1850), landhunger grew, reaching a peak among the Taranaki pioneers in the 1850s. Governor Grey (1845–53) tried to use the government as an intermediary in land sales, but in so doing he failed to satisfy the insatiable settler demand. After the introduction of responsible government among the colonists in 1855 the Maoris found themselves under increasing economic pressure, and the period from 1860 to 1872 was marked by constant warfare between natives and Europeans. By 1870 the British government had largely withdrawn from the situation, leaving the settlers to crush Maori resistance and introduce a 'free' market in land.

R. F. H.

Above: Scattering a hostile aboriginal tribe near Baines River, Northern Territory
Below: The Hobart Town chain gang, 1831

EXPLORATION, EXPANSION AND IMPERIALISM

Long before the Western advance into the undeveloped regions of the world was made irresistible by the emergence of modern industrial capitalism, the Portuguese, Spanish, Dutch, French and, eventually, the British (with more lasting success than any of them) had established a rather loose form of control over vast, remote regions. These ventures set the pattern for a continuous, if largely unnoticed, process of colonial expansion outside the Western world.

By the late 18th century expansion decelerated and, in some cases, even came to a standstill. Liberal economists no longer considered colonies to be of undoubted value to the mother country. Neither public opinion nor the governments of the day were much in favour of colonial expansion and all they were willing to tolerate was informal expansion and colonial rule by chartered companies at their own risk. Even so, during the early 19th century colonial expansion gradually gained momentum again and led to a wild scramble for territories overseas. The reasons for this about-turn were manifold. Initially, missionary work and the anti-slavery campaign had attracted the attention of the public to strange, but infinitely promising regions, in particular on the African continent. At the same time, individual explorers ignored hardships in opening up regions that hitherto had never been visited by any Europeans: between 1850 and 1880 the public was fascinated by the published reports from Rohlf, Nachtigal, Livingstone, Stanley, Burton and many other scholarly pioneers.

More important was the sub-imperialism of Europeans already settled on the African periphery who had a personal interest in the further expansion of their control. The Cape colonists continuously extended their sway to the north, no matter what the government at Westminster had to say. In the case of France, the military element was the main force behind expansion, beginning in 1831 with the long, bloody fight for the control of Algeria. Last but not least, economic interest groups such as the British East India Company extended their rapacious, though largely indirect, rule. In general, the European governments much preferred the methods of 'indirect rule', if possible, by seeking the cooperation of indigenous élites, as in the case of Egypt, Tunisia and Morocco. Finance-imperialist penetration either through huge state loans at enormous interest rates or private investments, and economic imperialism through the acquisition of economic privileges played more important roles than territorial aggrandisement.

During the early 1880s these older, informal methods began to fail, partly because the collaborating régimes came under fire from within. The British invasion of Egypt in 1882, which Gladstone had embarked upon as a mere political action, triggered off an accelerating process of imperialist expansion. The attempt by the Belgian king, Leopold II, to carve out for himself a huge central African empire, using the good names of Stanley and other European explorers for his rather dubious undertaking, signalled the end of 'indirect rule', which had not interfered much with the tribal systems of the indigenous populations. European governments gradually forced into submission the tribes and peoples of the hinterland who had hitherto been largely left alone.

The idea of imperialism took hold of the minds of the upper classes and even some of the working classes throughout Europe. From the 1890s governments were badgered 'to peg out claims for posterity' in all those regions of the world that nobody had yet formally annexed, in order to enhance the world position of the metropolitan nation. Growing economies were believed to require new markets to allow further continuous growth, and imperialism appeared to be the obvious answer to this. The new imperialist nationalism could also be used as a convenient strategy for the defence of the traditional order at home. All these factors together brought about that tremendous European expansion into the still 'free' regions of the globe that is described as high imperialism. The imperialist rivalries between the great powers, which came to a head during the First World War, may be considered the climax and the eclipse of classical imperialism. Since 1919 imperialism has been in retreat, even though it managed to hold its own to a surprising degree in many regions of the Third World up to the recent past. *W. J. M.*

Explorers, from top to bottom: Sir Richard Burton, Gustav Nachtigal, David Livingstone

The End of Imperial China

The Opium War

China's last imperial dynasty had begun to decline by the early 19th century. The tripling of the population to a figure of 400 million between 1400 and 1800 had triggered many social changes which strained the traditional pattern of rule. This also affected the response to the modern challenge of Western imperialism.

The introduction of opium on a large scale into the trade with China in the 1820s, increasing in the 1830s, had enabled the British to reverse an extremely adverse trade balance. The resulting social evils and the damage to the Chinese economy by the drain of silver led the Chinese authorities in 1839 to take drastic measures to stop the pernicious traffic. The manner of their so doing was regarded by Lord Palmerston as a provocation. The British government had long been irked by what were regarded as unwarranted Chinese pretensions and the high-handed manner in which foreigners were allowed to perch like pariahs on the outskirts of China's southernmost city of Canton. China had long regarded itself as the only repository of true values and civilization in the world. Since time immemorial the Chinese had always claimed with good reason to regard the less cultured foreigners on their periphery as barbarians of one kind or another. Naturally, Europeans and Americans were regarded in the same light. Moreover, adventurous British traders backed by thrustful manufacturers back home, were eager to reach 400 million potential customers in China. They never understood that the decentralized, self-sufficient Chinese economy was largely immune to substantial penetration by foreign goods, and accordingly, they always blamed their frustrations upon obstructionist Chinese officialdom.

The resulting war brought a swift victory to the British, who compelled the Chinese to sign the Treaty of Nanking in 1842. Hong Kong was ceded in perpetuity and five ports were opened to foreign traders where they were granted enclaves of extra-territoriality immune to Chinese law. Of these Treaty Ports, Shanghai was to become the most important. This war was followed nearly 20 years later by yet another which finally forced the reluctant Chinese into what Palmerston called the 'comity of nations'. By the treaties of 1860 the Chinese had to allow diplomatic missions in Peking and further concessions were granted to foreigners in China. Meanwhile, the Russians took advantage of Chinese weakness to compel the ceding of vast tracts of land in the north.

The Taiping Uprising

In the midst of the foreign challenge the Chinese Empire faced its greatest-ever threat from an internal rebellion which from 1850 to 1864 engulfed most of south and central China, and at one point even threatened the capital, Peking. Unlike previous peasant rebellions in Chinese history, this one was inspired by a communal ideology of a golden age of 'Great Peace' (Taiping), combining a curious mixture of Christian and traditional rebellious themes. This turned the uprising into a revolutionary challenge to the doctrines of Confucianism, which teach obedience and order as the basis of traditional rule. Basing itself initially on disadvantaged minority social groups in

Right: Popular woodcut of 'Boxers' charging a European firing line with bare blades

the south the rebellion spread like a prairie fire before the wind. The uprising was not subdued before the foundations of the empire had been thoroughly shaken and 20 to 30 million people had been slain, and the imperial armies had been destroyed. The rebels had been defeated in fact by regional forces raised, financed and controlled by leaders outside the direct control of the Imperial Court. Although it was not immediately apparent, political power had shifted decisively to the regions.

'Self-Strengthening'

The victorious regional leaders, notably Tseng Kuo-fan, were convinced Confucianists and in many ways the finest example of Confucian paternalism of their day. Combining with a progressive group in the Imperial Court, they recognized that the challenge from the West differed from any previous external threat. To defeat it, China would have to learn Western ways. Their concern, however, was not simply with the survival of China but rather with that of China's traditional system and values. China had to strengthen itself by learning to manufacture Western military technology but only so that its traditional values could endure. Although a number of successful enterprises were established from the 1860s onwards, such as the Kiangnan Arsenal, which in its day was the biggest in Asia, the attempt eventually failed. As reactionary Confucianists at Court were quick to point out, even the attempt itself challenged traditional precepts and undermined the social order. Moreover, Chinese

officials were poor managers of these new enterprises. Nor was there a vigorous independent Chinese bourgeoisie to take up the challenge. The ravaged Chinese countryside reacted with hatred and xenophobia to foreign missionary activity, thus creating successive incidents with foreign countries which left the 'self-strengtheners' with little breathing space. The *coup de grâce* was delivered by the humiliating defeat inflicted on the cream of China's new armies and navy by the hitherto despised Japanese in 1894. They, too, had been modernizing.

The Boxer Uprising

The defeat by Japan sparked off an abortive attempt to reform at Court, which only ended with the conservative dowager empress even more strongly in power. These events coupled with the high tide of imperialism in the West led to 'the battle for concessions' in China, which at one point threatened even the survival of the country as a unitary state. It was in this context that reactionaries in the Court sided with an atavistic peasant rebellion organized by a secret society called the Boxers (I Ho Ch'üan, The 'Righteous Harmonious Fists'), on account of their magic rituals involving the martial arts which supposedly made them invulnerable to bullets. This anti-foreign uprising culminated in the siege of the foreign legations in Peking from June to August 1900, and was put down by the imperialist powers acting in concert. A mixed force fought its way through from Tientsin, and the Summer Palace was looted. A huge indemnity was claimed and a

much chastened dowager empress tried to follow the path of reform. She died in 1908.

The End of the Empire

The last decade of the empire was accompanied by a number of the major reforms long urged by friendly foreigners as a key to survival. Paradoxically, these hastened the end. The abolition of the ancient examination system alienated millions of Chinese gentry whose claim to special social status rested upon this. The attempts to establish some kind of representative provincial assemblies so as to reach down to the people further alienated traditional supporters, without winning the support of new forces, such as the hundreds of thousands of educated people in foreign schools and countries.

Meanwhile, a genuine if still ineffective nationalist movement had begun among overseas Chinese and students abroad and was headed by Sun Yat-sen. The authority of the Imperial Court had been undermined throughout the century and the new reforms had accelerated that process. Real political power in China lay with the commanders of regional armies. In the end, in 1911, a misfired attempt at rebellion in Wu Ch'ang, a major city in central China, led to the local commander being forced to pick up the flag of republicanism. Abandoned by scheming regional commanders, the last emperor, a boy, had no alternative but to abdicate.   *M. B. Y.*

Nanking, 1911: A pigtail (symbol of Chinese servitude to the Manchu dynasty) cut off by a soldier

The Opening of Japan

Japan's seclusion, which had been prescribed by the strict ordinances of the feudal Tokugawa rulers for over two centuries, was broken by Commodore Perry of the US Navy carrying out the orders of his government. After a first, insistent visit to Tokyo Bay with his naval expedition in July 1853, he returned in greater force in March 1854. Reluctantly, in the face of such pressure, Japan granted the US and the other maritime countries treaties containing concessions: trading rights, the exchange of emissaries and the opening of 'treaty ports' such as Nagasaki, Yokohama, Kobe, Osaka and Tokyo. The Tokugawa ruler, the Shogun, already unpopular, was doubly criticized for offering foreigners special privileges. Those Japanese who were hostile to foreign incursions wanted to prevent any further extension of foreign trade. By threatening the safety of foreigners and their property, the anti-foreign party made life difficult for foreign nationals, though there was sometimes provocation enough from the unruly communities of the treaty ports.

This was only the foreign dimension to the disputes between the powerless emperor's court, which had for seven centuries been located at Kyoto, and the effective Tokugawa authorities at Edo (Tokyo), which were coming to the surface. The western, or 'outer', clans and other opponents of the Shogun banded together to form an emperor's party. The Shogun sent punitive expeditions against the rebellious clans so that a state of civil war de-

veloped. The clans realized that they stood to gain by foreign contacts and sent missions overseas in order to give assurances that they favoured an increase in trade. Although there was little scope for foreign intervention in this internal dispute, the powers were divided in their approach: France tended to favour the Shogun, and Britain the clan forces. In 1867 the Shogun was forced to resign and the 16-year-old emperor and his party were restored to government in 1868. The new emperor took the reign-name of Meiji, hence the restoration of the imperial system came to be described as the 'Meiji Restoration'. To indicate the change which was intended, the emperor moved his capital from Kyoto to Tokyo in 1869.

The new government adopted a policy of reform and consolidation in every sector. Between 1871 and 1873 a mission headed by Prince Iwakura and containing many cabinet ministers toured the world on the look-out for ideas suitable for transplanting to Japan from advanced foreign countries. They were able to observe at first hand the effects of the industrial revolution in Europe and America. In the general atmosphere of change, vocal elements were calling for elected legislatures on Western models. The government was cautious and showed great skill in choosing from abroad the political models which would not injure the Japanese state and the institution of the emperor. In 1882–83 the influential statesman Ito went to Europe to examine constitutional systems. Poli-

The 'black ships', 'Mississippi' and 'Susquehanna' steaming into Tokyo Bay, July 1853

tical parties were formed, and the 1880s saw modern politics come to life. Finally, a constitution was promulgated in 1889, and the first elections for the Diet and its first session took place the following year.

As Japan gained self-confidence and saw that she was not now likely to be invaded by foreign powers either singly or together, she announced her determination to renegotiate her existing treaties with the Western powers. Under the treaties she had given them consular jurisdiction in both civil and criminal cases and a fixed import duty of 5 per cent *ad valorem*. For two decades revision of the unequal treaties had been a major political objective of the Japanese. By the Anglo-Japanese commercial treaty of 1894 this inequality was for the first time dropped in return for the Westernization of the Japanese law codes. Other countries agreed that they, too, would drop their extra-territorial privileges. By 1899, Japan had to a large extent removed the more objectionable restraints which had been imposed at the time of her forcible opening.

The Korean kingdom had traditionally been tributary to China but had enjoyed virtual independence until the 1880s, when China tried to tighten her grip. In the 1890s, Japan detected the hand of Russia behind China's activities in Korea. While attempts at outside mediation were made, the Japanese were determined to put the dispute to the test of war. In August 1894, they sent an expeditionary force and won the land battles in Korea and Manchuria,

though their advance was then arrested by the severity of the winter. They also defeated the Chinese fleet. By the Treaty of Shimonoseki (April 1895), Japan imposed on China demands for an indemnity, the opening of ports and the territories of the Liaotung peninsula at the southern tip of Manchuria, the island of Formosa (Taiwan) and the Pescadores Islands. China leaked the terms to the European powers and complained that Japan's demands were excessive. Russia, France and Germany offered Japan the 'friendly advice' not to pursue her demand for the transfer of the Liaotung peninsula. The Japanese felt that they could not fight a naval battle against three European squadrons and contented themselves with an enhanced indemnity.

The Japanese found that China in her weakness after the war again turned to Russia, which now contested Japan's position in Korea and signed an alliance with China against Japan for 15 years. Moreover, Russia obtained the right to build a branch-line of her trans-Siberian railway across Manchuria. Meanwhile, Japan used the substantial indemnity extracted from China for increasing and modernizing her army and for building a first-class navy. Busy in this way, she did not play a major part in the demands the powers made on China in 1898, but, when the anti-foreign Boxer uprising broke out in 1900, Japan sent a substantial force, which proved crucial in the relief of the Peking legations.   *I. H. N.*

Westernization begun: sailor and Japanese girl (left); a railroad station (right)

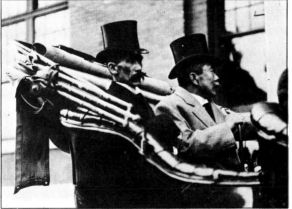

Westernization achieved: victorious Japanese envoys arrive for the Portsmouth NH peace talks, 1905

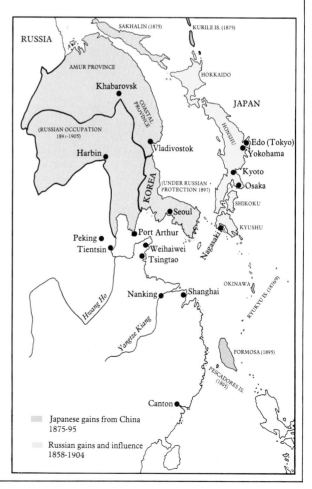

The Scramble for Africa

Until the beginning of the 19th century, the slave trade was at the centre of commercial relations between Europe and Africa. Because slaves, required mainly for the West Indian and American plantations, were supplied by powerful African or Arab middlemen who bought cheaply in the interior and sold expensively at the coast, European activity was confined to the African shoreline. The geography of the interior was consequently almost completely unknown. That Europe's ignorance of Africa was gradually overcome during the new century was largely due to the enterprise of individual explorers, missionaries and traders.

The first explorations of inner Africa were conducted under the auspices of the Association for the Discovery of the Interior of Africa, the forerunner of the Royal Geographical Society. In 1795, the 'African Association' (as it was called) financed the remarkable journey to the upper Niger River of Mungo Park, a young Scots surgeon, who established for the first time that, contrary to earlier belief, the Niger River flowed from west to east. The need to establish a new basis for commerce with Africa following the abolition of the slave trade in 1807 encouraged the British government to provide funds for further exploration. Dixon Denham and Hugh Clapperton crossed the Sahara from Tripoli to visit Bornu and Hausaland in 1823–25; in 1830 Richard and John Lander traced the course of the lower Niger River to the sea; and the German explorer, Heinrich Barth, also sponsored by the British government, visited the western Sudan between 1849 and 1855.

Missionaries played an important part in improving Europe's knowledge of the African interior. Two German members of the Church Missionary Society, Johan Krapf and Johannes Rebmann, travelled widely in East Africa and first saw the peaks of Mount Kilimanjaro and Mount Kenya. The most celebrated Victorian missionary-explorer was David Livingstone, who between 1851 and 1856 travelled north beyond the Cape frontier to the Victoria Falls, and from there westwards to Luanda in Angola and eastwards to the mouth of the Zambezi River. Livingstone's account of his journey, *Missionary Travels and Researches*, sold 22,000 copies in six months and made him a rich man. The Royal Geographical Society sent Richard Burton and John Speke to Lake Tanganyika in 1858, and Speke and James Grant to the upper reaches of the White Nile and Lake Victoria in 1862–64. Livingstone, meanwhile, continued his explorations. Lake Nyasa was discovered during his Zambezi expedition of 1859–64. Livingstone became so renowned that during his final African journey to the upper Congo in 1867–73 a young war correspondent, H. M. Stanley, was sent to find him by an American newspaper proprietor.

Leopold and the Congo

Until the 1870s, few explorers and missionaries saw themselves as pioneers of imperialism. European governments were uninterested in formal empire-building in Africa. There seemed to be no wealth in Africa which could possibly justify the enormous expense of establishing colonies, and each government was content with informal and often overlapping spheres of influence, provided that other nations exercised similar restraint. The beginning of a new era was marked by the entry upon the African scene of Leopold II of Belgium. Leopold's motives were ostensibly scientific and humanitarian, though his real intention was to create a vast monopoly trading area which to some extent would provide an outlet for his frustrated energies as constitutional ruler of a small and peaceable state. With the collaboration of Stanley, he concluded a treaty network with African chiefs in the Congo Basin between 1879 and 1884. The king's activities soon aroused the suspicion of other nations. A French explorer, Savorgnan de Brazza, believed the great potential wealth of the region could best be tapped by way of the Ogooué River rather than the Congo, and in 1880 de Brazza made a series of treaties with African rulers which purported to cede large territories to him as the representative of the French government. France later accepted these agreements as valid.

Following the British occupation of Egypt in 1882 and the subsequent ending of Anglo-French Dual Control of Egyptian finances, France sought to expand her interests elsewhere in Africa. She was encouraged to do so by the German chancellor, Bismarck, who wished to divert French attention away from Germany's annexation of Alsace and Lorraine in 1871. The 'gentlemen's agreement' between Britain and France not to encroach upon each other's interests in West Africa thereafter collapsed. Germany also began to develop an interest of her own in Africa, and between 1883 and 1885 she hurriedly acquired four colonies – South-West Africa (now Namibia), Togoland, the Cameroons and East Africa (now Tanzania). Germany's action precipitated a 'scramble' for African territory by the other European powers, for once one nation set up formal colonies, from which traders of other nations could be excluded, it followed that each government wanted to formalize its control of its own spheres of trading activity and political influence.

Anglo-French rivalry

The main axis of British colonization in Africa in the late 19th century was north–south in two movements: towards the centre of the continent from South Africa, and towards the source of the White Nile from Egypt. This movement inspired Cecil Rhodes to dream of a railway running entirely through British territory from Cape Town to Cairo. By contrast, the main axis of French expansion was west–east, from the Atlantic shore of West Africa to the Red Sea. The two axes met in the Sudan where, in 1898, the final dramatic scene of the 'scramble' was played out when Kitchener's Anglo-Egyptian army came face to face at Fashoda with Colonel Marchand's military expedition from the French Congo. War seemed likely, but France gave in and signed an agreement which left Britain in control of the Sudan and the entire course of the White Nile. By 1914, all but a tiny fraction of Africa had been partitioned by the European powers and only Liberia and Ethiopia remained independent under African governments.   *P. W.*

The depth of European influence on indigenous African cultures in the 19th century might depend on the degree of self-confidence retained in traditional values. For these Dahomey chiefs, visiting Paris in 1893, a top hat and western footwear did not compromise their dignity

The East Indies

Although the Dutch had been present in the East Indies since the end of the 16th century, their activities before the 19th century were largely confined to the Moluccas (the Spice Islands) and parts of Java. It was not until 1808 that European governments (the Dutch, as subjects of Napoleon, from 1808 to 1811, the British from 1811 to 1816, and the Dutch again thereafter) sought to impose direct colonial rule over the whole of Java. These attempts produced the Java War (1825–30), which cost at least 200,000 Javanese lives, out of an estimated population of perhaps six million.

The Java War broke the military power of the Javanese aristocracy and the Dutch were free to create a modern colonial state, which they did in two ways. First, they imposed upon Java one of the most purely exploitative systems in colonial history, the cultivation system (*cultuurstelsel*). This compelled the Javanese to produce crops (especially coffee, sugar and indigo) for export to Europe at an enormous profit to the Netherlands and a cost of great hardship to the Javanese. Second, they moved into the outer islands of Indonesia. Between 1818 and about 1912 the Dutch fought their way to Sumatra, Bali, Lombok, Makassar, Borneo (Kalimantan) and elsewhere. In the course of these wars, the Aceh War (1873–1912) stands as one of the most terrible and costly campaigns in the history of colonialism.

The cultivation system was progressively replaced after about 1870 by the 'liberal system', the aim of which was to open Indonesia to private rather than state enterprises. In 1900 the Dutch announced a new régime, the 'ethical policy'. This was to repay their 'debt of honour' to their Indonesian subjects through increased welfare projects, particularly education. The welfare measures were paltry when compared with Indonesia's population (by 1900 estimated at about 34 million), but increased opportunities for political expression did allow the growth of nationalist organizations. The most important of these were the Budi Utomo, the Sarekat Islam and the Indonesian Communist Party.

When popular protest began to assume more violent forms after 1919, the Dutch began to have second thoughts. The Communist Party launched an ill-prepared rebellion in 1926–27, and the Dutch returned to a policy of repression. Thereafter, Indonesian politics were quiescent until the arrival of the Japanese, except for the brief emergence of the Indonesian Nationalist Party in 1927, founded by the rising young demagogue Sukarno. He was arrested and exiled from Java.

The Japanese drove out the Dutch in 1942, and by the time of their surrender in 1945 the political environment of Indonesia was irrevocably changed. The Japanese had particularly needed two raw materials only developed in the 20th century: rubber and oil. To get them, they were even harsher than the Dutch had been, but they utilized nationalist leaders (especially Sukarno) to mobilize the population for their war effort. This gave the nationalists a chance to create a mass base for their movement. On 17 August 1945, before the Western Allies could reoccupy Indonesia, the nationalist leaders declared the independence of the Republic of Indonesia.

The Philippines

Whereas Dutch conquests were progressively sealing off Indonesia from the outside world, the Spanish Philippines were being opened up. Since the 16th century, the Spanish had ruled the islands (except for the southern Muslim provinces, which were only sporadically subjected) without exploiting their wealth. In the 19th century sugar, tobacco, hemp, indigo and minerals began to be developed, largely by British, American and other non-Spanish entrepreneurs.

The Filipinos themselves, and particularly the Filipino-Chinese mestizos, took an active part in this process, and a sophisticated indigenous middle class came into being. It called for reforms in the antiquated Spanish colonial structure, which was heavily influenced by arch-conservative clerical interests. The reformers did not seek independence, nor did they repudiate their Catholicism; they merely demanded the same rights as were given to Spaniards in Spain.

The colonial authorities were unwilling to make significant reforms and a secret rebel movement developed, with lower-class roots. This was the Katipunan, founded in 1892 by Andrés Bonifacio. Class tensions prevented a union of the lower and middle-class movements.

In 1896 the Katipunan was betrayed to the Spanish authorities, and was forced into a premature rebellion which spread widely, taking the colonial government by surprise. By 1897 there was a stalemate, and the revolutionary leadership had passed to Emilio Aguinaldo, who agreed a truce with the Spanish. For a large payment, he and his closest comrades went into exile in Hongkong.

In 1898, when the Spanish–American War broke out, Admiral George Dewey sailed into Manila and, to help him take the islands, brought Aguinaldo with him from Hongkong. Relations rapidly deteriorated and fighting soon broke out between the Americans and their Filipino allies. The Filipinos declared their independence and set up a republican government, but in 1901 Aguinaldo was compelled to surrender to the Americans.

Despite their ruthless suppression of the Philippine revolution, the Americans made it clear that their intention was to give independence to the Philippines as soon as they thought practical. Filipino leaders, particularly Sergio Osmeña and Manuel L. Quezon, had private doubts about the wisdom of independence, especially as expansionist Japan loomed ever larger on the horizon in the 1930s. None the less, after a series of self-interested manoeuvres among the Filipino leaders, an independence bill was passed by the American Congress and signed by President Roosevelt in 1934. Independence Day was fixed for 4 July 1946.

In 1935 a Commonwealth of the Philippines government was established. When the Japanese invaded at the end of 1941, the Commonwealth leaders left with the Americans. The Japanese proclaimed a sham independence under José Laurel as president, and, although they had little difficulty in finding collaborators, they could not arouse the anti-colonial fervour as they had done elsewhere, for the Filipinos knew their independence was already at hand. The American reconquest of the Philippines was complete by February 1945. In the 1946 elections Manual Roxas was elected president and the Philippines were declared independent on schedule. *M.C.R.*

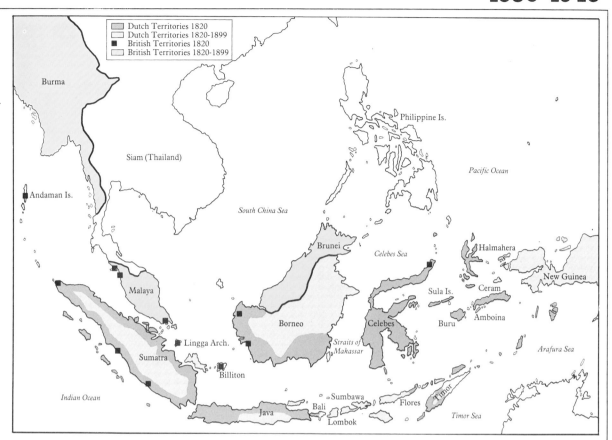

Legend:
- Dutch Territories 1820
- Dutch Territories 1820-1899
- British Territories 1820
- British Territories 1820-1899

Burma

Siam (Thailand)

Andaman Is.

South China Sea

Philippine Is.

Pacific Ocean

Malaya

Brunei

Celebes Sea

Halmahera

New Guinea

Sula Is.

Ceram

Buru

Amboina

Sumatra

Lingga Arch.

Borneo

Celebes

Straits of Makassar

Arafura Sea

Billiton

Indian Ocean

Sumbawa

Flores

Timor

Java

Bali

Lombok

Timor Sea

C.E. FRIPP.
CALUMPIT.
APRIL 27th '99.

US troops in action against Filipino insurgents in Manila, April 1899

Indochina

All the mainland parts of south-east Asia lying between India and China – comprising modern Burma, Thailand, Cambodia, Laos and Vietnam – were originally known as 'Indochina', although today the term usually refers to that part of the whole region that was known until the 1940s as French Indochina. In the early 19th century the two principal states in this region were the kingdoms of Siam and Vietnam (then known as Annam).

Both were authoritarian and bureaucratic monarchies, but with striking contrasts between their institutions, religion and culture. The Confucian civilization of China had for centuries deeply influenced Vietnam from the north, whereas Siam, with Cambodia and Laos, was part of the world of 'Theravada' Buddhism (the older, purer form also known as 'Hinayana' or 'Lesser Vehicle'). Politically, however, both recognized the superiority of China by sending regular tributary missions and by conducting their trade with China through those channels until the system was disrupted by the West after 1855.

Vietnam was first united to its present extent by the founder of the Nguyen dynasty in 1802. Its southern provinces had been conquered from Cambodia only since the 17th century, and were still being settled by Vietnamese throughout the period down to 1940, its 'frontier' areas contrasting sharply with the densely populated Red River delta of the north. In the 1830s the strongly Confucian emperor Minh Mang introduced government reforms and greater centralization, which provoked a rebellion in the south. The Siamese sought to take advantage of it, but their army was driven out; as a result, in 1836 the Vietnamese sent their own army to annexe a

large part of Cambodia, which had previously been under Siamese domination. The conquest was not permanent, and by 1850 a Cambodian rebellion had restored the former loose relationship with Bangkok, at the same time allowing for an equally loose relationship with Hué. The Siamese themselves were also expanding their power in this period. Both Vietnamese and Siamese expansion were interrupted by the beginnings of European control.

In 1855 the British and French decided to extend to this region the system of treaty trade they had begun to impose on China in 1842. For the British, Sir John Bowring secured a trade treaty with Siam, the provisions of which were then embodied in treaties with other Western powers, but the Vietnamese rejected a similar approach by the French and refused to enter into any Western treaties. Desire for trade, together with concern about the fate of Christian missionaries in the face of growing persecution in Vietnam, led the French to send a military expedition against Hué in 1858–59. It failed to capture the port of Danang, south of Hué, but succeeded in taking over Saigon. Under the treaty of Saigon of 1862, the French annexed three provinces of southern Vietnam; and in 1867 they seized another three, to form French Cochinchina. They also went on to impose a protectorate on Cambodia, which Siam was forced to accept by a treaty signed in 1865.

French rule was eventually extended over the whole of Vietnam, Cambodia and present-day Laos. In 1874 the Vietnamese had to allow the French to trade at Hanoi, even though the Europeans were obliged to abandon an attempt to take over Tongking (northern Vietnam) by force. In 1882 the French embarked on a more serious campaign against Tongking, which proved more costly than they expected and led them into war with China

---

Thai envoys with gifts visiting the court of Napoleon III (painting by J. L. Gérôme)

(1884–85). Only after the Treaty of Tientsin (1885) were they able to impose an effective protectorate over northern and central Vietnam. In 1887 France created the Indochinese Union, within which Cochinchina remained a colony, while Vietnam and Cambodia were nominally protectorates with monarchs and royal capitals but in practice under the rule of French Residents. The system of colonial rule was greatly strengthened under the governor-generalship of the later president of France, Paul Doumer (1898–1901). He also laid the foundations of a colonial economy and encouraged investment in railways, plantations and mines.

From the 1880s Laos became a bone of contention between the French and the Siamese. In 1885, moreover, upper Burma had been annexed by the British, so there were also problems of Anglo-French rivalry on the upper Mekong River. At first it seemed as though all of Laos would be incorporated into Siam, but in 1893 the French forced Siam to give up all territory east of the Mekong River. In 1896 the British obliged France to sign a convention that recognized the independence of the central parts of Siam, in return for a settlement of issues between them on the upper Mekong. The modern boundary of Siam in the north was finally settled by these international treaties. In the east, Siam subsequently lost two more Cambodian provinces to France in 1907; and in the south the British annexed Kedah and three other Malay dependencies of Siam in 1909.

Siam (renamed Thailand in 1939) nevertheless emerged from all this as an independent kingdom. While its economy was dominated by British banks, its administrative institutions were modernized under an independent monarchy, with the aid of Western advisers. In 1932, however, the monarchical system was virtually overthrown by a

The French concluding the Treaty of Tientsin

military coup. The king was allowed to remain as a constitutional monarch, but real power passed to a council made up of the coup-promoters. A constitution established a national assembly (not, as yet, democratically elected), but moves towards social and economic reform were short lived. The army proved the strongest element in the new system and in 1938 General Phibunsongkram became virtual military dictator. He was an admirer of Japanese nationalism and in 1941 took his country into the Second World War on the side of Japan.   *R. B. S.*

Canada

Canada's constitution, as embodied in the British North America Act of 1867, was a Canadian product forged principally from extensive debate and discussions among the founding fathers themselves, although with the British Colonial Office acting as scrutineer-in-chief. The constitution made the confederal government clearly dominant, but left to the provinces those matters that were then considered to be of purely local concern. The French and English languages were established in the federal parliament, its records and its courts, and the province of Quebec was also recognized as an officially bilingual province. Henceforward Canada was to have a federated parliamentary and monarchical form of government, operating according to the by then established British principles of cabinet government. The Parliament of Canada in the newly named capital at Ottawa was composed of the Crown's representative (the Governor-General) and a two-chamber legislature.

Although the Dominion of Canada of 1867 was made of a compact principally between 'East' and 'West' Canada (i.e. Quebec and Ontario), from the start its founding fathers intended that the national territory of the new nation should stretch from coast to coast, from the Atlantic to the Pacific Ocean. A first major step was the acquisition of the lands owned by the Hudson's Bay Company in the west. The first new province, Manitoba, was established in 1870 after a rebellion of *métis* (French-speaking half-breeds) in Red River, led by Louis Riel, was defeated. A year later the Pacific coast province of British Columbia entered the union on the promise that a transcontinental railway would be built. Two years later, Prince Edward Island, from the other side of the continent, came in. In 1874 the extensive lands between Manitoba and British Columbia were organized as the Northwest Territories. This area was the scene, in 1885, of a second uprising of *métis* and Indians, again led by Louis Riel. The ability to move troops rapidly by means of the Canadian Pacific Railway along newly completed track made it possible for the authorities to defeat the rebels. This time Riel was captured, tried and hanged for treason. Twenty years later, in 1905, the provinces of Saskatchewan and Alberta were added to the union. The last of the present ten provinces to join Canada was Newfoundland in 1949.

Three prime ministers bestrode the stage of Canada's national politics in its first hundred years. By the length of their periods of office and their personal ascendancies, these three, John A. Macdonald, Wilfrid Laurier, and William Lyon Mackenzie King, count as great and controversial Canadian leaders. Macdonald was the dominion's first prime minister and leader of the Conservative Party; the other two in turn led the Liberal Party. The long reign of each of them was based, however, on much the same kind of 'national' policy: involving the federal government actively in the encouragement of commerce, industry and the construction of railways, maintaining racial harmony between the British and the French by compromise and conciliation, and navigating carefully against the cross-currents of British and American power while tending Canada's growing national freedom and strength. Throughout most of Canada's history differences in social goals and principles have been submerged by the demanding task of making and maintaining the Canadian nation, in the never-ending task of reconciling or at least conciliating different provinces, peoples and priorities.

The Conservatives were in power in Ottawa from 1867 to 1873 and again from 1878 to 1896 with Macdonald as their leader until his death in 1891. For Macdonald, Canada's only counterweight to the US was Great Britain. None the less, Canada became in many respects a pioneer within the British Empire in developing an independent diplomacy. In 1880 Canada appointed its first high commissioner to London. Although the British government continued to conduct affairs for the empire as a whole, the Canadians were consulted whenever their interests were at stake. Many Canadians, however, saw drawbacks as well as advantages in membership within the British Empire. Indeed, some Canadians (especially some French Canadians) believed that their interests had been sacrificed in almost every Anglo-American agreement that affected British North America.

National integrity and autonomy first, but good relations whenever possible with Britain and the US, and particularly in times of crisis, were the practical axioms of Canada's great Liberal prime ministers – Wilfrid Laurier, the first *Canadien* prime minister, who held office from 1893 to 1911, and then Mackenzie King, who at various times between 1921 and 1948 served altogether longer than any other as Canada's prime minister.

During the First World War Canadian troops distinguished themselves in many battles. Throughout the years 1919 to 1939, both in the League of Nations and in the conference diplomacy of the Empire–Commonwealth, Canada played circumspect roles, eschewing either colonies or even Mandates for itself, being concerned to work out policies carefully without assuming predetermined commitments. Unilateral relations with Britain and the US within the North Atlantic triangle, and similar reticence in the League of Nations and the British Commonwealth, were backed by much psychological isolationism at home (especially in Quebec).

In the first 20 years of the 20th century Canada was transformed from a predominantly rural and small-town country into an industrial and urban society. The 1921 census showed that for the first time more Canadians lived in urban than in rural settings. Almost three million immigrants entered Canada in the decade and a half before 1914 to develop the virgin land of the west, to work in the new or enlarging factories in Ontario, or to develop the mineral and forest resources, especially of the northern lands. More immigrants came in the 1920s, but the Great Depression and the Second World War effectively stopped immigration between 1930 and 1945.

The world depression produced serious hardship and dislocations in Canada's economic and social life. Heavy unemployment and new movements of social protest limited and discredited the authority of the federal government. In Quebec discontent found partial expression in a new nationalist party called the Union Nationale. In the western provinces, the Social Credit (SC) and Co-operative Commonwealth Federation (CCF) parties made a marked impact with their radical and somewhat utopian economic programmes, winning power in Alberta and Saskatchewan. Eventually the demands of another world war stimulated the economy and restored the federal government to a predominant position. *P. H. L.*

Above: Pushing ahead with the CP track through Saskatchewan. Below: An engagement during Riel's Rebellion, 1885

Australasia

The rise of Australian nationhood after 1860 is, above all, connected with the great migration from the old industrial centres of Europe to developing areas offering wider opportunities and greater freedoms. Most of those who went to Australia in this period were not rural workers in background, and continued to live in towns and cities. Frequently, the more adventurous migrants became involved in the boom-and-bust pattern of the mining sector, some making great fortunes out of corporate successes such as the Broken Hill Proprietary Company, which began operations in 1885. Australian gold discoveries, as at Kalgoorlie in Western Australia during 1893, had a world-wide importance because they provided an expanding metal supply for international money transactions. Rural development also continued briskly through the 1870s and 1880s. After the advent of refrigeration in the same period, Australia supplied much of Britain's meat, while pastoralism was displaced in some areas by other agricultural activities, such as wheat production. It was through the medium of these commodities – gold, wool, wheat and meat – that the Australian economy became so tightly connected with the world trading system.

In the 1890s that system moved into a cycle of depression, causing considerable unemployment in Australia. The social conflict of this period (trades unions, for example, now emerged as powerful institutions) indicated a new political maturity in Australian life. Many of the social and economic problems had become so complex that they were beyond the resources of the individual states, so that in 1901 the latter were federated in the Commonwealth of Australia. This new structure of government inevitably affected political habits. Before 1901 there had been no clear-cut party system, so it was the rise of the Labour Party after federation that, by gradually forcing all opposed elements to combine, accelerated the growth of factional organizations. The Australian Labour Party proved to be moderate reformist, rather than revolutionary, in character, and a general consensus grew up between those engaged in Australian government and politics as to the objectives of policy: economic development protected by tariffs from outside competition, and a democratic sharing of wealth to involve almost all groups in the common task of nation-building.

Since the so-called 'mother country' was also Australia's best customer, there was no real opposition when Australia followed Britain into war in 1914. Australia's important contributions to the subsequent Allied war effort at Gallipoli, in Egypt and the Western Front played a vital part in cultivating a national consciousness. But the war had even more important economic effects. It had led to growth in both rural and manufacturing production, and during the 1920s Australian governments sought to project a 'development' image to gratify the forces of expansion created by the war. The Depression after 1929, however, modified these expectations. World agricultural prices fell very sharply, and Australia, as essentially a primary producer, suffered badly. By thus encouraging a shift towards the manufacturing of finished goods, the character of the Australian economy was critically altered at this time. The Depression also forced the federal government to take over powers previously held by the states, so centralizing the Australian political system.

'Canadian'-style cottage in gold-rush Gulagong, NSW, in the 1870s

'Don't shoot any more of your rubbish here, or you and I shall quarrel,' 'Punch', 1864

'Grim Evidence', a painting by Samuel Thomas Gill, shows the dangers of exploring the central desert of Australia

A New Zealand planter with his Maori servants at the turn of the century

Maori chiefs signing the Treaty of Waitangi, 1840, granting possession of their lands to the Crown

Gold miners' banking facilities in the 1880s, when they added to the settlers' pressure on unoccupied land

Despite these changes, Australia continued to follow British policy in the sphere of foreign relations. The threat of Japanese dominance in the Pacific region partly explains this undiminished reliance on British power. Consequently, in September 1939 Australia again followed Britain into a major conflict. This time, however, the effect was to weaken the Anglo-Australian connection. Britain was at first kept busy with home defence, and after the naval and military disasters of 1941–42 in south-east Asia, could no longer provide, alone, for the defence of Australasia against the advancing Japanese tide. This now fell to the US within the American strategy of the Pacific war. By 1945 Australia had become dependent, economically as well as militarily, on American assistance. This breaking free from the psychology of dependence on a British motherland and the more diversified economy produced by the war meant that the Australian state and nation had come of age.

New Zealand

The history of New Zealand in this period follows a similar pattern to Australia. With the Maori wars over, more lands were available for settlement, and the next two decades were characterized by migration, investment and the extension of the agrarian frontier. Political power in the years up to the 1890s was held by such development-oriented leaders as Julius Vogel. Expansion, however, meant dependence on foreign credit, so that New Zealand too was deeply affected by the world-wide financial crises that broke out in 1893.

These turn-of-the-century troubles led to the transfer of power from the old colonial oligarchy of large land-owners to more popular leaders, such as 'King Dick' Seddon. Small farmers and urban workers subsequently benefited from the introduction after 1900 of state welfare schemes. The 'state capitalism' so characteristic of New Zealand was extended by setting up marketing controls during the First World War. New Zealand, although very prosperous, still remained reliant on the level of international trade, and her farmers were badly hit by the 1930s Depression. This phase and the Second World War marked a difficult psychological adjustment for New Zealanders, who, more than most colonial societies, had looked to Great Britain for military and economic assurance. The dominance of the Labour Party after 1935 smoothed the way towards a more independent foreign policy and a diversified, controlled economy with widespread industrialization and state price guarantees for key farm products. By 1945 New Zealand had a highly developed social system based on a prosperous economy, and a burgeoning sense of identity, but she remained, like Australia, dependent, if no longer so much on Britain, then on the consumer markets and political support of the Western alliance.

P. H. L.

Egypt and the Sudan

Mohammed Ali

The French occupation of Egypt – nominally subject to the Ottoman Empire, in practice ruled by the Mamluk caste – lasted only from 1798 to 1801, after which they were driven out by an Anglo-Turkish expedition, but it made a lasting impression on Egypt's economic and political life. The technology and military effectiveness of the French impressed the Egyptians, some of whom advocated improvements of the same kind to bring Egypt up to date and strengthen its development as an independent nation. The Mamluks were overthrown in 1811 and in the power struggle that ensued, the victor was Mohammed Ali, an Albanian soldier whom the Ottoman sultan had recognized as Pasha (governor) of Egypt in 1805.

Mohammed Ali modernized the army by introducing conscription and employing European instructors and equipment. His reforms in administration and education led to the emergence of a small European-educated élite. He also imposed state controls on the economy, including a monopoly on the sale of cotton, Egypt's major export crop. At the sultan's request, his army fought a successful campaign in Arabia against the puritan Wahhabis (the sect in which the Saudi dynasty had its power-base) in 1811–18. He intervened to support the Turks in the Greek revolt from 1824 until the Turkish and Egyptian fleets were destroyed by a European squadron at Navarino in 1827. In 1830, Mohammed Ali's son, Ibrahim Pasha, invaded Syria, which Egypt continued to control until 1840. In settlement, the governorship of Egypt was made hereditary in Mohammed Ali's line.

Under his successors, Abbas I (1849–54), Said (1854–1862) and Ismail (1863–79), the European powers gained an increasingly strong position in Egypt which was bound, as part of the Ottoman Empire, by the special privileges ('capitulations') to European consuls and merchants. In the 1860s, a world cotton shortage caused by the American Civil War led to the expansion of Egyptian cotton production. This became Egypt's chief source of foreign revenue, but made it increasingly dependent on the fluctuations of the world cotton market.

The Suez Canal

In 1854, Said was persuaded to grant a concession to the French engineer and diplomat, Ferdinand de Lesseps, to build a canal through the Suez isthmus. By its completion in 1869, the European foothold in Egypt had been strengthened, while Ismail's lavish public and private expenditure plunged Egypt deeply into debt. He developed the country's network of canals, railways and telegraph lines, but by 1875 he had run into severe financial difficulties, which were temporarily mitigated by the sale to Britain of the shares in the Suez Canal co-held by Egypt. However, in 1876, Ismail (since 1866 titled Khedive, or Viceroy, of Egypt by the sultan) acknowledged Egypt's bankruptcy and direct international control of debt servicing was established. Britain and France imposed their advisers on the Egyptian Government to supervise financial affairs (known as the Dual Control). When Ismail resisted these measures, Britain and France persuaded the sultan to depose him in favour of his son Tawfiq in 1879. Affairs between Egypt and her creditors were controlled by the Law of Liquidation of 1880.

This humiliation generated a strong nationalist reac-

tion. By 1882, an army-dominated ministry under Urabi (Arabi) Pasha demanded reforms from Tawfiq and an end to foreign intervention. Anti-European riots in Alexandria followed, but of the powers involved – Britain, France, Italy, Germany and Turkey – only Britain was prepared to intervene. France and Britain staged a naval demonstration off Alexandria in May and June 1882, but after the French drew off, the British went on to bombard the city on the 11 July. A British force was landed at Ismailia and routed Egyptian forces at Tal al-Kabir (1882). Tawfiq's position was restored, but he was henceforth under British tutelage.

Various factors discouraged British withdrawal, among them the increasing importance of the Suez Canal in British strategic thinking, Britain's increasing economic stake in Egypt and rivalry with the French in North Africa. Furthermore, the consolidation of Britain's position in East Africa in the 1890s meant that Egypt, and particularly the Sudan, became important for the maintenance of British hegemony.

Internal affairs in Egypt in the period 1883–1907 were dominated by the first British agent and consul-general, Lord Cromer (formerly Sir Evelyn Baring), who was effective ruler of Egypt. Egyptian ministers were largely

The tribune from which the Empress Eugénie ceremonially opened the Suez Canal in 1869

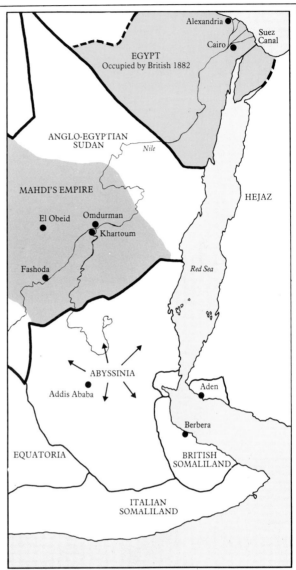

puppet figures dominated by their British advisers. Until the turn of the century, Cromer had to operate under the constraints imposed by British obligations to Egypt's foreign creditors. He reorganized Egyptian finances and enacted reforms such as the abolition of forced labour, developed transport and communications and enlarged the irrigation system to expand the production of cotton. Although benevolent, his authoritarian rule fuelled Egyptian resentment against British domination, especially after the accession of Abbas II in 1892. A new generation of nationalists expressed their opposition to Egypt's economic and political subservience to Britain.

After the outbreak of the First World War, when Turkey entered the war on Germany's side, Britain declared a formal protectorate over Egypt and assumed responsibility for the defence of the Suez Canal. The British used Egypt as a base for operations in the Middle East, including Allenby's campaign in Palestine. Permanent martial law and rampant inflation increased the antipathy to British rule.

The Sudan

The Sudan, as part of the Pashalik of Egypt, was nominally under Ottoman control from its subjugation in 1820 by Mohammed Ali until, in 1881, a revivalist Muslim religious leader known as the Mahdi rose in rebellion. In 1885, the Mahdi took Khartoum, where General Charles Gordon, sent to evacuate the Egyptian garrison, was killed two days before the arrival of the British rescue expedition. The Mahdi himself died soon after, but the movement which he created dominated the Sudan until 1898. The reconquest of the Sudan was only undertaken in 1896, when the British position in Egypt was more secure, and France and Italy were showing an interest in the area. In 1898, the Mahdist forces were defeated at Omdurman by an Anglo-Egyptian force under General Kitchener, who subsequently occupied Khartoum and advanced south to Fashoda (now Kodok) on the White Nile, where he confronted a French force advancing from the west. The French finally withdrew and in 1899 an Anglo-Egyptian Condominium was established, making Britain the effective ruler of the Sudan. *S. G. B.*

The Indian Empire : Congress v. Raj

Of the many British innovations in the economic sphere, modern means of transport and communication, and the commercialization of land were the most significant. The construction of railways began in 1849 and with metalled roads, post and telegraph gave unity and cohesion to India: the Indians were for the first time enabled to discover India for themselves. Commercialization of land was achieved mainly through various kinds of land revenue settlements, and legal reforms. In Hindu law land was inalienably vested in families and transferable only by inheritance within the blood line. Under the new civil law, land became alienable by individuals through commercial transactions or by will. Commercialization of land, however, did not go hand-in-hand with the industrialization of the country. As the commercial policy of the British Empire was to turn India into the producer of raw materials and consumer of goods produced by British home industries, the industrialization of India was not encouraged. In spite of this, Indians managed to get a modicum of their own industrialization started, particularly cotton mills, which increased from 51 in 1875 to 207 in 1908. In 1890 only 300,000 people were employed in factories and mines, and as a result the pressure on land continued to increase, which in turn intensified the problems of uneconomic holdings, subsistence farming and rural indebtedness.

While British reforms set India on the path of modernization, British scholar-administrators studied the ancient civilizations of the land and made middle-class Indians conscious, for the first time, of their heritage. Sir William Jones, who went to Calcutta in 1783 as a judge of the Supreme Court, discovered the richness and perfection of the Sanskrit language and literature, and first showed the world that the Indians were linked to the Europeans through the Indo-European family of languages.

The discovery of the 'glory that was India' emboldened the members of the new Indian middle class, the product of the educational, administrative, legal and economic changes the British had introduced, to dispel from their minds the idea of Western superiority. By 1885 English-educated Indians had come to realize that their interests were not at one with those of the British, and that the only way they could make the imperial government concede their demands for a larger share of power was by organizing themselves on an all-India basis. It was with this end that about 100 delegates from various provinces of British India assembled in Bombay on 27 December 1885 and formed the All-India National Congress, which would eventually turn into the main vehicle of the Indian nationalist movement. From 1885 until 1918 it drew its members exclusively from the upper and middle ranks of Indian society, and its leadership was predominantly liberal in the English sense. Its members were opposed to mass politics and believed in India's progress through collaboration with the British. At the end of the First World War the liberal leadership of Congress was ousted by 'militants and revolutionaries' headed by Mohandas K. Gandhi. The liberals parted company with Congress and formed their own party in 1918 – the National Liberal Federation of India. Gandhi gave Congress a constitution and turned it into a mass party with branches spreading down into rural areas. In 1929 the total membership rose to 477,440. Congress claimed to be secular and democratic, representing all Indians irrespective of their religion and race. In 1906 the All-India Muslim League was founded in opposition to Congress. This was a communal party consisting of upper-class Muslims, who demanded that in the event of some political power being transferred to the Indians, their community should have a share in it – a larger one than its numerical strength (21 per cent of the total population of British India) warranted. Until 1934, when M. A. Jinnah took over its leadership, the Muslim League remained an élitist party with almost no mass support.

Independence was not the objective of Congress until after 1918. Its liberal leaders had at first aspired to a junior partnership with the British in running the affairs of their country. Then, from 1918 to 1929, Congress stood for dominion status for India within the British Common-

A Sunday picnic near Simla in 1865, in the heyday of the British raj

wealth, and from 1930 onwards it agitated for complete independence. For Congress, however, independence was not the sole end of the nationalist movement. It was to be a means, as Jawaharlal Nehru visualized, of turning India into a democratic, secular and socialist state. Gandhi, on the other hand, wanted to mould India into his image of the ideal state – decentralized and based entirely on agricultural economy – which he believed had existed in ancient India. It was Nehru who ultimately won. Gandhi's Ram Rajya ('Rama's Realm', as he called his ideal state) was never officially endorsed by Congress.

In its first 20 years, under the liberal leadership, Congress relied on peaceful deputations for putting its demands, but, between 1905 and 1918 terrorism came into use by young and frustrated Indians. During the First World War the terrorists made contact with Britain's enemies, particularly Germany. In the end, however, it was Gandhi's non-violent method of *satyagraha* or 'agitation for truth' (which in 1919 gained the ascendancy over all other methods) rather than British repression that suppressed terrorism. Gandhi's way of fighting the British raj through non-co-operation and civil disobedience brought into being the politics of suffering.

Gandhi aimed at changing hearts, and he hoped he would raise the moral standards not only of his own countrymen, but also of the British. However, the degree of self-control Gandhi's method required of its votaries was missing as much among the leaders of Congress as among the millions now involved in the movement. Consequently, each of the two big mass movements Gandhi launched against the British raj during this period – the non-cooperation movement, 1920–22, and the civil disobedience movement, 1930–34 – became contaminated with violence. Much to his disappointment, Gandhi did not succeed in wiping out violence from the face of India.

During this period Congress alone was the vehicle of the nationalist movement, being the only party that stood for the transfer of power from British into Indian hands. The British, being most reluctant to think about the possibility of their total withdrawal from India even in the distant – let alone the foreseeable – future, began to treat Congress as an enemy, particularly after it came under Gandhi's leadership. The British sought support from the sectarian, feudal and liberal forces in India. It was when Congress became a little militant in 1905–7 and agitated over the partition of Bengal, that the governor-general, Lord Minto, lent a hand in founding the Muslim League, and secured an enlarged representation for Muslims in the central and provincial legislative bodies established under the Government of India Act of 1909. When, for the first and last time, Muslims and Hindus joined in Gandhi's 1920 non-cooperation movement, the government leaned on the liberals for support in implementing the constitutional reforms introduced by the Government of India Act of 1919. Again, when Congress alone did battle with the British in 1930, the government drew the Indian princes, Muslim leaders and the leaders of the National Liberal Federation to its side, and with their support went through the three Round Table Conferences held in London to formulate the new set of constitutional reforms eventually incorporated in the Government of India Act of 1935.

The British raj was not only concerned to browbeat or

Mohandas Gandhi in London, 1931

annihilate Congress. Its battles with Congress were fought in the context of the British asking themselves, in the first decade of this century, not when to wind up the raj, but, how best to preserve it. Except for diehard imperialists who still believed that an empire won by the sword must be preserved by the sword, the general consensus among policy-makers was for progressively associating Indians in the legislative and executive organs of the raj. The 19th-century British trust in the landed aristocrats as the natural leaders of Indian society had, by the 1900s, been reluctantly abandoned. Their place was taken by the lawyers, teachers, journalists, doctors, bankers, businessmen, and so on whom the British distrusted and despised, in spite of their being the creation of the British raj. As to how to associate them in government, British thinking took into account the divisions in Indian society based on race, religion, caste and education, and consequently prescribed all the three major modes of representation – territorial, class and communal. The controversial 'communal electorate' allotted to the Muslim community by the Act of 1909 (according to which they alone could elect Muslim members to the legislatures) went against the principle of democracy, and in some measure encouraged Muslim separatism.

As to how much power should be transferred into Indian hands, British policy was for gradualness: Indians were to be given responsibility first at the local government level, then in due course at the provincial level. The usual arguments – that because of the high rate of illiteracy and intense social divisions India was not ready for self-government – were unacceptable to the Congress leaders.

B. N. P.

Southern Africa

Following their departure from the Cape in 1836 and 1837 some Voortrekkers dispersed across the high veld, clashing with Mzilikazi's Ndebele (Matabele) people who were driven north across the River Limpopo. The main body of trekers led by Piet Retief crossed the Drakensberg Mountains eastwards to the rich grasslands of Natal to seek permission to settle there from Dingane (Dingaan), the Zulu king. Dingane, aware of the military threat posed by the emigrants, murdered Retief at his kraal. On 16 December 1838 at the Battle of Blood River, the Zulu army was destroyed by the Voortrekkers led by Andries Pretorius. A new republic was proclaimed, but its independence was short-lived for soon afterwards Britain occupied Durban (Port Natal), and in 1842 its hinterland was annexed to the Crown. Consequently, many settlers returned across the Drakensberg to begin a new life again.

The emigrant communities eventually came together in two major republics: the Transvaal or South African Republic, between the Vaal and Limpopo rivers; and the Orange Free State, between the Orange River and the Vaal. Their independence was recognized by Britain in 1852 and 1854. Although each republic assumed the trappings of a modern state with constitutions derived from Europe and America, an office of president and a rudimentary all-white parliament (Volksraad), in practice the Afrikaner states were composed of widely dispersed farming communities each of which effectively controlled its own affairs. The republics also remained extremely poor, compelled to compete with African societies for land and livestock, and only communicating with the outside world by the long ox-wagon routes to the coast.

Meanwhile, economic development in the south began to gather pace with the expansion of sheep-farming for the world market in the Cape, and the growth of sugar plantations in Natal worked by indentured Indian labour. The economy of the Cape was further boosted by the trade that resulted from diamond-mining which began at Kimberley in 1867. By contrast, the Transvaal was bankrupt and scarcely able to generate the resources needed to cope with the military threat posed by the Pedi, Zulu and other African societies of the interior. The Transvaal's poverty and consequent political vulnerability enabled Disraeli's Conservative government to annex the republic to the Crown in 1877. The annexation was intended to be the first step towards achieving a self-governing federation in South Africa that would be responsible for its own defence. But Britain underestimated the spirit of independence of the majority of Afrikaner settlers who, led by Paul Kruger, rose in rebellion in 1880. Their military victory at Majuba prompted Britain to abandon her design, and in 1881 the independence of the Transvaal was restored subject to limitations on its foreign policy.

In 1886 the discovery of immense gold deposits on the Witwatersrand revolutionized affairs in southern Africa. The possibility of finding further gold in the interior encouraged Cecil Rhodes, who became prime minister of Cape Colony in 1890, to prepare plans for white settlement beyond the River Limpopo. Rhodes, a fervent English imperialist who had made a vast personal fortune from diamonds, organized a pioneer column that set out north in 1890. Following bitter struggles with the Ndebele and Shona peoples in 1893 and 1896–97 a new British colony was established – Rhodesia.

Paul Kruger, president of the South African Republic from 1883 to 1902

A stirring moment at Isandhlwana, 1879, where the Zulus defeated the British

Further south, Johannesburg rapidly became a boom town with the arrival in the Transvaal of a new industrial community, called the Uitlander or 'Foreigners', many of them British, and whose numbers threatened to swamp the Afrikaner population. Kruger's government responded by rigidly controlling the mining industry and denying full political rights to members of the immigrant community. Gold created for the Transvaal a new source of abundant wealth, and the political authority that accrued to Kruger's government as a consequence of the shift northward of the centre of economic activity in South

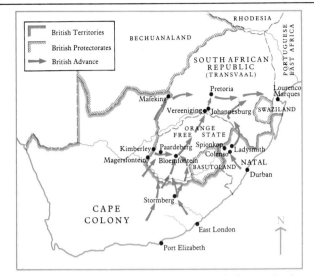

British Territories
British Protectorates
British Advance

RHODESIA
BECHUANALAND
PORTUGUESE EAST AFRICA
SOUTH AFRICAN REPUBLIC (TRANSVAAL)
Pretoria
Lourenço Marques
Mafeking
Vereeniging Johannesburg SWAZILAND
ORANGE FREE STATE
Kimberley Paardeberg Spionkop Ladysmith
Magersfontein Bloemfontein Colenso NATAL
BASUTOLAND Durban
Stormberg
CAPE COLONY
East London
Port Elizabeth
N

Africa threatened to undermine Britain's influence in the subcontinent and place at risk the security of Simonstown, the naval base on the Cape peninsula. Furthermore, the interests of British financiers and industrialists were hampered by the restrictive economic practices of the Transvaal Government. Relations between the two countries deteriorated rapidly during the 1890s. War seemed likely in 1896 following the Jameson Raid, a thoroughly mismanaged attempt by Rhodes, with the connivance of the British colonial secretary, Joseph Chamberlain, to engineer an Uitlander rebellion and the overthrow of the Kruger régime. Afterwards, relentless diplomatic and political pressure was brought to bear on Kruger to enfranchise the Uitlander community so that the political domination of the Transvaal by the Afrikaner oligarchy would be undermined. In October 1899 a final impasse was reached in negotiations, and Kruger chose to seize the military initiative by declaring war on Britain in defence of his republic's political independence.   *P.W.*

The 'Anglo-Boer War'

Boer strategy in 1899 was largely inspired by the 29-year-old lawyer, J. C. Smuts, later prime minister of the Union of South Africa and a leading Commonwealth statesman. The two republics could raise 45,000 men between them, including the State Artillery, a permanent unit of about 1200 well-trained gunners, and 1500 para-military police. Smuts believed the Boers must exploit this initial superiority by a bold drive to Durban and Cape Town. In October the Boers attacked the British garrisons of some 20,000 men, but since most Boer commandants lacked Smuts's boldness, they failed to seize any major port, contenting themselves with besieging the inland garrisons at Ladysmith, Mafeking and Kimberley. The need to relieve them dictated British strategy. General Sir Redvers Buller, who took command in Natal, split his army into three columns. All three commanders made elementary mistakes and met with humiliating defeats, the price of underestimating an enemy skilled in marksmanship and defensive tactics. On the left, Lord Methuen fell into a Boer trap at Magersfontein where he lost 1000 men and retreated. In the centre, Gatacre, who had failed to reconnoitre in advance, was beaten at Stormberg and lost over

700 men, mostly as prisoners. Worst of all, Buller, attacking across open ground at Colenso with guns exposed against entrenched Boers, lost over 1000 men and 12 guns. This trinity of disasters, falling between 10 and 15 December 1899, became known as 'Black Week'. In January, Buller's force advanced again on the River Tugela and was again beaten at Spionkop. Lord Roberts, with Kitchener as his chief-of-staff, was sent out to take over the command. Buller and his subordinates paid heavily for their tactical blunders, but their difficulties in a completely new kind of war dominated by long-range rifle fire in open country, should not be underestimated.

Roberts left Buller to relieve Ladysmith while his force advanced from Cape Colony into the Orange Free State. His opponent, Piet Cronje, allowed his column to be surrounded and captured after another mismanaged battle at Paardeberg in February 1900. This enabled the British cavalry to relieve Kimberley. Roberts advanced steadily to occupy the Boer capitals of Bloemfontein and Pretoria. Dividing his force into flying columns, Roberts hounded down the remaining Boer commandos, the last (under Prinsloo) capitulating on the Basutoland border in July. Meanwhile, Buller eventually relieved Ladysmith in February. Baden-Powell's besieged garrison in Mafeking was not liberated until 17 May.

With the Boers' field forces captured, all their main towns in British hands and a huge army guarding communications, the war seemed over by November 1900. Roberts thought so and returned home to a victor's welcome, leaving Kitchener in command. In fact, the Boers were far from beaten. Under several outstanding leaders, including Smuts, Botha, de Wet, Reitz and de la Rey they conducted hit-and-run guerrilla operations to which the British had no tactical answer. Kitchener gradually countered their superior mobility by a scorched earth policy, and by incarcerating prisoners in blockhouses. Concentration camps were set up, with the intention of isolating Boer civilians from the guerrillas, but poor sanitation and food led to many deaths. By May 1901 there were already 36 such camps, housing nearly 100,000 Boers, about half of them children. British popular opinion was bitterly divided on this issue. The Afrikaner commandos accepted defeat in May 1902 but their prolonged resistance won dividends.   *B.J.B.*

In the aftermath of war, Britain made vigorous efforts to encourage large-scale immigration to the Transvaal, and to destroy Afrikaner nationalism and reconcile Afrikaners to the British Empire by introducing a new educational system, creating an efficient professional bureaucracy, and promoting economic development. By 1906, however, it again became apparent that Afrikanerdom could not be destroyed by force of arms or by political domination, and self-government was restored to the former republics by the Liberal government of Henry Campbell-Bannerman. From the British point of view the war had not been fought completely in vain, for in 1910 a unification of the four settler colonies was achieved which, though dominated economically by the Transvaal and politically by the Afrikaner population of the Union, remained part of the British Empire and subsequent Commonwealth for the next half-century.   *P. W.*

The early Puritan settlers in America hoped that their 'New England' would be, in John Winthrop's words, 'as a city upon a hill' for the rest of the world to emulate and admire. This notion that America was something special, at the same time different from and superior to the old European world, persisted for a very long time. Even at the end of the 19th century the historian Frederick Jackson Turner published a celebrated essay in which he argued that America's uniqueness stemmed from the existence of enormous tracts of unsettled, free land. The egalitarianism and rough democracy of the frontier had moulded Americans, and made them different from Europeans. Ironically, as he wrote, the last reserves of free land were fast disappearing.

Growing cities, with large enclaves of foreign-born population, had little of the cohesiveness of small-town communities. Haphazard urbanization left in its wake a whole range of social problems, from housing slums, or 'ghettos', to the inadequate provision of basic services. By the end of the 19th century, indeed, American reformers had begun to realize that their cities lagged behind their European counterparts in providing for the amenities of a civilized, urban life. In the meantime, rapid industrialization, in particular the growth of enormous business trusts, brought with it increasing strife between employers and workers and hastened the appearance of distinct, hostile classes in what until then had been a relatively class-free America.

If American society had lost its uniqueness, so too had the policy of the federal government. In the 1890s, for the first time, the US committed itself to building up a large peace-time navy. In 1898 it went to war with Spain, the first hostilities with a European power since the end of the War of 1812 with Britain. In the aftermath of the Spanish-American War, despite strenuous internal opposition, the US

THE GREAT REPUBLIC

embarked on a brief policy of overseas expansionism, which, with the acquisition of Hawaii and the Philippines, made it for the first time a Pacific power. During the administrations of Presidents Roosevelt, Taft and Wilson a canal was built to link the Atlantic and Pacific Oceans across the isthmus of Panama. To protect that canal, successive American governments made frequent interventions in the domestic affairs of several Caribbean and Central American states. This new American imperialism brought with it many burdens and little glory. It further destroyed the illusion that the US was somehow different from older European states. By 1917 all that remained of the myth of American uniqueness was the traditional policy of avoiding entanglement in European affairs. That, too, disappeared in April 1917 when the US entered the First World War.   *M. S.*

USA, Coast to Coast

Early expansion

The peace treaty of 1783 left the newly independent US bordered by British North America to the north and Spanish possessions in Florida and Louisiana to the south and west. As the tide of American settlement washed over the Appalachian Mountains and on towards the Mississippi valley during the years of peace after 1783, it became increasingly likely that neither the southern nor western boundaries could be regarded as permanent.

So long as the area west of the Mississippi River was held by Spain, a comparatively weak power, Americans could console themselves with the thought that there could be little real resistance to further American expansion. This situation changed shortly after Thomas Jefferson came to the presidency in 1801, when it was learned that Napoleon had signed a treaty with Spain transferring the Louisiana territory back to France. Profoundly distressed, Jefferson instructed the American minister in Paris to begin negotiations to buy the key port of New Orleans from France.

Circumstances smiled upon Jefferson's initiative, for in March 1803, Napoleon decided to renew the war with Britain that had been temporarily halted by the Peace of Amiens. British seapower made it extremely unlikely that France would be able to maintain her hold on Louisiana. Moreover, a Negro revolt on the rich West Indian island of Santo Domingo – a revolt the French proved unable to suppress – destroyed Napoleon's dreams of renewing France's 'New World' empire. Rather than persist in a

doomed endeavour, he decided to finance the French war effort by selling the whole of Louisiana rather than just New Orleans to the Americans. For $15 million, the US effectively doubled its territory, acquiring an enormous 800,000-sq. mile tract of land for future settlement. A year later, when Spain entered the European war on the side of France, Jefferson also tried to purchase Spanish Florida. This attempt failed: western Florida was ceded to the US only in 1810, under Jefferson's successor, James Madison, while eastern Florida finally became part of the US by the Adams-Onís Treaty of 1819.

The south-west

With the revolt of the Spanish colonies in the 'New World', the US acquired a new neighbour in the west: the Republic of Mexico. The Mexicans proved just as powerless as the Spanish when it came to turning back the American settlers who flooded into the area of present-day Texas. In 1835, the Texans revolted against Mexican rule, and managed to secure their independence by defeating the Mexican army in the field, notably at the Battle of San Jacinto in 1836. For nine years thereafter, an independent Texas republic existed between the Rio Grande and Sabine rivers, in territory still claimed by Mexico. In 1845, the US offered to annex Texas to the Union and the Texans willingly consented.

With the annexation of Texas, the US inherited not only another vast area of land for settlement, but also a succession of boundary disputes and claims that finally brought

'Across the Continent', a famous Currier & Ives lithograph of 1869, showing the through train, New York-San Francisco, summing up the optimistic vision of America

about a war with Mexico in 1846. Although President James K. Polk used a border clash as his excuse to ask for Congressional approval to make war, there can be little doubt that the Mexican refusal to consider selling California to the US also played its part in his decision. In 1848, at the end of the war, defeated Mexico ceded not only California to the US, but also the present-day states of Nevada, Utah and Arizona, together with parts of modern Colorado, New Mexico and Wyoming. To this vast area must be added the small slice of land south of Arizona, bought from Mexico in 1853 to secure the best southern route for a transcontinental railroad and known as the Gadsden Purchase.

With the successful conclusion of the Mexican War, the US at last acquired a frontier on the Pacific Ocean. It is notable, however, that most American expansion from 1783 to the 1840s was at the expense of weak neighbours: the indigenous Indians, Spaniards and Mexicans. Only in the north-west did the US come into conflict with the power of Britain. After the war of 1812 between the two countries, both had asserted their rights to the Oregon territory, but in 1818 they had agreed on joint occupation. By the 1840s, the pressure of American settlement along the valleys of the Willamette and Columbia rivers had tipped the balance decisively in American favour. Wisely, the British government realized this, and the decade of the 1840s saw a series of agreements between the two countries on boundaries between Canada and the US. In 1846, British and American negotiators fixed the new boundary between Oregon and British Columbia by extending the 49th parallel as far as the Pacific. Four years earlier, the Ashburton-Webster Treaty had settled the boundary between Maine and New Brunswick and between Ontario and what is now Minnesota.

The 'Golden Spike'

The Civil War brought a temporary end to American expansionism, but the present boundaries of the US with Canada and Mexico had been established before 1860. The US was, indeed, a continental empire, stretching from coast to coast. With one exception, all the European powers had either withdrawn from North America or – like Britain – reached an accommodation with the US. That one exception was Russia, which still occupied the Alaska territory. In 1867, however, two years after the end of the American Civil War, Russia too fell into line by selling Alaska to the US for $7 million.

Ever since the 1840s, men had dreamed of a railroad that would cross the entire continent and finally link up the far-flung corners of the new US. Differences of opinion between northerners and southerners over the proposed route delayed the start of the project until this difficulty disappeared with the secession of the southern states in 1861. One year later, Congress chartered a Pacific railroad, to be built by two companies. The Union Pacific built westwards from Iowa, while the Central Pacific gangs constructed their railroad eastwards from San Francisco. On 10 May 1869, the two tracks joined at Promontory Point, Utah, and a golden spike was hammered into the ground to commemorate the event. That spike symbolized much more than easier continental travel: it was a final expression of the hopes of millions of pioneering Americans who in the years since independence had spread democracy and civilization over a whole continent, 'from sea to shining sea'.

M. S.

'Wild Bill' Hickok, painted from the life by Henry H. Cross in 1874, two years before he was slain

The meeting of the Union Pacific and Central Pacific railroads at Promontory Point in 1869

American Capitalism

Thomas Jefferson dreamed of the day when his country would be a great agrarian democracy, but the economic development of the US led it in a different direction. Spurred on by the stimulus of civil war, industrial production rose markedly during the 1860s, and by the 1890s the US was fast becoming an urban, industrial society. The process of economic change brought into prominence a new breed of American capitalists: railroad bosses like 'Commodore' Cornelius Vanderbilt and later Edward H. Harriman, financiers such as Jay Cooke, Jim Fisk and Jay Gould, bankers like John P. Morgan and industrialists such as John D. Rockefeller of Standard Oil and Andrew Carnegie of the Carnegie Steel Company. In an earlier period, the vast fortunes accumulated by these men would have been seen as a symbol of American democratic opportunity; by the end of the 19th century, they were being attacked as evidence of exploitation. Successful businessmen were no longer praised for their enterprise: they were criticized as modern 'robber barons', holding the rest of society to ransom for personal gain.

Some of the barons richly deserved the opprobrium that was heaped on their heads. Men like Fisk and Gould were not so much businessmen as speculators. They specialized in stock manipulation. While in control of the Erie Railroad, for example, Gould heavily 'watered' the stock to his own advantage, leaving the railroad vastly over-capitalized and in disastrously poor financial shape. He also lowered freight rates and fares to an uneconomic level, and thereby forced Vanderbilt's competing New York Central Railroad to buy up the Erie company. Although Gould himself made a fortune out of all these operations, he made no constructive contribution to the growth of the American economy. Far different was the case of men such as Rockefeller and Carnegie.

The trusts

There was no 'water' in the stock of Rockefeller's Standard Oil or the Carnegie Steel Company, for these were efficient industrial concerns. Criticism of them tended instead to focus on their size and the methods they used to attain commercial supremacy within their own industry. In 1870, Rockefeller formed the Standard Oil Company of Ohio. In the years that followed, he used a vast array of weapons that were unethical if not downright illegal to eliminate or absorb competitors. By secret bargaining with competing railroads, Standard Oil obtained rebates or freight-rate concessions for itself and even managed to extort additional rebates for Standard from freight payments made by competitors. Through industrial espionage and ruthless price-cutting wars, Rockefeller undermined his remaining competitors until, in less than a decade, Standard Oil reigned supreme.

Rockefeller's company was the first and best-organized industrial 'trust'; it was by no means the last. The process of combination within a particular industry grew more and more common until it climaxed in 1901 with the organization of the first 'billion-dollar trust': the United States Steel Corporation. US Steel had its origin in Carnegie's decision to sell out his steel interests and spend the rest of his life in philanthropic pursuits. The deal itself was engineered by J. P. Morgan's banking house, and highlighted the concentration of economic power into fewer and fewer hands.

Standard Oil and US Steel cut across the traditional American belief in free competition; so did other business corporations. While paying lip-service to the virtues of competition, men like Rockefeller and Carnegie were involved in a determined attempt to eliminate it wherever possible. Their reason for doing this was simple: the period from 1865 to 1900 was a time of great economic insecurity, with two great depressions in the 1870s and 1890s, during which many businesses failed. Only when a corporation had succeeded in eliminating all competition could it feel truly secure. The problem from the point of view of the American consumer was that the disappearance of competition removed the last check on prices.

The organization of labour

The rise of large industrial corporations also threatened the position of labour. Wages could no longer be decided informally between workers and an employer, who not infrequently knew all his men by name. Moreover, the increasing mechanization of industrial production brought with it an increasing division of labour. The factory worker found himself doing a boring, repetitive job as only one cog in an industrial machine. When labouring men tried to organize to fight for fair wages and better conditions, they met ruthless resistance from corporate directors who owed loyalty only to their stockholders and re-

Brown shading shows land owned by the railroad companies in the western USA, 1879

garded labour itself only as a commodity to be acquired as cheaply as possible. If workers went on strike or attempted to impose boycotts, businessmen responded with a whole array of weapons: lock-outs, blacklists of union leaders, private detectives, company police, court injunctions and – as an ultimate resort – military intervention. It was President Grover Cleveland's dispatch of federal troops to Chicago in 1894 that ended the Pullman strike and destroyed the American Railway Union.

American trade unionists laboured under a range of disadvantages, not the least of which was that trade unionism itself was widely regarded as being something profoundly un-American. The Knights of Labor, founded in 1869, tried to unite all American workers into one big union. Under the leadership of Terence Powderly, its membership had grown to nearly 750,000 by 1885. But in the following year, the Knights were unfairly tarred with anarchism and violence after an unsuccessful strike for the eight-hour day and the Haymarket bomb outrage in Chicago. By the end of the 1880s, after a succession of failed strikes, membership of the order had fallen to around 100,000. As the Knights declined, their place was taken by another organization, the American Federation of Labour (AFL). Under the leadership of Samuel Gompers, the AFL abandoned the idea of one large union of both skilled and unskilled workers. It concentrated instead on

THE PULLMAN STRIKE, 1894

The model town of Pullman outside Chicago was founded by the creator of the sleeping car in 1880, and run on paternalistic lines for his workers. In 1889 the residents rejected their 'company store' community in favour of incorporation in Chicago, and the company was ordered by the courts to sell all its non-industrial property in Pullman. The great strike and railroad boycott of May–July 1894 began in protest against wage cuts.

organizing skilled workers into several unions. Gompers astutely avoided any involvement in political activities and went to great lengths to present the AFL as a non-radical body. From a membership of $\frac{1}{2}$ million in 1900, it had grown to 2 million by the beginning of the First World War. The International Workers of the World, organized in 1905 to cater for non-skilled workers, was not as lucky: it won a series of spectacular strikes, notably that of textile-workers at Lawrence, Massachusetts, in 1912, but succumbed in 1917–18 to the suspicion that its activities were hampering the American war effort.   *M. S.*

A 1934 cartoon by Jacob Burke in 'New Masses', suggesting that 'robber baron' J. P. Morgan controlled Congress by virtue of his financial interests

Voices of Reform and Protest

The hard and complacent commercial civilization that grew up in the US during the years after the Civil War had its critics. Henry George, writing from California, could not at first understand how poverty proliferated as fast as wealth. In his book, *Progress and Poverty* (1879), he finally traced the source of inequality back to one class's power to pre-empt the wealth of society through its ownership of land. To remove this inequality, he advocated a 'single tax' on land values. During the 1880s, thousands of people joined 'single tax' clubs dedicated to the furtherance of George's ideas. In 1888, Edward Bellamy, a shy, retiring New Englander, published *Looking Backward*, a best-selling Utopian novel that criticized the principle of un-restrained competition in economic life and advocated socializing or 'nationalizing' industrial production. Many Bellamyite 'Nationalist' clubs sprang into being across the US. In 1890, Jacob A. Riis, a Danish immigrant to New York journalism, published *How the Other Half Lives*, a graphic description of life in the slums of New York City. Four years later, Henry Demarest Lloyd produced his *Wealth Against Commonwealth*, a detailed critique of Rockefeller's Standard Oil Company and the methods it used to attain commercial success.

Populism and progressivism

All these writers had one thing in common: they pointed out the deficiencies of the American economic system and underlined the fact that it operated in a way that was detrimental to the interest of many Americans. Perhaps the most obvious group to suffer exclusion from the bene-fits of an industrial society were the farmers. A long period of deflation, beginning in the early 1870s, trapped the American farmers into a vicious cycle of falling prices and increasing indebtedness. Exploited by railroads, ware-houses, grain elevators and mortgage companies, they slowly began to band together to seek redress for their grievances, first in the Granger movement and later in the Farmers' Alliance. When neither of the two major parties showed any sympathy for their plight, the farmers organized their own political party, the Populist or People's Party, which polled over a million votes for its presidential candidate in the 1892 elections. The Populists called for the government ownership of railroads, measures to expand the supply of credit in rural areas, and an inflationary expansion in money supply through the free coinage of silver as well as gold. In 1896, the Populists lost their separate identity as a political party when they also adopted the losing Democratic candidate, William Jennings Bryan. In the years that followed, as the long international depression came to an end and prices at last began to rise, Populism disappeared and was replaced by a new and more successful movement for reform: progressivism.

Populism was a revolt of producers discontented with their share of the economic cake in an increasingly in-dustrialized America; progressivism was very largely a movement of middle-class consumers. Populism was a rural movement; progressivism drew much of its strength from expanding cities. Populism was very largely confined to the west and the south; progressivism had a genuinely national constituency.

Progressivism operated politically at three levels. In the cities, reform mayors like Brand Whitlock of Toledo, Ohio, fought a long battle against corruption in local politics, in particular the corruption associated with the attempt of utility companies to protect their valuable franchise privileges. At the state level a succession of progressive governors from Robert M. La Follette of Wisconsin to Woodrow Wilson of New Jersey pushed through a legislative programme designed to secure greater democratic participation and began the long process of humanizing industrial society through law. At the national level, attempts were made to regulate the excesses of business corporations too large to be handled by state legislation. As president, Theodore Roosevelt was

Campaign poster of the United Labor Party, an early urban-leftist movement

US union label of the later 19th century

largely responsible for two pieces of legislation regulating the railroads, the Elkins Act of 1903 and the Hepburn Act of 1906. Roosevelt also sponsored a Meat Inspection Act and the Pure Food and Drug Act, both of 1906.

When Roosevelt retired from the presidency in 1909, his successor, William Howard Taft, proved too conservative to satisfy the Republican progressives. The Party itself split, with regulars supporting Taft and insurgents supporting Roosevelt, who in 1912 left the Republicans to found his own Progressive Party. The real contest in the 1912 election, in fact, was between Roosevelt and the Democratic nominee, Woodrow Wilson. Both had very different views on how to deal with large business corporations. Roosevelt, in his 'New Nationalism' programme, accepted big business but wanted it to be regulated by government. Wilson, advocating a 'New Freedom', believed in the virtues of free competition and wanted to keep both business and government on as small a scale as possible. Wilson won the election and tried to put his programme into operation, but the decades since 1912 have seen the triumph of Rooseveltian methods of regulation over the 'rural Toryism' of the 'New Freedom'.

The 'Progressive Era' lasted from around 1900 to America's entry into the First World War in 1917. It was a time of social innovation as well as political reform. Young college girls like Jane Addams established settlement houses in the slums of great cities, to bring back a sense of community to poor and wretched neighbourhoods. John Dewey pioneered new educational methods in Chicago while Judge Ben Lindsey, of Denver, Colorado, became the lynch-pin of a movement for the treatment of young offenders in separate juvenile courts. Muck-raking journalists like Ray Stannard Baker, Lincoln Steffens and Ida Tarbell exposed the ills of American society in mass-circulation magazines. Men like Gifford Pinchot fought for a less wasteful use of America's natural resources, such as timber.

American socialism

The middle-class American progressives very much resembled British liberals of the same period. But socialism in the US, unlike its counterparts in Britain, France and Germany, never became a powerful political force. The American Socialist Party (ASP) reached its greatest voting strength in the 1912 presidential election when its candidate, Eugene V. Debs, still ran a very poor fourth behind Wilson, Roosevelt and Taft. American socialists were even more subject to dissension and disunity than their European colleagues. Many of them were born abroad and had to contend with the suspicion that socialism was un-American, while the relatively classless society of the US left them at a disadvantage. Finally, the American Federation of Labor under Samuel Gompers, unlike trade union movements in Europe, remained resolutely anti-socialist. American progressivism, therefore, never had to face an effective opposition from the political left, as did the liberalism of men like Asquith and Lloyd George in Britain. *M. S.*

The Boston police strike, 1919: the proprietor of a department store and assistants prepare for eventualities

Founded in 1911, 'The Masses' was the leading left-wing intellectual vehicle. Hugo Gellert's cover expresses liberal elements in idealistic socialism

'Teddy' Roosevelt and the Big Stick

The USA went to war with Spain in 1898 for a variety of reasons: idealistic concern for the Cubans – so long oppressed by Spain – commercial ambitions for wider world markets, the strategic desire for more coaling stations, a genuine concern that if the US did not intervene in Cuba, other nations would, and last, but by no means least, a virulent campaign mounted by the 'yellow' press of Joseph Pulitzer and William Randolph Hearst. At the beginning of the war, comparatively few Americans visualized the nature of the peace that would follow the total defeat of Spanish forces in both the Caribbean and the Far East. The US emerged from the war if not yet as a great power, at least as an imperial one with worldwide responsibilities. Barred by the Teller Amendment from annexing Cuba itself, the US nevertheless established an informal protectorate over the island and formally annexed Guam, Puerto Rico and the Philippines from Spain. The new territories brought with them the burdens of empire as well as the advantages: dismayed by American refusals to grant independence to the Philippines, Emilio Aguinaldo, leader of the insurrection against Spain, led his people in revolt again. It lasted three years and cost over 4000 lives before it was finally suppressed.

The first president to really understand the changing role of the US in the world was Theodore Roosevelt, who came to office on the assassination of William McKinley in 1901. Roosevelt, an ex-assistant secretary of the navy, had led his own band of irregulars, the 'Rough Riders', against the Spanish forces on Cuba. He was an activist in foreign policy, an imperialist, and a devotee of the ideas advanced by Captain A. T. Mahan USN concerning the influence of sea power upon history. His policy in foreign affairs as president, he explained, would be to 'speak softly and carry a big stick'. This would involve not only building more ships for the navy, but also the construction of a canal across the isthmus of Central America for the easier ocean-to-ocean transfer of American naval power.

The Panama Canal

The Panama Canal affair of 1903 showed Roosevelt at both his best and worst. On the one hand he grasped the strategic arguments for building a canal under American auspices; on the other he was unconcerned over the methods used to attain such an end. When negotiations with the Government of Colombia for the lease of a 10-mile-wide strip of territory on which the canal would be built became difficult and prolonged, Roosevelt aided and abetted (if he did not actually inspire) a 'revolution' in Panama and its secession from the Republic of Colombia. A few days later, the US and the government of 'Panama' signed a treaty leasing the canal zone in perpetuity to the former. 'I took Panama', Roosevelt later boasted, unconscious of the effect this wielding of the 'big stick' had on both Colombia and the other republics of Latin America. Only in 1921 did the US at last pay Colombia $25 million in compensation for the territory seized in 1903.

In 1904, when the desperate financial state of affairs in Santo Domingo threatened to provoke the intervention of European powers on behalf of their creditors, Roosevelt took another step towards a policy of greater interference

'Punch's' view of Taft's nomination: 'I've fixed you up so they won't know the difference between us.'

Right: American visitors proudly observe the cutting of the Panama Canal, about 1912

Ex-President Roosevelt campaigning against Woodrow Wilson in New Jersey, 1913

in Latin American affairs by enunciating what became known as the Roosevelt Corollary to the Monroe Doctrine. While repeating Monroe's declaration of 1823 that European powers should not interfere in the Americas, Roosevelt now proposed that the US herself should assume responsibility for protecting and supervising the smaller American republics. The first constructive act under the new policy was the imposition of an American financial protectorate over Santo Domingo. Within two years, that debt-ridden and strife-torn island was transformed into a newly-prosperous country. But American intervention in Santo Domingo proved a dangerous precedent: indeed, so burdensome did the Corollary in time become, that the State Department officially repudiated it during the 1930s.

Roosevelt's appreciation of the realities of power in the world, which made it possible for him to interfere without scruple in the affairs of weaker neighbouring states, made him much more circumspect in his dealings with the great powers. While trying to maintain the principle of the 'Open Door' in China, as laid down by Secretary of State John Hay in his diplomatic notes of 1899 and 1900, Roosevelt was careful not to antagonize the expansionist Japanese. After Japan defeated Russia in the war of 1904–1905, Roosevelt was instrumental in bringing the two countries together and breaking the deadlock between them. The Treaty of Portsmouth, New Hampshire, signed by the belligerents in September 1905, preserved at least for a time the territorial integrity of China, but replaced Russians by Japanese in Manchuria. Conscious of the growing strength of Japan, Roosevelt realized that the preservation of the 'Open Door' in China, as well as American possession of the Philippines, depended in the final resort on Japanese goodwill. When relations between Japan and the US became threatened in 1906 and 1907, because of California's policy of discriminating against the growing number of Japanese immigrants to the West Coast, the president managed a diplomatic solution to the dispute through the so-called 'Gentleman's Agreement' of 1908. Japanese immigration was not prohibited, but the Japanese government itself undertook to discourage its subjects from moving to the US.

In Europe, unlike the Caribbean and the Far East, the US had no political nor territorial interests at stake. Nevertheless, fresh from his triumph in ending the Russo-Japanese war, President Roosevelt did intervene in the Moroccan crisis of 1905-6 between France and Germany. The president managed to persuade the French to attend a conference on the North African problem, and Henry White, the American representative, did much to ensure the success of the conference when it met at Algeciras, Spain, in January 1906. Whatever its weaknesses, the agreement reached then did preserve the peace of Europe for several more years. But American participation at the conference provoked a great deal of domestic criticism, and the Senate only ratified the Convention of Algeciras with the qualifying amendment that ratification did not involve any change in the traditional policy of the US over non-entanglement in European affairs. Roosevelt's initiative was, in fact, the first and last American political involvement in Europe until the First World War. *M. S.*

American Power

The rise of the USA to the first rank among world powers is not primarily a story of wars won and lost, for, unlike the great powers of Europe, America's military might was a comparatively late offshoot of her industrial supremacy. In 1860, for example, the entire US produced rather less than 1 million tons of pig iron. But by 1890, the production of iron and steel in American mills surpassed that of Britain; only 10 years later the US was making more steel than both Britain and Germany combined.

The American industrial revolution rested on a solid basis of almost inexhaustible natural resources. In 1858, Colonel Edwin Drake discovered oil near Titusville, Pennsylvania. In less than five years, the oilfields of Pennsylvania were producing more than 2 million barrels every year. During the decades that followed, new fields were discovered in Illinois, Kansas, Texas, Oklahoma and California. In iron ore, too, the US was equally favoured: the discovery and exploitation of the great reserves and the rich red iron-ore deposits of northern Michigan gave the American iron-and-steel industry an enormous advantage. Underneath the Appalachian Mountains lay huge reserves of coal, stretching from eastern Pennsylvania in the north down as far as Alabama in the south. By the 20th century, the US was producing a third of the world's coal and of this half came from the Appalachians.

The technical inventiveness and native ingenuity of many Americans made sure that this natural wealth would not be wasted. In the 30 years after 1860, the US Patents Office issued almost 500,000 patents for new inventions. Alexander Graham Bell showed off his new telephone at the Centennial Exhibition in Philadelphia in 1876, while Thomas A. Edison contributed a galaxy of inventions from electric lighting to motion pictures and the phonograph. American businessmen were also prepared to utilize foreign discoveries. Andrew Carnegie introduced a smelting process invented by an English engineer, Henry Bessemer, into the production of steel. Ironmaster Abram S. Hewitt later adopted the more costly Belgian method of open-hearth smelting, destined in time to supplant the Bessemer Process as a method of mass-producing steel. Other pioneering American industrialists found ways to make science pay. The first motor cars powered by an internal combustion engine made their appearance in the

1890s, but it was not until Henry Ford launched his famous 'Model T' in 1908 that a rich man's plaything started to become a means of transportation for millions. Ford managed to minimize costs through techniques of mass-production: by 1920, his factories in Detroit were turning out 6000 cars a day.

Better communications facilitated the American industrial revolution. In 1860, there had been some 30,000 miles of railroad track in the country. The fact that the North had 21,000 miles of this total, and the South but 9000, is one of the reasons why the North won the Civil War. The end of the war in 1865 signalled the start of a period of railroad mania: between 1865 and 1873 some 35,000 miles of track were laid, more than in the two preceding generations. By 1910, the American railroad network was largely complete, and nearly 250,000 miles of track were carrying 1 billion tons of freight each year. The farmers and small-scale manufacturers of the first half of the 19th century had, for the most part, produced their goods for a local market: with the coming of the railroads, the US for the first time had a busily expanding national market.

A plentiful supply of cheap labour kept the wheels of industry turning. Between 1815 and 1860, some 5 million immigrants had entered the US. During the decade of the 1880s alone, another 5 million entered. The depression of the 1890s checked this flood for a time, but it rose to over 8 million in the first decade of the 20th century. Whereas immigrants before the Civil War had tended to come from Britain, Germany and Scandinavia, and many had engaged themselves in agricultural pursuits, by the end of the 19th century most immigrants came from

Garment trade and rooming houses right under the 'El' (elevated train system) in New York City

Italian immigrants landing at Ellis Island, NY, in the 1890s, ready for life in the New World

Mediterranean and eastern European countries in search of factory jobs in the cities. Most native Americans of the time saw this foreign invasion as an asset to the American economy: only during the First World War did the immigrant come to be perceived as a threat to American society, and unrestricted immigration came to an end with the quota system of 1921 and in the Act of 1924, which stipulated the reduction of the number of immigrants by a 'national origins plan'.

Parallelling the flow of immigrants into industry, the last third of the 19th century saw a movement of almost as many native Americans away from the farms into jobs in the city. By the 1920s, over half of all Americans were urban dwellers. The economic depression of the 1870s and 1890s slowed down this movement to the cities, but frenetic expansion in other decades more than made up for it. Chicago, advantageously situated at the centre of a web of railroads, more than doubled in size between 1880 and 1890, when it reached the million mark for the first time. Denver, Colorado, already a good-sized city of 35,000 in 1880, had trebled in size a decade later. Industry tended to become increasingly urban in location. Milwaukee and Wisconsin, with its large German population, became a centre of German-brewed beers. Cleveland, Ohio, became the centre of the oil-refining activities of Rockefeller's Standard Oil Company. Great smoke-blackened cities appeared where only a generation earlier there had been farms and fields: Pittsburgh, Pennsylvania, became the centre of American iron-and-steel production. The US began the 19th century as an agrarian civilization with its population stretched out along the Atlantic coast; it finished the century as an industrial and increasingly urban society moving rapidly towards economic pre-eminence in the world.

The American industrial achievement was made possible only by raising large sums of capital, some of it from abroad. British investors, for example, had a large stake in the American railroad network. In the USA the operations of bankers like Jay Cooke and later, on an even grander scale, J. P. Morgan had an incalculable effect – for good or ill – on the American industrial revolution. It was the collapse of Cooke's Philadelphia bank in 1873 that plunged the US into the depression of the 1870s. Just over 20 years later the government itself looked to J. P. Morgan for help in the midst of another great depression. Morgan formed a syndicate that came to the rescue of the sorely pressed federal Treasury by lending it $65,000,000 in gold. When he died in 1913, one newspaper declared that 'Kings have died, conquerors have fallen, with less world concern than attended the dying of John Pierpont Morgan, a private citizen of one of the younger nations'. Morgan was a symbol of the enormous concentration of financial power in private hands that characterized the country's economic life as America entered the 20th century. When he died, the USA was a debtor country. By the end of the First World War, only five years later, this situation had been transformed. America was now a creditor nation, poised on the verge of a new financial course that would eventually make the 'almighty dollar' the principal prop of the world's economic system.   *M. S.*

Model-K Fords lining up outside the works on Piquette Ave., Detroit, in 1904. The Ford Motor Co. began operations in 1903. Inset: Founder Henry Ford and tyre tycoon Harvey S. Firestone

Mexico: from 'Porfiriato' to Revolution

Between 1876 and 1910 Mexico was rigidly controlled by the most ruthless dictator of her history, Porfirio Díaz, a Liberal general who had supported the Liberal Reform programme of the 1850s and the leadership of President Benito Juárez in the civil wars against the Conservatives, but who withdrew his support from Juárez' successor, Miguel Lerdo, and ousted him in a military coup.

Díaz consolidated himself in power through arbitrary means. He wooed his opponents with subordinate posts in his régime and destroyed those he could not co-opt. He built up a ruthless rural police force to curb peasant discontent and Indian revolt, and was responsible for transporting the Yaqui Indians from one end of the country to the other in order to quell a rebellion. Díaz secured his own unchallenged re-appointment at all elections except one, when he arranged the election of his brother-in-law.

The 'Porfiriato', as the period became known, brought an unprecedented prosperity to Mexico. Díaz gave generous concessions to foreign investors in mines, rail-ways and export-led agriculture. He employed a small group of able financiers, the *científicos*, whose job it was to shape economic policy and project an image of financial responsibility on behalf of the régime in both Western Europe and the USA.

By the 1900s the Porfiriato was in a crisis. New investments had been exclusively concentrated in the export sector and, in spite of rapid population growth, agriculture for domestic consumption had been starved of capital. The failure to invest in transport links between the Mexican regions made it impossible to carry foodstuffs from regions that enjoyed an abundance to those that suffered famine. At the same time there was growing discontent within the governing apparatus itself. Men from 40 to 60 years of age resented exclusion from senior posts, monopolized by men aged over 65. There was growing concern that Díaz was ageing, and there was latent competition between the *científicos* and the military wing of the Liberal Party for the succession.

Díaz himself broke the stalemate in 1908 by announcing

President Porfirio Diaz, the epitome of Victorian-style prosperity

Zapata, the rebel of the south, in 1913

elections and proclaiming the right to form opposition parties. The 'Porfiristas' organized hastily for the contest, but they were overtaken by the group surrounding Francisco Madero, a French-educated landowner from the north, who announced his candidacy and a broadly liberal programme that involved some concessions to the underprivileged groups. Madero triumphed despite 11th-hour resistance from Díaz, and Diaz left the country. In the confusion surrounding Madero's election several factions had organized and armed themselves. Three stood out: firstly, there was the peasant movement led by Emilio Zapata in Morelos that demanded the restoration of lands seized by the large landowners from the peasants and Indians over a long period; secondly, there was a movement led by Felio Díaz, the nephew of Porfirio, who was determined to restore the Porfiriato; finally, there was a faction of soldiers competing with Felio for the support of the 'Porfiristas'. Madero had few options: he had inherited the Porfirian apparatus and was unable to make concessions to one armed faction without antagonizing the other two. It was hardly surprising that Madero was assassinated on the orders of a treacherous general, Huerta.

The Huerta coup provoked the formation of new armed movements from the north: the constitutionalists, who had identified with Madero, and the violently anti-clerical bandit group of 'Pancho' Villa. The US was so alarmed at the ascendancy of Huerta that it used a trivial pretext to occupy the Caribbean port of Veracruz, thereby cutting Huerta off from his main source of revenue, the import and export duties. The US provided financial support and armaments for the Constitutionalists and Huerta was overthrown. The Mexican revolution lurched from left to right; it had no clear-cut direction, no single outstanding ideologue.

In 1916 the Constitutionalists tried to resolve factional differences peacefully by calling a convention to which all significant groups were invited. The convention, held in Mexico City and influenced by the urban radicals, drew up the 1917 constitution, which still governs Mexico. This constitution is significantly different from the American constitution: it did not lay down rules for immediate implementation, but established guidelines for a continuing revolution of uncertain duration. It included references to land distribution, an eight-hour working day, accident compensation and has acted as a yardstick for achievement by later régimes. *C. G. A.*

'Pancho' Villa, the rebel of the north

The popular artist Posada's view of the Mexican revolutionaries

INTELLECTUAL CLIMATES IN THE 19TH CENTURY

Much of 19th-century thought was a response to the challenging, and often conflicting, legacies of the 18th-century Enlightenment (the cult of reason) and of the Romantic movement (the cult of feeling). The '*philosophe*' and the 'romantic' of the late 18th century each repudiated much of the existing social and political order of their day, and their shared emphasis on individual self-expression (however differently interpreted) helped to promote the intellectual restlessness so characteristic of the decades ahead. The spirit of nostalgia for an idealized past that was so popular with the earlier romantics was less evident among the later ones. These tended to join the rationalist heirs of the Enlightenment in contemplating visions of a brighter future, which were spurring liberals, nationalists and socialists alike to greater effort in the political and social fields. The mid-19th century did produce, in such writers as Baudelaire and Kierkegaard, some notable prophets of anxiety or even of doom, but far the greater noise was made by the champions of progress.

About mid-century many succumbed to the temptation of idolizing natural science and of expecting from it some key to the ultimate riddles of the universe. There came into vogue the positivism of Auguste Comte, who argued that every form of intellectual and imaginative endeavour should be assimilated to the triumphant model of scientific method. Only against this background can we properly appreciate the diversity of such changes as the erosion of conventional religious belief, the rise of realism in art (Courbet, Daumier) and literature (Zola, Tolstoy), and the grandiose systems of social explanation elaborated by Karl Marx and Herbert Spencer.

The quest for security and synthesis, on this

or any other basis, was understandable amidst the unprecedented turmoil of mass society. Yet by 1914, the line of scientific certainty had failed to hold at its very centre, in physics. The generation of Max Planck and Albert Einstein shattered the classical imagery with concepts of 'discontinuity', 'indeterminacy' and 'relativity'. Evolutionary theory, too, had to accommodate an extra element of 'randomness' after the rediscovery of Mendel's genetics. In other realms men's modes of thinking and talking about the world were being radically transformed. Sigmund Freud was revolutionizing

From left to right, top row: Leo Tolstoy, Sigmund Freud, Marcel Proust; bottom row: C. W. F. Hegel, Karl Marx, Friedrich Nietzsche

the study of mind, and Max Weber that of society. In literature, Marcel Proust, in music, Arnold Schoenberg, and in painting, Vassily Kandinsky were pioneering the great break with the aims and conventions of the 19th-century masters. Intellectual life was assuming a new vitality by foregoing earlier illusions, particularly about progress. Confidence was waning even before the guns began to thunder.

M. D. B.

Scientific Enquiry

By the end of the 19th century, science and mathematics had become a professionally organized set of disciplines which were actively taught in secondary schools and universities; research was pursued by salaried scientists and mathematicians and encouraged by governments for reasons of national prestige and economic viability. In contrast, at the beginning of the century little science or mathematics was taught, governments were little interested, and both fields were mainly the pursuit of cultured amateurs – gentlemen, doctors and clergymen. The astonishing transformation in the fortunes of science, and the expansion of the scientific and mathematical communities during the century, helped to make many intellectuals, such as Auguste Comte and Herbert Spencer, sceptical of orthodox religious beliefs and to see in science a new religion and politico-social philosophy. This 'scientistic' view, which is usually called 'scientific naturalism', held that science, having so successfully solved its own internal problems, could solve society's as well. Scientific naturalism was based upon three major 19th-century ideas: atomism, energy and evolution.

The idea that matter is not continuous, or a field of force, but composed from sub-microscopic, discrete, uncuttable particles, or 'atoms', is an ancient one. It was first given chemical significance by J. Dalton between 1800 and 1810. By the 1860s, despite philosophical difficulties and confusions over the determination of atomic weights, atomism had explained and linked together an impressive variety of chemical and physical phenomena.

In 1800 the Italian Alessandro Volta had built the first battery, ushering in the investigation of current electricity. The intimate connection between electricity and magnetism was demonstrated experimentally by Hans Oersted and Michael Faraday in the 1820s and 1830s, and their connection with light theoretically by James Maxwell in 1873. Although Faraday established the principle of both the electric motor and the dynamo, investment in steam-engine technology and gas lighting delayed the dawning of the electric age until the 1870s, when the inventive genius of the American, Thomas Edison, was at its peak. In the same decade, using the tools of electricity and magnetism, the inner architecture of the atom began to be explored. By 1908, the work of Marie Curie on radioactivity (discovered by Antoine Becquerel in 1895), Sir Joseph Thomson on the electron (discovered in 1897) and Ernest Rutherford on atomic radiation and the atomic nucleus, had produced the planetary model of the atom, and transformed physicists' ideas of energy sources and their views on the age of the universe.

In the mid-19th century, the concept of energy had been introduced by a number of scientists independently. Their notion that the ultimate forces and powers of nature were all conserved, but quantitatively related, established the discipline of physics and its two most important classical theories of thermodynamics and the electromagnetic

Charles Darwin caricatured by 'Vanity Fair' in 1871, the year he published 'The Descent of Man'

K. F. Gauss, whose mathematical thinking provides the basis for the 'new mathematics'

theory of light. The conservation rules of thermodynamics disallowed spiritual forces and miraculous events.

Evolution was, of course, the theme that coordinated the biological sciences during the century. In its most general form, however, it implied that the universe had evolved slowly over millions of years by the rearrangement of atoms and energy. In the biological sphere, Charles Darwin explained the development of plants and animals in terms of selection for breeding of naturally occurring advantages found present in populations. In 1888, Darwin's cousin, Sir Francis Galton, developed statistical techniques whereby it could be guaranteed mathematically that one factor was definitely correlated with another, even if not causally related to it. He applied this to hereditary information in books like *Natural Inheritance* (1889), but failed to unravel the simple laws of inheritance which the Austrian Augustinian monk, Gregor Mendel, had deduced from experiments with pea plants between 1858 and 1865. Mendel's work, which was to form the basis of modern genetics and neo-Darwinism, remained virtually unknown until revived in 1901 by the Dutch botanist, Hugo de Vries, who introduced the term 'mutation'.

Astronomers had been interested in the evolution of the universe since the 18th century when William Herschel the Elder suggested that nebulae were stellar factories. In the 1870s, a series of solar eclipses, together with the use of new tools like the spectroscope (invented in 1859) and photography, permitted astronomers like Sir Joseph Lockyer to identify the elements in stars and to speculate about their internal structure. However, the classification of stellar spectra proved extremely complicated, and was only satisfactorily resolved by astronomers at Harvard Observatory in 1910 by using an evolutionary correlation between stellar magnitudes and spectral types which had been suggested by the Dane, E. Hertzsprung and the American, H. N. Russell. Though improved after 1920 by quantum mechanical considerations, the Russell–Hertzsprung Diagram (1913) was to be the cornerstone of 20th-century research on the formation and evolution of stars.

Although Euclid remained in favour with teachers of geometry for much of the century, projective geometry in the hands of G. Monge, J. V. Poncelet and M. Chasles in France, and Jakob Steiner in Germany, became a sophisticated subject. Steiner claimed that synthetic geometric methods were as adaptable as, and ultimately superior to, analytical (algebraic and functional) methods. This viewpoint was not sustainable, despite the emergence of non-Euclidean geometries from the versatile and peerless Karl Gauss in 1799, the Hungarian J. Bolyai in 1823 and the Russian Nikolai Lobachevski in 1826. Such new geometries led mathematicians like Henri Poincaré to view as a mere convention the way in which Euclidean geometry had been used traditionally by physicists to describe space, so undermining notions of scientific naturalism.

W. H. B.

Thomas Henry Huxley, the leading Victorian agnostic and Darwin's greatest disciple

A caricature of Marie and Pierre Curie in 'Vanity Fair' in December 1904

Romanticism and Nationalism

European thought at the close of the 18th century swung away from the hard-headed and cool reasoning of the Enlightenment. Convinced of the limitations of intellectual speculation as a mode of thought, thinkers and writers such as Jean Jacques Rousseau, Edmund Burke, Johann Schiller, Johann Goethe, Samuel Taylor Coleridge and William Wordsworth began looking at man and the human condition in terms of the emotions as much as of the intellect. In its fullest flowering, this movement (especially in the arts) is referred to as Romanticism.

The flight from the universalist rationalism of the *philosophes* and physiocrats was already evident in Rousseau's *First Discourse* (1750). By the time of his famous letter to d'Alembert (1757), he had clearly split away from the mainstream of the Enlightenment. His commitment to sensibility can be seen most clearly in his novel *La Nouvelle Héloïse*. In challenging the commonly held view that the best guarantee of morality was to identify self with collective interest, he questioned the belief of the Enlightenment that reason was the supreme guide to human behaviour. There are times, according to Rousseau, when it could ultimately be more beneficial for society if individuals took decisions with only their own happiness in mind. Rousseau was saying, in essence, that moral judgement could not simply be a matter of utilitarian arithmetic. Man, he insisted, had to listen to his inner voice, the only true arbiter of virtue.

The plea for the inner voice to be heard was being made in other languages. In English writing, it was first heard around 1760 in the work of Edmund Burke and Lawrence Sterne and culminated at the turn of the century in the lyrical ballads of Coleridge and Wordsworth. In Germany it gave birth to the literary movement named *Sturm und Drang* after a play by Friedrich Maximilian von Klinger. Romantic themes such as the tension between man and both nature and society and the emphasis on simplicity and the emotions are, although not fully developed, clearly identifiable in Goethe's *The Sorrows of Young Werther* (1774) or Schiller's *The Robbers* (1781).

Kant

It was in Germany that the cool rationalism and the classical models of the Enlightenment came most heavily under attack, yet it was the German philosopher Immanuel Kant who rescued the concept of rationality, or, let us say, defined the limits of its application.

In his *Critique of Practical Reason* (1788), moreover, he attempted to solve the dilemma of man trying to chart a moral course in a world he could only perceive through his own mind. Following Rousseau, he sought to find the answer within man himself. Although religion availed man of divine truth, it was his own mind that told him what was right and what was wrong, and presented him with what Kant called the 'categorical imperative'. The result of a struggle within the conscience of man, it was an agonizing rather than an easy process. Whether it produced the right decision was not, according to Kant, immediately discernible. Clearly, both the man of reason and the man of faith could accommodate themselves in his philosophy.

For some, especially after the French Revolution had entered its more radical phase, there was never to be any reconciliation with rationalism. They blamed the Enlightenment not only for not allowing the inner voice to be heard, but also for the excesses of the Jacobins and Napoleon as well. The convulsion in France acted as a catalyst for the widespread rejection of the idea of progress. It increased interest in the past, especially in the Middle Ages, and mysticism revived.

Herder

Although Rousseau had already cast doubt on the belief that greater knowledge paved the way for universal happiness, Johann Gottfried von Herder in 1774 rejected the notion that the contemporary age was the high point of human civilization and became the first major European thinker to challenge the 18th-century idea of steady universal progress. At first in his *Fragments of a New German Literature* (1767) and then in later writings, Herder argued that every people is intrinsically and peculiarly different, and none is superior to any other. Its singularity was manifest in its culture, of which language was the most important attribute, as well as in its customs and institutions. Each nation thus had its own proper folk-spirit (*Volksgeist*). In Herder's view, a people did not have to comprise a political entity in order to be recognized as a nationality. Apart from the submerged nationalities of eastern and northern Europe, with which he became familiar while residing in the Baltic lands, he had, no doubt, his own Germany in mind. Believing that the culture of a people existed in forms other than the written language and literature, Herder became an avid collector of folk-songs and legends, particularly amongst the Slavs. The influence of Herder was significant in that throughout Europe, writers began to show a keen interest in the oral tradition.

Partly as a result of his example, national revivals took place amongst the Slavs as well as in the Iberian Peninsula, in Ireland and in Iceland. These had been given impetus by, in some cases, the unifying, centralizing and standardizing policies of enlightened monarchs, and in other cases by the rationalist and homogenizing effects of the French Revolution and Napoleonic conquest.

Fichte

Perhaps more to the point, events in France and Napoleon's attempt to establish French hegemony over Europe played an important part in helping to convert the Romantic notion of cultural patriotism into political nationalism. By proclaiming the concept of popular sovereignty, the French Revolution first of all upset the concept of the state as merely the totality of persons in a given country under a single government. When the Abbé Sieyès wrote in 1789 that the Third Estate was nothing (that is to say, only the Church and nobility had political power) and yet ought to be everything, he was pleading that government should be a manifestation of the democratic will and that the state should be recognized as sovereign in the people. The state was no longer to be conceived of as an accident of territory or inheritance, but as an expression of the popular will. The idea of national self-determination had come into being.

The influence of France was not solely ideological. Often for reasons of military expediency, France actively encouraged national independence movements, such as those in Poland and Italy. Especially under Napoleon, France promoted the rise of nationalism in another way. The armies of France more often than not brought in

Scarcely anything that symbolizes romantic nationalism is left out of Girodet-Trioson's painting 'The spirits of France's fallen heroes welcomed by Ossian the Bard' (1801)

their wake, instead of revolutionary change, political domination and economic exploitation. In Germany, especially, French domination was seen in cultural as well as political terms.

This can probably be seen most clearly in the *Addresses to the German Nation* (1807–08) by Johann Gottlieb Fichte. Because Germany was, in his analysis, the only nation whose culture had not been contaminated by the Classical influence, she was destined to lead the fight against French tyranny. The struggle was against the Enlightenment as much as against its incarnation, Napoleon. Delivering the *Addresses* in the aftermath of the

Prussian defeat at Jena (1806), Fichte tried to make the German people, especially its rulers, realize that independence was worth preserving. He implied, furthermore, that Prussia should take the lead in forging German unity.

During the rest of the 19th century, nationalism became a potent political force throughout Europe and the Americas. By the middle of the 20th century it had enveloped the rest of the world. Although differing in some ways from nation to nation, the concept of nationalism clearly has its roots in the European Romantic era and in the French Revolution. It was from the start tied up with the movement for popular sovereignty. *M. R.*

Early Socialism and Anarchism

Although socialism as an idea goes back to thinkers of the Greco-Roman world, its development as a modern, coherent ideological force can be charted from the end of the 18th century. The upheavals of the French Revolution and the Napoleonic rule that followed had disturbed the fabric of European society, and the results of industrialization were seen at their worst in Britain, where it had all started and was most advanced. It was in Britain at that time that the beginning of spontaneous working class agitation (culminating in Chartism) and a heightened middle class social awareness (poor relief no longer seen as a solution in itself) manifested themselves.

The relationship of labour and capital to the means of production appeared to be the root of the problem to some writers, and they began to question the theory (put most clearly by Adam Smith in *The Wealth of Nations*, 1776) that the value added to a commodity during its manufacture or processing originated in the skilful use of capital. In 1827 the *Cooperative Magazine* proposed that since the value of a commodity consisted of the toil of the people who helped to produce it ('present labour') as well as the capital or stock of the entrepreneur or joint stock company ('past labour'), the ownership of the means of production ('capital') should be shared in common. In this article the term 'socialist' appeared for the first time.

Robert Owen, a successful cotton manufacturer, was thinking along similar lines. According to his *Report to the County of Lanark* (1821), capitalism, rather than industrialization in itself, was to blame for unemployment, pauperism, bad working conditions and long hours. His remedy took the form of experiments in communal living – although his own attempts to put them into effect in both Britain and the US failed. Behind his ideas, and those of William Godwin (see below), lay the emphasis that the English romantics – notably Coleridge – had put on the need for 'organic' communities. Others approached the problems of poverty from the 'utilitarian' point of view, inspired by the writings of Jeremy Bentham, seeing the workhouses as an answer and initiating the national control of the poor laws in 1834.

By the 1830s both strands of protest – the criticism of capitalism on largely moral grounds, and a furtive class conflict – were very much part of the British scene, without ever coming together. Owen's critique of capitalism and his collectivism were in no real way political. Some early trade unionists took up some of Owen's ideas, but Chartism, which became the focus of British working class protest, was devoid of any socialist element, notwithstanding Friedrich Engels' belief that the Chartists shared the aims of working class activists in France and Germany, many of whom had embraced socialist ideas by the 1840s.

In France a very different tradition nourished socialism as well as anarchism. For a start, industrialization was still in its early stages. Moreover, in the home of the 18th-century Enlightenment, all discussion of social ideas took place within an existing ideological framework. Even more important, the unfinished revolution gave social protest its strong political impetus to telescope social and political revolution at once. This applied more to Louis-Auguste Blanqui's 'communist' followers and to Louis Blanc's 'republican socialists' than to the two other dominant French influences, Charles Fourier and Henri de Saint-Simon.

Robert Owen

Like Owen, Fourier and Saint-Simon promoted their different visions of new ways of living in communities rather than thinking of overthrowing society, for which reason their more radical critics labelled them 'utopians'. Saint-Simon was never a socialist in the true sense, although his proposals implied some form of collectivism. His influence on later generations of social thinkers is due to his vision of progressive technocrats controlling a concerted effort by workers and employers towards industrial modernization, and to his fundamental regard for individual liberty.

In the eyes of more radical thinkers, all these utopian or democratic schemes – Fourier's 'Phalanstères', or Louis Blanc's 'national workshops' – seemed to restrict the critique of bourgeois society to the aspect of liberal economics only. This was the attitude of communists (Blanqui, Marx, Engels) and anarchists (Proudhon, Bakunin) alike.

For anarchists, the possibilities for the improvement of humans are limitless. This, coupled with the belief that society can be reformed by the application of rational principles, was derived from the Enlightenment, and Rousseau (although he did not hold that you could only reform society by violent upheaval) provided a concept that is vital to the spirit of anarchism: the 'noble savage'. The idea that society imprisons man and corrupts him, and that he could be rescued by nurturing the basic goodness and simplicity of humanity were essential to the anarchist programme.

The first expression of anarchist doctrine came from William Godwin in *An Enquiry Concerning Political Justice*, 1793. In his view, as mankind was very susceptible to outside influence, a just society could be created by simply reforming the educational system and teaching people that acquiring more than they basically needed leads to conflict in society. In his own time Godwin's influence was slight, and confined to the British Isles, but his work was appreciated and propagated by the poets Shelley and Coleridge, and through Robert Owen he made an impression on early British trade unionists.

Michael Bakunin   **Louis Blanc**   **Peter Kropotkin**

The French Revolution had shown that not only could a firmly entrenched régime be toppled, but also that the greatest opportunity for fundamental social and economic (as well as political) change existed when society is in disarray. The Revolution also provided anarchists with a myth: that of the opportunity lost. This belief was supported by the incident of Gracchus Babeuf's 'Conspiracy of Equals' (1796). Babeuf had seen his vision of a thorough-going land reform made impossible by the setting up of the Directory in 1795. He became convinced that the only way to bring about any fundamental change in society was to turn a political upheaval into a social and economic revolution through the forging of a tightly knit conspiracy. Babeuf rejected the concept of private property, but as a strong believer in positive state action to bring about a just and equal society he was not an anarchist in the true sense, but rather a 'conspiratorial collectivist'. Babeuf failed, and he and his colleagues were guillotined. His example might have been lost to posterity had it not been for Filippo Buenorotti, who not only took part in the plot, but also wrote its history after escaping to Switzerland.

In the radical sub-culture of the period after the fall of Napoleon (1815–48) the doctrine of anarchism came into its own. Its first true and comprehensive statement was produced by Pierre-Joseph Proudhon, best known for his pamphlet *What is Property?* (1840), in which he gave his often-quoted answer: 'property is theft'. In an exchange of views with Marx (1846–47) Proudhon envisaged an ideal society in which all but the most rudimentary form of government was eliminated, and that it would be achieved by the personal emancipation of its members: man must consciously defeat evil in himself before he could be free.

Michael Bakunin, a Russian aristocrat by birth and a revolutionary agitator, gave anarchism an organizational footing. Although disagreeing with Proudhon on several points, he came to have a deep regard for him as a social and revolutionary thinker. Bakunin and his followers grew increasingly committed to the idea of socialism, but they initially refused to join the Marx-led First International. Even when they finally did so, relations were not happy

and Marx contrived to get them expelled at the Basel congress in 1871. The leading light in the movement after Bakunin's retreat into private life in 1874 was Peter Kropotkin, who shared a similar background. The style of Kropotkin's views stressed evolution rather than violence, and in later years, especially after settling in England, he came to have a significant influence on William Morris and the Fabians. Views similar to Kropotkin's were expressed by the great Russian novelist Lev Tolstoy, whose anarchism – having Christian, pacifist and ascetic elements – won a following not only in Russia but also in Western Europe and America, and foreshadowed the 'non-violence' doctrine of Mahatma Gandhi.

Meanwhile, the revolutionary wing of the movement continued to attract support, especially in Spain and Italy. More significantly, it gave birth, first in France and then in the USA, to 'anarcho-syndicalism', a movement that held as an essential principle that the best way for the working class to gain control of the means of production is through the general strike. In 1902 the French *Syndicats* (industrial unions) and the *Bourses du Travail* (a combination of labour exchanges and workers' education societies) amalgamated in the *Confédération Générale du Travail* (CGT) – an organization that seemed to embody Proudhonist principles of autonomy and non-centralism. In 1906, while still representing only a fraction of the total French work-force, it took up the general strike as official policy.

Although some of the anarchist old guard, such as Errico Malatesta and Emma Goldman, feared that by uniting insurrectionist anarchism with trade-unionism the freedom of the individual would be lost, the syndicalist movement spread. In the US, it led to the founding of the International Workers of the World and, in turn, to the growth of the industrial unions. Syndicalist ideas found their way too, in a perhaps perverted form, into the 'corporativism' of Salazar's Portugal and Fascist Italy. The wave of strikes organized by the CGT before 1914 failed to overthrow French society, but the concept of the general strike as the working class weapon stayed alive.   *M. R.*

The Age of Exhibitions

From the middle of the 19th century, few years passed without some city in the world becoming the scene of an international exhibition of industrial products, new machinery and curious artefacts. Although most of these exhibitions were relatively small versions of the less frequent 'great' exhibitions, their existence is proof of the vitality of a movement which represents the essence of the age: a belief that man's great achievements in science and technology promised him progress to a future where all social questions could be solved.

Exhibitions of art and industry were known in both France and England before 1851. Under the Directoire, in 1798, there had been begun a series of national exhibitions which all succeeding French régimes maintained and developed. In England the Society for the Encouragement of Arts, Manufactures and Commerce, which since 1760 had maintained a 'museum of useful inventions', began to hold a series of annual industrial and applied-art exhibitions. Four years later, the Society planned an exhibition which would rival, if not eclipse, the till then unrivalled French displays. In June 1849 Queen Victoria's husband, Prince Albert, made the significant suggestion that the forthcoming exhibition should be an international one.

The Great Exhibition of 1851

In spite of opposition and public apathy, Prince Albert, by means of the Society of Arts and of a Royal Commission appointed by the government, secured financial support, a site (Hyde Park) in the most fashionable part of London and a prefabricated building of iron and glass (Joseph Paxton's 'Crystal Palace') ideally suited for its purpose.

From the opening ceremony on 1 May 1851 until the closure on 15 October the Exhibition was an outstanding success. For the first time in modern history nation states (40 were represented) had discarded their commercial and political jealousies and laid open to the world the secrets of their technological and artistic skills. The popular response from all classes of British society and the goodwill shown by the crowds so soon after the period of Chartist agitation and continental revolution marked the Exhibition as a turning point in the internal history of the country and as a suitable beginning for the great Victorian boom (c. 1851–c. 1871). For American machinery seemed to be farther advanced than had been imagined, and French decorative art to be overwhelmingly more skilful; the enormous British engineering exhibits ('the new and gigantic locomotives') promised many years of industrial superiority for the country. The concrete legacies of the Exhibition were its South Kensington, London, site for colleges and museums bought out of the profits (it was probably the only profitable international exhibition ever held), and the re-erected Crystal Palace in south London.

Paris 1855-1900

Napoleon III responded to the progressive and internationalist ideals displayed at London in 1851, while naturally anxious to assert French ascendancy and to increase the popularity of his régime. The Universal Exhibition held at Paris in 1855 was an even larger and more impressive affair than London's pioneer effort of 1851. Called a 'Temple of Peace' designed to bring 'all nations together in concord', its timing may have been inappropriate when the Crimean War (1854–56) was in progress.

Tenniel's title-page for a bound volume of 'Punch': the international character of Crystal Palace

The bold tunnel structure for the Hall of Labour, Turin, 1898

France and Britain were at the time allies, and Queen Victoria came to Paris with Prince Albert to see the exhibition. Anglo-French collaboration in the London International Exhibition of 1862 led directly to the Paris Exhibition of 1867, another triumph for Napoleon III in spite of the domestic and international problems which seemed to threaten his throne. One ominous exhibit was the new 50-ton steel cannon made by Krupp's of Prussia.

The recovery of Paris after the ordeals of the siege and Commune from 1870 to 1871 astonished the world. In 1878 a third great international exhibition was held in Paris, which 'affected everyone with the greatest wonder.'

To commemorate the centenary of the Revolution (1889) another enormous show was staged with the controversial steel landmark designed by Gustave Eiffel as its permanent memorial. Finally, in 1900, 'the end of a century of prodigious scientific and economic effort' was commemorated in an exhibition larger than any Europe had yet known.

The USA

Although the New York World's Fair of 1853 had given the United States a taste of the 1851 atmosphere, it was not until 1876 that America staged an exhibition which was truly international: the Centennial Exhibition held in Philadelphia. It was opened by President Grant in the presence of the Emperor of Brazil. The President and the Emperor ceremoniously turned on the steam of the giant Corlis Engine which worked the mechanical exhibits, a feature of this impressive display of American technology. Other important exhibits were the first sewing-machine, the first typewriter and Alexander Graham Bell's tele-phone. The World's Columbian Exhibition held at Chicago in 1893 and the St Louis exhibition of 1904 (commemorating the Louisiana Purchase of 1804) were further demonstrations of the growth of America to world status as an economic power. The St Louis exhibition in particular, showed the American desire for bigger and better products. There the zenith in size was reached with a 300-acre site which included an agricultural pavilion that incurred a nine-mile walk if the visitor wished to view all the exhibits. Also on display were five dirigible airships and 160 'horseless carriages'.

Central Europe

Vienna was in 1873 the scene of an international exhibition which had an atmosphere of glamour and éclat only equalled by the Parisian displays. Its special characteristic was the large number of exhibits from countries in the Near, Middle and Far East. The Japanese delegation included 66 engineers who, on their return to Japan, produced a 96-volume report which did much to speed the industrialization of their country. The citizens of Berlin, capital of the new German Reich, also felt that their city should be the scene of a great international exhibition, but the idea was rejected by Emperor Wilhelm II in 1892. Instead of a world exhibition, an unusually large, imposing trade fair, the *Gewerbeausstellung*, was held in 1896, which provided an impressive demonstration of Germany's industrial greatness. Her emergence as an international influence in the field of architecture and design, which was to be characteristic of the period of the Weimar Republic, was heralded by the first exhibition of the *Deutsche Werkbund* at Cologne in 1914.   D. G. C. A.

A Currier & Ives print of New York's Crystal Palace, which was built for the 1853 Exhibition of Industry of All Nations. Constructed of iron and glass, it covered six acres of land in New York City

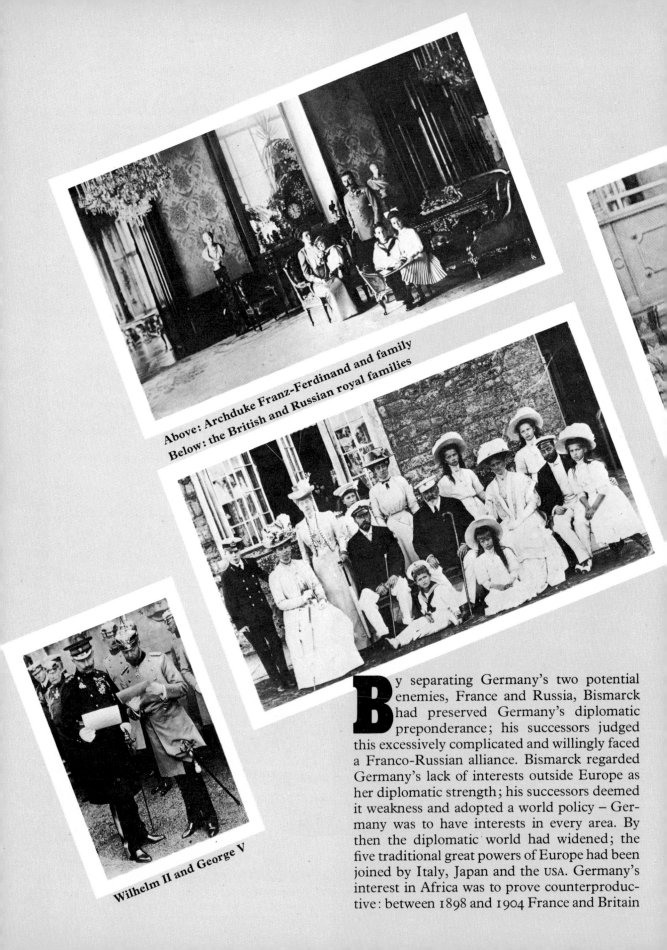

Above: Archduke Franz-Ferdinand and family
Below: the British and Russian royal families

Wilhelm II and George V

By separating Germany's two potential enemies, France and Russia, Bismarck had preserved Germany's diplomatic preponderance; his successors judged this excessively complicated and willingly faced a Franco-Russian alliance. Bismarck regarded Germany's lack of interests outside Europe as her diplomatic strength; his successors deemed it weakness and adopted a world policy – Germany was to have interests in every area. By then the diplomatic world had widened; the five traditional great powers of Europe had been joined by Italy, Japan and the USA. Germany's interest in Africa was to prove counterproductive: between 1898 and 1904 France and Britain

Queen Victoria and royal party

Edward VII and Wilhelm II

GREAT POWER RIVALRIES

Hungarian Empire. Unlike rivalry over Africa, the Balkans aroused real hostility between two great powers. When Turkey's European empire broke up, Russia and Austria-Hungary disagreed as to the area's future: Russia's aim was to foster Slav nationalism, Austria-Hungary's intention was to suppress it. In the two subsequent Balkan crises (1908–9, 1912–13) Russia was deserted by her allies. The French feared that a repetition would cause Russia to conclude a separate agreement with Germany.

Europe's war ministries believed that whoever assumed the offensive first would win speedily. Hence tight mobilization plans left the diplomats very little negotiating time. Wars occur when two sides are prepared to fight; this happened in July 1914. The crisis began when a Slav nationalist assassinated the heir to the Habsburg throne; a strong response by Austria-Hungary was predictable. The key issue was whether the form of Serbia's chastisement was internationally acceptable; it was not, as Russia objected, on Panslav grounds, and this time her allies supported her. The Russo-French and Russo-Serb exchanges were uncompromising. Germany had accepted a 'calculated risk' of war when she agreed to endorse the Austrian demands. A Slav-Habsburg confrontation, if resolved decisively in favour of either party, would have altered the balance of power, and therefore the powers were prepared to fight.

P. H. S. H.

settled their differences and cooperated to minimize German influence, especially during the Morocco crises. This settlement, together with German naval expansion, led Britain into closer alignment with the Franco-Russian alliance.

This and other shifts in allegiance had, by 1906, reversed Germany's former diplomatic predominance. Attempting to rebuild her position, she was occasionally tempted to stress German strength in a threatening manner. When war came, it was over a Balkan issue vital to the stability of her one firm ally, the Austro-

Britain and Ireland

In December 1905 the divided Unionist ministry finally resigned, and the Liberals took office and dissolved Parliament. Early in 1906 they won a landslide victory in the general election. Chamberlain's protectionist proposals were seen to have alienated many voters, who for once preferred the Liberals as the 'safer' party. Also, the nonconformist interest was now once more solidly behind the Liberals. Whatever reservations nonconformists might have had about Irish Home Rule, which to many had seemed far too favourable to Roman Catholicism, were now overridden by anger at the 1902 Education Act, with its policy of rate-aid for Anglican schools. Another factor was the performance of the infant Labour Party. Founded in 1900 to press for changes in the law relating to trade unions, it cooperated with the Liberals and won several seats in industrial areas.

The new Liberal government under Henry Campbell-Bannerman contained some notable personalities, Herbert Asquith, David Lloyd George and Winston Churchill, each of whom subsequently became prime minister. It was determined to reverse the policies of the previous years. In South Africa the Boer republics were granted constitutional government in order to reconcile them to British rule, and the steps were laid for the setting-up of the Union of South Africa (1910). At home, labour interests were aided by the repeal of the Taff Vale decision, which had curtailed the right to strike, and the Liberals also sought to amend the 1902 Education Act. But here they

The 'Welsh Wizard' David Lloyd George, sketched on the front bench by David Low

faced a serious challenge: however weak the Unionist Party might be in the House of Commons, it still dominated the House of Lords, and the upper chamber was therefore used to defeat Liberal legislation relating to education and to other matters as well. There was only one way round this situation. Certain necessary reforms could be implemented through the budget, with which, traditionally, the House of Lords could not interfere. In 1908 old age pensions were introduced for the first time in this way. In 1909 the need for money to pay both for pensions and for the new battleship programme in competition with Germany necessitated increased taxation, and Lloyd George, the chancellor of the exchequer, produced the 'people's budget', embodying a hefty rise in duties on income and land. At this the Lords threw precedent overboard, rejected the budget and thus forced the Liberal government to appeal to the country.

The constitutional crisis and the Irish question
Two general elections were held in the course of 1910. The first was fought on the question of the budget, the second on the Liberal plan to curtail the powers of the House of Lords. On both occasions the Liberals won approximately the same number of seats as the Unionists, but, enjoying the support of the Labour and Irish Parties, the Liberal government was able to stay in power. Any legislation to emasculate the House of Lords would, of course, have to be passed by that body as well as by the House of Commons. The only way to achieve this was by massive peerage creations, which only the king could sanction. George V was at first reluctant, but gave his consent after the second general election of 1910 had confirmed the Liberals in power. The Lords now capitulated rather than face such a dilution of their numbers, and by the Parliament Act of 1911 the veto of the upper chamber was limited to a maximum of two years.

These events made Home Rule for Ireland practical politics once more, for the strong and reorganized group of nationalists led by John Redmond now held the balance of power in the House of Commons, and they knew that the House of Lords could no longer forestall them as in 1893. Accordingly, the third Home Rule Bill was introduced in 1912, and it was expected to become law by 1914. Desperately, the Unionists sought another weapon with which to combat Home Rule, and they fixed upon Ulster for this purpose. Ireland's northern province, partly industrialized and predominantly Protestant, differed markedly from the Catholic and agrarian south. Unionist politicians now played on Ulster's sense of its history and traditions, and encouraged its population to resist, by force if necessary, any imposition of Home Rule, which would only, it was said, result in 'Rome rule'. From 1912 to 1914, as the third Home Rule Bill was making its way slowly through Parliament, tension was mounting in Ireland. Ulstermen made military preparations, thereby provoking other Irishmen to do likewise.

If the Irish nationalists were well organized, the Unionists, too, commanded forces that had barely existed in 1886. Under Sir Edmund Carson, the upper-class Protestant and Catholic Unionists of the south and the largely Presbyterian working-class Unionists of Ulster rejected any thought of a united, self-governing Ireland. Open arming and drilling by a massive Ulster Volunteer Force

John Redmond, the last of the great Irish parliamentarians at Westminster

(UVF), encouraged by British Unionists and army officers, and similar nationalist moves, raised the prospect of civil war. In the so-called 'mutiny' at the Curragh, the British military base west of Dublin, army officers voiced their intention of refusing orders designed to coerce Ulster. The Liberal cabinet, under Asquith, toyed with the notion of partitioning Ireland, but realized that this would be unacceptable to the Liberals' Irish nationalist allies. In reality, ministers had no firm idea what to do, and the coming of the international crisis in July 1914 was greeted almost with relief as a welcome distraction from the intractable problems of Ireland.

Social reform and social conflicts

The potential for violence in Edwardian Britain and the years before 1914 did not exist only in Ireland. The militant suffragettes indulged in arson and physical assaults on politicians in their efforts to obtain votes for women. Trade unions were also beginning to make their power felt in a major way. In 1910–14 the country was wracked by the most severe labour disputes it had yet known, including the first nationwide strike by the coalminers (1912). But the years of the last Liberal governments were certainly not wasted ones in terms of social construction. Lloyd George had introduced old age pensions in 1908, partly to trump Unionist proposals for social reform to be paid for by the imposition of tariffs and partly to remedy social conditions that, it was thought, put Britain behind rivals like Germany in terms of welfare and national efficiency. Similar motives prompted the other social reforms of this period, including the institution of school meals (1906) and compulsory medical inspection of schoolchildren (1907), the limitation of labour in the coalmines to a maximum of eight hours a day by the 1908 Act,

the establishment of minimum wages in the 'sweated' workshop trades of east London (1909), the provision (also in 1909) of a national system of labour exchanges in order to combat unemployment, and, most important of all, the monumental National Insurance Act of 1911. This last measure fell into two parts. One section dealt with unemployment insurance, which was now introduced for the first time in industries such as ship-building, iron-founding, and motor-car manufacture, where fluctuations in employment were rife. The other, and more significant, section provided for a comprehensive scheme of national health insurance. Government, employers and employees were all to contribute to a fund to ensure free medical treatment for 'panel patients', in general comprising the less well-off members of the community.

In many ways these reforms foreshadowed the emergence of the welfare state later in the 20th century: unemployment insurance was to be extended to most categories of the working population in the inter-war years, and free medical attention would be made available to all by the 1948 National Health Act, following the suggestions of the Beveridge Report of 1943. But the Liberal reformers of the pre-1914 era did not necessarily envisage constructing a new social order. They were acting much more in the piecemeal reforming tradition of their Victorian predecessors. Nor did their reforms necessarily prove popular with those whom they were designed to benefit. Trade unions were suspicious of the introduction of labour exchanges, which they feared might be used to organize blackleg labour for strike-breaking activities. Many also opposed the principle of insurance contributions in the Act of 1911, which they considered a form of regressive taxation. The Coal Mines Act of 1908, though designed to reduce hours of labour, necessitated a reorganization of the shift system, and made the coal owners anxious to extract increased productivity. It played its part in sparking off the great strike wave before 1914, which began with a stoppage in the South Wales coalfield in 1910. Inflation, however, and the consequent drop in working class living standards, was undoubtedly the most potent factor in the unrest.

The embittered social climate of this time raises the intriguing question of what might have happened to the Liberal Party had the First World War not intervened. It is dangerous to speculate too freely, but it was evident that the strikes and the consequent increase in trade union activities and membership would rebound to the benefit of the emerging Labour Party, although it was still a long way behind the Liberals in support among the electorate. From 1911 to 1914 the Unionists were winning by-elections chiefly because the Labour Party was intervening in seats where it usually only came third in the poll but managed at the same time to take enough votes from the Liberals to let in the Unionists. There was a growing possibility that the Liberals might be outflanked by Labour on the left. The Liberal reforming impetus had lost much of its momentum by 1914. Ministers disliked heavy government expenditure, and preferred to leave the old Poor Law still in existence rather than risk the expense that its abolition might entail. Lloyd George, radical demagogue though he was, could offer little more than the time-honoured Liberal policies of land reform and disestablishment of the Welsh church. *D. R. B.*

France: the Third Republic

With the defeat and capture of Napoleon III by the Prussians at Sedan in September 1870 the Second Empire came to an end. Nothing was less certain than that the new republic, proclaimed immediately in Paris, would survive. It failed to prevent defeat in the continuing war with Bismarck, and in February 1871, elections to a national assembly produced a large majority of monarchists. This assembly granted itself constituent powers and appointed as chief of the 'executive power' (not of the republic) Adolphe Thiers. His government immediately distinguished itself, in May, by the savagery of its repression of the Commune, which the people of Paris had set up in March. To many, the excesses of the Commune seemed the logical and terrible consequence of the whole principle of egalitarian republicanism. Thiers himself soon believed it was possible to combine republicanism with conservatism, but in 1873 the assembly replaced him by the monarchist Marshal Macmahon. Only two years later this same assembly established the Third Republic. The reasons for this lie partly in the deep divisions that separated the two monarchist claimants. Reconciliation came too late and by then many moderate monarchists were prepared to follow Thiers in his belief that a republic would guard against rather than encourage social dis-

order. By-elections after 1871 showed a steady progress of republican candidates.

The constitutional laws of 1875 provided for only one popularly elected branch of government, the Chamber of Deputies, to which a ministry nominated by the president of the republic was responsible. The president was appointed for seven years by Chamber and Senate sitting together, had extensive powers of appointment and, crucially, the right to dissolve the Chamber with the approval of the Senate. This constitution was expressly designed to check the alleged instabilities of popular assemblies, yet the Third Republic became known as the 'république des députés', a byword for weak governments and over-powerful legislatures. There were 108 ministries between 1870 and 1940 with an average life-span of only eight months, and it was very difficult to pass legislation of national, as opposed to local, importance. The presidency became largely ceremonial, and after 1877 none of its occupants ever dared to dissolve a Chamber before its allotted term was up. There was, therefore, no restraint on the Chamber's pre-eminence other than four-yearly elections.

The success of the Third Republic was that, for all its governmental weakness and for all the crises that periodically racked it, it survived longer than any régime since the revolution. The crises included the rise and fall of the would-be nationalist dictator General Boulanger in the late 1880s, well-founded allegations of political corruption by republican politicians in the 1880s and 1890s, and serious riots in the south in 1907. Above all, the accusations made during the Dreyfus Affair (1894–1902) made France seem irredeemably split into bitterly hostile republicans and anti-republicans. The latter included, on the right, powerful institutions like the Catholic Church (despite the social awareness of Pope Leo XIII) and, on the left, an anarchist, anti-republican trade union organization, the *Confédération Générale du Travail*. Yet the republic survived and even flourished. Governments in the 1890s and 1900s negotiated agreements with, respectively, Russia and Britain that ended the diplomatic isolation that had been so disastrous in 1870. At home there was fairly widespread prosperity and limited but real industrial growth after the 1880s. By 1914 the debate about France's political institutions had an academic air.

France remained a centralized state, and assiduous use was made by the republicans (whether moderate or radical) of the benefits that governments could provide at local level in the form of cash grants, provision of railways and so on. Successive ministers, notably Jules Ferry, established a network of state primary schools, which existed in part to provide a limited social mobility but more to inculcate republicanism, a sense of loyalty to the system and to the values of liberal democracy. These schools were part of the attack on the status (though not the existence) of the Catholic Church that culminated in the 1905 separation of Church and state. The 'mystique' of republicanism meant that, during the Dreyfus Affair and thereafter, many socialists were prepared to defend the system on political grounds even though it was socially regressive. For example, in the 1890s the conservative government of Méline passed a tariff measure that protected France's large, and largely inefficient, agricultural system from the rigours of foreign competition. Thus, a key section of the

Adolphe Thiers, historian of the revolution and of Napoleon, and first president of the Third Republic from 1871 to 1873

electorate was placated, and even left-wing governments dared not alienate the mass of small businessmen and professional people by a progressive tax system. The result was that the political system protected the interests of the majority of the population though it did not promote rapid economic growth. The Third Republic had become, as its founders had claimed it would, 'the system that divides men least'.   P. M.

Alfred Dreyfus, a French staff captain of Jewish origin from Alsace, was arrested on suspicion of supplying secrets to the German military attaché. Convicted by court martial in 1894, Dreyfus was sentenced to reduction to the ranks and a term of imprisonment on Devil's Island. His case was taken up in 1896 when evidence was found that incriminated another officer. Public pressure for a retrial became a major political issue. In 1898 it was proved that evidence used to convict Dreyfus had been forged, and Major Henry, the officer responsible, killed himself. A retrial was ordered but the new court martial convicted Dreyfus again, and only in 1906 was he finally exonerated and reinstated in rank.

The accused Captain Dreyfus leaving the court-martial at Rennes, 1894

Jean Jaurès, leader of France's Socialists, speaking from the tribune of the Chamber of Deputies, 1903

Wilhelmine Germany

Following elections in 1890, Bismarck lost the majority on which he had depended in the Reichstag. One month later he was dismissed by the young Kaiser Wilhelm II. The political instability of subsequent years was not, however, the result of Bismarck's successors – Caprivi, Hohenlohe, Bülow and Bethmann – being 'lesser men', although they certainly lacked his political acumen. Nor did it derive simply from the kaiser's desire for 'personal rule', although his autocratic wilfulness and petulant outbursts were certainly destructive in both internal and external affairs. Bismarck had simply not reconciled the many contradictions of imperial politics, he had only suppressed their symptoms. His successors, oscillating between repressive and cosmetic policies, were unequal to that task.

The powers of the kaiser, the three-class franchise in Prussia, the influence of the Prussian army and the entrenched position of the Junker landowners, all appeared more blatantly anachronistic as Germany's industrial advance quickened. Opposition in the Reichstag grew, and the idea of abolishing universal suffrage was toyed with in ruling circles in the 1890s and then again in 1912–1913. Largely, however, governments sought to neutralize opposition in various ways. In the first place, they tried to unite middle class and aristocracy, business and agriculture, to save the 'marriage of iron and rye' which Bismarck had solemnized. Secondly, they attempted to buy off opposition by satisfying the various demands of economic, naval and nationalist pressure groups, as well as those of the Catholic Centre Party. Thirdly, they followed the aggressive course of naval construction known as the 'Tirpitz Plan' (which is described below).

These policies were, on the whole, unsuccessful. Business and the middle-classes generally became increasingly hostile to the Junker aristocracy, as the latter stubbornly resisted constitutional, economic and tax reforms. The smoothing over of these differences became more difficult. The attempt to satisfy conflicting interest groups frequently proved self-cancelling, and appetites were fed rather than satisfied. Nor did an aggressive foreign policy serve as an effective lightning rod for domestic opposition. As the German diplomatic failure during the second Moroccan crisis showed, there was again a danger of raising expectations which had to remain unfulfilled. And not all sections of German society could, anyway, be won over by such means. The anti-militarist Social Democratic Party, for example, continued to grow, and at the 1912 elections became the largest party in the Reichstag.

The central problem of imperial Germany was the gap between rapid economic and social change on the one hand, and atrophied political institutions on the other. The development of mass parties, the political press and advanced electioneering techniques served only to point up this discrepancy. The circumstances under which Germany was unified created the problem: Bismarck and his successors aggravated it by tackling only its symptoms. After 1912 their room for manoeuvre was narrowed still further. On the eve of war, constitutional, political and financial crises raised seriously the question of whether the Reich was governable in its existing form.

Between the early 1890s and 1912 the German army was not expanded. It was feared that growth would fill the ranks with socialist workers and entail a bourgeois dilution

Bismarck the 'tourist' with colonial 'souvenirs', as seen by 'Punch'

Carl Peters (1856-1918), explorer and promoter of German colonies in Africa

of the aristocratic officer corps. Expansion came only with the return of German interests to the European continent, and with general intensification of the arms race.

A major element in this arms build-up among the great powers was the Tirpitz Plan: the German decision to build a battle fleet which would be a symbol of German 'world policy' ambitions. Like German colonial policy, the Tirpitz Plan had domestic and international origins. A powerful navy would, it was hoped, help domestic heavy industry, win business support generally, and act as a vehicle for rallying popular enthusiasm behind the imperial government. It was, at the same time, a direct challenge to British naval supremacy, a blunt indication that Germany would not be thwarted by alleged British trade rivalry in her search for a 'place in the sun'.

It failed on both counts. Working-class enthusiasm was not forthcoming, and rapid naval construction in fact proved politically divisive. Moreover, by challenging Britain at her most sensitive point, Germany helped to bring about that very encirclement which she feared.

Bismarck was generally hostile to what he once described as 'German colonial humbug'. Yet between 1884 and 1886 Germany acquired protectorates in South-West Africa, East Africa (Tanganyika) and West Africa (Togoland, the Cameroons), as well as in the Pacific.

Diplomatic considerations provided part of the motive. Bismarck wished to exploit Anglo-French hostility over Egypt by seeking a quarrel with Britain in Africa, thereby cementing German friendship with France. At the same time, both the economic recession of 1882–86 and the founding in 1882 of the German Colonial Association created demands for overseas expansion. The acquisition of colonies would serve both as an economic and as a political safety valve. In particular, conflict with Britain would serve as an acceptable 'national' issue with which to attack the left in the 1884 Reichstag elections.

Within two years Bismarck had lost interest. By the end of the decade the African protectorates had, it is true, been formally taken over by the state as colonies, but principally because the private interests were unwilling to meet the costs of communications and defence.

D. G. B.

The irrepressible Kaiser, on manoeuvres, shares a joke with Graf Fürstenberg and the Austrian military attaché, while his English friend Lord Lonsdale observes it all from nearby

Italy: Growing Pains

The continued existence of division within Italian society was, at least in part, a consequence of the economic policies followed after unification. Italy's weakness compared with other European powers was widely recognized, and it was felt that only the rapid development of Italian industry would remedy it. The free trade policies adopted after unification provoked a crisis through much of Italian industry, which suffered from the competition of her stronger rivals. In the south, where industry had been heavily protected by the Bourbon régime prior to unification, the shock of competition was too great and such southern industry as there was collapsed, never to recover.

Northern industry was less severely affected, but, in the first two decades after 1861, found expansion difficult. Capital was short and the high taxation imposed by Italian governments on the population reduced spending power and limited the home market. Increasingly, industry came to rely on the state. The state could provide capital, through loans, and – more important – could also purchase many of the products of industry, particularly in the case of those heavy industries involved in the railway-building boom of the 1870s, arms production and ship-building.

The Italian economy began to grow more rapidly during the 1880s, but the brief period of expansion was halted by the effects of the international agrarian crisis, consequent on the arrival in Europe of large quantities of cheap grain from the USA. In Italy the crisis was met with calls for protectionism. Northern industrialists argued that the young Italian industry needed a period of respite from foreign competition in order to become strong enough to withstand that competition in the future, while southern landowners were clearly terrified that cheap imported grain would ruin their backward and inefficient grain-producing estates. Capitalist industrialists of the north and pre-capitalist landowners of the south thus came together to pass a protectionist tariff in 1887. As a consequence, northern industry and the more efficient capitalist agriculture of the north continued to expand. In the south, however, protectionism meant simply the continuation of backwardness, since landowners were not compelled by competition to become more efficient in their methods of production. The uneven development between north and south (the 'Southern Question') was thus accentuated by the introduction of protectionism. The price of this policy was expensive bread and highly priced industrial products.

The appointment of the dynamic Sicilian Francesco Crispi as prime minister in 1887 underlined the conservative and authoritarian trend of Italian politics. Previously, in 1882, Italy had severed her traditional links with France and formed the Triple Alliance with Germany and Austria–Hungary. Italy's new colonial pretensions and her rivalry with France in North Africa, especially over Tunis, provided one motive, but colonial ventures were to prove remarkably unsuccessful. In 1887 Italy suffered a humiliating defeat at the hands of Eritrean tribesmen at Dogali, while in 1895 the defeat of 15,000 Italian troops at Adowa in Ethiopia ended the political career of Crispi, the main advocate of military expansion.

The economic difficulties of the last decade of the century were reflected in growing social protest. Risings in Sicily in 1893 (the *Fasci siciliani*) and in Carrara in the same year were repressed with severity. In 1898 the army

Giovanni Giolitti outside the parliament building, Rome

used artillery to disperse a bread riot in Milan. The threat posed to existing institutions by popular unrest and, in particular, the Italian Socialist Party, formed in 1892, gave rise to calls for an authoritarian solution to the crisis. The rejection of such proposals reflected the appreciation on the part of the more advanced sectors of Italian capitalism that some sort of understanding with the working class was essential if Italy were to participate in the cycle of European economic expansion that had begun in other countries about 1896. The principal exponent of this view was the Piedmontese statesman Giovanni Giolitti, in office (with intervals) between 1903 and 1914. His conviction that the industrial proletariat of the north and the industrial entrepreneurs would benefit equally from cautious reformism and an improvement in the condition of the working class led him to try to convince both the reformist wing of the Socialist Party and the industrialists that their interests lay in co-operation. Although partially successful prior to 1907, the policy foundered with the economic crisis of that year and the long period of stagnation that followed. Employers became less disposed to make concessions to the workers and after 1907 Giolitti's role as mediator between the Socialist Party and the employers became less effective as both parties passed to more direct tactics of confrontation. Efforts to regain support for the 'system' of compromise were made in 1911 with the conquest of Libya, intended to please the opponents of socialism, and in 1912 with the granting of universal male suffrage, which failed, however, to reduce the increasingly revolutionary stance of the Socialist Party. By the outbreak of the First World War, the division in Italy between right-wing nationalist opinion, to some extent backed by the industrialists, and revolutionary socialism appeared complete. *P. R. C.*

The unmistakable clerical politician Don Luigi Sturzo (right), with colleagues Stefano Cavazzoni and (left) Alcide De Gasperi in 1921; 24 years later De Gasperi would head Italy's government. Inset: De Gasperi in 1948, after the sweeping victory of the Christian Democrats

The Russo-Japanese War

Russo-Japanese rivalry

The control of Manchuria and Korea was the issue at stake. Russia had leased Port Arthur on the Liaotung peninsula from a cowed China in 1898, and after the suppression of the Boxer Rising in 1900 (in which both Russia and Japan played a part), Russia maintained a military occupation of Manchuria. Japan called for its withdrawal in 1901, and in January 1902 entered into an alliance with Britain. Britain shared Japan's distrust of Russia in north-east Asia, and looked for the backing of Japan's new naval power once the Japanese building programme had been fulfilled in 1901. Shortly after the alliance was published, Russia promised to withdraw from Manchuria, but by 1903 the later phases of withdrawal were halted. Six months of inconclusive negotiations ended on 8 February 1904, when Japan attacked the carelessly exposed Russian naval squadron at Port Arthur, without a declaration of war.

The war

The conflict was significant not only as a trial of strength between an Asiatic and a European power, but also as a testing ground for new weapons and tactics. In many respects, including that of trench warfare, it foreshadowed the First World War. Communications played a decisive part in the outcome. Japan retained command in the Yellow Sea, thus preventing the Russians from uniting their Port Arthur and Vladivostok squadrons. The battle theatre was devoid of good roads and poor in food supplies, and the Russians, operating over 5000 miles from Moscow, depended heavily on the single-track, uncompleted trans-Siberian railway. At the outset they had only 108,000 troops east of Lake Baikal (including fortress garrisons) whereas Japan could mobilize nearly 300,000. Nevertheless, in Western eyes Japan began as the underdog.

Japanese strategy was determined by the need to divide her armies between Port Arthur, and the main Russian field army concentrating at Liao-yang. The former planned to land three armies in North Korea which would advance towards Liao-yang while a fourth rapidly captured Port Arthur before joining them. These calculations were upset when the fortress of Port Arthur proved far too strong to rush and had to be besieged.

By the beginning of June the Japanese had won control of Korea by its First Army's victory at the Yalu River on 1 May and had cut off the land approaches to Port Arthur. However, their four armies were so dispersed that they risked defeat in detail from a bold opponent. Field-Marshal Alexai Kuropatkin, the Russian commander-in-chief, attempted such a defeat but failed in the first important battle at Te-li-ssu on 14 and 15 June. He also

appeared to be winning the great battle at Liao-yang in August but after a fortnight's fighting withdrew towards Mukden. Throughout the summer and autumn of 1904 Nogi's Third Army attacked at Port Arthur with ever greater desperation and sustained enormous casualties (58,000 killed as against 31,000 Russians), but the fortress held out until 2 January 1905. It had been one of the longest and most bloody sieges in modern history. Meanwhile, Russian hopes rested chiefly on their Baltic Fleet, but when it eventually reached the Sea of Japan after a hazardous voyage round the world it was annihilated at Tsushima in the Korea Strait on 27 May 1905, in the most decisive naval battle since Trafalgar.

When the last and greatest land battle began at Mukden on 23 February 1905, each side had approximately 300,000 men. The Japanese attempted to outflank the Russian right and Kuropatkin eventually withdrew, giving up Mukden with its huge supply depot. He had sustained 85,000 casualties as against 70,000 by the Japanese. These defeats triggered off strikes and riots in St Petersburg, and as Japan was also nearing exhaustion both sides were ready to accept mediation by President Theodore Roosevelt. Negotiations began at Portsmouth, New Hampshire, in August and the peace treaty was signed in September.

The peace

Russia escaped lightly, transferring to Japan the rail and other rights she had in southern Manchuria, together with the rolling-stock, and giving up the Liaotung peninsula, including Port Arthur, but refusing to pay an indemnity. Both powers agreed to evacuate Manchuria, but Korea became a Japanese protectorate (which Japan annexed as a colony in 1911).

Heavily indebted as a result of the war, Japan felt embittered at winning no indemnity, and to guarantee her security against a Russian war of revenge, she concluded a revised Anglo-Japanese alliance in August 1905, which was again renewed in 1911. The outcome of the war clearly signalled Japan's arrival as a great power poised to challenge for hegemony in the Far East, but still unsure of getting her own way among the other powers.

I. H. N./B. J. B.

A Japanese print (1905) of the Russian Baltic squadron being wiped out in the Straits of Tsushima by Admiral Togo

183

Russia in Crisis

Discontent had been stirring for some years among all classes, especially as the war in the Far East was going badly by early 1905, but what sparked off the 1905 revolution was a peaceful demonstration of St Petersburg workers on 9/22 January, led by the priest Gapon. Trying to reach the Winter Palace to present a petition to the emperor, they were fired on by troops and more than a hundred were killed. News of this 'Bloody Sunday' massacre spread quickly, and strikes and demonstrations broke out all over Russia. The climax was the general strike of October 1905, which started in the Moscow railway workshops and soon covered most of the country. A new feature of the workers' movement was the formation of councils (*soviets*), systematically representing factory employees, to co-ordinate the strikes and negotiate with the authorities. The St Petersburg soviet came to be seen as speaking for the whole Russian workers' movement, and when the government arrested its entire membership at the beginning of December, the Moscow soviet took over the banner and organized an armed uprising that had to be suppressed with considerable bloodshed. The Socialist Revolutionaries (SRs), Bolsheviks and Mensheviks, who were at first surprised by the vehemence of the revolutionary movement, became increasingly involved in it, and took a leading part in the organization of the soviets.

The workers' movement was paralleled in the countryside by peasant unrest, aimed principally against the landlords, some of whom were driven off their land and deprived of their property by the village communes (*mirs*). Some later returned, others accepted defeat and sold off their estates. In general, order was restored gradually during 1906–7.

The government was able eventually to overcome the revolutionary movement for two reasons. Firstly, because the army, on the whole, remained loyal (despite considerable unrest in the navy). Secondly, because the government made concessions to the demands of the *zemstvos* and professional associations for a constitutional monarchy. At the height of the October strike, the emperor issued a manifesto promising civil liberties for all his subjects, and the establishment of a genuine legislative assembly elected by all classes of the population. These promises went far to satisfy the demands of the newly forming liberal political parties, which had hitherto supported the workers' and peasants' movement. Witte, the new prime minister, was nevertheless unable to draw any of the liberals into his cabinet, which had, therefore, to be made up of bureaucrats. The government was simultaneously having to crush the revolution and promote new political structures dependent on popular participation. As the elections to the first parliament (*duma*) were taking place, involving most of the population, police and officials were fining newspapers, closing trades union branches, flogging peasants, exiling recalcitrant workers, and standing by while pogroms devastated Jewish quarters in the western cities. The death penalty was frequently applied, especially under Witte's successor, Stolypin. It is not surprising that government and duma found it difficult to co-operate. Both the first (1906) and the second (1907) dumas were dissolved within a few months of meeting. The parliamentary majority, centring on the radical liberal Kadet Party (so called from the initials KD for con-

stitutional democrats), constantly denounced governmental violence and lawlessness in the repression of the revolution and called for a large-scale compulsory expropriation of land in favour of the peasants. The government could not accept this, but Stolypin did not abandon the idea of parliaments altogether. Instead, he altered the electoral law in June 1907 to reduce the voting strength of workers, peasants and non-Russian nationalities in favour of the nobility.

In the third duma (1907–12) the focal position was held by the Union of 17 October (the date of the imperial manifesto of 1905), which was committed to working with the government for reform in the agrarian field, civil rights, education, workers' insurance, justice and local government. Stolypin's agrarian reform, passed irregularly under emergency decree in 1906, was endorsed by them. It dealt with the peasant land shortage by facilitating the break-up of the *mir*. Those peasants who wanted to leave the countryside could now do so without hindrance, while those who wanted independent smallholdings could demand their share of the communal land as private property. The reform was only in operation effectively for less than a decade. During this time, some 10 per cent of all households transferred to smallholdings, but in the central, and most crowded and poverty-stricken, regions of European Russia, communal landholding proved very durable.

The nobility, which had supported Stolypin's agrarian reform, opposed him on a number of other issues where they felt their interests or that of the monarchy threatened, and they used their dominant position in the upper house, the 'state council', where many of the reform measures adopted in the duma were blocked. Stolypin was assassinated in 1911 in mysterious circumstances that suggest the possible complicity of his own security police. If the duma had few successful reforms to its credit, it did change enormously the climate of Russian politics by bringing official abuses out into the open, and by forcing public discussion of contentious issues.

From 1912 there was a resurgence of the workers' movement following the massacre of protesters at the Lena gold mines in Siberia. Ultimately, this led to the erection of barricades and to street fighting in St Petersburg on the eve of the First World War. *G. A. H.*

Revolutionary Russian ladies exiled to Siberia in 1905: Gitzenko, Izerekaya, Fialka, Shrolnik, Spiridonova and Izmailovich. Inset: The slaughtered in the Lena gold fields, 1912

New Perceptions

The decade and a half preceding the outbreak of the First World War was possibly the most prolific and concentrated in artistic and scientific innovation that the world had ever seen. Everything that is 'modern' about 20th-century art, style and thought was already on the scene by the summer of 1914. A new architecture of functional forms constructed from industrial materials – steel, sheet glass, reinforced concrete – had appeared. Louis H. Sullivan in Chicago (1904) and Auguste Perret in Paris (1903) had built concrete-framed, multi-storey blocks. In central Europe Walter Gropius had designed the Fagus factory (1913) and Adolf Loos the cube-like Steiner House (1911) in Vienna. The 1914 exhibition at Cologne of the group of German industrial designers called the 'Werkbund' presented a model factory (by Gropius and Adolf Meyer), which, with its curved glass walls and clean, structural lines, could have been lifted from the film set of *Things to Come*. Le Corbusier, in the same year, published his design for a standard construction module for houses and flats, the Dom-Ino. Cubism, in the hands of the Paris avant-garde – Picasso, Braque, Juan Gris – had between 1905 and 1910 given painting and sculpture a completely new direction. Experiments in Munich and elsewhere in central Europe resulted in the unheard-of development of abstract painting. Wassily Kandinsky painted his first entirely non-figurative watercolour in 1910. The antics of the publicity-conscious 'futurists' around Marinetti in 1909–10 celebrated the beauty of machine forms and functional industrial design.

Debussy's innovative tone poem *La Mer* was heard in 1905, and the key compositions of 20th-century music – the atonal unpredictability of Arnold Schönberg's *Pierrot Lunaire* (1912) and the harsh primitiveness of Igor Stravinsky's *Rite of Spring* (1913) – followed each other with sensational effect in consecutive years. Syncopated ragtime had permeated American entertainment music by the time of the St Louis Fair of 1904. Piano-rolls and travelling bands carried it to the ballrooms and *thé dansants* of Europe. By 1914 young people in Western society were dancing to the foxtrot. In literature, 1913 saw both the first publication of Guillaume Apollinaire's technical experiments with poetry in *Alcools* – the printed letters on the page being used to create evocative shapes and associations – and the appearance of the first of the 16 volumes of Marcel Proust's *A la recherche du temps perdu*, a vast project that instead of sticking – as novels were still supposed to do – to telling an entertaining story, embarked the reader on a capricious stream of consciousness in the recall of the author's past experiences.

In science, 1900 was a turning point. Following the publication in that year of Max Planck's quantum theory in physics, all previous work – from Newton to the end of the 19th century – was to become known as 'classical' physics. 'Modern' physics quickly made giant strides. The highly increased accuracy of measurement at both the microscopic and the astronomic scales, made possible by late-19th-century technology, had disclosed unforeseen discrepancies as against the predictions of classical physics. In 1905 Albert Einstein published a paper in which, applying the quantum theory, he propounded a 'special theory of relativity' – a complex mathematical explanation of the riddles posed by the evidence from physics and astrophysics. Einstein's theories (which he continued to de-

velop, publishing his 'general theory of relativity' in 1915) on the fundamental relationship between matter, mass and energy came to be understood in ways that had far-reaching philosophical and technological consequences. One of the latter, of course, was 20th-century mankind's unique achievement: the making of nuclear bombs.

Thus, by 1914, behind a façade of triumphant continuity with the fin-de-siècle, late-Edwardian world, with its confident values and opulent social show, a quite new world of perception and analysis was already in existence.

If for the educated élite, 'modernism' in every area of creativity was shortly to become a weapon for fighting the pre-1914 establishment, there were, for the newly literate masses, other influences at work that were changing public perceptions of what was happening in the world. The new mass-circulation press brought current events closer to their readers, while the last major shrinking of physical distances – by air travel – was taking place in a rush. The first developable powered aircraft was flown by the Wright brothers only in 1903, yet by 1910 there was a flourishing aviation industry in France, and by 1913, in technologically backward Russia, Igor Sikorski had built and flown giant four-engined military biplanes.

By 1905 five per cent of Americans were using the telephone, and Marconi's 'wireless telegraphy' had become commonplace for ship-to-shore communication. With the patenting of the Armstrong circuit in 1913, long-range radio reception became feasible.

Albert Einstein in about 1905

To the instantaneous – or at least, overnight – publication of world news *via* the telegraph was added the transmission of photographs by wire. In the illustrated daily press, which had started to appear in America and Europe in the 1890s, photographers had totally superseded illustrators and engravers by 1910. Photo-journalism in weekly magazines was first developed by the efficient German printing and publishing industry in Leipzig. Expanding in the home market created by Bismarck's new Reich, magazine publishing gradually shifted to the nearby capital, Berlin. By 1914 German magazines had established the punchy style of journalism that was to become familiar in English, two decades later, in *Life* and *Picture Post*.

Movies were familiar entertainment in the early years of the 20th century, and with them there appeared newsreels, recording important state occasions. By 1914 millions of citizens in the advanced Western countries had got to know the mannerisms of their own and foreign countries' leaders on the silent screen. Film of battleships steaming in line ahead through heavy seas excited British audiences with patriotism, and impressed foreign or backward nations with a majestic image of British naval power. Political attitudes of the masses were for the first time being moulded through moving pictures, an opportunity that governments were slower to grasp than press lords and revolutionaries.

As great events do not happen daily, newspapers needed filling, while they grew in extent and number. Personal stories, gossip and crime-reporting were found to be the circulation builders. The telephone made the civilized world a private club for the pressman.

In most leading nations the newspaper-reading public had decisive voting rights. Up to 1914 it had not yet grown cynical about what the papers say. The special correspondent's despatch, the evidence of the camera, which 'cannot lie', the resounding phrases of an editorial column – all seemed to warrant truth and responsibility. Fast-moving in its search for interest stories and in its competition for readers, the press had become a major social and political weapon in national and international affairs. Profits for the press came through selling advertising space, and the winners of the circulation battles won the advertising prizes. Sensationalism was stepped up as a result. The techniques of advertising were themselves used in news presentation. Headlines read like advertising slogans, and politicians laboured to say something that would make a good headline. Those politicians who had the ear of the popular press could swing public opinion, and a new kind of journalist-politician was a typical product of the time. President Theodore Roosevelt was one adept; another was the aspiring young Winston S. Churchill, making a name with his reports from the battlefields of the imperial frontiers before entering Parliament in 1900. *B. L. M.*

Above: newsreel cameramen await the Kaiser, 1913
Right: German home movies poster, 1913

The Last Summer

Grey and the British Position

Around 1900, British naval supremacy and a European balance of power were considered the keys to British prosperity and security. Germany became Britain's greatest rival in only a couple of decades, and Britain sought to contain her by understandings with France (1904) and Russia (1907). Just as the Anglo-Japanese alliance (1902) had been designed to minimize the possibility of British involvement in Far Eastern conflicts, so these friendly arrangements gave Britain greater security in areas of long-standing friction with France (Egypt) and Russia (Persia and India). Britain was enabled to concentrate her fleet nearer home, giving the French added confidence and emphasizing to Germany Britain's refusal to be bullied by a programme of battleship-building. It was not anti-German feeling, widespread in the Foreign Office and the services, that dominated Sir Edward Grey, the foreign secretary from 1905 to 1916. He had authorized military conversations with France but had always refused guarantees as to whether or on what terms Britain would support France in a war with Germany. This attempt to restrain possible French impetuousness may have been unwise, but it paralleled his efforts between 1912 and 1914 to ease tension by negotiating with Germany – over Persia and the Portuguese colonies. He also worked to resolve Great Power disputes on matters not directly involving Britain. Assuming that any British military engagement on the Continent would be small, and that any Anglo-German conflict would be naval, military planning had centred on creating a small British Expeditionary Force (BEF) for rapid dispatch to aid a Continental ally, while naval expansion was undertaken from 1908 onwards. Fleet dispositions and the military conversations may have created a moral obligation for Britain to aid France if Germany attacked without provocation, but Britain's only definite commitment – partly by treaty, but largely for security reasons – was to Belgium's neutrality. This the Cabinet confirmed on 2 August 1914. Germany's invasion of Belgium provided the ostensible justification for British entry into the war on France's side. *A. N. P.*

Sarajevo

Serbia's victories in the Balkan wars against Turkey in 1912 and against Bulgaria in 1913 increased not only her territory but also her ambitions. These were now directed towards absorbing the predominantly Slav areas of Austria–Hungary (Bosnia, Croatia, Slovenia) within a greater Serbia. The Serbians increased their anti-Habsburg and pan-Serbian propaganda within the empire. Many Austrian officials, including Leopold von Berchtold, the Austro-Hungarian foreign minister (1912–15), feared that unless Austria–Hungary acted decisively against her vexatious neighbour, she would face the prospect of the eventual collapse of her multi-national and unstable empire.

The opportunity for Austrian action was provided by the assassination of the heir of the Austro-Hungarian throne, the Archduke Franz Ferdinand, on the morning of Sunday, 28 June 1914 by a Bosnian terrorist, Gavrilo Prinčip, during an official visit by the Archduke to Sarajevo, the capital of Austria's recently annexed and unruly province of Bosnia. Prinčip and his co-conspirators were given support by Serbian army and customs officers, but the Serbian government was not involved in the plot.

German forebodings, spring 1913: the forces of life plead against the dark god of winter and war
Right: Visible proof of Britain's security and world power – the fleet reviewed at Spithead, 1914

Berchtold needed the approval of the German and Hungarian governments before he could move against Serbia. German support for Austria was essential if Russia came to the assistance of her protégé, Serbia. The German government feared that unless Austria–Hungary took a firm stand against Serbia, Austria would be doomed as a great power, and that if the Habsburg Empire collapsed as a result of Serbian-backed internal convulsions, Germany would, as a result, lose her only reliable ally on the Continent. Indeed, the chief of the German general staff since 1906, Helmuth von Moltke, hoped that a Russo-German war would ensue in view of Germany's alarm about the increase in Russian military strength. He considered that a German victory would be more likely to result in 1914 than in a war undertaken later. Of course, Germany was taking an even greater gamble, since under the Schlieffen plan Russian mobilization must lead to the immediate invasion of France by Germany through Belgium, which, in turn, might result in British intervention under the treaty of 1839 guaranteeing Belgian neutrality. On 5 July the German emperor, Wilhelm II, promised Austria that German support would be forthcoming.

During this period Berchtold struggled to convince his colleague in the Dual Monarchy, the Hungarian prime minister, Count Stephen Tisza, of the need for immediate Austro-Hungarian action against Serbia. Tisza was worried about the prospect of Russian intervention, but he gave way on 14 July, mainly under strong German pressure. He insisted that the turbulent Serbs should not be annexed by Austria, but either divided among other Balkan neighbours, or reduced to an Austro-Hungarian satellite state. A 48-hour ultimatum was presented to Serbia on 24 July, containing not only demands for guarantees of future Serbian good behaviour towards Austria–Hungary, but also for Austrian police collaboration within Serbia in investigating and punishing those officials implicated in the assassination plot. No sovereign state could accede to such a demand, which would have amounted to placing itself under Austrian tutelage. Serbia's reply was conciliatory, accepting all but the last demand, but Berchtold rejected it and declared war on Serbia on 28 July.

Throughout the crisis Germany had been pressing Austria to present the ultimatum quickly. By 24 July European indignation about the assassination had subsided. Furthermore, Russia was faced on 28 July with the stark choice between abandoning Serbia to her fate, and a war with Germany as well as Austria, unless Austria agreed to a compromise that would maintain Serbia's independence and territorial integrity. But Austria would not draw back and, after some hesitation by the Russian emperor, Nicholas II, Russia proclaimed general mobilization to begin on 1 August. This precipitated a simultaneous German mobilization. A German ultimatum to St Petersburg to demobilize her army or face war with Germany, and a German demand that France remain neutral in the event of a Russo-German conflict were, as Berlin anticipated, alike rejected.

On 2 August Germany declared war on Russia and, after making false accusations of French violations of the German frontier, declared war on France the next day. An ultimatum to Belgium on 2 August to allow the unimpeded passage of German troops across her territory into France was rejected by Brussels, also on 3 August. Belgium appealed to Britain for support, and this resulted in the British ultimatum to Germany to respect Belgian neutrality. When German troops entered Belgium on 4 August, Britain declared war on Germany. Ironically, Austria–Hungary did not declare war on Russia until 6 August (despite German appeals to her to do so), in the vain hope of occupying Serbia before becoming involved in fighting on the Russian front.   *M. L. D.*

Franz Ferdinand and his wife enter the car in which they will die, Sarajevo, 28 June 1914

THE FIRST WORLD WAR

The war of 1914–18 can be called a world war only because countries in every continent were legally at war. Nearly all the fighting took place in Europe among European powers. Neither the United States nor Japan was heavily engaged. The main US effect on the war was to make hopeless a German continuation of the war into 1919; that of Japan was peripheral. It was a European great war and its effects were felt in Europe.

The war lasted much longer and was much more murderous than governments and soldiers expected when it began. None of the European countries involved would have gone to war if they could have foretold the consequences. So far from victory being won by a series of quick and decisive manoeuvres in the autumn of 1914, slow attrition generated protracted bloodshed on every front. Countries won or lost according

Winston Churchill

David Lloyd George

to the size of the population they could mobilize, the extent of their industrial resources, and the spirit of endurance and self-sacrifice they could induce in their serving men, rather than through any brilliant strokes by military masterminds. One effect was the suffering caused by sudden death and lingering injury. Everywhere in Europe death destroyed expectations and stunted the lives of survivors. Above all, large numbers of women were condemned to lonely infertility. Among nations where the falling birth-rate was already reducing the size of the active population, losses of the war made dangerous gaps in the productive part of the people – an effect most evident in France.

Compulsory military service in varying forms had been familiar in every European country except Britain: the war caused its extension, even in Britain, to compulsory participation in mass slaughter. Simultaneously, governments had to attempt the organization of economic life for war. Hence the scope of governmental power and the extent of state interference in private life was greatly increased.

Governments had to persuade large numbers of their subjects that it was sensible for them to risk injury and death. The easiest way was to give them a high moral purpose, to argue that the enemy was evil or that the war was to defend liberty or to end all wars. One result was to make negotiated peace settlements between equals impossible, so extending the slaughter yet again. Another bribe sometimes appeared: warriors would win a better life at home. The war aroused hope for prosperity at home and peace abroad.   *R. A. C. P.*

Woodrow Wilson

Field Marshal Hindenburg and General Ludendorff

Stalemate in the West

The Schlieffen Plan

The failure of the plan devised by the then German chief of general staff in 1906, Alfred Count von Schlieffen, determined the whole nature of the war on the Western Front for the next four years. The object of the plan was the overwhelming of France in the six weeks before Germany switched her armies eastward to deal with Russia. The idea was to make the main thrust through Belgium, wheel down the Channel coast and swing round to encircle Paris from the west. The German centre and left wing were deliberately left weak in the hope (fulfilled in 1914) that the French would attack there and so help close the trap behind them. It was a bold gamble dependent on first-class communications, an iron-nerved commander and luck. Apart from the French reaction, none of these conditions was fulfilled.

The German right wing, numbering some 750,000 troops, outnumbered the French opposite them by three to one, but the British Expeditionary Force (BEF) of 120,000 was fortuitously well placed to fight delaying actions at Mons in Belgium on 23 August and Le Cateau on 26 August which prevented the French from being outflanked. Though beaten in the frontier battles, the French, Belgian and British forces retreated towards a good road and rail network, whereas the Germans weakened as they outpaced their supplies in the scorching summer heat.

By the end of August the German chief of general staff, the 66-year-old 'younger' Moltke (nephew of the great field-marshal of Bismarck's day), was approaching nervous and physical collapse, and failed to control his Army commanders. When the commander on the extreme right wing, General August von Kluck, turned south-east on 30 August Moltke did not intervene. The grandiose aims of the Schlieffen Plan were abandoned. The French commander-in-chief, Joffre, ordered an about-turn and counter-attacked on 6 September. Though the Allies failed to exploit their opportunity on the River Marne to the full, the Germans began to retreat on 9 September to take up a strong defensive position behind the River Aisne. The Germans' only hope for a quick victory now lay in outflanking the Allies to the north but neither side had the mobility to win this ponderous 'race to the sea'. By the end of the year, after fierce fighting around Ypres which virtually annihilated the original BEF, the rival armies faced each other in shallow defensive lines all the way from the Swiss frontier to the English Channel. Both began to entrench and prepare for an unexpected and long war of siege. Although the Schlieffen Plan had failed, the Germans had won great advantages. Virtually the whole of Belgium and nearly a tenth of France was in German hands including 80 per cent of the French coal industry and practically all her iron-ore resources. Germany could therefore afford to strengthen her defences and let the Allies do most of the attacking while she concentrated in 1915 in knocking out Russia. In fact, so superior were the Germans' defensive tactics that, despite persistent Allied offensives, the lines of the great siege never changed as much as ten miles until March 1918.

Trench warfare

Only gradually and at great cost in lives did the Allied commanders realize in 1915 that, lacking open flanks, it

was impossible to break through simply by accumulating more men and guns at the selected point. Ammunition was then inadequate in quantity and quality, the accumulation of material forfeited surprise and it proved to be impossible to break through quickly and deeply enough to prevent the enemy from rushing up his reserves and counter-attacking. The battles in the spring of 1915 – Neuve-Chapelle, Aubers Ridge and Festubert (and Loos in the autumn) – also underlined the inadequacies of communications since higher commanders were dependent on vulnerable telephone lines and runners. The generals could not keep abreast of conditions at the front and hence failed to direct reinforcements to the right place when fleeting opportunities did occur. Instead, the gruesome tactics of attrition were adopted: faith was placed in killing more of the enemy than one lost; reserves were used to repeat attacks that had failed; and ground was never willingly yielded.

Whereas the Germans developed sophisticated defences and defensive tactics based on holding the front trenches thinly but with support from machine guns and artillery, the Allies discovered no new means to break *through*, rather than merely *into*, the enemy trench system. Various methods were employed using existing weapons, including heavier and longer artillery preparations, and the 'creeping barrage' by which gunfire lifted in stages just in front of the advancing infantry. Unfortunately, the communications available simply did not allow precise

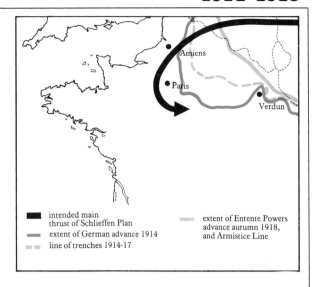

intended main
thrust of Schlieffen Plan

extent of German advance 1914

line of trenches 1914-17

extent of Entente Powers
advance autumn 1918,
and Armistice Line

Left: War artist C. W. R. Nevinson's image of the costly horror of trench warfare in Flanders – 'The Harvest of Battle', in which British and German casualties are mingled (detail)

The Germans' last fling

The Germans were the first to break the trench deadlock in their March 1918 offensive, which nearly succeeded in taking Amiens and driving a wedge between the British and French armies. This short-lived success was particularly impressive because the attackers had only a handful of tanks. They relied instead on exploiting fog and smoke, and used skilful infiltration tactics by small highly-trained commando groups. In the remaining months of the war the Allies also displayed considerable skill in combining infantry, artillery and tanks aided by virtually complete control in the air. The victory at Amiens in August, spearheaded by about 400 British tanks, and the breach of the Hindenburg Line in September, were particularly impressive. Thus the war ended in November 1918 with the tank again in the ascendant but with its full potential far from fulfilled. *B. J. B.*

timetables to be followed. Air observation from balloons and aircraft also greatly improved but the combination of wire, deep trench and pillbox systems, machine guns and supporting artillery remained impregnable.

The difficulty of breaking through into open country was nowhere better illustrated than in the British Somme offensive (from July to November 1916) which was undertaken to relieve German pressure on Verdun. When the offensive had already got bogged down in mud the first tanks were used (in mid-September) but only about 40 were available, and these early types were clumsy, slow and liable to breakdown. Their impact was consequently limited and their revolutionary potential not grasped by the High Command. There was even less opportunity for the cavalry, although it remained assembled in readiness until the end.

Apart from the detonation of enormous mines under the German front trenches in June at the Messines Ridge, 1917 was characterized by the continuation of attrition methods in the Passchendaele campaign (from July to November) in which both sides suffered losses of about 200,000 men for the exchange of a few square miles of what looked like a lunar landscape. The British used tanks more imaginatively at Cambrai in November, but failed to occupy the ground gained sufficiently quickly and were driven back to their original lines by fierce counterattacks.

Dismemberment of the Ottoman Empire

The Dardanelles

The Dardanelles campaign of 1915 was prompted by an urgent Russian request for a diversion to help their hard-beset forces in the Caucasus. After a purely naval operation had failed in its efforts to force the Narrows on 18 March, a hastily improvised military force comprising British, Indian, Anzac and French troops under the command of General Sir Ian Hamilton was given the task of seizing the Gallipoli Peninsula. Dramatic landings took place on 25 April at Cape Helles and Anzac Cove, while the French created a diversion at Kumkale, but the Turkish defenders – with a stiffening of German officers – managed to confine the invaders to tiny beach-heads. Siege operations reminiscent of those on the Western Front rapidly set in and persistent Allied offensives throughout the summer failed to break the Turkish lines. On 6 August Hamilton launched a second major offensive in which the Anzacs were to seize the heights of the Sari Bair Ridge assisted by a new landing at Suvla Bay. Complete surprise was achieved, progress was made on all sectors and the Anzacs briefly occupied the crest of the ridge. Unfortunately, elderly and ultra-cautious commanders wasted vital time so enabling the Turkish reserves, commanded by the brilliant Mustapha Kemal (later Kemal Atatürk), to counter-attack successfully. By the end of August the offensive had clearly failed. Hamilton was removed and an alternative theatre opened at Salonica. It was decided not to risk the hazards of winter. Ironically the withdrawal, completed in January 1916, went like clockwork. The Turks had suffered heavily but were encouraged by their remarkable success.

Mesopotamia

The Mesopotamian campaign began with the limited objective of safeguarding the Anglo-Persian oil pipeline by occupying Basra with a brigade from India. In March 1915 the British government of India decided to take the whole province of Basra with the capture of Baghdad as the ultimate objective. Although Kūt-el-Amāra was taken by a skilful manoeuvre on 2 October the advance was already putting a strain on the precarious river supply line. At Ctesiphon, 16 miles south of Baghdad, 20,000 Turks awaited Sir John Nixon's 12,000 veterans in a well-prepared position. In the battle on 22 November the British lost about 4500 troops – only half as many as the Turks – but the field commander, General Townshend, decided to retreat to Kūt. There he was besieged and the Turks, aided by rain, mud and flooding, defeated all attempts to relieve him. When even an airdrop of food failed, starvation forced Townshend to capitulate on 29 April 1916. Nearly 10,000 troops entered captivity; less than a third survived Turkish brutality.

In contrast to its policy over the Dardanelles the British Government decided against cutting its losses. The excellent new commander, Sir Stanley Maude, took no chances. With a numerical superiority of four to one and supported by a flotilla of river boats he out-manoeuvred the Turks and entered Baghdad in March 1917. Maude died of cholera in November 1917 and it was left to his successor to drive the Turks from the remainder of the country by the Armistice.

Palestine

After a Turkish attempt to attack the Suez Canal in January 1915 had been easily defeated, the British assembled a garrison of nearly 300,000 troops in Egypt and prepared to invade Palestine. By the end of 1916 El Arish and the whole Sinai Peninsula was in British hands. Under pressure from Britain to secure a 'political victory' Sir Archibald Murray bungled two attempts to take Gaza and was replaced by the dynamic cavalry commander, Sir Edmund Allenby. The latter executed a bold encircling manoeuvre on 31 October 1917 to seize Beersheba and isolate the Gaza garrison. Jerusalem, too, was occupied by the end of the year.

Meanwhile, the numerous Turkish garrisons east of the River Jordan were mercilessly harassed by Arab irregulars under the inspiring leadership of Colonel T. E. Lawrence. In his culminating battle of Megiddo, Allenby entrusted to the Arabs the cutting of the rail junction at Deraa which would sever communications with Damascus. On 19 September 1918, vastly superior ground and air forces overwhelmed the dispirited Turks; the cavalry cut off retreat by covering 70 miles in 34 hours; and the Arabs not only took Deraa but also massacred an isolated Turkish army. The fall of Damascus on 2 October heralded the end of Turkish resistance, her capitulation being hastened by Bulgaria's surrender a few days earlier. Turkey's military defeats resulted in a harsh post-war settlement in which she was deprived of virtually all her territory in the Balkans and the Middle East.   *B. J. B.*

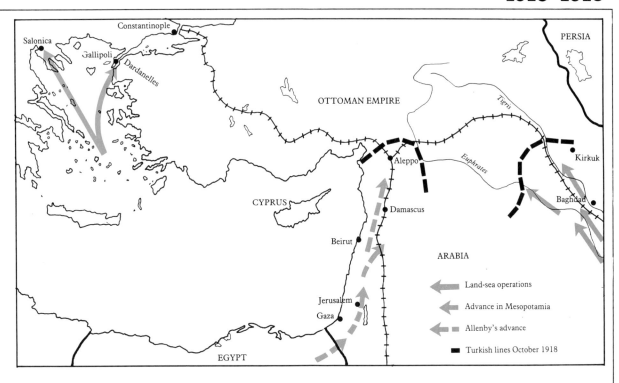

Salonica
Constantinople
Gallipoli
Dardanelles
PERSIA
OTTOMAN EMPIRE
Tigris
Aleppo
Kirkuk
Euphrates
Baghdad
CYPRUS
Damascus
Beirut
ARABIA
Jerusalem
Gaza
EGYPT

Land-sea operations
Advance in Mesopotamia
Allenby's advance
Turkish lines October 1918

Anzacs simulating an attack for the camera at Gallipoli, 1915

Colonel T. E. Lawrence in his post-war incognito of Aircraftman Shaw

Italy Comes In   1915   The Easter Rising

Despite her treaty obligations to Germany and Austria–Hungary under the Triple Alliance, Italy intervened in the war in May 1915 on the side of the Entente. The decision, justified publicly on nationalist grounds as continuing the struggle against the old enemy, Austria, was prompted more by Italy's extreme economic dependence on raw materials supplied through the straits of Gibraltar and the Suez canal – both routes controlled by the British. Any other choice threatened to prove disastrous for the Italian economy. The promises of territorial concessions in the Trentino, Alto Adige (South Tyrol), and on the Adriatic coast made to the Italians under the Treaty of London (1915) served to clinch the change of alliance.

With the war, divisions within Italy became more acute. The period of neutrality prior to May 1915 saw bitter clashes between a nationalist minority intent on forcing intervention and a Socialist Party opposed to intervention in what was judged to be a war between competing imperialisms. As the war dragged on, the Socialist attitude – summed up in the phrase 'neither support nor sabotage' – aroused enormous resentment among moderate and middle class opinion, which was prepared to accept 'patriotic' appeals, and by 1917 the Socialist Party was increasingly subjected to vitriolic attacks against its alleged 'defeatism'. Yet, for the ordinary soldiers, many of them peasants, the Socialist position earned considerable sympathy, and the hatred of the trenches and the officers was slowly transformed into a hatred of the political class that had taken Italy into the war. Low morale among the troops resulted in the rout of the Italian army at Caporetto in November 1917, a humiliation only partly compensated for by the success of the Italians (bolstered by French and British units) against the Austrians at Vittorio Veneto in the final days of the conflict.

On the home front the needs of the war produced an unprecedented expansion in many sectors of Italian industry. Just as important, the exceptional conditions of the war greatly reinforced the position of the industrialists *vis-à-vis* the state. In many cases, industrialists were taken into government and responsibility for allocation of contracts and for pricing passed directly into their hands. The state assumed responsibility for the provision of raw materials for industry and legislated to impose rigid discipline among the labour force in the factories and to control wages. The favourable conditions created for many of the major industrialists by the virtual symbiosis of state and economic interests would be recalled with nostalgia during the 'red' years of 1919 and 1920.   *P. R. C.*

A scene from the film 'A Farewell to Arms'

In the 60 years leading up to 1916, Irish Nationalist sentiment and party organization had grown, encouraged by the heightened patriotic feelings of Irishmen abroad, especially in North America, and by the willingness of liberal-minded Englishmen to concede to the Irish a distinct ethnic or cultural identity which deserved extensive institutional recognition. This Nationalist movement was stimulated by, and in its turn periodically encouraged, the violent tradition of Catholic agrarian peasant protest against an élite of landlords whose religious and economic power was seen to depend on British rule. This violent strain in Irish Nationalism was greatly enhanced by the crisis of 1912–14. Only the threat of violence by Ulstermen and British Unionists had seemed to stand in the way of Irish self-rule, and early in 1914 it was seen as having been successful in diverting the policy of a British government. No greater incentive could have been given to Irishmen to follow the same path, and Irish Volunteer forces grew rapidly. The corollary of this was the declining importance of the Irish Nationalists' parliamentary wing. As ever, only the Liberals could deliver anything the Irish wanted. Failing that, they had no constitutional alternative. The Home Rule Act of 1914, at John Redmond's insistence, did not exclude Ulster, but in suspending its operation, Herbert Asquith also renounced for ever the use of force against Ulster. Seeing the drift of events, an extreme minority in the Volunteer movement challenged Redmond's leadership, splitting the movement between moderates and irreconcilables. It was from among the latter that the rebels of 1916 were drawn. They sought German aid, and, as drilling continued in Ireland, Sir Roger Casement tried with poor results to recruit troops from among Allied prisoners of war in Germany. Easter Sunday 1916 was the symbolic date set for the rising, but when the Germans failed to put the promised arms ashore, Volunteer plans were cancelled. On Easter Monday, however, a small force seized the General Post Office in Dublin and proclaimed an Irish Republic. It lasted five days. Its occurrence in wartime, Volunteer negotiations with Germany, and the fact that (despite disillusionment with Britain's handling of the Home Rule issue) the rising did not win support elsewhere in Ireland, all encouraged the British to suppress it very harshly. Casement was tried and hanged for treason, the Volunteer leaders, with the exception of Eamonn de Valera (who was American-born), were shot. The Rising had failed, but its results were lasting. The British government considered implementing Home Rule straightaway, and Lloyd George negotiated with the two sides, devising a settlement whereby 26 Irish counties would receive Home Rule at once, and the six counties of Ulster would remain for reconsideration after the war. Certain Conservatives then pressed for its revision, and the government weakly agreed. Redmond understandably refused to negotiate further, and thus by its own actions the British government ended the Nationalist parliamentary tradition. As British rule continued in Dublin, Irishmen re-evaluated the Rising, and many concluded that the Republicans had after all taken the only hopeful course.   *A. N. P.*

Above: Captured Irish Volunteers under escort, 1916. Right: Prisoners in Richmond Barracks. Inset: Eamonn de Valera speaking, 1917

America In, Russia Out

America enters the war

At the outset of hostilities in Europe, America's entry seemed unlikely, but her neutrality was increasingly strained by the war at sea. In February 1915, in response to Britain's draconian blockade policy, Germany proclaimed the seas around her enemy a war zone which neutral ships would enter at their peril. On 7 May a U-boat torpedoed the great Cunard passenger liner *Lusitania* off southern Ireland without warning. Germany was obliged to modify her submarine offensive in the face of President Woodrow Wilson's anger at the loss of more than 100 American lives. The offensive was suspended altogether in April 1916 after further American warnings. Early in 1917, however, Germany's military leaders, Paul von Hindenburg and Erich Ludendorff, successfully pressed for renewal of unrestricted submarine warfare, gambling that British merchant-shipping losses would force her to surrender before American participation became effective. In the short run the policy promised success as monthly statistics of tonnage sunk rose sharply.

However, America's declaration of war on the Central Powers in April 1917 at once affected the war at sea. The cooperation of the Royal Navy converted the latter's blockade into a complete stranglehold which was no longer hampered by respect for neutrals. Britain belatedly introduced convoys in April 1917 and by September the addition of American destroyers enabled transatlantic shipping to be escorted for the whole voyage in both directions. American ships also played a crucial part in the anti-submarine offensive. Germany seldom had as many as 50 submarines operational at one time and her offensive could not be sustained against two major navies employing new anti-submarine devices and tactics.

The impact of America's entry on the land war was longer delayed because her army had to be recruited, trained and transported, and even then she depended on her allies for much of the necessary equipment. The problem was whether America's armies could be deployed on the Western Front in time to offset Russia's defection, which seemed imminent from mid-1917. Another delaying factor was the Americans' nationalist determination to enter battle as an independent army, but in the crisis of March 1918 their commander, General John Pershing, relaxed this demand, stipulating only that they should fight as complete divisions. By July 1918, seven American divisions were in action with 14 more in reserve. More impressively, from April 1918, 300,000 Americans were arriving in France every month: the longer the war lasted the more formidable they would become in contrast to the waning effort of the European belligerents. The German generals realized that they must win by mid-1918 or never, hence their persistence with the offensive long after its momentum had been lost. In mid-September the Americans, in their first battle as an independent army, erased the notorious St Mihiel salient. Inexperience caused them heavy casualties, but it was clear to both sides that this 'blood transfusion' signified ultimate victory for the entente.

B. J. B.

The Eastern Front

The Russian Army suffered tremendous reverses in 1914 and 1915, but thereafter recovered and held its own on the

keep these off the U.S.A
Buy more LIBERTY BONDS

Charlie Chaplin on a Liberty Bond drive. Inset: An anti-German poster with the same message

Eastern Front between the Baltic and the Carpathians. War production was put on a sounder basis in the rear, but Russia's social structure was under severe strain. Peasants were mobilized in millions, given weapons and taught how to use them, while being for the first time concentrated in huge numbers where revolutionary propaganda could reach them. The disruption of agricultural production and transport led to inflation and shortages in the cities. The liberal press ruthlessly exposed corruption and incompetence, and even insinuated that the imperial family (the empress was German-born), under the influence of the unorthodox 'holy man' Gregor Rasputin, did not support the war effort.

The February Revolution of 1917 (which occurred in March, by the Gregorian calendar) began in the food queues of the capital, Petrograd, as St Petersburg had been renamed in 1914. It was not inspired or even supported by the army, the grievances of the soldiers being almost entirely military. In view of Russian loss of life (over a million casualties in 1914 alone) and poor leadership, it is remarkable that the army was still fighting in 1917, yet the soldiers were prepared to fight on, provided that conditions (including wretched food and clothing, poor leave arrangements and brutal treatment by officers) were improved, and futile offensives were called off. There was a strong 'front-line' mentality, which gave soldiers little sympathy for any civilians, even if they were revolutionary factory workers. On the other hand it is remarkable how quickly Russia's élites were persuaded that the emperor, Nicholas II, and indeed the Romanov dynasty, must abdicate.   *G. A. H./B. J. B.*

Above: The baleful hold of the late Grigory Rasputin over the tsar's household – the cartoon appeared in a bourgeois magazine after the revolution

The dough-boys 'cross the pond' to the European theatre of war in their tens of thousands during 1918 (painting by Thomas Derrick)

The American Revolution marked the emergence of the New World that was destined to play a vital role in the future of the old centre of Western civilization, Europe – not least by its decisive intervention in two wars. The French Revolution led to the consolidation of middle class dominance in Europe and to the establishment of liberal principles of government. The Russian Revolution in 1917 – the collapse of the Romanov dynasty, followed eight months later by the seizure of power by the Bolsheviks from the weak, idealistic, incompetent and inexperienced liberals and socialists – marked the beginning of a new trend in the destinies of mankind.

The Russia that emerged was a mass society, in which the state controlled the economy, and a small self-appointed élite manipulated the destinies of the population in accordance with a dogmatic view of what was the right course to pursue. To challenge this official outlook became increasingly dangerous for the individual. In return for conformity, the population was given the opportunity for strictly organized and controlled democratic participation. The Soviet peoples were also provided with improved material conditions, although at a heavy cost in life and liberty.

The new pattern of manipulated mass democracy invented by Lenin has since been imitated in many parts of the world. There is, of course, an obverse to the coin. On the one hand, in those territories that were for long under colonial rule, new, nominally independent,

RUSSIAN REVOLUTION

countries have emerged. On the other hand, the older industrial societies of western Europe have witnessed considerable improvements in social justice and in the material conditions of the underprivileged class. This development must, in part at all events, be attributed both to fear of revolution and to the results of Soviet propaganda. For the new Bolshevik (later Communist) state proclaimed itself from the first to be the champion of the poor and oppressed everywhere – even if its practice did not always live up to its precepts so far as those actually subject to its own rule were concerned.

After 1945, the USSR emerged on the world scene as a military giant second only to the USA, with an aim – the establishment of manipulated mass democracy of the Soviet type on a world scale – that had remained constant since 1917. The extension of its influence in Europe, Africa, Asia and America, strengthened by the faith that 'history' is on the side of revolution, made this ambition look less fanciful thirty-odd years later. As against these advantages, the Soviet leaders have been faced abroad with the military and economic might of the USA and western Europe, the rivalry of Communist China and divisions among Communist Parties, and at home with national and political dissent, and persistent economic backwardness in spheres other than the military. Whatever future historians may have to record about the 20th century, they will not underestimate the influence of the Russian Revolution upon it.   *L. S.*

From February to the Death of Lenin

The downfall of the monarchy signalled the beginning of general disintegration. In cities all over Russia, the prisons were flung open, councils (*soviets*) of workers and soldiers were created, sometimes to maintain order, sometimes to exploit the economic, military and political chaos.

In the army, soldiers' committees sprang up to express the will of 'soviet democracy'. In mid-March the soviet of the capital Petrograd (ex-St Petersburg) issued its Order Number 1, stipulating that the Government's orders must not conflict with its orders, that the committees keep all arms under their authority, and that soldiers not observe distinctions of rank while off duty.

The implicit undertakings of the new government were to do better in fighting the war than the tsarist régime had done, to end the food shortage, relieve transport, satisfy the peasants' land-hunger and the workers' demands for better wages and conditions, and grant self-determination to the nationalities of the old empire. But it could do nothing without the approval of the Petrograd soviet, itself an increasingly chaotic institution.

In May, the soviet was flooded by returning professional revolutionary exiles, including Trotsky and many Bolsheviks, whose party had been led by Lenin, since his return from exile in Switzerland via Germany in April. From the moment of his return Lenin urged opposition to the Provisional Government and to the continuation of the war.

This worsened the Government's job of keeping the troops at the front, a task which from May fell upon Alexander Kerensky, the new minister for war and an orator of legendary powers.

Alexander Kerensky, last head of the provisional government of the Russian republic, photographed in the gardens of Tsarskoye Selo

Supporters of the October Revolution in Khabarovsk in the Far East demonstrate against the Allied intervention forces

Lenin the orator, sketched by Leonid Pasternak, father of the novelist Boris Pasternak (author of 'Dr Zhivago')

A major crisis occurred in July. On the 14th four liberals resigned over Kerensky's apparent concession of self-determination to the Ukrainians, which the liberals saw as pre-empting the job of the forthcoming Constituent Assembly. Simultaneously, the Russian offensive in Galicia collapsed, with the troops in full flight and utterly demoralized. On the 16th, thousands of workers, armed soldiers and sailors, poured into the streets of Petrograd shouting Bolshevik slogans for the overthrow of the Government and all power to the soviets. The Menshevik (social democrat) leadership of the soviet denounced the demonstration as dangerous to the revolution, and the mobs became violent at this soviet 'cowardice'. Lenin considered whether to lead the demonstration in a bid for power, but decided he was not strong enough to aim the mob against the Government's forces. The 'July Days' fizzled out as suddenly as they had erupted, leaving a number dead and many injured.

Kerensky now decided to charge Lenin with receiving German money to finance his defeatist campaign. Lenin fled in disguise to nearby Finland. Some Bolsheviks were arrested and the mood of the mobs turned against them. The Bolshevik Red Guards were disarmed. Kerensky, now prime minister, and his army commander, General Lavr Kornilov, resolved to make a show of strength in the capital. At the last moment, Kerensky changed his mind, fearing a coup by Kornilov, who still sent his troops towards the city. They were halted and disbanded by railway dislocation and persuasion, though not before the soviet, backed by Kerensky in a panic, had rearmed the Bolsheviks.

By late October, Kerensky's Government was impotent. Lenin was back, promising the people 'land, peace, and bread' and urging his followers to organize the armed uprising, which, under Trotsky, they launched on 7 November. The Government dissolved and Kerensky fled abroad. Next day, Lenin proclaimed that all land belonged to the people, a formula which was understood by the peasants, especially those in the army, to mean it belonged to them. Instant demobilization ensued.

Lenin next decreed that peace negotiations must begin. The Allies would not hear of it, so Lenin sought separate peace with Germany. But before making peace, Lenin had to deal with the long-awaited Constituent Assembly, elected on 25 November under pre-Bolshevik arrangements, and convoked on 18 January 1918 under the new régime. The Bolsheviks had won less than a quarter of the seats, half going to the Socialist Revolutionaries. This 'problem' was solved by the forcible dissolution of the Assembly after its first session. The 'dictatorship of the proletariat' had been installed in Russia.

Lenin had less success over peace, in exchange for which the Germans demanded a third of Russian territory in Europe. When indignant Bolsheviks urged Lenin to launch a 'revolutionary war', he pointed out that the soldiers had already voted for peace 'with their feet'. Trotsky's solution was to ignore the German demands, whereupon the Germans occupied the Ukraine. Lenin conceded defeat and signed the 'indecent' Treaty of Brest-Litovsk.

'White' (anti-Bolshevik) armies came into being in various parts of Russia in 1918 and, when Germany was finally beaten, Western forces were sent to Russia to reinforce the Whites. Until the end of 1920, civil war raged, at times coming close to extinguishing Lenin's régime. Trotsky organized the Red Army, making use of ex-tsarist officers, the powers of propaganda and ruthless coercion. The White armies were unco-ordinated, and their leaders disunited, and although neither of the Red or White armies was ever popular, the peasants felt their land less threatened by a Bolshevik victory, and in the end the Reds won.

In 1920, the Poles attempted to reconquer their historic territories in south-west Russia. They were defeated and pursued into Poland, Lenin trusting that the Polish workers would rally to the Red Flag, and even spark off the long-expected German revolution. The Polish workers rallied instead to the Polish flag and the Russians were defeated, ceding great areas of territory in the process of making peace.

Civil war and famine had ravaged the economy. To feed the Army and the factory workers, the régime had forcibly wrung produce from the peasants. Since December 1917, the régime had applied the Red Terror (through the Cheka, the Bolshevik political police) to achieve its aims. With the external and civil wars over and discontent rising among workers and soldiers over the harsh economic and political conditions, Lenin abandoned his socialist programme and introduced, through his New Economic Policy (NEP), a return to market trading. Merchants, peasants and artisans were encouraged to enrich themselves.

On the eve of his death, which occurred in January 1924, Lenin acknowledged that the system he had begun to install had recreated many of the worst features of tsarism – excessive bureaucracy with violent powers, and isolation of the government from the people. The characteristics of the old underground Bolshevik Party had become institutional traits of the new Communist system, and Lenin died disappointed, and anxious for the Party's future under its General Secretary, Joseph Stalin.   *H. S.*

Trotsky and Stalin

Lenin died without specifying who should follow him as leader of the Party, and hence, in effect, of the state. He did not think there was anyone up to the task. In a secret memorandum to the Central Committee, written at the end of 1922, he noted that Trotsky and Stalin, the two most serious contenders, each had faults – Trotsky's an inclination towards authoritarianism ('administrative methods'), and Stalin's an indifference, if not worse, towards the views and feelings of others, and the disposition to abuse his great power of patronage as general secretary of the Party. Stalin was responsible for, among other things, the recruitment and deployment of personnel throughout the apparatus, and was thus the dispenser of patronage that brought him personal allegiance.

At the 13th Party Congress, held in May 1924 after Lenin's death, Stalin's supporters agreed to suppress Lenin's 'testament', with its urgent advice that Stalin be replaced by a more tolerant, but unspecified, figure. On the contrary, the Congress retained Stalin as general secretary, together with Zinoviev and Kamenev as a collective leadership, to frustrate any attempt by Trotsky to don Lenin's mantle. The Congress also further isolated Trotsky by reviewing his past conflicts with Stalin, to which Trotsky retaliated by publishing his own account of 1917 (*The Lessons of October*), showing himself as in-dispensable to the success of the revolution. Trotsky's self-defence backfired because it implied that only he had been in harmony with Lenin, and this outraged the present leadership, which proceeded to destroy him politically.

By this time all revolutionary efforts in Europe had failed, and Trotsky's doctrine of 'permanent revolution', as the necessary condition for the survival and development of socialism in Russia, was discredited in favour of Stalin's slogan of 'socialism in one country', a more palatable ideology consistent with Russia's isolated efforts to restore her economy while still surrounded by the hostile forces of the capitalist world.

Though he proclaimed the inevitability of world revolution, Stalin asserted that only a secure, socialist USSR could help other revolutions, and, therefore, it was incumbent on the Soviet workers to build socialism in their own country first. The so-called 'left opposition' of Zinoviev and Kamenev, both identified with the policies of the Communist International (Comintern), the vehicle of world revolution, lost ground as all revolutionary efforts failed in Europe (and in 1927 in China as well), and Stalin, who had engineered a personal predominance in the Politburo, the Party's highest authority, was able to enhance his own position at the expense of his recent allies.

With Trotsky, Zinoviev and Kamenev defeated, Stalin

During the power struggle – Stalin with friends (left to right) Ordzonikidze, Kalinin, Kuibyshev, Felix Kon, on the temporary Lenin Mausoleum, November 1926

turned his attention to his rivals on the so-called 'right', of whom the most significant was Bukharin, a close and favoured comrade of Lenin and the most brilliantly intellectual of the Party leaders. Bukharin, responsible for agriculture and protagonist of Lenin's 'new economic policy', which had been designed to restore agricultural and small production through private enterprise, was now attacked by Stalin for helping the prosperous farmers – the kulaks – to survive and grow rich. This hostile class was now to be removed through the collectivization of agriculture. Collectivization would also abolish the 25 million smallholdings that since 1917 had formed Soviet agriculture, and bring the peasant population under Communist Party control. The details of collectivization had barely been discussed when, in 1928, an unexpected grain shortage gave Stalin the opportunity to accuse the kulaks of sabotage, and to order immediate, forced collectivization. Resistance by the peasants was overcome by armed force and police terror, but not before peasants throughout Russia had destroyed their crops, slaughtered their livestock and smashed their implements, acts that carried the death penalty. The resulting famine and suffering of 1932–33 were extreme, and up to 15 million peasants died, one way or another.   *H. S.*

Top right: The oppositionists (left to right) – Trotsky, Zinoviev, Radek

The genial Secretary-General of the Party among Uzbek farmers

THE INTER-WAR YEARS

Leon Blum

Between the two great wars economic instability caused political disturbance that indirectly helped to create new wars. The European war of 1914–18 broke a long and relatively stable pattern of economic growth based on the exchange of the industrial products of western Europe for the raw materials and food of the outside world. The war curtailed industrial exports during the war and increased demand for food and raw materials during and immediately after the war. Thus the less industrialized countries went through a boom, checked when European agriculture recovered. Increased production of food and raw materials led to falling world prices, which weakened the demand for industrial products. At the end of the 1920s this process worked together with a cyclical slump in the United States to set off a world depression of unprecedented scale.

Everywhere economic instability led to domestic disturbance. The effect was least in those countries that had not been defeated in the war (so that economic sufferings could not be blamed on foreigners) and in those countries where traditions of representative government were firmly established (so that governments were experienced in techniques of winning support). Britain, however, had to endure the general strike and the coal strike, the USA succumbed to the demagoguery of Franklin D.

From left to right: Baldwin, Ramsay MacDonald, Hindenburg, Franco, Stresemann, Mussolini

Roosevelt, and France suffered deep political conflicts in the 1930s. In Japan and Germany economic crises led to formidably aggressive militarisms. In Japan the increasing protectionism of the British Empire and the USA led to an armed struggle for control of markets and the raw materials and food to maintain Japan's industries and rising population; in Germany economic disaster drove the conservative classes to work with an uncontrollably fanatical exponent of racial struggle through armed conquest, Adolf Hitler.

In retrospect, the inter-war years were a brief truce. Curiously though, in the 1920s, post-war optimism remained. The world seemed to be growing more stable: Europe continued securely dominant in Asia and Africa; Chinese nationalism remained weak; Japan could be checked by Britain and the US; Africa and the Near East (except Palestine) were quiescent under British and French control. Britain and France still seemed great world powers – the US abstained from interference; Russia did not resume the path to industrialized greatness until Stalin's rule; Germany was artificially weak. Now the world dominance of France and Britain, which reached its peak in the 1920s, seems ephemeral and accidental. *R. A. C. P.*

Versailles and the Peace Conference

The decisions of the Versailles Peace Conference (January–June 1919) – with its associated treaties of Saint-Germain (Austria), Trianon (Hungary), Neuilly (Bulgaria) and Sèvres (Turkey) – were the heart of the post-First World War settlement. The major leaders involved had striven to invest its proceedings with the tone of a liberal millenium: it had been the 'war to end war', the 'war to make the world safe for democracy'. Even the smaller powers were supposed to have an important influence on decisions through their representatives on the constituent committees. But it soon became clear that hegemony lay with the 'Big Four' – the USA, Britain, France and Italy – who discussed crucial matters on their own. American military power in Europe and her creditor status made President Woodrow Wilson the most impressive single force at the outset. Wilson's objective was to stabilize Europe. To that end he did not wish to destroy completely the existence of a powerful (but not dominant) German state. Lloyd George, the British prime minister, would have preferred the same approach, but the anti-German hysteria of his own propaganda machine, culminating in the 1918 general election, had so moulded British public opinion as to make this impossible for him. The biggest obstacle for Wilson, however, was Georges Clemenceau, prime minister of the French Republic, whose priority was not the stabilization of Europe, but the security of France. In the French view, this security necessitated the destruction of German military and economic strength. Clemenceau's insistence meant that

the German clauses of the treaty were harsh. Germany was disarmed and very low limits set to her forces in future. A liberal gloss was put on this by the accompanying declaration that all other powers would shortly follow suit – which they never did. Germany was also informed that she would have to pay huge amounts of financial reparations. The motive here, significant for both British and French industrial interests, was to create a financial lever that could be pulled on if the German economy threatened to become too competitive. Ostensibly as a guarantee for these money payments, the Saar coalfield was internationalized and its production allocated to French manufacturers. In fact, the objective was to limit German economic growth by fuel shortages. France also received back Alsace-Lorraine, which she had lost in 1871.

Although Wilson did not approve of most of these measures, even he could not withstand the forces of hatred that had permeated the European democracies. But the German problem was only part of the Versailles Conference. One of Wilson's major aims was to take nationalism out of European politics. To do so he advocated the principle of self-determination, and the result was the patchwork of 'successor states' that took the place of the rambling Austro-Hungarian Empire. The Czechs and Slovaks, for example, attained statehood at this time, but the ethnic complexities of eastern Europe meant, inevitably, that large minorities remained in the various new states – Poles in German Silesia, Germans in the internationalized city of Danzig, Ukrainians in Hungary,

The victorious Allied leaders in session at the Quai d'Orsay, 6 May 1919. Left to right: Clemenceau, Wilson, Lloyd George, Orlando (sketch by Edouard Requin)

among others. The establishment of new nation-states also set the scene for an acute competition to dominate the resources of the area, which had not been nicely distributed in proportion to racial categories. Self-determination was thus the root of a new set of future troubles.

It was not only the defeated who felt aggrieved at the Conference conclusions. Italy expected to receive large territorial gains as a reward for joining the Allies, but Prime Minister V. E. Orlando was quickly reduced to protest and tears. Neither Wilson nor Lloyd George felt that the danger of a nationalist reaction in Italy was important enough to risk destabilizing Austria or the Balkans, where most of Orlando's claims lay.

Versailles was essentially concerned with European questions, but it did at points have to consider the outside world. It sought to amend the colonial system by introducing the concept of a 'mandate', a territory to be administered in trust by an imperial power whose sovereignty was, in theory, to be internationalized and vested in the League of Nations. Germany's colonies were 'mandated' to other nations: South West Africa to South Africa, Tanganyika to Britain and Western Samoa (a source of copra) to New Zealand. In the Middle East mandates were intended to help Syria, Iraq and Palestine come to terms with the end of Turkish suzerainty, but all soon developed internal complexities beyond the controls of the trusteeship system. Finally, in an important episode, the Versailles Conference was seen to embody Anglo-American racial superiority. Japan, who as one of

the Allies had emerged as the chief power in the Pacific, demanded a clause asserting the principle of racial equality. This clashed directly with the discrimination central to the economic and social policies of many European nations, above all in the essentially racialist policies of the British Dominions. Japan's proposal was turned down, and this served to alienate her from Europe.

The main Allied protagonists at the Conference were clearly out not to 'solve' problems, but to patch together the necessary fabric of stability to permit revived economic activity. In a context of deep internal crisis in almost all advanced societies, and with the Soviet menace evident in the violent Communist take-overs in Bavaria and Hungary during the Conference period, this desire for normalization was intensely felt. As such, the victorious leaderships grasped hold of short-term expedients, dressed them up as principles and promoted them as a 'world settlement', and in this deception lay the materials of future war. *R. F. H.*

Below: The humiliations of the defeated are meted out to the Socialist chancellor of Austria, Karl Renner

Right: The anti-parliamentary appeal of the extreme left threat to the Weimar republic

Britain between the Wars

Although Britain had already felt her economic decline, relative to Germany and the US, before 1914, her situation was far worse after the war. Wartime disruption of trade prompted overseas customers both to seek supplies elsewhere and to develop their own industries. With the rapid post-war recovery of her rivals, demand for Britain's coal, iron, steel, ships and textiles slumped at a time when her capacity in these goods – partly stimulated by wartime requirements – greatly exceeded peace-time needs. Technological changes overseas, not so readily adopted in Britain, also made these basic industries uncompetitive or – with oil replacing coal – further reduced demand. Old staple industries were therefore seriously depressed, and in south Wales or industrial Scotland, unemployment remained high after 1921. Elsewhere, especially in the south, newer developments – cars and various light industries – were successful. Here, contrary to popular mythology, there was slowly rising prosperity – the Depression and the Jarrow Hunger March notwithstanding. Real wages rose as prices of imported food and raw materials fell, and consumer spending, especially on housing, expanded with the help of hire-purchase schemes. By the late 1930s these factors and rearmament were stimulating the older staple industries, steel and certain textiles. Economic growth and recovery owed little to planners or politicians.

Politicians and recovery

The widespread post-war wish was to recreate the pre-war world of 1914. While this prompted politicians to look at the difficulties of the old industrial areas, it narrowed their remedies for the unemployment problem. In wartime there had been government control of industry to an unprecedented degree, but the peace-time political exigencies of the coalition government encouraged rapid decontrol. When a depression set in during 1921–22 it was widely held to be only temporary, and although optimism eventually evaporated, only familiar pre-war expedients were resorted to. In the shadow of a National Debt swollen by war, borrowing was avoided if possible and budgets were balanced annually. Welfare provisions, notably unemployment relief and insurance schemes, were haphazard and meagre. Governments frequently preferred piecemeal changes or to live in hope, relying on local government somehow to muddle through. Conservative and Labour governments were as bad as each other. The Conservatives in 1925 returned to the gold standard at the pre-war parity; this briefly restored London's role as world financial centre, but damaged British exports by over-valuing the pound. Labour's Cabinet majority in August 1931 preferred to reduce unemployment payments rather than face a larger budget deficit or abandon the gold standard. Not until 1937, when unemployment was falling anyway, did the operation of the 1934 Unemployment Act really ease matters. That little was done for the unemployed and less for the economy was the more tragic because constructive alternatives were available. John Maynard Keynes, David Lloyd George, Oswald Mosley, and some younger Conservatives, all supported forms of public borrowing and planned expenditure to stimulate investment and consumption. The most that governments did was to revive obsolete dreams of imperial economic development and cooperation. After being muted for most of the 1920s, the concern for still cheaper raw materials and larger markets came into the open again with the Labour government's 1929 Colonial Development Act, and the Imperial Economic Conference at Ottawa in 1932.

The political parties, despite similarities in their approach to economic questions, were otherwise sharply at odds in the 1920s. The collapse of Lloyd George's wartime coalition government in 1922 made the decline of the Liberal Party plain for all to see. Some Liberals drifted into the Conservative Party, others joined Labour; those who remained were bitterly divided between supporters of Herbert Asquith and Lloyd George. From 158 seats in 1923, they dwindled to 59 in 1929. Labour, to the alarm of many, emerged as the major Opposition party and formed minority governments in 1923 and 1929. Their socialist ideals succumbed to the necessities of parliamentary dependence on the Liberals, to inexperience in government, and to the need to prove their respectability to the electorate. Labour's internationalism and attempts to normalize relations with Communist Russia awoke the worst Conservative prejudices. The prosecution of a Communist newspaper editor for inciting troops to mutiny, and the publication of a letter apparently from the head of the Comintern, Grigori Zinoviev, to the British Communist Party about plans for revolution, contributed much to Labour's defeat in 1924. The Conservatives then precipitated the General Strike in 1926 by failing, like earlier governments, to tackle comprehensively the problems of the coalmining industry and insisting on wage reductions to meet the industry's difficulties. This strike was the weapon of those who felt that all governments had failed them, but it was pursued only hesitantly and soon collapsed, to be followed by a decline in industrial militancy for the remainder of the inter-war period.

Peace and appeasement

When they did think about foreign affairs (which most did only rarely), the British were not unnaturally anxious to avoid another war. The death and waste of 1914–18 haunted the national consciousness. Some felt it would destroy the greater affluence they were beginning to experience; others that it would destroy their hopes of sharing in economic recovery. During the 1920s, international disarmament and cooperation at the League of Nations seemed capable of preserving peace. After Japanese aggression in 1931, it became clear that disarmament had failed, and that the League was unable to restrain aggression without risking war. Few were even prepared to support a 'just' war on behalf of the League, and of this Japan, Italy and Germany showed they were well aware. Reluctantly, the British government therefore began to re-arm in 1935, although most politicians wished to avoid both the expense and the appearance of being warmongers. Neville Chamberlain, prime minister from 1937, fully shared these views. Fearing that another European war would find Britain involved but unsupported by America and the Dominions, and convinced that he could preserve peace by direct negotiation with the dictators, he offered them concessions to obtain security. Although this 'appeasement' failed, Chamberlain's policy was in tune with much popular opinion, appealing to self-interest and to moral instincts in stressing that in any circumstances modern war was the greatest evil. *A. N. P.*

The 'National' government of 1931 takes a stroll into the garden at No. 10 Downing Street. It contains all the prime ministers of the years 1929–40: Ramsay Macdonald (in front), Stanley Baldwin (coming down the stairs) and Neville Chamberlain (at the top of the stairs)

France: Versailles to Vichy

France greeted the First World War with the same immense enthusiasm as did other countries; unlike them, France had a precise territorial goal, the recovery of Alsace-Lorraine from Germany. The bulk of the fighting took place on French soil, doing tremendous material and human damage, and 1.4 million men died out of a total population of only 40 million. This represented a greater percentage loss than that suffered by any other of the major combatants and contributed to the paralysing sense of inferiority that was to grip French politicians and soldiers in the 1930s. These enormous losses and the serious mutinies in 1917 did not, however, break French morale. Georges Clemenceau (prime minister 1917–20) personified a will to resistance that culminated in the victory of November 1918 and in the recovery of Alsace-Lorraine. At the peace conferences of 1919 France failed to achieve the separation of the Rhineland from Germany, but did obtain short-lived guarantees of American and British protection against a future German attack. Although French policy towards Germany in the 1920s fluctuated between intransigence (Poincaré's occupation of the Ruhr, 1923) and conciliation (Briand's agreements with Stresemann), neither was the result of weakness.

Marshal Pétain, who recommended an armistice and became head of the Vichy government

If France appeared strengthened, so too did the political system. The Republic had won back what the Second Empire had lost. Charles Maurras' attempts to popularize monarchism made much noise but had little effect, while the formation of a Leninist Communist Party in 1920 out of the majority of the old Socialist Party did not, despite widespread social unrest, bring about a revolution. Political power in the 1920s was in the hands either of conservative republicans like Poincaré (prime minister 1922–1924, 1926–28) or of centre-left politicians, usually members of the Radical Party. The Socialist Party under Léon Blum refused to participate in what it regarded as bourgeois governments, but this did not prevent it forming electoral alliances with the Radicals and other centrist groups. There was also a decline in the intensity of the contest between clericals and anti-clericals. Economic reconstruction made progress and, after periodic runs on the franc, financial stability was achieved in 1926. In 1928–29 French exports reached record levels and the depression that struck the USA and Britain in 1929 largely passed France by.

The 1930s faced France with a triple crisis – diplomatic, economic and ultimately institutional – which the political system could not resolve and which resulted in the national collapse of 1940. The rise of Hitler accentuated the limitations of France's strategic position, her low birth-rate and the feebleness of her alliances with small East European states. After 1931 the effects of the international economic crises were felt with increasing severity, and the old protectionist measures proved incapable of dealing with them. Industrial production fell sharply; tourist revenue melted away as the Americans followed Scott Fitzgerald back across the Atlantic; agricultural prices collapsed. The cascade of short-lived centre-left governments that followed the 1932 election offered no response to the crisis other than deflation. The result was that for the first time since the Boulanger Affair in the 1880s there was an economic basis for mass political protest. A number of right-wing ex-veterans' leagues sprang up, more or less modelled on fascist movements elsewhere, and ready to attack what they saw as inefficient, corrupt parliamentary democracy. The revelation of a financial scandal involving prominent Radical politicians (the Stavisky Affair) led to violent anti-parliamentary demonstrations in Paris on 6 February 1934, leaving 14 dead. To many, including Blum, it appeared that the Republic's existence was threatened by fascism.

In the short run the threat was averted. Between 1934 and 1936 an alliance known as the Popular Front was formed between the Communists, Socialists and Radicals to defend Republican institutions, and was victorious in the 1936 elections. For the first time a Socialist (Blum) became head of a government that relied in part on Communist votes. It nationalized the Bank of France and passed a number of long-overdue social reforms, including holidays with pay. These actions aroused intense hostility among conservatives and many centrist Radicals, but what destroyed the Popular Front, and ultimately the Republic, was once again the problem of Germany. Public opinion and the parties were split over the proper reaction to Nazi expansionism. Some on the right regarded acceptance of Hitler as preferable to acceptance of Communists, and even Socialists, as 'good Frenchmen'.

The necessity for war in September 1939 was recognized by most Frenchmen, though without the enthusiasm of 1914. The Communists followed Stalin's instructions to oppose the war, but more serious was the opposition which continued to be shown by prominent politicians and soldiers. When Marshal Pétain, France's most prestigious soldier, told the War Cabinet of which he was a member that the German assault of May 1940 could not be stopped and that an armistice must be sought, his moral authority was so great that no civilian politician could resist him. Similarly, when Pétain declared that the political system itself was responsible for the defeat, the deputies and senators, many of whom had been elected in 1936 to defend the Republic, accepted his analysis of their failings. The prestige of a 70-year-old Republic proved weaker than that of an 84-year-old Marshal. At Vichy, on 10 July 1940, the Chamber and Senate voted overwhelmingly to abolish the Republic and to entrust Pétain with the drawing up of a new, authoritarian and anti-democratic constitution. *P. M.*

Right: Edouard Daladier, premier in 1934
Below: A mass meeting of Communists

The World Depression

The Great Depression of 1929–33 is commonly dated from the New York Stock Exchange crash of 24 October 1929. The low point was reached in the last quarter of 1932. Thereafter a generally weak recovery started, partly induced by national recovery programmes. Nationalist economics was accompanied (and partly caused) by rising international tensions until the remains of the Depression were swept away in the Second World War.

The statistical story of the Depression can soon be told. Taking 1925–29 as 100, the volume of world production fell to 96 in 1930, 84 in 1931 and 69 in 1932. The volume of world trade fell to 93 in 1930, 84 in 1931 and 73 in 1932; its value to 81, 58 and 39 respectively. Unemployment rose from about 5 million in 1929 to 35 million at the end of 1932, with totals of 15 million in the United States, 6 million in Germany and 3 million in Britain. How did the Depression originate, and what caused it to be so severe and prolonged?

One big debate about the first question is: did the downturn of 1929 start in the US or in the primary sector? Most writers believe it started in the US. The two critical factors here were the contraction of US foreign lending after mid-1928, and the US economic downturn from the middle of 1929. After the First World War, America had taken over from Britain as the world's chief capital exporter. From July 1928 American investment funds were diverted to the New York Stock Exchange boom, with the result that the debtors (which included Germany, whose industry had been refloated on American loans) could no longer service their debts and started to lose gold. From mid-1929 indices of American business activity turned downwards. The great American boom of the 1920s – mainly in automobiles, real estate and share speculation – was unsupported by adequate purchasing power and ran out of steam. The Stock Exchange collapse registered and accelerated business contraction.

These American developments dealt primary producers a mortal blow. Since the war there had been agricultural overproduction. Technical improvements, increased acreage (especially in Europe) and a succession of good harvests had increased supply, while high tariffs and sluggish industrial growth had limited the world market. The downward pressure on prices had been offset by creating buffer stocks financed by foreign loans. The decline of US lending forced primary producers to unload stocks and try to increase exports to service their debts at the precise moment when the US recession reduced American demand for Latin American, Asian and Australasian imports. The

Three typical street scenes from the USA in the 1930s

result was a spectacular collapse of commodity prices in 1929–30.

The rest of the industrial world felt the impact of both the Americans' and the primary suppliers' loss of income. This diminished exports of manufactured goods, producing mass unemployment in Europe. Once industrial depression had started, it became cumulative as domestic demand contracted as well. The first eight months of 1931 were dominated by the European financial crisis, which culminated in Britain leaving the gold standard on 20 September 1931. The US, too, suspended gold convertibility early in 1933. Quite simply, output was no longer enough to sustain the financial structure of governments, firms and banks. Following the financial crisis of 1931, the multilateral payments system and free trade both came to an end, as countries embarked on protectionist roads to recovery.

Why was the Depression so severe and so prolonged? Most classical economists assumed business cycles as a fact of life. The question that concerned them was why 'natural forces' were failing to produce a recovery. The answer they gave was that these natural, or market, forces were prevented from operating by all manner of interferences: unions and unemployment insurance kept wages too high; rings of producers tried to keep up prices; governments raised tariffs; the gold-exchange standard enabled countries for too long to live beyond their means. These things prevented the necessary adjustments in wages and prices coming soon enough, and thus made the downswing far greater than it need have been.

There are also three different types of explanation which have all been influenced by the theories of the British economist, John Maynard Keynes. Together they provide the elements of a comprehensive explanation of the Depression's severity. According to Kindleberger, a less than fluid international economy requires an 'underwriter' to offset inevitable strains, for example, between industrial nations and primary producers – an underwriter who will maintain a flow of unruffled, long-term lending, keep an open market for imports and discount in a crisis. This role of coordinator in the world's economy was played by Britain in the 19th century; the US was to assume it after 1945. But between the wars Britain was unable, and America unwilling, to do so. Between 1928 and 1930, the US cut down simultaneously on both lending and imports. As Kindleberger put it, the US Hawley-Smoot tariff of 1930 'made it clear that in the world economy there was no one in charge'.

Orthodox Keynesian theory would attribute the severity and length of the Depression to government policies that mistakenly aimed to adjust incomes to reduced output, or reduce surplus capacity to keep up prices, instead of increasing incomes to reverse the fall in output. In most countries governments tried to balance budgets at a lower level of revenue by cutting spending and the salaries of public employees, when what was needed was direct stimulation of investment and consumption. In a depression, Keynesians would say, government needs to offset the contractionary forces of a private economy, not add to them.

Monetarists blame the severity of the Depression on the failure of the authorities to maintain a sufficient quantity of money to ensure the purchase of output at full employment. By reducing the money supply, they reduced the amount of money people had to spend on purchases of goods and services. According to Milton Friedman, 'when the United States embarked on deflation and proceeded to reduce its money stock, the rest of the world was forced into a major catastrophe.'   R. S.

The Roosevelt Era

In the years that followed the Wall Street 'crash' of 1929, American capitalism faced its gravest crisis. The prosperity of the 1920s endured only as a memory. By 1932, at least twelve million Americans were unemployed, one-third of the entire workforce. Industrial production had fallen to a fraction of 1929 levels. In the presidential election of November 1932, American voters expressed their lack of confidence in the Hoover administration's capacity to deal with the depression by electing Hoover's Democratic opponent, Franklin Delano Roosevelt, whose platform called for a 'New Deal' for the American people.

The new president had a daunting task. On 4 March 1933, when he took the oath of office, the financial system of the United States was on the point of collapse. So many banks had failed that 40 states had closed all banks to wait and see what Roosevelt would do. Boldly declaring in his inaugural speech that 'the only thing we have to fear is fear itself', he summoned Congress into special session and proclaimed a national bank holiday. When Congress met, it took only seven hours to pass Roosevelt's banking bill, which extended federal assistance to the banks. In the first of his 'fireside' chats to Americans over the radio, the president declared that under the new act it was safer to keep money in the banks than hidden away at home. So quickly did Roosevelt establish public confidence in his leadership that when the banks opened the next morning, deposits exceeded withdrawals. The President and his advisers now turned their attention to other problems.

Between March and June of 1933, during the celebrated first 'hundred days' of the Roosevelt Administration, Congress at the prompting of the president passed more important legislation than in any other comparable period of American history. A Civilian Conservation Corps was established to provide open-air relief work for young men. The Farm Credit Administration protected farmers from having their property foreclosed for non-payment of debts. A Home Owners' Loan Corporation was created to refinance mortgages on private homes. The Securities Act of May 1933 sought to prevent any repetition of the stock-market 'crash' of 1929 by bringing the marketing of stocks and bonds under federal control. In June, a more permanent reform of the banking system was instituted by the Glass–Steagall Act, which provided for federal insurance of bank deposits up to a certain sum.

The New Deal

The most important of all the early measures of the New Deal were the Agricultural Adjustment Act passed in May, and the National Industrial Recovery Act which Roosevelt signed into law in June. The 'Triple A' (as it quickly became known) tried to increase prices by subsidizing farmers to limit output. This policy of deliberate crop reduction prompted the bitter taunt that the New Deal was trying to solve the problem of poverty in the middle of plenty by doing away with the plenty, but the AAA did mark a distinct step forward for many American farmers. The National Industrial Recovery Act (known as NIRA) sought to help business stabilize price levels by drawing up codes for their industries. These codes needed government approval to become effective, but were then exempt from anti-trust proceedings. Within a year, 500 codes had been adopted and another 200 were in preparation. Under the NIRA, a Public Works Administration was

FDR – the most commanding and interesting political figure in 20th-century America

Franklin Delano Roosevelt

1882	born 30 January, Hyde Park, NY, the fifth cousin of Theodore Roosevelt
1905	married Anna Eleanor Roosevelt (1884–1962), niece of Theodore Roosevelt
1910	elected (Democrat) to NY State senate
1913–20	Assistant Secretary of the Navy
1921	contracted polio, legs paralysed
1928	elected Democrat governor of New York State
1932	elected president of the USA (22 million votes to Hoover's 15 million)
1936	re-elected for second term (27 million votes to Landon's 16 million)
1940	re-elected for third term (27 million votes to Willkie's 22 million)
1944	re-elected for fourth term (25 million votes to Dewey's 22 million)
1945	died in office, 12 April

established, with funds of over $3 billion to spend on putting unemployed men to work. In clause 7(a), the Act also for the first time recognized the right of American labour to collective bargaining.

There was something in the New Deal programme for almost every group in American society. Farmers had the 'Triple A' and security for their farms. Middle-class home-owners had the protection of the Home Owners' Loan Corporation. Businessmen had the NIRA and its codes. Organized labour had clause 7(a). The unemployed had relief work under the Public Works Administration and, when that seemed inadequate, a supplementary programme of aid under Harry Hopkins' Civil Works Administration. So many people were indebted to the New Deal and the Democratic party that Roosevelt's policies effected a revolution in American politics. Just as the Republican party had dominated national politics from the end of the Civil War to 1932, the period since 1932 has seen the ascendancy of the Democrats. Not until 1946 did the Republicans again win control of Congress, and that proved only a temporary recovery. Between 1932 and 1976, the Democrats lost control of the House of Representatives at only two elections.

The Supreme Court fight

The New Deal might have been successful politically, but by 1935 there was still little hard evidence of economic recovery. Voices to the left of Roosevelt – Dr. Francis Townsend, Father Coughlin, and Huey Long of Louisiana – had begun to demand more radical remedies. To add to Roosevelt's troubles, the United States Supreme Court destroyed the core of the New Deal programme by ruling the NIRA unconstitutional in May 1935, and then overturning the AAA in January 1936. All these pressures combined to drive Roosevelt himself further to the left. He supported a large new programme of public works, the introduction of old-age pensions and unemployment insurance in the Social Security Act of 1935, and approved the Wagner Act of 1935, which confirmed the rights of labour included in clause 7(a) of the NIRA legislation.

Roosevelt's triumphant re-election to a second term in 1936 was in many ways both the climax and the close of the New Deal. A year later, the president involved himself in a futile attempt to 'pack' the Supreme Court with justices more sympathetic to his own point of view. The failure of the plan was a devastating blow to his personal prestige. Soon after the Court fight, the president found himself more and more enmeshed in the foreign policy problems that would occupy him for the remainder of both his presidency and his life. He paid less and less attention to economic problems as time went on. He seems, in any case, never to have understood the connection between federal expenditure and economic recovery. In 1937, when the economy seemed to be improving, he cut relief-rolls. The result was a sharp recession as the economy adapted to the reduced stimulus of federal money. Chastened, the Administration went back to its earlier policy of 'pump-priming'. But the New Deal never did manage to solve the problem of mass unemployment during peace-time. Only the Second World War, with its heavy demand for manpower and great stimulus to industrial production, finally brought full employment.   *M. S.*

NRA day parade in NY, 1933: 250,000 marchers from all walks of life took part

The blue eagle emblem of the National Recovery Administration, set up in June 1933

The Atatürk Revolution

The end of the First World War saw the Turks stripped of their empire. More, the victorious Allies had agreed among themselves to carve up the Turkish homeland, Anatolia. Although the sultan acquiesced in the proposed dismemberment of his country, guerrillas took up arms against the French, Italian and Greek invaders. The leadership in the nationalist struggle was assumed by Mustafa Kemal, the only Ottoman general never to have lost a battle. Undeterred by being declared a rebel against the sultan, he led his forces to victory, compelling the various invading armies to withdraw.

An elected Grand National Assembly abolished the sultanate (1 November 1922), moved the capital from Istanbul to Ankara (13 October 1923) and proclaimed a republic with Mustafa Kemal as its president (29 October 1923). He then set about making Turkey into a modern westward-looking state. This meant dis-establishing Islam. Over the next five years the caliphate was abolished, the religious courts and schools were closed, the dervish orders suppressed, western legal codes supplanted the existing mixture of Islamic law and edicts of the sultans (an immediate result was to make polygamy illegal), and the Arabo-Persian alphabet was replaced by the Latin letters. Female emancipation made rapid strides: the first woman judge was appointed in 1932, and in 1934 women were given the right to vote in national elections and to be candidates for election. In 1935 surnames were introduced, and it was then that Mustafa Kemal became Atatürk ('Father-Turk').

The basis of foreign policy was Atatürk's slogan 'Peace at home and peace abroad'. During the war of independence the Turks' only support had come from the Soviets, but centuries of Russo-Turkish conflict had not predisposed them to perpetuate this state of affairs. After Turkey's independence was recognized in the Treaty of Lausanne (24 June 1923), friendly relations were established with many other countries, including Greece. On 18 July 1932 Turkey joined the League of Nations.

Turkey in this period was not prosperous. Most of the Greek and Armenian businessmen had left during and immediately after the First World War. The country's rulers, having witnessed the economic servitude of the Ottoman Empire in its final years, were hostile to foreign investors. At the same time, they were determined that Turkey must exploit her industrial potential to the full (she is fairly rich in minerals, including iron and coal). The state therefore took the lead in financing and developing industry, at the expense of agriculture, which formed the livelihood of the majority of the Turks. Atatürk, well aware of the widespread discontent and eager for Turkey to be ultimately a parliamentary democracy, tried twice (in 1924–25 and 1930) to institutionalize opposition to the ruling Republican People's Party by allowing a rival party to be set up. Both experiments had to be called off when it was seen that they were premature. Those who opposed not just the economic policy but the whole idea of a secular republic were using the new party as a front for insurrection. When Atatürk died, on 10 November 1938, Turkey was still a one-party state. *G. L. L.*

Mustafa Kemal before the westernizing reforms, speaking at Bursa, 1921

Kemal Atatürk as modernist president of Turkey

Spain

The Break-down of Oligarchical Rule

In 1910, the new Liberal leader, José Canalejas, formed a government, determined to reform the system. He gave the Catalans a mild form of local government and introduced minor social reforms, but his efforts to save the system were doomed. On 12 November 1912, he was assassinated in retaliation for suppressing a strike by the newly formed anarcho-syndicalist union, the National Confederation of Labour (CNT). The gulf between the system and the classes excluded from it was now irrevocable. This was illustrated by the effect of the First World War which not only unleashed the pressures which were eventually to destroy the restoration system, but also witnessed the final division of Spanish society into the forces which were to fight the civil war.

As an exporter to both sides in the First World War, Spain enjoyed a tremendous boom in both industry and agriculture, together with shortages and galloping inflation. Impelled by rising prices, the socialist General Union of Workers (UGT) and the anarchist National Confederation of Labour (CNT) were drawn together in early 1917 to take strike action. At the same time, the political representatives of Basque ironmasters, Asturian coalmine owners and Catalan textile magnates began to protest at the political monopoly of the landed oligarchy. The northern industrialists were enraged by the prospect of having to pay taxes on their war profits. Coincidentally, middle-rank army officers began to protest at low wages, antiquated promotion structures and political corruption. Since the military protest was couched in the language of 1898 'regenerationism', the dissidents were acclaimed as figureheads of the great national reform movement. Workers, officers and industrialists temporarily coincided in their calls for reform, but their interests were ultimately contradictory and the system survived by skilfully playing on their differences. The Conservative prime minister, Eduardo Dato, conceded the officers' demands. He then provoked a strike of socialist railway workers, forcing the UGT to act before the CNT was ready. Now at peace with the system, the army was happy to defend it in August 1917 by crushing the strike with considerable bloodshed.

Yet again, the bourgeoisie had abandoned its political ideals and allied with the landed oligarchy out of fear of the lower classes. Its success was short-lived. The urban socialists had been defeated, but the assault on the system was not over. Between 1918 and 1921, the 'three bolshevik years', the anarchists of the south, inspired by the Russian example, took part in a series of risings which were only defeated because of anarchist disorganization. At the same time, urban anarchists were also coming into conflict with the authorities. In the post-war depression, Catalan industrialists were determined to put an end to the irritation of trade unionism. They countered strikes with lock-outs, backed up by hired gunmen. The anarchists retaliated in kind and between 1919 and 1923 the streets of Barcelona witnessed a spiral of terror and counter-terror. The restoration system was on the verge of collapse. The final crisis came in 1923 when a parliamentary commission investigating another military defeat at Annual in Morocco in 1921 seemed likely to incriminate senior army officers and even the king, Alfonso XIII.

To prevent the commission presenting its findings, a military coup was organized by General Miguel Primo de

General Primo de Rivera, dictator of Spain

Rivera on 13 September 1923. As Captain-General of Barcelona and intimate of the Catalan textile barons, Primo was fully aware of the anarchist threat to them. Equally, as a large landowner from the south, he also had experience of the peasant risings of 1918–21. He was thus the ideal defender of the coalition of industrialists and landowners which had been forged during the great crisis of 1917. Initially, his dictatorship had two advantages – a general disgust with the chaos of the previous six years and a context of economic growth. He crushed the anarchists and made a deal with the socialists whereby the UGT was given a monopoly of trade union affairs. A massive public works programme allowed Primo to substitute prosperity for liberty.

However, Primo was never able to use the economic breathing space to build a lasting political replacement for the restoration system. A genial eccentric, he governed by personal improvisation and, after an early triumph in settling the Moroccan question in 1925, gradually alienated all the groups which had previously supported him. As a military nationalist, he soon alienated the regionalist Catalans. He even upset his fellow landowners by trying to set up rural wage arbitration committees. His attempts to standardize promotion machinery offended army officers. Finally, when the depression began to hit the economy, he lost working-class support. Primo resigned on 26 January 1930, a broken man. Unable to return to the pre-1923 political system, the king turned in desperation to another dictator, General Berenguer. However, the monarchy was now discredited, even among the upper classes. The 1920s had seen a considerable growth of republicanism and Berenguer's régime was bedevilled by republican plots, strikes and even military sedition. When he held municipal elections on 12 April 1931, republican and socialist candidates swept the board in all the main towns and monarchists won only in the rural areas where the *caciques* were still powerful. Alfonso XIII decided to bow out gracefully before he was thrown out forcibly. The Second Republic was founded on 14 April.   *P. P.*

Republican China

Warlordism

Following the Imperial abdication a republic was proclaimed and Sun Yat-sen declared the first president. Almost immediately he gave way to the greatest regional military leader, Yüan Shih-k'ai, who was dominant in the north. The nationalists headed by Sun totally lacked power and organization, and soon withdrew to Canton. Yüan made an attempt to declare himself emperor only to give way in the face of united opposition by the swirling cliques of warlords who came to dominate China. Yüan died a broken man in 1916. As warlords vied for influence and foreign patronage the country lost such little cohesion as it had had. Different cliques from time to time assumed the title of government, but effective power rested with regional and local warlords. The oppressed peasantry of the countryside was dominated by venal landlords and moneylenders.

Cultural and national awakening

Both China and Japan formally joined the First World War on the side of the Allies. Japan was the more important ally from the Western point of view, even though the main activity of the Japanese in the war was to enforce their claims to the former German concessions at Wei-hai-wei in Shantung Province and, indeed, to try to turn China into a Japanese protectorate. This was resisted principally by mammoth street demonstrations by students and other nationally-awakened groups in the cities. The main resurgence of a national feeling occurred in the wake of the Versailles peace conference when Chinese expectations of self-determination were brusquely disappointed as a consequence of the Allied commitment to Japan. The news reached Peking on 4 May 1919. It immediately sparked off demonstrations in all the major cities and blew the fire of a movement which had been quietly smouldering in the modern universities; what was then needed was a complete revolution in culture in order for China to solve its national problems. Under the slogan 'down with the Confucian shop', traditional values were attacked. The traditional literary language of the scholars was rejected in favour of writing in the style of modern speech so as to bridge the gap between the educated élite and the masses and create a genuine political community. All schools of Western thought came under scrutiny. The Bolshevik Revolution seemed to offer China's young radical nationalists a way of getting rid of domestic reaction, standing up to the imperialist powers and releasing the latent energies of the people. The 'liberal' nationalists soon lost influence. It became common ground that China required a social revolution, modernization and the establishment of a new kind of national unity. Above all, what was required was the ending of foreign imperialist privilege, symbolized by the unequal treaties under which territory had been ceded and extra-territorial rights had been granted.

The countryside was hardly touched by this obviously urban movement. Effective power was still diffused among the warlords and their armies.

The Nationalist-Communist united front

The Kuo Min Tang (KMT), the party founded by Sun Yat-sen, being confined to Canton, had not figured greatly in this nationalist cultural awakening. However, as the

Symbol of the revolution: warlord-president Yüan Shih-k'ai has his pigtail removed

An early republican poster, displaying phoenixes arising around the new flag

Chiang Kai-shek, on Taiwan (Formosa), aged 67

Comintern in Moscow was looking for a bourgeois national party in China as an ally against the imperialist powers, the KMT was the only candidate. Sun, meanwhile, had been disillusioned by the lack of support from the West. The two sides met in 1923 and the Russians agreed to help with the organization of the KMT and above all to train an effective military force which could march north and unify the country. It was also agreed that the members of the nascent Communist Party of China (CPC), founded in 1921, could join the KMT on an individual basis as a united front from below. The revamped KMT was committed to land reform and friendship with Russia as well as nationalism and democracy. Sun died in 1925, to be succeeded by Chiang Kai-shek. Relations between the KMT and the CPC were uneasy, and eventually, when the military 'Northern Expedition' was launched, with great success, Chiang finally turned against the Communists. After entering Shanghai in April 1927, he had them slaughtered in their thousands. This ended the CPC as a party with an effective urban base. Its future was to lie with a revolutionary armed struggle in the countryside under the aegis of Mao Tse-tung. Chiang, meanwhile, established his government in Nanking.

The Nationalist interlude 1928-1936

Having turned against the Communists, Chiang was embraced by the Western powers. Henceforth, support for the KMT came from the Western-oriented mercantile groups of the coastal cities and from the landlord class in the countryside. Although some success was registered in developing industry, precious little was achieved in agriculture and the social problems worsened. Chiang's dictatorial rule depended on manipulating various cliques and on ensuring that appointees to high office were personally loyal. Efficiency and genuine reform were the first casualties. Moreover, despite its nationalist and anti-imperialist rhetoric, the régime was extremely dependent on Western goodwill. Two major problems plagued the Chiang Kai-shek régime. First, the Northern Expedition had been halted before total conquest of China had been achieved, leaving influential warlords in the north and to the western periphery unsubdued. Secondly, the Communist challenge. During this period, the Communists had built a 'red base' in Kiangsi under Mao's leadership, based on land revolution and a people's army. After five extermination campaigns, Chiang managed to dislodge the Communists, who then began the epic Long March of 6000 miles which brought a depleted force to their north-west redoubt of Yenan.

The Sino-Japanese War

Although the Japanese had invaded and taken over Manchuria in 1931, their main impact on Chinese history came with the invasion of China proper in 1937. The Communists in Yenan succeeded in compelling Chiang to agree to establish a national united front against the Japanese. Chiang Kai-shek's main forces withdrew to the south-west in the face of the fierce Japanese onslaughts on Peking, Shanghai and Canton and after 1942 began to prepare for the day when, after the Japanese had been defeated by America, the KMT could finish off the Communists once and for all. For their part, the Communists expanded in the north-west. Politically awakened by the ravages of the Japanese invaders and by the social revolution engendered by the Communists, the peasantry became a political and military force for national resurgence and revolution. While the KMT atrophied in its southwestern redoubt centred on Chungking, the Communist forces under Mao's leadership developed their own way of making revolution and provided a convincing alternative to the KMT.

The Civil War

At the time of the Japanese surrender in August 1945, the KMT had a superiority on paper over the Communists to the order of four to one in manpower, war material and territory. Even Stalin advised the Communists to avoid a civil war. Chiang Kai-shek was America's ally and the Americans were clearly committed to him, but they also wished to avoid a civil war and sought to mediate between the two sides, while at the same time extending aid on a vast scale to the KMT. Despite US efforts, Chiang was determined to wipe out the Communists while he still had this superiority. Moral decay, bad generalship, lack of popular support, and the earlier abandonment of the radical reforms which had been at the heart of Chinese national aspirations now took their toll. Although materially weaker, the Communists under Mao were effective in all these respects and, after three mammoth battles in the north, the KMT crumbled. On 1 October 1949 Mao proclaimed the establishment of the People's Republic. Chiang Kai-shek, meanwhile, fled to Taiwan with a huge treasure chest and a million dispirited men. China's national aspirations for unity, dignity and social change had finally been achieved by the Communists.

M. B. Y.

Stalin and the Five Year Plans

By 1929 all contenders had been overcome, and Stalin possessed absolute power. At once he launched the first Five Year Plan for the massive industrialization of the USSR. Industrialization was rapid, but also reckless. Industrial life was dominated by the 'quota', which always had to be 'over-fulfilled'. The result was low standards of workmanship, safety, productivity and hence low morale. To fulfil, or over-fulfil, the Plan, all means were justified. Under such pressures, Soviet workers performed heroic feats of labour and endurance in competition with each other and with those rare workers who could set standards far above the average, the shock-workers or Stakhanovites. The primary aim of the Plan, that of laying the heavy industrial base of the Soviet Union's national defence, was achieved, and by the completion of the second Five Year Plan (1937), the USSR had a strong industrial economy.

The hierarchical structure of the Communist Party had made Stalin's rise to absolute dictatorship possible, and dictatorship demands conformity above all. Experimentation in the arts, sciences and education, which had given the USSR its revolutionary cultural image in the 1920s, conflicted with this demand and, once Stalin was in sole charge, modernism came under attack and traditional forms were reinstated. The internationalist message of the revolution was played down and the image of a besieged, heroic Russia, with her pious habits of loyalty and obedience to her one leader, was projected everywhere, in poetry and prose, in films and classrooms. Rewards for toeing the Party line were attractive, for along with modernism Stalin had also thrown out the egalitarianism of the 1920s and introduced 'socialist competition', which yielded differential rewards and status for services to the socialist fatherland. Marxism became Marxism–Leninism–Stalinism, and in every field of Soviet endeavour the inspiration of 'Stalin the genius' was acknowledged. Above all, the history of the revolution was rewritten, and invariably referred to the Bolshevik leadership as 'Lenin and Stalin' in one undifferentiated entity.

Since December 1917, the Extraordinary Commission for Combating Counterrevolution and Sabotage (the *Cheka*) had used harsh repression against the régime's political enemies. Likewise, since the early years, the Party itself had conducted a succession of self-cleansing operations, or purges, to maintain its high standards of militancy and commitment. From 1935 to 1938 these two activities combined, and political purges were conducted with the most savage police measures. To liquidate all potential opposition and to create an utterly obedient following, and hence to secure his own position in the event of a difficult conflict with Germany, Stalin launched a series of show trials that struck down virtually the entire leadership of 1917 and the top echelons of the party, state apparatus and armed forces. Without warning or trace, people disappeared overnight.

For leading party functionaries, it was enough to hint at a foreign contact or a trip abroad to bring down a charge of spying for foreign powers. (This placed the whole Comintern personnel in jeopardy.) The main charge at the trials and prison interrogations was of 'Trotskyite deviation', a term devoid of meaning, an incantation less real even than that of 'bourgeois nationalism', which at least could be levelled against tens of thousands of detainees from the non-Russian nationalities. Trotsky, the alleged architect of every plot to murder Stalin and overthrow socialism in the USSR, had been deported in 1929. His informed attacks, published in his *Bulletin of the Opposition*, riled Stalin, who had him hunted down and at last murdered in August 1940.

That the Soviet state did not fall to pieces during Stalin's mass terror was due to the inner dynamics of the terror itself: as each echelon was cut down, its place was

The first Five Year Plan is typified by the Magnetostroi steel plant (1931)

taken by new generations of 'apparatchiks', officers, managers, engineers and professors, eager to occupy the vacated posts and trained in a more Stalinist climate, less inclined to independent thinking than to surviving.

Since its beginning, the Soviet state had been making agreements with neighbouring and other states. Once it seemed clear that, for the foreseeable future, revolution in Europe had failed, the rate of foreign trade and diplomatic treaties picked up rapidly. The year of Lenin's death saw diplomatic relations established with Britain, Italy, China, France and several other states. A full treaty with Germany had already been signed at Rapallo in 1922, under which the two ruined powers of the First World War undertook various forms of economic and military cooperation, and renounced all mutual claims to war reparations.

The Communist International (Comintern) was composed, since its formal foundation in Moscow in 1919, of national Communist Parties, regarded as 'sections' of the Comintern and dealt with by its central, Moscow-based apparatus.

From its inception in 1919, the Comintern had instructed its foreign 'sections' (the national Communist Parties) to agitate for pro-Soviet causes, whether trade agreements or diplomatic recognition. As the need of the USSR for peaceful and profitable foreign relations became clearer, so the Comintern became more blatantly a tool of Soviet foreign policy. The drive for conformism in Russia was reflected in the policy Stalin laid down for the Comintern: Communists everywhere were to avoid alliances with all other parties, especially social democrats. He repudiated the 'united front' tactics of the 1920s, which had been needed to win friends for the USSR of the NEP period, when ideology was being played down. In 1934, when Stalin realized that in Germany his tactic of no alliances had helped Hitler into power by dividing the left-wing vote at elections, he gave a new direction to the party-line

The chief prosecutor at the great show trials, 1935–38: Andrei Vyshinski

in the 'popular front'. Communists were now to find all possible allies to unite against fascism, in other words, to defend the USSR. At the same time, the USSR entered the League of Nations and began to search for viable military alliances in the event of a war. Since Hitler was the chief potential aggressor, Stalin crowned his alliance-seeking by signing a non-aggression pact with Nazi Germany itself, in August 1939, only weeks before Hitler's invasion of Poland. Stalin blamed the Western Allies for the war, but it gave him the chance to occupy half of Poland, and soon after to annex the Baltic republics of Latvia, Lithuania and Estonia, thus practically restoring the frontiers of the old Russian empire. *H. S.*

The Weimar Republic

The Treaty of Versailles was signed in June 1919, and the constitution of the Weimar Republic completed two months later. These events did not, however, end the period of post-war political instability in Germany, which continued with revolutionary and counter-revolutionary initiatives until 1923.

The pre-1914 splits on the left were further exacerbated by war and revolution. In November 1918, the majority Social Democratic Party (SPD) made a pact with the army to maintain order against the Spartacist left in Berlin. From December through to March 1919 the Social Democrat Noske used the ultra right-wing Free Corps to crush the Spartacists (in the course of which Rosa Luxemburg and Karl Liebknecht were murdered), and to put down socialist governments in Brunswick, Saxony and Bavaria. This repression, coupled with SPD unwillingness to dispossess the Junkers, reform the bureaucracy or institute more rapid socialization of the economy, led to disillusion on the left. The Independent Social Democrats (USPD), who stood half-way between the SPD and the Spartacists, began to increase their working-class support relative to the SPD; and in early 1920 almost a third of USPD members joined the new Communist Party (KPD), founded in 1919, making the latter a rival mass party to the SPD on the left. As the SPD floundered and lost its pivotal role in the Reich government, the KPD attempted to realize a Russian 'October' in Germany; but uprisings in 1921 and 1923 failed. The élan of the left had disappeared by 1923. More important for the future, the years since 1918 had created a lasting division and legacy of bitterness.

The German 'white terror' was brutal, especially in Munich, but counter-revolution as a whole was unsuccessful, at least to the extent that the Republic survived. The Kapp putsch of 1920 was brought down by a general strike, while the Munich 'beer-hall putsch' of 1923, led by Hitler and Ludendorff, was unpropitiously timed and irresolutely executed.

The right, in disarray in 1918, nevertheless recovered strongly. Those among the middle class and peasantry whose wartime grievances had led them not to oppose revolution, returned to the nationalist political parties, which rebuilt their organizations and increased their electoral strength. Resentment over the terms of Versailles and economic instability, culminating in catastrophic inflation, gave a fillip to this process, for both were unfairly laid at the door of republicans and the left. Above all, the bureaucracy, army and judiciary remained essentially unreconstructed. The risible sentence passed on Hitler for his part in the Munich putsch was symptomatic. *D. G. B.*

Poland

At the outbreak of the First World War in August 1914 Russia promised, though in equivocal terms, to give the Poles some measure of independence in the future. The successful German and Austrian offensive in 1915, however, placed most of the Polish territories in their possession. A Council of Regency was later established (12 September 1917), which set up a Council of State (4 February 1918), so that the nucleus of a Polish state existed before the Central Powers' collapse in 1918. The Treaty of Versailles (1919) fixed the frontiers of Poland in the west, providing also for the Free City of Danzig as a free trading port and for plebiscites in Upper Silesia, Warmia (Ermeland), Mazuria and the territories on the right bank of the lower Vistula (Powisle) – which gave results unfavourable to Poland. In Upper Silesia successive Polish revolts (1919–21) led to the Allies' decision to partition the province between Germany and Poland. Polish Silesia was given autonomy with its own regional parliament. The Polish frontiers with Soviet Russia were established after the Polish-Soviet War of 1920 by the Treaty of Riga (18 March 1921), which placed the eastern frontier far to the east of the 'Curzon line', which had been recommended by the Council of Ambassadors in December 1919. The new state therefore contained large non-Polish minorities: Germans in the west and Lithuanians, Byelorussians, Russians and Ukrainians in the east. This created a grave weakness. Of Poland's population in 1931, only 68.9 per cent (22 million) were Poles.

Poland was primarily an agricultural country with 60 per cent of the population deriving a living from farming. Some industrial progress was made, but the world slump of 1929 retarded advancement.

The constitution of March 1921 set up a parliament (*sejm*) and a senate, with the legislative organs enjoying a marked superiority over the executive. Politics were complicated by the multiplicity of parties. In May 1926 a coup d'état was carried out by Marshal Josef Pilsudski that established a more authoritarian system. In April 1935 a new constitution came into existence that gave the president, Ignacy Moscicki, dictatorial powers.

Poland was formally allied with France (19 February 1921), but the Polish-German Non-Aggression Agreement (26 January 1934) led to an egocentric policy under the foreign minister, Colonel Jozef Beck. In October 1938,

Cartoon on Noske's crushing of the Spartacists: 'Cheers, Noske! The proletariat has been disarmed!'

Poland   1918-1944   Greece   1919-1940

after the Munich agreement, Poland took her share of Czechoslovakia: Cieszyn (Teschen) in Zaolzie (Czech Silesia). When Hitler made demands on Poland for frontier rectifications in 1939, neither the British guarantee of Polish independence (March 1939) nor the alliance of 25 August 1939 could physically save Poland. Germany invaded Poland on 1 September 1939, and the country was partitioned by Germany and the USSR under the terms of the Nazi-Soviet Pact (23 August 1939). Part of the Polish territories were incorporated into Germany, while central and southern Poland were administered like a colony. The territories occupied by the USSR were incorporated in the Byelorussian and Ukrainian Soviet Socialist Republics.

A Polish government-in-exile was established first in Paris and then in London (1940) under General Wladyslaw Sikorski. At the outbreak of war between Germany and the USSR (June 1941) a Pact of Mutual Assistance and Non-Aggression was signed with Soviet Russia, but frontier questions remained unresolved, the USSR claiming that the 1941 frontiers were valid and not those of 1939. Relations worsened and in April 1943 the Soviet government broke off diplomatic relations with the government-in-exile. A communist revival in occupied Poland followed the despatch from the USSR of the 'Initiative Group' in December 1941. On 1 January 1944 the communists established the National Committee of the Homeland (KRN) in liberated Lublin to challenge the underground authorities owing allegiance to the government-in-exile. On the eve of the Soviet offensive of June 1944 there were thus two elements contending for the control of the future post-war state of Poland.   *R. F. L.*

The catastrophe that followed the Greek occupation of western Asia Minor soon after the end of the First World War was the most far-reaching event in the history of modern Greece. It began in 1919, when the prime minister, Eleftherios Venizelos, who had led his country into the war on the Allied side, against considerable domestic opposition, sought his reward in the creation of a 'Greater Greece' – a dream long cherished by Greek nationalists. This was to contain the areas, now in Turkey, that were the historical province of Ionia, and still had a substantial Greek population – especially in its chief city, Smyrna (now Izmir). In the partitioning of the defeated Ottoman Empire, the Allies agreed to the occupation, but the resurgent Turkish nationalist armies, inspired by Mustafa Kemal (Atatürk), fought back and counter-attacked in 1922. Abandoned by the Allies, who had increasing doubts about the whole venture, the Greeks were overwhelmed. Not only was all the territory lost, but also there followed a compulsory exchange of Muslims in Greece for Orthodox Christians in Turkey. Some $1\frac{1}{2}$ million of the latter, mostly destitute, flooded into Greece, an impoverished country with a population of some five million. This massive influx had important consequences for the social and economic development of Greece.

Defeat in Asia Minor prompted a military revolution and ushered in a period of considerable confusion during which Greece was declared a republic (1924–35). In 1935, however, George II was restored to the throne and under his rule General Ioannis Metaxás installed a quasi-fascist dictatorship the following year. In October 1940 Greece valiantly held off an Italian invasion, but in April 1941 the country was occupied by the Germans.   *R. C.*

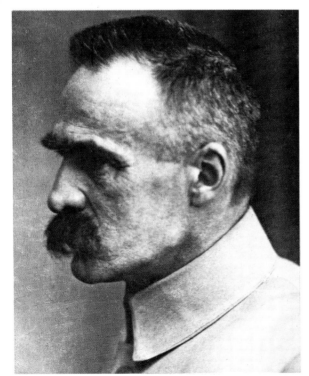

Josef Pilsudski, a major force in re-establishing independent Poland in 1918, and dictator 1926–35

Eleftherios Venizelos, many times premier between 1910 and 1935, and leading anti-royalist

The Fascist Régime in Italy

By the end of the First World War Italy was polarized between a rapidly expanding socialist movement, inspired by the example of the Russian Revolution, and a nationalist middle class. Nationalism fed on resentment at what seemed ungrateful treatment of Italy at the Peace Conference and on d'Annunzio's theatrical occupation of Fiume – the Adriatic port secretly promised to Yugoslavia by the Allies, but claimed by Italy as spoils of war – in September 1919. Against socialist advances, nationalism appeared powerless, yet Italian socialism failed to work out a coherent political strategy. By the autumn of 1920, with the inconclusive end to the occupation of the factories in Turin, the movement had clearly lost momentum. Reaction against the fading Socialist Party was spearheaded by the Fascist movement. Founded in March 1919, but notoriously unsuccessful in its first year, the Fascist movement began to expand only when it assumed the characteristics of agrarian reaction in the autumn of 1920. Fascist squads, recruited largely from ex-servicemen and financed by the big landowners of the Po Valley, and enjoying the active collusion of the state authorities, scored immediate successes against the confused Socialists. Workers' organizations were disbanded, wages reduced and hours of work increased. The Fascist leader, Benito Mussolini, a renegade Socialist who had moved rapidly to the right during the course of the war, exploited the weaknesses of the liberal state and the miscalculation of liberal politicians about his objectives in order to pose a direct threat to the state by 1922. The 'March on Rome' of October 1922, although represented by the Fascists as a coup d'état, was in reality little more than an exercise in choreography. Faced with the alternative of turning an army of doubtful loyalty against the Fascists, the liberal politicians could only recognize the reality of Fascist power and invite Mussolini to form a government.

Fascism did not immediately assume the attributes of a dictatorial régime. Mussolini's first efforts in government were directed towards a 'normalization' of the political situation, but the murder by Fascists of the Socialist deputy Giacomo Matteotti in 1924 and the subsequent wave of revulsion from fascism compelled Mussolini to accept the logical consequences of Fascist violence and crush all opposition. In 1925 and 1926 opposition parties were banned and a Fascist special tribunal set up to deal with enemies of the régime. Police action effectively removed most opposition. Many liberals and Socialists went into exile and only the Italian Communist Party, formed in 1921, continued with clandestine activity within Italy during the Fascist régime.

Support for Fascism came from diverse sources. The urban petit bourgeoisie, grateful for financial stability and enthusiastic supporters of the nationalist and populist themes of Fascist propaganda, provided the backbone of the Fascist movement. Catholic sentiment within Italy (and elsewhere) was encouraged to look with favour on Fascism by the Concordat of 1929, by which the 70-year-old conflict between the Italian state and the Vatican was finally resolved. But the key to Fascist power lay in continued support by industrial and financial interests, and both northern and southern landowners. Rigid disciplining of the labour force was the fundamental condition of this support, but Fascist policies helped these interests in other ways. Large landowners benefited from agricultural protectionism, from the much-publicized 'battle of wheat' to boost grain production, and from the land reclamation programmes (the Pontine Marshes). Industrialists also looked to the Fascist state to help them through the lean years of the world economic depression. The creation of the state holding companies IMI and IRI in 1932 and 1933 was one of the ways by which the state channelled capital towards industry and prevented financial collapse. The ideology of the corporate state, which claimed to end the conflict between capital and labour and reconcile private interest with national priorities, in no way concealed the sectional interests served by Fascism.

Foreign policy and the Second World War

The weakness of the régime was revealed above all by its foreign adventures. The highly militarist tone fundamental to fascism found expression in 1935 with the attack on Abyssinia. The war was carried to a successful conclusion, but the employment of modern methods of warfare against a virtually defenceless population earned Italy the condemnation of the League of Nations for her aggression. The imposition of economic sanctions tended to harden Italian attitudes and rally support for Mussolini, whose determination to pursue an active foreign policy was reinforced. Eager to avoid unfavourable comparison with the rapidly growing power of Hitler (the informal Rome–Berlin Axis having been created in 1936), Mussolini sent troops to Spain in 1936 to fight on the side of Franco and occupied Albania in 1939. The degree of bluff involved in Fascist posturings was revealed, however, with the Second World War. Mussolini, tied to Hitler under the 'Pact of Steel' (1939), at first declared Italy's non-belligerency and only intervened in June 1940 when a German victory seemed assured. Italian troops, largely unprepared and ill-equipped to fight a long war, were sent to fight in Greece and North Africa, where they endured humiliating set-backs, and on the disastrous Russian front, where they lost 100,000 men. By the spring of 1943 the Anglo-American armies were advancing through Sicily and military defeat was imminent. Having lost the confidence of even his closest collaborators, Mussolini was arrested in July on the orders of the king. He was subsequently rescued by the Germans, formed a puppet Fascist state in the north of Italy (*Repubblica sociale italiana*) and was captured and shot by partisans in April 1945.

P. R. C.

Mussolini flanked by his henchmen at Naples, ready for the so-called 'March on Rome'

L'ILLUSTRAZIONE
ITALIANA

Anno LXIII · N. 41   11 ottobre 1936 · A. XIV

Per tutti gli articoli, fotografie e disegni pubblicati è riservata la proprietà artistica e letteraria, secondo le leggi e i trattati internazionali

The Ascent of Hitler

The years 1923–29 were years of only superficial stability in Germany. In foreign policy, for example, Stresemann's accommodating posture towards the west was matched by his intransigence towards the east, and by the continuing pursuit of German expansion eastwards by economic means. Hostility towards reparations and the desire for a 'revision' of the Treaty of Versailles were general; the National Socialists were merely to cast common resentments in a violently extreme form.

These resentments were fed by undercurrents of social discontent. Broad sections of the middle class blamed Versailles and the republic for a decline in their own positions, for their narrowing differentials with regard to the working class, for the declining availability of servants and for the overcrowded professions such as medicine, and in the universities, where the new competition of women created an additional sense of grievance. Among the lower middle class, which had been the particular victim of inflation, there were related fears that changing earnings' patterns were undermining the distinction between their own status and that of the manual workers.

At the political level, the Weimar system was widely discredited as a result of the frequent parliamentary stalemate and changes of ministry, the blatant horse trading of the parties and the prosaic contrast which this was held to afford with the imagined 'greatness' of imperial times. The continued existence of an army, bureaucracy and judiciary whose values remained those of imperial Germany could only reinforce this disenchantment with republican democracy.

Economically, too, despite the curbing of inflation after 1923, the stability of the republic was partly an illusion. There was a great industrial spurt, but the rationalization which accompanied it created a reservoir of disaffection among the small businesses who had suffered as a result. The dependence of this recovery on American capital was also potentially dangerous, as the extremely severe effects in Germany of the Wall Street 'Crash' were to show.

Economic depression heightened previously existing discontents and added new ones, like the fear of the working class and Communism bred by unemployment which topped 6 million. The National Socialists exploited the crisis to offer all things to all men. They promised the peasantry guaranteed markets and prices and a new dignity. Small businesses were offered cheap credit and freedom from both large-scale competition and trade unions. To the middle class and lower middle class in general the Nazis portrayed themselves as a bulwark against Communism and a party which would get things done. For these groups, as for big business, the image of dynamism was a seductive one. Finally, they promised work to the unemployed, a slogan which had particular success among the young who had never held jobs.

Anti-semitism fused these disparate appeals. Through skilful propaganda the Jew was depicted, in turn, as the heartless, manipulative capitalist, the fomenter of working-class unrest, the professional man who robbed Aryans of work and the rootless cosmopolitan who poisoned German culture and undermined morale. Virulent nationalism, anti-Communism and hostility towards Versailles augmented these appeals.

Working-class and Catholic voters largely resisted Nazi blandishments; but the Protestant middle class, lower middle class and peasantry provided an electoral base which enabled the party to increase its representation in the Reichstag from 12 to 107 seats between 1928 and 1932. Faced with this, the politicians of the republic failed. Between 1930 and 1933 a succession of authoritarian chancellors – Brüning, Papen, Schleicher – sought to rule without the Nazis, by-passing parliament when necessary. Then, in January 1933, President Hindenburg appointed Hitler chancellor, believing – like the Junkers, key elements of big business, the army and others on the right – that he could be 'tamed'. In this immediate sense, and in the more general sense that they had created a consensus which made the Nazis more respectable, the right (and the Catholic Centre Party) bore a heavy responsibility for the legal 'seizure of power'.

The left also failed to offer resistance. Large-scale unemployment made it impossible to consider a general strike; and SPD and KPD were chronically divided. The SPD was thrown on the defensive, its unimaginative leaders hamstrung by a rigid, legalistic mentality. This attitude, in turn, further antagonized the KPD, 85 per cent of whose members were unemployed in 1932, and which (in line with Comintern orthodoxy) branded the SPD as 'social fascists'. The left, like the right, had its own brand of myopia. The SPD believed that dictatorship could not last long, while the KPD saw Hitler's appointment as the inevitable final stage before working-class revolution.

D. G. B.

Adolf Hitler with his stormtroopers at Gera, Thuringia, after winning control of the provincial government, 6 September 1931

IN IHREM GEIST VORWÄRTS IM KAMPF
GEGEN KRIEGSGEFAHR, FASCHISMUS, HUNGER
UND FROST, FÜR ARBEIT, BROT
U. FREIHEIT

IM ZEICHEN DES LENINISMUS
LENIN
LIEBKNECHT
LUXEMBURG
WÄHLT ROTE BETRIEBSRÄTE
STÄRKT DIE REVOLUTIONÄRE
GEWERKSCHAFTS-OPPOSITION

Top: Stormtroopers parade outside the Communist party hq. in Berlin on 22 January 1933, eight days before Hitler became chancellor

Above: Chancellor Hitler with Reichs President von Hindenburg at the Tannenberg battle commemoration seven months after achieving power

The Spanish Civil War

The Spanish upper classes had hoped that by sacrificing the king, they might divert left-wing desires to tamper with the existing balance of social and economic power. In fact, the relatively honest elections of the republic allowed political power to pass to the middle class republican lawyers and intellectuals and their working class allies, the socialists. They intended to use this power to create a modern Spain by destroying the reactionary influence of the Church and the army, by improving the lot of the wretched *braceros* on the southern estates and by meeting the demands of Catalan and Basque regionalists. This constituted a massive challenge to the great oligarchical coalition which had hitherto dominated Spanish politics. Coming at a time of world depression, with agricultural prices tumbling, the republic's proposed social reforms could only infuriate the landowning classes, as these mild reforms could not be absorbed by increased profits.

Between 1931 and 1933, a coalition government of republicans and socialists introduced a thorough-going programme of reforms. Social reforms were resisted at a local level by the *caciques*. At a national level, the attempt to defend oligarchical privilege took two forms. The Catholic, authoritarian, Spanish Confederation of Autonomous Rightist Groups (CEDA), used massive propaganda depicting the republicans' attempts to break the social power of the Church as religious persecution, thereby mobilizing mass support among the conservative smallholders of northern Spain. That support was used to get CEDA deputies into parliament to obstruct agrarian reform. Some aristocrats and army officers found this

method too slow, but an attempted coup on 10 August 1932 failed, leaving the CEDA as the main right-wing bulwark against reform.

So successfully did the CEDA block reform that many socialists lost faith in the possibility of changing Spain by parliamentary methods. In their disillusion, they broke their alliance with the left-wing republicans and fought the November 1933 elections alone. In a system which favoured coalition lists, this handed victory on a plate to a combination of the CEDA and the right-wing republican Radical Party. Immediately the social and religious reforms of the first two years were overthrown. Wages were slashed and the *caciques* reasserted their power. Gradually the left came to the conclusion that the CEDA leader, José María Gil Robles, aimed to set up a fascist state and smash the unions. In an attempt to stop this, socialists, anarchists and Communists took part in an uprising in Asturias in October 1934. It was defeated by the army, but with so much difficulty that Gil Robles was forced to slow down his plans to reintroduce the pre-1931 social order protected by an authoritarian political system. Moreover, the experience of right-wing government between 1933 and 1935 reunited the left. In the February 1936 elections, despite a huge right-wing propaganda effort, the left's Popular Front won a narrow victory and immediately readopted the reforming plans of 1931.

The 1936 elections marked the end of the legalist attempt to defend the interests of the landed and industrial oligarchies. Monarchist landowners and industrialists financed a small fascist party, the Falange, founded by

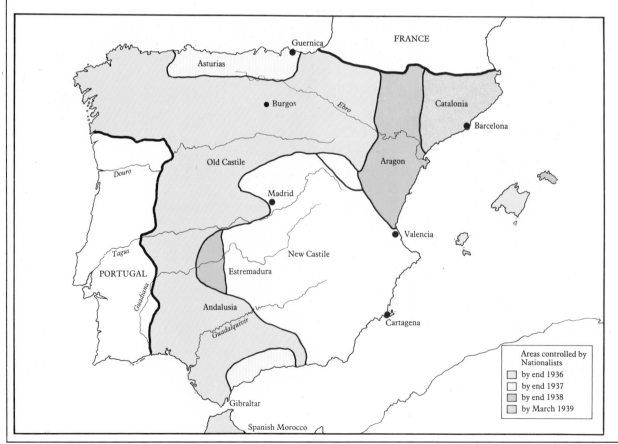

Primo de Rivera's son, José Antonio. Its militants began to destabilize republican politics by acts of terrorist provocation designed to provoke leftist retaliation. This created the atmosphere which was used to justify the military rising which had long been planned. The socialists, divided between parliamentary moderates and revolutionary activists, took no part in the government and the republican cabinet could do nothing to stop the slide into disorder. Meanwhile, military conspirators were arranging for a rising of the army garrison in each provincial capital. Things were made easier for them by the murder of the monarchist leader, José Calvo Sotelo, on 13 July. On 18 July, the garrisons rose.

The revolt was successful in the conservative towns of rural Castile but was defeated in the industrial towns by spontaneous working-class resistance. The rebels' most substantial force, the Moroccan army under General Franco, was stranded on the wrong side of the Straits of Gibraltar. In fact, it was the aid of Hitler and Mussolini in providing transport aircraft that turned a *pronunciamiento* that was going wrong into a full-scale civil war. Franco's army of the south swept north through Extremadura, reaching Madrid in November. The rebels, or Nationalists as they called themselves, were halted there by the determined defence of the *Madrileños* backed up by the anti-fascist volunteers of the International Brigade and tanks and aircraft bought from Russia. Stalemated in Madrid, the rebels spent most of 1937 mopping up large areas of republican territory in Andalusia and northern Spain. On 26 April 1937, the market town of Guernica was totally destroyed by German bombers as part of a deliberate ploy to terrorize the Basque country into surrender. Attempts to cut off Madrid were defeated at the battles of Jarama and Guadalajara, but the Republicans were always on the defensive. Their offensives regularly broke down in the face of the material superiority of the Nationalists. In April 1938, the rebels reached the Mediterranean coast and split the Republican zone. A desperate attack was launched across the River Ebro in order to join the two halves again, but fierce fighting between July and November saw the Republicans pushed back completely exhausted. The rebels captured Barcelona on 22 January 1939 and on 1 April entered Madrid.

While Hitler and Mussolini were unstinting with their aid, the Western democracies, Britain and France, stood aside, fearful of helping a left-wing régime. Russian assistance was costly, both financially and in terms of Soviet interference in Republican affairs. Anxious to appease the democracies, Stalin used the Spanish Communists to crush the revolutionary gains made by the workers in the Republican zone. The forcible dismantling of industrial and rural collectives demoralized and divided the left-wing forces. The Nationalists, on the other hand, enjoyed a unified command, especially after General Franco became head of state on 27 April 1937. All resistance in the Nationalist zone was brutally crushed as the old order was re-established by the military. *P. P.*

Catalan-language poster of the Socialist party: 'No to Fascism!' (1937)

Gen. Francisco Franco, commander of the 'Army of Africa', with Gen. Emilio Mola, leader of the insurrection, at Burgos in 1936

Towards the Second World War

The Liquidation of the Versailles System

The internal consolidation of the Third Reich was rapid. The Reichstag fire was used as a pretext to introduce the Enabling Act, for which all parties but the Social Democrats voted (the Communists had already been banned). This gave the régime dictatorial powers. Parties other than the National Socialists were outlawed and concentration camps were opened to hold political prisoners. At the same time, public works programmes like motorway construction and the large-scale provision of credit to private industry began to soak up unemployment.

In foreign affairs, however, Hitler was initially circumspect. The conservative Neurath was appointed foreign minister, out of deference to Hindenburg. A Concordat was signed with Rome in July 1933 and a non-aggression pact with Poland in January 1934. Reactions abroad to the Austrian Nazis' attempted putsch of 1934, in which German complicity was widely suspected, underlined the need to proceed cautiously.

Germany nevertheless withdrew both from the Geneva disarmament conference and the League of Nations in 1933, and rearmament was set underway immediately, as Hitler had promised local army commanders in a meeting only four days after becoming chancellor. Between January 1933 and the end of 1934 the army grew from 10 divisions and 100,000 men to 24 divisions and 240,000 men. The improvement in the German balance of payments over this period encouraged further rearmament, and this, in turn, created the basis for a more forward-looking foreign policy.

Hitler's more confident and aggressive stance was marked by the plebiscite over the future of the Saar in January 1935. When, in March, Göring told a British newspaper reporter that Germany now had an air force, the revelation caused so little surprise that the powers failed even to protest. It is true that the announcement in the same month that conscription was to be introduced brought British, French and Italian protests, and condemnation from the League of Nations, but no action was taken. The Anglo-German naval convention of 1935, moreover, encouraged Hitler to maintain his belief that Britain could be won over, while the war in Abyssinia distracted the attention of the western powers and created a stronger Italian need for German support.

Exploiting favourable circumstances – in particular, Italian vulnerability, British military weakness and France's internal crisis – Germany re-occupied the Rhineland in March 1936. This was a major diplomatic victory over the western powers, who could only protest ineffectually, and it prepared the way for an aggressive policy towards the east. Germany's forward foreign policy nevertheless aggravated domestic conflicts. The minister of war, Blomberg, was nervous about Hitler's haste. There were also economic problems. The return to full employment had already brought labour discontent and the danger of inflation. The speed and scale of rearmament pre-empted raw materials, cost valuable foreign exchange and threatened to distort the pattern of economic recovery (which was by no means based just on rearmament).

While the régime reaped propaganda from the holding of the 1936 Olympic Games in Berlin, that summer saw the build-up of a crisis. Hitler was faced with advice, particularly from the 'financial wizard' Schacht, to proceed more conservatively. He characteristically disregarded these cautious counsels. In April, Göring had taken over responsibility for raw materials and foreign exchange; in August the period of conscription was increased to two years; and in the following month an economic Four Year Plan was announced, with Göring as overlord. This marked a new interventionist phase in Nazi economic policy, but was designed less to deal with the problems which worried Schacht than to prepare Germany economically for war.

While friction continued between Göring and Schacht over economic policy (Schacht resigning in 1937), Germany's international position strengthened. The Anti-Comintern Pact was signed with Japan in November 1936 and Italy joined the Pact the following year. The Rome-Berlin Axis had been created. Britain could not be won for the Pact, and indeed the tempo of British rearmament increased in 1937. With France in domestic crisis, however, and British statesmen like Halifax susceptible to anti-Bolshevik arguments, Germany possessed the diplomatic initiative. Further military preparations in the autumn of 1937 suggested that this would be exploited.   *D. G. B.*

Czechoslovakia

Czechoslovakia is a product of the First World War. Founded in 1918 after military defeat had dissolved the Austro-Hungarian Empire, its leading peoples, the Czechs of Bohemia and Moravia and the Slovaks of Hungary, had long had national movements. Before 1914 these had aimed mainly at achieving autonomy within the Empire; only the war and the activities of T. G. Masaryk (president 1918–35) made complete independence thinkable. Czechoslovakia became the industrial workshop of central Europe. It was efficiently run and had excellent systems of education and national security. It maintained a stable democratic system of government until external pressure destroyed it. Czechoslovak democracy was less perfect than it has sometimes been depicted, but it was more solid than that of neighbouring countries such as Germany, Poland and Austria, all of which succumbed to dictatorships. Even so, a basic weakness of inter-war Czechoslovakia was its multinational population. From its foundation, the republic suffered from internal divisions and uncertain loyalties. There were sizeable Ukrainian, Hungarian and German minorities. Even the Czechs and Slovaks, who were supposed to form one nation, had no previous experience of political co-existence. The Czechoslovak nation was a myth, for in practice people divided into either Czechs or Slovaks. To a large extent the Slovaks maintained their own political parties, the strongest of which – the People's Party – demanded greater Slovak autonomy than the central government would concede. The largest minority, the Germans, numbering over three million in a total population of 15 million, lived mainly in the outer areas of Bohemia–Moravia, which could not have been detached from Czechoslovakia at its foundation, precisely for strategic and economic reasons.

Since 1848 there had been serious political antagonism between the Czechs and German–Austrians of Bohemia–Moravia, and the latter found the new state difficult to accept. At first there was widespread German refusal to cooperate politically with the Czechoslovak republic.

Later, between the mid-1920s and 1930s, the Germans – whose rights had been generously defined and on the whole scrupulously observed – became reconciled and co-operative, but Hitler's coming to power in 1933 changed everything. From 1934 onwards Berlin financed and directed a German movement inside Czechoslovakia intended to subvert the state. In response, Eduard Beneš – foreign minister 1918–35, and subsequently president – tried to create security through alliances. This policy culminated in the 1935 treaties whereby the Soviet Union undertook to aid Czechoslovakia if attacked, provided that France did so. France, however, was prepared to act only if Britain assisted, and the British had no treaty obligations towards Czechoslovakia. These considerations formed the key to the crisis of 1938. The Munich Agreement arising from this crisis crippled Czechoslovakia militarily and economically. The Germans were not the only ones to gain Czechoslovak territory, for Poland and Hungary also made annexations, while Slovakia became autonomous in October 1938. In March 1939 an independent Slovakia was established under German aegis when Hitler occupied what remained of the Czechoslovak state (15 March 1939). The whole Czechoslovak economy was thereafter geared to the German war effort. Resistance was less effective than in Poland or Yugoslavia except for an heroic but premature Slovak rising in 1944, crushed by the Germans. _T. V. T._

Munich 1938

Adolf Hitler had begun to gear Germany for war the moment he came to power in 1933. By November 1937 he could tell his senior military commanders of his intention to expand Germany eastwards, beginning with Austria and Czechoslovakia by 1942 at the latest. His policy of quietly subverting Austrian independence from within blew up in his face in March 1938 when he learned of the Austrian chancellor's plans to call a plebiscite to demonstrate Austrian opposition to absorption by Germany. Swift action secured the overthrow of the Austrian government and Austria's annexation by Germany. The failure of Britain or France to act encouraged Hitler to step up pressure on Czechoslovakia. He hoped that an alliance with Italy would further distract Britain and France, but when he visited Italy in early May 1938 Mussolini rejected him. His humiliation in the weekend crisis of 21–22 May, when a partial Czech mobilization against rumours that he was about to attack them forced him publicly to deny any such plans, in fact determined him to attack Czechoslovakia that year. And he ordered the leaders of the Sudeten German minority in Czechoslovakia to provide him with an excuse for war. The British and French governments were conscious of their military weakness and vulnerability to air attack. The British therefore, reviewing the situation after the annexation of Austria by Germany, determined to prevent the internal Czech–Sudeten German dispute from growing into full-scale war by pressing the Czech government to negotiate with the Sudeten leaders and urging France, Czechoslovakia's ally, not to encourage any Czech intransigence. Thus they refused France staff talks in April 1938, warned

The Czechs show their anger at the Nazi invasion, March 1939, which also killed appeasement

Hitler that he could not count on British neutrality in the May 'weekend' crisis, and forced the Czechs in June to accept a British mediator, Lord Runciman. Lord Runciman's mission failed when disorders in the Sudeten areas were followed by Czech military action to restore order. Fearing an immediate German intervention, Neville Chamberlain, the British premier, surprised both Hitler and the world by flying to summit meetings with Hitler at Berchtesgaden and Godesberg. Hitler, intent on war, tried to raise his terms, but when the German people and army demonstrated their lack of enthusiasm for war and Mussolini intervened, he was forced to accept a settlement at a third summit meeting with Mussolini, Chamberlain and Daladier, the French premier, at Munich. This destroyed Czechoslovakia's defences, awarding the Sudeten areas to Germany, but it robbed Hitler of his war. Chamberlain was universally acclaimed by all who feared an all-out war, but those who felt Britain's honour had been betrayed and believed (rightly as it turned out) that the peace secured by the Munich Agreement would at best prove fleeting, attacked him bitterly, giving the word 'appeasement' the bad taste it has today. _D. C. W._

Neville Chamberlain makes a point to Benito Mussolini during the Munich conference, 1938

Japan was involved in a 14-year war with China which started with the Manchuria Incident (1931–33) and did not end until 1945, but it is probably true to say that Japan viewed the Manchuria Incident as being separate and distinct from the North China Incident which began in 1937.

After her victory over Russia in 1905, Japan had acquired residual rights in the Russian railway system in southern Manchuria, re-named the South Manchurian Railway. Over two decades, the railway was renovated and expanded until it became the central institution in the Manchurian economy and part of a vast, efficient mining and industrial complex. Japan had meanwhile been acquiring considerable rights in this region, described by the Chinese as their Three Eastern Provinces. By 1931, neither the Manchurian warlord nor the central government in Nanking was able to ensure the law and order necessary to enjoy these rights. The commanders of the Japanese Kwantung Army, taking the law into their own hands, provoked an incident at Mukden on 18 September 1931 and proceeded to expand their sphere of influence in south and central Manchuria by military advances. The Nanking authorities made little effective resistance, relying instead on an appeal to the League of Nations and on boycotting Japanese goods and factories in China proper. The League, finding no ready solution, sent a commission of enquiry under Lord Lytton to investigate on the spot.

The Chinese boycotts led the Japanese to retaliate in January–February 1932 when they sent more than two divisions to the Shanghai area until the situation was patched up by an armistice in May. The Lytton Report, published in October, while it was critical of China, condemned the setting up of an independent government of Manchukuo and urged that members of the League of Nations should not recognize it. Japan, however, had already done so and offered her resignation from the League (March 1933). This was followed by a lull in hostilities, which resulted from the Tangku truce.

Trouble with China began afresh with a small incident at the Marco Polo Bridge, near Peking, in July 1937. The war increased in scope when the fighting spread to Shanghai (captured September), Nanking (December), Suchow (May 1938) and Hankow (September). The Nationalist government under General Chiang Kai-shek withdrew to a new capital at Chungking whence it presided over China's war effort until 1945, mainly an elaborate guerrilla campaign. Though the Japanese commanded the coastline, they failed to reach an accommodation with Chungking, either by military victory or by peace overtures. Eventually Japan created a new Nationalist government under Chiang's rival, Wang Ching-wei, at Nanking in March 1940. In order to win the hearts of occupied Chinese and of Asia in general, Japan issued the declaration on a New Order in East Asia (1938) and the Great East Asia Co-prosperity Sphere (1940). Japan's declaration of war against the US and Britain in December 1941, and the promise of American loans and supplies by the Burma Road and by airlift from India gave those at Chungking new hope. The China war became deadlocked, with Chiang content to keep battling on and Japan preoccupied with campaigns elsewhere. In the Allied campaigns against Japan, which from 1943 onwards were aimed at the main islands themselves, the war in China was largely by-passed. *I. H. N.*

The Munich Agreement determined Hitler to alter his plans. He would drive Britain from the Continent before turning his armies eastwards. This meant knocking out France so as to deny the British a continental base. With that aim he embarked on a new armaments drive, giving the German navy priority, and sought a triple alliance with Italy and Japan to distract British power elsewhere. In the east, he tried to ensure Poland's subservience by an agreement over Danzig and the Polish 'Corridor', while at the same time mopping up the remains of Czechoslovakia on 15 March 1939. The last was so clumsily done as to turn everyone against him, negotiations with the Poles over Danzig and the Corridor were fruitless, and he had to settle for a simple alliance with Italy. But by the time the Pact of Steel with Italy was signed (22 May 1939), a new agreement seemed possible: with the Soviet Union.

The Soviet leadership, well aware that Hitler's immediate plans did not threaten them, decided to see what Germany had to offer, a decision no doubt strengthened by the British lack of enthusiasm shown when, in mid-April 1939, the Soviets offered them an alliance. British policy had swung steadily against Germany after Munich, and fears of a German attack in Holland and Belgium swung the decision to commit Britain's army to a continental war. But in the panic that swept Europe after Hitler's destruction of Czechoslovakia and occupation of Memel (lost by Germany to Lithuania after 1918), British policy was still focused on the idea of deterring Germany, and its ally Italy, by a series of guarantees of Poland, Rumania, Greece and Turkey – seemingly the next targets of aggression. Implementation of these guarantees would, however, require Soviet support, and this, it gradually emerged, would only be forthcoming on terms unacceptable to Poland and Rumania: the Soviets demanded the right to intervene in those countries in the event of pro-German developments. The Anglo-French-Soviet talks were thus doomed to failure. In the meantime, Hitler fomented a crisis between Poland and Danzig, in the belief that British and French nerves would crack for fear of war. The Poles believed Germany was bluffing and hoped that a major French offensive into western Germany would save them should it come to war.

When Hitler finally unmasked his plans, signing a non-aggression pact with Russia on 23 August 1939, with a secret protocol dividing Poland, the Baltic states and Rumania between them, his expectations were once more disappointed. The Italians, furious at Hitler's deceit, made it clear they would be neutral, and Britain, with France, signed an alliance with Poland on 25 August. The German armies poised to attack Poland upon a faked pretext had to be recalled to their barracks while Hitler frantically sought for a new pretext for a war that, by throwing the blame on Poland, would (so he hoped) give Britain and France an excuse for ignoring the alliance they had just signed. This time Britain was, psychologically if not militarily, ready for war and refused to force the Poles into agreement. When Hitler duly went ahead with his attack on Poland at the end of August, only French reluctance delayed the British and French declarations of war on Germany until 3 September 1939. *D. C. W.*

Above: Maxim Litvinoff, dropped as Soviet foreign minister in May 1939
Left: the British ambassador in Moscow during the Anglo-French talks, Sir William Seeds

Stalin shows up for the signing of the German-Soviet non-aggression pact, 23 August 1939. Molotov signs, with von Ribbentrop looking on

THE SECOND WORLD WAR

Rommel

Dönitz

Eisenhower and Montgomery

When the Second World War began, it was confined to Europe. It has been called the 'last European war'. America and Russia, the future super-powers, remained neutral, with America favouring Britain, and Russia favouring Germany. Germany, after early victories, dragged in Italy as an ally and Russia as an enemy; Japan, long embroiled in her own drive for empire in the Far East, dragged in America. The war settled two quite different issues, according to whether it was being fought in the Pacific and Asia, including the Middle East, or in Europe. In the non-European battlefields it enormously accelerated the ebb of European supremacy. Native anti-European movements in many cases supported the Japanese; where they turned against them, as in Burma, Indonesia or Malaya, it was the experience of Japanese overlordship or ties with China, rather than loyalty to European culture, that drove them. In the Middle East nationalist leaders were divided and Britain to many seemed preferable to Germany, France or Italy. But war, as in Egypt, nurtured new anti-British feelings. In Europe the issues were quite different. Two political traditions, absolutist authoritarianism, justified by faith, fought conditional, pluralist, parliamentary, law-based democracy, and lost. Much of eastern Europe was lost politically to the Soviet Union, the embodiment of an increasingly non-European authoritarianism. Even in eastern Europe the Soviet victory rested on force alone, and elsewhere the democratic tradition triumphed.

The war forced technological and social development. Mass air transport, radio location and television took giant strides forwards. Medical science advanced to the point where the conquest of bacterial infection was in sight. Atomic power, both as a weapon and as a potential source of power for industry, was mastered. Jet and rocket propulsion became practicable. In social matters, apart from the effects of the control of both epidemic and endemic disease, Britain pioneered the idea of the welfare state in a democratic society with the Beveridge Report (1944). These were, however, effects that were only to be felt in the long run. In the short run the war cost at least 60 million lives, starved and impoverished Europe and the Soviet Union. Only the United States thrived on the war, displaying an industrial productivity undreamed of before.   *D. C. W.*

The Triumph of Blitzkrieg

Poland, Norway and France

In the opening, or European, phase of the Second World War, Germany enjoyed a remarkable run of successes by exploiting new methods of ruthless, swift-moving operations known as Blitzkrieg. Victories were due as much to the psychological as to the military unpreparedness of her opponents. But this style of campaigning was heavily dependent on strategic surprise leading to a quick decision. It was not a magic formula for victory and could not be endlessly repeated. From 1942, Germany became engaged in total war against enemies with a far superior production capacity in which her commanders' operational brilliance was at a discount.

The conquest of Poland in September 1939 was so one-sided that Hitler's war machine was not fully tested. Bravely though the Poles fought, they had a 2000-mile frontier to defend with a hostile Russia in their rear. In aircraft they were outnumbered by 450 to 1300 and in tanks by 660 to 2800. Germany's spearhead comprised six panzer divisions supported by motorized divisions but the bulk of the infantry divisions still had to march and were dependent on horse-drawn transport. The Luftwaffe played a decisive part, attacking key points behind the enemy's front in close cooperation with the ground forces.

The second wave of conquests involved the overrunning of Denmark and Norway in April 1940. The seizure of Norway was a brilliant demonstration of combined operations carried out under the nose of a superior enemy navy. The Anglo-French Expeditionary Force managed to hang on at Narvik for a few weeks but this did little to save face in a badly mismanaged campaign.

The German conquest of France and the Low Countries, in May and June 1940, was the greatest triumph of Blitzkrieg. It was achieved with approximate parity in ground forces (including tanks), but with a decisive advantage in the air. By sending seven of their ten panzer divisions through the lightly-defended Ardennes the Germans surprised the defenders on the River Meuse, effected a crossing and virtually decided the war within five days. The Allies' line of communications was severed on 19 May and by 4 June the evacuation of Dunkirk was completed.

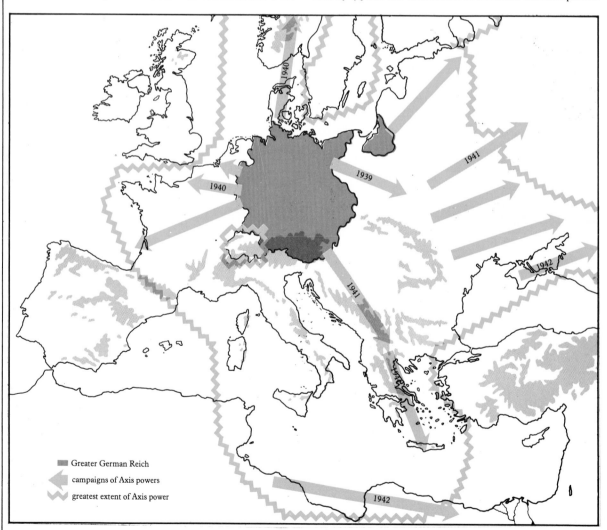

Greater German Reich

campaigns of Axis powers

greatest extent of Axis power

Symbol of Blitzkrieg: a Junkers 87 Stuka howls down on its target

'The Return from Dunkirk - arrival at Dover', drawn by Muirhead Bone

Britain saved the bulk of her troops but abandoned her weapons and vehicles. France accepted defeat on 22 June.

Allied blunders and disagreements helped to convert the initial German success into a catastrophe for themselves. The panzer spearheads were extremely vulnerable to counter-attack after crossing the Meuse, but Britain had not a single armoured division available, while the French squandered theirs in piecemeal efforts. Hitler and his High Command showed a tendency to panic and issue confused orders in a crisis. Finally, the Luftwaffe, so dominant when operating from its home bases, grew less effective as the campaign developed, and failed at Dunkirk.

Britain alone
So rapid was Hitler's triumph in the west that he was unprepared to complete the débâcle in France by invading Britain. How seriously Hitler and his service chiefs contemplated a seaborne invasion of Britain in the summer of 1940 is disputed. Such an operation stood little chance without complete command of the air and that was denied them by the RAF. The Luftwaffe's difficult task was made harder by Hermann Göring's vacillation between knock-ing out airfields to eliminate RAF Fighter Command and bombing London. German losses over the latter were so great that the offensive was called off in mid-September, never to be seriously resumed.

Meanwhile, the collapse of France had caused Italy to abandon her neutrality and attack, with little success, across the French Alps in June. She also began to build up her forces in Libya for a ponderous advance towards Egypt. Furthermore, by bungling an attack on Greece from Albania in October, Italy unintentionally opened up a new area of German conquest in the Balkans. In the spring of 1941, Germany drove through Greece and also captured Crete, though with crippling losses to her airborne forces.

At sea, Germany's strategic situation with regard to Britain was greatly enhanced by her conquest of bases in Norway and, even more important, by her ability to operate U-boats further out into the Atlantic from captured bases along the French coast. Also, long-range Focke-Wulf Condor aircraft from Bordeaux reconnoitered for the U-boats, and attacked shipping. The new tactic of massed attack on convoys by surfaced U-boats, known as 'wolf-packs' was developed. In October 1940, two homeward-bound convoys were virtually annihilated without a single U-boat casualty. Fortunately for Britain, there were less than 30 U-boats operational so that such 'kills' were followed by welcome lulls. By May 1941, improved defensive discoveries, such as the equipment of escorts with a primitive type of radar and the basing of ships and aircraft in Iceland, forced the wolf-packs to operate further west. By August 1941, Admiral Karl Dönitz had 80 U-boats operational and 198 in commission, but after a further 'happy time' in the western Atlantic, Hitler ordered him to direct all available submarines to the Mediterranean. Then, on 7 December, Germany's declaration of war on the USA opened a whole new complex of vulnerable trade routes from the Caribbean to Canada. Once again, the sea wolves could wreak havoc.

'Barbarossa'
Hitler's final Blitzkrieg offensive, Operation 'Barbarossa', opened on 22 June 1941 with spectacular territorial advances and huge 'bags' of prisoners. There were now 21 panzer divisions (equipped with Mk III and Mk IV tanks) but the bulk of the 163 infantry divisions were still unmotorized. Despite repeated warnings of the impending attack, the Russians were badly surprised. Their ground forces were numerically impressive but poorly trained and too densely deployed in the forward zone. Stalin temporarily lost control and, but for the vast size of the country, Russia might have shared France's fate. Guderian's panzer group, for example, advanced 250 miles in six days encircling whole Russian armies: 650,000 troops were captured at Vyaz'ma alone. Even in this first successful phase, Hitler interfered with operations, removing the panzer forces from the thrust towards Moscow and switching the main efforts towards Leningrad and the Ukraine. When winter set in the Germans were far from achieving their goals and their appalling logistical miscalculations were revealed. Ferocious Russian counterattacks in December 1941 showed that the Blitzkrieg phase was coming to an end. *B. J. B.*

Rommel in Africa

In February 1941, General Erwin Rommel was sent by Hitler to Tripoli to reinforce the Italians with, initially, only two German divisions. Finding the British over-extended after their victory over the Italians at Bedafomm and weakened by the diversion of units to Greece, Rommel promptly attacked at the end of March. By 11 April he had retaken Benghazï, Bardia and Sollum, but with Tobruk holding out in his rear this was the limit of his advance. In June 1941 Field-Marshal Earl Wavell mounted a counter-attack (Operation 'Battleaxe') but when this failed he was replaced by General Claude Auchinleck. The latter's offensive (Operation 'Crusader') took until mid-November to prepare but after a long and confused battle the Axis forces retreated. The largely Australian garrison of Tobruk was relieved by the New Zealanders on 10 December and by Christmas Benghazï was again in British hands. By the end of the year Rommel had taken up a defensive position at El 'Agheila about 50 miles beyond Bedafomm. The Allies had advanced some 300 miles but distances in the desert meant little; proximity to fuel, stores and repair workshops and better air cover were far more important than ground occupied.

Rommel quickly proved this by counter-attacking again at the end of January 1942. Benghazï changed hands for a fourth time, and the Axis forces halted at a line from El Gazala on the coast to Bir Hacheim. Here the German commander paused until the end of May in the vain hope that Axis air attacks would knock out British bases on Malta and so greatly ease his supply problem. Rommel resumed the offensive by sending his armoured forces round the open southern flank to threaten the British rear and Tobruk. The British in turn counter-attacked forcing the German centre onto the defensive in the midst of the Allied minefield. Rommel's impetuous leadership from the front added to the confusion, but after 16 days of heavy fighting his daring paid off when Auchinleck decided to retreat to El 'Alamein. There was, however, a major difference from the previous summer: despite Winston Churchill's rhetoric, Tobruk had not been rendered impregnable and this time it capitulated.

This doubtless influenced Churchill in his decision to replace Auchinleck with Alexander as Commander-in-Chief Middle East while General Bernard Montgomery took command of the Eighth Army. Before these changes occurred, however, Auchinleck had decisively checked the Axis advance at the El 'Alamein line in July 1942. Another reason for Auchinleck's removal was his insistence that a counter-offensive could not be mounted before the autumn.

In the event, Montgomery took even longer to build up and train his army, being certain that, after his defeat of Rommel's last desperate attack on 'Alam el Halfa early in September, he could, with his marked superiority in ground and air forces, win a decisive victory. If the final battle of El 'Alamein (from 23 October to 4 November) did not achieve all that Montgomery hoped, it nevertheless dealt Rommel a fatal blow. Forced to retreat to Tunisia and then being hemmed in by General Dwight Eisenhower's Anglo-American forces in Algeria, Rommel put up a stubborn resistance, and even won an ephemeral victory against the Americans at the Kasserine Pass in February 1943. Soon afterwards, Rommel handed over command to General Achim von Arnim who, on 13 May, surrendered the entire Axis army.   *B. J. B.*

Erwin Rommel, commander of the Afrika Korps, in the Egyptian desert, July 1942

The Nordic and Baltic Lands

The Nordic lands

By the end of the First World War the Social Democrats in Denmark, Norway and Sweden were strong but far from having a majority in parliament, and their socialist ideology made cooperation with parties to the right of them difficult. On the non-socialist side, the parties were mutually suspicious, and during the 1920s there was a succession of short-lived minority governments. A change took place during the 1930s. Stable governments, based on cooperation between the Social Democrats and a non-socialist party, came to power in all three countries. The need to devise measures to meet the effects of the world economic depression that began in 1929 made lasting inter-party cooperation possible. In Denmark the Social Democrat Torvald Stauning was prime minister from 1929 to 1942. His counterpart in Sweden, Per-Albin Hansson, was prime minister for almost exactly as long (1932–46). The relative success in coping with the economic crisis and the Social Democrats' renunciation of socialism as an immediate goal in favour of moderate reformist policies laid the foundation for their political hegemony after 1945.

A similar development did not occur in Finland. Independence upon the collapse of the tsarist empire in 1917 had been followed by a civil war in 1918 between 'Reds' and 'Whites'. The latter won, but the bitterness engendered by defeat, and White reprisals, helped to create support for the Finnish Communist Party that has made it the strongest in the Nordic countries to this day and has divided the Finnish labour movement into fairly evenly balanced Social Democratic and Communist sections. During the inter-war years the Whites set the tone and the Finnish left was therefore not integrated into political life in the same way as its Nordic counterparts.

During the First World War, Denmark, Norway and Sweden had succeeded in remaining neutral and by the inter-war period a foreign policy of neutrality was an established tradition. Finland's position was more ambiguous. The dominant political groups distrusted Russia, but by the end of the 1930s Finland was trying to pursue a policy of neutrality in cooperation with her Nordic neighbours. At the outbreak of the Second World War the Nordic area was quickly involved by conflicting great-power interests. Russia feared – and Germany hoped – that Finland could be used as a base for attack on Leningrad. The result was the Russo-Finnish Winter War of 1939–40 and Finnish involvement (1941–44) in Germany's war against Russia. Finland was able in the end to make a separate peace, but on terms that included the loss of one-tenth of her territory. Conflicting German and Anglo-French attempts to exploit Scandinavia for their strategic purposes led to the German invasion of Denmark and Norway on 9 April 1940 and their occupation by Germany for the remainder of the war. Only Sweden succeeded in remaining neutral, but at the price of accommodating whichever belligerent had the upper hand at any one time. *T. M.-P.*

The Baltic lands

Estonia, Latvia and Lithuania also achieved independence in 1917, but the subsequent Russo-German treaty of Brest-Litovsk (March 1918) gave control of the Baltic provinces to Germany. Complete independence was only

Extreme winter conditions provided Finland's best defence against Stalin's superior forces in 1939–40

assured after the expulsion of invading Soviet forces and German irregulars in 1919. The economies of all three states were markedly agrarian. There had been little industrial development in Lithuania before 1914, and industrialization in Latvia and Estonia was severely affected by the cutting of ties with the Russian hinterland. A series of short-lived and weak coalition governments in the 1920s gave way to authoritarian régimes established by leading figures in the struggle for independence – by Smetona in 1926 in Lithuania, and by Ulmanis (Latvia) and Päts (Estonia) in 1934. Jewish minorities were freed from the restrictions of the tsarist period, and played a prominent part in the academic and cultural life of the new states. Land reforms of the early 1920s and majority ethnic rule deprived the old Baltic German upper class of its dominant rule in Estonia and Latvia, but the Baltic Germans continued to play an active role until their evacuation to Germany in 1939–40.

The Nazi-Soviet Pact in August 1939 placed the Baltic states at the mercy of the two great powers. All three were compelled to sign mutual assistance treaties with the USSR in the autumn of 1939. Red Army units were stationed within the republics, but relations with Moscow remained cordial until the spring of 1940, when further demands were made. Under Soviet pressure, new national assemblies were hastily elected and these voted for incorporation into the USSR in August 1940. Less than a year later German troops occupied the Baltic areas, which remained under German administration until the restoration of Soviet control in 1944–45. Although a degree of autonomy is vested in the Soviet Baltic republics, Moscow has remained firmly in control of the affairs of the Baltic peoples ever since. *D. K.*

The Tide begins to Turn

The world at war

On 7 December 1941, while negotiations were continuing in Washington, Japan attacked the American base at Pearl Harbor in the Hawaiian Islands. Achieving complete surprise, 353 carrier-borne aircraft destroyed 18 warships and over 300 aircraft, but they missed the vital prize of the four American aircraft carriers, which were all at sea. Simultaneously, the Japanese attacked Hong Kong, Malaya, the Philippines and the three American-held Pacific islands of Midway, Wake and Guam.

The Japanese war plan had two purposes. First, to capture and occupy south-east Asia and the Dutch East Indies with their abundant supplies of oil, rice and rubber; second, to secure a vast defensive perimeter which would render a counter-offensive extremely difficult. The first aim was achieved remarkably quickly and cheaply. By the end of December 1941, they had captured Guam, Wake and Hong Kong. Rangoon fell on 8 February 1942 and a week later Singapore capitulated – the greatest disaster in British imperial history. The Dutch East Indies were overrun in March and on 9 April Ceylon was attacked from aircraft carriers. India itself appeared threatened. Finally, in May, America's humiliation was underlined by the loss of the Philippines. In just five months Japan had conquered a vast Pacific empire. Could she retain it?

Meanwhile, in Europe and the Mediterranean, Japan's assumption that the Axis powers would win began to seem questionable in 1942. At the final battle of El Alamein (from 23 October to 4 November) General Bernard Montgomery slowly but surely defeated Rommel's forces and ended the threat to Egypt. Simultaneously the Anglo-American landings in French North Africa (Operation 'Torch') cut off the Axis forces' retreat.

Stalingrad and El Alamein

Though El Alamein was an important victory for the Allies, it was small in scale compared with Stalingrad. Although this city on the west bank of the Volga was important as a major manufacturing centre and commanded the main communications network of southern Russia, its capture and destruction seemed to have a symbolic significance for Hitler. By the autumn of 1942, von Paulus's Sixth Army had driven Chuikov's 62nd Army into the city, where every building was stubbornly defended. The former's communications with Army Group A in the Caucasus were precarious, yet Hitler removed generals who attempted to warn him of the danger. As autumn turned to winter, von Paulus concentrated his German troops in Stalingrad itself, leaving his flanks to be defended by Rumanians. Meanwhile, General Zhukov was assembling no less than 12 armies for a massive counter-offensive.

On 19 and 20 November, when the ground was frozen and suitable for tanks, Zhukov launched an enormous pincer movement north and south of Stalingrad which smashed through the Rumanian lines. Three days later the encircling armies linked up on the Don. The besiegers now became the besieged: von Paulus, and 250,000 men were cut off. Hitler ordered von Paulus to stand firm, accepting Reichmarshal Hermann Göring's assurance that the Sixth Army could be supplied by air. In mid-December Field-Marshal Fritz von Manstein, commanding Army Group B, attempted to relieve von Paulus by

attacking from the west, but the faint chance that this would succeed disappeared when Hitler forbade von Paulus to fight his way out. As only a fraction of Göring's promised supplies got through, the German defenders suffered increasing privation. Hitler ordered von Paulus to refuse all invitations to surrender and promoted him to field-marshal in order to strengthen his will to resist. After his defences had been cut in two, von Paulus disobeyed, and surrendered on 2 February 1943. By then some 70,000 Germans had died in the siege and nearly 100,000, including 24 generals, became prisoners. Few survived their captivity.

Terrible though these losses were, they did not sum up the full extent of the catastrophe. For the first time, a major German formation had been utterly defeated, not merely as a result of attrition by larger forces, but by being encircled in the same way as the Germans themselves had outmanoeuvred the Russians in 1941. Although the Germans fought a long rearguard action, punctuated by counter-offensives, they never regained the strategic initiative on the Eastern Front.

Above: Besieged Leningrad, 1942 – 'Death to the Child-Murderers!' on the poster
Left: Pearl Harbor under Japanese attack, as re-enacted in the 1970 film 'Tora Tora Tora!'

The Battle of the Atlantic

The Battle of the Atlantic started to go badly for Germany at approximately the same time. With America's entry into the war in December 1941, the U-boats enjoyed their second 'happy time', sinking as many as 360 merchant ships in American coastal waters between January and July 1942. Shipping losses continued at a high rate throughout 1942, to the point where even Prime Minister Winston Churchill feared they might cause Britain's defeat. March 1943 marked the zenith of U-boat successes, with 43 ships sunk in three weeks, but with the introduction of a more effective type of radar the Allies thereafter regained the ascendancy. Not a single Allied ship was lost to submarines in the Atlantic between mid-May and September 1943, whereas Admiral Karl Dönitz had to advise Hitler that submarine losses were now unacceptably high. Dönitz kept the battle going, but even with new inventions, such as the acoustic torpedo, his submarines never regained the upper hand.

The Allied bomber offensive

Finally, in the aerial bombing campaign it took even longer for the scales to tilt decisively against Germany but when at last they did so, the effect was truly devastating. When the war began, the British (and later the Americans) wrongly believed their strategic bombing to be accurate. Both were slow to accept that it was not. By the autumn of 1941, forced by German air and ground defences to operate at night, RAF Bomber Command chiefs realized that only large towns presented realistic targets. Numerous navigational and bombing inventions enabled Bomber Command to cause great destruction in the Ruhr and to Hamburg. On the other hand, losses to night-fighters mounted steadily throughout 1943. Meanwhile, the American Eighth Army Air Force based in England joined the air offensive in 1942. Using heavily-armed B-17 Flying Fortresses, they attempted to carry out precision bombing in daylight. This proved disastrous when they flew beyond their fighter escorts, as in the raids on Schweinfurt in October 1943. The Allied bombing offensive might have been abandoned altogether but for the introduction of the excellent long-range Mustang fighter in the spring of 1944. With the Americans bombing by day and the British by night, the strategic air offensive at last began to pay dividends. *B. J. B.*

The Pacific War

Japan checked

Encouraged by their easy victories in the first few months of the war, the Japanese decided to extend their perimeter to include Papua New Guinea and the Solomon Islands, thus posing a direct threat to Australia and her communications with the US. Three land and sea actions in the summer and autumn of 1942 showed that the Japanese had over-reached themselves.

In attempting to capture Port Moresby in Papua New Guinea and the small island of Tulagi, the Japanese were drawn into the Battle of the Coral Sea. This was the first sea battle to be fought exclusively by the rival carrier-borne aircraft without the fleets sighting each other. American aircraft from the carriers USS *Lexington* and USS *Yorktown* intercepted the Japanese invasion force en route for Port Moresby. They sank one of its three accompanying carriers, badly damaged another and shot down 40 aircraft. The *Lexington* suffered an internal explosion and had to be sunk, but all her planes were saved. Since the invasion force turned back, this could be counted an American victory.

The Battle of Midway on 3 and 4 June was a more clear-cut Japanese defeat. With eleven battleships and four carriers, Admiral Yamamoto set out to capture the Midway Islands and complete the destruction of the American Pacific Fleet. Opposing him, Admiral Chester Nimitz had only three carriers (including the damaged USS *Yorktown*) and no battleships, but to offset this numerical weakness the Americans had broken the enemy code. The sea and air battle was conducted with the fleets even further apart than in the previous encounter. Although the *Yorktown* was lost, all four Japanese carriers were sunk or disabled. It was a crippling blow from which the Japanese never fully recovered.

'Island-hopping'

Early in August 1942, US Marines carried out the first of innumerable amphibious landings when they established beach-heads on Tulagi and at Guadalcanal in the Solomon Islands. The Japanese ferried reinforcements from their main base in the area, Rabaul, in New Britain, and between mid-August and November carried out repeated counter-attacks with characteristic ferocity. Early in 1943

they accepted defeat and withdrew from Guadalcanal; simultaneously the long struggle in the mountain jungles of Papua New Guinea ended with Japanese withdrawal from Buna.

Since they were too weak to attack Rabaul, Admiral William Halsey and General Douglas MacArthur spent the second half of 1943 winkling out the Japanese from their bases in the Solomon Islands and Papua New Guinea respectively. MacArthur's forces, assisted by air supply and paratroop landings, had captured Lae, Salamaua and Finschhafen by October. Meanwhile, Halsey's task-forces steadily approached within striking range of Rabaul by taking New Georgia, Bougainville and Green islands.

As the MacArthur–Halsey operations would be slow to affect Japan herself, it was decided to undertake supplementary operations against the enemy's inner defensive ring of islands, with the aim of striking at her cities directly with long-range B-29 Superfortress bombers.

This campaign, which was characterized throughout by heavy American losses in the face of fanatical resistance, began in November 1943 with the capture of the Tarawa Atoll in the Gilbert Islands, and early in 1944, four islands in the Marshall Islands were secured. By July 1944, Nimitz's force was in possession of Saipan, Guam and Tinian in the Mariana Islands. The systematic destruction of Japanese cities now began, although the B-29s could not yet be given fighter escort.

On Eniwetok Island (Marshall group), February 1944: waiting to go

Post-VE Day propaganda, calling for a final effort to win the Pacific War

GET THE JAP
AND GET IT OVER!
Work where you're needed
SEE YOUR U. S. EMPLOYMENT SERVICE
WAR MANPOWER COMMISSION

The Philippines regained

In September 1944, MacArthur and Halsey made the bold decision to go straight for the southern Philippine islands of Mindanao and Leyte, leaving the Japanese garrisons of the Dutch East Indies to be mopped up later. American landings in Leyte Gulf on 20 October provoked the naval battles which virtually eliminated the Japanese fleet. The Japanese sent two powerful squadrons to destroy the American covering force and attack the precarious beach-head. Admiral Nishimura's squadron, approaching from the south-east, was caught by Admiral Oldendorf's squadron moving through the Surigao Strait in line ahead. In the last classic surface ship battle of the Pacific war, the Japanese squadron was ambushed by superior forces and virtually annihilated by gunfire at ranges of eight to ten miles. Admiral Kurita's task-force approaching from the north through the San Bernardino Strait constituted a greater menace, particularly when Halsey despatched his main carrier group northward in the mistaken belief that Kurita's whole force was withdrawing. The only covering force between Kurita's ten capital ships and the beach-heads was Admiral Sprague's inferior force of light escort carriers and destroyers. At the Battle of Samar Island on 25 October, Sprague's smaller and slower ships fought heroically and, although five were sunk, Kurita decided to withdraw. This was a more decisive victory than the Americans realized at the time.

MacArthur regarded the recapture of the Philippines as essential to provide the main base for a gigantic invasion of Japan towards the end of 1945, but in the event she was bombed into submission before this hazardous operation was attempted. The price paid in American lives was nevertheless high, for the Japanese fought almost literally to the last man to prevent the establishment of fighter bases on the tiny volcanic atoll of Iwo Jima and on Okinawa. Iwo Jima took five weeks to conquer instead of the expected four days. Few of the 23,000 defenders survived and the Americans lost about 6000 men. Okinawa's garrison of 100,000 held out from early April to mid-June 1945, assisted by suicide-plane attacks from land bases.

The Bomb

By the spring of 1945, it was clear to all but Japan's most fanatical leaders that her defeat was imminent. Although she still had large armies in the field, particularly in China, her navy and merchant shipping had been destroyed and her cities were being flattened. When on 26 July an Allied call to surrender was ignored, it was decided to drop an atomic bomb. The first fell on Hiroshima on 6 August and three days later a second was dropped on Nagasaki. Russia's declaration of war underlined the hopelessness of further resistance and the Emperor ordered a ceasefire. MacArthur accepted the formal surrender aboard USS *Missouri* on 2 September.   *B. J. B*

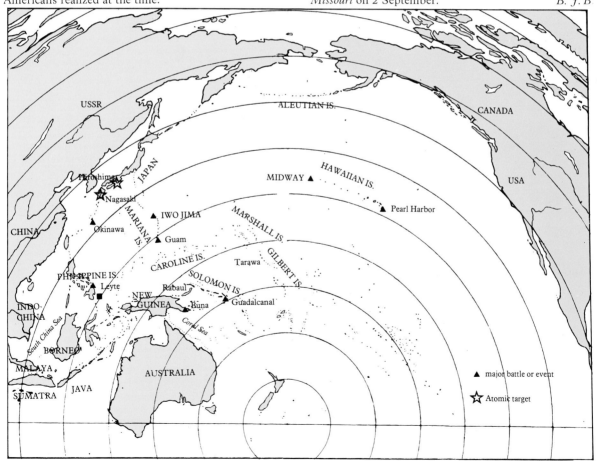

The Axis Smashed

With Japan's attack on America in December 1941, the war had become truly world-wide. Japan's empire at its greatest extent included pro-Japanese governments in occupied China, Thailand, Burma, the Philippines, Indochina and Indonesia. Malaya remained a Japanese colony. Hitler's Europe was divided into Greater Germany (including Austria, the Sudetenland, north-west Poland, with Alsace-Lorraine, Luxembourg, Bialystok, Slovenia and after 1943, the south Tyrol marked for eventual inclusion), quasi-colonial territories (Bohemia-Moravia, the Baltic states, central Poland, White Russia and the Ukraine), countries under military occupation (Norway, Denmark, the Netherlands, Belgium, France, the Channel Islands, Greece and Serbia) and the satellites (Finland, Bulgaria, Rumania, Hungary, Slovakia, Croatia and, after 1943, the rump of Mussolini's fascist Italy).

Against these were ranged Britain, the Empire and Dominions (save Eire) and the governments-in-exile of Poland, Czechoslovakia, Norway, the Netherlands, Belgium, Greece, Yugoslavia and the Free French. Behind America were ranged the Latin American states, in varying degrees of bellicosity, united in the declaration of Rio de Janeiro (January 1942) and the Act of Chapultepec (March 1945). The Soviet Union at first lacked any equivalent coterie of allies and satellites. In May 1942 it concluded an alliance with Britain and in December 1943 it was to conclude an alliance with the Czechoslovak government-in-exile.

Up to the end of 1943 there were persistent reports of clandestine Soviet-German peace feelers. The Soviet Union, alone among the anti-Nazi forces, played with a Free German movement, while Britain and the US, by contrast, rejected all approaches from the various internal anti-Nazi groups in Germany. At Casablanca, in January 1943, President Roosevelt and the British premier, Winston Churchill, announced that German surrender must be unconditional.

The Soviet Union remained deeply suspicious of Britain and America, and in 1942 and 1943 the Soviet leadership pressed their allies desperately to invade western Europe and open a second front that would relieve the German pressure. Britain, locked in a life-and-death battle with the German submarine fleet for the control of the Atlantic, managed to persuade the Americans into invading North Africa in November 1942 and moving on against Sicily and Italy, postponing the invasion of France until 1944. Their reward came in September 1943 when the Italians, having dismissed Mussolini six weeks previously, surrendered. German troops, forewarned, occupied northern Italy and the Italian-occupied areas of the Balkans, taking over the desperate fight against the Yugoslav partisans, led by the communist, Josip Tito. Mussolini, rescued from his Italian captors by German commandos, became head of the Repubblica Sociale Italiana. In November 1943 the new Italian government declared war on Germany and a largely Communist-led partisan movement sprang up in northern Italy.

The main issue between Britain and the USA stemmed from American anti-colonialism in the Far Eastern theatre, and from American antipathy to General De Gaulle. No alternative could be found, and De Gaulle easily took over the Committee of National Liberation set up in January 1943 in Algiers. On the eve of D-Day, it was recognized as the provisional government of France and in October 1944, after the liberation of France, De Gaulle was recognized *de jure* as the president of a French ally who on British insistence was given her own zone of occupation in Germany and Austria.

Relations between the so-called Big Three remained awkward throughout the war. On the military and administrative side of the European war, Britain and America functioned as one, with integrated command and supply organizations. In south-east Asia and the Pacific, the British effort was largely separate from the American and, where it overlapped, as on the Sino-Burmese border, relations were strained at best.

Military relations with the Soviet Union hardly existed, the main instrument for reconciliation of the views of the Big Three being conferences of foreign ministers and, on three occasions, meetings of the three war leaders (at Teheran in November 1943, at Yalta in the Crimea in February 1945 and at Potsdam in July 1945, after the German surrender). Britain and America, convinced of the need to incorporate the Soviet Union in the arrangements for a post-war international peace-keeping organization, played the wooer in much of this. Churchill took part in several bilateral meetings with Roosevelt (at the Atlantic Charter meeting, August 1941 – when both leaders subscribed to a set of political principles for world

The alliance that was forged against the Axis powers had the overwhelming superiority in industrial potential

peace – at Casablanca, January 1943, at Quebec, August 1943, at Cairo, November 1943 and again at Quebec, September 1944). In October 1944 Churchill met Stalin in Moscow on his own to conclude an agreement dividing south-eastern Europe into British and Soviet zones of influence. The principal area of difference lay in eastern Europe, beginning inevitably with Poland. In April 1943 relations between the Polish government-in-exile and the Soviets broke down irretrievably after the discovery of a massacre of Polish officers at Katyn some time after the Soviet occupation of eastern Poland in 1939. As the Red Army swept through Poland in the spring of 1944, supporters of the government-in-exile were suppressed and the Lublin Committee of Polish Communists and fellow travellers put in their place. In August 1944, largely to forestall the Soviets, the Polish Home Army controlled by the government-in-exile rose against the Germans in Warsaw. The Soviets watched its elimination by the Germans unmoved, and remained static in Poland for another eight months, the main Red Army thrust swinging into south-east Europe to anticipate any western thrust of the kind Churchill was vainly urging on his American allies.

The Soviet thrust took Rumania and Bulgaria out of the war in August and September 1944. That same month Finland signed an armistice and Russian troops broke into Slovakia, too late to save a Slovak rising against the Germans, and linked with Tito's forces in Yugoslavia. A German coup in Hungary forestalled a Hungarian attempt to follow Rumania out of the war. British forces entering Greece found themselves embroiled in an attempted armed seizure of power in Athens by the Greek communists, which they suppressed. At Yalta many of the issues between the Big Three were temporarily settled, but with Roosevelt's death in April 1945 relations began to deteriorate again. At Yalta the Soviet Union had yielded to American pressure on her to enter the war against Japan, and a Polish government with a few elements from the government-in-exile had been accepted. But Soviet determination to control the governments of the east-European states they had occupied aroused old suspicions of long-term Soviet aims in Britain and the USA. Almost from the start, four-power relations in occupied Germany were bedevilled by the issue of the level of reparations, with the Russians ranged against the rest. De Gaulle had allied himself in December 1944 with the Soviet Union and, having been excluded from Yalta and Potsdam, refused to be bound by their decisions. Then in August 1945 atomic bombs were dropped on Hiroshima and Nagasaki. On 14 August Japan surrendered unconditionally. The Second World War was over.   *D. C. W.*

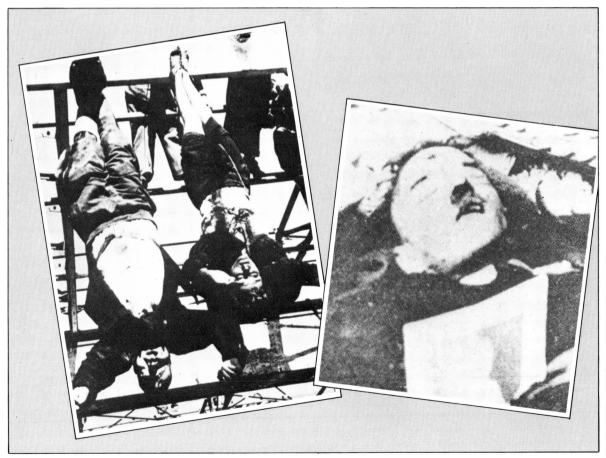

Nemesis: (left) Mussolini and his mistress in Milan, 29 April 1945; (right) a unique East German photograph, claimed to show Hitler after his suicide, 30 April 1945

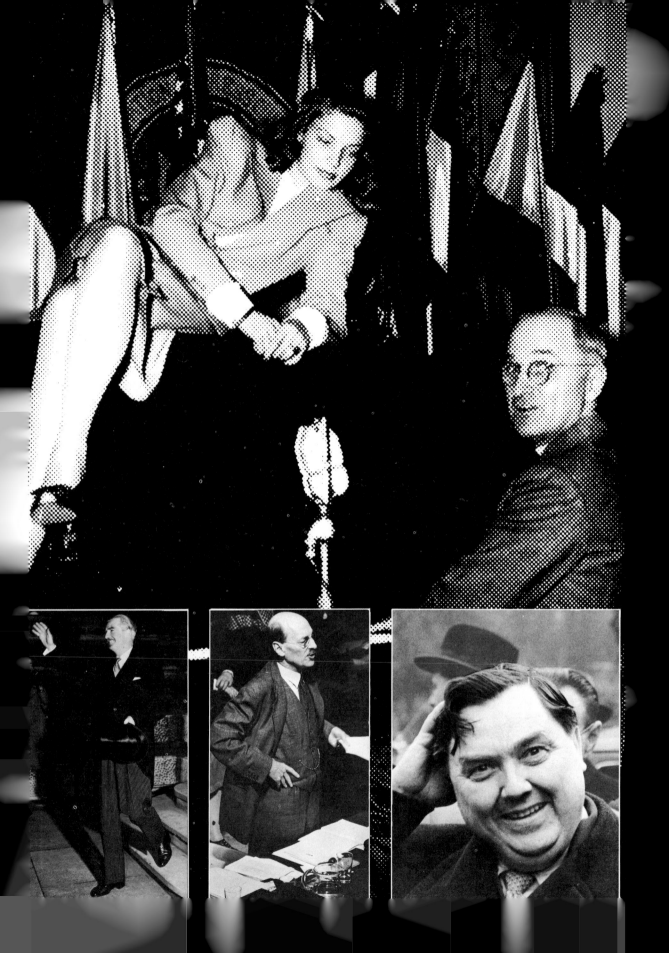

THE POST-WAR WORLD

Konrad Adenauer

After the Second World War the world seemed at first to belong to the super-powers, which swiftly became locked in confrontation in Germany, the Balkans, Iran and Korea. The degree to which this was so made it impossible for them to police or control the rest of the world, as the remains of Europe's overseas empires either took or were granted their independence. Apart from the super-powers and their largely European allies and satellites there was to develop an increasingly large group of non-aligned states, intent on eliminating the last traces of European political colonial rule, but only too conscious that the backwardness of their economies made them continue in dependence on the industrially advanced powers – the USA, the major countries of western Europe and Japan.

This so-called 'Third World' included some states whose monopoly control of resources essential to the industrial world (such as oil) put them among the 'have' nations. But for the large majority, anti-colonialism and a desire for international control over the trade, aid and investment policies of the industrial powers provided a unifying factor. Apart from that, they fought among themselves in a way that only their dependence on arms deliveries from the major industrial powers could contain. Besides numerous wars of 'decolonization' or liberation, there were post-colonial wars – some of them, like the Arab–Israeli and Indo–Pakistani conflicts, seemingly become endemic. There were, too, post-colonial civil wars, as in the Biafran affair in Nigeria, the Eritrean and Ogaden wars in Ethiopia, the Mauritanian fighting, the Kurdish wars in Iraq, the Yemeni civil war, the Hutu–Tutsi massacres in Ruanda, the repeated trouble in the south of Zaire

(Congo) and so on. Sometimes the super-powers were drawn in, as America was into Vietnam. The Soviet Union on three occasions, in East Germany in 1953, in Hungary in 1956 and in Czechoslovakia in 1968, used force to maintain pro-Soviet governments.

The high-technology arms race between the super-powers was central to their relationship and represented an investment of national wealth that only the two of them could afford. Other powers – Britain, France, China – either lagged behind or dropped out. In both super-powers there were internal elements (military, scientific and political) that had a vested interest in breaking up any temporary accommodation that showed signs of weakening their own positions. Fear, however, of a nuclear holocaust kept the super-power leaderships from allowing their occasional confrontations to get out of hand, and gave them the will to control international disputes that threatened to escalate into something worse. Over it all, the new institutions of the UN functioned, however imperfectly, to preserve a semblance of the international order that all peoples wished for.

D. C. W.

Actress Lauren Bacall watches President Harry Truman. Inset, left to right: Sir Anthony Eden, Clement Attlee, Georgi Malenkov.

249

Years of Hope

The peoples of the world could hope, after the defeat of the Axis in 1945, that the 'Grand Alliance' that had won military victory would remain united in peace as well. The USA under Roosevelt and then Truman, the Soviet Union under Stalin, and Britain under Churchill and then Attlee were all publicly committed to the concept of democracy, and were all members of the United Nations Organization. This body, established in 1945, seemed to have much better prospects than the abortive League of Nations set up in 1919: not only did it have all the world's leading powers among its members, but it also had a Security Council potentially much better equipped than the old League Council to preserve peace, and its specialized agencies were dedicated to removing the economic, social and psychological causes of international conflict.

The bright prospects of 1945 proved to have little basis in the underlying and deep-seated conflicts between the Western Allies and the Soviet Union. Ideology was one major source of conflict: what the West meant by 'democracy', based on free elections and a free economy, could not be reconciled with the Soviet Union's Marxist–Leninist view that true democracy requires one-party working-class control and the abolition of private property. There were also conflicts arising from the traditional workings of the international balance of power. When the destruction of German and Japanese military might in 1945 left one power vacuum in Europe and another in Asia, the US and Soviet Russia were almost inevitably drawn in to take their place.

East–West conflicts soon emerged in the Middle East, the Balkans and central Europe. In Iran a dispute arose from the Soviet Union's unwillingness to evacuate the northern part of the country, occupied in 1941, and it was only after strong criticism in the United Nations that the Soviet occupation was ended in 1946. In Germany, at the same time, the elaborate arrangements for joint control by the four occupying powers – the USSR, the USA, Britain and France – proved unworkable. The Potsdam Agreement of 1945 had laid down that occupied Germany would be treated as a single unit, and that each of the four Allied powers would apply the same policies in its zone of occupation. However, deep differences soon appeared: in all the zones the occupying powers dismantled industrial equipment and removed some of it for their own use, but this policy was carried to extremes in the Soviet zone. In the Western occupied zones political life began again with the development of a wide range of political parties, but in the Soviet zone, the ruling Communist Party forcibly incorporated the Social Democratic Party, and the Socialist Unity Party that resulted from this merger thus took over power in a one-party régime. Between 1945 and 1947 there were several conferences between the Soviet and Western governments to try to reach agreement on re-unifying Germany, but the gap of mistrust could not be bridged, and by early 1947, at a meeting of Foreign Ministers in Moscow, it was clear that total deadlock had been reached.

Apart from the mounting conflict of interests in Germany, President Truman and his Secretary of State, General Marshall, were increasingly aware of tensions in the eastern Mediterranean, where the Soviet Union was putting pressure on Turkey to concede territory and naval rights, and was also involved in the bitter civil war in

· ALL OUR COLOURS TO THE MAST ·

An optimistic poster, promoting the Marshall Plan and European unity

President Harry S. Truman with the architect of European post-war recovery, George C. Marshall, and, far right, Averell Harriman

Greece between Communists and anti-Communists. France and Italy had powerful Communist Parties that posed an acute challenge to weak governments struggling with the problems of post-war reconstruction. In Britain the Labour government under Clement Attlee was faced with not only the economic and industrial weakness caused by the war but also, in 1946–47, the harshest winter for many years. This was the background that led Attlee's Foreign Secretary, Ernest Bevin, to send an urgent warning to Washington in February 1947: Britain's economic plight would not allow her to support Greece and Turkey for more than a few weeks longer, and American help was essential. Truman's response was quick and effective: on 12 March he went before Congress to proclaim the 'Truman Doctrine' – that the US would lend powerful economic and, if necessary, military support to Greece, Turkey and other countries facing Communist pressure.

The Truman Doctrine was a first clear commitment of American power to the East–West balance in Europe, and it was followed three months later by General Marshall's announcement of the European Recovery Programme (the Marshall Plan). This massive American economic aid for the rebuilding of Western Europe led in 1948 to the setting-up of the Organization for European Economic Co-operation (OEEC), followed by the military Western European Union pact and the civilian Council of Europe.

The establishment in 1947 of the Communist Information Bureau (Cominform) – as a successor to the Comintern, dissolved in 1943 – increased Western fears that Russia's aim was world revolution. In February 1948 a political crisis in Czechoslovakia ended that country's long struggle to remain neutral between the opposing camps. The Czech Communists were able to take power despite their minority support in the country, and a few months later, in June 1948, a conflict between the Soviet Union and the Communist leader of Yugoslavia, Marshal Tito, showed the nature of Stalin's intentions towards the satellite countries. Tito resented post-war Soviet attempts to dictate his country's policies, and in June 1948 Yugoslavia was expelled from the Cominform.

The most serious East–West conflict of 1948 developed at the same moment on the issue of Berlin. The agreements between the wartime Allies had left Germany's former capital as an enclave within the Soviet zone of occupation, in the expectation that reunification would soon follow. Instead, the division of Germany was mirrored in a split between East and West Berlin, with the Western sectors of the city occupied by the Americans, British and French, and dependent on them for fuel, food and other supplies. In June 1948 the Soviet and East German authorities tried to cut West Berlin's links with the West by blockading all transport by road, rail and canal, leaving the two million inhabitants entirely dependent on the ensuing 'air-lift' of 1948–49, in which the Western Allies flew a huge tonnage of essential supplies into the blockaded city. The division of both Germany and Europe into two hostile blocs, separated by the 'Iron Curtain' (a phrase first used by Churchill in a dramatic speech in 1946), was confirmed. *R. M.*

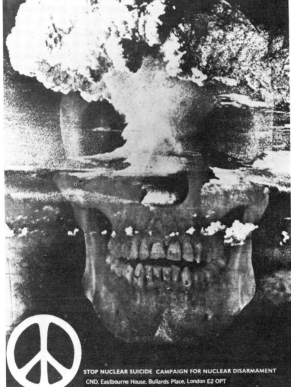

STOP NUCLEAR SUICIDE CAMPAIGN FOR NUCLEAR DISARMAMENT
CND, Eastbourne House, Bullards Place, London E2 OPT

The answer of many idealists to the threat of the bomb was to campaign for nuclear disarmament

The 'Cold War'

The direct East–West confrontation of the Berlin blockade, in 1948–49, hardened the division of Europe into two blocs, and the term 'cold' war was invented to describe a state of conflict that stopped only just short of shooting. The Berlin crisis, which ended with a Soviet climb-down after nearly a year of blockade, speeded up the creation of two rival German states: in the West, the Federal Republic was formed from the British, American and French zones of occupation, and in the East the Russians turned their own zone into the German Democratic Republic. Each of these bitterly hostile German states was incorporated into the alliance-bloc led by its super-power sponsor: the Federal Republic was set from the beginning on the path that would make it a full member of the North Atlantic Treaty Organization (NATO), and the German Democratic Republic would in due course join the Soviet-led Warsaw Pact.

America's strategic commitment to the European power balance, confirmed by the North Atlantic Treaty in 1949, was consolidated by events in Korea in the early 1950s. Even though Korea was remote from Europe, the American administration saw the outbreak of war there, in June 1950, as part of a world-wide trial of strength between Communist and anti-Communist forces. Korea, like Germany, had been divided after 1945 between the two rival camps, and Communist North Korea's attack on the anti-Communist South Korean state appeared to threaten a similar conflict between East and West Germany. The Korean War was ended by 1953, though not without savage and bloody fighting between the forces of the United Nations Organization (commanded by the impetuous American General Douglas MacArthur, who had to be dismissed by President Truman for pressing the counter-attack too heavily into North Korea), and the Communist forces, including massive reinforcements from the Peoples' Republic of China.

Even though the Korean crisis was managed by the outside powers in a way that prevented a direct escalation of the conflict, its impact was felt in many ways, including the pressure for the rearmament of West Germany. The newly created Federal Republic was intimately aligned with the Western bloc, but any idea of rearming Germany so soon after the war was anathema to large sections of British and French opinion, and also to the majority of Germans. Under the impact of the Korean War, however, the United States pressed strongly for a German contribution to Western defence, and this was finally agreed on when the Federal Republic joined NATO in 1955. The simultaneous involvement of the East German state in the Warsaw Pact only hardened the division of Germany. Even though the neutralization of Austria, which also took place in 1955, produced a fleeting hope that Germany too might be neutralized and reunified, the realities were different.

The Korean War had seen the emergence of Communist China on the world scene, following the Communist victory in the civil war against Chiang Kai-shek's Nationalist government in 1949, and China also played a part in the next major Far Eastern crisis, the war in French Indochina. This conflict, which had begun in 1946 with a local revolt against French colonial rule, lasted until 1954, when the strength of the Indochinese independence movement, with massive Chinese aid, led to the crushing defeat of French forces at the battle of Dien Bien Phu. Although the new American administration under President Eisenhower and Secretary of State Foster Dulles was alarmed by this victory for Communist-supported nationalists (and the use of American nuclear bombs to support France was suggested by Eisenhower's vice-president, Richard Nixon), the United States finally accepted the ending of French rule in Indochina, on terms that in theory left an independent South Vietnam free of Communist influence.

If the political map of Asia was liable to violent shifts, like those in China, Korea, and Vietnam, the dividing-line between East and West in Europe remained fixed once the trial of strength of the Berlin blockade was over. There were rumblings within the Communist bloc that suggested that new forces of change might take the upper hand, particularly after the personal domination of Stalin was removed by his death in 1953. However, these stirrings produced no major risk to the stability of the East–West balance. The Western powers took care not to intervene either when the East Germans demonstrated against Soviet influence in 1953, or when the Poles under Gomulka took the same course in early 1956, or even when the Hungarians, under Imre Nagy, defied the might of the Red Army in bloody street-fighting in November of the same year.

There was renewed East–West conflict over Berlin from 1958 onwards, culminating in the building of the Berlin Wall by the Russians and East Germans in August 1961 – a move that showed that the Eastern side was determined to cut off the flow of East German refugees to the West, and to seal the division between the two Germanys. Again the Western governments did nothing to prevent the Eastern action (the new American President Kennedy correctly saw that any Western obstruction to the building of the Wall might escalate into a major international conflict) and Western governments turned instead to the concept of détente or relaxation – of making the inevitable gap between the Eastern and Western blocs less dangerous and less harsh to live with.

The search for détente was sharply interrupted by the Cuban crisis of October 1962, when Kennedy had to face the challenge of Russian missiles installed on the Communist-ruled island of Cuba, less than a hundred miles from the American mainland. After a tense confrontation, which for a time looked like producing a third world war, the Soviet leader Khrushchev agreed to remove the missiles, and the terrifying experience of this narrowly averted war encouraged the two super-powers on the path to détente that they were to follow, with many hesitations and setbacks, in the 1960s and 1970s.

R. M.

More in sorrow than in anger, 'Krokodil', the Soviet satirical weekly, assumes the role of critic of American democracy, December 1951. Inset, left: Senator Joseph R. McCarthy in full cry on coast-to-coast TV, 6 April 1957. Inset, right: Conclusive evidence – a medium-range missile base on Cuba, photographed by the US Air Force

MISSILE ERECTOR

THEODOLITE STATION

5 TRUCKS UNDER CAMOUFLAGE NETTIN

A Watershed: Suez and Hungary

Suez

British interests in the Middle East – oil, 28 per cent of the trade as well as the route through the Suez Canal, and strategic defences against the Soviet Union – were of long standing. In the disturbed conditions of Arab–Israeli conflict, they were also difficult to protect. However, in October 1954, Britain made an agreement with the Egyptians, by which she undertook to withdraw her troops from the Suez Canal Zone within 20 months while retaining certain rights to use her old bases there especially in wartime, and the Egyptians promised to maintain the freedom of the Canal to all ships at all times. Many people in Britain, especially Conservatives, criticized this settlement for weakening her position; however, Sir Anthony Eden, then foreign secretary, defended it strongly and finally secured Parliament's approval. In April 1955, Eden succeeded Winston Churchill as Conservative leader and prime minister, but continued his direct interest in foreign affairs. He now found President Nasser moving rapidly away from Britain and the West in his bid to give Egypt leadership of the Arab world, apparently aligning himself with Communist countries, and accepting Russian aid for the Aswan Dam irrigation project. An Egyptian arms deal with the Soviet Bloc, and doubts about Nasser's ability to complete the Aswan programme, led Britain to follow the US in withdrawing her support for the scheme. Nasser's response was to nationalize the canal. Eden was furious. He saw Nasser's behaviour as a personal affront, making his defence of the 1954 agreement seem foolish and shortsighted. In the light of his memories of the 1930s, he also saw it as a new example of fascist behaviour in Nasser's unilateral rejection of international agreements and obligations. For Eden, appeasement was not to be repeated. Britain could not allow her prestige or international security to be weakened, nor was Eden willing to see his own leadership called in question. When international action failed to change Nasser's course, Britain went ahead – negotiating secretly with the French and Israelis, encouraging an Israeli attack on Egypt, and then invading the Canal Zone on 31 October 1956 with the excuse of separating the Egyptian and Israeli forces. International opinion was outraged, and Eden, instead of crowning his political career, annihilated it. The operation was a fiasco, and Britain's forced withdrawal a humiliation. Eden and his closest colleagues, R. A. Butler and Harold Macmillan, had seriously misread the international situation in expecting support for their action. The greatest effects were felt at home. Eden's action, although it provoked little open Conservative opposition, divided the Party. He therefore resigned on grounds of ill-health in January 1957, and was succeeded by Macmillan. The Liberals led by Joseph Grimond were strongly critical, moved into Opposition, and began a revival of their Party. The considerable degree of post-war bi-partisanship on foreign policy existing between Labour and Conservative was finally broken. The Suez adventure, having made plain the limitations of Britain's international strength, also hastened the slowly growing public feeling that Britain needed to re-think her role as a power in the world.

A. N. P.

Satellite view of the theatre of war, from Suez to Tiran

British public opinion was deeply split over Suez: an anti-Eden rally, 2 October 1956

Hungary

A late Stalinist comeback took place in Hungary in March–April 1955, when the feared, Moscow-trained ex-premier Mátyás Rákosi resumed power after engineering the dismissal of his more moderate and popular successor, Imre Nagy. Subsequently, Nagy was expelled from the Party, but many of his associates were left inside it. The unpopularity of Rákosi and his clique was growing in the country, and this led to tension and a critical debate between the influential Writers' Association and the Party leadership. This process was speeded up when Khrushchev's denunciation of Stalin in February 1956 became known to the Hungarian Party. Rákosi was cast off by the Soviet leaders in July 1956, and lost the leadership to Ernö Gerö. The rehabilitation of Imre Nagy was strongly opposed by Gerö, but this was precisely what was demanded by a faction within the Party, the writers and the public with increasing insistence. The reburial of one of Rakosi's opponents, László Rajk, executed in 1949 and now rehabilitated, touched off a public demonstration on 6 October directed against the Stalinists in the régime. It was, however, the reports of events in Poland later that month (the recall of Gomulka as Secretary-General under pressure of popular demonstrations) that finally triggered off the much larger student demonstration on 23 October. There were clashes with Soviet armour, and the government gave in. On 24 October Nagy was reappointed prime minister and, under popular pressure, he agreed to introduce the multi-party system, leave the Warsaw Pact and turn to the UN for help in making Hungary a neutral state like Austria.

Soviet forces were withdrawn from Budapest on 31 October and negotiations were begun between the Nagy government and the Soviet authorities for the eventual evacuation of all Soviet troops from Hungary. However, on 4 November the Soviet army moved back and fought its way to the centre of Budapest against heavy resistance by young volunteers. The government was deposed and the insurrectionists dispersed. Imre Nagy was arrested while under safe conduct from the Yugoslav embassy, and later tried in secret and executed. Meanwhile, the world was informed that a new government had been set up under János Kádár, and had asked for Soviet help against the 'counter-revolutionaries'. Kádár reorganized the Party as the Hungarian Socialist Workers Party, ruthlessly suppressed all opposition, and reconstructed the régime, while preserving the principle of collective leadership.

The Hungarian rising and its crushing by Soviet tanks, though not dissimilar to events that had already been witnessed in East Berlin in June 1953 and in Poland in October 1956, made a far deeper impression on world opinion, particularly on many veteran Communist Party activists in Western Europe and America. In the crisis of conscience caused by the sight of a popular uprising brutally put down by Russian armed force, a number of the latter left the party or became inactive. The determination of the leaders of the USSR to hold on at all costs to what they had acquired in 1945, in total disregard of the wishes of the people or of world opinion, was made clear by the outcome of the Hungarian October.   *L. P.*

The Hungarian struggle against Russian force: demonstrators dismantle the huge statue of Stalin

Britain after Churchill

After the mid-1950s Conservative and Labour governments aspired to similar goals – industrial growth, reduced unemployment, rising real incomes especially for the lowest paid, and improvement of the welfare state. They recognized that these goals necessitated controlling inflation, increasing exports, and economic planning. All, however, failed to achieve their objects for very long, and staggered from economic crisis to recovery to renewed crisis, for two chief reasons. First, Britain's industrial and export performance was never so generally good as that of her principal rivals, the US, Germany and Japan. Lack of success in foreign and domestic markets produced a trade deficit, and contributed to the decline in value of the pound sterling. The second was the reluctance of politicians to admit that their goals were frequently conflicting, and therefore could not be permanently reconciled. Industrial growth, for example, necessitated extensive investment, which could only mean at least temporarily less real wealth either for distribution as personal income or for public expenditure. Governments had therefore either to muddle along, or try to establish 'priorities'. In their propaganda, Conservatives emphasized privately-financed industrial expansion, higher personal incomes and investment, taxation and governmental activity kept to a minimum; Labour talked more of redistributing wealth, expanding the welfare state, and the necessary role of government in directing not only the economy as a whole but also particular sectors of industry. In practice, differences were less marked. Conservative victory again in 1959 was followed, despite Harold Macmillan's slogan 'You've never had it so good', by their testimony to government's unavoidable interventionist role: Selwyn Lloyd, chancellor of the exchequer, brought trade unions, industry and government together in 1961 in the National Economic Development Council (NEDC, or Neddy), and experimented with incomes policy. Although Labour added ineffective price control to incomes policy, such regulation and consultation was only intensified by the crises of 1966–68 and 1975–78. Both parties tried and failed (1969–74) to ease their problems by bringing trade unions firmly within a legal framework governing industrial relations. Conservatives under Edward Heath found it impossible to avoid state-financing of important industries. Questions of degree rather than principle were involved in inter-party disputes.

Entry into the EEC

One answer to Britain's economic difficulties was sought in membership of the European Economic Community (EEC), for which Macmillan's government applied in August 1961. Closer links with Europe had been rejected by Winston Churchill as incompatible with British traditions, especially her American, Commonwealth and imperial ties. By 1959 this position was being questioned. Britain's trade with the Commonwealth, while important, was growing only slowly if at all; by contrast, trade with the EEC countries grew by 43 per cent between 1958 and 1961. Unrestricted access to this large market, and a share in the rapid industrial growth, prosperity and low unemployment levels of the Six, seemed very attractive. Pressures on Britain from the US – anxious to foster a stronger Europe – and Britain's need to reduce overseas commitments (of which Macmillan's decision in 1959–60 to hasten the process of decolonization was a major sign) pushed her in the same direction. Although the first round of negotiations from October 1961 to January 1963 failed due to French opposition, entry remained the goal of later governments. The Labour Party was never wholly sympathetic to the idea of joining this 'rich man's club', with its largely conservative governments and the growing power of international 'big business'. In May 1967, however, despite opposition from its left wing, the Labour government applied again for membership, influenced by continuing economic troubles, and the inability of Britain's partners in the European Free Trade Area (EFTA) to match EEC growth. Again Britain's Commonwealth trading links and agricultural policies were stumbling-blocks, and again the French president, General Charles de Gaulle vetoed her entry. Only after the General's retirement in April 1969 was headway possible. Britain finally joined the EEC, after retreating extensively from her insistence on protecting Commonwealth food producers and her own cheaper sources of food, and after Harold Wilson's Labour government held an unprecedented national referendum in order to defeat the opponents of membership (June 1975).

Devolution

After 1960, the activities of central government affecting the lives of ordinary people seemed to become more obvious and irritating. This paralleled the growth of a more liberal and 'permissive' society, with the result that traditions of dress and ethics, respect for authority or institutions, were widely and readily questioned. The greater size and remoteness of government and its lack of responsiveness were felt particularly in Wales and Scotland, notwithstanding some decentralization of public departments. The late 1960s witnessed, among other forms of protest, the growth of separatist movements in the north and west. Plaid Cymru and the Scottish Nationalist Party were both able (unlike, say, disgruntled Tynesiders) to appeal to distinct nationalist traditions. They could also point to continuous discussion of devolving government responsibilities to these regions, at least since the 1880s. Devolution had actually occurred in Northern Ireland, albeit with questionable success. Welsh arguments for devolution rested on the existence of a distinct Welsh language and culture, and manifested themselves most obviously in demands that equality be given in education and common usage to both Welsh and English languages. Cultural protest in Wales became the preserve of more than a small intellectual élite because it was fuelled by a sense of economic grievance, and in Scotland the latter was always far more prominent. The feeling persisted that England took more than it returned. Since 1972, growing nationalism has forced the Westminster parties to espouse devolution. In particular, the Labour Party, trying to preserve support crucial to its future parliamentary strength, tried to pass a Devolution Bill in 1977. This failed, and in 1978, again with scant respect for Parliament or good legislation, Scottish and Welsh devolution bills were introduced.   *A. N. P.*

Right: In 1955 Sir Anthony Eden, now prime minister, says good-bye to his great predecessor, Sir Winston Churchill

Former prime ministers: (above) Sir Harold Mac-millan, (top) Sir Alec Douglas-Home, (middle) Edward Heath, (bottom) Sir Harold Wilson

US Economic and Foreign Policy

When Dwight D. Eisenhower was inaugurated as President of the USA in January 1953, the Korean War was still in progress. Communist China, the most populous country on earth, was unrepresented in the UN: the only Chinese government recognized by the US was General Chiang Kai-shek's Nationalist régime based on the island of Formosa. French forces were fighting a bitter colonial war in Vietnam. One year earlier, with American approval, six European countries had joined together to form the European Coal and Steel Community, forerunner of the present European Economic Community (EEC). Russia under Stalin was still engaged in what seemed an almost unending 'cold war'. In Africa, the European colonial empires were still largely intact. In the Middle East, the five-year-old state of Israel existed uneasily in the midst of a sea of hostile neighbours.

The 25 years after 1953 saw many changes in the world situation confronting American policy makers. One of the most dramatic was the rise of the defeated powers, Germany and Japan, to a position of economic strength that made them serious competitors to the US in world markets. Without American aid in the first place, it is unlikely that they would have attained their subsequent economic pre-eminence so quickly. American support for the idea of a more integrated Europe can similarly be seen as working to the long-term disadvantage of the US. In 1958, the six nations which had signed the agreement setting up a European Coal and Steel Community broadened their collaboration by establishing the EEC. By the early 1960s, so threatening had this Common Market become in competition with the US that the Kennedy administration promoted the so-called 'Kennedy round' of negotiations for reducing tariffs.

Since 1949, NATO has been the core of US European policy. It was in order to strengthen NATO that the US, less than a decade after the end of the Second World War, actively promoted German rearmament. This provoked a response from the Soviet Union and the countries of Eastern Europe, who in 1955 signed the Warsaw Treaty Organization (the Warsaw Pact) for their own defence.

American relations with Russia alternated, during the 1950s and 1960s, between cold hostility and guarded optimism. The Geneva summit meeting of 1955 brought about a new spirit of restrained cordiality, which vanished abruptly with the brutal Soviet suppression of the Hungarian rising in the autumn of 1956. Arrangements for a further summit meeting in the spring of 1960 collapsed as a result of the U-2 affair. Despite calls by the post-Stalin Russian leadership for 'peaceful coexistence', a series of confrontations took place between the two super-powers. The last and most serious of these, the Berlin crisis of 1961 and the Cuban missile crisis of 1962, seem to have had a chastening effect on Soviet policy. One year after the world reached the very edge of nuclear catastrophe over Cuba, the great powers signed a Nuclear Test Ban Treaty. After Nikita Khrushchev's fall from power in 1964, Russian policy was in the hands of more cautious men who believed in the need to relax international tensions in order to secure the help of western technology. Thus was born the policy of détente. In 1969, America and Russia began to negotiate limitations on strategic or nuclear armaments, signing the first Strategic Arms Limitation Talks (SALT) agreement in 1972.

Left: A 1952 campaign poster, wry reading in post-Watergate times

Not only did the 'cold war' come to an end, many of the assumptions on which American foreign policy was based after the Truman Doctrine of 1947 either changed or were seen to be false. After the Sino-Soviet split of 1963, it became increasingly clear that world communism was not a single, monolithic threat. In February 1972, President Nixon ended over two decades of hostility to the People's Republic of China by visiting Peking. The US at last recognized Mao Tse-tung's Communist régime as the real government of China, and withdrew its opposition to China's admission to the UN. Other events in Asia brought into question the capacity and will of the US to sustain the world-wide role as the defender of freedom.

The Geneva Conference of 1954 left Vietnam divided into two parts. By the end of the 1950s, the southern pro-Western part was coming under increasing attack from Communist guerrillas. Since the French had withdrawn from Indochina, the US stepped in to supply the threatened régime of Ngo Dinh Diem with weapons and training facilities. By the end of Eisenhower's presidency, there were 800 American advisers in South Vietnam. Three years later, that figure had reached 16,000. President Lyndon B. Johnson decided in 1965 to commit American combat troops. By 1968, there were over half a million American soldiers in Vietnam.

The war in Vietnam split American society. By the time President Nixon ended American participation in the war in January 1973, it had cost 60,000 American lives. Vietnam also prompted a public debate on the limitations of American power. Many congressmen and political commentators began to advance the view that after 25 years of world leadership and the expenditure of almost $150 billion in overseas aid, the time had come for the US to follow a more modest and realistic path in its foreign policy. This lesson was underlined by the October 1973 war in the Middle East and the oil embargo imposed by the Arab states. By the 1970s, a large proportion of the oil used in the US was imported from the Middle East. The enormous financial and political power this gave Middle-Eastern rulers could no longer be ignored. The US, chastened by the Vietnam experience and running a large balance of payments deficit because of its dependence on imported oil, faced the question of whether the shift of wealth and power from Western industrialized societies, headed by the US, to the resource-rich countries of the Third World is irreversible.   *M. S.*

Two Democrat presidents – J. F. Kennedy and Vice-President L. B. Johnson in November 1961

Détente extended – Chairman Brezhnev on the White House balcony with his host President Nixon

Above: Détente in Vienna, June 1961 – President Kennedy greets Chairman Khrushchev

De Gaulle and After

In 1944 France had just passed through four traumatic years of German occupation that had resulted not only in widespread material and human losses, but also in the discrediting of large sections of her social and political élites, which were accused of collaboration with the Nazis. Charles de Gaulle was unable to capitalize on his prestige as head of the Resistance and his position as head of the provisional government (1944–46) to obtain the kind of constitution he wanted. In the referendum of June 1945 the French massively rejected a return to the Third Republic, but the Fourth Republic that replaced it a year later was even more biased towards legislative dominance over the executive. Governments fell after 1947 at least as rapidly as they had done before 1940. In 1951 the two political forces with most votes, the Communists and the Gaullists, were both openly hostile to the political system.

Yet it was in the Fourth Republic that changes began. For the first time in a hundred years the population started to increase steadily and in the 1950s the predominance in the economy of a largely inefficient agricultural sector weakened. Thanks in part to the early application of planning techniques, linking the goals of industry and government, France entered a period of sustained economic growth. By 1957 the government felt able sufficiently to disregard its old protectionist impulses to commit France to membership of the EEC.

What the politicians could not cope with were the problems arising from the dismantling of France's large overseas empire. Military defeat at Dien Bien Phu forced France out of Indochina in 1954. By 1958 sections of the armed forces were in open revolt against Paris in support of the determination of French settlers in Algeria not to tolerate Algerian independence. In May 1958 De Gaulle emerged from a morose retirement to form a government, which, it was hoped, would prevent a military take-over in France itself and somehow 'save' French Algeria.

De Gaulle had other ideas. By 1959 he was prepared to concede the principle of Algerian independence and in a series of referenda obtained support for a French withdrawal from North Africa. His chief interest lay in the establishment of a new institutional framework that would at last guarantee the stability and authority of government. The constitution of the Fifth Republic, overwhelmingly approved by a referendum, maintained the principle of governmental responsibility before the legislature (National Assembly) but greatly altered the distribution of political power. A whole series of clauses limited the means by which the Assembly could challenge government; above all, the authority of the president of the Republic was increased. It was originally thought that in normal circumstances the prime minister could determine government policy with the president acting as 'supreme arbiter', but in 1962 De Gaulle instituted a constitutional amendment providing for the direct election of the president. For the first time since 1848 the president had the political authority that comes from universal suffrage.

In the early days of De Gaulle's own political movement, about 1946, his bid for power aroused bitter hatred on the left. De Gaulle was not recalled to rule France until 1958

Brilliant propaganda graphics were generated by the student protests of July 1968: 'The police are on the air every night at eight'

Valéry Giscard d'Estaing, third president of the Fifth Republic, speaking to a joint session of the British Parliament, June 1976

For 10 years, 1959–69, De Gaulle proudly presided over the Republic he had created. Using the services of a highly competent and interventionist inclined civil service, the governments of Debré (1959–62) and Pompidou (1962–69) pressed on with economic growth and technological change. French economic performance first equalled and then surpassed that of Great Britain. Abroad, De Gaulle's conviction that the nation state was the only possible political unit enabled him to appear as the champion of Third World independence against super-power (notably American) interference and successfully to oppose Britain's attempts to enter the EEC.

In 1968, however, his régime underwent its most severe test. Economic growth had not reduced the marked inequalities within French society, and young people in particular were facing difficulties both of finding employment and of surviving France's notoriously inadequate higher educational system. These problems combined with a generalized sense of frustration at the stiflingly authoritarian nature of the political system to produce a massive outburst of hostility against the régime in May 1968. Violent demonstrations occurred in Paris and elsewhere, and there was a spontaneous, widely followed strike movement. For a few days the government appeared helpless and De Gaulle's vaunting of a new French stability ridiculous. Yet De Gaulle survived. Helped by the powerful Communist Party, which had no desire to see its leader-

ship of the French working class usurped by youthful leftists, he managed to contain the protest by means of new general elections (June 1968). These produced a huge majority for the Gaullist party as the guarantor of order and stability.

In 1968, however, De Gaulle resigned after losing a referendum on regional reform. His successor was Georges Pompidou, a cautious, conservative Gaullist who was willing to accept British membership of the EEC but otherwise maintained the Gaullist stress on national independence through economic growth. The 1970s saw a marked revival in the electoral fortunes of the Socialist Party under its leader François Mitterrand. Following Pompidou's death in 1974, his finance minister Valéry Giscard d'Estaing narrowly defeated Mitterrand in the ensuing presidential election. Thereafter it looked likely that the Socialists and Communists could challenge the presidential pre-eminence that has characterized the Fifth Republic, but internal divisions within the Left ensured that the expected electoral victory did not take place in 1978.

P. M.

Total defeat in 1945 and Allied occupation in the years that followed mark a caesura in modern German history. The Federal Republic, formed in 1949 out of the former American, British and French zones, was the Western, capitalist variant of the attempt to complete a decisive break with the recent past.

The 1950s were dominated by the figure of Dr Konrad Adenauer, whose Christian Democratic Party (CDU/CSU) improved its position in successive elections up to the landslide victory of 1957. Projecting himself as father figure and 'strong man', Adenauer anchored the Federal Republic within the Western alliance system, initiated re-armament and achieved recognition abroad as a major European statesman. In addition, his 'chancellor dictator-ship' succeeded to a great extent in identifying the stability of the state with the rule of the CDU/CSU. The hegemony of the Christian Democrats was further underpinned by the 'economic miracle' presided over by Ludwig Erhard, whose belief in a 'social market economy' stressed the role of private enterprise and rejected state interference.

Change came in the following decade. Adenauer's pro-tracted attempt to block Erhard's succession as party leader helped to discredit the CDU/CSU. More funda-mentally, the building of the Berlin Wall in 1961 cast serious doubts on the efficacy of Adenauer's virulent anti-Communism and his preoccupation with the Western alliance at the expense of an 'Eastern policy' (*Ostpolitik*). The growing awareness of social problems also con-tributed to an undermining of Christian Democratic popularity. The Social Democratic Party (SPD) in the same period had adopted its Godesberg Programme (1959) and sought to convince the electorate that it was reliable as an alternative 'party of government'.

Recession in the mid-1960s stimulated the rise of the neo-Nazi NPD; it also led to Erhard's fall, and the forma-tion of a 'grand coalition' of Christian and Social Demo-crats – by far the two largest parties – under Kurt Georg Kiesinger (CDU). The dangerous anti-democratic implica-tions of this coalition (and Kiesinger's Nazi past) were not lost on the left, and in response a powerful 'extra-parlia-mentary opposition' (APO) emerged in the late 1960s.

The SPD was the chief beneficiary of the 'grand coali-tion', and since 1969 has formed the government, together with the small Free Democratic Party (FDP). This 'social-liberal coalition' has tackled the backlog of social reforms which accrued during the unbridled pursuit of private affluence in the 1950s, and has given support to industrial co-determination. Above all, the *Ostpolitik* of Willy Brandt and Walter Scheel marked a definitive rejection of German claims in Eastern Europe, and a recognition that two German states existed.

'Bonn is not Weimar': the decline of the neo-Nazis and the success of the *Ostpolitik* testify to this. Yet self-confidence in democracy is less than complete. The threat posed by urban guerrillas has prompted a rabid response in parts of the press, which tend to identify criticism with terrorism. The government, moreover, together with the prime ministers of the individual *Länder*, has since 1972 been vetting the political views of applicants for public posts. The economic reconstruction of the 1950s has con-tinued to bear fruit; but the intolerance of critical dissent that was then nurtured continues in the 1970s to revenge itself on democracy in the Federal Republic.   *D. G. B.*

Wohlstand für alle Ludwig Erhard CDU

Top: The reassuring features of Ludwig Erhard, the father of Germany's 'economic miracle', put-ting over his party's electoral message. Above: Seven years after unconditional surrender, Chan-cellor Konrad Adenauer concludes the treaty that restored most of West Germany's sovereignty

The surrender of Leopold III with his army in 1940 was to bring great problems in the post-war period. The king, unlike other European sovereigns, saw himself as commander-in-chief and not as ruler, and so considered himself a prisoner of war. Hence the Belgian government-in-exile in London was without its sovereign. The German occupation ran its usual course; collaborationists emerged, there was deportation of the Jews, and there was also a highly organized resistance movement.

Totally liberated by 1944, Belgium faced the problems of both political and economic reconstruction. The latter proved much the easier since the industrial structure was mostly intact, and a massive influx of US dollars came partly in aid and partly through the use of Antwerp as the main Allied forces port of entry. Also, the entire economy was, until 1960, supported by revenues from the Congo. By the 1950s Belgium was one of the most prosperous of the European states, with one of the strongest currencies. Even after the loss of the Congo, Belgium benefited from being a founder member of the EEC, and so was able to take advantage of the general continental European growth that occurred in the 1950s and 1960s.

The country fared less well in the political sphere. The return of Leopold III after 1944–45 led almost to civil war. Constitutional tradition suggested the attempt to settle the matter by referendum and a parliamentary vote, which went in the king's favour, but on his return in 1950 serious disturbances occurred, and Leopold abdicated in 1951 in favour of his son, Baudouin. Since then, in spite of occasional sharp bursts of criticism, the position of the monarchy has been secure.

Much more disruptive was the revival in a harsher form of the linguistic 'Fleming/Wallon' question. This had been exacerbated by the feeling that the Flemings had been less hostile to the Germans during the occupation and also because, in Belgium as elsewhere, the war had tended to shake old party and political loyalties, making politics less predictable and sometimes more violent. The loss of the Congo tended to sharpen all political problems. In an attempt to end the linguistic dispute, a virtual language frontier was established in 1962–63. In the north, Flemish became the official language; in the south, French. Brussels became bi-lingual, while the east has a small German-speaking area. Unofficially, a quasi-federal state had been produced.

Paradoxically, although occupied with domestic difficulties, Belgium has, since 1945, played a very important role in the whole concept of the EEC and also in the NATO alliance system. As part of the Benelux group, Belgium has a strong economic base within the wider European framework, but the aim is that of a fully integrated and united Europe, not simply for economic advantages. Brussels is in many ways a 'European' capital, since it houses so many of the Community's organizations. Problems arising from their own cultural and linguistic diversity perhaps make the Belgians more aware of others' problems. One thing remains constant: founded by international consent, Belgium remains international in outlook.   *W. H. S.*

Top: The bitterness of the referendum campaign shows in this defacing of a pro-Leopold poster. Right: Leopold III with his sons; Baudouin is on his right

Italy

The Allied landing in Sicily in July 1943 sounded the death knell of fascism. After the removal of Mussolini, Marshal Badoglio formed a government that ostensibly was going to carry on the fight. Secretly, an armistice was negotiated, and was signed in September to coincide with the Allied landing at Salerno. The armistice provided for unconditional surrender and an Allied administration in Italy. The country suddenly found itself cut in two by the front line: the south under the Allies and the north under the Nazi Germans. The anti-fascist parties, which had been formed clandestinely during the war, emerged to form Committees of National Liberation. They joined the king's government in Salerno after the celebrated switch (*svolta*) in the Communist Party line announced by its leader, Palmiro Togliatti, on his return from Moscow, and they started a partisan struggle to speed the liberation of the north. Of the six anti-fascist parties, three had mass support: the Christian Democrats, led by De Gasperi, a party formed of various Catholic groups and supported by the church; the Socialist Party, led by Nenni, formed from a merger between various socialist groups; and the Communist Party, which had been the only party to remain active in the country throughout the period of the Fascist régime. Three minor parties were the Liberals, the Action Party and the Labour Democrats.

After the liberation, to which the general partisan uprising of April 1945 behind the German lines made a major contribution, a new government for the whole of Italy was formed, led by the partisan leader Parri. This, it was hoped, would fulfil the general desire for political and social renewal, but profound disagreements rapidly under-mined the precarious unity of the Resistance leaders and set the pattern for post-war Italian politics for almost 30 years. On the one hand stood the Communists and Socialists, whose mass support came from the industrial proletariat of the north and the sharecroppers of central Italy, and who wanted a progressive, popular democracy and a programme of social transformation (workers' management committees, land reform, etc.). On the other hand stood the Christian Democrats, whose support came from the peasants and the urban petty bourgeoisie, and the Liberals, representing the high bourgeoisie, who feared a Communist take-over and wished to reconstruct a liberal market economy.

The Parri government fell after six months and was replaced by the first of Alcide De Gasperi's eight governments (1945–53), which were to see the proclamation of a republic by referendum and the election of a constituent assembly before the differences between left and right provoked by the Cold War became such that De Gasperi expelled the Communists and Socialists from the government. As a result, reconstruction of the Italian economy proceeded on orthodox liberal lines. Under the Marshall Plan, massive investment was directed towards the advanced sectors of the economy, which were streamlined to become competitive in international markets. Fascist foreign trade restrictions were removed and an export-led growth mechanism was created that produced the 'economic miracle' of 1958–62, at the price, however, of low wages and poor conditions for the working class.

This socially divisive economic policy might have destroyed the fragile Italian democracy if the Christian

De Gasperi's January 1947 visit to Truman and Acheson, which produced substantial US aid for Italy

Democrats and their allies had failed to muster the support of all the other sectors of society. Political consensus was achieved by forging the middle classes into a power bloc of provincial bosses. A cautious land reform and the policy of subsidizing development in southern Italy through the fund called the 'Cassa per il Mezzogiorno' were inspired by the same logic: to tie by means of a patron–client system whole populations to the government *via* subventions from the Treasury. It was a system that accorded with Italian traditions of personal allegiance within the comparatively new and weak nation-state.

Although this system created the 'economic miracle' of the 1950s, its underlying inconsistency became apparent in the early 1960s. Industrial expansion in the north had created full employment for skilled labour. This gave the unions a bargaining power that they had not known for a decade and the result was a wages explosion. To avoid the confrontation to which this could lead, the Christian Democrats invited the Socialists to share the government with them. This was the 'opening to the left' (*apertura a sinistra*) of the Aldo Moro governments of 1964–68, which had the object of carrying out a programme of democratic reforms, both to satisfy industry and benefit the working class. It failed because the support of the advanced sectors of industry was only half-hearted. Moreover, the Communists, an essential element of any successful reformist alliance because of their working class support, were kept out for reasons of international policy. Indeed, some Christian Democrat leaders had hoped the alliance would weaken the Communist Party. At the same time, any reforms that seemed to threaten the interests of the middle classes were vetoed in parliament by that very bloc of provincial bosses who owed their position of power to the earlier strategy of the Christian Democrats.

The failure of the centre–left coalition to do what it promised was the immediate cause of the crisis that Italy has endured for almost a decade. High wages won in the 'hot autumn' of 1969, without corresponding social reforms, resulted in a profits squeeze and the drying up of private investment. Competition for markets between Italian and foreign firms became ever more intense, and this led to mounting antagonism between various sectors of Italian industry. Public investment was increased as a cure-all, but most of the spending went into an ever-expanding state bureaucracy. Small firms faced bankruptcy or take-over by state holding companies. The economic recession became prolonged and the growth of the previous two decades came to a grinding halt.

This continuous crisis of the 1970s can be traced to the contradictions in the post-liberation mechanism that was set up to create political consensus in the late 1940s, but long stood in the way of change. That change had been taking place was made clear by the 60 per cent in favour of divorce in the 1974 referendum and by the results of the 1975 regional and 1976 general elections, which showed large Communist gains. The fear of change led neo-fascist extremists to launch terrorist violence as a 'strategy of tension' designed to mobilize the 'silent majority' in support of an authoritarian response to leftward trends. The increased support for the parliamentary system by the Communist Party under Enrico Berlinguer, and its availability for deals with the Christian Democrats (the 'historic compromise'), prompted leftist terrorists into a similar campaign to provoke the authoritarian response – but as a prelude to proletarian revolution. In March 1978 the Christian Democrats agreed to form a government enjoying the parliamentary support of the Communists, for the first time since 1947. The day it was presented in parliament, Red Brigade terrorists kidnapped and later murdered the former Christian Democrat Prime Minister Moro in the gravest challenge to the state's authority since the fall of fascism.   *P. A. A.*

After 30 years of democracy in Italy: a once unthinkable pro-divorce rally in Rome, 1974

The Partition of India

The forces that led to the partition of the sub-continent were first activated with the passing of the Government of India Act of 1935. Into its making had gone the report of a constitutional commission, the deliberations of the three Round Table Conferences (held in London between 1930 and 1933), and over two years of parliamentary debates, punctured here and there by the delaying tactics of Winston Churchill, who, as always, was obstinately opposed to the transfer into Indian hands of even a fraction of the imperial power. The 1935 Act provided for the establishment of almost full responsible government in the 11 provinces of British India. Based on the British parliamentary system, government in these provinces was to be conducted by Indian ministers, who were to be responsible to the elected legislatures of the provinces. The federal part of the Act, which was never implemented, transferred only a portion of the central power into Indian hands. In addition, a federation, consisting of British India and 562 Indian states, was to come into existence only when at least half of the total population of all states had voluntarily acceded.

Although the 1935 Act for the first time brought the Indian states close to the political arena, the power-game continued to be played mainly between three parties, the British Raj, Congress and the Muslim League. Up to 1939

'Quaid-i-Azam' Mohammad Ali Jinnah, leader of the Muslim League and first president of Pakistan

the British were mainly occupied in securing the full implementation of the 1935 Act. The earlier enthusiasm of the princes for joining the federation had subsided, and Lord Linlithgow (Governor-General, 1936–43) had made very little progress when the war broke out and the federal scheme had to be put into cold storage.

The Muslim League, seeing that the proposed federation, and for that reason any central government in India, would be Hindu-dominated, was opposed to the federal provisions of the Act, but it was willing to accept the provincial part under which it could be reasonably assured of running the government in five provinces – Sind, Baluchistan, North West Frontier Province, the Punjab and Bengal – where Muslims were in the majority. Congress was opposed to the whole Act on the grounds that it did not grant India full independence or even dominion status. However, in order mainly to measure its strength against the sectarian and feudal forces, Congress decided to contest the 1937 elections, which were held for the implementation of the provincial part of the Act. Congress was jubilant at its victory, not only for winning eight provinces, including the Muslim inhabited NWFP, but also because the Muslim League failed to capture any of the five Muslim provinces. The Congress leader, Jawaharlal Nehru, saw this as the collapse of the Muslim League and of the sectarian and reactionary forces it had represented so far, and rejected the League's demand to share one-third of the power in the Congress-governed provinces. The League had been revived as a party only just before the election and while Congress ruled the provinces from 1937 to 1939 its leader, Mohammad Ali Jinnah, raised the cry of 'Islam in danger'. In spite of the fear of the common Muslims, that their culture, livelihood and freedom were at stake in a Hindu-dominated political system, Jinnah's Muslim League would not have emerged as a powerful force but for the support the British began giving it after October 1939. Congress had resigned the provincial ministries in protest against being dragged into the war without consultation and without being given any assurance that India would be made independent immediately after the war. To undermine Congress's claim that it represented all communities and classes of India, Linlithgow supported Jinnah in grooming the Muslim League as a powerful counter-force in India's national life. In March 1940 the League passed the 'Pakistan resolution', asking for Muslim majority provinces to be turned into independent states, and the vision of a separate homeland gradually came to acquire a hold on the Muslim mind. In August 1940 Linlithgow made it clear that there would be no constitutional change without the consent of the Muslim League. Sir Stafford Cripps's plan of 1942, by implication, offered to the Muslim provinces of India the option of Pakistan if they did not wish to remain in the Indian union. In July 1942, two months after the failure of the Cripps mission, Congress launched a mass civil disobedience campaign (the 'quit-India movement') and was consequently banned and its leaders imprisoned, leaving the Muslim League with the political arena to itself. In 1942–45, while Congress was in the wilderness, the League gathered some strength under the aegis of Churchill, who saw in the 'Muslim minority problem' the last hope of retaining the British Empire in India. At the Simla conference of Indian leaders, called in June 1945 by Lord

Wavell, who had succeeded Linlithgow in 1943, Jinnah pitched his demands high. The League was offered as many seats as Congress in the proposed provisional government of India, but Jinnah further demanded that the Muslim League be accepted as the sole representative of the Muslims of India, and that Congress must not be allowed to nominate any Muslim from its allotted quota to the government. Jinnah's demand was fiercely opposed by Congress, for not only had Congress a large number of Muslims among its rank and file, but also its president for the year was a Muslim. Wavell was prepared to go ahead without Muslim League cooperation, but Churchill would not endorse any scheme that did not have Jinnah's approval.

Although the British Labour Party had a bias in favour of Congress, it could no longer ignore the Muslim League when Clement Attlee became British prime minister in July 1945, soon after the failure of the Simla Conference. To ascertain the relative strength of the parties, Attlee called for an Indian general election, which was held in the winter of 1945–46. The results showed that there were only two parties to reckon with: Congress, which had captured all the general seats, and the Muslim League, which had won all the Muslim seats in the central legislature. It was, therefore, to negotiate with these two parties for a final settlement that, in March 1946, Attlee sent the Cabinet mission (Lord Pethick-Lawrence, Sir Stafford Cripps and A. V. Alexander) to India. Failing to induce the parties to arrive at a negotiated settlement, the Cabinet mission made its own awards. While rejecting Jinnah's demand for two separate and sovereign states, the Cabinet Mission Plan laid down provisions under which Jinnah's six 'Pakistan provinces' could be organized into two groups, and exercise autonomous powers in all matters except foreign affairs, defence and communications, over which the Union Government was to have control. Within this framework the Constituent Assembly was to draft the constitution for the Indian Union, provinces and groups. While the constitution was being framed, an interim government of India, consisting mainly of the Congress and Muslim League nominees, was to be set up. Jinnah accepted the awards, which made Congress more apprehensive about the implications of the 'grouping of the provinces'. Congress leaders feared that if ever the 'Pakistan provinces' broke away from the Indian union, they would be taking with them Assam and large parts of Bengal and the Punjab, which were Hindu majority areas. Indecisiveness and loud-thinking on the part of the Congress leaders provoked Jinnah into retracting his original acceptance of the Cabinet mission awards, and he called for 'direct action' or civil war to commence on 16 August 1946.

The appalling civil war that began in Calcutta on that date soon spread over the whole country and took several million lives. The Muslim League and Congress, while jointly running the interim government since September 1946, proved their incompatibility. The Congress leadership, dedicated to preserving the unity of India, now felt obliged to let Jinnah get away with his Pakistan, but it was determined to prevent Hindu majority areas from being swallowed by a Muslim state. Congress demanded on 8 March 1947 the division of the Punjab and Bengal on religious lines. India's partition was thus already established

Jawaharlal 'Pandit' Nehru, first prime minister of independent India

before the last viceroy, Lord Mountbatten, arrived in Delhi on 22 March. Mountbatten was sent by Attlee with a mandate to wind up the 182-year-old British Indian Empire in 15 months by June 1948, but as the top Congress leaders, excepting Gandhi, had already accepted the division of the country as the only way to end the civil war, Mountbatten succeeded in doing his job earlier than stipulated. Through his interviews conducted with the Indian leaders, Mountbatten reached the conclusion that India had to be divided and that Jinnah had to be content with a 'moth-eaten' or truncated Pakistan. On 2 June 1947 the leaders of all parties concerned accepted the partition plan, according to which the people of the 'Pakistan provinces' were themselves to decide whether they wanted a partition of the country. The people made their decision between 20 June and 17 July. The Punjab and Bengal were divided; West Punjab, East Bengal, part of Assam, together with Sind, Baluchistan and the NWFP opted for Pakistan; the other provinces and territories remained with India. The princes, who had been given the option to join either of the dominions or to stay independent, were persuaded by Mountbatten to accede to India or Pakistan only on external affairs, defence and communications. By 15 August all the Hindu-majority states, except Hyderabad and Junagadh, and all the Muslim-majority states, except Kashmir, had acceded to India and Pakistan respectively. Junagadh and Hyderabad eventually acceded to the Indian union, but a war had to be waged between India and Pakistan over Kashmir, the UN had to intervene, and with the ceasefire agreement reached on 1 January 1949, 32,000 square miles of its territory remained occupied by Pakistan and 54,000 square miles by India.

B. N. P.

Decolonization (I)

Since 1945 'decolonization' – the dismantling of overseas empires and the consequent formal ending of colonial status – has wrought major transformations in the main types of government prevailing throughout the world. By decolonization, vast areas that were part and parcel of the once very extensive overseas empires of the west European powers (especially Britain and France, but also Holland, Belgium, Portugal and Spain) have become independent nation-states. In 1939 there were more than 90 separate colonies and dependencies, comprising over one-third of the population and land area of the world. By the late 1970s almost all of these overseas empires of the west Europeans had been dismantled, either (as in a few cases) because of eviction following a war of independence, or (in the great majority of cases) as a result of a negotiated transfer of power.

Three main phases can be distinguished: (1) From 1945 to 1949 decolonization was confined to the southern flanks of Asia and achieved rather differently in its three main sub-regions. (a) In south-west Asia, Britain and France gave up their former mandates over Palestine, Syria and Lebanon, and the state of Israel was born in 1948. (b) From south Asia, Britain evacuated entirely, and India, Pakistan, Burma and Ceylon consequently each became independent states. India under Nehru became the exemplar for new states in the late 1940s. Ceylon achieved independence more quietly, and Burma chose not to join the Commonwealth. (c) Within south-east Asia, the Philippines achieved independence by peaceful transfer of power from American rule on 4 July 1946, whereas Indonesian nationalists won actual independence (without West Irian, which was not obtained until 1963) by waging guerrilla warfare and mobilizing diplomatic support for some four years after proclaiming their independence on 17 August 1945. In marked contrast, Malaya and Singapore remained British colonies, while the Vietnamese national struggle against French control, spearheaded by Ho Chi Minh's Communists, escalated steadily after independence was proclaimed in 1945.

(2) From 1950 to 1957 very little decolonization took place except in North Africa (Libya, Morocco, Tunisia and Sudan) and three-quarters of Indochina (North Vietnam, Cambodia and Laos). Even so, in the first half of the 1950s, mainly as an assertion of independence and as a reaction against the prevailing deadlock between two Cold War camps organized into rival alliance systems, the relatively few countries that were outside the power systems – notably India, Egypt and Yugoslavia – began to encourage the idea of non-alignment and a 'Third World'. The Bandung Conference held in April 1955 in Indonesia gave a tremendous fillip to such ideas.

(3) From 1957 to 1960 decolonization got rapidly under way in Africa south of the Sahara, and quickened in pace and intensity elsewhere, beginning with Ghana and Malaya in 1957 and Guinea in 1958. 1960 was the climactic year for decolonization, reaching a peak when almost all the remaining French African colonies became independent, as well as Nigeria and the Belgian Congo. In February 1960 the British prime minister, Harold Macmillan, spoke in Capetown of 'the wind of change' of rising national consciousness throughout Africa. In June 1960 De Gaulle's government started negotiations with the Algerian provisional government with a view to independence. These changes were reflected in the much expanded membership and changed political atmosphere of the UN, and were symbolized by Resolution 1514 of the General Assembly in December 1960, sometimes called 'the Anti-Colonialist Declaration'.

Subsequently, Portugal's remaining overseas empire fell piecemeal, due to the revolution in Lisbon (1974) and wars of national liberation in the colonies themselves. By the late 1970s only southern Africa retained the white man's minority rule.

Decolonization gathered momentum from the 1960s onwards because of its preceding successes and from the consequent addition to the number of voices of newly independent states. It even applied to some miniscule remnants of empire and an age of many mini-states (especially in the Caribbean, the Persian Gulf, and the Indian and Pacific oceans) dawned.

The causes of this rapid and wide-reaching imperial evacuation are still being sharply debated by historians. How much is due to the loss of will for empire at particular times by the ruling élites of western Europe, to the declared anti-colonialism of both the Russians and the Americans, or to the growth of nationalism within the erstwhile colonies? Was the use of violence in achieving decolonization intrinsic and inescapable? Or has it not been remarkable that so much of the administration of large overseas empires has been transferred without any violence at all? Some contemporary writers citing not only Kwame Nkrumah, but Lenin's pamphlet of 1916, *On Imperialism*, charge that the formal transfer of political power is usually only a charade and that, as long as economic subordination continues, a situation of neo-imperialism or neo-colonialism exists. This is widely alleged and believed in the Third World. Since the mid-1960s China's leaders have in turn accused the Soviet leadership of 'social imperialism' and neo-colonialism, and the Cubans as their accomplices.   *P. H. L.*

African nationalism

In 1945, less than 50 million African people lived under black governments; by the mid-1960s this figure had increased to over 250 million. A number of factors account for the rapid decolonization of Africa: the post-war weakness of the two most important colonial powers, Britain and France; the development of liberal international political principles; the influence of powerful anti-colonial groups in Europe; and, above all, the rise of African nationalist movements. African nationalism grew from a common feeling of weakness, oppression and negritude. Its intellectual roots lay in the ideas of socialist writers and black American leaders such as the publicist W. E. B. Du Bois and the flamboyant Jamaican Marcus Garvey (who first used the slogan 'Africa for the Africans'). African nationalists drew inspiration, too, from the political traditions of the main colonizing powers themselves, for the principles of freedom, equality and democracy were part of the political heritage of both Britain and France, and could be turned against them.

On 6 March 1957 the Gold Coast achieved its independence under the new name of Ghana, the first British colony in tropical Africa to reach such status. Ghana's leader, Kwame Nkrumah, dedicated himself to leading the rest of Africa to nationhood. In Nigeria the course

Prime Minister Kenyatta of Kenya and President Nkrumah of Ghana in London, July 1964

Dr Hastings Banda, when nationalist leader of Nyasaland (now Malawi), in 1962

towards independence had been firmly set in the early 1950s, but the process took a little longer than in the Gold Coast because of the differences in education, wealth and outlook of the three regions in the country – north, east and west. Nigeria achieved independence in 1960 with a federal system of government dominated by the most backward region, the north. Sierra Leone became independent in 1961 and the Gambia in 1965.

In East Africa decolonization proceeded less smoothly, since Britain's territories here were economically poorer, educationally more backward, and in Kenya there existed a politically influential white settler community. Britain was also slow to realize that the emergent African nationalism in her West African colonies would quickly spread to those in the East. In Kenya, a savage insurrection by the Kikuyu people broke out in 1951. The Mau Mau rebellion began with the murder of a number of isolated white settlers and the mutilation of their cattle. Panic soon spread among the white farming community, troops were called in, and the nationalist leader, Jomo Kenyatta, a Kikuyu, was arrested and imprisoned. The revolt was eventually suppressed, though the intensity of the feeling that lay behind it showed that Kenyan independence could not be postponed indefinitely. The evidence used to convict Kenyatta had been flimsy, and in 1961 he was released. In 1963 Kenya became independent, a year after Uganda, and two years after Nyerere's Tanzania.

Nyasaland achieved independence from Britain in July 1964, taking the name Malawi, and three months later Northern Rhodesia became the Republic of Zambia, with Kenneth Kaunda as its first president. Both followed the collapse of the settler-dominated Central African Federation in the previous year. White settlers in Southern Rhodesia proclaimed their Unilateral Declaration of Independence (UDI) in 1965. Two of the three former British High Commission territories in southern Africa, Basutoland and Bechuanaland, won their independence in 1966 as Lesotho and Botswana. The third, Swaziland, became an independent kingdom in 1968. All three coun-

tries remained heavily dependent economically on the Republic of South Africa.

'L'Afrique francophone'

Under France's post-war constitution her colonial empire was transformed into the French Union (*l'Union Française*), in which her overseas territories became partners in a new 'Greater France'. All Africans became French citizens and thereby were entitled to participate in French parliamentary elections. In Africa, elected assemblies came into being in each colony. A number of political parties emerged, the most important being the *Rassemblement Démocratique Africaine* (RDA), an inter-territorial organization led by Félix Houphouet-Boigny of the Ivory Coast. The RDA soon faced competition from locally-based nationalist parties, and in 1956 when Houphouet-Boigny became a minister in the French socialist government he was instrumental in drafting an outline law (*loi cadre*), which gave to each of France's African territories a considerable degree of self-government. The two basic principles of French colonial policy – assimilation and centralization – were thereby discarded, and the two large federations, French West Africa and French Equatorial Africa, virtually dismantled. However, a number of nationalist leaders, in particular Sékou Touré of Guinea and Léopold Senghor of Senegal, believed that 'francophone' (French-speaking) Africa was being fragmented into units too small to be truly free of French control. Following the establishment of the Fifth Republic in 1958, De Gaulle offered all of France's tropical African colonies a choice of complete independence or autonomy as separate republics within a French 'Community'. Only Guinea chose to leave at first. In 1959 Senegal and the French Sudan (Mali) became independent but stayed within the Community. Shortly afterwards the Ivory Coast, Niger, Dahomey and Upper Volta secured complete independence from France. By the end of 1960 all the former colonies of French West Africa and French Equatorial Africa had achieved independence.   *P. W.*

Decolonization (II)

Algeria

The French position in Algeria differed from that in her protectorates Morocco and Tunisia: it was constitutionally part of metropolitan France and by the 1950s had a European settler population of about a million. Algeria had been loosely under Ottoman control until the French invasion of 1830, mainly designed to gain prestige for Charles X's faltering régime. The French easily subdued the coastal areas but by 1832 faced a holy war (*jihad*) launched from the interior by Abd al-Qadir (Abd-el-Kader), son of a famous holy man from the Atlas Mountains. He established control over the western and central interior until the French began a systematic and ruthless conquest of his territories in 1841. Abd al-Qadir was killed in 1847 and the suppression of his revolt left a legacy of bitterness between colonizers and colonized. Colonization by the French and other Europeans (mainly Spanish and Italian) expanded to 181,000 in 1857 and 350,000 by 1880. Much of the best agricultural land fell into the hands of wealthy individuals and institutions. The 'colons' (colonists) maintained close links with France, and Algeria

was made part of metropolitan France in 1848. As citizens of France, the colonists exercised a disproportionate influence in French politics. Later, rights of citizenship were offered to Algerians, but only if they abandoned Muslim law for French law. Only a small élite of Muslims became assimilated to French culture.

In 1945, a revolt against French authority in Sétif was savagely repressed. In the years following Sétif, some nationalists saw no hope of achieving independence by constitutional means, as France could not be persuaded to consider independence for Algeria, although it was to grant independence to Morocco and Tunisia in 1956. In 1954, the Front de la Libération Nationale (FLN) was formed to guide an armed struggle, and a guerrilla campaign was begun in the Aurès Mountains. This initiated a ferocious war that was to last nearly seven years.

Successive French governments, under pressure from the colonists and their friends at home, were unable even to compromise with the FLN. Despite setbacks, including internal divisions and the imprisonment of many leaders, the FLN formed a provisional government in Tunis in

1958. In the same year, De Gaulle returned to power in France, ostensibly with the support of the colonists in Algeria. De Gaulle foresaw, however, the inevitability of independence and opened negotiations with the FLN. It then took four years to reach the Evian Agreement of March 1962 with the Algerian provisional government.

Meanwhile, a second rebellion by colonists and dissident Army officers had developed, directed mainly against De Gaulle's government. Revolts in Algeria occurred in January 1960 and April 1961 and their failure led to the formation of the Organisation de l'Armée Secrète (OAS). The OAS launched a terror campaign which only ended with the mass exodus of colonists when Algeria finally became independent in July 1962.

Tunisia

The Beylikat (regency) of Tunis was nominally part of the Ottoman Empire, but after the French invasion of Algeria (1830), the bey sought the support of the British to counterbalance French and Ottoman influence in the area. The Tunisian upper class succeeded, with the assist-

ance of the British and French consuls, in persuading the bey to issue a constitution (1861) although this did not curtail his power to any great extent. With British and German approval, the French occupied Tunisia in 1881. The bey and his government continued to function under French supervision, although French officials came to dominate the Civil Service. French and Italian colonists came to Tunisia, though in much smaller numbers than to Algeria (about 200,000 by the 1930s). During the early part of the 20th century, the Destour (Constitution) Party represented a wealthy Tunisian élite, but in 1934 a younger, more radical group led by Habib Bourguiba broke away to form the Neo-Destour Party, which demanded more power and representation for Tunisians. The Neo-Destour faced repression from the French until after the Second World War, since both the colonists and the French officials resisted any idea of independence for Tunisia on strategic as much as political grounds. By the end of the 1940s, there seemed to be a possibility of independence within the French Union but by 1952 a tougher policy, favourable to the colonists, again prevailed in Paris. Bourguiba was arrested and many other nationalists fled the country. However, after the outbreak of the war in Algeria in 1954, the French will to maintain their position diminished and in March 1956 Tunisia became independent. A treaty with France was concluded, which included the maintenance of French bases.

Morocco

Until the 19th century Morocco was an independent kingdom ruled by sultans who frequently had difficulty in maintaining their authority over rebellious tribes, particularly in the High Atlas Mountains. However, the country was not free from European intervention. When Abd al-Qadir (Abd-el-Kader) rose against the French in Algeria in 1832, Morocco supported him and clashed with the French, being severely defeated. In 1906, the economic and political rivalries of the great powers over Morocco culminated in the Algeciras Conference which gave France a free hand in Morocco. After a period of informal intervention, the French occupation of Fez to quell a local rebellion in 1911 provoked Germany to send a gunboat to Agadir, thus causing a major international crisis. In 1912, the French declared a protectorate over Morocco, with the exception of a northern zone in the Rif Mountains, where Spanish military rule was established. The first French Resident-General, Marshal Lyautey, set out to bring all areas of Morocco not previously under the sultan's control under French administration. In the 1920s, his 'pacification' was interrupted by the Rif wars, when Berber tribes rebelled against Spanish rule in the north. This revolt was led by a former Muslim judge *qadi*, Abd al-Krim, and spread to the French zone. It was finally put down only in 1926. Nationalist activity developed in the 1930s and in 1943 the Istiqlal (Independence) Party was founded with the support of the young Sultan Muhammad V. Deposed by the French in 1953, he was restored in 1955 after widespread unrest. Morocco became independent in 1956 under a government headed by the sultan and including the Istiqlal Party.   *S. G. B.*

The fight against the French, from the film 'The Battle of Algiers'

Malayan society, being almost evenly balanced in numbers between the indigenous Muslim Malays on the one hand and on the other the Chinese and Indians, lacked cohesion. This, among other things, accounted for the country acquiring its independence as late as 31 August 1957. As national unity could not be based on a fusion of cultures, the élitist leaders of Malaya evolved a non-communal approach to political problems in order to bring about cooperation between the three major communities. As a result, an alliance of three political parties was formed in 1955. It was through the Alliance that Malaya presented a united front to the British and acquired its independence. Under the able Malayan leadership of three prime ministers, Tanku Abdul Rahman (1957–70), Tun Abdul Razak (1970–76) and Datuk Hussain Onn (since 1976), the Alliance has been in power ever since. It has always kept its doors open for any important opposition party to step in. In 1974 it became a wide-based national front of 10 political parties. The pattern of Alliance politics at the federal level has been also followed in the states, and the system has come to dominate the entire political life of the country, providing almost all politicians of the coalition parties with an opportunity to wield power at federal or state level. While the Alliance system is mainly responsible for the continuous functioning of Western-type democracy in Malaysia, the country's increasing prosperity has been another stabilizing factor.

But all has not been plain sailing for democracy in Malaysia. The country faced its first big problem soon after becoming the Federation of Malaysia in 1963. This 'greater Malay' federation included for the first time the two states of North Borneo (Sarawak and Sabah) and Singapore. As most of Borneo (Kalimantan) belonged to Indonesia, the merger of the north-western coastal area into Malaysia made the two countries next-door neighbours, and aroused President Sukarno's apprehensions. He saw in it the rise of neo-colonialism. Sukarno called his people to 'crush Malaysia', and the 'confrontation' between Indonesia and Malaysia began in 1963 and lasted until Sukarno's fall from power in 1965. The expanded federation, however, shrank in 1965, when Lee Kuan Yew (prime minister of Singapore since 1959), finding no room in Malaysian politics for his style of leadership, took Singapore out of the federation.

Two other factors – the Communist insurgency and racial riots – have continually overstrained the political order and occasionally forced Malaysian governments into resorting to emergency measures. In 1948 the Malayan Communist Party, with an overwhelming Malayan-Chinese membership, was banned and the Communist guerrillas took to the jungles. After independence some of them surrendered, but a faction continued to conduct guerrilla warfare. Since the fall of the Indochinese states into the Communist fold in 1975 their hopes have been raised. Racial tension, mainly between the affluent Chinese community and the relatively poor majority of Malays, arises out of two factors. First, the government's economic policies, aimed at erasing the wealth gap, meant giving preferential treatment to the Malays. Second, the government's decision to make Malay the sole national language also gave a decided advantage to Malays.   *B. N. P.*

Following the fall of France to the Germans in May 1940, Japan established an independent relationship with the pro-Vichy régime that emerged in French Indochina under Admiral Jean Decoux, and by September they had secured the right to station troops in northern Vietnam. In July 1941 the Japanese decision to occupy also the southern half of Indochina marked the beginning of their advance into south-east Asia. At the time of Pearl Harbor and the Malayan campaign (December 1941) neither the French nor the Thai government of the militaristic Phibunsongkram put up any resistance to the Japanese advance. Thailand entered the war on the side of Japan in 1942, although its ambassador in Washington refused to deliver the declaration of war against the USA. The Thais were encouraged by the Japanese willingness to permit them to recover provinces lost to the French in Cambodia in 1907, as well as several of the Shan and Malay states that had been annexed by Britain – territory that had to be handed back again after VJ day. In Indochina the Japanese permitted the French administration to continue provided it met Japan's economic and military needs. On 9 March 1945, when the Vichy government was in exile in Germany, the French rulers were interned and the Japanese took direct control. They allowed the Vietnamese, Cambodian and Laotian rulers to proclaim token independence by renouncing their treaties with France.

The situation was transformed by the Japanese surrender in August 1945, but it was also complicated by the fact that the Western Allies were not agreed about the future of the region. Not until July 1945 was it decided that Thailand and southern Indochina should be part of Lord Mountbatten's south-east Asia command, while northern Indochina should be part of the China theatre. When the war ended abruptly in August, British troops accepted the surrender of Japanese forces in their area, while the surrender in northern Vietnam and northern Laos was taken by the Chinese nationalists of Chiang Kai-shek. In Thailand the military occupation lasted only until 1946. In southern Indochina, however, the British assisted in the restoration of French control.

The Chinese presence in northern Indochina, on the other hand, permitted a quite different pattern of events. During the war some Vietnamese nationalists had collaborated with the Japanese, but others, notably the Communists, had set up a resistance movement. By mid-1945 the pro-Communist Viet-Minh (founded by Ho Chi Minh in 1941) had established a small army and a number of base areas in northern Tongking, and had entered into contact with the American OSS. Immediately after the Japanese surrender, they entered Hanoi and on 2 September 1945 Ho Chi Minh proclaimed the independence of the Democratic Republic of Vietnam. The Chinese armies, which occupied the north from September 1945 to spring 1946, allowed the Viet-Minh provisional government to continue. In the summer of 1946 it was the Viet-Minh who negotiated with the French at Fontainebleau, and who secretly prepared for war against France in case that conference failed. In December full scale war broke out. The Viet-Minh withdrew from Hanoi and began the long 'revolutionary guerrilla war' that culminated in French defeat at Dien Bien Phu in May 1954.   *R. B. S.*

Ho Chi Minh, founder of the Viet-Minh and leader of the fight for Vietnamese independence

The Vietnam War

The Geneva Agreements of 1954 brought an end to the war and established a *de facto* partition of Vietnam at the 17th parallel. The North was taken over by the Viet-Minh, and began to undergo a socialist revolution under Ho Chi Minh. The South was administered by the government that had been created under French auspices in 1949 and was now given independence. Under the premiership of Ngo Dinh Diem (who was president, 1955–63), American influence supplanted that of France, and the US became committed to the maintenance of an independent South Vietnam. Meanwhile, Cambodia became independent under Prince Norodom Sihanouk (in power till 1970), while Laos was supposed to form a similarly neutralist area, but was in effect partitioned between a royal government and the pro-Communist Pathet Lao. Thailand by this time was again under the rule of General Phibunsongkram, after a phase in 1944–47 under the civilian Pridi Panomyong. Phibunsongkram was now strongly pro-American, as were his successors, General Sarit (1958–63) and General Thanom (1963–73).

In 1958–59 the Communist régime in Hanoi appears to have decided on a campaign to weaken and eventually destroy American influence in both Laos and South Vietnam. In Laos the Americans responded by covert

Ho Chi Minh in 1964, greeting a Buddhist priest

The price of an unwinnable war: wasted lives, terrified children and, finally, the enemy takes all

action and an attempt in 1961–62 to re-establish formal neutralization under their own and Soviet guarantee; when that failed, a largely secret war was conducted there until 1973, but the Americans failed to prevent the Vietnamese Communists from using the 'Ho Chi Minh Trail' through Laos as a supply route from North to South Vietnam. In Vietnam itself there was a progressive expansion of guerrilla warfare from about 1960, to which the US responded by developing their own campaign of 'counterinsurgency'. By 1964, this had failed to defeat the Communists, but the Americans were then openly committed to the defence of the South as a separate state. Moreover, political stability crumbled after 1963, when the Americans sanctioned the overthrow of Ngo Dinh Diem by a military coup, after a concerted Buddhist revolt against his rule. Stability was not restored to South Vietnamese politics until the emergence of Nguyen Van Thieu, who ruled as president from 1967 to 1975. By then, as a result of decisions taken under President Johnson in 1964–65, the US had entered the war with regular forces. A bombing campaign against North Vietnam from 1965 to 1968 was accompanied by the commitment of over 500,000 ground troops in the South, but still the war was not won. The North Vietnamese sent their regular forces to the South from 1965 onwards. In January–February 1968 the Communists tried to break the stalemate by their 'Tet (New-Year) offensive' which severely shook American morale and, in conjunction with the American anti-war movement and a severe financial crisis, forced President Johnson to start winding down the war in March 1968. But negotiations did not produce any result, and in 1969 the Nixon administration decided to continue the war on the principle of 'Vietnamization': American withdrawal combined with massive military aid to Nguyen Van Thieu. In 1970 Nixon sanctioned the overthrow of Sihanouk in Cambodia, followed by the extension of the war to that country under the anti-Communist régime of Lon Nol (1970–75).

In 1972 a further large-scale Communist offensive again shook American confidence, although militarily it merely confirmed the stalemate situation, with renewed American bombing of the North. Finally, in autumn 1972 secret negotiations between the Communist Le Duc Tho and Henry Kissinger culminated in a draft agreement, which was finally signed in Paris in January 1973. Its signature was preceded, however, by the heaviest bombing of the war in North Vietnam. Between January and March the remaining American forces withdrew from Vietnam and their prisoners were released from Hanoi. The next two years saw an uneasy peace between the two sides in Vietnam, punctuated by frequent outbursts of fighting, and a continuing struggle in Cambodia. In Laos a ceasefire permitted American withdrawal and the emergence of the Pathet Lao as a political force.

The end came in 1975. In March the Communists made so much progress in the northern part of South Vietnam that Nguyen Van Thieu ordered his army to evacuate the region. The withdrawal quickly became a rout, and on 30 April 1975 Saigon fell to the Communists. After a period of six months during which the South was administered by a separate Communist authority, the formal reunification of the country was begun in November and completed in 1976. In Cambodia, meanwhile, the Communist forces

known as the 'Khmer Rouge' seized Phnom Penh in April 1975 and immediately began to evacuate its inhabitants. As subsequently became clear, the new rulers were no mere pawns of the Vietnamese Communists, and their ruthless suppression, and perhaps mass execution, of all opposition elements was designed to give them unassailable control of the country. In Laos the Pathet Lao finally seized control in December 1975 and proceeded to establish a 'special relationship' with Hanoi that made Laos virtually a dependency of Vietnam. It was this status that the Cambodian Communists sought to avoid by forming a close alliance with China, and by 1978 the Vietnamese and Cambodian régimes were virtually at war.

Thailand during this period had maintained close ties with the US, but after the American withdrawal from Vietnam in 1973 the situation changed. In October 1973 the military dictatorship was overthrown and the country, with students taking the lead, embarked on another constitutional experiment lasting until 1976. By the time the military resumed control, Thailand was faced with its own internal security problems. Diplomatically, the new Thai régime was anxious to play down its conflicts with China and with a reunified Vietnam, and in this it was assisted by the development of the Cambodian–Vietnamese conflict. *R. B. S.*

Vietnam's unique lesson in protest: the first voluntary fire-death, Saigon, 11 June 1963

Indonesia and the Philippines

South-east Asia: the islands

The Dutch returned in 1945 and expected to re-occupy their empire, but found that the newly established republic had wide support. Fighting soon broke out. The republic's main centres were in Java and Sumatra, and in 1947 and 1948 the Dutch undertook major 'police actions' in these areas. They also established other states in non-republican areas, in the hope of creating a federal 'United States of Indonesia' within a Dutch–Indonesian union, which would be subject to continuing Dutch influence and in which the republic would be only one of several elements.

Indonesian resistance and international pressure, particularly from the USA, proved too strong, and in 1949 the Dutch were obliged to negotiate and to recognize Indonesia's independence. Shortly after, the federal states abolished themselves and merged into a unitary republic. Conflicts within Indonesia became more serious after independence. Notably, in 1948, just when the republic seemed most threatened, elements of the Indonesian Communist Party (PKI) staged a rebellion against the government. This was crushed by republican troops, and left a legacy of suspicion towards the PKI in the army and in strict Muslim circles.

Initially, a democratic form of government was created, with a cabinet responsible to a legislature. The conditions were poor for maintaining a democracy, however, with a large and growing population (surpassing 120 million by the 1970s), low income and literacy levels, and a tradition of élite politicking in the capital with little reference to the countryside. The functioning of the state was also increasingly threatened by regional military take-overs in the outer islands.

By 1956, disillusionment with democratic forms of government was widespread, and President Sukarno proposed a new system of 'guided democracy'. This was to be an authoritarian form of government, but with formal consultative bodies to represent popular interests. The army supported the idea, but the other major political force, the PKI, was reluctant. In 1959 'guided democracy' was formally inaugurated. The PKI adapted to the new environment and its membership grew to about 20 million by 1965. Sukarno's political style became increasingly leftist, and the economy was in ruins.

In 1965 an abortive coup occurred in Jakarta. The roles played by Sukarno, the army and the PKI are still unclear, but the coup led to the deposition of 'Life President' Sukarno, the annihilation of the PKI (involving the killing of at least half a million people) and the emergence of General Suharto as president in 1966.

The economic chaos of the 'guided democracy' years was eliminated, but there have been accusations that some 100,000 political prisoners have been held, in many cases for as long as 12 years.

The Philippines

American tutelage had made a large part of the populace familiar with democratic norms, literacy was high (72 per cent of those over 10 years of age in 1960) and, despite a large variety of languages, many people spoke either the national language, Tagalog (44.5 per cent), or English (39.5 per cent). But social and economic inequalities were extreme and the democratic structures were often merely vehicles by which a small and extremely wealthy élite manoeuvred for power. Social and economic problems, especially those on the densely populated island of Luzon, received little attention from the government. Rural guerrillas who had fought against the Japanese under left-wing leadership had found themselves no better off after independence. Their continued discontent led to the Hukbalahap Revolt of 1948. Although the Huks, as they were known, ceased to be a major military threat to the state by 1954, the agrarian problems that spawned the rebellion were never resolved.

Of all the presidents of the Philippines before 1972, only Ramon Magsaysay (1953–57) seemed sincerely committed to an attack on the inequalities of Filipino society. His death in an air crash ended such hopes as had existed.

By 1972 internal security seemed near to collapse, the relationship with the US was due for revision, the press (in the hands of the wealthy élite) had turned against President Ferdinand Marcos (1966–   ), and the constitution forbade him from standing for a third term in the 1973 elections. Marcos' response was to suspend the constitution and institute martial law in September 1972. His so-called 'democratic revolution' has entailed the confiscation of large amounts of the wealth held by other élite families, and the security of the state has been improved by the dismantling of private armies and curbs on firearms, although it has been threatened by armed resistance in the southern Muslim provinces.   M. C. R.

President Sukarno in August 1961

Ferdinand Marcos, president since 1966, and strongly supported politically by Imelda, his wife

Manuel Quezón, first president of the Philippine Commonwealth

Ramon Magsaysay, president of the Philippines 1953-57

Canada

At the start of the Second World War the Canadian government faced the difficulty of bringing a divided nation into the war. Isolationist sentiment was strong, especially in opposition to conscription in Quebec. There were also acute problems of coordination with Britain, especially before Churchill succeeded Chamberlain, and for the first two years of the war with a neutral US. These matters were compounded by trade problems, difficulties over wheat sales and munitions orders. As early as August 1940, however, at Ogdensburg on the American side of the St Lawrence, Mackenzie King announced the establishment of a Permanent Joint Board on Defence for the North American continent. Throughout the war Canada showed that she could produce soldiers, sailors and airmen second to none, and could organize her productive resources so energetically as to become one of the main arsenals and granaries of democracy. Canada undoubtedly grew in world stature during the years 1939–45.

If unilateralism (avoidance of blocs and multiple alliances) backed by isolationism had characterized much of Canada's external policies before 1939, the last years in office of Mackenzie King (he retired in 1948) saw the development of a more active multilateralism within the UN and the Commonwealth. These trends were confirmed and defined by Mackenzie King's successors as Liberal leaders and prime ministers – Louis St Laurent, Lester Pearson, who became prime minister after a long and successful career as a diplomat and then minister of external affairs, culminating in his scheme for a UN peace force in Suez after 1956, for which he was awarded the Nobel Peace Prize; and Pierre Trudeau. Only John Diefenbaker's volatile leadership of the Conservative government (1957–63) interrupted the long years of Liberal rule in Ottawa, during which time there were four federal elections, including the landslide in his favour in 1958. When Canada joined NATO in 1949, this membership in a military alliance in Europe was as big a diplomatic revolution for her as for Britain and the US. It was a step taken deliberately in conjunction with these two main allies, and with France. Throughout the 1950s and early 1960s Canada was one of the leading participants in UN peacekeeping endeavours in various trouble-spots.

Canada was the first country in the Commonwealth to adopt its own distinct, legally defined national citizenship, by the Canadian Citizenship Act of 1947. Subsequently, this Act had many revisions; one, which became law in 1977, was designed among other things to grant legal equality to men and women, and to aliens and British subjects. Canada's citizenship policies are facilitated and implemented by a number of programmes concerned with such matters as multiculturalism, native citizens (especially Indians and Eskimos), official language minority groups and women's rights.

The 1971 census showed that 44.6 per cent of Canada's population was of British origin, 28.7 per cent French and the remaining 26.7 per cent of other linguistic origins. In October 1971 Prime Minister Trudeau announced the federal government's policy of multiculturalism in response to recommendations of the report of the Royal Commission on Bilingualism and Biculturalism on the status of the various cultures in Canada. The government promised support to programmes aimed at retaining, developing and sharing these cultures on a larger scale. Since the Parti Québécois won power in Quebec in November 1976 it has forcefully initiated policies to promote the French language in its province.

Maurice Duplessis, Prime Minister of Quebec, and leader of the Parti Québécois

De Gaulle stirring it up in 1967: 'Vive le Québec libre!' from Montreal City Hall

About ten and a half million immigrants have been admitted to Canada since the beginning of the Confederation in 1867, more than four million of them since 1945 – 25.2 per cent of these were from Great Britain, 10.1 per cent from the USA, 7.9 per cent from West Germany and 4.4 per cent from the Netherlands. Today a points system is used to assess the capacity of independent applicants to establish themselves if admitted to the country. Canadian citizens and landed immigrants may sponsor dependants or nominate non-dependent relatives.

Canada is a very large country with a relatively small population (about 24 million in the late 1970s), and is dependent on foreign markets for its goods and services to a greater degree than many other countries of its size. In the middle 1970s Canada exported per capita on average twice as much as the French and three times more than the Americans, the British or the Japanese. Exports provide almost 23 per cent of Canada's gross national product – as compared with 7 per cent for the US, 12.3 per cent for Japan and 23.8 per cent for the countries of the EEC. In September 1976 a Framework Agreement for commercial and economic cooperation was signed between the EEC and Canada – the first such agreement the Community had made with a rich, non-member country.

By the late 1970s about 80 per cent of total foreign direct investment in Canada was owned by US residents, making many of Canada's industries branch plants of US parent companies. Investment owned by British residents continued to be about 10 per cent of the total. Canada in the late 1970s is beset with economic difficulties, though its energy and mineral resources are considerable assets.

No all-Canada society existed in 1867, and the provinces were expected to be relatively free from extensive controls even by their individual governments. Over a century later, not only the federal government but also each of the provinces and the main municipalities (Toronto, Montreal and Vancouver) of Canada consist of considerably governmentalized and bureaucratized societies, interwoven with each other in relations of competitive interdependence. By the year 2000, and perhaps before, it is projected that nine out of every ten Canadians will be living in an urban community if urban growth continues at its present rate.

No appreciation of contemporary Canada can be adequate without due regard to the intensely regionalized interests and outlooks of each province. Quebec is not unique in asserting provincial interests and individuality. At times Ontario behaves towards the federal government like a proud and obstreperous vassal, which is not entirely surprising perhaps from a province that generates about 45 per cent of the gross national product. Alberta, which supplies 80 per cent of Canada's oil and gas, is often critical of the pricing, taxation and pipeline policies of the federal government. Even revenue deficit provinces, such as the Maritimes, can be fiercely critical and resentful of particular policies of the federal government. Undoubtedly, however, the fundamental question of whether Canada could stay a single country was most sharply posed when the electoral victory of the Parti Québécois installed a party with an avowed separatist leadership in power in Quebec.   *P. H. L.*

John Diefenbaker in 1963

Pierre Trudeau, Canada's world-class premier

Australasia

The immediate post-1945 years were a time of austerity. The war experience had produced a hardy leftism in the Labour Party, and its leader, Ben Chifley, set about reconstruction with radical intentions, attempting, for example, to nationalize the banks. This government was destroyed by the social tensions of the post-war period. Chifley was forced to use troops to break key strikes in 1949, and in the 1951 elections the Liberal–Country coalition under Robert G. Menzies won a convincing victory. A long period of conservative predominance followed, continuing into the 1970s and possibly beyond. This hegemony was partly due to the political shrewdness of Menzies, who dominated the parliamentary scene until his retirement in 1966; partly to the material prosperity of the times; and partly to the acute divisions within the Labour Party, which broke into internally competing fragments in 1955 over the question of Communist influence within the trade unions. During the 1960s, however, the Liberal–Country coalition was not without its problems. Country Party politicians tried to extend their party's political base beyond rural interest-groups and so challenge the Liberal monopoly of political and bureaucratic patronage. It was, however, only the advent of a new phase of structural economic difficulties in the early 1970s that broke the status quo and brought a new group of men to power, this time a Labour government led by Gough Whitlam. Whitlam's radical policies were opposed both by business and by the Liberal–Country majority in the Senate. When the Senate took the plunge in 1975 and denied his government financial supply, the Governor-General, exercising constitutional rights, called on the opposition to form an administration and so avoid an immediate general election. Although there were good legal precedents for this move, it caused bitter political divisions. When elections finally took place in 1976, the new Liberal government under Malcolm Fraser won a decisive victory.

The Australian economy underwent vital changes in this period, partly due to internal growth, but also partly imposed from outside. American pressure after 1945 had meant that Australia had to reduce her tariff levels, while Britain's later entry into the EEC forced Australian producers to look for new markets. The growth of a dynamic mining sector (iron ore in Western Australia, for example) led to close connections with Japanese manufacturers. By the later 1960s both Japan and the USA had become much more significant trading partners for Australia than Britain. Since rapid population growth after 1945 had created a large local market for mass consumer goods, secondary industry became an even more important element in the overall economy. Meanwhile, rural industries and primary products declined in proportion. Although wheat sales kept up, the once proud wool industry slumped badly in the later 1960s. The Australian economy had at last come 'off the sheep-run'.

Australia's greater involvement in the regional affairs of the Pacific was partly due to this economic diversification, but also to Britain's withdrawal from an imperial role in the area, leaving Australia to accept larger responsibilities and making her dependent on American power. Her foreign policy became deeply coloured by anti-Communism, and this culminated in Australian participation in the Vietnam War. The following débâcle on the Asian mainland discredited the idea of 'forward defence', and since then Australian diplomatic and military thinking has exhibited more tentative qualities. Finally, it must be

Sir Robert Menzies inspecting Australian troops in Malaya, 1959

Gough Whitlam opens Labour's election campaign in Sydney Opera House, November 1976

noted that, while American cultural influences (TV, films, magazines) have tended to standardize the increasingly bourgeois style of Australian life, the ethnic character of her population has become more varied. Some 2.5 million migrants arrived between 1950 and 1970, and of these approximately one-half had non-British origins.

New Zealand

Political and social development in New Zealand during this period again resembled the Australian pattern. A Labour government attempted to cope with post-1945 reconstruction through a process of radical change, extending state welfare into such critical areas as health, only to find that the drift of national consensus after 1949 brought prolonged power to the conservative National Party. The National Party has, none the less, continued to develop a planned economy under essentially state direction. These controls have proved very necessary since New Zealand's continued reliance on primary exports has made the economy vulnerable. Britain's entry into the EEC made New Zealand's need to locate new markets even more urgent than Australia's. Industrialization has also been a feature of economic life, not least because persistent balance of payments difficulties have limited importing power, but there are real limits to this, given the restricted size of the local market. In foreign policy New Zealand, like Australia, has accepted American leadership. Involvement in the Vietnam War was perhaps the first really divisive foreign policy issue to intrude into New Zealand domestic politics, but after the end of the war, in the face of international uncertainties, there were signs of closer

A New Zealand protest yacht alongside nuclear warship USS Truxton at Wellington, August 1976

New Zealand–Australian co-operation than for some time past. New Zealand society remains isolationist in its basic attitudes, protected by, and happy in, the levelling uniformity of its middle-class life-style. So long as the large industrial populations elsewhere remain rich enough to require high-quality food imports, New Zealand's economic and political security is not endangered. *R. F. H.*

Sydney Harbour Bridge and Sydney Opera House – modern emblems of a modern nation

Japan

Following the surrender of the Japanese in August 1945, their islands were occupied by the armies of the US and the British Commonwealth (Australia, Britain, India and New Zealand). While their civilian government continued in existence, its activities were closely supervised by an American military government presided over by the Supreme Commander Allied Powers, General Douglas MacArthur. During the immediate post-war years Japan was a sad country where food and fuel were in short supply, and the yen was unstable, but from 1949 onwards the economy improved. Overseas trade was re-started and industry re-established, especially when the 'special procurement' policies of the UN forces during the Korean War (June 1950–July 1953) pumped money into the country.

President Truman's administration, therefore, decided to push ahead with the peace settlement with Japan in 1950, whether or not this secured the approval of the Soviet Union and China. After many-sided negotiations, the treaty of peace between Japan and the Allies was signed at San Francisco on 8 September 1951. Representatives of the Soviet Union and its satellites attended the conference but refused to sign, while the governments of Peking and Taiwan were not invited.

The treaty was accompanied by a security agreement between Japan and the US. Because it provided for Japan's security, it compensated for the new constitution she had accepted in 1946 which contained a clause renouncing war. When the occupation came to an end in 1952, the US was permitted to maintain bases on Japanese soil for ten years afterwards; but the pact gave rise to many disagreements, mainly from the left wing who resented the American attempts to increase Japan's contribution to her own defence. Eventually, Japan agreed to renew the pact on a revised basis, whereby the Allies would consult each other whenever major changes in the deployment of American armed forces in her islands took place. The socialist opposition tried to prevent ratification of the treaty in June 1960, but was unsuccessful.

Economic revival

The Japanese economy returned to its pre-1937 level in 1955 and grew in the peaceful atmosphere of the following decade. There were serious cyclical fluctuations, but Japan began to enjoy a new-found affluence as during the boom of 1959–61. Private companies were investing in modern plant and equipment on a lavish scale, while the government introduced its plans for doubling national income in 1961. These measures bore fruit in the large export surpluses which Japan attained in the later 1960s when she became an 'economic superpower'. In the political arena, conservative coalition governments had been in office since 1947, and the Liberal-Democratic Party (LDP) since 1955. They reaped the benefits of the improved state of the country; and industry became an important political force, because it had played such a large part in economic recovery. The left-wing parties and the trade unions, while they could cause upsets, were too divided to constitute a challenge to the LDP during much of the 1960s.

Optimism gave way to depression in the 1970s. This change was heralded by the twin 'Nixon shocks' of 1971: President Richard Nixon's announcement of his visit to China in July, and of his emergency set of economic

measures, including the surcharge on imports. In the case of the Peking visit, the Americans had given no advance warning as provided for in the security treaty. They claimed that the need for secrecy prevented this, but the Japanese were stung by this evident weakening of their American alliance. Over the economic measures, they agreed, after many months of hard bargaining, to introduce orderly marketing procedures, ie voluntary restrictions in various selected commodities under dispute. These two issues of 1971 were to be the precursors of important changes.

Japan and China

In the first place, the Japanese took up a more independent stance in international affairs. As soon as Nixon visited Peking, Japanese public opinion – knowing that China had, in the 1950s and 1960s, been a useful, ex-

The genesis of post-war Japan's economic recovery and world power lay in total defeat. Here, a Nagasaki doctor, victim of atomic radiation, contemplates his obliterated city in September 1945

joint communiqué with Premier Chou En-lai on 29 September which declared the abnormal relationship of the two countries to be terminated forthwith. Cautious over the prickly question of Taiwan, Tanaka stated that Japan 'fully understands and respects the stand of the government of the People's Republic of China that Taiwan is an inalienable part of its territory'. These negotiations were followed by increased trade and reinforced by the conclusion of four working arrangements relating to trade, fisheries, airlines and shipping. The most fundamental agreement, a Sino-Japanese peace treaty, still remained unconcluded at the beginning of 1978, partly because of opposition by the Soviet Union.

World economic power

In the second change, Japan found herself increasingly isolated and under attack in the world of economics. This became manifest first during the oil crisis of 1973, which revealed the dependence of Japan's post-war industrial success on oil, and on Middle Eastern oil in particular. On 17 October 1973 the Arab oil producers announced their embargo against countries which supported Israel. By reason of her American alliance, Japan was initially assumed to fall within this category. After a month of diplomacy, Japan was designated as a 'friendly nation'. Oil supplies were resumed and the domestic crisis was overcome. Senior Japanese statesmen toured the Middle East, offering aid. Since international oil prices were quadrupled, the result for Japan was a steep increase in overall commodity prices and a savage inflation which took some years to control.

Since the oil crisis, Japan has encountered resentment abroad over her export performance. Certainly her growth in recent years has appeared to be export-led, and her exporters have not always been sensitive to the consequences of their actions in the recipient countries, which have complained that Japan has been 'exporting unemployment' in certain industries. The US, Japan's leading trading partner, made frequent complaints in 1976 and 1977 about 'market disruption' caused by the import of Japanese cars, steel and colour television sets. Member countries of the European Common Market (EEC) made similar protests. Confronted by these, Japan has attempted to take remedial action in order to avert the growth of protectionist measures against her.

Since the Sato cabinets of 1964–72, the fortunes of the governing LDP have declined because of the Lockheed scandals and rivalry between factions within the party. At the election for the lower house of the Diet in December 1976 the LDP won 249 seats (265 at dissolution). The Japan Socialist Party, the leading opposition party, won 123 seats (112 at dissolution).

Post-war Japan has gradually established herself as a world power, yet with only a few of the characteristics which would normally be found in great powers. She has a limited defence capability and has renounced the use of nuclear weapons, and is dependent on foreign sources of energy and raw materials. Her standing in the world comes from her industrial success – her productive capacity and international trading acumen. In three decades Japan has risen from the literal ashes of 1945 to a place in the world where she has to be regarded with respect by the world's leaders.   *I. H. N.*

panding trading partner – called for normalization of Sino-Japanese relations. It was claimed that the political problem had only remained unresolved in the past because of the American alliance. It appears that China declined to negotiate with Premier Eisaku Sato, and it was left to his successor to set things in motion. In July 1972, the Chinese leaders invited the new Japanese premier, Kakuei Tanaka, to their country. After an intense period of talks between the political factions in Japan, and with the governments of Taiwan and the US, Tanaka visited China in September and offered the apologies expected of him for the China 'incidents' of the 1930s. He issued a

Economic Communities in Europe

The 'Common Market'

The European Economic Community was established in March 1957 by the Treaty of Rome. In this treaty three major continental countries – France, Italy and the German Federal Republic – and three smaller ones – Belgium, the Netherlands and Luxembourg – committed themselves to creating new institutions to deal collectively with problems of economic and commercial policy, and to seeking closer unity in politics. The same six countries had already placed a vital sector of their national economic life under a European authority through the Coal and Steel Community established in 1952, and had committed themselves to joint development of a new energy source through the European Atomic Energy Community (EURATOM), which they set up at the same time as the EEC.

Together, these three European Communities were designed by some of their pioneers (for instance, the Frenchman Jean Monnet and the German Walter Hallstein) to be the embryo of a federal United States of Europe. This aim was reflected in the institutional structure of the Communities: as well as a Council of Ministers, representing the member-governments, and a parliamentary Assembly representing the public, the EEC was provided with a Commission, an independent body of nine members (later thirteen) with the task of defining the collective interests of Europe and guiding the Community forward towards closer unity.

Because of hesitation about these political aims, as well as a different view of economic priorities, some important European countries, including Britain, preferred at the beginning not to join the Community. When Britain changed her mind in 1961 and applied to join, the negotiations for entry broke down in 1963, largely because of President De Gaulle's view that Britain was too pro-American to be 'European' in his sense. Thus it was only in January 1973 that Britain, along with Ireland and Denmark, joined the EEC. This expansion of the Six into the Nine was marked by a summit conference of the nine heads of government in Paris, which committed the EEC countries to achieving 'European union' by the year 1980.

This ambitious aim was brought nearer to realization in some ways, for instance by the decision to hold direct elections to the European parliament in 1979, but at the same time the economic recession unleashed by the energy crisis of 1973 tended to drive the Nine further apart. The stronger national economies drew further ahead of the weaker ones among the Nine – the Germans being distinctly in the lead, and the British and Italians very much in the rear – and this made it difficult for the Commission in Brussels to keep the Community together in the pursuit of full economic and monetary union.

The Nine cooperate closely in matters of foreign policy, and have all agreed in principle to the admission of three further members – Spain, Portugal and Greece. But the resulting Community, though a powerful economic unity, is a long way from developing into the United States of Europe of which the pioneers of the European movement dreamed.   *R. M.*

Above: The signing of the Treaty of Rome, 25 March 1957
Right: The cipher of the European parliament

The European parliament in session at Strasbourg

Comecon

Comecon (the acronym for the Council for Mutual Economic Assistance) was established at a conference of representatives of the governments of Bulgaria, Czechoslovakia, Hungary, Poland, Rumania and the USSR in Moscow in January 1949; Albania was admitted the following month, and the German Democratic Republic in September 1950. Membership remained restricted to European countries (under Article II(2) of its first charter, 1960), but was widened in 1962 to any state 'which shares the purposes and principles of this charter'. Mongolia was thereupon introduced (June 1962), but the membership of Albania, with whom the USSR broke diplomatic relations in December 1961 in the wake of the Sino-Soviet dispute, was deemed to have lapsed in December 1962. Cuba was admitted in July 1972. Yugoslavia was invited to certain meetings between 1956 and 1958 and received formal observer status in September 1964. As a consistent instrument of Soviet external economic policy throughout its existence, Comecon has in the light of that policy accorded informal observer status at various times to Angola, China, North Korea, Laos and Vietnam.

The first three decades of Comecon's history divide into four parts, separated at 1956, 1964 and 1971. So little overt activity marked its initial seven years as to justify the contention that it had been established merely as a formal response to the Marshall Plan (and its west European implementing agency, the OEEC), but with the resources flowing from the smaller members to the protecting superpower – in contrast to the dollar aid furnished to OEEC members by the US. The demonstrations of national independence by Hungary and Poland in 1956 were important factors in the next eight years, up to 1964, which created a working organization. Permanent commissions for individual industries and international functional relationships were established, starting in 1956; its 'Basic Principles of the International Socialist Division of Labour' were agreed in 1961; an executive committee was introduced in 1962 and its financial arm, the International Bank for Economic Co-operation (IBEC), opened for business in 1964. Soviet pressure for supra-nationally directed integration within Comecon (supported by the more industrialized members who feared discrimination in their trade with the West by the erection of the Common External Tariff of the EEC) was contested by Rumania. A declaration of April 1964 by the Rumanian Communist Party opposing such tendencies ushered in a period of relative quiescence, while Comecon's internal mechanisms adjusted to a new political environment. Economic relationships were also under revision as its members, between 1964 and 1969, applied, in varying degrees, some devolution to their previous highly centralized planning. The Soviet-led invasion of Czechoslovakia in August 1968 led to domestic recentralization in all members save Hungary, and renewed efforts at mutual integration by all except Rumania. Comecon's members having accorded the organization none of the supra-national powers exercised on behalf of EEC states by the Commission of the European Communities, no formal agreement between the two organizations was reached in sporadic discussions during 1973–78. *M. K.*

THE RED EAST

Before 1945 'socialism' in the Russian revolutionary sense existed in one country alone, the USSR. Between 1945 and 1949 it was established by Soviet 'persuasion', if not by force, throughout eastern Europe and in North Korea. Only the Yugoslav and Albanian régimes in Europe and the Chinese in the Far East were established by native revolutionary movements. In the same

period risings took place in Greece, Malaya, Indonesia and Annam (North Vietnam). The first three were suppressed, the last established in power (with Chinese and Soviet aid) by the Geneva South East Asian Conference in 1954. During his lifetime the Soviet leader Joseph Stalin insisted on subservience, both political and economic, to his leadership, through the Cominform, an organization set up in 1947. Only the Yugoslavs, under Marshal Tito, rejected this and were expelled from the Cominform in 1949. After Stalin's death in 1953, however, and the process of de-Stalinization begun by Nikita Khrushchev, the concept of 'polycentrism' took hold of Communist movements throughout the world. Resistance to this unorthodoxy was led originally by the Chinese leadership, who broke relations finally with the USSR in 1963, moving gradually from doctrinal

Soviet leaders at the 25th anniversary of Lenin's death, from left to right: **Mikoyan, Kuznetzov, Beria, Saslov, Malenkov, Kosygin, Voznessensky, Molotov, Bulganin, Voroshilov, Popov, Stalin, Ponomarenko, Shkiryatov, Shvernik, Budyenny, Parfenov, Zholnin, Rodinov, Selivanov, Burylichev, Kozlova, Sarycheva, Popova. Pospelov is at the left delivering a tribute to Lenin.**

breach to a state of latent but armed hostility. Few Communist countries followed Chinese leadership apart from Albania, but they were equally reluctant to take part in the Soviet-Chinese ideological conflict. The Soviet Union consolidated its hold over Eastern Europe by the Comecon, an economic planning organization and the Warsaw Pact, a military organization. Soviet forces were used ruthlessly to suppress the East German rising in 1953, the Hungarians in 1956, and the Czechs in 1968. On this last occasion Leonid Brezhnev, the Soviet leader, pronounced that it was the Soviet duty to intervene where a bourgeois counter-revolution seemed about to succeed. The Soviet action was widely denounced by the Communist movement in western Europe, especially in Italy and Spain, where writers on Communist dogma spoke of a new form of 'Eurocommunism', which Soviet writers strongly denounced. Whatever the differences between the 'Eurocommunist' thinkers and Soviet ideologists, and some of the differences were very abstruse, it was clear that doctrinal control from Moscow and doctrinal unity within the 'socialist' or Communist bloc of states was as dead as the political unity between the Soviet Union and China, especially after the death of Mao Tse-Tung and the defeat of his widow's efforts to take over the leadership of China. *D. C. W.*

The USSR after Stalin

When Stalin died on 5 March 1953, a struggle for power among not only individuals but also powerful bureaucratic agencies ensued. The main potential leaders were Georgi Malenkov, who, as chairman of the Council of Ministers, headed the governmental machine; Lavrenti Beria, the minister of the interior and head of the political police; and Nikita Khrushchev, who early emerged as the *de facto* leader of the party and in September 1953 was accorded the title of party first secretary. Both the party and governmental leaders saw eye to eye on keeping the political police in a much more subordinate role than it had played during the last two decades of Stalin's life, and on the need to get rid of Beria. The hated police chief was arrested in the summer of 1953 and shot before the end of the year.

The struggle between Khrushchev and his rivals within the leadership took longer to resolve. Malenkov was demoted in 1955 and replaced as chairman of the Council of Ministers by Bulganin, but the conflict reached its climax in the so-called 'anti-Party group' crisis of 1957, when Khrushchev found himself outvoted in a meeting of the Politburo (or Praesidium of the Central Committee, as the Politburo was known, 1953–66) and carried the fight to a plenary session of the Central Committee of the party, which supported him against the majority in the Politburo. This victory enabled Khrushchev to strengthen his position by the removal from the leadership (1957–58) of such senior figures as Malenkov, Molotov, Kaganovich and Bulganin and their replacement by his protégés. In 1958 Khrushchev himself became chairman of the Coun-

cil of Ministers and from then until his own removal from office in October 1964 he headed both the party and government.

One of the causes of the conflict between Khrushchev and other leaders was the long speech that he had delivered to the 20th Congress of the Communist Party of the Soviet Union in February 1956, in which he gave details of many of Stalin's crimes. Although Khrushchev limited himself to criticisms of the purges of Communist Party members (with the notable omissions of Trotsky and Bukharin) and showed little apparent concern for the fate of non-party members, his shattering of the Stalin image had momentous consequences. His relative frankness contributed to a freer intellectual atmosphere within the Soviet Union itself, but his revelations came as a great shock to many Communists and helped to stimulate unrest in eastern Europe (notably in Hungary and Poland) and dissension within the international Communist movement. Nevertheless, Khrushchev returned to the de-Stalinization theme at the 22nd Party Congress in 1961 and said in open session things that he had uttered only in closed session in 1956.

Khrushchev was a bold and impulsive leader and his frequent administrative reorganizations, once he had secured his supreme authority, did not endear him to party and state bureaucrats. In foreign policy he took the important step of recognizing that war between states with 'different social systems' was not inevitable, and he was very conscious of the destructive power of nuclear weapons. At the same time, his heavy emphasis on nuclear

Khrushchev with Ulbricht in East Berlin, 1963, declares that communism would reunite Germany

rather than conventional forces helped to lose him the support of the Soviet military. From the point of view of the KGB (state security police) as well as of conservative party officials, Khrushchev was also opening up dangerous possibilities by permitting attacks on Stalin and his period.

In other areas of policy Khrushchev combined reformist initiatives with a tendency to push particular policies too far and with inconsistency. He upgraded the status of agriculture within the Soviet economy, but his frantic agricultural campaigns and unrealistic targets achieved less than the more sober agricultural policies of his successors. In literature, alternating periods of freeze and thaw were symbolized by the refusal, on the one hand, to publish Boris Pasternak's novel, *Doctor Zhivago*, and, on the other, by Khrushchev's personal approval for publication of Alexander Solzhenitsyn's *One Day in the Life of Ivan Denisovich*.

Khrushchev's style of rule also helped to lose him the support he had earlier built up. He took many important decisions on his own and latterly he frequently put more reliance upon his personal advisers than upon officials within the appropriate party and government agencies. Some of his personal initiatives – above all, the decision to put missiles in Cuba – were also fraught with danger and when they turned out to be less than wholly successful, it was clear where responsibility lay.

A coalition of Khrushchev's disgruntled party colleagues, with the evident support of other élite groups, such as the military and the KGB, finally brought his remarkable political career to an end at a plenary session of the Central Committee on 14 October 1964 – ostensibly on the grounds of Khrushchev's age (he was 70) and failing health. That same day, Leonid Brezhnev was elected to the party first secretaryship (retitled general-secretary in 1966) and a day later Alexei Kosygin was appointed to the chairmanship of the Council of Ministers. What followed was a period of greater political and administrative stability than had previously been known in Soviet history, exemplified by the fact that in the late 1970s these two top posts were still held by Brezhnev and Kosygin, now themselves (with more than a third of the Politburo members) in their 70s.

Many of Khrushchev's policies were modified or even reversed by the new leadership. Military expenditure was increased and attacks on Stalin and the Stalin period became virtually forbidden. The attitudes of Brezhnev and Kosygin and their colleagues in cultural as well as political matters were more conservative than those of their ebullient predecessor. In foreign affairs a policy of extending Soviet influence without taking undue risks was pursued, and the early 1970s saw a substantial improvement in Soviet relations with the USA and with western European countries. The signing of the Helsinki Agreement (the Final Act of the Conference on Security and Cooperation in Europe) on 1 August 1975 marked the achievement of an important Soviet goal – the official acceptance by Western powers of the division of Europe and the borders that had existed since 1945. The provisions of the agreement on human rights, cultural co-operation and dissemination of information, however, caused the USSR some embarrassment, especially after the election of Jimmy Carter as US president in 1976 and the stress that he chose to lay on the human rights issue in international relations.

Alexei Kosygin addressing an election meeting

Party congresses, held in 1966, 1971 and 1976, were less exciting occasions than those presided over by Khrushchev. Brezhnev's political style was very different from that of Khrushchev. Yet in Brezhnev's case, too, a gradual strengthening of his authority within the leadership took place. By the early 1970s he had virtually supplanted Kosygin as principal Soviet spokesman on foreign policy, and in 1977 he succeeded Nikolai Podgorny as chairman of the Praesidium of the Supreme Soviet, so adding the headship of the Soviet state to his general-secretaryship of the party. This was not so powerful a combination of offices as that held by Khrushchev from 1958 to 1964, but a sign that Brezhnev had become something more than a first among equals within the collective leadership. A new constitution, containing few surprises, was adopted in 1977 to replace the Stalin constitution of 1936, and this set a seal on Brezhnev's incumbency as Soviet leader. The constitution, with its emphasis on the Communist Party as 'the leading and guiding force of Soviet society and the nucleus of its political system', corresponded more closely to political reality than did the Stalin constitution, which devoted no more than half an article to the party, near the end of the text.

Comparing the first 25 years after Stalin's death with the last 25 years of his life, there are important continuities within the political structure, but the change in atmosphere is very great. Though overt criticism of the existing political system has not been legitimized, and open political dissenters continue to be punished, people have ceased to be afraid to speak frankly on political matters among their family and friends. Outward conformity of political behaviour has been largely maintained, but there is ample evidence, thanks to the measure of relaxation in the post-Stalin years (compared with what had gone before), that the values and norms of official Marxism–Leninism are by no means as fully accepted within the USSR as might have appeared to be the case in 1953.　　　　　　　　　　　　　　　　*A. H. B.*

Formally, the establishment of the German Democratic Republic (GDR or DDR) in 1949 followed the founding of the Federal Republic in the West. In practice, two divergent states had already come into existence under different occupying powers. As the Federal Republic was brought within the economic and military framework of the Western powers, so the GDR was incorporated into the economic and defence system of the Eastern bloc.

In the period before the construction of the Berlin Wall in 1961, the GDR was characterized, first, by a policy of de-Nazification far more vigorous than that pursued in the Federal Republic, embracing the economic as well as the political sphere, and extending to the educational system and the judiciary. 'Anti-fascism' played (and plays) a prominent part in the official ideology of the GDR. Secondly, after massive 'dismantling' by Soviet occupation forces, the economic system was reconstructed by means of central planning, collectivization of agriculture and step-by-step socialization of industry and trade. Rates of growth were high; but planning was inflexible, and living standards were substantially below those in the West. The arbitrary raising of work targets was, in particular, responsible for sparking off the rising of June 1953 in East Berlin, which spread to other cities before it was put down by Soviet tanks. Economic discontent was also partly responsible for the movement of 2.7 million of its citizens, almost all of working age, as refugees to the Federal Republic between 1948 and 1961.

Politically, too, there was a transformation in the 1950s of the Socialist Unity Party (SED), the effective governing party founded in 1946 from the amalgamation of the Social Democratic and Communist parties. From 1948, under its first secretary, Walter Ulbricht, the SED became increasingly a Stalinist, cadre-type party, organized along the lines of a strictly interpreted 'democratic centralism'. Despite the continued existence of other parties, these features of rigid central control were the ones which also formed the character of the state itself.

The building of the Berlin Wall prevented emigration. Paradoxically, however, the Wall made possible a relaxation of political repression. At the same time, the disadvantages of over-rigid economic planning were recognized by the authorities; greater autonomy for local plants and more consideration for consumer demand were the outcome. These developments, together with increased internal mobility, began in the 1960s to generate a distinct sense of loyalty and identity among citizens of the GDR, which defined itself not only against less economically developed Eastern bloc partners, but also against the Federal Republic and its 'arrogance'. This new sense of identity manifested itself in a literary revival, and also in the new pride taken in the particular achievements of the GDR in the fields of health and welfare provision, the occupational equality of women, education and sport. Recession, inflation and general uncertainty in the capitalist countries also brought home the advantages of guaranteed employment, fixed prices of basic requirements and comprehensive social security.

Under Erich Honecker, who succeeded Ulbricht as first secretary of the SED in 1971, economic liberalization has continued. The new generation of specialist cadres, distinct from the older, purely political, élite, has confirmed this trend, yet much of the oppressive puritanism of the official ideology remains, as indicated by the exiling of prominent dissidents in 1977.   *D. G. B.*

The German Democratic Republic's trade-mark to the world: the Berlin Wall, erected in 1961

Poland

In the absence of diplomatic relations with the USSR the leaders of the underground Home Army (AK), owing allegiance to the government-in-exile in London, called a rising in Warsaw on 1 August 1944 in order to receive the advancing Soviet forces as representatives of a sovereign state. The Soviet forces were halted on 3 August by a German counter-attack and the rising was crushed. Authority in liberated areas was thereafter exercised by the pro-Soviet Polish Committee of National Liberation (PKWN) set up on 21 July 1944, which converted itself into a provisional government on 31 December 1944.

As a result of British and US pressure, it was replaced by the Provisional Government of National Unity (26 June 1945), which included politicians from home and abroad, but effective control of the administration remained in the hands of the pro-Soviet leaders. With the virtual elimination of the Peasant Party (SL), real power has lain with the Polish United Workers' Party (PZPR), founded on 15 December 1948 by a merger of the communist Polish Workers' Party (PPR) and the Polish Socialist Party (PPS).

A constituent assembly met on 19 January 1947, modified the constitution of 1921 then in force and adopted the 'Little Constitution'. The Constitution of the Polish People's Republic came into force on 22 July 1952, with a single-chamber parliament (*sejm*) electing a Council of State presided over by the president. This constitution has been changed frequently.

The eastern frontier of Poland was based upon the 'Curzon Line' (1919) with modifications of a few miles in favour of Poland. The western frontier, on the line of the rivers Oder and Neisse, including Szczucin (Stettin) and almost all of East Prussia, was placed 'under the administration of the Polish state' by the Potsdam Conference (1945). This proved a bone of contention between

Wladyslaw Gomulka

the Federal Republic of Germany and Poland and the question was not settled until the treaty between them was signed (7 December 1970, ratified 4 June 1972). Poland is a member of the Warsaw Treaty Organization and in foreign affairs adheres strictly to the policy of the Soviet bloc, but has good relations with Britain and West Germany, who are important trading partners.

Within its new frontiers Poland has experienced one basic problem. The population in 1946 was approximately 23 million, most of whom were Poles, but growth has been very high, amounting to 19 per cent in the years 1950–56, but dropping slightly thereafter. Provisional figures for December 1977 put the population at 34.86 million. The Polish government, being committed to a policy of full employment, has adopted the course of investment in industry in order to provide jobs for school-leavers. By the late 1970s about 51 per cent of the population had employment in urban areas. To provide the capital for expansion, the government placed emphasis upon the export of agricultural products, which often resulted in a shortage of food in the urban areas. Furthermore, Polish export trade has been at the mercy of fluctuations of trade in the capitalist world.

Crises have therefore arisen. The policy of heavy capital investment in industry resulted in the crisis of October 1956, when Wladyslaw Gomulka, passed over in 1949 for his insistence upon a 'Polish path to socialism', was made secretary-general of the party. Difficulties again arose in December 1970, when food prices were raised in order to encourage the peasants to increase their deliveries. Riots occurred in Gdansk (Danzig), Gdynia and Szczucin. As a result, Gomulka was succeeded by Edward Gierek and the price increases dropped. In June 1976 increases in food prices led to further riots. Discontent has also been apparent among the intellectuals, for whom the strict discipline imposed by the state has been a source of irritation. The economic difficulties of Poland have been rendered more severe by heavy borrowings in the capitalist countries and the consequent burden of interest and repayments. *R. F. L.*

Czechoslovakia

On 9 May 1945, the day after VE-Day, the Red Army entered Prague and completed the liberation of Czechoslovakia from German occupation. Later in May, the new Czechoslovak government was installed: Beneš returned as president with a coalition ministry of Communists and non-Communists. At the first post-war elections in May 1946 the Communists emerged as the largest single party; and their leader, Gottwald, formed a new coalition government under his premiership. The coalition fell apart in February 1948 when 12 non-Communist ministers resigned. Under extreme Communist pressure, Beneš was forced to accept a new and predominantly Communist government. Constitutional forms were outwardly observed but in fact a coup had taken place. Beneš resigned in June 1948 to be succeeded by Gottwald. Soon a complete Communist system on the Soviet model was established. In 1953 Gottwald was succeeded as president by Zapotocky, whom Novotny succeeded in 1957. Novotny combined for the first time the highest government and party positions and used his power to resist all reforms.

By 1960 the Czechoslovak economy began to falter. The rapid increase in industrial production since 1948 ceased and by 1963 showed a decline, as did agricultural production. Economic reforms had finally to be introduced in 1966 to make economic management more flexible. In the wake of economic failure other problems came to the surface. Intellectuals, and especially writers, demanded more freedom of expression, the Slovaks wanted the autonomy that had effectively been denied them since 1948, and by 1967 there was strong student discontent. These combined pressures, operating within as well as outside the Communist Party, drove Novotny from power. In January 1968 Dubček, a Slovak and leader of the Slovak Communist Party, succeeded Novotny as Czechoslovak party leader. The main intention of the Dubcek reforms was to make the Communist system more liberal and humane. Although there was no question of displacing the Communist system these proposed reforms seemed to the Soviet leadership dangerously radical and a threat to Communism in eastern Europe. When other methods failed they used force to stop the reforms. On 20–21 August 1968, Soviet troops invaded and quickly occupied Czechoslovakia. Dubček and his fellow reformers were arrested and taken to Moscow where, under duress, they signed an agreement (26 August) that meant the end of reforms. Dubček was reinstated in office, but had to accept the permanent stationing of Russian troops in Czechoslovakia. On 17 April 1969 he was replaced by Husak and the 1968 reform programme was abandoned. The only item that was implemented was federalization, which created separate Czech and Slovak governments within a federal framework (1969); by 1971 Slovak autonomy was again reduced. Under Husak, a conservative Slovak, who became president as well as party leader in 1975, a comprehensive purge of 1968 reformers in the party and in all positions of influence was conducted. At the same time the economy has improved and more and better consumer goods made available. A small group of dissidents challenged the government, which replied with repression. In 1977 the dissidents formed the 'Charter 77' movement to publicize their cause at home and abroad.

T. V. T.

Alexander Dubček at the height of the 'Prague Spring' of 1968

Soviet tanks bring the 'Prague Spring' to an end, August 1968

In the spring of 1945, Hungary was defeated as an ally of Germany by the Russian army which completed the occupation of her territory. War damage was considerable and the whole social and political order based on the dominance of the land-owning classes crumbled. Land was distributed among the landless, economic reconstruction started and political life became democratized. Elections, held in November 1945, produced a majority for the Smallholders' Party – a non-Marxist peasant party in existence before the war. It now mopped up the votes of all those in the urban middle classes who feared left-wing policies, no right-wing parties being permitted by the Soviet-dominated Allied Control Commission (ACC). In spite of the result, the ACC insisted on the appointment of a coalition government of the Smallholders, the Communists, the Social Democrats and the National Peasant Party, headed by Zoltán Tildy, the Smallholders' leader. Hungary became a republic in February and Tildy, who became president, was replaced by another Smallholder, Ferenc Nagy. The non-Communist government had much less power than the Allied Control Commission, the Soviet army of occupation and the new police controlled by the Communists. A series of show trials of Smallholder politicians, Cardinal-Primate Mindszenty and even veteran socialist and Communist leaders, was used to soften up all non-Communist forces. The Communists gradually built up a monopoly of power, and Hungary was turned into a one-party state run by a group who had spent their years of exile in Moscow. Over them, Rákosi, the party boss and later premier, established personal autocracy.

The 1949 Constitution declared Hungary a peoples' democracy and its social order socialist. Industry had already been nationalized and peasants were now compelled to give up their land to form co-operatives. An ambitious five-year plan introduced in 1950 promised to turn the mainly agricultural country to one of 'iron and steel'. Factories were built but living conditions deteriorated. After the death of Stalin, Imre Nagy became premier in July 1953, promising improvements in living standards and the end of police terror. Rákosi had a spectacular comeback in March 1955 when he ousted Nagy, only to be deposed by Khrushchev in the summer of 1956.

The country was now seething with discontent and the unprecedented happened: a Communist one-party state was overthrown by a popular uprising. This event is described in more detail on page 255.

After the reprisals for the uprising, the former Stalinists were expelled from the party in 1962 and the régime became surprisingly tolerant. It is true that the peasants were forced into co-operatives but, that apart, individual rights became more respected, living standards improved, foreign travel was allowed and a liberal cultural policy was introduced. In January 1968 the economic management of the state was reformed: market forces were allowed to operate to some extent and enterprises became less dependent on central control. Reforms created disparities in income and some discontent among hard-line Communists, leading to the removal of some 'liberals' from office in March 1974. As Kádár is an unflinching supporter of Soviet foreign policy, he has retained the backing of the Soviet leadership while enjoying considerable popularity in Hungary. *L. P.*

János Kádár, leader of the régime in Hungary since it was installed by Soviet tanks

Mátyás Rákosi (at the front), old-guard Stalinist, ousted from power in Hungary in 1956

Rumania, Bulgaria, Albania

The Balkan lands exhibited all the signs of underdevelopment when they gained their independence in the 19th century or added the territories that their governments came to rule in the 20th century. These included far-reaching political illiteracy and inexperience, the exclusion of the bulk of the population from practical politics, the survival of the overwhelmingly peasant population at starvation level, and government by shifting coalitions drawn exclusively from within a ruling élite.

Rumania

The Rumanian state profited considerably from the Balkan Wars (1912–13) and the First World War in terms of territory, and expanded to virtually the maximum of nationalist demands by adding southern Dobruja, the Bukovina, Bessarabia and Transylvania. The consequence was that almost all the individuals who could be claimed for the Rumanian nation were citizens of the Rumanian state, together with substantial minorities of non-Rumanians. Although there was some economic growth during the inter-war period, the great bulk of the population lived in miserable conditions. Rumanian politics became a by-word for corruption, and the constant changing of governments was eventually ended by the dictatorship of King Carol. The frustrations of the population tended to be channelled into the right-extremist Iron Guard movement, until it was crushed in 1940 after an attempted rising. The Second World War found Rumania an ally of the Nazis and, at the same time, resentful over the loss imposed by Germany of northern Transylvania to Hungary, Bessarabia and northern Bukovina to the Soviet Union and southern Dobruja to Bulgaria. The hope of regaining these territories led the Rumanian government to participate in the invasion of the Soviet Union on the side of the Wehrmacht, but when the tide of battle had turned, the king mounted a royal putsch and executed a turn-about in the country's alignment. This led to the involvement of Rumanian armies now fighting on the side of the Allies and the recovery of northern Transylvania.

The Communist Party was extremely weak in Rumania, but with Soviet support it gained a monopoly in the country's political life. From 1948 until the early 1960s, Rumania, under the leadership of Gheorghe Gheorghiu-Dej, was a model satellite of the Soviet Union. Dej skilfully steered the country first through the massive build-up of pressure during the Stalinist period, which involved the formulation of very ambitious plans for industrialization, and subsequently through the minimum of de-Stalinization necessary. His reward was the withdrawal of Soviet occupation forces in 1958. By the early 1960s, however, the Rumanian leadership had seemingly reversed its policies and began a cautious, but unmistakable, campaign to free the country from excessive dependence on Soviet tutelage.

In the first place, Dej resisted Khrushchev's plans for the transformation of Comecon into a supra-national planning agency, whereby Rumania would have been left as an agricultural supplier to the European Communist area. Secondly, the leadership began deliberately to use Rumanian nationalism as the primary source of its power. To some degree, open coercion was abandoned and during the 1960s some cautious steps were taken towards liberalization. In 1968 Rumania, now led by Nicolae Ceauşescu, supported the right of Czechoslovakia to determine its own future under Alexander Dubček but without showing much enthusiasm for liberalization. In the same period Rumania attracted increasing attention by an independent foreign policy, which led it to become the only Warsaw Pact state with a diplomatic mission in Israel. It broke ranks in establishing relations with West Germany in 1967, and it sought to establish a position for itself as a developing country to some degree involved with the non-aligned movement. It also maintained cordial relations with China at a time when Sino-Soviet relations were deteriorating. Perhaps the high point was President Nixon's visit to Bucharest in 1969, the first visit by a US president to a Communist country. In the 1970s Rumania's independence declined in importance as East–West relations improved under détente, but within the Communist world the Rumanians backed the right of the Euro-communists to develop their own doctrine.

Internally, however, Ceauşescu presided over an increasingly repressive régime that was meeting grave difficulties with its economic plans, low level social unrest and growing alienation of the country's two million-strong Hungarian minority, excluded as it was from Rumanian nationhood. Ceauşescu's style of leadership had turned into an almost unparalleled personality cult by the mid-1970s, and his style of rule involved many members of his family in high positions, while a complex bureaucracy ran the country with the methods of a police state.

Nicolae Ceauşescu on a visit to Britain in 1978

Bulgaria

Bulgaria emerged as a loser from the Balkan Wars and the First World War and has ever since been haunted by the vision of re-establishing the 'Greater Bulgaria' of the 1877 San Stefano Treaty. After a brief flirtation with a populist government in the 1920s, the traditional political élite settled back into running the country in the time-honoured fashion. Bulgaria joined the Axis and temporarily re-occupied Macedonia, but in 1944 the Communist-dominated Fatherland Front seized control and led Bulgaria into alliance with the Soviet Union against Nazi Germany.

Communist control was rapidly established and, after the death of Georgi Dimitrov, one of the great figures of the international Communist movement, Vǔlko Chervenkov established himself as the country's undisputed ruler. With the onset of de-Stalinization, Chervenkov gradually lost power, but it took from 1954 to 1962 for his successor, Todor Zhivkov (the current leader), to oust all rivals. Under Zhivkov the country has enjoyed a modest, but not unimpressive, rise in the standard of living and a political stability that in the 1970s began to resemble stagnation. The Bulgarian leadership began increasingly to rely on nationalism for buttressing its legitimacy and put great pressure on Bulgaria's minorities – Turks, Pomaks, Macedonians – to assimilate. At the same time, the Macedonian issue led Bulgaria into constant friction with Yugoslavia, for the Bulgarians deny the existence of an independent Macedonian nation and argue that Macedonians are Bulgarians. Bulgaria's very close relations with the Soviet Union, in a country where pro-Russian feelings have traditionally been strong, has been the government's principal external support.

Albania

Albania was given its independence in 1912 in the course of the Balkan Wars and in the inter-war period King Zog ruled the country largely as a client of Italy's, which eventually occupied the country in 1939. After confused fighting during the Second World War, the Communists emerged as the strongest political group under Enver Hoxha. However, Albania was only saved from incorporation into Yugoslavia by the quarrel between Stalin and Tito, after which Hoxha relied on the Soviet Union for protection. Soviet–Yugoslav reconciliation in the 1950s eventually led Albania to turn to China, a relationship that lasted until 1977, when it ended over Albania's disapproval of Peking's unacceptable moderation in foreign policy. Externally pursuing a policy of isolation, internally Albania has one of the most repressive régimes in the world under Hoxha. Control by the party extends over all areas of life and in 1967 Albania became the only state in the world to ban all organized religion. In the post-war period Albania's economy has grown and modernization is the target of the régime, which it pursues with determination verging on ruthlessness. *G. S.*

Enver Hoxha, leader of the world's most isolated Communist state, Albania. A diehard Stalinist and Maoist, he has bitterly criticized both the USSR and China

Yugoslavia

The establishment of Yugoslavia in 1918 as a single state of the South Slavs was both the fulfilment of the aspirations of the nations constituting the country and the source of friction in which a relationship that fully satisfies all of them has to be found. The dominant nation proved to be the Serbs, who had won their independence from the Ottoman Empire by stages from 1804 onwards, through armed struggle. It was the Serbian monarchy that headed the new Yugoslav state and, to a substantial extent, Serbian traditions of centralization that formed the basis of its organization. The second largest national group, the Croats, had cut their political teeth in the very different traditions of a legalistic struggle with Hungary and Austria and had expected extensive self-rule in the new state, something that the Serbs never accepted. The entire inter-war period was envenomed by the burgeoning Serb–Croat conflict, one incident of which was the assassination of the Croatian peasant leader Stjepan Radić actually during a session of the parliament. The outbreak of the Second World War found the country divided and in 1941, after the German invasion, Croatia was set up as an independent state under German tutelage and an internecine Serb–Croat conflict led to the massacre of large numbers of Serbs. The other nations – Slovenes, Macedonians, Muslims – also had their reasons for distrusting the Serbian-dominated state. This was the background against which the communist partisans under Josip Broz Tito fought a war of liberation against the foreign occupation forces and against non-communist domestic forces. In 1945 Tito emerged victorious, but the country's war losses were enormous – 11 per cent of the population dead. Tito's control of the country was complete and he enjoyed genuine popularity.

Tito was alone among communist leaders in Europe – Albania excepted – to have come to power without the full backing of the Red Army, and by 1948 he clashed with Stalin over the degree of Soviet control over Yugoslavia. Tito was determined to rule the country without interference from outside, the Soviet Union included, and successfully held off the challenge. From then on, Yugoslavia was a non-aligned communist state, seeking a middle position between east and west that would guarantee the country's long-term independence. At times relations with the Soviet Union deteriorated, at others a reconciliation was effected, but at no point could the Yugoslavs be certain that Moscow genuinely accepted their defection from the Soviet sphere of political, ideological and military influence.

These two threads have run through Yugoslav affairs since the war. In foreign policy, Tito has earned world-wide respect as an elder statesman and founder of the non-aligned movement. Yugoslavia has fair relations with the West and accepts that up to a million Yugoslavs work there as temporary workers. Relations with the Soviet Union, while seemingly cordial at times, are characterized by a sense of unease. This has been intensified by the existence of Yugoslavia's competing Marxist ideology, developed over the years, and based on the principle of democratization through self-management, a concept never accepted by the Soviet Union.

In internal affairs strict central control was maintained by the party, backed by the coercive apparatus, in the 1950s and early 1960s. In the mid-1960s a breakthrough

Tito (right) in 1944 at partisan hq. with comrades-in-arms

was achieved and decentralization followed in politics and economics, with the power of the secret police broken in 1966. Decentralization led to the resurgence of nationalist aspirations, above all in Croatia, where communist centralization was identified with Serbian domination. The Croatian national movement was judged unacceptable by Tito and the rest of Yugoslavia and was stifled at the end of 1971. Tito then proceeded to purge the other republican leaderships and to restore greater central control by the Party. He placed renewed stress on the principle of self-management as the dominant ideology in Yugoslav life and, at the end of 1977, he formally acknowledged the

The shrewd pilot who charted Yugoslavia's road to communism, Josip Broz, better known as President Tito, photographed in 1957

society on a reasonably equitable basis. The relative political stability and economic prosperity of the post-war period may be ascribed to Tito's unique model of communism that has acquired a degree of authority and popular support so far unparalleled in the communist world. At the same time, Titoism has generated a certain amount of opposition and the authorities have at times dealt harshly with dissidents. The best known of them, Milovan Djilas, spent nine years in prison for publicly calling for more democracy. The *Praxis* group of left-wing philosophers, who have argued that there can be nothing sacred in a Marxist Yugoslavia and that all aspects of the Titoist system should be subjected to the criticism of everyday practice, had their journal (called 'Praxis') suspended and some members of the group were suspended from their academic jobs. Pro-Soviet dissidents, known as Cominformists, have been imprisoned, as have those charged with Croatian, Albanian and other kinds of nationalist activities.

G. S.

role of the armed forces as the guarantors of the political integrity of the state. These moves may be regarded as having been preparations for the difficult period after Tito's death. He has so dominated Yugoslav politics for a generation that the succession will be a source of concern and anxiety.

Under Tito, Yugoslavia has made enormous strides economically. The developed republics of Croatia and Slovenia have achieved Western standards of living, and the poor south has also benefited, but the gap between the two remains. Political development has lagged somewhat, but there is no doubt that, when compared with its neighbours, Yugoslavia enjoys greater political freedom, and the existing dispensation recognizes the need for differentiation and provides for the mediation of conflict in

The People's Republic of China

After a century of division and humiliation, the Chinese people had, with the establishment of the People's Republic in the words of Mao Tse-tung, 'stood up'. Little time was lost in extending control to all the outlying provinces, including Tibet. The victory of the revolution was consolidated in the countryside through a land reform movement. This was carried out with the Communists' well-tested methods of using it as a vehicle for social revolution, rather than by simply dividing the land. It was a preparatory stage for moving towards a more collective agriculture. The cities and the problems of industrialization raised new and unfamiliar problems for the Chinese leaders, and in this area predominantly they began to lean heavily on the Soviet experience.

Because of the Cold War, US hostility and an ideological affinity with the Soviet Union, Mao had declared in the summer of 1949 that the new China would lean to the Soviet side, from which he also looked forward to receiving genuine aid. After unexpectedly tough negotiations, a Sino-Soviet alliance was signed on 14 February 1950. The main benefit to China was strategic security from possible American threats. The initial aid offered was more limited than might have been expected, but at least the Chinese now had access to Soviet expertise. Indeed, their administrative structures, economic, education and other systems were modelled directly on the Soviet example. Mao Tse-tung had accepted for China initially something of the role of a junior ally. Stalin had mistrusted Mao's independence and had thought of him as potentially another Tito. He therefore insisted on maintaining a Soviet presence in Manchuria and in the western province of Sinkiang. It was only with the Korean War that Stalin eventually trusted his Chinese allies not to make a deal with the Americans.

The Korean War was a watershed in Chinese history. Although they had played no part in its outbreak, Chinese forces ended up taking the brunt of the fighting. It was the first war in modern Chinese history in which Chinese armies had been able to inflict defeats upon modern Western armies. At the end, China emerged as an acknowledged great power in her own right in world affairs. Domestically, the war had given an opportunity for establishing full Communist control over the urban bourgeoisie and for extirpating the remaining cultural influence of the West. However, the war also brought renewed American intervention in the unfinished Chinese civil war. The American Seventh Fleet was interposed between mainland China and Taiwan to prevent a military conquest by the Communists. In December 1954 a mutual security pact was signed between the United States and the Chiang régime, which still claimed to be the Republic of China. Sino-American relations were then locked into continual hostility until President Nixon's visit to Peking in 1972.

After the Korean War and the death of Stalin, China became an independent and almost equal ally of the Soviet Union. Although Soviet aid flowed in greater quantities (more than 140 modern industrial plants were built with Soviet assistance), Chinese conditions differed from those of the Soviet Union, and problems began to arise in the application of the Soviet model. On their side, the Chinese leaders – and especially Mao – had the experience of the more democratic Yenan model to fall back on. From the

The people salute Chairman Mao, and wish him 'long life'.

Propaganda painting of peasants gathered on a traditional stove-bed to draw up a production plan, advised by a party activist

middle 1950s, despite the misgivings of some party leaders, Mao began to move away from the Soviet model. The climax came with the 'Great Leap Forward' of 1958, when, with the mobilization of hundreds of millions of people, communes were established in agriculture and the careful administrative planning and controls for running the economy were shelved. The communes were designed as largely self-sufficient, decentralized units of several

Mass meeting of soldiers and workers in the stadium after the setting up of the Peking Municipal Revolutionary Committee during the Cultural Revolution. The score-board repeats the greeting to Chairman Mao seen opposite

tens of thousands of people each, in a three-tiered structure of 'commune', 'brigade' and 'core village'. Combining both industry and agriculture, communes were also to be units of local defence and local government. In a euphoric atmosphere it was claimed that a unique way to communism had been discovered. Exaggerated claims of economic output led the leadership to proclaim that China's food problem had been solved once and for all. In fact, although much had been achieved, the dislocations had been great and the disorder engendered left the people ill-prepared for the following three years of exceptionally bad weather. In the period 1959–62 policies of severe retrenchment were followed. The commune system was retained because of the flexibility of allocating resources and responsibility within it. Thus, by 1961 the core village had become the basic accounting unit, the brigade was a group of villages with responsibility for larger scale economic activities, and the commune became mostly a unit of administration.

The break with the Soviet Union
The Sino-Soviet dispute broke out during the pursuit of the 'Chinese way' to communism. Ideological and strategic factors were perhaps the most important. Starting with Khrushchev, the Soviet leaders were, in the Chinese view,

more interested in finding a strategic accommodation with the USA than in exploiting the changing balance of world forces to restrain the USA from acting in a high-handed, imperialist way in Asia, Africa and Latin America and, of course, towards China. A corollary of the Russian position was that revolutionary conflicts in any part of the world must not be allowed to endanger the Soviet-American détente. It was this, in the Chinese view, that led Khrushchev to argue against Lenin that a socialist revolution could come about peacefully. It did not take Mao long to argue that the reason the Soviet leaders were following revisionist policies was because they were themselves revisionists. As a result of these quarrels, the Soviet Union began to side with bourgeois India against socialist China and in 1960 suddenly withdrew all aid and experts from China. By 1962 Mao had decided that the Soviet leaders were nothing but fascist dictators. The actual breaking point coincided with China's independent acquisition of nuclear weapons.

The Cultural Revolution
Divisions in the Chinese leadership as to the correct socialist path for China, and Mao's concern lest the Chinese revolution be betrayed from within on the Soviet pattern led Mao to identify his domestic opponents as revisionists too. Suspecting that power-holders in the Communist Party were 'following a capitalist road' while mouthing socialist language, Mao used his prestige and authority to reach down to the masses, especially the urban young, urging them to rise and seize power from the Party bosses. The main target was the head of state, Liu Shao-ch'i, who in Mao's mind symbolized the revisionist attitude. Soon almost the entire Party establishment was overthrown, and by 1968 chaos and anarchy loomed as Red Guard student factions fought pitched battles with each other. The course of this revolution was influenced by bitter struggles for supremacy in the Political Bureau. In 1971 Mao's named successor, Lin Piao, was put to flight and his conspiracy to restore the Soviet link exposed. Lin Piao and his associates died in an aircraft that crashed mysteriously in Mongolia while heading for the USSR. Following Mao's death in September 1976, his own widow and her close supporters were imprisoned and pilloried as the 'gang of four' who had opposed modernization.

Before his death, Mao had presided over a massive change in China's foreign policy, which saw China assume its rightful place in world affairs at the United Nations. Following American setbacks in Indochina and the subsequent decline of US power from 1968 onwards, paralleled by the rise of the USSR as an aggressive super-power, Mao in his last years initiated better relations with the USA. After the removal of the 'gang of four', China's policies were re-directed to the goals Mao had espoused in the 1950s: building up China rapidly into a modern, powerful, socialist state. The current commitment to modernization while maintaining an authentic, independent identity should not be taken lightly, as this is perhaps the deepest Chinese aspiration in its modern history since the challenge of the West began with the Opium War in 1840.

M. B. Y.

THE NON-ALIGNED WORLD

Early in the 1950s as the number of new states admitted to the United Nations from former colonial status began to increase, it became clear that a number of them did not wish to commit themselves to supporting either the North Atlantic or the Soviet bloc. Meeting at Bandung in Indonesia in 1955, they declared themselves neutralist. The epithet 'non-aligned' was adopted at a subsequent conference meeting at Belgrade in 1961.

These states, it emerged, had more than neutrality to bring them together. All were in some sense or other socialist; *étatiste* would perhaps have been a better way of putting it, since all relied on state direction of the economy and large scale enterprises. They were also largely united in thinking anti-colonialism the main issue at the United Nations, by which all but a few, mainly Islamic, states meant hostility to the receding tide of European colonial power, rather than to the Soviet bloc. At the United Nations these non-aligned states joined to play two other roles. They insisted on being represented at arms control and disarmament negotiations, including those designed to put an end to nuclear tests and to limit the world-wide stationing of nuclear weapons; nuclear-free zones were negotiated for Africa and Latin America. And they played an increasingly important role in world economic discussions. Despite the vast capital gains that accrued to those states that could exert near monopoly control of a single raw material, as it might be at various times oil, cocoa, tin, copper or rubber, they were in the main comparatively undeveloped, dependent on the industrial nations of Europe, America and Japan for development capital, imports of capital goods and markets for their products. They developed a common interest in using their combined voting power to influence special economic gatherings, organizing themselves under titles such as the 'Group of Seventy-Seven'. They were often, of course, divided among themselves by bitter sources of conflict such as Kashmir, the Ogaden, Katanga or the Sahara. Many were afraid of China; most went through periods of dependence on Soviet arms. Regional organizations absorbed much of their political energy. But for all of them the United Nations was the centre of their foreign policy; much more so than for the major powers of Europe, America or the Far East. *D. C. W.*

President Sukarno of Indonesia making the opening address at the African–Asian Conference at Bandung in April, 1955. Inset, from left to right: Archbishop Makarios of Cyprus, Pandit Jawaharlal Nehru of India, Emperor Haile Selassie of Ethiopia.

South America: the Major Economies

Venezuela

In 1945 Venezuela was already established as the leading oil-producer of Latin America and her output exceeded that of all the other countries of the continent combined. Venezuelan oil has been particularly important to the US because it is not subject to the political uncertainties in the Middle East.

From 1945 to 1948 Venezuela was governed by a progressive movement, Democratic Action, led by Romulo Betancourt, which set out to redistribute some of the profits of oil to the urban working class and the peasantry. Democratic Action embarked upon an ambitious programme: it reviewed oil concessions and raised the taxes (previously minimal) paid by the international oil companies, set out to redistribute under-used land on large estates to the landless peasantry, promoted trades unions, and introduced reform in education. The reform programme, supported by progressive military officers, was resisted by an alliance of large landowners, urban employers, multi-nationals and the Church and, in 1948, the precarious Democratic Action Alliance was finally overthrown by a right-wing military coup. One of the most brutal dictatorships in Latin American history then followed. Led by Marcos Pérez Jiménez, it benefited only a small minority of the upper class, loyal military officers and the international firms. In spite of half-hearted attempts to woo the urban workers, the Church and even the Communists, the dictatorship succeeded only in antagonizing all groups in turn, and became increasingly reliant on the use of coercion to maintain power. When support from within the Army crumbled as a consequence of Jiménez' capricious promotion policy, an alliance of civilians and progressive military assumed power.

Since 1958, Venezuela has enjoyed a series of democratic governments and regular elections and has twice undergone a peaceful transition of power from one party to another. The dominant force remains Democratic Action. In the early 1960s this maintained a liberal, progressive stance. It launched an apparently comprehensive reform programme but by 1970 it was clear that its entrenched leadership had neither the will nor the administrative capacity to implement the programme fully. Popular discontent, fanned by inflation and a population growth-rate exceeded only by China, culminated in an election victory in 1970 for the opposition party, a Catholic reformist movement called the COPEI, led by Rafael Caldera.

During the oil crisis from 1973 to 1974 Venezuela emerged as the leader and most articulate spokesman of the group of oil-producers. She had already enjoyed considerable success in her nationalization of the oil industry and the replacement of foreign technicians by Venezuelans has been accomplished smoothly. Venezuelan tactics in dealings with the oil companies were particularly intelligent; the Government did not deny them compensation, but based it upon the tax returns of the companies, whose practice of evasion was common knowledge. The new profits from oil have turned Venezuela into one of the foremost Latin American nations. There is little evidence of the benefits to be seen in the shanty-towns which surround Caracas, but it is clear that Venezuela is using the new revenues to expand her influence in the Caribbean and Central America.

Colombia

Colombian politics have been dominated by two parties – the Conservatives and Liberals – since their formation in the 1840s. Though relationships between the two parties have often been bitter, the respective members have contrived through a subtle blend of manipulation, co-option and coercion to preserve their joint ascendancy.

The post-war period in Colombia has witnessed some economic expansion, rapid urbanization and growing maldistribution of income. Post-war inflation and intense competition between the traditional parties exploded during the 1948 Inter-American Conference held in Bogotá in a tragic sequence of events known as the *violencia*. This was a period of undeclared civil war between Conservative and Liberal peasants when perhaps 200,000 peasants were killed while Conservative and Liberal leaders were still on cocktail party terms. A wide range of grievances had accumulated over two or more decades: quarrels over the spoils of office, abuse of police powers, the failure of the Liberal régime of the 1930s to execute a promised land reform, encroachment upon the land and water supply of small proprietors and tenant farmers by larger proprietors, anti-clerical violence and clerical retaliation. Rural protest was too disparate to be co-ordinated in a single peasant movement, yet it rendered Colombia virtually ungovernable for long periods between 1949 and 1958. Only a Liberal–Conservative coalition, established in 1958 brought the *violencia* to an uncertain conclusion in 1964.

The Conservative–Liberal coalition continues to exist. Adept at political manipulation, its leaders have secured the interests of the small upper class. The coalition has been challenged from all sides – by dissident Liberals and Conservative leaders, rural guerrillas, small, evanescent urban leftist groupings, and by a populist movement headed by the former military dictator, Gustavo Rojas Pinilla. The most spectacular (and the most ineffective) opposition came from a young priest, Camilo Torres. Torres, influenced by the Second Vatican Council, became increasingly impatient with the Colombian bishops who, despite the liberalization of the Catholic Church over most of South America, clung resolutely to the ultramontane and pro-Franco position which they had held in the 1930s. Camilo Torres, concluding that social justice could be achieved in Colombia only through revolutionary violence, joined the guerrillas and was killed in armed action in 1967. Since then, most younger priests have diverted their energy from political action to social work.

Economic expansion has provided the surplus which has financed the co-option and neutralization of most critics of the coalition régime. In the 1970s Colombia enjoyed an exceptional economic boom made possible by a record international price in coffee and a bonanza of illicit drugs exports. The new prosperity has, however, hardly percolated through to the peasantry and the urban workers. Proposals for agrarian and urban reform and for improvements in education and health facilities have barely been implemented. In spite of inflation and unemployment, no organization has been strong enough to use the seething unrest to overthrow the régime. A military coup has been widely predicted, but the combination of military dissension and civilian manipulative skills has confounded the experts.

Peru

Peru has always been a deeply divided and rigidly stratified society. The most pronounced cleavage is geographical: on the one hand, there is the Pacific coastline and the city of Lima which have both been susceptible to international trends; on the other, the Andean highlands, where remoteness and distance from the capital have enabled primitive labour systems to survive to the present.

In 1968 the military coup which overthrew a civilian régime at a moment of acute upheaval when Peru was virtually ungovernable, was in sharp contrast with those in most other Latin American countries in the post-war period. It was led by progressive officers, who viewed themselves not as the champions of tradition against the forces of revolutionary change but as progressive nationalists who would gnaw at Peruvian dependence upon foreign capital and remove the stranglehold of the national oligarchy. The military régime led by General Velasco adopted a programme of nationalization of the multi-national enterprises (notably in oil and minerals), redistribution of land to the landless peasantry, urban and educational reform, and industrialization based upon locally assembled capital. The Government found allies among nationalist elements in the middle class and in certain trades unions. After some initial successes, the reform programme began to falter in the early 1970s. Industrialization was slower than had been hoped and inflation and unemployment combined to foment urban unrest that forced the army into a repressive posture. The agrarian reform failed to capture the imagination of the peasantry imposed from above without local consultation. Civilian discontent found a response within the army and power slowly shifted from the progressive faction surrounding Velasco to the conservative officers. Velasco's death in 1978 seemed to symbolize the entrenchment of the conservative faction of the military in power.

Brazil since 1945

The authoritarian, corporatist régime of Getulio Vargas, the *Estado Novo* of 1937–45, had been modelled on the Salazar régime in Portugal. The army, returning from Italy where it had been fighting on the side of the Allies, threatened to overthrow Vargas. The army was not proposing a military dictatorship; indeed, the army had been embarrassed at being identified with a corporatist régime that had more in common with Italian Fascism than with the Western democracies, and was afraid that the US might impose sanctions against Brazilian exports. Vargas, hypersensitive to changes of national mood, opportunely allowed political parties to operate freely and announced forthcoming elections. Thus began what has hesitantly been known as the 'democratic experiment' in Brazil from 1945 to 1964. The political parties that emerged were not, with the exception of the Communist Party, ideologically defined as in France, Italy or Chile, but were personal clienteles and coalitions that embraced a wide range of ideological positions and were cemented only by a common interest in political and administrative spoils. The victors in such a system were the politicians most adept at manipulation; the losers were the electorate who were offered no genuine choice at the polls. Vargas, who unashamedly founded two parties in order to guarantee his position, was outmanoeuvred and committed suicide.

By the early 1960s mounting popular discontent in Brazil was fuelled by high levels of unemployment and hyperinflation. Successive presidents had promised handsome concessions to the underprivileged classes in exchange for their votes, and had failed to live up to expectations. João Goulart, vice-president and a prosperous cattle-rancher, unexpectedly rose to the presidency when the incumbent president died. Because he had never campaigned as a presidential candidate, Goulart was not a nationally known figure and lacked the support of a broad coalition. He, therefore, set about constructing an alliance of discontented groups, notably the peasant leagues and urban trades unions. The propertied classes and Congress became increasingly restive as Goulart failed to resolve the economic crisis and continued to promote popular mobilizations. By 1964, Brazil was virtually ungovernable.

The military, angered at interference by Goulart in internal matters of promotion, stepped into the political vacuum. The military's involvement was welcomed by most civilian politicians as a temporary expedient to restore public order. Gradually, the apparatus of a democratic society was dismantled: Congress was closed, the press was censored and trades unions, peasant leagues and student groups were suppressed. The military régime tantalized civilian leaders with the carrot of a return to 'democratic normalcy', and even maintained a façade of regular presidential elections (of military candidates). But, by 1968, it was clear that the army had no intention of withdrawing from politics even in the medium term.

This was not, however, an exclusively military régime. It was true that the army did assume all responsibility for matters of public order, but it left matters of economic development to allies among the technocrats who saw an authoritarian régime as an essential prerequisite of economic development. The military also established something of a constituency among the urban middle class who were the main beneficiaries of the 'economic miracle' and the leading customers for new consumer goods. By the mid-1970s the Brazilian economy was again in crisis. The Brazilian market was incapable of absorbing continued expansion of industrial goods because the purchasing power of the urban workers and peasants was so low. At the same time, there were few opportunities for expanding industrial exports as a result of the world recession. The military régime responded to renewed urban unemployment and widespread deprivation by applying increasingly repressive measures. The only critics of the régime who can escape official repression are the liberal bishops, led by Dom Helder Camara, Archbishop of Recife, who have repeatedly condemned the practices of harassment and torture employed by agents and allies of the régime.

Brazil seems set to be a world power. It is building up its naval strength in the South Atlantic and has consolidated the jungle frontier (at the expense of the jungle Indians). Also, its military power is regarded as a threat in Venezuela and Argentina. The US has, certainly since the 1960s, treated Brazil as the second power in the Western hemisphere, and there is growing involvement by Brazil in Africa, mainly for reasons of linguistic and cultural fraternity, in the former Portuguese colonies of Angola and Mozambique. *C. G. A.*

By the mid-1920s most internal differences in Mexico had been smoothed out, and the country emerged from the revolutionary upheaval to enter a long period of slow recovery. The revolutionary programme embodied in the 1917 constitution was applied only slowly and incompletely. Its most ardent supporter was the reformist president Lazaro Cárdenas (1934–40), who took significant steps to shift funds towards industrial development, expropriate foreign-owned oil-wells, redistribute land to peasants and strengthen trade unions. The pace of reform between 1935 and 1938 was unsurpassed in any previous or subsequent presidency. Indeed, Cárdenas himself had to put a brake on the reform programme in the last years of his presidency in the face of growing militancy from the propertied classes.

With the Second World War, the pace stepped up again. Mexico's industries – iron and steel, chemicals, paper, textiles – expanded at a rate that was unthinkable in the 1930s. Her cities have swelled alarmingly: in the early 1970s, Mexico City overtook Tokyo to become the largest city in the world and, on present United Nations predictions, is set to become the focus of an agglomeration of 30 million people by the year 2000. Industrialization has been accompanied by a fierce drive to modernize agriculture. Several dramatic changes are visible: rural credit has been expanded, much infertile land has been irrigated, the quality of agrarian education has been improved immeasurably, the mechanization of the countryside has been accelerated, and farmers have access to fertilizer, insecticide and modern methods of veterinary surgery as never before. Success has, however, been achieved at the expense of the shanty-town dwellers and the rural labouring class. Economists reckon that national income in Mexico is even more inequitably distributed than in India.

A long period of political stability has made economic expansion possible. The revolutionary factions of the 1910s and 1920s were, in 1928, consolidated by President Calles in one political party, which has governed Mexico continuously since that date. The single party, known since 1946 as the Institutionalized Revolutionary Party (PRI) has aimed at containing political and social tensions and promoting peaceful economic change. The PRI has channelled the aspirations of organized pressure groups – trades unions, professionals, peasants, urban workers, businessmen and commercial farmers – and has diffused information from the centre to the periphery. It has maintained regular elections and the democratic apparatus of Congress, regional assemblies and municipal councils, and has professionalized the civil service. It has also tolerated opposition parties and factions so long as they have not posed a serious challenge at the polls.

The PRI has made several dramatic shifts in policy in order to co-opt critics from the various interest groups, and where it has failed to absorb them, it has suffocated or isolated their opposition. All civilian pressure groups have been reassured by a consistent policy of low spending on the military: the Mexican armed forces have enjoyed a smaller proportion of the national budget than the military in all other Latin American countries except Costa Rica. Low military spending has enabled the government to invest substantial resources in unprofitable but essential sectors of the economy, such as transport, where the

Modern Mexico's deep roots in history exemplified by the Plaza of the Three Cultures: pre-Columbian, Spanish colonial and 20th-century buildings cheek by jowl

private sector has been reluctant to invest. The government has so regulated the economy as to ensure a subtle blend of the interests of the private and public sector; and has, at the same time, placated Mexican nationalists by establishing a state agency to control the flow of foreign investments and to monitor the activities of the international firms. The PRI has contrived, with some success, to implement the reforms envisaged in the 1917 constitution – improved education, social security benefits and pensions, for example – without sacrificing the goals of economic growth. A radical foreign policy, attracting attention by praise for the Cuban revolution and support for the Group of Non-aligned Countries, has given some substance to the revolutionary image cultivated by the PRI. Nevertheless, in domestic policy, the party has often been unashamedly conservative, showering benefits upon the urban middle class and neglecting the underprivileged.

For all its talk of a revolutionary commitment and democratic practice, the PRI is dominated by an exclusive circle of perhaps 30 men – the 'revolutionary family' – who control appointments, policy and propaganda. This is a system characterized by controlled participation, central manipulation and general apathy. Since 1945 disparities in wealth and administrative competence between central and local government have been accentuated. Few *municipios* have sufficient funds to embark on local projects more ambitious than street-paving. Consequently, much time is spent in bargaining between local PRI bosses and their patrons in Mexico City over allocations of funds to local government. Dissatisfaction with the inefficiency and inequitability of the political system culminated in a series of violent outbreaks in the 1960s, yet no coordinated movement of opposition to the PRI régime emerged. The opposition forces did not cohere even in the heady, optimistic months of 1968–69, when events in Paris reverberated across Mexico. Meanwhile, conservative groups within the PRI regrouped and consolidated themselves, reasserting the ascendancy of the single party. *C. G. A.*

Chile achieved a stability rare among Hispanic-American republics in the 19th century. She adhered to orderly, democratic procedures with a faithfulness uncommon even in Western Europe. The military coup of 1973 was a sharp break with the past in a country where a civilian political culture was so thoroughly established.

The Great Depression of 1929–33 hit the Chilean economy with a severity unequalled in Latin America; the price of her leading export commodity – copper – fell by 80 per cent. Chile has never fully recovered. Her population has expanded at a rapid pace (it now stands at about 10 million, of whom 10 per cent – a conservative estimate – are in exile) and industrialization has failed to keep pace with urban growth so that shanty-towns have mushroomed on the outskirts of the leading cities. Food supplies have been inadequate because agriculture has been starved of investment, and the disparity in wealth between the city and the countryside has become increasingly pronounced. Inflation and high rates of unemployment have contributed to recurring economic crises and social unrest.

It is hardly surprising that the Chilean electorate has experimented with different modes of government in the hope of finding the way to sustained economic growth. From the 1930s to the 1950s, Popular Front, conservative, radical and coalition régimes were elected (and there was one interlude in which the military seized power) but no government had more than limited success in solving the most pressing problems. By 1964 Chile was ripe for radical change. The Christian Democratic Party, founded after the Second World War roughly on the Italian and German prototypes, won power in an electoral landslide. Its leader, Eduardo Frei, promised a middle path on Catholic lines between capitalism and Communism – the pursuit of social justice combined with a programme of economic growth. But by 1968 the Christian Democratic promise had become tarnished. The government had both antagonized the business interests for failing to achieve sustained growth and failed to satisfy the expectations of the underprivileged classes of a dramatic redistribution of wealth from the rich to the poor.

The left-wing parties seized the initiative. The candidate of the Marxist coalition of socialist, Communist and radical parties, Salvador Allende, won the 1970 elections in a three-cornered fight against the Christian Democrats and the National (Conservative) Party. The 'Popular Unity' coalition launched a dramatic programme that included expropriation of the multi-nationals in copper and banking, an accelerated redistribution of land to the landless, expansion of health and education facilities and state encouragement to industrialization. In 1970–71 the Allende government was remarkably successful in expanding the economy and reducing unemployment. But in 1972 the boom faded, because the US and the international lending agencies resident there responded to the expropriation of foreign concerns by denying credit to Chile.

Left and right in confrontation
External pressures coincided with internal confrontation. The opposition parties, which controlled both Congress and the media, sustained a vitriolic campaign that delayed legislation and heightened middle-class anxieties about the government's intentions. The constitutionally elected parties lost the initiative to extra-parliamentary groups. Peasants and urban workers, again frustrated by the slowness of change, were encouraged by the extra-parliamentary left to seize land and occupy factories. The extra-parliamentary right responded by unleashing a campaign of terrorism and sabotage. Allende resorted to expedients to calm and contain the situation. He recruited military figures into the government as mayors. state governors and even one as minister of the interior. This resourcefulness was rewarded by an improved showing in the mid-term elections, but it did nothing to relieve the economic crisis which was deepened by hyperinflation, renewed high levels of unemployment and a flourishing black market. By mid-1973, Chile was virtually ungovernable and the parties so polarized that reconciliation between the government and the official opposition was impossible. Accordingly, the military members of the government resigned under pressure from the opposition.

The Pinochet régime
In September 1973 the stalemate was resolved by a brutal military coup led by General Auguste Pinochet, during which President Allende was killed. Pinochet constructed a ruthless security apparatus, outlawed all political parties and trade unions, reversed the reform programmes of his predecessors and gave generous concessions to foreign investment. Measures to reactivate the economy were financed by reducing the incomes of the urban workers and peasantry. A return to civilian rule in Chile does not appear likely in the foreseeable future. *C. G. A.*

Salvador Allende, president of Chile from 1970 to 1973, when he was killed in a military coup

Demagogue Dictators: Castro and Perón

Cuba under Castro

Cuba had a long tradition of external dependence and of radical opposition to it. Nationalist armies had twice fought protracted wars of independence against Spain in the 19th century, but they had only been assured of victory when the US intervened decisively in 1898. The war left a vacuum in Cuba that US capital soon filled. In 1933–34, at the beginning of the Roosevelt era of 'good neighbour' policies, disparate left-wing and nationalist groups aligned together in an abortive attempt to oust the imperialist power, but what successes they had were soon reversed by subsequent governments.

In the mid-1950s a new nationalist guerrilla movement, led by Fidel Castro, his brother Raúl and an Argentine doctor, Ernesto 'Che' Guevara, established itself in the Sierra Maestra Mountains in the east of the island. The Castroite movement aimed at overthrowing the corrupt dictatorship of Fulgencio Batista and nationalizing foreign-owned enterprises. The small guerrilla army – the 26 July Movement – was remarkably successful at resisting the Batista offensives. The guerrillas were more mobile than the military and knew the terrain better, they were prudent in enlisting the support of the local peasantry and were skilful in propagating their case across the island through the rebel radio station, Radio Rebelde.

In 1958 the Army began to crumble. There was low morale in the Officer Corps because Batista promoted officers on grounds of personal loyalty and not merit, and disenchantment among the rank-and-file. In 1959 Castro entered the city of Havana and assumed power.

In a short period Castro nationalized the international companies, expropriated large Cuban-owned estates, launched major campaigns against malaria and illiteracy, and reshaped public administration. The multi-nationals and right-wing Cuban exiles financed a lobbying campaign in the US and persuaded the Kennedy administration to impose an embargo on Cuban exports and on US imports. Expatriate elements with CIA support undertook an unsuccessful invasion of Cuba at the Bay of Pigs which served only to stiffen the resistance of the revolutionary régime. The closure of the US market compelled Cuba to look elsewhere for customers for her sugar cane. The west European market was saturated by locally produced sugar beet and by sugar cane from the European colonies. The Soviet Union, eager for a Caribbean ally, came to the rescue. In exchange for a generous price for her cane exports Cuba agreed to allow the installation of Soviet military equipment in the island.

In the early 1960s Cuba had several bargaining counters in her dealings with the Soviet Union. She was set on an ambitious programme of industrialization and had gone ahead with a policy of exporting guerrilla-led revolution to mainland Latin America that ran counter to the Soviet policy of supporting Communist factions that competed for power through the ballot box. Cuba even flirted with transferring her allegiance from the Soviet Union to China when the Sino-Soviet dispute was at its peak, but gradually Cuban fragility was exposed. The industrialization

Through the power of the word and with inflexible sense of purpose, Fidel Castro stirs the masses of Cuba into action on a Marxist-Leninist course

policy backfired, the programme to export revolution came to nothing, and it was decided that China had little to offer Cuba. Cuban dependence on the Soviet Union increased and the Communist Party in the island gathered strength because it was the main link with Moscow. Castro himself declared his commitment to Marxism-Leninism. In the 1962 missile crisis, Khrushchev lost nothing by agreeing with Kennedy to dismantle ground-to-ground missile sites in Cuba without consulting Castro. By the late 1960s the Soviet Union was reckoned to be pouring aid into Cuba at the rate of a million dollars a day.

Castro had few new domestic achievements to offer his electorate. Isolation in the late 1960s had imposed a policy of austerity, enforced by a growing regimentation of society. In 1970 Cuba failed to achieve the much-vaunted production target of 10 million tons of sugar cane, despite two years of exhortation and distortions of other sectors of the economy. In the mid-1970s Cuba became heavily involved in African politics. Some commentators argue that Castro is acting as a client of the Soviet Union, others that he is determined to find some achievement with which to convince an increasingly apathetic electorate, others that Castro simply responded to President Neto's plea to send troops to assist the MPLA in Angola. What is beyond doubt is that the policy of exporting revolution is consistent with Cuban policy in the 1960s and that a deep sense of identification is felt by Cuban blacks of African ancestry for what they understand to be a struggle by revolutionary comrades in a situation comparable to their own.

'Perónismo'

The outstanding feature of Argentine politics since 1945 has been '*Perónismo*'. This was the movement established by Juan Perón, an ambitious officer who, after a military coup in 1943, emerged as Secretary of Labour and in 1945 was catapulted to power by an alliance of dissident soldiers and the trades unions. Perón pursued a policy of nationalization of foreign enterprises, locally capitalized industrialization, distribution of social security benefits to the urban workers and the improvement of working and living conditions for the Army. Supported by his charismatic wife, Evita Duarte, a radio announcer whose talents were not exclusively political, Perón made use of the press, radio and mass rallies to develop a personal rapport with the populace in the absence of an effective party organization. No other politician was able to compete with Perón's populist appeal (which Europeans, whose attitudes were shaped by the Second World War, mistook for Fascism). Slowly, Perón's appeal wore thin. By the early 1950s inflation, unemployment and the failure of his industrialization policy combined to promote popular discontent. After a Navy-backed coup by the middle-class establishment, Perón was sent into exile, eventually settling in Madrid. No subsequent government had any greater success than that of Perón. A series of radical, military and coalition régimes failed to break through the vicious circle of economic stagnation and public disorder.

In 1973 Perón was again elected president. The *Perónista* movement consisted now of a broad-based coalition ranging from the extreme left to the extreme right. The urban workers rallied to Perón, recalling his first administration as the only period when they had enjoyed substantial new welfare benefits. Segments of the upper and middle classes looked back upon his government as a period of relative tranquillity. Left and right hoped to manipulate Perón. Discontent was already mounting when Perón died at the age of 79, leaving his second wife, Isabel – a cabaret singer from Panama – as his successor. Isabel had none of Evita's political acumen. She survived in office only because she was the one symbol that united the *Perónista* movement. As the government lurched to the right, so urban guerrillas from the left – some of them recruited from the ranks of disenchanted *Perónistas* – took to armed action. Right-wing terror squads retaliated. Isabel's régime, tainted by corruption, was unable to contain pressures inside and outside the *Perónista* movement and Argentina became ungovernable. The stage was set for a coup, but the Army hesitated. Internal divisions and the memory of the failures of earlier military régimes meant that the officer corps deferred intervention until the country was in a state of undeclared civil war.

The future of Argentina remains uncertain. The military government has been widely criticized for its brutal disregard for human rights and for tolerating indiscriminate killings by right-wing terror squads. Tensions between careerists within the Army, between the Army and the Navy, and civilian rightists and the Officer Corps, prevent the formation of an efficient authoritarian régime on Brazilian lines. At the same time, the authoritarian right is too well armed and the left too factionalized for the latter to make substantial headway. The centre, in this polarized context, is discredited.   *C. G. A.*

Eva Perón at the microphone, with her husband President Juan Perón, in 1945

Independent Africa

The new nations of Africa were largely created from societies which had been brought together for the first time under colonial rule. Their peoples often spoke a number of different languages and did not share the same cultural traditions. The economies of almost all the independent African states were weak because of the poverty, or lack of development, of their natural resources. Furthermore, African peoples entered upon their independence with high expectations for the future – expectations which the new African governments soon realized they would be unable to fulfil. The difficulties of the post-independence era were revealed most tragically in Zaire (formerly the Belgian Congo) and Nigeria.

In 1960 Patrice Lumumba became Zaire's first prime minister under President Kassavubu, but his ability to govern depended on the parliamentary support of a number of different political groups. His government was dependent, too, on the help of Belgian army officers and civil servants. Only six days after independence an army mutiny occurred. Fighting broke out between various tribes soon afterwards, Lumumba was murdered, and Zaire's most wealthy province, Katanga, seceded under its local political leader, Moïse Tshombe, supported by Belgian mining interests. Troops from other African states under UN control entered the country and in 1963 finally succeeded in ending the Katangan secession and imposing some semblance of order upon affairs. When the UN soldiers and officials withdrew, however, President Kassavubu's government was immediately faced with armed resistance from various dissident groups. The ex-rebel Tshombe was invited to become prime minister, and he managed to establish a ruthless control over most of the country through the use of the national army and white mercenary troops. The unpopular government of Kassavubu and Tshombe was eventually overthrown in 1965 by the commander of the Zairean army, General Mobutu, whose military régime ultimately re-established stable government in the country.

In 1966 the Nigerian federal government of Sir Abubakar Tafawa Balewa, dominated by Fulani-Hausa politicians from the Muslim north, was overthrown by General Ironsi, largely supported by Ibos from the eastern region. Only a matter of months later, however, Ironsi and many leading Ibo officers were killed in an army mutiny, and General Gowon, a Christian northerner, assumed control of Nigerian affairs. In the north thousands of Ibos, who dominated the bureaucracy and commerce of the region, were murdered. Perhaps as many as a million Ibos returned home. Gowon's scheme to end the federal system of government in the country, which involved the division of the east into three separate provinces, seemed designed to weaken further Ibo influence and strengthen that of the Muslim peoples of the north. In June 1967 Colonel Ojukwu declared the secession of the Ibo-controlled eastern region as the independent state of Biafra, and a month later a bloody civil war began. The conflict lasted for 30 months until early in 1970, with the Biafran economy ruined and its inhabitants starving, Ojukwu fled and the secessionist movement collapsed.

In both Zaire and Nigeria civilian governments were replaced by military régimes. In many other African states military coups have taken place since independence – in the Sudan (1958, 1969); Algeria (1965); Burundi, the Central African Republic and Upper Volta (1966); Ghana (1966, 1971); Mali, Congo (Brazzaville) and Togo (1967); Libya (1969); and Uganda (1971). Dahomey has suffered a series of coups and counter-coups since 1963, and the military have twice intervened in Sierra Leone politics. Elsewhere, the constitutional systems set up by Britain

Presidents Kaunda (Zambia), Khama (Botswana), Machel (Mozambique) and Nyerere (Tanzania)

and France during the final years of their rule in Africa have undergone profound changes. Most independent states have established one-party systems of government designed to promote national unity and give political stability. 'African socialism' has provided the inspiration for most government programmes intended to combat poverty and ill-health. In Tanzania, one of the poorest African countries, dispersed rural communities have been resettled in larger villages, thereby making possible an increase in food production and an improvement in the health of the population through collectivization and the more effective application of scientific, technical and medical aid. Other countries, such as Kenya and the Ivory Coast, have relied more upon private enterprise and a 'liberal economy' to raise their living standards.

African peoples achieved an impressive unity during the final years of colonial rule. It naturally became of major concern to the newly independent states to build upon this mutual understanding and cooperation, and to transform negative anti-colonialism into a positive sense of nationalism. Pan-Africanism was given formal expression in the establishment of the Organization of African Unity (OAU) in Addis Ababa in 1963. Inter-state rivalry, however, has intensified rather than diminished since then. The former British and French colonies have not found it easy to work together in either the economic or political field, and in 1964 the *Union Africaine et Malagache*, comprising most of the former French territories, was reconstituted (following its dissolution in the previous year). Relations between the three former British colonies in East Africa – Kenya, Uganda and Tanzania – have been difficult, especially since General Amin's military coup in 1971. Following Portugal's decision to withdraw from Africa in the train of the Lisbon coup of April 1974, the three rival nationalist groups in Angola, the FNLA, MPLA and Unita, were each given political support and military aid by different African states.

African rivalry has been particularly keen in the Horn of Africa, where the Ethiopian state of Emperor Haile Selassie included within its frontiers both Eritreans and Somalis. When the emperor was deposed in 1974 the Eritrean separatists intensified their liberation struggle, and the independent state of Somalia invaded Ethiopia to claim possession of the Ogaden Desert, inhabited by nomadic Somali peoples. The Somali forces, supplied with Soviet weaponry, took possession of most of the Ogaden. The USSR, however, switched its support to the revolutionary government in Addis Ababa, and with the assistance of Soviet armaments and Cuban troops Ethiopia restored its position in the region early in 1978. *P. W.*

Idi Amin, ruler of Uganda, addresses the Organization of African Unity, 1977

Haile Selassie I, who died in the Ethiopian revolution

Moise Tshombe of Katanga and (right) his victim, Patrice Lumumba

India

During the 17 years of his prime ministership, Jawaharlal Nehru laid the foundation of the world's largest democracy by bringing into existence the Indian Constitution of 1950, which embodied all the basic principles of liberal democracy. He fought, by democratic means, the religious, separatist and militarist forces that raised their heads soon after independence. He held India's first three general elections, each a colossal experiment in view of the size of the electorate, which rose from 173 million in 1951 to 210 million in 1962 (it went up to 320 million in India's sixth parliamentary election held in March 1977). Each of these elections was won by Nehru and his ruling Congress Party. Never gaining the opportunity to wield power, the parties in opposition became increasingly frustrated, but their politics, by and large, did not degenerate into the opportunism that was to characterize their political style in the post-Nehru era.

Nehru pioneered the economic system of mixed economy and planned growth, which came to be adopted by most of the 'third world' countries. The three Five Year Plans implemented during Nehru's era created the infrastructure of the world's tenth largest industrial nation, which India was to become in the 1970s. However, this 'revolution by consent', as Nehru called it, failed to obtain the people's co-operation in one vital sector: all land, upon which 75 per cent of Indians depend for their livelihood, is privately owned, and some necessary agrarian reforms could not be carried out.

In India's international relations Nehru set the new trends of non-alignment, non-intervention and co-existence. Although he consistently opposed the defence pacts and Anglo-American interventions in Asia (Baghdad Pact, SEATO, Suez) and displayed a temperamental abhorrence towards brute force, he was most unwillingly compelled to wage two defensive wars, the first in 1947 against Pakistan over Kashmir, and the second in 1962 against China over the disputed territories that lay along 2600 miles of India's border with China.

The short-lived administration of Nehru's successor, Lal Bahadur Shastri (June 1964–January 1966), spanned the second Indo-Pakistan war over Kashmir, which ended in a draw. After the sudden death of Shastri, the Congress Party barons chose Mrs Indira Gandhi, daughter of Nehru, to be his successor. They thought she would be easier to handle than Morarji Desai, who was feared for his inflexibility and self-righteousness.

During her 11 years' rule (January 1966–March 1977) Mrs Gandhi introduced no radical changes in her father's economic and foreign policy models. Non-alignment continued to be the general norm in foreign policy, but Mrs Gandhi, believing more in physical than moral power, had to strike a closer association with the Soviet Union (the Indo-Soviet Friendship Treaty, August 1971) before going to war with Pakistan over Bangladesh. She further departed from her father's moorings in allowing the testing of India's first nuclear bomb in May 1974.

In the political sphere Mrs Gandhi was driven by a determination to rule the country in her own right and not as the daughter of the great Nehru or as the puppet of the Congress bosses who had put her on the throne. She altered the entire structure that her father had built and sustained. She began the demolition first in her own party and by 1969 succeeded in driving out the old bosses. The more she enhanced her power and the strength of her party (Congress swept the polls in 1971), the more irresponsible the opposition leaders became. As a result, the politics of both the ruling and the aspiring élites became destitute of ideology, and acquired, in the period 1972–75, a market-place style, particularly at state level.

Most of the opposition parties united under the leadership of an old nationalist, J. P. Narayan, and, in 1974, launched a mass movement against the state governments of Gujarat and Bihar. When in June 1975 the Allahabad High Court found Mrs Gandhi technically guilty of 'corrupt electoral practices' (using some government facilities while canvassing in her constituency in 1971) and disqualified her from contesting an election for the next six years, the opposition planned to begin a nationwide movement demanding that she quit her office at once. Instead of relinquishing office until her appeal to the Supreme Court was decided, Mrs Gandhi declared India in a state of emergency.

During the state of emergency (26 June 1975–22 March 1977) almost all the leaders of the opposition were kept in prison, 26 political organizations were banned, censorship was imposed, the independence of the judiciary was abridged and the central government acquired overriding powers over state governments. Most of these measures were sanctioned by parliament, the majority of whose members, belonging to the ruling Congress Party, acted throughout as a rubber-stamp for Mrs Gandhi's fiats. However, to acquire legitimacy for her rule, Mrs Gandhi had to go to the polls. At the end of 1976 she felt confident enough to win if the election was held within two to three months. On 18 January 1977 she announced that the election would be held in March. Opposition leaders were released and the emergency was relaxed, but not lifted. Four of the non-communist opposition parties united and launched the Janata Party under the leadership of 81-year-old Morarji Desai. The election results were as surprising to the Janata leaders as they were to Mrs Gandhi. The Janata Party won by absolute majority, gaining over 300 of the 542 Lok Sabha seats. Mrs Gandhi and some of her close associates lost their seats. The defeat of Mrs Gandhi and Congress can be attributed to many factors. The degree of coercion used in implementing some of the emergency schemes, particularly the sterilization campaign, alienated the common people, but most importantly, all sections of the community had come to fear and distrust her. The emergency had made the Indian intelligentsia realize the value of freedom and democracy.

On 24 March 1977 Morarji Desai became India's fourth prime minister, and 30 years of Congress rule came to an end. The Janata government cancelled all the authoritarian measures taken during the emergency, and formulated constitutional devices to make it difficult for any government to declare internal emergency in future. Mrs Gandhi, as the leader of her faction of Congress, regained some lost ground and virtually became leader of the opposition.

B. N. P.

Mrs Indira Gandhi, prime minister of India, 1966–1977, photographed by Lord Snowdon. Inset: Mrs Gandhi with her father, Prime Minister Jawaharlal Nehru, in 1962

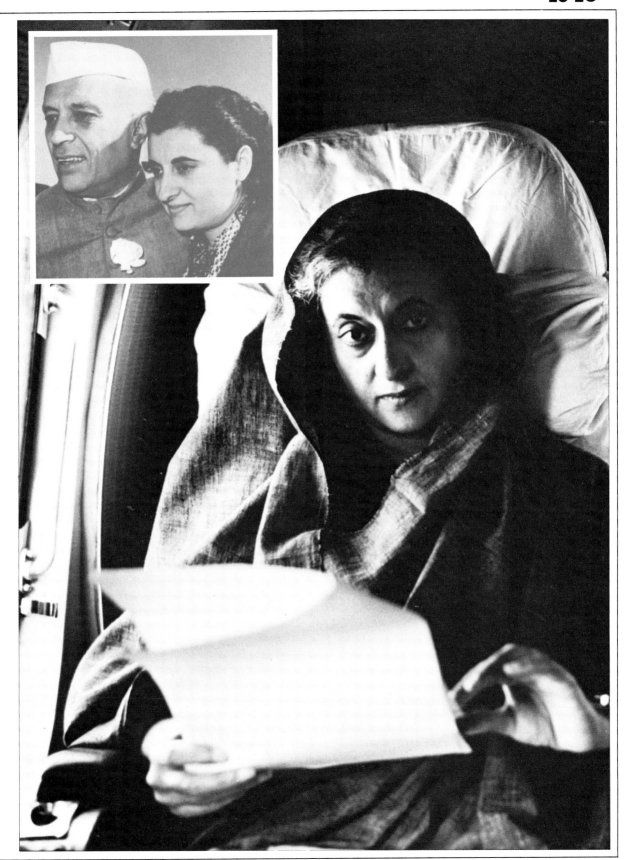

Pakistan and Bangladesh

The democratic order in Pakistan staggered for a decade until 1958, when it was sent packing by General Ayub Khan, since when the country has undergone four phases of authoritarian rule: Ayub Khan, 1958–69; General Yahya Khan, 1969–71; Zulfikar Ali Bhutto, 1971–77; General Zia ul-Haq since July 1977. The lack of a political leadership fully committed to the system was perhaps the most important of the many factors responsible for the failure of democratic experiment in Pakistan. Mohammad Ali Jinnah, the creator of Pakistan, was a strong leader but an autocrat by force of circumstances and by temperament. While he lived the last year of his life as governor-general of Pakistan, he ruled the country as a constitutional dictator. After his death, Liaquat Ali Khan held the fort until October 1951 when he was assassinated. Pakistan was left with no leader of national standing, no party of any strength, no constitution and no general election so far on record. The partyless civilian politicians presented a sad spectacle in 1951–58. One of the reasons for this was that the ruling élites were refugees from what was now the separate state of India (eight million Muslims had emigrated from India to Pakistan in 1947–51), and having no political base in their adopted country, they were most reluctant to go to a people they hardly knew and hold general elections.

Another important factor was East Pakistan, populated by Bengalis who outnumbered the population of West Pakistan by over eight million. Under full democracy, the Bengalis were bound to rule the whole country. But from the very beginning of independence, the reins of power were zealously guarded by the West Pakistani élites. The West Pakistan Act of 1955, by which the four provinces of West Pakistan were merged into one unit and given parity with East Pakistan in the central legislature, made East Pakistan's numerical strength ineffective. Whenever the Bengalis tried to reach for their 50 per cent, a West-Pakistani-dominated authoritarian régime intervened.

Ayub Khan was the first dictator in south and southeast Asia seriously to evolve a substitute for western democracy. The system was imposed upon the nation on 27 October 1959 and later embodied in the constitution of 1962 – Pakistan's second since independence, the first of 1956 having been abrogated in 1958 when Ayub began his martial law régime. 'Basic democracy' was a four-tiered structure at the bottom of which were the village and town councils, whose members were elected on the basis of universal adult franchise. There was no direct election at the upper levels. The members of these councils, called Basic Democrats, were to elect members for the district councils and for provincial and central legislatures. The 80,000 or so Basic Democrats were also to elect the president.

Carried away by his popularity, Ayub lifted the ban on political parties in 1962. With their revival, the gradual decline of Ayub's régime began and, combined with four other factors, brought about his downfall in 1969: failure to achieve economic goals, Bhutto's persistent opposition, East Pakistan's movement for regional autonomy under the leadership of Sheikh Mujibur Rahman, and his own illness. On 25 March 1969 Ayub Khan handed over power to the army commander-in-chief, General Yahya Khan. Yahya abrogated the constitution of 1962, declared martial law and assumed the presidency.

In November 1969 Yahya announced direct elections for 1970, dissolved West Pakistan into its old four constituent provinces and gave East Pakistan representation on the basis of population. Yahya hoped that no party would win a majority and that he would be able to prolong his 'caretaker military administration'. But this was not to be. In December 1970 Pakistan went to the polls for the first time since independence. Mujibur Rahman's Awami League won 53 per cent of the National Assembly's seats; Bhutto's People's Party came second, capturing 27 per cent. If national unity was to be maintained, this result demanded the termination of military rule and the transfer of power to Mujibur Rahman, but Bhutto argued that it by no means constituted a 'national verdict', on the grounds that the Bengalis had voted en bloc for Mujibur Rahman, and West Pakistanis for his own People's Party. In effect, two nations had voted separately for their respective national parties. Negotiations between Yahya, Bhutto and Mujibur Rahman lasted until March 1971, when Mujibur Rahman opted for complete independence, and Yahya's army began ruthless repression in East Pakistan. By December 10 million East Pakistanis had fled to India. The refugee problem helped to force India into armed intervention on 16 December 1971. The three-week war ended with the surrender of the Pakistani army at Dacca.

Soon after the loss of its eastern wing, Pakistan was plagued by separatist forces. Bhutto, having taken over the government from Yahya Khan, continued to rule under the state of emergency that had been declared on the eve

President Ayub Khan of Pakistan in 1962, when he lifted the ban on political parties

of the last Indo-Pakistan war. To ensure against the possibility of being deposed by 'political dwarfs' or 'discredited generals', Bhutto brought into being the constitution of 1973 (Pakistan's third), adopted by the National Assembly in April. It provided for a parliamentary form of government and vested the prime minister with almost absolute power. Bhutto thus ruled Pakistan as a constitutional dictator. Like Mrs Gandhi of India, he believed that his régime had the full support of the people, and early in 1977 he decided to go to the polls. Nine opposition parties joined hands to fight his People's Party, but Bhutto won the March 1977 election. The frustrated opposition, alleging that Bhutto had organized a widespread rigging, launched a civil disobedience movement. When, in the course of his confrontation with the opposition, Bhutto began to rely heavily on the army, he became vulnerable. On 5 July 1977 he was overthrown by General Mohammad Zia ul-Haq, the army chief of staff.

General Zia announced that elections would be held in October 1977, after which he would transfer power to the civilian authority. When the election campaigns revealed that Bhutto was still a political force and might win the election, Zia declared it was essential that the electorate be fully aware of the 'true face of all candidates'. The election was postponed, Bhutto was arrested and charged with a murder that had been committed in 1974. His trial lasted until 19 March 1978, when the Punjab High Court found him guilty and sentenced him to death.

Bangladesh

In spite of the popular and powerful leadership of Sheikh Mujibur Rahman, the newly born state of Bangladesh could not maintain parliamentary democracy for more than three years. Subversion, lawlessness and economic havoc together with a split in the ruling party induced Mujib to opt for the authoritarian system. Early in 1975 he replaced the parliamentary system with an amalgam of American-style presidential structure and Soviet-style party cadres. This one-man, one-party rule left no room for any peaceful change of government to take place in future. However, the coup of 15 August 1975, in which Mujib was assassinated, was the work of a handful of misguided young army officers, excited by personal grievances against him. The senior military officers, who were as much taken by surprise as the people at large, stepped into the power vacuum that was created, and the net outcome of the whole grisly episode was the replacement of Mujib's personal rule by the military dictatorship of Major-general Ziaur Rahman, who through two further coups in November 1975 assumed supreme power as president. General Rahman has so far made no promise to revive democracy in Bangladesh. The election promised for 1977 was postponed on the grounds that the politicians had not yet sunk their past differences, and that, consequently, as many as 50 parties had asked for recognition. Instead, Rahman acquired a vote of confidence for himself by national referendum in May 1977.   *B. N. P.*

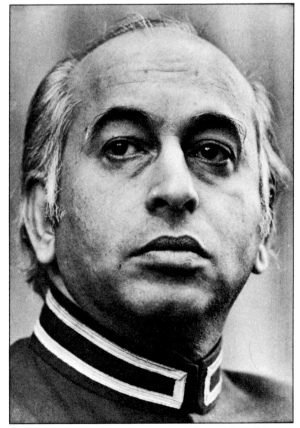

Sheikh Mujibur Rahman, president of Bangladesh, in 1972. He was assassinated in 1975

Zulfikar Ali Bhutto, prime minister of Pakistan, 1973-77. He was tried for murder in 1978

Burma and Sri Lanka

Burma

When Burma began its independent life on 4 January 1948 and opted to remain outside the British Commonwealth, it was encumbered with a political army raised and trained by the Japanese to fight a Burmese war of independence against the British. This did not have an adverse effect on the country's political life for the first 10 years of its independence, when Burma experimented with a Westminster-type of democracy under the able leadership of Prime Minister U Nu. The factor that weakened his government was the recurring armed insurgency of the communists, and of the ethnic minorities – Karens, Mons, Shans, Kachins, Chins – who, having experienced British protection from the dominant Burmans in the days of the Raj, now demanded autonomous states for themselves. In 1958 U Nu's ruling party – the Anti-Fascist People's Freedom League (AFPFL) – split and the prime minister had to hand over power to the military. Although the caretaker military administration of General Ne Win returned power to U Nu after the February 1960 election, in which the U Nu faction of the AFPFL won the majority of seats in parliament, the military continued to keep the government under surveillance. When in March 1962 the U Nu government seemed to be weakening under the Shans' threat to secede, the army intervened. This time General Ne Win overthrew the constitutional government by

arresting its members, dismissed the parliament and abolished the 1947 constitution.

The system of 'socialist democracy', which the military rulers of Burma evolved between 1962 and 1973, though savouring of Marxism, was by no means a communist order. In fact, one of the main objectives of the régime throughout has been to suppress communist insurgency, and to steer, in Buddhist fashion, a middle path between the rightists (represented by the deposed U Nu) and the leftists (comprising Burma's two communist parties). The declaration of a political philosophy (*The Burmese Way to Socialism*, issued on 30 April 1962) decried Western democracy and theoretically committed Burma to Marxist socialism. On 4 July 1962 an official political party was founded: the Burma Socialist Programme Party (BSPP), most of whose members were from the armed forces. On 4 January 1974 a new constitution was announced, providing for a one-chamber legislature – the People's Assembly – of 450 members directly elected by the people. The first elections under the new constitution were held early in 1974. No other political party being allowed to exist, the government-controlled BSPP's candidates were returned. The People's Assembly met in March 1974 and elected the State Council, with Ne Win as its chairman and ex-officio head of the state. That same day it was officially declared that the revolution begun on 2 March 1962 had ended and power was now transferred to the people. In reality, however, Burma continued to be ruled by the military junta headed by President Ne Win.

Burma's image of political strength is partly due to the isolationist policy rigidly followed since 1962. Burma has been the only non-communist country in this region to appear unconcerned about the West and Western values, and has pursued economic, social and political self-reliance to a chauvinistic extreme. However, Burma's strength, whether reality or myth, has not yet enabled her to resolve the basic problems. In February 1977 the general secretary of the BSPP admitted that economic self-sufficiency could not be attained without capital investment and technical assistance from abroad. In September 1977 the tempo of nationalization was relaxed. In the political arena opposition to Ne Win's régime persisted among the national minorities, operating from hide-outs on the Thailand border, and among the communist guerrillas, operating on the north-eastern border with China. When in 1976 the Chief-of-Staff and Defence Minister, General Tin U, was sacked, and brought to trial with 14 young army officers for plotting to assassinate Ne Win and overthrow the government, the Burmese system appeared to lose its distinguishing feature – security based on the unity and loyalty of the armed forces. *B. N. P.*

Mrs Bandaranaike became prime minister of Sri Lanka (and the world's first woman head of government) in 1960, succeeding her assassinated husband in office in under a year

Sri Lanka

The uniqueness of Sri Lanka's political development since independence on 4 February 1948 lies in the running of the Westminster-style democracy on a two-party system. Since its independence, the island has been governed alternately by the United National Party (UNP) and Sri Lanka Freedom Party (SLFP): by the UNP in 1948–56, 1965–70 and since July 1977; by the SLFP in 1956–65 and

1970–77. In fact, there had been over six parties working in opposition during the first long spell of UNP rule. In 1956, however, they joined to form the single SLFP. The alliance or merger of opposition parties that happened in

U Nu in 1960. First prime minister of independent Burma, he was in and out of power until 1962

General Ne Win, head of the military régime in Burma

India and Pakistan in 1977 had already taken place in Sri Lanka almost 20 years before.

There were other factors that made it possible for parliamentary democracy to have plain sailing in Sri Lanka. Nowhere in Asia was the nationalist movement so élitist, constitutional and peaceful as in Sri Lanka. As a result, the country slid gently through a series of constitutional reforms into independence. As the masses had not been involved in the national movement, post-independence politics continued to be the preserve of the élite, the leaders of both the UNP and SLFP sharing identical social and educational backgrounds. The two-party system gave the opportunity of actually wielding power to both, and the party in opposition had an interest in behaving responsibly. Another factor is Sri Lanka's electorate, which, being more educated and more politically conscious than that of, say, India or Pakistan, has displaced more governments since independence than any other country in southern Asia. Sri Lanka was the first British colony in Asia to have universal adult franchise introduced – as early as 1931 – and 92 per cent of people under 24 can read and write. Above all, Sri Lanka is the only country in southern Asia to become a welfare state with free education and medicine, subsidized food and protective labour laws.

However, in spite of such assets, Sri Lanka had to resort to a state of emergency many more times than any other state in south and south-east Asia. These emergencies were declared in order to fight forces that threatened the integrity of the state. The continuing tension between the Hindu Tamils of Indian origin and the indigenous Buddhist Sinhalese often burst into communal riots. Of the five states of emergency the country has so far endured, the last (1971), declared by Mrs Sirimavo Bandaranaike, was the longest and most controversial. Though accused of displaying an authoritarian bent, Mrs Bandaranaike did not go as far as Mrs Gandhi. Her one constitutional change was the replacement of the 1948 dominion constitution by a republican constitution (framed in December 1971 and implemented in May 1972), which retained the parliamentary form of government. The prolonged state of emergency, however, made Mrs Bandaranaike unpopular, and when she went to the polls in July 1977, her SLFP secured only 8 seats in a 168-member parliament (in 1970 her party had won 91 seats). The UNP was returned to power with an overwhelming majority, but its leader, J. R. Jayawardene, was committed to rejecting the country's Westminster form of government, on the grounds that the fickleness of parliamentary factions had made for weak government, and substituting in its place a French-style presidential form of government. The constitution was accordingly amended, and in February 1978 Jayawardene became the country's first executive president. Jayawardene may have been further impelled to create a strong and independent executive by Tamil separatism: in the 1977 election the Tamil United Liberation Front gained more seats than the SLFP and was agitating for an independent Tamil state, carved out of the northern and eastern provinces of Sri Lanka.

B. N. P.

THE MIDDLE EAST AND THE ARAB WORLD

For centuries before its emergence into independence after the Second World War, the Middle East and the Arab world had been dominated by alien rule, first by the Ottoman Empire and then by its French and British successors. Under this alien rule, its institutions, Islamic and non-Islamic, its city notables with their clients, and its village and tribal sheikhs with their followers, had come to function perfectly. Although they lacked independent authority, their legitimacy was accepted by all.

Arab nationalism, as it emerged in the 19th and 20th centuries, adopted its vocabulary from Islam, postulating an all-embracing political unity of Arabic-speaking peoples for which there was neither geographical, economic nor political warranty. The emergence after both world wars of separate Arabic-speaking states, each with its governing amalgam of army officers, city dignitaries and technocrats, confronted the new governments with the problem of legitimizing in the people's eyes their claims to an authority that had hitherto been wielded by traditional Arab overlords. Monarchies, save in Arabia proper, fell swiftly out of favour, until by 1965 only Jordan and Saudi Arabia survived, together with the sheikhly families of the small but immensely wealthy 'oil states' of the Gulf. The army leaderships were often drawn from social groups that had been excluded from status or influence (let alone power) by the structure of traditional society, and could maintain themselves only by severe repression and pandering to the rhetoric of Arab unity.

This rhetoric came to define Arab unity in

Moshe Dayan

King Hussein

Colonel Khadaffy

Anwar Sadat and Yassir Arafat

terms of hostility to Israel, whose existence was depicted as the latest manifestation of non-Arab imperialism – a development encouraged by the leaders of the Arab Palestinian refugees from the 1948–49 fighting. Fears for their own status as a minority made Arab Christians and members of Islamic sects more extreme in their Arab nationalism than most – save only in the Lebanon, where a delicate compromise between Muslims and Christians made the latter extreme only in their hostility to Arab nationalism itself, plunging the Lebanon into violent civil war in 1958 and again in the mid-1970s.

The control of oil exercised by the Arab-dominated monopolist Organization of Petroleum-Exporting States (OPEC) gave the whole Middle East enormous capital assets, but the oil states were reluctant to invest their capital in Egypt or Syria, where it was most needed, preferring to send it abroad. The need to seek legitimacy through hostility to Israel made for enormous armed forces and dependence on Soviet arms supplies. Only Egypt felt strong enough to defy these compulsions and the question of peace with Israel remained central even for Egypt. *D. C. W.*

Israel: Political Issues

When the British Mandate for Palestine expired on 14 May 1948 and the state of Israel simultaneously proclaimed its independence, the foundations for the transition to a parliamentary system of government were already prepared. The existing people's council and people's administration became respectively the provisional council of state and the provisional government of the independent state of Israel. These bodies organized elections to the constituent assembly that met in February 1949 and passed what became known as 'the small constitution', which has ever since remained the effective instrument of government. It provided for a democratic republic with a parliamentary system of government and a strong cabinet. A number of political parties formed the Knesset (parliament) of 120 members elected on a basis of proportional representation. A president, elected by the members of the Knesset, served as head of state with largely honorific functions.

After the elections to the constituent assembly, David Ben-Gurion, as leader of the largest party, Mapai (moderate Labour), was called upon by President Chaim Weizmann to form the first regular government. This resulted in a coalition dominated by Mapai, but with representatives from the religious parties and the Progressives (and later, the Independent Liberals). This coalition pattern – with minor changes depending on the inclusion of this or that minor party, so that the government should always enjoy a majority in the Knesset – formed the pattern for all subsequent cabinets until 1977. The work of

the first Knesset was dominated by the Law of the Return, which recognized the right of every Jew to settle in Israel. The government fell through a combination of dissatisfaction over food and commodity shortages and disputes over religious education.

In the subsequent elections the right-wing General Zionists made the expected gains, but not sufficiently to upset the central role of Mapai in the new coalition. Education, reparations from Germany and defence policy were the main subjects of controversy. None the less, the second Knesset lasted out its constitutionally allotted span of four years (1951–55). In the life of its successor, internal politics were marked by the emergence of Herut – the right-wing 'freedom' party – as principal opposition under the leadership of Menachem Begin. However, foreign affairs claimed an unusual degree of attention through the Sinai campaign of 1956, which brought Ben-Gurion to a peak of popularity, and through the proposal to sell Israel-manufactured arms to West Germany. The years 1955–59 were also marked by riots by new immigrants in Haifa and Beersheba, which jeopardized relations between immigrants from Europe and those from Muslim countries, who alleged discrimination and unfavourable treatment as compared with that extended to their western counterparts. Even so, in the elections to the fourth Knesset (1959–61) none of the ethnic lists representing bodies of non-European immigrants won a seat. Mapai, in fact, won the greatest victory in its political existence, gaining from the rise in the standard of living and the improved

Dr Chaim Weizman raises his right hand as he takes the oath of office when he is sworn in as the first president of Israel, 16 February 1949

David Ben-Gurion, first prime minister of Israel, 1948–53, and again 1955–61

Voting in an election in Israel under the Middle East's only true parliamentary democracy

security situation as shown in the reduced number of border incidents. However, the new government came to grief in 1961 – only two years through its four-year term – following internal dissensions within the ruling Mapai Party over the so-called 'Lavon affair'. This stemmed ultimately from controversy over responsibility for a failed security operation of 1954 – details of which have never been officially revealed, but which was conducted while Pinchas Lavon was minister of defence. In the end, the animosity between Ben-Gurion and Lavon (now secretary of the general federation of trade unions – the Histadrut) made it impossible for Mapai to continue in office.

The most notable developments of the following decade were, first, the formation of a cabinet of national unity in May 1967, in view of the threat exercised by Egyptian concentrations in Sinai and the resulting Six Day War; and, second, the alliance or alignment of all Labour Parties in 1969, which gave Labour an absolute majority in the Knesset – 63 seats, or 67 with affiliated Arab lists. It was the first time any party or even governing bloc had enjoyed an absolute majority, and the transformation contributed to a certain consolidation of political life. This was noted, for example, in a package deal between government, labour and management to limit increases in taxes, wages and prices as a means to offset the inflationary effects of rapid economic growth and the increased burden of defence. However, this deal did not prevent a considerable worsening of the balance of trade. Only the receipt of foreign loans and increased contributions from Jewish appeal funds made good the drain on Israeli reserves. Another worrying problem continued to be the type of policy to be implemented in the territories in Judea and Samaria (the 'West Bank') occupied during the 1967 war.

By 1973 the economic boom was still in full swing, though at the cost of rapid inflation, labour unrest and increasing inequality, particularly evident in the economic position of the oriental communities. Not surprisingly – and especially so when seen in conjunction with the impact of the Yom Kippur War of October 1973 – the elections at the end of that year weakened the Labour Alignment and simultaneously created an opposition bloc of unprecedented strength. The former, with 51 seats, still remained the largest single party, but the right-wing Likud, led by Menachem Begin, gained eight, making a total of 39. The prime minister, Golda Meir, now had difficulty in re-forming her cabinet, which, in fact, collapsed after a few weeks. She was replaced by Yitzhak Rabin, whose new cabinet received a vote of confidence from the Knesset in June 1974.

In May 1977 Labour lost the political hegemony it had enjoyed for the 29 years of the state's existence and was replaced by Begin's Likud grouping. The cause of the Labour defeat was widely reputed to be the financial scandals that had involved certain members of the party (including Premier Rabin) and a continuing swing to the right by the oriental communities. Another feature of the election was the phenomenal success of the Democratic Movement for Change, Israel's first grass-roots political movement. This was a further symptom of disenchantment with the traditional political scene.   L. K.

Israel and the Arab World

The League of Nations mandate (confirmed in 1922) under which Britain took control of Palestine included the obligation to allow the development of a 'Jewish national home' in Palestine, in fulfilment of the Balfour Declaration (1917), the wartime promise made by Arthur Balfour, the foreign secretary, on behalf of the British government. In the period of British rule from 1920 to 1948 political and economic conflict intensified between the rapidly augmenting immigrant Jewish community and the indigenous Arab Palestinian population. The Arab rebellion of 1937–39, headed by the Grand Mufti of Jerusalem, was directed not only against Jewish settlement and land buying, but also increasingly against British rule. British policies, caught between the needs to maintain its position in the Arab world and to fulfil pledges to the Zionists, fluctuated on the crucial issues of Jewish land buying and quotas of Jewish immigrants. While the Jews pressed for greater immigration, particularly as Nazi pressures developed in Europe after 1933, the Palestinians feared this would lead to a Jewish majority and Jewish political domination.

In the closing years of the war the Zionist authorities pressed for massive immigration of displaced Jews from eastern and central Europe. Extremists resorted to increasingly violent terrorist tactics when the British refused. The UN attempts to solve the problem of Arab–Jewish conflict by partitioning the country proved unacceptable, particularly to the Arabs, and the British, unwilling to impose a solution by force, surrendered the mandate to the UN and withdrew from Palestine in May 1948. The Jewish leadership immediately proclaimed the state of Israel. Fighting, which had already broken out between Arabs and Jews before the British left, developed into the first full-scale Arab–Israeli war. Five Arab armies from surrounding states invaded Palestine, but after almost a year of fighting, punctuated by short-lived cease-fires, Israel had made substantial territorial gains. These *de facto* borders established by the final cease-fire were not confirmed by peace treaties. In the course of the war about 700,000 Palestinians had fled to neighbouring states and most remained there as refugees, since the Israelis allowed only a few to return, despite repeated UN resolutions calling for their repatriation. Since this time, the two interrelated questions of the dispossessed Palestinians and the recognition of the state of Israel by its Arab neighbours have dominated Middle Eastern politics.

Britain, France and the US initially made a tripartite agreement (1950) on arms sales to maintain a balance of power between the opponents. This was undermined from 1954 onwards by French arms sales to Israel, which combined with a massive Israeli raid on Gaza (1955) in retaliation for *fidayin* (commando) incursions into Israel, and the return as Israeli prime minister of the militant David Ben Gurion, induced President Nasser of Egypt to turn to the Soviet bloc for arms, which he could not obtain on acceptable terms from the West. In 1956 the crisis generated by Egypt's nationalization of the Suez Canal culminated in an Israeli invasion of Sinai, co-ordinated with the Anglo–French Suez operation. The Israelis withdrew from Sinai after this second Arab–Israeli war, but not before clearing the Gaza Strip of *fidayin* bases and opening the strategically vital Straits of Tiran to shipping destined for Eilat.

During the next decade Israel substantially increased its Jewish population through immigration, mainly from the Soviet bloc, and developed its economy. Palestinian Arabs living within Israeli borders remained under military government until 1967, though they were permitted to take a limited part in the political process. After 1956, the Russians developed ties with the more militant Arab states – Egypt, Syria and (after 1958) Iraq – and became their main source of arms supplies, while the USA drew closer to Israel, providing most of its arms and aid. In 1964 an organized Palestinian movement, the Palestine Liberation Organization (PLO), was established under Arab League auspices. Other more militant Palestinian groups emerging at this time saw armed struggle as the only way to restore a Palestinian homeland. These often uncoordinated groups carried out raids on Israel, particularly from Syria and Jordan, which provoked massive retaliation from the Israelis. Arab fears of a full-scale Israeli attack led Nasser to close the Straits of Tiran to Israeli shipping and order the UN Emergency Force out of the Egyptian–Israeli border zone. The Israelis then launched the lightning 'six-day war' (June 1967), in which they took the Golan Heights from Syria, the West Bank from Jordan, and the Gaza Strip and Sinai from Egypt, thus considerably extending their territory, but at the same time bringing under their rule a large number of hostile Palestinians. The Israelis refused to comply with the UN Resolution 242, which called for the withdrawal of Israeli forces from territories occupied in 1967, as well as for recognition of Israel's right to exist. An Arab summit conference in Khartoum (1967) affirmed non-recognition

Above: At the 'Christmas summit' in Jerusalem, 1977: Israeli Premier Begin and Egyptian President Sadat

of Israel and the right of Palestinians to return to their country. It also arranged for the Arab oil-producing states to provide aid to the 'front-line states'.

From 1967 to 1970 the Israelis and Egyptians kept up a limited war on the banks of the Suez Canal. In 1970 the fighting was ended, but no peace settlement was achieved. From the late 1960s onwards Palestinian groups resorted to increasingly violent tactics, especially after being driven out of Jordan in 1970–71, staging a series of raids and hijackings. In October 1973 Nasser's successor, President Sadat of Egypt, in alliance with Syria and Jordan, launched an offensive to recover the territories lost in 1967. Although unsuccessful in that aim, this fourth Arab–Israeli war pushed the Israelis back from the Canal.

The Arab oil embargo on the West after the war made the industrialized countries acutely aware of their need to maintain good relations with the Arab world. Increased pressure was put on Israel to make concessions and the UN recognized the PLO as the sole representative of the Palestinian people. However, the PLO – now the main 'umbrella' organization of the Palestinians – and other more radical groups outside its control, have found it increasingly hard to maintain bases in Arab countries, which (as in Jordan and Lebanon) have come to see the militant Palestinians as a threat to their own security.

The courageous initiative of President Sadat in visiting Premier Begin in Jerusalem at the end of 1977 was historic in the sense that it would have been unthinkable at any time since 1948, but its diplomatic and political fruit may take years to gather. *S. G. B.*

Top: Prime Minister Golda Meir with General Moshe Dayan on the banks of the Suez Canal

Egypt and the Sudan

In 1919, a new nationalist party, the Wafd ('delegation'), led by the moderate anti-British politician Saad Zaglul, demanded independence. The British refused and there were civil disturbances, but the 1922 treaty recognized Egypt as an independent sovereign state but maintained British control over defence, the protection of foreign interests, the administration of the Sudan and the security of British imperial communications. A further treaty (1936) allowed British troops to be stationed in the Suez Canal Zone for another 20 years and maintained the status quo in the Sudan.

In the interwar period, the Wafd Party usually commanded electoral majorities but its governments were frequently unacceptable to either the king or the British high commissioner. Economically, the country remained heavily dependent on its cotton exports at a time when world prices were generally declining. Industrial development began on a small scale and expanded during the 1940s, mainly in response to the needs of the British war effort in the Middle East.

During the Second World War, British control of Egypt and the Suez Canal was crucial to Allied strategy. Some Egyptian politicians, and King Faruq (who came to the throne in 1936), were not wholeheartedly committed to the Allies, and in 1942, when it seemed that Rommel's army might threaten Cairo, the British high commissioner threatened the king with force if he refused to accept a pro-British prime minister. After the war, discontent with a corrupt monarch and weak governments, representing mainly conservative nationalists who made little attempt at social reform, increased. Popular support went to the radical parties of the right and left, such as the Muslim Brotherhood and the Communist Party. A brief economic boom after the war soon gave way to stagnation and a decline in cotton prices after the collapse of the boom induced by the Korean War.

The Egyptian defeat in the 1948 Arab–Israeli war was the death-blow to the régime. A group of young army officers who had formed the 'Free Officers' Movement' began to plot its overthrow. In the early 1950s the government was rapidly losing authority and when no agreement was reached over the status of British forces in Egypt, some guerrilla attacks were launched against the British base at Suez. In July 1952, members of the Free Officers' Movement staged a coup and deposed King Faruq, who went into exile. Initially, General Naguib, an associate of the Free Officers, was the figurehead of the régime. In June 1953, Egypt was declared a republic, with Naguib as president. A power struggle developed between him and Colonel Gamal Abdul Nasser, the leader of the Officers' Movement, and Naguib was finally relieved of the presidency in 1954. In January 1953, all political parties except the Muslim Brotherhood had been banned and the Brotherhood itself was outlawed in 1954 after attempting to assassinate Nasser. Nasser was elected president by a plebiscite in 1956.

The new régime instituted a land reform (1952) which curbed to some extent the power of the landowning class, and negotiated agreements with Britain for Sudanese independence (1953) and the withdrawal of British troops from the Canal Zone (1954) which was completed in June 1956. In 1955 the Western powers began to press Egypt to join the Baghdad Pact and to align openly with the West.

Nasser resisted and strongly advocated 'positive neutralism' at the conference of non-aligned nations at Bandung.

However, Nasser felt the need to build up his defence forces, particularly as Egypt was bearing the brunt of Israeli retaliation. After the heavy Gaza Raid (March 1955), Nasser's requests for arms to offset secret French sales to the Israelis were not met by the West on terms he could accept. He turned to the Eastern bloc and signed an arms deal with Czechoslovakia in September 1955.

Nasser's largest domestic project was building the High Dam at Aswan which was substantially to increase Egypt's cultivable land area and provide power for industry. Western interest in financing this vast scheme diminished with the Czech arms deal and Nasser's recognition of Communist China. (The dam was eventually financed by the Russians.) The US and Britain withdrew their offers in July 1956, and the immediate result was Nasser's nationalization of the Suez Canal Company. Although the canal stayed open to all except Israeli and Israel-bound shipping, Nasser's action was seen by Britain and France as a serious threat to their strategic interests and to political stability in the area. A series of conferences failed to establish agreement on international control over the Canal. President Dwight D. Eisenhower and Secretary of State John Dulles of the US were opposed to using force against Nasser, but France and Britain secretly planned a tripartite military operation with Israel to re-establish control over the Suez Canal and, if possible, overthrow Nasser. On 29 October 1956, Israel advanced into Sinai towards the Canal. Britain and France issued a hypocritical ultimatum demanding that both Egypt and Israel withdraw 10 miles from the Canal (which was inside Egyptian territory). The UN General Assembly demanded a cease-fire but on 5 November the Anglo-French occupation began. This advance lasted only until 6 November when first Britain and then France gave in to heavy pressure from the US to end the occupation. Nasser emerged from this crisis with his prestige in the Arab world much enhanced and his popularity confirmed.

In 1958 he embarked on a hasty and ill-prepared union with Syria – the United Arab Republic (UAR). It was ended by a conservative military coup in Syria in 1961.

The year 1962 marked the beginning of a new phase in Nasser's internal policy, mainly due to his disillusion with the development of the economy under predominantly private capital. Until then, reforms had been piecemeal – land reform, nationalization of foreign-owned companies and the expansion of education and social services. Nasser's National Charter (1962) announced more comprehensive reforms, including the extension of State control over many industries and financial institutions and more stringent provisions for land reform. The Charter also established the Arab Socialist Union as Egypt's only political party. At the same time, Egypt became increasingly dependent on Russia for arms and aid.

In 1963, Egypt intervened on the republican side in the civil war in the Yemen. Saudi Arabia supported the Imam of Yemen and two years later, King Faisal and Nasser agreed to end the fighting, though the Egyptians did not finally withdraw until after the 1967 war.

Early in 1967, with tension increasing between Israel and the Arab states (particularly Syria and Jordan), Nasser ordered the UN Emergency Force out of Sinai and closed

Gamal Abdul Nasser, president of Egypt (United Arab Republic), 1956-70

Egyptian mourners reach out their hands in homage to touch Nasser's coffin, 1 October 1970

the Straits of Tiran to Israeli shipping, in an attempt to divert Israeli military attention from Syria. The Israelis replied with a lightning war (July 1967) in which Egypt and her allies were decisively defeated, leaving Sinai and the east bank of the Suez Canal in Israeli hands. Nasser resigned but was reinstated by popular pressure. Several senior army officers were made scapegoats for the military débâcle. In 1970, Nasser died suddenly, perhaps the victim of stress and political disappointment. One of his aims, to rectify an impoverished one-crop export economy by diversification and development of industry, social services and land reform, had met with a limited success, but its benefits were being cancelled out by population growth, arms expenditure and foreign debt. The prestige of his régime had depended to a considerable extent on his

handling of foreign policy, especially the successes of the early years.

Once his successor, Anwar al-Sadat, a member of the original Free Officers' Movement, had consolidated his own position, he began to move away from Nasserite policies in both internal and foreign affairs. Although he signed a friendship treaty with the Soviets in 1971, Sadat fell out with them and in 1972 expelled all Russian personnel from Egypt. The 1973 Arab–Israeli war, in which Egypt took the initiative by attacking Israel across the Suez Canal, strengthened Sadat's position. He achieved closer relationships with the US and Saudi Arabia, and in 1976 abrogated the treaty with the Soviet Union. A union with Libya, Sudan and Syria ended in failure in 1972–73. In domestic affairs, he dismantled part of the state's control over industry and instituted his open-door policy of lifting restrictions to encourage foreign investment. However, inflation, increasing indebtedness, economic stagnation and the cost of maintaining military preparedness, drained funds from development and led to popular unrest. Economic pressure and the hope of American support were major factors in Sadat's peace initiative to Israel in 1977.

The Sudan

From 1899 to 1955 the Sudan was ruled as an Anglo-Egyptian condominium, in which Britain had effective control. Sudanese nationalism, which gathered momentum in the 1930s, was initially directed against the British rather than the Egyptians. However, after the Second World War there was a split between a group which saw Britain as the primary enemy and accepted unity with Egypt was a possible means to rid themselves of the British; and those who viewed such a union with hostility. The British and Egyptians did not come to an agreement on the future status of Sudan until 1953, after the Free Officers' coup in Egypt, when it was agreed that Sudan should become an independent state. In the same year, elections gave victory to the pro-Egyptian party. However, before independence in January 1965 an army mutiny in the south sparked off general unrest there. The British administration had concentrated on Arab northern Sudan and neglected the largely non-Arab south, thus reinforcing incipient cultural and religious differences. This pattern was perpetuated after independence. From 1956 to 1958 Sudan was governed by a series of shifting parliamentary coalitions but in 1958 a military coup substituted a Supreme Council of army officers under General Abboud. The situation in the south worsened during his rule, since the government pursued a policy of repressive Arabization. In 1964 popular unrest helped to bring down Abboud's régime and civilian rule was re-established. After elections in 1965 a coalition government again emerged which had little success in coping with the country's increasing economic difficulties; attempts to negotiate a settlement in the south also failed.

In 1969 another coup brought General Jaafar Numairi (Nimeiry) to power, proclaiming a policy of 'Sudanese socialism'. Political parties were dissolved, and banks and some companies were nationalized. The régime announced that the south would be granted regional autonomy within a federal framework under the Addis Ababa Agreement of 1972.   *S. G. B.*

Turkey since Atatürk

In July 1939 Turkey enlarged her territory to its present extent by occupying Hatay (Alexandretta), the north-western corner of French-ruled Syria. France acquiesced in its annexation to Turkey, hoping thereby to win Turkish support in the imminent war against Germany. The skilful diplomacy of Ismet Inönü, Atatürk's former chief of staff and his successor in the presidency, kept Turkey out of the hostilities, however. It was only in February 1945 that she declared war on the Axis powers, thus qualifying for membership of the UN. Turkey's neutrality had brought the country considerable wealth, with the consequent rise of a new class of Turkish entre-preneurs, who wanted an end to the state's domination of the economy. At the same time, rising prices had made life harder for wage-earners, who were legally forbidden to strike. The religiously minded masses bitterly resented the attitude of the Republican People's Party, which was that their existence was an anachronistic disgrace to the secular republic. In the post-war euphoria, moreover, liberty and democracy were in vogue, and Inönü knew that change must come. He therefore raised no objection when, in January 1946, Adnan Menderes and other dissi-dent ex-members of the RPP formed the Democrat Party. Although the 1946 elections had been blatantly rigged against the new party, it swept into power in 1950.

In the ensuing Democrat Party decade agriculture boomed, thanks to generous American aid and a run of unprecedentedly good harvests. So did industry, both state and private, but at the price of huge foreign indebted-ness, with a resulting inflation that brought great hardship to those on fixed incomes. Unfortunately for Menderes, they included the officers of the armed forces, who were further incensed by his connivance at breaches of Ata-türk's secularist reforms: turbans had reappeared, as had polygamy. Menderes, who was pathologically intolerant of criticism, manipulated the law so as to muzzle the judi-ciary, the press and the opposition in the Assembly. On 27 May 1960 a group of officers seized power, 'in fulfil-

ment of their legal duty to safeguard the republic and the constitution'. Menderes and his ministers were put on trial; he and two others were hanged in 1961. A new con-stitution created a second chamber and a constitutional court, in the hope of checking any future Menderes before he went too far. In October 1961 elections were held and the officers scrupulously handed power back to the Assembly. The new Justice Party inherited most of the support previously given to the Democrat Party, now out-lawed, but no party won a clear majority and for the next few years the country was ruled by a series of coalitions.

Meanwhile, with the steady expansion of industry, particularly in the private sector, working people were becoming more politically aware. Another factor was that from 1958 on, Turkish workers had been answering West Germany's need for foreign labour (the *Gastarbeiter*). Their remittances home helped the Turkish economy, but when they came home on leave, or after having made their pile, they had tales to tell of the outside world that opened the eyes of their stay-at-home friends. In 1961 the Turkish Labour Party was founded and in 1963 a law was enacted recognizing the right to strike. In an attempt to steal the Labour Party's thunder, Inönü announced, just before the 1965 elections, that his RPP was now 'left of centre'. In fact, its share of the vote dropped, from 37 per cent in 1961 to 29 per cent. Many Turks were scared of the word 'left', connoting as it did their ancient enemy, Russia, and the conservative Justice Party, under Süleyman Demirel, won an absolute majority. The Labour Party won only 3 per cent of the votes, and some of its supporters, with financial backing from outside the country, resorted to violence. Student and trade union demonstrations and counter-demonstrations became a feature of urban life, and rival factions did not stop short of murder. In March 1971 Demirel resigned after an ultimatum from the service chiefs, impatient at what they saw as his timid failure to

Ismet Inönü, ex-president and Atatürk's stalwart ally, campaigning in 1961 at the age of 77

1978 saw Ecevit as prime minister, his cabinet including a number of independents. The economic situation was parlous, with inflation at well over 40 per cent per annum. The population, at 40 million, had almost doubled since 1950. The solidarity of NATO was threatened by America's continued refusal to restore the military aid that had been cut off after the Cyprus invasion, and the Turks were letting it be known that they might have to turn towards Russia. On a more positive note, it is worth mentioning that Turkey is one of the handful of countries outside Western Europe whose governments can be changed by a free vote of the people. *G. L. L.*

Both a pledge of westernization and a reminiscence of ancient Asiatic power: the Atatürk mausoleum, Ankara

maintain order. Succeeding governments did little better. Between 1975 and 1977, 200 people were killed and over 4000 wounded in political clashes, and most universities were closed more often than not.

A major event of 1977 was the admission by Bülent Ecevit, leader of the RPP, that the party had been guilty of an 'historical misjudgement' in failing to see the essential part played by Islam in the life of the people. In other words, the party recognized that Atatürk had acted too swiftly and too radically in imposing secularism. This admission meant that reactionary parties could no longer hope to monopolize the votes of the religious, as respect for religious sentiments was now common ground.

In foreign affairs, true to Atatürk's policy of joining the Western world, Turkish troops took their full share in the UN action in Korea in 1950–53 and Turkey joined NATO in 1952. Relations with Greece continued to be amicable until the Cyprus troubles began in 1954. When the Republic of Cyprus was created in 1960, Turkey joined Greece and Great Britain as its guarantors. It was in this capacity that Turkey claimed to be acting when she invaded the island in July 1974. The situation was exacerbated in 1976 by conflicting Greek and Turkish claims to the right to prospect for oil in the continental shelf of the Aegean Sea. While maintaining diplomatic and commercial ties with Israel, Turkey worked at improving relations with her Arab neighbours, partly for economic reasons and partly in the hope of winning their votes in the UN. Relations did improve, but with little reward to Turkey.

Officially scorned, Turkey's Islamic past looms over contemporary daily life

The Fertile Crescent

Syria: the French Mandate

After the short-lived attempt in 1919 by the Hashemite Prince Feisal, encouraged by T. E. Lawrence ('Lawrence of Arabia'), to set up the independent greater Arab state based on Damascus, which British policy had seemed to promise as the reward for rebelling against the Turks, Syria and Lebanon were handed over to France in 1920. The area was designated a League of Nations 'mandate', following secret wartime pacts between the Allies. Traditional French interests – especially in the coastal area with its Christian minorities – were traded for British interests in the oilfields of Iraq. French rule met with some resistance: the Druze mountain people rebelled in 1925, and after 1928 the National Bloc began to demand independence from France. In 1936 the French signed a treaty promising independence within three years, but delayed its ratification with the approach of the Second World War. In 1940 Syria and Lebanon remained under Vichy control, but in 1941 were invaded by British and Free French forces. The French reluctantly granted independence in 1946 under strong nationalist and British/American pressure.

Syria after independence

From 1946 until 1949, Syria was ruled by old-guard nationalists who resisted any radical economic or political changes. Syria's defeat in the first Palestine War (1948) exposed the inadequacy and corruption of the régime. The army, resenting its role as a scapegoat for civilian incompetence, seized power amid increasing civil disorder. A series of short-lived military and quasi-military régimes followed. In 1954 civilian government was restored, but the army remained a force in political life. During the period 1949–58 there was intense discussion whether Syria should merge with Egypt or with Iraq and Jordan. This culminated in union with Egypt as the United Arab Republic (UAR) (1958–61). The small but influential Ba'ath Party initially favoured the union, but Egypt's dominant position under Nasser soon aroused Syrian resentment. The union was ended by a conservative military coup in Syria. The 1960s saw the consolidation of the Ba'ath Party's power. The régime of 1966–70 was dominated by radical Ba'athists who curtailed the power of landowners and undertook widespread nationalization. General Assad, the Ba'athist air force commander who seized power in 1970, softened these policies and reopened trade with the West. Ba'athist régimes have generally taken a militant stand against Israel but Assad severely limited the independence of Palestinian groups in Syria and sent his army to intervene in the Lebanese civil war (1976) to limit the Palestinians' power there.

Lebanon after independence

The Lebanese National Pact of 1943 was based on a division of power between the main religious groups – the Christian majority (Maronites, Greek Orthodox and others) and the Muslim minority (Sunni, Shia and Druze), whose separate identities had been encouraged under the French. The president was always to be a Maronite Christian, the prime minister, a Sunni Muslim. The president's position was, in fact, more powerful, since he appointed the prime minister. Civil service appointments were also divided proportionally on a confessional basis,

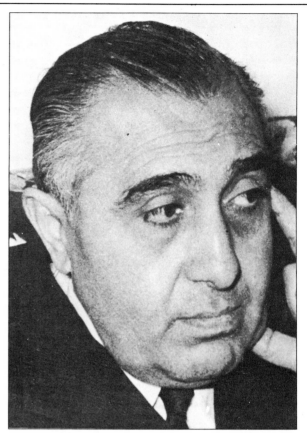

Founded in 1943 by Michel Aflaq and (above) Salaheddin el Bitar, the Ba'ath Party is a major constituent of governments in Syria and Iraq

factors which established Christian predominance. Within each community, landowners and businessmen exercised patronage over their co-religionists and political 'bossism' was a common feature of Lebanese political life. After 1946 Lebanon became the prosperous banking capital of the Middle East, but tensions built up under presidents Khuri and Shamoun. The Muslim population was increasing faster than the others, unbalancing confessional representation, and a fierce struggle for power between various leaders led to a civil war in 1958, when Shamoun called in US Marines to help restore order. His replacement, General Shihab (Chehab), strengthened the administrative apparatus and instituted limited reforms, which were continued under President Helou but President Franjieh returned to more laissez-faire policies. The problems of urban and rural poverty, confessional tension and the presence of the Palestinians, and both the impoverished refugees and the commandos operating against Israel, remained unsolved in the 1970s.

Iraq: the British Mandate

After driving the Turks out of Mesopotamia (Iraq in Arabic) between 1915 and 1918, the British were slow to grant independence to the Arab inhabitants. After a brief rebellion by impatient nationalists in 1920, British rule was confirmed by the Treaty of Sèvres in 1922. Iraq became a British League of Nations mandate with Feisal

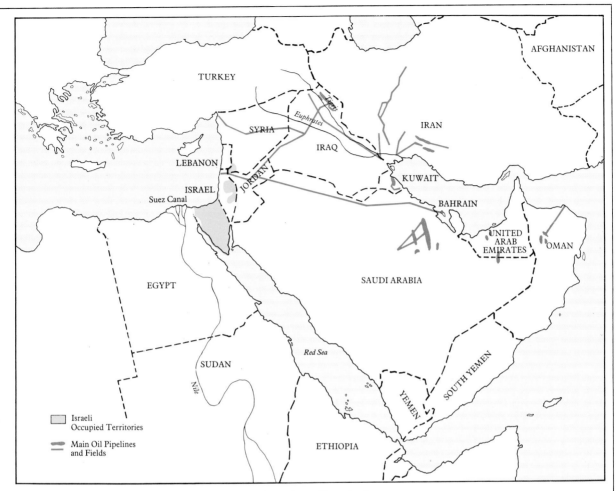

Israeli
Occupied Territories

Main Oil Pipelines
and Fields

(ousted from Damascus) as king. Influential British advisers to the Iraqi government attempted to unify the country, particularly by controlling the powerful tribal groups, and helped to establish a small usually pro-British, ruling oligarchy. This élite, in which the best-known figure was Nuri es-Said, remained the dominant force in Iraqi politics until 1958.

After the Anglo-Iraqi Treaty (1930) Iraq was nominally independent but the British retained bases and control over defence and foreign policy. There was, however, intermittent violent opposition. In 1936 Bakr Sidqi staged a short-lived military coup. In April 1941 – when the possibility was in the air that the Axis powers might, with Vichy French aid, oust the British from the Middle East – Rashid Ali al-Ghailain siezed power in Baghdad. The British, determined to hold on to their air bases, sent in reinforcements and in May repelled Rashid Ali's attacks. By June, the British had regained control of Iraq and re-installed the pro-British regent, Abdul-illah. In 1948, Iraq rejected a proposed modification of the 1930 treaty because it set no date for British withdrawal, but Britain still exercised some influence on external policy – Iraq was the only Arab country to sign the British-sponsored Baghdad Pact of 1955 between Britain, Turkey and Iraq (later the Central Treaty Organization (CENTO), with Iran and Pakistan as members).

Revolution

The downfall of the old pro-British régime was provoked by Nuri es-Said's ill-judged attempt in February 1958 to create an Arab union, consisting of the two Hashemite-ruled states of Iraq and Jordan, in competition with Nasser's new UAR (Egypt and Syria). In July 1958 King Feisal II and Nuri es-Said were killed in an army coup led by Colonel Qasim (Kassem). A power struggle ensued over union with the UAR, which was opposed by Qasim but favoured by Iraqi Nasserists and Ba'athists. The influential Communist Party was initially Qasim's main ally, but he subsequently restricted its growing power. Qasim was overthrown in 1963 by an alliance of army officers and Ba'athists, and later in the year, Colonel Abdu'Salam Arif expelled the Ba'athists from the government. They only returned to power in 1968 in a coup led by Ahmad Hassan al-Bakr. The Ba'ath Party then established itself more firmly in power than previous régimes had done, and embarked on a policy of statist economic development based on oil revenues. In 1973, the Iraq Petroleum Company was nationalized.

One of Iraq's main internal difficulties since 1958 has been persistent Kurdish insurrection in the northern provinces. In 1975, agreement between Iraq and Iran (which previously gave sanctuary to the Kurds) to end their border dispute curtailed the rebellion. *S. G. B.*

Northern Africa

Libya

For 125 years prior to 1835, the Karamanli dynasty (composed of Arabs and Berbers) controlled much of what is now known as Libya – Tripolitania, Cyrenaica and parts of Fezzan. In 1835, the Ottoman Turks reasserted their previously nominal authority over Tripoli and the coast. From the mid-19th century, control of Cyrenaica and the interior went to the Sanusi religious order, which also controlled the important trans-Saharan trade route through their territory. In 1911–12, the Italians occupied the coastal areas of Tripolitania and Cyrenaica with minimal Ottoman resistance. In the interior, however, they were opposed by the Sanusi and their Bedouin allies who, after the First World War, launched a guerrilla war with the support of much of the population. This was only subdued in 1931 by the use of aerial bombardment and concentration camps. During the Second World War, the British eventually occupied Tripolitania and Cyrenaica, and the Free French held Fezzan. The British made an alliance with Sayyid Idris, the temporal head of the Sanusi order, whom they subsequently supported for kingship of the whole country. Libya remained under British and French rule with UN supervision until 1951, when it became independent under King Idris I. Britain provided most of Libya's arms and aid and, with the US, maintained military bases there. The discovery of oil in the 1960s led to rapid but uneven economic development.

In 1969, a group of young army officers overthrew the corrupt and pro-Western régime of King Idris and installed a Revolutionary Command Council led by Colonel Mu'ammar Khadafi (Gadaffi). He rapidly assumed a dominant position in the régime, which combined a statist economic policy with an attempt to make Islam its guiding political and cultural force. Colonel Khadafi has also taken an active role in foreign affairs, both in Africa and the Middle East. He has generally been hostile to the West though not pro-Communist, supporting militant Palestinian groups and advocating the use of oil as a political weapon. His régime nationalized foreign oil interests in Libya and pressed for higher oil prices. Khadafi's efforts to achieve union with Egypt, Sudan and Syria in 1972 and 1973 ended in failure.

Tunisia

Relations with France became strained after independence by Tunisian support for the FLN in Algeria and by President Bourguiba's demand in 1961 for the evacuation of French troops from Tunisia. Fighting broke out which lasted until October 1962 when the French agreed to evacuate. French settlers' land was subsequently nationalized and after initially following liberal economic policies, the government embarked on a period (1963–69) of more interventionist policies for a planned economy. Political opposition was suppressed and Bourguiba's position became entrenched. Tunisia has maintained a generally pro-Western orientation, dependence on Western aid and an open-door policy towards foreign capital, as well as providing a large-scale migration of labour to Western Europe. Its relations with other Arab states have fre-

Habib Bourguiba, first president of independent Tunisia

Colonel Khadaffy of Libya (left) and President Sadat of Egypt briefly united their states in 1973

Ahmed Ben Bella (left) was ousted from power by Houari Boumedienne (right)

quently been strained, particularly over the question of Israel, on which Bourguiba has on occasion taken a more compromising stand than other Arab states.

Algeria

At independence in July 1962, consequent upon the Evian Agreement of March with De Gaulle's Fifth Republic, dissensions arose between the various groups making up the FLN. Ahmad Ben Bella, who had been a prisoner of the French for much of the war, emerged as first prime minister of the Algerian republic. His régime lasted until 1965, when Colonel Houari Boumedienne, previously commander of the Liberation Army, staged a coup that put Ben Bella back in detention. Algeria faced a difficult economic situation – shortage of skills as Europeans left, high unemployment and stagnant agriculture, although the country was rich in oil and natural gas. The state took a 51 per cent share in two major French oil companies in 1971 and initiated a programme of agrarian reform. Under Ben Bella, Algeria had been a strong advocate of Afro-Asian solidarity, and in general the country has avoided close relations with the Western powers. However, economic ties with France remain: Algeria has a large adverse trade balance with France and many Algerian migrants work in Europe.

Morocco

Muhammad V was succeeded on his death in 1961 by Hassan II. The king and his supporters have been in continuous conflict with these more radical elements (including the Union National des Forces Populaires led by Mehdi Ben Barka) which broke away from the Istiqlal Party and which wanted to reduce the king's power. By 1972, the king had survived two attempted coups and had consolidated his position by direct rule and the periodical suspension of the Moroccan parliament. He won some support by the 'Moroccanization' of foreign-owned property and some land redistribution. He was also successful in appealing for unity over the Moroccan occupation of part of the former Spanish Sahara.

The Western Sahara

The Western Sahara was under Spanish rule from 1884, although Spain only controlled a small coastal enclave. In 1960, the whole territory was made a province of Spain. Spain's subsequent decision to decolonize the Sahara (1974–75) opened a struggle for control of its rich phosphate deposits between Morocco. Mauritania and the Saharan liberation movement (Frente Polisario) supported by Algeria. In 1975, a UN investigating committee reported the majority of Saharans to favour independence. After this decision, King Hassan of Morocco launched the peaceful 'Green March' of 350,000 Moroccans across the border of the Western Sahara. This was followed by a Tripartite Agreement between Morocco, Mauritania and Spain for partition of the territory. Mauritania, a very poor country, which had become independent of France in 1960, obtained a share in the phosphates, most of which are found in the Moroccan zone. Morocco occupied the sector assigned to it in December 1975. Both governments have been opposed by the Polisario guerrillas.   *S. G. B.*

The 'Green March' of the Moroccans into the ex-Spanish Sahara, led by King Hassan

Desert Arabia

Jordan

After the First World War, the area (mostly desert) to the east of the River Jordan was administered as part of the British Mandate for Palestine. Another son of the Hashemite Sharif Husain of Mecca, Prince Abdullah, younger brother of Prince Feisal, was installed as ruler in 1923. The British gradually increased Trans-Jordan's autonomy while remaining in control of foreign affairs, finance and defence – the mainly Bedouin Arab Legion being led by a British officer, Glubb Pasha. In 1946, the independent Hashemite Kingdom of Jordan was proclaimed by Abdullah. In the first Palestine War, the Arab Legion secured a portion of the west bank territory for King Abdullah, including Jerusalem, where he was assassinated in 1951. His son Talal succeeded briefly, to be replaced by his grandson, Husain, in 1953. The kingdom maintained close ties with Britain and the USA, though it refused to join the Baghdad Pact in 1955, and dismissed Glubb from command of the Arab Legion in 1956. In 1958, however, Husain had to call in British troops to support his faltering régime after the short-lived union with Iraq had provoked the revolution in Baghdad.

The conflict with Israel has deeply affected Jordan's internal politics. Jordan had occupied the west bank in 1948 and annexed it in 1950, and also received an influx of Palestinian refugees. In 1967, Israel recaptured the west bank and more refugees fled to Jordan, which was becoming a major base for Palestinian guerrilla activities against Israel. Clashes between the Jordanian army and Palestinian commandos led to a hard-fought war in 1970–1971, after which Palestinian activities in Jordan were suppressed.

The Gulf States, South Arabia and Yemen

In the 19th century, the Persian (or Arabian) Gulf was dominated by Britain as a safeguard to its trade and strategic route to India. At first the treaties (or 'truces') were aimed mainly at curbing piracy by the coastal sheikhdoms. A further series of agreements was made in the 1880s and 1890s with the 'Trucial' sheikhdoms, along with Bahrain and Kuwait, giving Britain effective control over their external affairs. In this century, strategic interests were reinforced by the discovery of oil in this area. The richest of the states, Kuwait, which became independent in 1961, could afford to establish an extensive welfare state under a government still largely controlled by the hereditary ruling family. Most of the Trucial States (Abu Dhabi, Dubai, Ra's al Khaymah, 'Umm al-Qaiwain, Ajmān and Fujaira) combined to form the United Arab Emirates (UAR) in 1971 in the wake of the general British military withdrawal from the Gulf. Bahrain also became independent in 1971 after a UN investigation. All of these states have maintained close relations with Britain and the US. Further south, in Oman, the Sultan of Muscat and Oman was receiving assistance from British advisers and Iranian troops in the mid-1970s in quelling a guerrilla war in Dhofar province.

Aden was an important British staging post on the route to India, and gradually the British established control over its hinterland. After the British evacuation of Suez in 1956, Aden became a major British base, and the government was reluctant to let it become independent. After abortive attempts to establish a Federation of Aden and its hinterland and a period of armed resistance by Aden nationalists, the British finally withdrew in 1967, after

Arab summit at Rabat, Morocco, October 1974: King Hussein of Jordan (left) and Sheikh Zayed ben Sultan, ruler of Abu Dhabi and president of the Supreme Council of the United Arab Emirates

which a radical régime set up the People's Democratic Republic of Yemen, aligned with the Soviet bloc, thus confirming Britain's worst fears.

Aden's northern neighbour, the Arab Republic of Yemen, was set up after a civil war from 1962 to 1969, in which monarchist forces with Saudi backing, supporting the former ruler, the Imam of Yemen, were defeated by republican forces backed by Nasser's Egypt.

Saudi Arabia

Early in the 19th century, the Wahhabis, a militant fundamentalist Muslim sect originating in Najd, central Arabia, began to expand north and west into the Ottoman domains and were only checked by Mohammed Ali, Pasha of Egypt, sending his army to the Hijaz (western Arabia) in 1811–18. The Wahhabis retained their control over parts of central Arabia and in 1902 they captured Riyadh, the capital of Najd. Their leader, Abdul-Aziz Ibn Saud, received a subsidy from Britain during the First World War to ensure his neutrality, although the main British support went to Sharif Husain of Mecca, who led a revolt in the Hijaz against the Turks from 1916. Increasing rivalry between Ibn Saud and Husain culminated in the conquest of the Hijaz by Ibn Saud's forces in 1925. Ibn Saud proclaimed himself King of Hijaz and Najd in 1926. In the period up to the Second World War, Ibn Saud consolidated his régime (naming his kingdom Saudi Arabia in 1932), by subduing tribal groups who opposed him.

Until the enormous oil resources discovered in the 1930s could be tapped, mostly by the American-owned Arabian-American Oil Company (Aramco), the Meccan pilgrimage was the main source of revenue for this poor,

largely desert country. When a decline in pilgrim revenue set in, before the Second World War, Saudi Arabia's economy was badly hit. During the Second World War, the country had to be supported by loans from Britain and the US. On Ibn Saud's death in 1953, King Saud came to the throne, but after 1958 his authority was increasingly taken over by his brother Faisal, who finally became king in 1964 when Saud was deposed. Faisal followed a policy of alliance with the West and development of the economy, along with very cautious social reform, reflecting the extremely conservative nature of the ruling family and of Saudi society in general. Saudi Arabia's vast oil wealth has made it a major contributor of aid to the Third World and a powerful force in oil politics, although its basically pro-Western orientation has made it relatively cautious in using the 'oil weapon'. In 1975 King Faisal was assassinated and succeeded by Crown Prince Khalid, without any major changes in Saudi policy.   *S. G. B.*

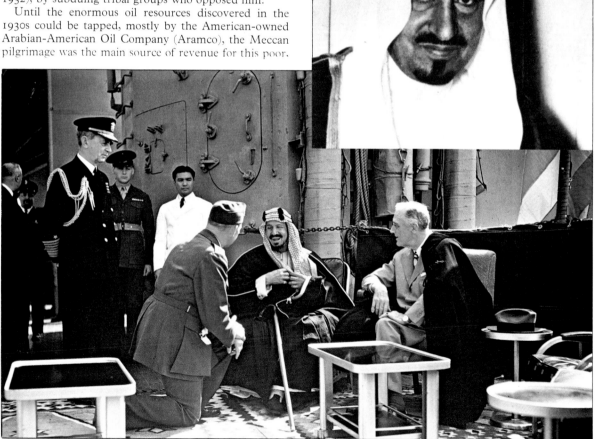

King Ibn Saud, the founder of Saudi Arabia, talks to President Franklin D. Roosevelt after the Cairo summit, November 1944. Inset: King Khaled, the third successor of Ibn Saud as ruler of Saudi Arabia

Iran

During the 19th century, Iran, weakened by centuries of Mongol and Turkish invasion and economic decline, experienced European penetration on an increasing scale, principally by the Russians in the north and the British (from India) in the south. By the end of the century, many of the country's resources were in foreign hands. Theoretically an absolute monarch, the shah's power was in fact curtailed not only externally but also by the accumulation of local power in the hands of provincial governors and religious leaders (*mujtahids*). A constitutionalist movement had been formed by the 1890s, leading to the establishment of a national assembly (*majlis*) and a constitution (1906). However, in 1908 the shah's attempts to reassert his authority led to political chaos, after which Britain and Russia took a hand. Both powers had signed the Anglo-Russian Agreement (1907) which allocated a sphere of influence to each, separated by a neutral zone. The discovery of oil in the south further enhanced British interests there. During the First World War, Iran was a battleground for Russia, Britain and Germany, mostly operating through subservient local forces. Only after Reza Khan, a former officer in the Russian-controlled Cossack Brigade, seized power in 1921 did Soviet Russia agree to end all intervention in Iran. The British were then also obliged to withdraw. By 1926, the exiled shah was deposed and Reza crowned himself shah, founding the Pahlavi dynasty. His régime was strongly nationalist, opposed to any form of foreign influence, and attempted to implement some economic and social reforms.

During the Second World War, Iran was officially neutral, but was occupied in 1941 by the Soviet Union and Britain to maintain Allied supply lines to Russia. They deported Reza Shah, who was succeeded on his death in 1944 by his son, Muhammad Reza Pahlavi. Both powers withdrew after the war, the Russians after some delay.

In the late 1940s Iran was the largest oil-producer in the Middle East, but control of the industry was still in the hands of the British-owned Anglo-Iranian Oil Company. A confrontation developed over the proportion of oil revenues allocated to Iran. A strongly nationalist group headed by Dr Muhammad Musadiq (Mossadegh), chairman of the *majlis* oil committee, favoured nationalization, which was implemented in 1951, and Musadiq became prime minister despite the shah's opposition. The dispute continued until 1953, with the British contesting the nationalization and blocking the sale of Iranian oil on international markets. Then the shah, with army backing, overthrew Musadiq and settled the dispute by setting up a consortium of foreign oil companies to work the oilfields on behalf of the new Iranian National Oil Company. After a period of instability, the shah gradually asserted his supremacy through army support and severe repression of all opposition. In the 1960s, the 'white revolution' – a programme of controlled reform from above – was launched. It was designed to redistribute land from large landowners to peasants, develop industry based on rapidly expanding oil revenues, and promote health and literacy, while maintaining strict control over political opposition to the régime. Iran's expanded role in the Persian Gulf region since British withdrawal in 1971 led to a rapid build up of its armed forces, purchased mostly from the US, with whom the régime has close relations. *S. G. B.*

When oil was discovered in the Middle East in the decades before the First World War, western oil companies obtained concessions which allowed them to prospect for, extract, refine, transport and market oil. The producer countries, with no facilities of their own for exploiting their mineral riches, had little say in these activities and received a fixed royalty and rent. By the late 1940s, the high profit levels of the major oil companies provoked Saudi Arabia, Iraq and Kuwait to insist on a greater share of these profits. Iran, failing to achieve an adjustment, nationalized the Anglo-Iranian Oil Company in 1951. Since the oil-producing states needed their oil revenues for economic development, they kept up the pressure for a bigger share of profits and, more fundamentally, for control over pricing and rates of extraction of this valuable but diminishing resource. In 1960, Saudi Arabia, Iran, Iraq, Kuwait and Venezuela (joined later by other oil producers) formed the Organization of Petroleum Exporting Countries (OPEC), to act collectively for these ends. OPEC's influence increased in the late 1960s and early 1970s, mainly due to the demand for oil from the West, particularly the US. During the 1973 Arab–Israeli War, Arab members of OPEC, by imposing an oil embargo on the West in combination with a series of rapid price rises, demonstrated their ability, at least in the short term, to use oil supplies vital to Western economies as a political weapon. The increased influence of OPEC has been accompanied by the phasing out of the concession system and the expansion of the producer-states' control over their oil resources by agreement or nationalization. The massive revenues accruing to major producers such as Saudi Arabia, Iran, Libya and Kuwait have given them immense financial leverage in international politics and finance. Poor in most other respects, they carry great weight in the power struggles of the present.   *S. G. B.*

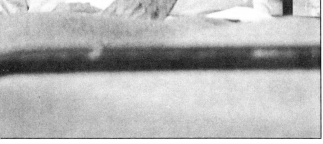

Above left: The Shahinshah of Iran visiting Washington, DC, in 1977
Above: Saudi Arabia's oil minister, Sheikh Yamani, in jovial mood at an OPEC conference, 1976
Left: Dr Musadiq as the world knew him in his days of power, 1951–53 – interviewed in bed

Top: Londonderry youth
Above: First photo of Mars' surface

Top: Alexander Solzhenitsyn
Above: Henry Kissinger

THE 1970s

As an account of contemporary history approaches the events that were happening at the time the final pages of the text were being written, it is fitting to change the focus, and move back a little from the most up-to-date developments to a view of a more generalized 'present' that embraces the *next* few years as well as the *past* few years. Otherwise, not long after publication, there is the danger of a stale taste about the last entries, and possibly a quite mistaken emphasis on what seemed important at the moment. But that change of focus can also lead one into just as mistaken speculations about what is likely to happen to the world beyond the last sentence in the book. Nevertheless, it is upon the knowledge of the immediate past, seen in a perspective of longer term trends, that any attempt to extrapolate into the future must be based. It seems to me that this is the foundation of all rational action, and that therefore this exercise is well worth undertaking.

It is fashionable on the *laissez-faire* right to decry any kind of prediction as a basis for any kind of planning on the grounds that the future is inherently unknowable. That, of course, is true but trite. What is also true is that all of us have to decide whether to buy a new overcoat, whether to buy a new car, whether to buy a house, and the electricity industry has to decide

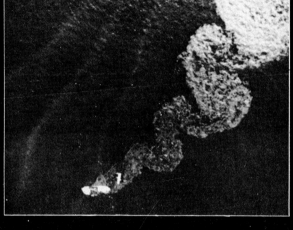

Top: Viking photo of Martian moon
Above: Richard M. Nixon

Top: Mao Tse-Tung lies in state
Above: Oil pollution from a tanker

whether to build power stations. All of these are decisions about the future, and when the decision is taken some view has also been implicitly or explicitly adopted about the course of future events. Thus the extreme know-nothingness of the *laissez-faire* position is in itself implausible.

A great deal of the future is known, in the sense that in the absence of a nuclear catastrophe, or some similar disaster, the size and structure of the population, for example, is within broad limits already determined well into the 21st century by the fact that everybody who will be 23 or more in the year 2000 has already been born, and that sets an upper limit to the size of the world population of 23 and above in the year 2000.

But who can possibly predict whether or not by 1980 there will still be a Soviet government in its present form, or whether by 1984 Iran, under the recently concluded agreement with President Carter, may not be a major nuclear power under a different leader from its present shah? All these speculations, interesting or not, have very little to do with the actual basis of the whole exercise, which is the wisdom or otherwise of the decision whether or not a new power station should be built based on coal, or oil, or nuclear energy. One needs to know what one thinks about the future in order to build a road or a power station, but to convert these hunches into a science of 'futurology' is, it seems to me, a little presumptuous, and in the end not very satisfying. *J. E. V.*

The Return of Democracy

Greece

Resistance to the Axis occupiers after April 1941 was increasingly dominated by the Communist-inspired EAM/ELAS, which was much the largest of the resistance movements. Even before the liberation of Greece in October 1944, fighting broke out between rival resistance organizations. In December 1944 the Communists, in an apparent bid for power, tried to seize Athens. This insurgency was put down by British troops, Churchill and Stalin having agreed in October 1944 that Greece should fall to the British sphere of influence. Atrocities were committed by both Communists and anti-Communists and the country drifted towards a civil war that lasted from 1946 to 1949. The Communist 'Democratic Army' received assistance from its Communist neighbours Yugoslavia, Bulgaria and Albania, and achieved considerable successes, but in 1949 the national government and army prevailed, thanks in part to substantial US military aid consequent to the Truman doctrine. Another factor in the defeat of the Communists was the closing of the Yugoslav border to them by Tito in 1949 in the wake of the Yugoslav–Soviet split.

In 1951 Greece was admitted to the NATO alliance. The end of the civil war was followed by a period of conservative and somewhat authoritarian rule, although considerable strides towards reconstruction were made under the premiership of Constantine Karamanlis. In 1963, his National Radical Union was defeated in elections by George Papandreou's Centre Union, which held out the prospect of greater liberalization. By July 1965, however, Papandreou was embroiled in a conflict with the young King Constantine II over control of the army and was obliged to resign. The ensuing 18 months of political turmoil gave a group of relatively junior army officers, known collectively as the Colonels, their chance to impose a military dictatorship in April 1967. Colonel George Papadopoulos emerged as the strong man of a régime that soon became known for its brutality and incompetence. In December 1967 King Constantine launched an ineffective counter-coup, following which he went into exile, to be replaced by a regent. In June 1973, following an abortive naval mutiny, Papadopoulos abolished the monarchy and had himself elected in July as president of the republic for an eight-year term. His attempt to give his régime a spurious façade of democratic respectability met with strong resistance from the university students and, following the bloody suppression of the occupation of the Athens Polytechnic in November 1973, Papadopoulos in turn was ousted by Brigadier Ioannidis, commander of the military police. Ioannidis's eight-month rule culminated in the disastrous coup against President Makarios of Cyprus on 15 July 1974, as a result of which Turkey occupied nearly half of the island. In the ensuing chaos Karamanlis was called back from self-imposed exile.

In democratic elections in November 1974 Karamanlis secured a large majority, and in a referendum the following month there was a substantial majority against a restoration of the monarchy. In 1975 a new constitution was introduced and the ringleaders of the Colonels' dictatorship were sentenced to long terms of imprisonment. Relations with Turkey continued to be soured by the Cyprus problem, and by a dispute over rights to search for mineral resources under the Aegean seabed. *R. C.*

Portugal

After being established by a formal constitution in 1933, the corporative régime (*Estado Novo*) went through a series of adaptations that sustained rather than altered its basic architecture. The first adaptations were due to mainly international factors: as support for Franco in the Spanish civil war led the Portuguese régime to a short-lived 'fascistization', so the defeat of the Axis in the Second World War led to a liberal window-dressing in the late 1940s. The cold war that followed made it possible for the régime to maintain its authoritarian features. Economic and social change, although still contained within the framework of corporativism, contributed to mass opposition to the dictatorship during the presidential campaign in 1958. The opposition candidate, General Delgado, was officially declared the loser in the ballots, but the anti-fascist movement did not cease to grow and threaten the régime until suppressed by harsh measures in 1962.

Despite the régime's survival, the early 1960s were a turning point. The outbreak of colonial wars, first in Angola (1961), later in Guinea (1963) and Mozambique (1964), added a new and growing challenge to the stability of the dictatorship. Portugal was meanwhile undergoing economic and social modernization. The régime was forced to open the economy to international influences, including foreign investment, while quantities of poor peasants migrated to Western Europe, disrupting the home labour market and undermining the corporative control of the official trade unions.

The political death of Salazar after a stroke in 1968 (he survived until 1970) favoured an attempt to liberalize the régime under the new premier, Marcelo Caetano, a militant fascist of the 1920s and former top official of the corporative system. Liberalization at home and a political solution in Africa seem to have been contemplated favourably by Caetano and his advisers about 1970. However, increasing economic difficulties and social unrest, and the clearly radical orientation of the opposition activists led the régime to restore complete authoritarianism at home and to continue the military effort overseas.

By 1973 discontent was growing among junior officers faced with an endless colonial war and the prospect of an inglorious defeat by the nationalist movements. At a later stage, the discontents made contact with both the anti-fascist forces and the liberal wing of the régime, now sponsored by high ranking officers like General Spínola. It was this broad alliance, which had failed to materialize behind Delgado in 1958, that overthrew the dictatorship on 25 April 1974.

The moderate first provisional government fell and, shortly afterwards, in September, General Spínola was removed. The Portuguese revolution was on an increasingly left-wing trend. Nationalizations, farm and factory seizures, Communist control of trade unions and the mass media led, in their turn, to a conservative reaction that eventually, on 25 November 1975, brought about the fall of premier Vasco Gonçalves and the end of the revolutionary period. Political divisions in the officer corps had contributed to the instability of that period. Now, with the colonial wars wound up, most army factions could be consolidated under President Ramalho Eanes, and this led to a phase of stability favourable to the development of the new Portuguese democracy. *M. V. C.*

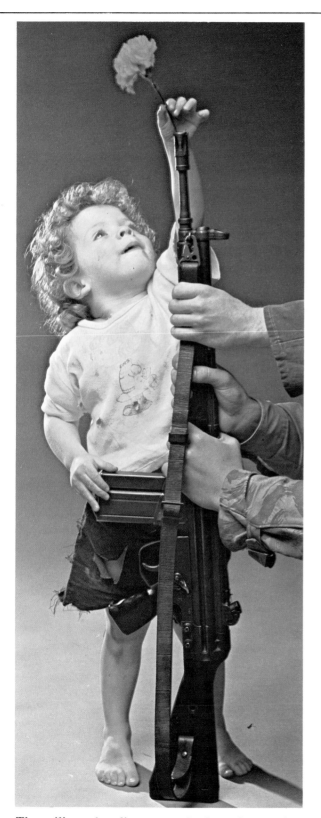

The military handing power back to the people – the potent image of the Portuguese revolution of 1974

Spain

The Spanish Civil War was won by a rightist coalition which arose in response to the reforming aspirations of the Second Republic. Accordingly, the first objectives of General Franco's new régime had been the maintenance of the existing structure of landed property and the strict control of the defeated working class and peasantry. Paradoxically, the repressive political structures of the Franco régime were eventually to preside over social changes which removed the justification for their existence. The destruction of the unions facilitated a slow accumulation of capital by the upper classes even in the hungry 1940s. By the early 1950s, Franco's fiercely anti-Communist régime had become a bulwark of the Western defence works and thus a recipient of massive American aid. When the great European economic boom began in the late 1950s, Spain with its repressive labour legislation and consequently high profit margins was very attractive to foreign investors. Moreover, Spanish migrant workers went to work in northern Europe and their remitted savings constituted an important source of foreign currency, on a par with the income from a tourist boom which began in the early 1960s.

Large numbers of peasants migrated to the towns to become industrial workers. Industrialization marked the end of the economic dominance of the old landed oligarchy which, by the late 1950s, lagged behind a dynamic, modern capitalist sector. Relative prosperity had changed the nature both of the oligarchy and the lower-class threat to it. With the emergence of a new proletariat with relatively high levels of skill and income, sophisticated productivity agreements came nearer to the requirements of continued economic progress than Franco's police terror. Moreover, by 1970, many powerful industrialists came to feel that the Franco régime was an obstacle to continued growth, which demanded entry into the European Economic Community (EEC). In 1973, Franco appointed the hard-line Admiral Carrero Blanco as prime minister to guarantee the unchanged survival of his régime. When Carrero was assassinated by Basque revolutionaries on 20 December 1973, his successor, Carlos Arias Navarro, tried to liberalize the régime to meet the demands of industrialists and a growing wave of working-class agitation.

Effective attempts to deal with the crisis of obsolescence of the Francoist political system only became possible after the death of the dictator on 19 November 1975. His successor, King Juan Carlos, was aware that important sectors of Spanish capitalism were anxious to ditch the political mechanisms of Francoism and that, by boldly opting for such a solution, he would be assured of wide popular support. However, unsure of the reaction of the army, the young king stepped cautiously. Once it had been made clear that Arias Navarro's government was incapable of introducing major changes, and impelled by a massive wave of popular militancy throughout 1976 in the form of strikes and amnesty demonstrations, Juan Carlos grasped the nettle. At the end of June, he dismissed Arias and replaced him with the dynamic Adolfo Suárez, who quickly introduced plans for serious democratization. Political prisoners were amnestied, the Communist Party was legalized and, undeterred by acts of right-wing terrorism, elections were held in June 1977. In 1978 the two main parties began drawing up a new constitution. *P. P.*

The White Rearguard in Africa

During the years after 1945 when the rest of Africa began moving progressively towards independence under African governments, most of southern Africa moved still further in the opposite direction. In 1948 the Afrikaner National Party swept to electoral victory in South Africa, its political philosophy one of protecting the interests of the white population (and in particular its predominant Afrikaner constituent) through a policy of racial separation or 'apartheid'. With further electoral victories in 1953 and 1958, the government's philosophy was relentlessly put into practice. The race of every individual was classified, mixed marriages prohibited, all amenities segregated, and separate residential areas formally assigned to each racial group. The remaining non-white voters in Cape Province were disenfranchised, the existing pass laws extended, many skilled occupations reserved for whites, and African education taken over by the state and its curriculum designed to accord with the role of Africans in the apartheid society that was being created. In 1959 Prime Minister Hendrik Verwoerd enunciated the ideal of giving Africans self-government and, ultimately, independence in their own homelands or 'Bantustans' – the scattered, impoverished and overcrowded reserve areas of South Africa that make up only 13 per cent of the country's land area. In 1960 South Africa became a republic, and in the following year left the Commonwealth.

As the apartheid programme developed so, too, did the opposition of the African, Asian and 'coloured' communities which make up 80 per cent of the country's population. The main African political organizations were the African National Congress (ANC) led by Albert Luthuli, a Nobel Peace Prize recipient, and the Pan-Africanist Congress (PAC) of Robert Sobukwe and Potlako Leballo. Passive resistance campaigns were mounted and mass demonstrations organized – to which the government responded vigorously. Assemblies were broken up by the police, and legislation enacted that provided the government with almost dictatorial powers to crush all extra-parliamentary opposition. In 1960 a peaceful demonstration against the pass laws at Sharpeville was ruthlessly dispersed by the police, leaving 67 Africans shot dead and 186 wounded, an event that shocked world opinion. Both the ANC and the PAC were afterwards declared illegal. With all normal channels of opposition effectively closed to black people, two groups – Umkonto we Sizwe and Poqo – went underground seeking to effect change through revolutionary means. Both organizations were rapidly suppressed.

Independent Rhodesia

It was not only in South Africa that white settlers took the initiative to stem the tide of African nationalism. White politicians in Northern and Southern Rhodesia revived plans to create a Central African Federation, comprising the two Rhodesias and Nyasaland. Such an arrangement, it was argued, would further liberate settlers from British control, enable them to frustrate African political aspirations, and would lead to accelerated economic development. The Federation came into being in 1953, but its life-span was short, for the nationalist aspirations of

B. J. Vorster, prime minister of South Africa since September 1966

Right: Flight and fatal casualties under police gunfire at Sharpeville, 21 March 1960

Ian Smith, prime minister of Rhodesia since April 1964

Africans in Northern Rhodesia and Nyasaland, both of which colonies had smaller settler communities than Southern Rhodesia, could not be indefinitely postponed. New constitutions were therefore introduced, and in 1964 Northern Rhodesia and Nyasaland became the independent republics of Zambia and Malawi.

A new, more extreme, white political party emerged, the Rhodesian Front (RF), which tried to secure complete independence from Britain. When negotiations broke down, Prime Minister Ian Smith unilaterally declared Rhodesia's independence on 11 November 1965. Smith's action led to the enforcement of economic sanctions against his régime by the UN, though the effects of sanctions were lessened by the assistance Rhodesia received from South Africa. Further British attempts to reach a settlement with Rhodesia failed in 1966, 1968 and 1971, and the main African nationalist organizations, Zimbabwe African People's Union (ZAPU) and Zimbabwe African Nationalist Union (ZANU), whose leaders Joshua Nkomo and the Rev. Ndabaningi Sithole were held in detention, began a war of liberation.

The sharpening conflict

Affairs in southern Africa were revolutionized by the overthrow of the Caetano dictatorship in Portugal in 1974 and the subsequent independence granted to Portugal's African colonies. The establishment of a revolutionary government in Mozambique made possible an intensification of the guerrilla war in neighbouring Rhodesia. The consequent instability north of the River Limpopo encouraged the South African prime minister, Balthazar Vorster, to begin a cautious dialogue with African leaders such as Kenneth Kaunda of Zambia with a view to assisting an orderly transfer of power to a moderate black government in Rhodesia. Even more surreptitiously, South African troops intervened in the Angolan Civil War in an attempt to prevent the Marxist (MPLA) movement achieving power. With Soviet and Cuban military assistance, however, the MPLA emerged victorious, and South Africa's policy of détente with black Africa collapsed when the scale of her involvement in Angolan affairs became known. The upheavals in the north, and South Africa's humiliation in Angola gave inspiration to the new generation of urban blacks in the republic, resolutely opposed to the apartheid society into which they had been born. In June 1976 a student rebellion broke out in the Johannesburg township of Soweto, quickly spreading to other urban centres. Only after ruthless action by the authorities was the situation in the townships brought under control. In the following year Steve Biko, the leader of the new black-consciousness movement in South Africa, died from injuries sustained in police custody.

Meanwhile, in Rhodesia, following the failure of efforts by Britain and the US to achieve a political settlement acceptable to all the parties concerned, Smith set out to win an agreement of his own with the moderate African nationalist leaders, the Rev. Ndabaningi Sithole and Bishop Abel Muzorewa. An agreement between the two sides for the achievement of black majority rule was announced early in 1978, though the guerrilla fighters operating from bases outside the country, many of whom look to Joshua Nkomo and Robert Mugabe for political leadership, pledged to continue the armed struggle.   *P. W.*

Inter-Communal Wars

Northern Ireland

Since 1921 Northern Ireland has returned MPs to Westminster while also possessing a local parliament at Stormont dominated by the Ulster Unionist Party. In 1968 a predominantly Catholic Civil Rights movement began to criticize the largely Protestant authorities for discrimination against Catholics in housing, local government and the police force. Clashes in October 1968 with Protestant extremists led by the Rev. Ian Paisley produced riots in Londonderry. Violence spread, especially in Belfast, and in August 1969 British troops were sent to keep the peace. The British Government hoped initially to hold the balance while Ulster politicians worked out solutions. This they failed to do. The Unionists split, moderates like O'Neill and Faulkner being anxious to remedy the worst injustices, extremists like William Craig refusing to accept any civil rights arguments. The violence originated in traditional Catholic/Presbyterian religious rivalry (reflected in segregated housing and separate schooling) and was exacerbated indirectly by high unemployment and low standards of living. Protestant extremists appealed to the preservation of union with Britain, Catholics to the cause of Irish unity. A Protestant Ulster Volunteer Force (UVF) and the Vanguard Movement faced Catholic Irish Republican Army (IRA), which split into two wings: a minority leftist 'official' IRA and a majority nationalist-sectarian 'provisional' IRA. Hooligans, criminals and thugs flourished on both sides. The British government, to avoid further unreformed Protestant domination and the break-up of the UK, suspended the Stormont government. Under direct Westminster rule, suspected terrorists were interned and constitutional schemes promoted for sharing power between the two communities. These foundered upon Catholic fears and Protestant insistence on their democratic rights as the numerical majority. The British army, hampered by political considerations, unable to keep the warring factions apart, and provoked beyond endurance, especially by IRA shootings and bombings, also failed to retain much popular confidence. In 1976–77 the general weariness was expressed in a widespread peace movement, but violence continued and political solutions seemed no nearer. *A. N. P.*

The Lebanese Civil War

By the 1970s tensions over the apportionment of government and civil service posts between Christians (Maronites, Greek Orthodox and others) and Muslims (Sunni, Shia and Druze), which had been essentially to protect the Christians, were heightened by social discontent. The gap between rich and poor was increased by rapid inflation and generally *laissez-faire* government policies. Beirut flourished as a financial centre, with blatant affluence, while Shia peasants in the south and migrant workers in the towns grew increasingly resentful. The influx of Palestinians expelled from Jordan after 1970 added to the poverty-stricken population of Palestinian refugee camps. These disadvantaged groups with their shared grievances began to cooperate, undermining the influence of the more conservative Sunni urban middle class and the traditional Shia leadership in the south. The Cairo Agreements (1969) defined Palestinian rights to operate and carry arms in certain parts of Lebanon, and made the country the main Palestinian commando base. However, Palestinian raids brought Israeli retaliation, which was resented particularly by the Maronite community.

In March 1975 a fishermen's demonstration in Sidon led to violent clashes between local people and Palestinians on one side and the army on the other. Soon afterwards, clashes in Beirut between Palestinians and members of the powerful Maronite Phalangist Party sparked off fighting in other parts of the country between the mainly Muslim groups – Nasserists, Communists, Shias, Palestinians and, later, Druze followers of the Socialist Party leader and landowner, Kamal Jumblat – and mainly Maronite Christians, particularly the Phalangists and the National Liberal Party.

The conflict continued sporadically throughout 1975. The government of the Maronite President Frangiya was paralysed by rivalries and confessional divisions, and the army, divided on religious lines, could not intervene without breaking apart. By the end of 1975 Christian militias were in retreat in Beirut itself and the army, which eventually intervened in their support, afterwards disintegrated into factional groups. In 1976 the conflict spread to most parts of the country except the south. In June the failure to make any cease-fire last, combined with the leftist and Palestinian successes in Beirut and attacks on Christian strongholds elsewhere, led to military intervention by Syria, with Arab League blessing. The Syrians occupied most of the country and gradually checked the fighting, but in 1977 another front opened in the south, where Christian militias, backed by the Israelis, fought the Palestinians and their allies.

As refugees fled from previously mixed areas, the Lebanese population became still further polarized geographically on religious lines, and some Christians demanded a formal partition of the state. Syrian intervention could not solve the basic problems that caused the civil war, but merely stifled the operations of the Palestinians and other militias, except in the south. *S. G. B.*

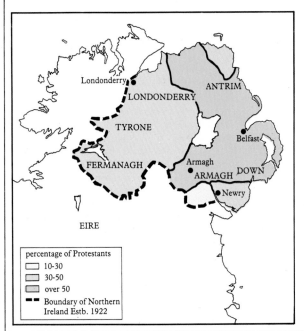

Londonderry
ANTRIM
LONDONDERRY
TYRONE
Belfast
FERMANAGH
Armagh
ARMAGH
DOWN
Newry

EIRE

percentage of Protestants
10-30
30-50
over 50
Boundary of Northern Ireland Estb. 1922

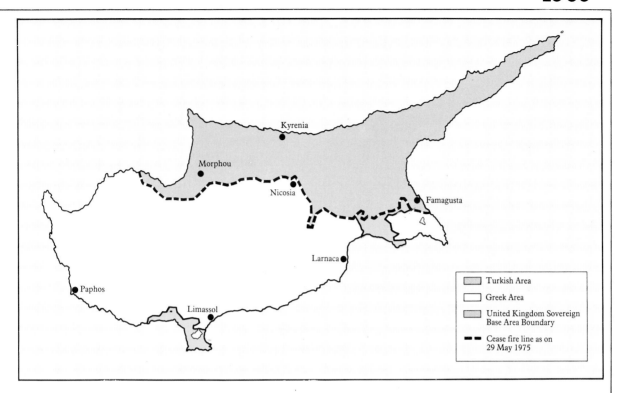

Turkish Area

Greek Area

United Kingdom Sovereign
Base Area Boundary

Cease fire line as on
29 May 1975

Cyprus

Between 1571 and 1878 the island of Cyprus formed part of the Ottoman Empire. By the Cyprus Convention of 1878, which was part of the settlement at the Congress of Berlin of that year, the Ottoman government agreed to British administration of the island, the surplus of revenue over expenditure being remitted to the Porte. Until 1914, when the Ottoman Empire entered the First World War on the side of the Central Powers, Britain recognized Ottoman sovereignty over the island. By the Treaty of Lausanne of 1923 Turkey in turn recognized British sovereignty and in 1925 the island became a Crown colony. Rioting by the pro-*enosis* faction, those Cypriots seeking union with Greece, resulted in the burning of Government House in 1931, whereupon the British authorities dissolved the Legislative Council, with whose assistance the governor had ruled the island. In the 1940s *enosist* sentiment revived and in a poll organized by the Orthodox Church Greek Cypriots voted overwhelmingly for union. The British government, however, insisted that, for strategic reasons, British sovereignty over Cyprus could never be relinquished. As a result Colonel George Grivas established the National Organization of Greek Fighters (EOKA) to fight for *enosis*, and the armed struggle began in March 1955. The British authorities unsuccessfully tried to resolve the conflict by both repressive and conciliatory measures, and invoked the Turkish community, who comprised approximately one-fifth of the total population of some 600,000, as a counterweight to Greek Cypriot demands. After four years of bitter struggle, the Greek and Turkish prime ministers agreed with Britain that the island should become an independent republic within the British Commonwealth. Archbishop Makarios, the head of the Orthodox Church on the island, somewhat reluc-

tantly agreed and became the first president in 1960. The constitutional settlement of 1960 guaranteed 30 per cent of positions in the public service and police to the Turkish minority, together with significant veto powers in the new government. These constitutional arrangements broke down in inter-communal fighting in 1963 and in the following year only pressure by US President Lyndon Johnson prevented a Turkish invasion of the island. Further tension in 1967 resulted in the withdrawal of large numbers of mainland Greek troops who had been infiltrated into the island. In the following years inter-communal talks between the leaders of the two communities produced little result. In July 1974 Makarios accused the Greek military régime of plotting against him. The junta's response was to launch a coup against Makarios, who was forced to flee the island. The coup prompted Turkey to launch its long-threatened invasion of the island on 20 July, a move that precipitated the collapse of the Athens junta. By mid-August the Turkish army had occupied some 40 per cent of the north of the island, including most of the best agricultural land. Some 200,000 Greek Cypriots fled to the south, and before long almost all the Turks in the south moved to the Turkish-occupied north of the island. In February 1975 the northern part of the island declared itself the 'Turkish Federated State of Cyprus' although, with the exception of Turkey, the rest of the world continued to recognize Archbishop Makarios as president of the Republic. Sporadic negotiations between representatives of the two communities resulted in little practical progress, with the Turks insisting on a bi-zonal federation with weak central government. In 1978 prospects for a settlement on the strife-torn island appeared remote, although the Greek Cypriots in the south had made a remarkable economic recovery.   *R. C.*

Political Terrorism

The 1970s witnessed a wave of terrorist actions such as bombings, aircraft hijackings, kidnappings and assassinations. It was a wave that affected every country in the world in one way or another, but not always in a way that the perpetrators of terrorist actions expected.

A single year – 1970 – saw an extraordinary growth of terrorist activity. In Guatemala the West German ambassador was kidnapped and killed. In Brazil the Japanese consul general was kidnapped, and then released when the government gave way and freed five prisoners; an exchange repeated on a larger scale three months later, when the kidnapped West German ambassador to Brazil was released after no less than 40 prisoners were freed. In Argentina three left-inclined urban terrorist groups started their activities in 1970: the People's Revolutionary Army (ERP), the Revolutionary Armed Forces (FAR) and the Montoneros, who kidnapped and murdered ex-President Aramburu. In Uruguay the Tupamaros began to kidnap diplomats, and they shot dead Dan Mitrione, an American police adviser, after the Uruguayan government had refused to make concessions.

The upsurge in terrorist and urban guerrilla activity in that year was far from being confined to Latin America. In India some pro-Chinese Communists turned towards urban violence. In the USA, a nihilistic group called The Weathermen (a name derived from the words of a Bob Dylan song), which had gone underground in December 1969, organized or inspired numerous acts of sabotage and terrorism. In Canada the Front de Libération du Québec (FLQ) kidnapped a British diplomat, James Cross, and a minister in the Quebec provincial government, Pierre Laporte. Laporte was strangled but, after some very limited concessions by the Canadian government, Cross was released. In Britain the first communiqués of a group called the Angry Brigade appeared in the wake of bomb attempts. In Northern Ireland the Provisional IRA (Irish Republican Army) initiated its campaign of bombing. In West Germany the Rote Armee Fraktion (RAF) – better known as the Baader-Meinhof gang – put bombs in various German institutions and US army installations.

The largest terrorist action of 1970 was organized by Palestinian guerrillas in September. Three aircraft (Swiss, British and American) were hijacked to a disused airfield in Jordan, providing over 400 hostages. The hijackers demanded the release of Palestinian prisoners in several countries as a condition for releasing the hostages. Some of their conditions were accepted, and in the end all the hostages were released or rescued, though all three aircraft were destroyed. Immediately afterwards, through massive military action, King Hussein of Jordan drove the Palestinian guerrillas out of Jordan.

To avenge this violent expulsion, a new Palestinian organization called Black September was formed, and in 1972, during the Munich Olympic Games, Black September kidnapped 11 Israeli athletes, all of whom, along with five of their kidnappers, were killed after police opened fire at Munich airport.

In the years after 1970 political terrorism continued, but did not follow any uniform pattern. In some countries, such as Canada, it largely fizzled out; in other countries, such as Uruguay, it led to the collapse of a liberal-democratic political system, which was replaced by a military-authoritarian one. It was most persistent, and

The earliest major political air-hijack, and one of the most spectacular: the end of the three jetliners on Dawson's Field, near Amman, Jordan

came closest to success, in some situations where modern terrorist methods were harnessed to violent and frustrated nationalist feelings – such as those of the Irish republicans, or of the Palestinians, a people who have not much in the way of a home of their own, let alone a sovereign state.

Some of the most fanatical terrorist groups of the 1970s were in Japan and West Germany. It was three Japanese terrorists who, on 30 May 1972, opened fire in the crowded baggage hall at Lod Airport in Israel, killing 24 people and wounding 72. The fact that many terrorists came from the two states – Germany and Japan – that had been defeated in the Second World War led to speculation about the causes of this extremism: could the fact that an elder generation had failed, and that democratic political systems in these countries had been brought in from outside, have contributed to such extreme rejection by a younger generation? Had the economic miracles of Japan and West Germany been performed at an unacceptable moral cost? The events surrounding the kidnapping and murder of the German industrialist Dr Hanns Martin Schleyer in 1977 raised these uncomfortable questions again.

The overall increase in terrorist activity required other explanations. One important cause was the perceived failure of other methods of achieving political change. In many countries rural guerrilla movements had failed – the most symbolic instance being the capture and murder of the legendary 'Che' Guevara in Bolivia in 1967. Elsewhere, as in France in 1968, revolution in the streets seemed to have failed. Or, as in Czechoslovakia later the

to terrorist methods, including torture. Others used the pretext to abolish civil liberties or attack opposition groups. In many west European states there was, after about 1972, a growing governmental reluctance to make concessions to terrorists, and an increased emphasis on special precautions, eg airport baggage checks, and specially trained armed units to discourage or defeat certain types of terrorist action.

Terrorism and urban guerrilla warfare can easily become a habit. If started by the left, it may be continued by the right, or vice versa, as happened in many Latin American countries. Once begun in a cause with a reasonably realistic goal, it may be taken up by others with a less attainable mission: the train hijackings of the South Moluccans living in Holland were unlikely to persuade the Indonesian government, on the other side of the world, to grant independence to their native islands. High-minded and dedicated individuals may be the first to launch acts of terrorism, which may be imitated by the criminal or the demented. By the mid 1970s there was evidence that in most instances terrorism was not breaking through the supposed limits on other means of achieving political change, but rather was proving relatively ineffective. It did attract large headlines, and it could, as in Lebanon in early 1978, spark off small wars, but it did not for the most part mobilize people for revolutionary action to the extent that the theorists of terrorism had hoped.   *A. R.*

same year, the attempt to achieve non-violent political change and to defend it against armed invasion had ended in retreat.

There were other causes of the increase in terrorism, including a growing belief that governments and social systems were themselves violent and terrorist – a belief that had been reinforced by the almost daily television spectacle of massive destruction in Vietnam. The Leninist argument that capitalism was responsible for the under-development of the Third World, and that capitalist states were by definition imperialist, provided an additional moral basis for terrorist action. Moreover, the fact that modern urban societies presented the terrorist with numerous tempting targets, and also with the means of destroying them, made the resort to terrorism comparatively easy, even if the consequences were not.

Perhaps the most significant new feature of the terrorism of the 1970s was the international scope of operations. Different groups in different countries often had broadly similar ideas and ideologies, and they tended to copy each other's actions. Thus, such actions as snatching ambassadors and hijacking aircraft occurred in 'clusters' in fairly short periods of time. In addition to such informal sharing of ideas, or imitation of actions, there were some formal contacts: international meetings, joint planning of actions, supply of arms, and so on. Thus, at Lod Airport in 1972 three Japanese, trained partly in North Korea and Lebanon, provided with false passports in West Germany and with East European weapons in Italy, travelled on a French aircraft to shoot down Puerto Rican pilgrims in Israel – a multi-national effort.

Terrorism as a whole was not entirely new, and it did not find governments entirely defenceless. Some governments, in order to defeat terrorism, themselves resorted

Presiding over most Palestinian guerrilla and terrorist groups – Yassir Arafat, seen at the Rabat summit, 1974

The Space Programmes: USA and USSR

The fruits of the first two decades of man's venture into space – with dramatic advances in almost all fields of science and technology – were not envisaged in the late 1950s, when the space programmes of the USA and USSR were motivated primarily by political and military considerations. America's early superiority in space technology produced a massive Soviet response, which actually overtook the American effort. The resulting technological rivalry culminated in the 'moon race' and the magnificent Apollo landings. The cost of these efforts was staggeringly high. At its peak in 1965 the space programme of the USA accounted for approximately 6 per cent of the total federal budget. Obviously, such costs could only be borne by the most wealthy nations.

Since the signing of non-proliferation agreements, greater emphasis was placed on science and technology, with the accompanying bonus of international prestige. The 1970s have seen a more business-like approach to space, with applications satellites increasing in importance. The same period has also seen more than 20 countries and organizations operating their own satellites.

Applications satellites are of many types. Of major importance are those concerned with communication (the Soviet Molniya and Intercosmos, and the American Intelsat), which can relay thousands of simultaneous telephone and television signals between continents. In the future we can expect to see more of the Soviet Ekran type of satellite, which broadcast directly into the home, so linking remote countries without the complication of a local receiving station. Other applications are navigation and meteorology satellites, such as Nimbus (USA) and Meteor (USSR), which are playing an increasing role in weather-warning and route-planning for aircraft and shipping.

Even more promising are the Earth resources satellites of the Landsat type, the orbital photography of which has numerous applications in geology, cartography, forestry, agriculture and many other fields. It is this type of satellite more than any other that financially justifies people's involvement in space.

The 1980s and after

A future application that is already approaching the detailed planning stage is that of space-based solar power plants. These would collect energy by using solar panels and beam it down to Earth, probably by a development of laser technology. An advantage of this system over land-based solar panels is that, being above the Earth's atmosphere, it should be possible to tap powers of 10,000 megawatts – equal to several atomic power stations' output.

Science is the second major space activity. It uses not only specialized Earth-orbital and interplanetary satellites, but also those of Earth-resources and meteorology. The immediate magnetic and particle environments of the Earth have been investigated by missions such as European Space Agency (GEOS) and Proton (USSR). The sun has been monitored from multi-instrument platforms, and space-based telescopes have enabled stars and galaxies to be examined in light not accessible to Earth-bound observatories due to atmospheric interference. A major advance in this field is planned for 1983 with the launch of the large US–European Space Telescope, which will be able to see seven times deeper into space and detect objects 50 times fainter than is presently possible.

The most spectacular effort of space science continues to be planetary exploration. Spacecraft have flown past Mercury (Mariner 10), Jupiter (Pioneer 10 and 11) and have successfully touched down on Venus (Venera 9 and 10) and Mars (Viking). American Voyager spacecraft are on their way to Jupiter, Saturn and Uranus. Future missions will include atmospheric probes, sample return missions and the landing of surface rovers similar to the Lunokhod vehicles used to explore the moon.

Although most of the space projects of the next few decades will be accomplished by automatic spacecraft, people have a role to play. Even with today's sophisticated computers, the human being is still supreme in the ability to react to the unpredictable. The future of manned space-

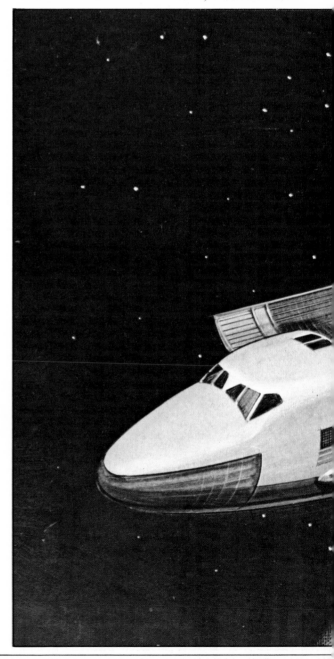

flight will be determined within the next decade. People have shown the ability to work effectively in space for up to three months, but whether they can adapt to the prolonged weightlessness envisaged for space stations of the next century, or planetary journeys, will be demonstrated by experimental stations such as Salyut (USSR).

A revolutionary change in space exploration is scheduled for the early 1980s with the introduction of re-usable spacecraft. The Space Shuttle currently under test and development by the US is an aircraft-like vehicle that will be launched vertically but return to land like a normal aircraft. The large cargo bay of the Shuttle will be used to transport satellites to and from orbit, and as a base from which to conduct experiments such as those of the Euro-pean Spacelab. The main advantage of this system is its re-usability, with an expected reduction in costs from the present $10,000 for every kilogramme placed in orbit, to $1000/kilogramme.

The next few decades of space exploration should see humanity reaping the benefits of the vast investment in resources used in the earlier years. Reductions in launching costs and increasing economic returns – e.g. from the Earth-resources satellites – will not only justify more applications, but will also indirectly pay for both the un-manned and manned scientific programmes necessary to push development forward.   *P. S. B./J. F. P.*

Artist's impression of the US Space Shuttle

World Population and Resources

One-quarter of all the people who have lived since the dawn of civilization are alive today. Never before have there been so many people living on planet Earth, yet the world's population today is probably the smallest it will ever be again.

Until the beginning of the industrial revolution late in the 18th century the number of people in the world had increased only slowly since the emergence of mankind. At the time of Christ, according to historical and archaeological estimates, the human population had reached 250 million. Fifteen hundred years later, at the time Columbus reached the new world, it was about 450 million. Only after 1800 did the Earth's total population begin building up, reaching 1650 million at the start of the 20th century. Since then the human population has nearly trebled and only a disaster of appalling magnitude could now prevent its reaching 6000 million by the end of the century.

In March 1976 human numbers exceeded 4 billion (4,000,000,000) and they are increasing by about 175,000 every day. By the year 2019 world population will have doubled to 8 billion unless in the meantime there is a dramatic decrease in the birth rate and a tragic increase in the death rate. According to the United Nations, the population of the world will most probably continue to grow for another 70 years until it has reached about 11 billion – nearly three times the 1976 figure.

Throughout history only a fraction of all babies grew to maturity. While six to eight births per woman were once necessary to maintain human numbers, today only two children per woman (replacement level) are necessary to maintain a stable population. Children and young people under the age of 15 now account for 36 per cent of the world's population. This increases the proportion of young people who are producing babies at a faster rate than their parents or grandparents are dying. This process of 'population momentum' will continue, with increasing effect, until the age structure changes to one that contains about as many old people as young. The 1.5 billion children in the world today under the age of 15 have been called 'the gunpowder of the population explosion'.

Today 94 per cent of the population of the world live in countries with family planning programmes provided by governments or voluntary family planning associations, contributing to the fact that between 1965 and 1974 birth rates dropped in 127 countries. There are even countries that in addition to providing family planning services have established population policies that stimulate the founding of smaller families by taxation policy and by encouraging later marriages. China, which comprises more than one-fifth of the world's total population, has included family planning in its constitution.

Yet despite dramatic and impressive progress as many as two-thirds of the world's couples do not practise family planning. This means that at any one time about 361 million women are exposed to ill-timed or unwanted pregnancies. Abortion – the main method of birth control world-wide – is perhaps the clearest evidence for the need for greater access to facilities for family planning. It is estimated that one in three pregnancies in the world is terminated by legal or illegal abortion. The fact that such a high proportion of women are prepared to face the risks of abortion, often without access to modern medical services and with little means on hand to deaden pain, indicates both how common and how passionate can be the wish to avoid an unwanted birth.

No matter what advances in technology and social organization remain possible, people will ultimately be restricted by the limitations of the Earth. The attempts to increase food production, for example, will tend to accelerate the deterioration of the environment and further deterioration of the environment will eventually reduce the capacity of the Earth to produce food.

Fertile land and fresh water are two basic resources essential to human life. In spite of the efforts being made to expand the world's cultivated area, in many regions the cultivated area is actually declining. It is estimated that millions of acres of crop land throughout the world are being lost each year to transportation, recreation, housing, industrial development, soil erosion and the spread of deserts. And although three-quarters of the Earth's surface is covered by water, only 2 per cent of the total water mass is available fresh water. The remaining fresh water is trapped either deep underground or in polar ice caps. One-quarter of the world's population lacks an adequate and accessible supply of safe water.

The overall impact of the modern rise in world population and the rapid consumption of non-renewable and limited resources has changed the physical face of the Earth. During the last 25 years the consumption of non-renewable resources quadrupled, which is more than the total value and the total volume of energy ever used by mankind. The amount of energy used every day by the world's 4.2 billion consumers, for everything from heating water to running the most sophisticated computers, is rapidly increasing. Each increment in demand is another claim on shrinking reserves.

We live in an age when a Boeing 707 flying from New York to San Francisco uses up more energy than would be required to feed 140,000 people for a day. Modern civilization has been made dependent on a resource that will soon be exhausted: fossil fuel. The risks involved in nuclear technology are at present a matter of fierce controversy. In the future people may find less expensive and less energy-consuming methods of harnessing power from the Earth's renewable energy resources: from the sun, the winds and the ocean tides. Of course, even if they do, the energy from a tidal wave cannot smelt lead or iron, or propel a Boeing 707.

The need to maintain a balance between demand and resources is one of the most fundamental problems of today's world. On one side of the scales is a more-or-less measurable amount of resources and on the other the two main elements of demand – numbers of people and standards of living.   *E. M./E. B.*

Mothers and children wait their turn in a clinic in Ethiopia where UNICEF drugs and food for malnourished children are distributed. Inset: Early family planning clinic poster in Pakistan

We women know that the LOOP is the best way to PROSPERITY

EAST PAKISTAN FAMILY PLANNING BOARD, DACCA.

Further Reading

Readers wishing to enlarge their knowledge of the history that is compactly presented in this book can consult the books listed below. Dealing with their subjects in greater depth, they have been selected and recommended by the contributors to this book, and are grouped for easy reference under headings by country or period.

The authors, titles and dates of publication are given, and this will be sufficient to locate all of them in public libraries. The publishers are not named since there are often separate American and British editions of the same book.

AFRICA
Davenport, Rodney *South Africa : A Modern History* 1977
Davidson, Basil *Discovering Africa's Past* 1978
Denoon, Donald *Southern Africa since 1800* 1972
Oliver, Roland & Atmore, Anthony *Africa since 1800* 1972

ALBANIA
Logoreci, Anton *The Albanians : Europe's Forgotten Survivors* 1977

AUSTRALIA
Clark, Manning *A Short History of Australia* 1969
Crowley, F. (ed.) *A New History of Australia* 1974

BRITAIN AND IRELAND
Blake, R. *Disraeli* 1966
Blewett, N. *The Peers, the Parties, the People : the General Elections of 1910* 1972
Briggs, A. *The Age of Improvement* 1959
Lyons, F. S. L. *Ireland Since the Famine* 1971
Pelling, H. *Modern Britain 1885–1955* 1960; *Winston Churchill* 1974
Perkin, H. *The Origins of Modern English Society 1780–1880* 1969
Rowland, P. *The Last Liberal Governments, volume 1 : The Promised Land 1905–10; volume 2 : Unfinished Business 1911–14* 1968, 1971
Shannon, R. T. *The Crisis of Imperialism, 1865–1915* 1974

BULGARIA
Oren, Nissan *Revolution Administered : Agrarianism and Communism in Bulgaria* 1973

BURMA
Donnison, F. S. V. *Burma* 1970

CANADA
Brebner, J. Bartlet *Canada : A Modern History* 1960
Creighton, Donald *The Story of Canada* 1959
McNaught, Kenneth *The Pelican History of Canada* 1969
Story, Norah *The Oxford Companion to Canadian History and Literature* 1967
Woodcock, George *Canada and the Canadians* 1973

CHINA
Hinton, William *Fanshen* 1979
Hsu, Immanuel C. Y. *The Rise of Modern China* 1976
McAleavy, Henry *The Modern History of China* 1967
Schram, Stuart R. *Mao Tse-Tung* 1970
Snow, Edgar *Red Star over China* 1972

COMECON
Kaser, M. *Comecon : Integration Problems of the Planned Economies* 1965, 1967

THE DEPRESSION 1929–1933
Davis, Joseph S. *The World between the Wars 1919-1939 : An Economist's View* 1975
Friedman, M. and Schwartz, A. J. *The Great Contraction* 1966
Kindleberger, Charles P. *The World in Depression 1929-1939* 1973
Rees, Goronwy *The Great Slump : Capitalism in Crisis 1929-1933* 1970
Skidelsky, R. *Politicians and the Slump* 1967

EUROPE
1848
Grenville, J. A. S. *Europe Reshaped, 1848-1878* 1976
Jennings, Lawrence *France and Europe in 1848* 1976
Mosse, W. E. *The European Powers and the German Question, 1848-1871* 1958
Taylor, A. J. P. *The Struggle for Mastery in Europe* 1954

1914
Anderson, M. S. *The Eastern Question* 1966

Bridge, F. R. *From Sadowa to Sarajevo : The Foreign Policy of Austria-Hungary 1866-1914* 1972
Koch, H. W. (ed.) *The Origins of the First World War : Great Power Rivalry and German War Aims* 1972
Lowe, C. J. and Dockrill, M. L. *The Mirage of Power : British Foreign Policy 1902-1914* 1972
Steiner, Zara S. *Britain and the Origins of the First World War* 1978
Tuchman, Barbara *The Guns of August* 1962

THE EUROPEAN COMMUNITY
Morgan, Roger *West European Politics since 1945 : The Shaping of the European Community* 1973
Pryce, Roy *The Politics of the European Community* 1973
Wallace, Helen and others (eds) *Policy-making in the European Communities* 1977

EXHIBITIONS
Allwood, J. *The Great Exhibitions* 1977
Gibbs-Smith, C. H. *The Great Exhibition of 1851 : A Commemorative Album* 1950
Luckhurst, K. W. *The Story of Exhibitions* 1951
Masor, G. *Imperial Berlin* 1971

FRANCE
Behrens, C. B. A. *The Ancien Régime* 1967
Cobban, Alfred *A History of Modern France* 1969-1970
Frears, J. R. *Political Parties and Elections in the 5th French Republic* 1977
Hampson, Norman *The French Revolution* 1975; *A Social History of the French Revolution* 1963
Hoffman, S. *France : Decline or Renewal* 1974
Sydenham, M. J. *The French Revolution* 1965
Weber, E. *Peasants into Frenchmen* 1977
Zeldin, T. *France 1848-1945* 1973-1977

GERMANY AND AUSTRIA
Carr, W. *A History of Germany 1815-1945* 1969
Dahrendorf, R. *Society and Democracy in Germany* 1968
Taylor, A. J. P. *The Course of German History* 1962; *The Habsburg Monarchy 1809-1918* 1964

HISTORY OF IDEAS
Joll, James *Europe since 1870* 1976
Kedourie, Elie *Nationalism* 1974
Lichtheim, George *A Short History of Socialism* 1975
Woodcock, George *Anarchism* 1970

HUNGARY
Macartney, C. A. *The Habsburg Empire 1790-1918* 1968; *Hungary : A Short History* 1966
Zinner, P. E. *Revolution in Hungary* 1962

INDIA
Hardgrave, Robert L. *India : Government and Politics in a Developing Nation* 1975
Nanda, B. R. *Mahatma Gandhi* 1958
Pandey, B. N. *The Break-up of British India* 1969
Spear, Percival *A History of India* 1965

INDOCHINA, THAILAND, VIETNAM
1800-1945
Duiker, W. J. *The Rise of Nationalism in Vietnam* 1976
Hall, D. G. E. *A History of South-east Asia* 1968
Jeshurun, Chandran *The Contest for Siam* 1977
McAleary, H. *Black Flags in Vietnam* 1968
Marr, D. G. *Vietnamese Anticolonialism 1885-1925* 1971
Smith, R. B. *Vietnam and the West* 1968
Steinberg, D. J. (ed.) *In Search of South-east Asia* 1971

1945-
Buttinger, J. *Vietnam : A Dragon Embattled* 1967
Chen, K. C. *Vietnam and China 1938-1954* 1969
Colbert, E. *South-east Asia in International Politics 1941-1956* 1977
Kalb, M. and Abel, E. *Roots of Involvement : The US in Asia* 1971
Lancaster, D. *The Emancipation of French Indochina* 1961
Wilson, D. A. *Politics in Thailand* 1962

INDONESIA AND THE PHILIPPINES
1830-1945
Agoncillo, Teodoro A. *A Short History of the Philippines* 1969
Benda, Harry J. *The Crescent and the Rising Sun : Indonesian Islam under the Japanese Occupation 1942-1945* 1958
Friend, Theodore *Between Two Empires : The Ordeal of the Philippines 1929-1946* 1965
Furnivall, J. S. *Netherlands India : A Study of a Plural Economy* 1939
Van Niel, Robert *The Emergence of the Modern Indonesian Elite* 1960

1945-
Agoncillo, Teodoro A. *op. cit.*
Grossholtz, Jean *Politics in the Philippines* 1964

Legge, J. D. *Sukarno : A Political Biography* 1972
Polomka, Peter *Indonesia since Sukarno* 1971

INTELLECTUAL AND SCIENTIFIC ISSUES
Bernal, J. D. *Science and History* 1969
Coleman, W. *Biology in the Nineteenth Century* 1971
Eiseley, L. *Darwin's Century* 1959
Knight, D. M. *Atoms and Elements* 1967
Lambert, R. *Sir John Simon 1816-1904* 1963
Pearce Williams, L. *Michael Faraday* 1965
Reid, R. *Microbes and Men* 1975
Turner, F. M. *Between Science and Religion* 1974

INTERNATIONAL AFFAIRS 1945-1962
Bell, C. *The Convention of Crisis : A Study in Diplomatic Management* 1971; *Negotiation from Strength* 1962
Hudson, G. F. *The Hard and Bitter Peace* 1966
Luard, D. E. T. (ed.) *The Cold War : A Reappraisal* 1964
Morgan, R. *The Unsettled Peace : A Study of the Cold War in Europe* 1976

ISRAEL
Lucas, N. *Modern History of Israel* 1974
Sachar, H. M. *A History of Israel* 1977
Segre, V. D. *Israel : A Society in Transition* 1971

ITALY
Allum, P. A. *Italy : Republic without Government?* 1973
Kogan, N. *A Political History of Postwar Italy* 1966
Lyttleton, Adrian *The Seizure of Power : Fascism in Italy 1919-1929* 1973
Mammarella, G. (ed.) *Italy after Fascism* 1967
Procacci, G. *History of the Italian People* 1969
Seton-Watson, C. I. W. *Italy from Liberalism to Fascism* 1967
Wiskemann, E. *Italy since 1945* 1974
Woolf, S. J. *The Rebirth of Italy 1943-1950* 1972

JAPAN
Allen, G. C. *Japan's Economic Expansion* 1965
Beasley, W. G. (ed.) *Modern Japan* 1975
Langdon, F. C. *Japan's Foreign Policy* 1973
Olson, L. *Japan in Postwar Asia* 1970
Pempel, T. J. (ed.) *Policy-making in Contemporary Japan* 1977
Stockwin, A. A. *Divided Politics in a Growth Economy* 1975

LATIN AMERICA
Bazant, J. *Mexico* 1977
Furtado, C. *Economic Development of Latin America* 1977
Stein, S. and B. *The Colonial Heritage of Latin America : Essays on Economic Development in Perspective* 1970
Thomas, H. *Cuba, or the Pursuit of Freedom* 1970

MALAYSIA
Means, G. P. *Malaysian Politics* 1970

THE MIDDLE EAST AND THE ARAB WORLD
Hourani, A. H. *Arabic Thought in the Liberal Age* 1962
Kirk, G. E. *A Short History of the Middle East* 1948
Knapp, W. *North-west Africa : A Political and Economic Survey* 1977
Monroe, E. *Britain's Moment in the Middle East* 1963
Robinson, M. *Israel and the Arabs* 1968

NEW ZEALAND
Sinclair, K. *A History of New Zealand* 1959

THE NORDIC LANDS
Andersson, Ingvar *A History of Sweden* 1970
Derry, T. K. *A History of Modern Norway 1814-1972* 1973
Mead, W. R. *Finland* 1968
Oakley, Stewart *The Story of Denmark* 1972

PAKISTAN AND BANGLADESH
Feldman, Herbert *Pakistan 1969-1971* 1975
Singhal, D. P. *Pakistan* 1972

POLAND
Bethell, N. *Gomulka, his Poland and his Communism* 1969
Ciechanowski, J. M. *The Warsaw Rising of 1944* 1974
Dziewanowski, M. K. *Poland in the Twentieth Century* 1977
Gieysztor, A. and others *History of Poland* 1968
Leslie, R. F. *Polish Politics and the Revolution of November 1830* 1956; *Reform and Insurrection in Russian Poland 1856-1865* 1962
Leslie, R. F. (ed.) *A History of Poland since 1863* 1979
Polonsky, A. *Politics in Independent Poland 1921-1939* 1971
Roos, H. *A History of Modern Poland from the Foundation of the State in the First World War to the Present Day* 1966
Wandycz, P. S. *The Lands of Partitioned Poland 1795-1918* 1974

POLITICAL TERRORISM
Alexander, Y. and Finger, S. M. (eds) *Terrorism : Interdisciplinary Perspectives* 1977

Clutterbuck, Richard *Living with Terrorism* 1975
Laqueur, Walter *Terrorism* 1977
Moss, Robert *Urban Guerrillas* 1972
O'Brien, Conor Cruise *Herod : Reflections on Political Violence* 1978

POPULATION AND RESOURCES
Braun, E. and Collingridge, D. *Science and Survival* 1977
Foley, G. *The Energy Question* 1975
Hartley, S. *Population : Quantity or Quality* 1972
Sutulov, A. *Minerals in World Affairs* 1973

PORTUGAL
Marques, A. H. de Oliveira *History of Portugal* 1972
Wheeler, Douglas L. *Republican Portugal : A Political History 1910-1926* 1978
Wiarda, Howard J. *Corporatism and Development : The Portuguese Experience* 1977

THE RAILWAYS
Adler, D. R. *British Investment in American Railways 1834-1898* 1970
Cameron, R. E. *France and the Economic Development of Europe 1800-1914* 1961
Reed, M. C. (ed.) *Railways in the Victorian Economy* 1969
Robbins, M. *The Railway Age* 1962
Simmons, J. *The Railway in England and Wales 1830-1914. I : The System and its Working* 1978

RUMANIA
Fischer-Galati, Stephen *Twentieth Century Rumania* 1970

SOUTH-EAST EUROPE (general)
Lendvai, Paul *Eagles in Cobwebs : Nationalism and Communism in the Balkans* 1970
Stavrianos, L. S. *The Balkans since 1453* 1958
Wolff, Robert Lee *The Balkans in Our Time* 1974

SPACE PROGRAMMES
Booker, Frewer and Pardoe *Project Apollo : The Way to the Moon* 1969
Gatland, Kenneth *Manned Spacecraft and Robot Explorers* 1976
Smolders, P. L. *Soviets in Space* 1973
Turnill, Reginald *The Observer's Book of Unmanned Space Flight* 1974

SPAIN
Brenan, Gerald *The Spanish Labyrinth* 1950
Carr, Raymond *Spain 1808-1939* 1966
Gallo, Max *Spain under Franco : A History* 1973
Jackson, Gabriel *The Spanish Republic and the Civil War* 1965
Preston, Paul *The Coming of the Spanish Civil War* 1978

SRI LANKA
Ludowyk, E. F. C. *The Modern History of Ceylon* 1966

TURKEY: THE OTTOMAN EMPIRE
Anderson, M. S. *The Eastern Question 1774-1923 : A Study in International Relations* 1966
Kinross, Lord *Atatürk : The Rebirth of a Nation* 1965
Lewis, B. *The Emergence of Modern Turkey* 1961
Lewis, Geoffrey *Modern Turkey* 1974
Mango, André *Turkey* 1968

USA
Hofstadter, Richard *The American Political Tradition and the Men who Made It* 1962
Link, Arthur S. with Catton, William B. and Leary, William M. Jnr. *American Epoch : A History of the United States since the 1890s* 1963
Morison, Samuel E., Commager, Henry S. and Leuchtenburg, William E. *A Concise History of the American Republic* 1977
Nevins, Allan and Commager, Henry S. *America : The Story of a Free People* 1976

USSR
Deutscher, Isaac *Stalin* 1970
Deutscher, Isaac *Prophet Armed : Leon Trotsky 1879-1921 ; Prophet Outcast : Leon Trotsky 1921-1929 ; Prophet Unarmed : Leon Trotsky 1929-1940* 1970
Shukman, Harold *Lenin and the Russian Revolution* 1977

The USSR After Stalin
Brown, Archie and Kaser, Michael (eds) *The Soviet Union since the Fall of Khrushchev* 1978
McAuley, Mary *Politics and the Soviet Union* 1977
Medvedev, Roy A. *On Socialist Democracy* 1975
Schapiro, Leonard *The Government and Politics of the Soviet Union* 1977
Talbott, Strobe (trs. and ed.) *Khrushchev Remembers : The Last Testament* 1974

YUGOSLAVIA
Pavlowitch, Stevan K. *Yugoslavia* 1971
Rusinow, Dennison *The Yugoslav Experiment 1948-1974* 1977

Recommended Films

Probably more people see films on historical subjects than ever read books on the subject, and probably more 'history' is absorbed by cinema and television audiences than by book readers. It seems useful, therefore, to append a list of feature – or fiction – films (with a few documentaries) that from time to time may appear on the screen, and which do not, from the factual point of view, present a totally inaccurate picture of historical events or social life of the period covered by this book. Many of the films listed here have been selected because they manage to transmit something of the 'feel' of a period or of a particular society, and others because their propaganda angle is a statement of a régime's political and social outlook.

The list of recommended films has been compiled with suggestions from the contributors to this book and with advice from Yvonne Renouf and Professor Paul Smith.

AUSTRALIA
The Back of Beyond John Heyer 1953
Eureka Stockade Harry Watt 1947
The Overlanders Harry Watt 1946
The Sundowners Fred Zinnemann 1960

BRITAIN
The Angry Silence Guy Green 1960
A Chance of a Lifetime Bernard Miles 1950
The Charge of the Light Brigade Tony Richardson 1968
Disraeli Alfred E. Green 1930
This Happy Breed David Lean 1944
Love on the Dole John Baxter 1941
The Prime Minister Thorold Dickinson 1940
Saturday Night and Sunday Morning Karel Reisz 1960
Sixty Glorious Years Herbert Wilcox 1938
The Stars Look Down Carol Reed 1939
The Young Mr Pitt Carol Reed 1942
Young Winston Richard Attenborough 1972
Waterloo Sergei Bondarchuk 1969

CHINA
One Fourth of Humanity Edgar Snow 1969
The Good Earth Irving Thalberg 1937
The Struggle for China Tony Essex 1969
The White-Haired Girl Wany Pu/Shui Hua 1950

FRANCE
A Propos de Nice Jean Vigo 1930
Le Chagrin et la Pitié Marcel Ophuls 1969
César Marcel Pagnol 1936
The Day of the Jackal Fred Zinnemann 1973
Les Enfants du Paradis Marcel Carné 1945
Fanny Marcel Pagnol 1932
Lacombe Lucien Louise Malle 1974
La Marseillaise Jean Renoir 1937
Marius Marcel Pagnol 1931
Mr Klein Joseph Losey 1976
Napoleon Abel Gance 1925
La Règle du Jeu Jean Renoir 1939
Section Spéciale Constantine Costa-Gavras 1975
Stavisky Alain Resnais 1974

GERMANY
The Blue Angel Joseph von Sternberg 1930
The Cabinet of Doctor Caligari Robert Wiene 1919
The Confessions of Winifred Wagner Hans Jügen Syberberg 1976
Double-Headed Eagle Lutz Becker 1973
Doctor Mabuse the Gambler Fritz Lang 1922
The Eternal Jew Fritz Hippler 1940
Fear Eats the Soul Rainer Werner Fassbinder 1974
Germany Year Zero Roberto Rossellini 1947
Murderers Are Amongst Us Wolfgang Staudte 1946
Olympia Leni Riefenstahl 1938
Triumph of the Will Leni Riefenstahl 1934
Yesterday Girl Alexander Kluge 1966

La Grande Illusion

Z

GREECE
The Travelling Players Theodor Angelopoulos 1975
Z Constantine Costa-Gavras 1968

HUNGARY
Agnus Dei Miklos Jancsó 1970
The Red and the White Miklos Jancsó 1967
The Round-Up Miklos Jancsó 1965

INDIA
Autobiography of a Princess James Ivory 1975
Bhowani Junction Pandros Berman 1955
Charulta Satyajit Ray 1964
Pather Panchali Satyajit Ray 1955
Shakespeare-Wallah James Ivory 1965
The World of Apu Satyajit Ray 1959

ITALY
Black Holiday Marco Leto 1973
Bicycle Thieves Vittorio de Sica 1947
The Conformist Bernardo Bertolucci 1970
La Dolce Vita Federico Fellini 1959
Illustrious Corpses Francesco Rosi 1976
The Leopard Luchino Visconti 1963
Mafia No! John Irvin 1967
Le Mani sulla Città Francesco Rosi 1963
The Mattei Affair Francesco Rosi 1972
Padre Padrone Taviani Brothers 1977
Rocco and his Brothers Luchino Visconti 1960
Senso Luchino Visconti 1953
La Terra Trema Luchino Visconti 1948
Uomini Contro Francesco Rosi 1970
1900 Bernardo Bertolucci 1977

JAPAN
The Burmese Harp Kon Ichikawa 1956
Children of Hiroshima Kaneto Shindo 1952
The Human Condition Masaki Kobayashi 1959-61
Minamata Noriaki Tsuchimoto 1971
Ugetsu Monogatari Kenji Mizoguchi 1953

LATIN AMERICA
Black God, White Devil Glauber Rocha (Brazil) 1964
Cuba Si! Chris Marker 1961
Death Day Upton Sinclair
The Frozen Revolution (Mexico) 1970
La Hora de los Hornos Octavio Getino/Fernando E. Solanas (Argentina) 1968
John Reed, Mexico Insurgente Paul Leduc (Mexico) 1972
Lucia Humberto Solas (Cuba) 1969
Memories of Underdevelopment Tomas Alea (Cuba) 1968
Los Olvidados Luis Buñuel 1950
Queimada! Gillô Pontecorvo 1968
The Ragged Revolution Tony Essex (Mexico) 1970
Viva Zapata! Elia Kazan 1952

THE MIDDLE EAST
The Cow Daryush Mehrjui (Iran) 1968
Exodus Otto Preminger 1961
Hill 24 Doesn't Answer Thorold Dickinson (Israel) 1955
Kafr Qassim Borhan Alaouie (Lebanon/Syria) 1974
The Palestinians Rory Battersby 1977
The Struggle for Israel Michael Deakin 1970

Recommended Films

NORTH AFRICA
The Battle of Algiers Gillo Pontecorvo 1965
Hyena's Son Rihda Behi (Tunisia) 1977

POLAND
Ashes and Diamonds Andrzej Wajda 1958
A Generation Andrzej Wajda 1954
Kanal Andrzej Wajda 1956
Passenger Andrzej Munk 1963

PORTUGAL
Deus, Pátria, Autoridade Rui Simões 1976
Tras os Montes Antonia Reis/Margarida Martins Cordeiro 1976
Viva Portugal! Various directors 1975

RUSSIA; USSR
Battleship Potemkin Sergei Eisenstein 1925
A Day in the Life of Ivan Denisovitch Casper Wrede 1971
The Fall of the Romanov Dynasty Esther Shub 1927
October Sergei Eisenstein 1927
Three Songs of Lenin Dziga Vertov 1934
War and Peace Sergei Bondarchuk 1967

SOUTHERN AFRICA
Cry, The Beloved Country (African Fury) Zoltan Korda 1951
A Luta Continua Robert Van Lierop 1971
When Bullets Begin to Flower L. Malmer/I. & L. Romare 1974

SPAIN
Caudillo Basilio Martin Patino 1977
L'Espoir André Malraux 1938
For Whom the Bell Tolls Sam Wood 1943
Las Hurdes Luis Buñuel 1932
Legion Condor Karl Ritter 1939
The Long Holiday of 1936 Jaime Camino 1976
Mourir à Madrid Frédéric Rossif 1962
Spanish Earth Joris Ivens 1937
The Spirit of the Beehive Victor Erice 1973

SWEDEN
Adalen 31 Bo Widerberg 1969

Paths of Glory

Lawrence of Arabia

All the President's Men

USA
All the King's Men Charles Rossen 1949
All the President's Men Alan J. Pakula 1976
The Birth of a Nation D. W. Griffith 1915
Citizen Kane Orson Welles 1941
The Devil's Disciple Guy Hamilton 1959
The Emigrants Jan Troell 1970
Gone With the Wind Victor Fleming 1939
The Grapes of Wrath John Ford 1940
In the Heat of the Night Norman Jewison 1967
Intruder in the Dust Clarence Brown 1949
A Lion is in the Streets Raoul Walsh 1953
Little Big Man Arthur Penn 1970
Medium Cool Haskell Wexler 1969
On the Waterfront Elia Kazan 1954
Vietnam Journey Haskell Wexler/Jane Fonda/Tom Hayden 1968
Westward Ho the Wagons William Beaudine 1956
Wilson Henry King 1944
Young Mr Lincoln John Ford 1939

THE FIRST WORLD WAR
All Quiet on the Western Front Lewis Milestone 1930
A Farewell to Arms Frank Borzage 1933
La Grande Illusion Jean Renoir 1936
Journey's End James Whale 1930
King and Country Joseph Losey 1964
Lawrence of Arabia David Lean 1962
Morgenrot Gustav Ucicky 1933
Paths of Glory Stanley Kubrick 1957
Westfront 1918 Georg Pabst 1930

THE SECOND WORLD WAR
Ballad of a Soldier Grigori Chukhrai
Baptism of Fire Hans Bertram 1940
La Bataille du Rail René Clement 1946
The Bridge on the River Kwai Sam Spiegel 1957
Catch-22 Mike Nichols 1970
Un Condamné à Mort s'est Echappé Robert Bresson 1956
The Cranes are Flying Mikhail Kalatozov 1957
The Dam Busters Michael Anderson 1954
Fires on the Plain Kon Ichikawa 1959
From Here to Eternity Fred Zinnemann 1953
In Which we Serve Noël Coward 1942
The Last Bridge Bernhard Wicki 1959
Nuit et Brouillard Alain Resnais 1955
Paisa Roberto Rossellini 1946
Rome : Open City Roberto Rossellini 1945
Target for Tonight Harry Watt 1941
Tora! Tora! Tora! Richard Fleischer 1970

POLITICAL TERRORISM
Black Sunday John Frankenheimer 1976
La Chinoise Jean-Luc Godard 1967
Germany in Autumn Collective 1978
Nada Claude Chabrol 1974
Targets Peter Bogdanovich 1967

TRENDS AND PROJECTIONS
A Nous la Liberté René Clair 1932
The Great Dictator Charles Chaplin 1940
Kameradschaft Georg Pabst 1931
Metropolis Fritz Lang 1927
Modern Times Charles Chaplin 1936
Things to Come William Menzies 1936
2001 : A Space Odyssey Stanley Kubrick 1968

Acknowledgements

The illustration on pages 72–73 is reproduced by the Gracious Permission of Her Majesty the Queen.

The Publishers gratefully acknowledge permission to reproduce the following illustrations:
Abu Dhabi Petroleum Co. 316–317; *Acme* 217t; *American History Picture Library* 139b; *American Philosophical Society, Philadelphia* 27; *Associated Press* 15bl, 235tl, tr, 256–257, 259l, 275, 278r, 323b, 334bl, 335tl, tr, br; *The Australian Information Service, London* 140t, 280; *Barnabys Picture Library* 141c, 202b; *Bibliothèque Nationale* 31, 189, 225r; *Bisonte Archive* 26, 39r, 50–51, 54b, 59, 60, 65, 79t, 87, 88, 129, 131cr, 133, 137, 145, 146b, 159, 160, 161, 162b, 169r, 170r, 180, 181, 182, 188l, 200–201, 205l, 207c, r, 218t, 220t, 226, 227, 231r, 244r, 247, 250b, 261l, 264, 293b, 296–297, 298, 301, 331, 347tl; *Photo Blauel/Neue Pinakothek* 63; *BBC Publications* 236bl; *British Library* 94tl, tr; *The Trustees of the British Museum* 128; *Camera Press Ltd* 6–7, 12r, 17br, 215r, 236–237, 239t, 265, 278l, 279b, 290–291, 292t, 295, 299, 300–301, 311, 313r, 317c, bl, 319b, 321, 325, 326, 328bl, 332, 335bl, 338t, 338–339b, 339t; *Campaign For Nuclear Disarmament* 251b; *Robert Descharnes/Salvador Dali Museum, Cleveland : Collection Mr & Mrs A. Reynolds Morse* 2–3; *De Witt Collection* 95, 258l; *European Commission* 284t; *European Parliament* 284–285, 285t; *Fotomas Index* 18l, 19, 54t, 112l, 173t, 174; *Thomas Gilcrease Institute of American Art* 151l; *Photographie Giraudon* 1, 32–33; *Ronald Grant* 242; *Estate of George Grosz* 224; *Sérgio Guimarães* 337; *The Imperial War Museum* 190–191, 192–193, 194–195, 199, 239b; *Internationaal Instituut voor Sociale Geschiednis, Amsterdam* 209b; *Keystone Press Ltd* 233t, 307; *Kobal Collection* 196, 270–271, 350, 351; *Kunsthãlle, Hamburg* 83; *Lauros-Giraudon* 43, 76, 167; *Library of Congress* 93bl, br, 94c, 97bl, br, 131b, 153, 157t, 198l, 215l; *Lichtbildstelle Deutsches Museum, Munich* 186; *London Midland Region (British Rail)* 52–53; *Louisiana State Museum* 99; *Mansell Collection* 10c, 13bc, br, 15r, 17c, 21b, 34, 35, 36–37, 39l, 42, 46, 55, 58, 61, 62, 64, 64–65, 67, 68, 69, 74, 75, 78, 79b, 80, 81, 90, 92, 100–101, 104, 105t, 107, 114, 115b, 116b, 118–119, 125b, 126, 135, 136–137, 140, 142–143, 150, 151r, 162t, 163, 164, 168, 169c, 175, 176, 177t, 178t, 191l, 200l, 209b, 220b, 225l; *Mexican National Tourist Council* 304; *Musée Carnavalet* 84; *Musée de l'Armée* 40; *Musée des Deux Guerres Mondiales* 208; *Musées de Versailles* 211t, 38; *NASA/ Johnson Space Center* 344–345; *National Gallery of Victoria, Melbourne* 140b; *National Maritime Museum* 49; *National Portrait Gallery* 7, 102t; *National Railway Museum, York* 52b, 53b; *New York Historical Society* 29; *New York Public Library* 24; *Novosti Press Agency* 47t, 113, 185r, 200r, 201, 203, 204–205, 241, 243, 259br, 289, 306; *Orbis Picture Library* 93tr, 130, 152, 154, 155, 156t, 158, 170l, 216, 253; *Picturepoint* 18, 25, 28–29, 49tl, 93, 97t, 122, 125t, 165r, 171, 187r, 274b, 281b; *Popperfoto* 10l, 11, 12l, 13l, tc, tr, 14, 16, 17l, r, 91, 105b, 108, 112r, 115t, 126c, 139t, 141t, b, 144, 146t, 148–149, 148, 149, 165l, 172, 173b, 178b, 179, 181tr, 187, 190, 191r, 195r, 197, 202t, 205b, 206–207, 206, 207l, 212, 213, 214, 218b, 219, 221, 222–223, 223, 228, 229b, 233b, 236cl, br, 240, 248, 249, 253l, r, 254b, 259tr, 260, 261r, 262, 263, 266, 267, 269, 273, 274, 276, 277, 279t, 281t, 286–287, 288, 291, 292b, 293t, 297, 300t, b, 305, 309, 311tl, 312, 313l, 314, 315, 317t, br, 318, 319t, 320–321, 323t, 324–325, 324, 328tr, br, 329, 330, 331r, 332–333, 333, 334tl, tr, br, 338–339c, 342–343, 343; *Press Association* 294; *Radio Times Hulton Picture Library* 12tc, 15tl, 30, 103r, 111, 126tr, 255b; *Snark International* 19r, 82, 85, 87r, 169l, 177b, 235b; *Space Frontiers/NASA* 254–255; *Photo Rodney Todd-White/by courtesy of the Victoria & Albert Museum* 116–117; *Topix* 211; *Photo Eileen Tweedy/by courtesy of the Victoria & Albert Museum* 116t, 117c; *Ullstein Bilderdienst* 185, 229t, 231l; *UNICEF/Photo Campbell* 347; *US Army* 241l; *US Information Service* 250–251; *US Military Academy* 246; *US National Archives* 157–158, 217b, 282–283; *US Signal Corps* 198; *Vickers Ltd* 188r; *Victoria & Albert Museum* 50l, 52, 102b, 103l, 116, 121; *His Grace The Duke of Wellington* 47b; *Werner Forman Archive* 131cl; *Werner Forman Archive/India Office Library* 120; *Zambian High Commission* 308.

Original illustrations by Peter Till on pages 56–57 and Tony Randall on pages 44–45 and 70–71

The Zenithal Equidistant Projection of the map on page 245 was courteously provided by John Bartholomew & Son Ltd, Edinburgh.